CLAIRE PETULENGRO

LOVE STARS

A GUIDE TO
ALL YOUR RELATIONSHIPS

D1364417

PAN BOOKS

First published 2002 by Pan Books

This edition published 2003 by Pan Books
an imprint of Pan Macmillan Ltd
Pan Macmillan, 20 New Wharf Road, London N1 9RR
Basingstoke and Oxford
Associated companies throughout the world
www.panmacmillan.com

ISBN 0 330 48770 1

Copyright © Claire Petulengro 2002

The right of Claire Petulengro to be identified as the
author of this work has been asserted by her in accordance
with the Copyright, Designs and Patents Act 1988.

1 3 5 7 9 8 6 4 2

A CIP catalogue record for this book is available from
the British Library.

Typeset by SX Composing DTP, Rayleigh, Essex
Printed and bound in Great Britain by
Mackays of Chatham plc, Chatham, Kent

133.581

For my family

My son, Paris. (Whoever would have thought life could create such a special little boy and place him in my life!) I love you, baby.

Eva, the best mum, my best friend and my mentor, thank you for being you, you're simply the best.

Gaggie, no words are necessary.

My uncle, Leo Petulengro, a wise, funny, loving and very individual person, EP, you're one in a million.

Greg, T-bone, for being such a great brother and a great uncle. Sarah for her help and support.

And last but never least, Bradley . . .

Sometimes life is too short to stop and say the things that we are really thinking. However, I have to tell you, Bradley, that without you I don't think I could have got where I am today. The love, help and encouragement you give me, together with the endless research that you do for me, means more to me than I say, even though I shout and rant and ask you to do a job in a minute when you've got a million things of your own to do. You are one in a million. I love you and can I have that research yesterday, please?

Thank you from the bottom of my heart.

And last but never least this book is also for my loving Libran dad, Johnny, who I know is watching from above and who never got to see the success that his time and patience with me over all the years created. I did it, Daddy!

Claire

(Madam M) And I'm not just talking about the furniture!

Acknowledgements

To my Cancerian manager, Melanie Cantor, who always speaks from the heart and tells it as it is, thank you for seeing my visions all those years ago and helping me to achieve my dreams, and, my Taurean literary agent, Vicki McIvor, who when seeking a publisher for me so cleverly made a decision to start at the very top and helped create the happiest working relationship of my life.

To Gordon Wise for his faith in me at the beginning and for being such a special man. Many thanks also go to Mari Roberts and to all at Pan, Charlie Mounter, Lucy Henson, Clare Harington and others too numerous to mention.

Contents

How to Find What
You Are Looking For

WHAT ARE YOU looking for in a relationship? Is it companionship, sex, or security? Perhaps you are not sure. Whatever it is, you are bound to have tales to tell of how your instincts have been wrong and your hopes misplaced, of how you felt the first flutter of love but did not know how to handle it. But don't give up, help is at hand. You are about to learn how to assess your true needs and desires, and how to spot the tell-tale relationship signs. You will find out how to identify, get and keep the man or woman of your dreams, and also how to recognize when the person you are with is simply not for you.

We all need certain things from a partner, but each individual has their own needs too. Of course you want someone who sees when you are feeling down. But do you want them to tread lightly round you or grab you by the arm and take you out partying? And partners are not only found in our love life. We also have to establish an understanding with our children, colleagues, boss, mother, father, friends and, of course, in-laws. Many ingredients go into successful relationships. How can this be revealed by the stars? Well, reading about your star sign is not just a matter of finding out what kind of a day or week you are going to have. It goes far deeper than that. It is about how the stars affect you as an individual.

Try this. Think of the people around you and try to remember when their birthdays are. You may well find that the people who are closest to you both professionally and personally are born under the same sign. Or maybe you surround yourself with the same element: Fire, or Earth, for example. Maybe you look for an element that is lacking in your own sign. Perhaps your imagination feels constricted and so you surround yourself with Water signs Cancer, Scorpio and Pisces to delve deeper into life (and at the same time make up for lack of Water in your chart). Can't stay grounded? Maybe you look for Earth signs Taurus, Virgo or Capricorn to show you how. Can't talk about your problems? Bet your best friend has lots of Air in his or her chart and can get your worries out of you. Maybe you are harbouring a deep dark secret and so you find the Fire signs, Aries, Leo and Sagittarius, irresistible. They can't keep anything under wraps for long. There is method in everyone's madness, and here you can find yours.

Here you can find out which signs you are compatible with in love, work and play. Who you should be going to for solace and who you should be going to for a party. Which sign will give you a one-night stand and which sign will give you a lifelong commitment. You can even learn the top ten dislikes of each sign so that you know what to avoid. Ever wondered why some signs leave you dumbstruck and unable to find the words you want to say? Why you stand and stare as your mouth moves but no words come out? Now you can also discover what the different signs are like in conversation. Are they listeners or talkers, and just which friends are likely to spill the dirt on you or even seduce your partner behind your back? You may have thought your best girlfriend had dropped a fork under the table but she could just be playing footsie with your other half. Get the inside information and find them out before they give themselves away. You also need to know where to go to find the man or woman of your dreams. You may have spent the last ten years in nightclubs when you should have been in the supermarket. Driving down the road in summertime with windows open? Find out what kind of music you should play to attract the man or woman of your dreams, and what hobbies and foods they like too.

And we are going to get down to the nitty-gritty too. What you also want to know is what the person you are after is like in bed: how passionate they are, whether they are wild and fervent or predictable and boring. This is a no-holds barred book and it has been written to let you know the things other books didn't dare tell.

Introducing the Planetary Influences

EACH PLANET HAS a different job to do in your horoscope. Let me tell you what each of the planets can do for you and which part of your life and personality they represent before you read the Sun sign chapters. Remember that you will have to get your chart drawn up by an astrologer or over the Internet to find out where each of these planets is in your chart. Everyone has his or her own individual pattern to explore. Your Sun sign you already know, of course, and maybe (clever you) you've found out where the other planets are in your chart too so that now it's just a matter of interpreting and understanding them.

YOUR RISING SIGN

Rising signs can tell us a lot about a person. The rising sign, or ascendant, is the degree of the zodiac that appears on the eastern horizon of your horoscope. It can have more of an effect than you realize. This is the feel of the fabric of your life. It describes the clothes you wear and the first impressions people get of you. Your rising sign is the face the world sees.

YOUR SUN SIGN

Your Sun sign is your true self. It is the essence of you and your conscience. It is very revealing about you, which is why we astrologers use the Sun sign when making general predictions in the magazines and newspapers. Moon signs would be no good for a public paper, for the Moon governs our hidden side. Which of us will admit how easily we get jealous, or that we are never first to the bar when we walk into a pub with friends? The darker sides of our personalities are for reading only in the privacy of a book, and are not for the public gaze of a newspaper. But we are happy to read about our Sun sign and to share the reading with others, for we are much less inclined to want to deny the truth of our outward personalities. The Sun sign is there for all to see.

YOUR MOON SIGN

You know when someone says something to you and you cannot help but give a quick quip back, or when your partner comes in late for dinner with a smirk on their face (or if they're a Pisces or Scorpio they possibly don't turn up at all) and you end up pouring the dinner into their favourite pair of shoes – well, that's your Moon sign. Put simply it is how you intuitively and instinctively react and respond. It is about the one thing that none of us is truly in control of: our emotions. The more you read up on your Moon sign, the more you will discover how to avoid the pitfalls, but beware – no amount of preparation can stop you from doing what your Moon sign deems irresistible.

The Moon rules those born under the sign of Cancer and so has an extra strong effect on these people. You can sometimes tell them from their round faces. These characters really are brilliant at coming out with witty comments just when you least expect it. Look up your Moon sign in the Sun signs section to find out what's pulling on your emotional strings.

YOUR MERCURY SIGN

Mercury is the planet of communication. Where Mercury is in your chart will govern how you put your message across to the world. It is the fastest-moving planet, and it rules the signs of Gemini and Virgo. Did you ever fail to get your homework in on time at school because you had done so much more than what was asked of you, questioning people who knew the topic and even joining the local society before you were satisfied that you knew enough? If so, your Mercury sign is probably Pisces and you can't help but go all out on a project. You will also be able to talk until the cows come home. Look up your Mercury sign in the Sun sign section and pick up some hints on where your powers of persuasion and your communication skills lie. It could just give you that extra power to seduce the person of your dreams.

YOUR VENUS SIGN

I'm sure you can guess what your Venus sign governs. Yes, that's right – love and romance and sex all come into this lovely part of your horoscope. How you handle love and what you seek in a partner can all be found here. Taurus and Libra share Venus as their ruling planet and you will find that these people will do anything for their lovers. These signs fall deeply in love and find it very hard to get out of it. Look up your Venus sign in the Sun sign section so you can get an idea of how you behave when good old Cupid gets a bull's eye with his arrow. The woman dressed impeccably in a business suit with a red G-string concealed beneath is probably a Libra with Venus in Scorpio. If she's a Pisces with Venus in Scorpio, she probably even has the stockings to match.

YOUR MARS SIGN

This is a great one. This is how you fare in an argument and how you handle conflict. The restaurant food that is off may not be a problem to the waitress who gives you a cocky and uninterested look but she'd better watch out if your Mars is in Aries because you may just turn the plate up over her head. Mars rules Aries and Scorpio, and so if you have both your Sun and your Mars in Aries or Scorpio you will be a force to be reckoned with. What you want you get, no matter how long it takes, and no one will be able to tell you any different.

YOUR JUPITER SIGN

Your Jupiter sign shows how you will grow and progress in life, and can help you to create opportunities where none existed. It will reveal how good a chance you have of getting the person you desire at the pace you desire, and it will tell you a lot about what beat you dance to, whether you salsa or whether a slow number is more your style. I mean your pace of seduction and your moves in life, rather than what you are like on the dance floor – but you realized that, of course.

Jupiter rules Sagittarius and Pisces and these characters have the strength to make plans succeed, as much for others as for themselves. They make great agents and supporters.

YOUR SATURN SIGN

This is the most distant and slow-moving of the planets. Ever had all day to do your shopping but once you got to the supermarket checkout started moaning and complaining that the person in front was taking for ever? You were battling it out with your Saturn influence, feeling hindered whether or not you were hindered in reality. This planet rules Capricorn and Aquarius and these people are always trying to get things done to a schedule. If you can't seem to get where you want as quickly as you would like it is probably because of Saturn. Saturn deals with restrictions in life, real and imagined. It is also about luck and fate and is a most interesting part of our charts and our characters.

THE NEW PLANETS

When I call these planets 'new', I mean new in terms of astrology. Uranus, co-ruler of Aquarius, was discovered in 1781. Let me see: Neptune was discovered in 1846, and Pluto was discovered in 1931. Pluto is all about regeneration, while Neptune governs our fantasies and sacrifices. Pluto is the co-ruler of Scorpio and is where this sign often gets its fascination with drink and drugs from. Pluto changes signs only every fifteen years and this is where the age generations start to find some common ground, and where phases and fashions meld together – not always, I'm afraid, on a constructive level. Uranus, co-ruler of Aquarius, was the first new planet discovered beyond Saturn and is all about resistance and dissociation. We still have a lot to learn about these planets.

How the Elements
Look at Love

THE ZODIAC IS made up of twelve star signs but we also have what is known as the triplicities, which may be more familiar to you as the elements. If you do not know which is your element, here they are:

FIRE	Aries	Leo	Sagittarius
EARTH	Taurus	Virgo	Capricorn
AIR	Gemini	Libra	Aquarius
WATER	Cancer	Scorpio	Pisces

Here is your quick guide to finding out what each of the elements is like and how they relate to each other in sex, friendship and business.

FIERY PASSION

Fire signs are quick to grasp a situation. These are the people who find a mate in a strange place – they are not frightened to tell the gorgeous stranger what they think. Just look at fiery Posh Spice Victoria Beckham. She is reported as having told her husband David Beckham when they first met that he had a nice arse. Now you wouldn't get an Earth sign saying that so soon! Fire signs act in an instinctive way and inspire the other less volatile signs in the zodiac. When Fire teams up with another element you will often hear friends comment about how much the other element has changed since the relationship began with Mr or Ms Fire sign. Fire signs push both life and love to the limit. They are confident, outgoing and warm-hearted, and will do anything for their close ones, and I mean anything. They are generous in spirit and generous with their money, although not always in their own best interests. Bear in mind that when they argue, they really argue, and if you can hear the neighbours through the walls it's likely to be a Fire sign that is screeching the loudest. This is how they deal with things, you see. It is only when they go quiet that you should start to worry, for something will definitely be brewing.

These are people who crave excitement and like nothing more than twists and turns in a relationship – though they are unlikely to admit this out loud. If Fire decides to hook up with Fire you can be sure that life will never be boring. Each will find it incredibly hard to guess the other's next move. Be careful if you are two Fire signs that you don't rush through your life together. Remember to savour the moments you have together – and try not to make yourselves travelsick. Fire and Earth together is a bit of a difficult match. Earth may try to restrict Fire too much and Fire may end up taking drastic action to avoid its biggest fear: life becoming mundane and predictable. Join Fire up with Water and you should have fun but remember that Water can put out Fire. On the other hand unextinguished Fire's need to be naughty and experiment could break the couple up. However, Fire will be attracted to the emotions of the Water signs and will find them truly inspiring and magical people. Fire and Air – now there's a head-turning combination. They are sure to find plenty to talk about and their sex life is also likely to be on the rather wild and experimental side.

EARTHY SENSUALITY

The Earth signs of the zodiac are more factual about life and love than the other elements and they deal in tangibles rather than concepts. They are the most practical of all the signs too so don't be surprised to be asked on a first date what your intentions and aspirations are, right down to the 2.4 kids bit. They see life in straightforward and somewhat material terms. These are the guys who will have their pension plans sorted out, so get in there, girls! They also like to discuss things in a rather long drawn-out manner which can be rather difficult for the shorter-fused Fire and Air signs, who will say they don't have the time that dear old Mr or Ms Earth has got but who may in fact be hiding from unpleasant realities. If you can attract Earth and make him or her fall in love with you, then you will have a mate who is loyal, resilient and constant. Tony Blair is Taurus, and even while leading the country as Prime Minister at Downing Street, insists that his family sit down each morning at the breakfast table so that they can start the day together. Routine is essential to a successful family life for him.

Earth with Earth has a very good chance of success but you are unlikely to find any real spontaneity between these two and they could end up becoming the boring set. They like their routine together and become upset if anyone tries to change it. Don't knock it, though. Once you are in this union you are sure to be very happy indeed, no matter what those looking in from the outside may see. Indeed, there will be plenty between you that neither I nor anyone else should ever see, including that kinky underwear drawer!

AIRY ROMANCE

The Air signs of the zodiac love to talk, about everything, anything and nothing, but don't even think about trying to raise anything sensitive with them for they will react to real emotional issues as they would to last week's milk. They'll even pull the same face. They can, however, spend absolutely hours talking about the trivial things in life and they are a mine of useless information. It will take these dear old souls a while to realize you fancy them for they are so busy living in tomorrow that they don't always get to enjoy today. They are, however, great flirters, particularly Libra, and they can spend too much time chasing and not enough time enjoying what they have.

There is an element of interchange about them, a circulation and connection about how they operate.

Cerebral, detached and impersonal are key concepts for them. They subject everything to reason and are logical, cool and rational when it matters. They work hard but don't always get to enjoy the benefits of their labour. Before they can start to spend their money they are out earning more. Very often they have two jobs instead of one. They have also been known to have more than one relationship on the go at the same time, especially the Geminis of this element. They don't mean to, it is just second nature to them. If you are a parent to an Air sign, you will be saving their future spouse a lot of pain if you allow them to get this tendency out of their system while young.

Air will argue its side of a problem very well, even if it is in the wrong. Excellent as an agony aunt to friends, Air signs will scream abuse at the name of the person who has done you any harm, even though they may have done the very same thing only last week. These signs are great fun to be with and you can be absolutely sure that life will never be boring. You just have to make sure you have the energy to keep up with them. You might get on OK if you are Fire. Air fans a good flame out of Fire, but it does get rather bored by Earth. Mix Air and Water and you get bubbles – which can be good, and can be bad. Air with Air and you just have to watch that the pair of you don't drift away up into the clouds. You could talk each other to death too. But you understand each other very well. Michael Douglas and Catherine Zeta Jones are both Libra. By marrying in November 2000 they proved that Air signs can make a strong pairing, and don't need to be of a similar age to find each other interesting.

WATERY MYSTERY

The Water signs of the zodiac are powerful and deep. These are the signs most in tune with their subconscious. They respond on both a feeling and a compassionate level and are imaginative and sensitive lovers. When two Water signs get together, however, they can lead each other down a very sticky path indeed and it is not unusual to see them experiment with drink or drugs. But if they then decide as a unit to become healthy and kick any bad habits you can be sure that they will give it 100 per cent – before long they'll be the top sportspersons in their community. These are definitely not people to do anything by halves. Multi-millionaire Bill Gates is proof of that.

Pisces Bruce Willis married Scorpio Demi Moore in 1987 and the press wrote about what a turbulent relationship these two Hollywood heart-throbs had. Demi herself admitted on chat shows that when things were good they were very very good and when they were bad they were horrid. So good were the best years that they produced three lovely children, Rumer, Scout and Tallulah, but so bad were the other years that the relationship ended in divorce in October 2000. This is not always the case, of course, and I have many clients of Water sign couplings who are still holding hands in their nineties. I certainly intend to: my husband Rob and I are both Scorpio. We are approaching the ten-year mark and he still says thank you when I cook him dinner. (Good job too or it would be on his head, with my Moon in Pisces!)

Success is about not keeping too much from each

other, which Water signs all too often decide to do. Couple Water with Earth and you get a lovely secure unit, one likely to produce more than the average number of offspring. Water and Fire don't mix too well. Fire gets Water bubbling away and these two will be in conflict unless they make a constant effort. They are better as friends, unless willing to give and take. Water and Air is a mess, really, but it is a fun one and is sure to have crowds gathering for many years to come.

THE QUADRUPLICITIES

Here's some more technical stuff: the quadruplicities or modes. Each sign has a particular mode or operating style, being either Cardinal, Fixed or Mutable.

CARDINAL
Aries, Cancer, Libra and Capricorn

The cardinal signs are initiators of action. Eager and impatient of delay these are the people who like to forge ahead and be in charge. They are forceful, feeling, bright, and full of ideas, ambition and drive.

FIXED
Taurus, Leo, Scorpio and Aquarius

Fixed signs have strong staying power. They take the cardinal signs' discarded bright ideas and make them work. As you can imagine this works brilliantly for the two together in business.

MUTABLE
Gemini, Virgo, Sagittarius and Pisces

These guys and gals have a flexible, adapting influence and are happy to negotiate with others to achieve the desired end result. They are easy-going as a rule. Their motto is often: 'Anything for a quiet life!'

POLARITIES

More technical stuff. Stick with me. It's all part of the picture. The signs in the zodiac are further subdivided into polarities.

These do not imply any sexual nature or predisposition: Yang (masculine and positive) and Yin (feminine and negative) describe yet another layer of our personalities. Let me first make it completely clear that being a negative sign does not mean in any way that you are of a negative disposition. It's all about energies, and creating the balance that we need for the world to work. As you can imagine, Yin and Yang come into play when finding the right partner in love. You will often find too that opposites attract and when some people say they have found their other half it is often a Yang that has found his or her Yin.

POSITIVE (MASCULINE) YANG
The Fire and Air signs:

Aries
Gemini
Leo

Libra
Sagittarius
Aquarius

NEGATIVE (FEMININE) YIN
The Earth and Water signs:

Taurus
Cancer
Virgo
Scorpio
Capricorn
Pisces

Take into account the triplicities and quaruplicities and you'll see that each sign is unique and unreplicated in nature or character or style by any other sign. That is what makes this world and the people in it so interesting.

Aries
March 21 to April 20

HEADSTRONG, OPINIONATED, ACTION initiator, leader, loyal to a cause, egotistical and passionate: these are the key words to describe Aries. People born under this sign are lucky to possess exciting personalities and a great deal of personal magnetism, yet sometimes they have an almost shy and reserved air about them, especially at first meeting. People soon realize that a strong character lies beneath this exterior and the Aries quiet confidence makes others keen to follow their lead. Others are bold from the word go, however.

Aries people can sniff out a good party instinctively and are always ready to go on in search of fun. They have a stimulating effect on others and, possibly because of this, are inclined to dominate and want their own way. Another aspect of the Aries paradox, however, is that they tend to need someone to lean on. For this reason, Aries are inclined to marry at an early age. They need a partner, need to feel wanted, and rejection is almost unthinkable. The women of this sign need to be constantly reassured of their partner's affection, and are inclined to be possessive. Mr Leo is an ideal partner for Ms Aries because he has the strength she needs and is generally charming and attentive.

Ms Aries makes a good mother and a loyal friend. Mr Aries is courageous with a sense of adventure and enjoys unusual enterprises. He is a fluent and ready speaker with strong views, which he enjoys expressing, and he shines whether in an argument or a calm debate. In a quarrel he will almost always emerge the victor for he is not a person to be trifled with and his tongue can be as sharp as a sword.

One of the things I love about this sign is that no matter how much you may argue with them they will always remain your friend at the end. Even after the most bitter of disputes you can see a smile begin to emerge, as if your Aries friend means to say, it's going to be all right, I still like you!

All Aries share a love of the sea; it has a very strong attraction for them. They are artistic in many ways, usually with an extremely good sense of colour. Many have a deep appreciation of classical music, although the younger ones are unlikely to admit this out loud. They are anything but lazy, but their energy does tend to vary with their interest in what they are doing. It is not unusual for Aries, especially the men, to be slow at making up their minds about what they want to do with their lives, but once they have they are dedicated to their profession. They do not always seek to make a fortune, no matter what they say. If you look at the jobs and professions of Aries people around you, you will see that it is nearly always work that is hard and requires dedication and commitment. Ideally, it is work that also allows a degree of escape. I know a lot of air stewards and stewardesses of this sign – they manage to lead an exciting, if laborious, life of travel for a fraction of the price because earning money is not their main priority in life but excitement and variety is. (Indeed, most of us are more likely to lie awake worrying about the little money problems than about how to make a fortune. Perhaps I need to write a book on how to be a millionaire for your star sign!) Many Aries find themselves drawn to computers, and either work in the electronics industry or dabble with computers as a hobby.

Aries can be led into something, but refuse to be driven. The very perceptive know that they can influence the ram by gentle flattery. Aries people are particular in their choice of friends, as indeed they are in most things in life. Their standards are high and they expect the same of those they care for.

Victoria Beckham, also known as Posh Spice, is an Aries woman who goes out of her way to look good, showing off the typical Aries sense of style and artistic flair, regardless of others who sometimes knock it for its boldness. She is a born leader who is not afraid to be different. In her marriage to David Beckham, who is a Taurus, she is likely to be the one who keeps the relationship constantly moving forward, ensuring that life will never become staid or boring.

This is a passionate sign which cannot fail to live life to the full. Aries must have passion and without it can become withdrawn and bitter. Aries does not want to have a hundred partners; one will suit the ram just fine so long as both have the same sexual appetite, and one that is as strong in fifty years' time as it was in the first year. Aries must be careful of being too selfish, though. This is a trait the ram knows it possesses but always strongly denies. Aries people think that whatever they want is the most important thing in the world, and no matter how much they love someone they do tend not to prioritize their partner's wants and needs.

This is also a sign that can be a little foolhardy at times. If they cheat on someone, it will come out in a conversation within twenty-four hours, be it to the local newsagent or the person they have betrayed. They are no good at keeping things in. Fire signs in general are lousy at keeping secrets; they just don't know how to. The pressure of staying silent about something gets too much for them to bear and eventually the lid flies off. It would kill them not to share that piece of oh so valuable information with those around.

Here's an example. I have a brother who is an Aries. When he was young I always knew way before any of his girlfriends did when he was going to chuck them. First he would lose his sense of humour, and a ram is nothing without his dry wit. Aries people need feedback, and I knew as soon as I made a cutting remark and did not get an immediate retort that I had better start cooking an extra dinner because I was going to have a houseguest. Then his emergency resources would kick in and he would start to flirt, usually with my friends!

Otherwise – when not falling out of love – he is a typical Aries, always watching for an opportunity to come out with a clever and quick remark, one which often borders on the unacceptable. Most people would never understand some of the jokes we share about life. You see, we have the same ruling planet. Mars governs both Aries and Scorpio (that's me). We both find it easier to laugh at disaster than to cry over it, which you can imagine those around sometimes find inappropriate. I even remember him making me laugh at funerals. We both knew that if we didn't laugh then we would start crying and would not be able to stop. He doesn't like to plan what he is going to do but everything always works out for him at the last minute. Friends call him jammy; I just call him an Aries. Not only is he quick-witted but he is also able to stop an argument by cracking a joke that will make the hardest-faced break into a smile. He is my best friend. After all, who could want anything more than someone who can make you smile in the face of disaster and can also find the best parties at a moment's notice. I would not, however, ask him how I looked if I was getting ready to go out. He would say 'Fine!' without even looking in my direction. It is to my meaningful and very Watery husband that I turn. He pays the sort of detailed attention that helps me get the whole look instead of just a whisper of an effect.

May I give a word of advice to you very attractive Aries – try to be a little more thoughtful, because it is in your sign to have a tactless streak. You find yourself saying hurtful things that you almost certainly immediately regret, and this often upsets you more than the person to whom the comment was directed because you are generous and kind-hearted and are desolate when you realize the effect of something you've said. You talk before you think, but this can also do you favours for you rush in where others fear to tread (even if you do regret it later). Other people spend time thinking about what they want to do but you, well, you just go ahead and do it anyway, and this gives you a better chance of success. You will just have to get used to spending a lot of your time making apologies. And you can take offence too, as well as cause it.

If your friend or partner is an Aries you can be sure of a mate who is fun to be with and who will make the world a more colourful place. Read on to find out more about what Aries are like as friends, partners, colleagues – even as your mother-in-law. But don't forget that whichever role they play these are people who will be a valuable asset in your life for years and years to come. Don't let yourself be the one who is asking, Why did I let them go? Chances are, if you do let them go out of your life, you will regret it.

SECRETS OF THE SEXES

So how do the males and females of the species differ then? Let's have a look.

Ms Aries

This woman needs a lot of love and affection. You must always support her and make her decisions with her.

She is funny and clever and can turn her hand to most things in life successfully. She can also be unpredictable, though, and needs to be kept on a fairly short leash with the credit cards. She collects friends easily and you'll be glad to hear that she will fit in easily with yours too. She's not frightened to make friends or to make an effort, and she is sure to look good too, which is always an asset in a partner. Don't try to push her, though. She simply won't stand for it. All she will end up doing is putting you down in front of your friends with some clever and cutting remark, probably to do with sex. Her love of adventure is strong so keep plenty of variety in your social rounds. She is generous with her money and will spend it on you rather than on herself. This can be a problem when you live together for she will continually come home with a new dressing-gown or a sexy scent for you, and it is only later that you will discover the mortgage wasn't paid. Her argument will be that at least you will smell good and be ready for bed.

Don't take advantage of this woman. I once had a client born under this sign who found out her husband was cheating on her. She found out while he was away on business, which gave this Fire sign time to calm down and to collect her thoughts. She continued to live with him for the following six months, during which time she drained his bank accounts and seduced his two best friends, so that the man was left penniless without even friends' floors to sleep on. Her sting can be even worse than the scorpion's.

What she wants from a relationship is attention and lots of it. If you dare for even one minute to ignore her then you can be sure that she will be off flirting with someone else. She knows she is worthy of attention and she will not hesitate to remind you of this.

She likes sex. Well, more accurate would be to say that she loves it. But she gets taken advantage of time and time again. If you have the right line then you can get under the skin of the darling Ms Aries. She can give as good as she gets, though. As a Fire sign she needs sex as and when she says and if you even think about pulling away your affections as a punishment then you can be sure that she will be off within a minute to find someone who is interested. She knows how to dress and she knows how to seduce. Put these two together and you have a femme fatale capable of getting the most resistant of signs to let his defences down. She is also very good at telling you your faults and so the fight and the flirtations begin.

This sign has been known to err on the rougher side of life and if she even thinks about getting into drinks or drugs then she is on the road to destruction. She doesn't do anything by halves and that includes the no-go areas.

But she is a fine lover. She knows how to make love to someone and leaves very little to the imagination. This, indeed, is the woman who will tell you what she wants, how she wants it, and when you should be doing it, although she would be thoroughly insulted if you asked the same of her. She loves children but is in no hurry to have her own. She will wait until she is ready to bear your offspring and will not give in to any outside pressures from friends and close ones.

Do not think you can pull the wool over her eyes in love. She will know what you are thinking of doing before you have even worked it out yourself. A word of advice. Once you try to play her games she will never trust you again or give herself to you completely for she hates to be thought of as a fool – so don't even try.

Mr Aries

This is an artistic man who likes to have a try at most things in life. He likes to impress people but never in an underhanded way. He doesn't care too much for routine. He is a great one for surprises though but also a great tease. As he likes security, he will make a good husband and will provide for his close ones and their family, but he does like to mix business with pleasure. Don't try to keep anything from him. He will like to tell you what to wear and may even try to mould you and change your appearance to his taste. He doesn't do so in an obvious way but will more than likely drop enough hints that you would have to be both hard of hearing and sight not to notice.

He is sexy, though, there is really is no denying that. There is no escaping the fact that this man is absolutely gorgeous and can flirt up there with the best of them. To prove the point, here are a few famous Aries men: my brother (OK, maybe some sisterly bias there), Dennis Quaid, Omar Sharif, Andy Garcia, Warren Beatty. You get the idea. These are people full of drive and with strong leadership qualities. They are always looking for new interests and new ideas. They won't think twice about taking chances and you can bet that the success they experience is not down to playing it safe. They inspire all around them. Women are often bowled over on first meeting by the charismatic charm these men possess.

However, they can be a bit weak as far as loyalty is concerned, so the only way to keep them I'm afraid is on a very short leash. They are quick and impulsive and can spring great surprises on people when in the early throes of passion. They know how to make love to a woman and instinctively know when to leave her alone too. They will come to you and engage you in witty chat – it's much less likely that you initiate the conversation with them – and nine times out of ten it works. I've seen this in motion many times. When an Aries man comes to me for a reading, I ask him how he met his last or current partner and he always has a tale to tell about how he charmed her with his silver tongue.

You could be forgiven for thinking he is arrogant, but you should think again because what you see is what you get. He won't put on any airs or graces, for you or anyone else in your life. He might try to put on an act but it won't last five minutes before that naughty smile comes out and his true self is revealed.

He can be mean with his words if he wants to, but it is usually only through drink or tiredness. As for you, don't hesitate to compliment him. He loves it. Forget to give him attention for a couple of days and you may as well pack your bags, for he will be off looking for fun faster than you can say the word 'gorgeous' – which I might mention is one of his favourites!

You will have to wrestle with this man to train him to your ways, but do you want to know a secret? He can and has been tamed and the way to do it is simply to let him think that he has tamed you. He will be so proud that he will not dare give up his prize trophy to anyone else. 'Think' is the keyword here, ladies and gentlemen, for as we all know, this gorgeous creature needs a very firm hand to keep him on the straight and narrow. You just mustn't let him see that it is you who is holding him up.

SEXUAL NEEDS

Aries are incredibly sexy people, but don't be fooled; they need that touch of romance too. One-night stands and casual sex are not something they will get involved in often, for most rams cherish every single new relationship as an adventure to be both relished and remembered. Saucy sex is no good unless with a familiar and much-loved face. Once they have a permanent partner they will not be afraid to experiment sexually but until then it will take an awful lot of alcohol!

The ram will not hesitate in telling you that you look good, and the stranger that compliments you in the street is probably a dear old Aries obeying an age-old instinct. The ram is attracted by physical appearance and reputation rather than just a good brain. You don't have to be a model to attract the ram but you need to have something slightly unusual and sexy about you. Aries likes to feel involved with someone before sleeping with him or her though later may admit that it was just pure and lustful sex after all. Aries hates to hurt other people's feelings and sometimes can be seen as being ruled by a partner. However, if the ram does follow the partner's lead all the time it will lead to boredom, which makes them an easy target for a new lover or a new flirtation. Surprisingly, Aries can sometimes be indifferent to sex, and this can be an issue of control. They like to be in control in a relationship and if they feel they are not they may cool off. When their sex drive is high it is very very high but when it is low it is non-existent.

You will probably have been attracted to your Aries by the movement of his or her mouth. Whatever shape the lips, Aries tends to make the sort of pout that gives you 'come and get me' signals. If, on the other hand, Aries doesn't like you as you approach then you will get the coldest of stares and will be made to feel you don't even exist. Watch this sign when on the drink. They tend to develop a bit of a wink, but it's usually all just harmless fun. It could also be the nervous reaction that most people born under this sign experience from time to time.

Let's get down to the nitty-gritty then. Are they any good at it? Yes, is the answer to that one, you'll be pleased to hear. 'When they are in the mood' is the other answer, I must add, because if they don't want it then you are not going to get it, it's as simple as that.

Aries people need in a partner someone who is as warm and loving as they themselves are. They also need someone with a high sex drive. Sex is one of the most important things in a relationship to the ram and I have known them to stay in relationships far longer than was really sensible just because the hanky-panky was to their liking. Try playing hard to get and stay a little aloof, for nothing will arouse Aries' curiosity more. They also need someone who is willing to try out new things, so if your idea of good sex is restricted to the bedroom then you'd better forget it! Planes, trains and automobiles are all possible places for passion in the Aries rulebook.

Be warned, though, that if there is something you do when making love that he or she does not like, you will be told, right down to the most personal of details. But if you try to do the same then you won't see them for dust. All in all sex with this sign is not an easy game and one must have a sense of humour to even think about entering into it!

TRUEST NEED AND DESIRE

HEATED AND SPONTANEOUS SEX

Marriage Partners at a Glance

This is just a taster. For more detail, turn to the chapter called Between the Sheets.

BEST BETS

ARIES gives you what you need and will understand how you feel about life, love and of course sex, but selfishness between the two of you could well become a problem in the bedroom.

GEMINI will stimulate Aries' mind and body and both usually crave changes in life at the same time.

LEO will make the ram feel attractive and this pair will still have their hands all over each other when they pass 100.

LIBRA is the ram's polar opposite and will provide all that has been missing in life, both mentally and physically.

SAGITTARIUS can stimulate and annoy at the same time, so a little in small doses is what is required here. The sex can be fantastic.

FAIR CHANCE

CANCER will give Aries the sex life the ram desires but may put too many demands on this forward-thinking sign.

SCORPIO is sexy but may try to take the lead a little too much. Aries, mind you, just can't resist the pull and helped along by their shared ruling planet Mars they will taunt each other to distraction.

CAPRICORN is sensual to the ram but a little too predictable. Duties that take away the goat's attention are not always acceptable for the limelight-craving Aries.

AQUARIUS will provide the support and the class that Aries needs, and will also boost their social life beautifully too.

HEAVY WEATHER

TAURUS is just too much of a stick-in-the-mud and will also put a rein on finances.

VIRGO will be too staid and boring and won't allow the ram's wild side to come out. They rub each other up the wrong way once too often.

PISCES is too much. It's all right to have one wild

partner but both of you? Could just be a recipe for disaster.

Top Ten Turn-offs

1 Planned weekends. Aries wants to explore.
2 Partners who have to work late at night.
3 Smelly feet.
4 Dirty underwear.
5 Cheap perfume or aftershave.
6 Presents that have been asked for. Aries wants and needs surprise.
7 People who snort when they laugh.
8 Broken promises.
9 Heart-to-hearts. Aries will speak when ready to.
10 Smokers. Aries can smoke but you can't.

HOW TO SEDUCE ARIES

The first thing you need to do is make sure that you smell nice – and expensive. Aries can't stand cheap smells and will avoid you if he or she thinks that you are a cheap date too. Pick somewhere different and interesting. You'll score top points if you can pick a location that even well-informed Aries has never been to before.

Show that you are interested in many things in life. Predictable, boring and staid lives don't impress Aries. Say that one day you could imagine just packing up and taking off round the world and adventure-loving Aries will jump for joy that you are the perfect playmate. You may also want to try offering a nice head massage. Aries rules the head and this is a very sensitive part of the body. Who knows where it could lead if you play your cards right!

Don't be frightened to talk about yourself. Aries are always interested in other people's life stories. But don't moan – no sob stories please. Keep the conversation light and unpredictable. And keep an open mind about the date. You could just as easily find yourself at the local airport bar talking about exotic holidays as you could down the local pub.

The ram does, I have to say, like money. If you want to spread a bit of the old dosh around it won't go down badly. Aries loves to think up get-rich-quick schemes, but don't even think of suggesting that you go into business together. Love and work do not mix success-fully long-term, never have and never will.

I must make a serious point here. If you are embarking on your first date with Mr or Ms Aries, take their selfishness in hand from day one or you will never have any control. It is no use five years down the line saying that you never liked the way they started eating their meal before yours arrived or how you've always hated them squeezing the toothpaste from the wrong end – it's too late then.

Dates are great fun to Aries. You mustn't expect the phone call afterwards, even if your Aries declared undying love or managed to seduce you into the bedroom. Unpredictability is what it's all about for this sign. You would be far better to leave it mysterious from your end too, and then you are more likely to return home and find a dozen messages on your answering machine. Better still, try not to sleep with them on the first date. I know a million Aries are going to hate me for saying so but unless you leave them with something else to find out about you then there is no real reason for them to call again. If you want to know a magic trick for your first date with an Aries, then here it is. You must ask your date lots of questions. Interrogate him or her about likes and dislikes. But softly softly. Don't delve too deep too soon or you'll only get a barrel of lies. Subtlety and genuine interest will soon draw the information from these very delectable lips.

Make sure that you let Aries know your intentions, whether by a lingering touch on the shoulder or a whisper in the ear. Give some sort of a signal to send your date away dreaming of you. Oh and one last hint: leave something behind for them to look at and to mull over later. But make it something tasteful – not underwear, please.

Tell-tale Signs that Aries has Fallen

Aries sometimes walks with the head sticking out in a distinctive way. Aries in love walks around with the head sticking out even more, looking around to make sure that everyone is watching. Aries people are proud of their partners and even a woman of this sign will usher her partner into the room first as if presenting a prize trophy. Don't always expect them to talk highly about the love of their lives though. It is not unknown for the ram to talk like a baby to their partner when they are on their own and then to trash them to high heaven when backs are turned. It's a little bit of a pride thing and they don't want friends around them to think that they have been shot in the heart with cupid's arrow. They prefer to give the impression that they are in control and that they could finish with this person whenever they chose, though the truth is probably that they depend on this person's every word for their reason to live.

You may think that the partner you see Aries with is an odd match, but you would be wrong, for Aries' taste is extremely individual. The ram does not suffer fools gladly, and you can be sure that these two wouldn't be together if the ram didn't want it that way.

If you are the partner, don't expect Aries to get home from work on time, no matter how much he or she loves you. The ram will run into a thousand and one problems on the journey home and the stories could range from helping an old lady home with her shopping to saving the world from an evil villain. Aries are terrible time-keepers, but the good news is that they often arrive home with a surprise gift. If it's underwear, don't be fooled. It's for their pleasure not yours. But you've probably already worked that out. And don't be surprised to be taken shopping and convinced into buying things you wouldn't have even thought about trying on. Aries is in love with you, so you must go along with it. If you want to keep Aries in love with you then don't ever tire of the ram's excitement for life and the need constantly to explore and experiment. Maybe you have got each other on a leash, but the whole point of a union with this sign is that neither of you should ever admit it.

Aries can be tight with money but there is usually a

good reason for it. This sign knows how to have fun without drawing hundreds of pounds out of the bank. Once a friend of mine with an Aries partner said to me, 'It's wonderful. We could have fun together waiting at a bus stop. That's when I realized that a relationship is about who you're with, not just where you go with them.' I've repeated this many times to friends who complain their boyfriends never take them anywhere expensive or flash. Of course, Gemini is always unimpressed by this comment, but Pisces and Libra know exactly what I'm talking about.

ARIES PEOPLE IN YOUR LIFE

This section tells you about the people you work, rest and play with.

Aries in the Workplace

The Aries boss is always in a hurry and tends to hand out important or vital work at the very last minute. Expect to arrive home late from work many a night. Fortunately, the ram loves people, is very under-standing and has the patience of a saint, so is mostly good to work with. Aries bosses get involved in your problems and do whatever possible to help. If you want to change your holiday or take time off for a wedding, they will always fix it. Need a loan for a problem you've run into? If the funds are there (and are not their funds to hand out) then you can be sure they'll give them to you. It is a bit different if it is their own money. Catch them on a good day with their money and you are well away but catch them on a normal day and you would have more luck getting money from a stranger.

Aries are great in social jobs, somehow always managing to find the right words to say at the right time. As an inventor or an innovator they are likely to succeed but I cannot guarantee that they will keep the money they make. The idea is more important than the longevity of a project so they'd be better off selling their idea so that someone else could see it through to the end.

You often see lecturers that are born under this sign. They could talk the hind legs off a donkey! I would be a little bit careful if I were you, though, for you cannot always be sure that what they say is 100 per cent gold-plated truth.

Motor mechanic is a good job for an Aries – but not in the local garage. It would have to be somewhere exciting such as the pit at a Formula One race.

Aries can see through false flattery or praise and prefer those who are loyal to them. Betray them and you may as well leave immediately. They need to know that those around them are allies, and one lie or betrayal is as bad as twenty. Sometimes they are unwise in business, seeing only as far as they want to. Large areas of responsibility can be left completely untouched.

The Aries sense of humour is likely to be much appreciated in the workplace and is one of the things that makes them so popular. They can laugh publicly at their own mistakes and have even been known to help out colleagues by taking the blame for things they haven't done. They tend not to keep proper hours with their work. If they like their job they will stay all night if necessary. If they don't like it they will skive off better than any teenager can, and will not understand what happened when they get given their marching orders.

Aries people in the workplace can be the biggest asset or the biggest liability, but you can't help loving them anyway.

The Aries Mother-in-law

This is a woman who will let you know whether or not she likes you the first time she meets you. She may not even have to say a word. Everything she is thinking will be written all over her face. Or she may come out with one of her classic comments, like, 'So you are actually thinking of staying in England then? You don't fancy somewhere else, like Mars?' She would rather her son or daughter played the field before settling down. If you married your Aries spouse young, be prepared for a mother-in-law who suspects you of having pushed her child into marriage.

She will be a great grandmother. She knows all the best places to take the grandchildren to and she'll buy them the trendiest and newest gear at Christmas. This will make them popular at school, something she understands the necessity of. There is a downside as well as an upside, of course. Her grandson will get the latest football strip, but she'll also convince him that he can play for England if he keeps in with her. She won't keep every promise she makes, but she will keep most of them, which is the main thing.

She is great fun. She'll party with the best of them, be the star turn at Christmas and birthdays, and always be ready with a dry quip to make you laugh when you are feeling down. She may say things she doesn't mean at times, so try to let any negative comments go over your head. It's really not worth getting into any bother for. Her sense of humour will see you through the darkest of days and she will always help you out of a crisis. She won't, I'm afraid, help you out of a scrape. Only major crises will do.

If she asks you round for dinner, don't expect it to be served on time. If she tells you she's cooking steak, then get your mouth juiced up for fish because she's bound to change her mind at the last minute. You'll love it when she's had a drink or two for she will come out with how tenderly she really feels towards you and will even confess the things she's done wrong to you over the years. But don't even think about expecting her to admit it the next morning.

She will, I'm sorry to say, report bad things about you to her friends, but that's her job. She wouldn't be an Aries mother-in-law if she didn't tell people how bad you are at washing your sheets or how your children have needed new shoes for at least a month, but she'll be showing her friends pictures of your new three-piece suite and kitchen units at the same time. Life with an Aries mother-in-law can be heaven and hell at the same time, but with the great gifts she'll get you for Christmas it's sure to be worth the bother. If she remembers to turn up on time, that is. And don't give her too much mulled wine or she'll convince herself that Aunt Susie would much rather have the tickets for Rome she's bought you and you would much rather have a new corset with silk lining she'd bought for Aunt Susie.

Aries Children

These slightly clumsy children like plenty of attention. If they do have a tantrum, it is unlikely to last long as Fire signs use up their energy quickly. As quickly as they start to scream they will flake out from using up so much vigour.

They will have plenty of friends and a sympathetic ear for tales of woe. Birthday parties will prove expensive for there will be a wide range of different personalities coming to share in the fun. The teenage years can be tricky. They will be either very good or very naughty, depending on which friend is influencing them at that time.

At around age eleven they start revealing what sort of a teenager they will be. This is a good time to curb any bad habits. They are unlikely to want to listen to advice from parents since they prefer to learn their lessons in life the hard way. You need to use clever tactics. To encourage them to learn you should provide them with incentives for they are all too quick to get bored. Support and persistence are essential if you are to see them through to the success.

During the school years, think of getting them some private lessons in public speaking. They are likely to have a flair for it and if you can perfect this you might have the next Prime Minister on your hands.

They are naturally good with their hands and a keyboard is also an essential tool for them to master, even if only for personal use. They are sure to get hours of pleasure from tapping away and this is probably the only means of guaranteeing that you get to hear from them in later years, especially as I have yet to see an Aries who is brilliant with pen and paper. Keyboards of the musical kind would also be a great gift for them, since they have a natural flair for music. Aries Lord Lloyd Webber is proof of this.

I must warn you that they are not quiet children. If you are planning to try to make an Aries baby, be aware of the pitfalls. They will not only speak when spoken to, but will come out with deadly comments at the worst moment, such as when they tell your mother-in-law that Daddy and Mummy had an argument about her today because she comes round too often. This kind of comment will roll off the tongue of the young Aries child.

However, they don't always express their own feelings very well when young. You may get a letter from school one day informing you that your little Tommy beat up Maisie in class today. What you don't know, however, is that lovely little Maisie has been taunting Tommy about his glasses for several months now. Aries children are like an explosion waiting to go off, but once they have done what is necessary they calm right down again.

They do give things their best shot. Try not to force them into things they don't like, but do encourage them to stick to the hobbies and sports you know they have an interest in or a knack for. Don't spend a fortune on accessories for their hobbies before you've established that their enthusiasm is genuine. Give it a month to make sure their keenness is real and save yourself a fortune.

Aries

Aries Friends

You can trust your Aries friends with secrets but you may not be able to count on them to be there when they say they will. What sounds great to do one day may not seem so tempting the next and so you may have to phone and double-check if you are expecting them to pick you up.

The great thing about this sign is its sense of humour. Aries friends always have the right words to say to make you feel better and the right words to say to make you laugh too. If you phone them in a crisis, they will go to great lengths to make sure you are OK. Although you can trust them with your secrets, don't be surprised to hear them told back to you and a crowd of friends a few months later with the names changed to protect the innocent.

They will hold many great parties and their house is sure to be a social one, unless they have picked a partner who refuses to pander to their whims. Then the late night at work will be a night down the local disco. Don't be embarrassed when Mr or Ms Aries still wants to go clubbing when well into their fifties. They want to be nosy and see what everyone else is doing and what the latest look is so that they can copy it when they get home.

I wouldn't say your Aries friends are trendy but they do have a certain je ne sais quoi about them that can turn heads. You won't be embarrassed by them but you may not be impressed either. They are bound to own one very expensive item of clothing or jewellery, the price of which they will happen to tell you every time they see you.

They adore children, and will get on great with your younger siblings or, if you have them, your children. If you are married then watch out. This sign can lead you astray very quickly. They won't talk about this directly but they'll drop the odd hint. They won't keep completely quiet about it, but once again names will have been changed to protect the innocent.

When Aries becomes your friend they will act as though they have found their other half and will call you twice a day just to make sure you still like them. Don't be shocked when they back off after a few months. You may think they no longer crave your company but that would not be true. They have found other new things to occupy them and you are still important but have just moved out of the limelight for a while – unless of course you hit crisis time, when they will be back on form like a real trouper.

They will spend their money on you but will expect you to spend double in return. They will trust you with some very dark secrets and it is no use telling them not to. They will tell you they have cheated on their loved ones but expect you to maintain your friendly loyalty to them. The cheek of it! Indeed, cheeky is a great word to sum up these friends, who are sure to provide you with years of entertainment. You may see them for five years and then not again for ten, but don't worry, they'll be back – and with a list of new places they are just dying to venture out to with you.

Taurus

April 21 to May 21

STUBBORN, SENSUAL, LOYAL, affectionate, materialistic and security-demanding: these are the key words to describe Taurus. Sincerity is also important to them and their warmth and genuine interest in the people around them make them a very popular companion, particularly to the opposite sex. They fairly exude dependability. They are utterly reliable, whether as a romantic partner, friend, confidant or in business, and no one need doubt that their word really is their bond. They are deep thinkers, avid seekers of knowledge, lovers of good literature, and very easy and interesting conversationalists. Their powers of persuasion are great and people usually love to hear them talk. Taurus, incidentally, is often an excellent after-dinner speaker, and great at wedding speeches, too. Taurus is the one who says the things the rest of us wouldn't dare. The reason they are such good speakers is partly to do with their enquiring minds. They like to know a lot about a wide variety of subjects and therefore are never at a loss for something interesting to say, and can say it with some conviction too. Actually, Taurus the bull is really rather clever, because it has mastered the art of quiet domination. Helpless on the surface, great powers of perseverance lurk beneath. When in a tight corner, Taurus can fend for itself very well indeed. This is another reason why Taurus is so attractive. Mr Taurus with his somewhat shy, helpless manner brings out the maternal urge in women, and Ms Taurus has the little-girl air about her which immediately makes men want to take care of her.

Personalities as warm, generous and attractive as these must also have drawbacks, albeit only smallish ones. One of these is that they are inclined to be possessive and suffer from jealousy. This is because they put a great deal into personal relationships. Their love or friendship is not given easily and they treasure the reciprocal feeling. I also have to say that they are a little moody at times. Never mind, for they have a generous disposition which applies both to money matters and to people, and their general outlook on life is broad. Theirs is not always a logical mind, as they tend to think and act on impulse. Their impulsiveness changes somewhat when they decide to marry or to move in with someone. Then they start to give more thought to their actions and become conscious of their responsibilities.

Fond of expensive clothes, Taurus's appearance is sometimes marred by lack of the artistic touch. They tend more often than not to be conservative about the way they dress. They are ultra-sensitive about just about everything, especially the impression they give to others. This is a sign that can often marry young as it is very hard for them not to get too serious too soon. Although they like to have fun, you won't often find men or women of this sign going for one casual relationship after another. They tend to go for characters who are very different from themselves, people you wouldn't expect them to be with.

They need stability and security, so if you can't handle your finances then forget it. That would be just as bad as cheating, to dear old Taurus. They need to know that they can come home to their favourite belongings and not see the bailiffs carrying them out. More often than not they end up living in the same town in which they were brought up and it would have to be some pretty swish surroundings to tempt them to pull up those roots and start anew. They are extremely sexy characters, though, and could talk their partners into doing almost anything with the sultry way they cock their head and look at you. They often have unusual voices and it could have been the voice that first attracted you. Look at a couple of famous examples: actors George Clooney and Jack Nicholson both use their sexy voices to woo women. Footballer David Beckham has an unusual voice too. The voice is often where the initial attraction to Mr or Ms Taurus sparks off. Another of the things that may attract you to Taurus is that he or she smells really good. Taurus knows how to wear a scent and can more often than not be found by following your nose.

Taurus really is one of the greatest flirts in the zodiac and anything that the bull has got in life has usually been acquired by a quick flutter of the eyelashes – this is from both the male and the female of the species. Taurus is pretty sharp at spotting a lucky opportunity too. The bull loves its work and an unhappy Taurus is one that is in the wrong career. Famous bulls in showbiz, sports and politics will often claim that they wanted from childhood to do what they are doing so successfully now. Actors Michelle Pfeiffer and Tori Spelling, tennis player André Agassi and Prime Minister Tony Blair are all famous examples.

Taurus likes to be boss. They have all at some time or another tried to take control of their careers by being the decision-maker, not just the loyal worker. But what I really love about these people is their ability to make a good home. They are brilliant at raising children. They create a safe and loving home environment in which the kids thrive, helping them to do really well both in and out of school. But I wouldn't like to cross the bull. When Taurus gets angry it charges like a bull and doesn't mind who gets hit in the process. You should be able to detect when Taurus is unhappy, though. You will see the steam is coming out of the bull's ears!

Don't be frightened to talk to Taurus. They can look pretty fierce when you first approach them but the best thing is to treat them as your equal. It is often only a fear of being disliked that makes them put up such a fierce front. They like consistency, and can find it hard to let go of the past. A former love is bound still to be in their phonebook or on their Christmas card list, which can make it rather hard if you yourself are the jealous kind.

A possible pitfall is that Taurus does like to have its routine, and for you it can be boring to come home and know that because it is Tuesday there will be cottage pie for tea. And Taurus does like food rather a lot, tending to put on a bit too much round the middle with age. The kindest way to stop this happening is to help the bull find a sport it likes, so that the extra pounds laid down thanks to that sweet tooth and that love of traditional meals and second helpings can be burned off.

Be good to the bull and you will be treated like royalty, but cause hurt and the bull will be downright rotten, and will not think twice about calling you vicious names in public. Taurus likes to look at life straight on. These people refuse to wear rose-tinted glasses as many of the other signs do. They are productive people, who are also likely to have green fingers. Indeed I have a Taurus friend who visits our Scorpio home and she does a very good job of saving the beautiful plants that my husband and I have lovingly overwatered. Taurus enjoys the simple things in life. Even the famous bulls still like to cook their own food. There is nothing to them like taking out their own dinner from the oven. And they don't think twice about bringing friends round for dinner when you are planning on a cosy meal for two, but don't worry, there will be much whispering about plans for later that night when you are alone again. This is not a person to break promises, and if they do then they will go to the ends of the earth to make it up to you. As lover, friend or even just an acquaintance, this is sure to be a person you can count on – unless of course you hurt their pride. Then you can forget about it, at least until Christmas or birthdays come around when they just won't be able to stop themselves from picking up the phone. So that may well answer an old question of yours. Who did call on your birthday but didn't leave a message? Just remind yourself which old Taurus friend you are no longer in contact with and ring them straight back. They will be very happy to hear from you.

SECRETS OF THE SEXES

So how do the males and females of the species differ then? Let's have a look.

Ms Taurus

This woman can have a very nasty temper when the mood takes her, or if you do something wrong such as flirt with someone she doesn't like. You can flirt with a person she does like, strangely, but that is where it all gets confusing. She generally oozes personality and you will have a hard job catching her, but once you do you will have her for ever. She may talk about marriage and children on the first date, but don't worry, you haven't found a clinger, you've simply found a sign that was built for marriage and children and she is sussing out if you are a suitable mate. You would be well advised not to dally with her affections unless you are serious. Once she has set her sights on you then you haven't got a chance, so don't smile in her direction if you don't mean it. I am not saying she can be obsessive but I am saying she can be determined. You have only yourself to blame if you go in with your eyes closed. Once she is sure of you she will be in no hurry to get down the aisle. It is usually the men who are begging Ms Taurus to go down the aisle after the five-year mark. She will only have talked about marriage during the first year. Don't get me wrong, she does want to do it. It's just that she's too busy organizing your lives together to get down to the necessary details of booking the church. That will be down to you to do, but then she will come up with the colour scheme all worked out, right down to the napkins – even though she won't be able to tell you the name of the vicar.

She has a rather domineering streak, and you ought to control this from the beginning or you will find it hard to get out of the submissive role. Those people you have seen being shouted at by their spouses to hurry up and get the shopping in the car are probably married to Ms Taurus, but she will then proceed to take fifteen minutes to fumble and find her keys to start the car.

She is sensitive, so do your best not to hurt her. A warm and wonderful mother she makes, and she will not be afraid to get involved with her children's lives. Her children will have the kit they want way before any of the other kids because she will have been planning it for months. She is a talented woman so don't try to tie her to the house.

The flirting she does with your friends is to her completely acceptable. She expects you to know that she is only having fun. You see, the flirting is what I would call a surface characteristic with this woman. By that same token, though, she can have created quite a reputation for herself in her young days. I cannot say whether or not she took it further than flirting, but I know a lot of young bulls who did, though they may be more the exception than the rule. Ms Taurus goes from one extreme to the other. First of all she wants to go out with everyone, and then as she grows older she wants only one mate, and that mate has to be best friend, lover and a good cook all rolled into one.

Her career is extremely important to her and she will not take criticism about it lightly. If you say you don't think she is all that good at selling things then she will do a marketing course just to make sure that you cannot level the same accusation at her again. She is usually a brilliant cook and many Taurus people who make money like to open up restaurants with their spare cash. Jack Nicholson is a famous example of how even an actor couldn't resist putting his money where his mouth is. Food always lurks somewhere in Taurus's life. One little secret about this woman – she smells good and you should make sure that you smell good too. She just adores a man who wears a good strong scent. It's got to have quality and class, mind you. No cheap stuff.

She is usually a keen walker. Many men who have met their Taurus partner by chance have literally bumped into her. Don't expect a quick courtship. She will need to know all about you, and she will go to any means to find things out, even ringing your friends and family. Watch that address book. You never know where she may end up getting her information from.

Mr Taurus

Mr Taurus is one for the other boys of the zodiac to watch out for. This is the guy that women will pick out in a crowd because he will have that shine that the others don't. You know when you look at a man and think, that's the kind I'd marry, well, that's Mr Taurus. But be warned, ladies, because a few seconds later he'll be off charming someone else. He likes to work the room, does our single Mr Taurus.

He is a patient man, practical, artistic, conservative, honest, passionate and graceful. If you don't have enough money to go out then he will go to great lengths to cover your costs for you. He is without doubt one of the gallant men of the species. The man in the movie who throws his coat down in a puddle, that's Mr Taurus. He's a charmer, but he is also practical enough to know that he can't put it back on again, whereas Mr Scorpio or Mr Pisces would forget. He has a proud streak that many people mistake for vanity. But that's not to say that he isn't vain too. He likes to spend a lot of time and money on grooming and that face mask you find in his bathroom cabinet doesn't belong to an ex, it really is his. So don't throw it out or he'll be furious.

Taurus men make great husbands as they are even-tempered (at least until you upset him). If you do make him angry then watch out. He is a bull and an angry bull is a dangerous thing.

He is inclined to push you into the limelight and stay in the background himself. If he takes a shine to you he will be determined to get you and although he always has an appreciative eye for a pretty face, this is usually just to keep you interested. He likes to feel you are jealous; he thinks it keeps things fresh. He will even flirt with your best friend, though he will make sure that everyone knows it's just fun.

The first few months spent with this man can be just magical. He will treat you in a way that no other man has even dreamt of doing. But he will expect you to be ready when he picks you up, even if he is three hours late. I'm afraid that you are unlikely to be able to talk him into taking you very far afield on your adventures together. You see, practicality is his middle name. If it's raining he may even suggest that you stay in and eat, but watch out, this man has a habit of mixing food and sex – his two favourite things – so be careful what you order as a take away because it could get very messy indeed.

You may get looks from other people as this man ushers you in and out of a room as if you were a possession, but this is partly because of his natural dominance, and also a sign of love. He is clever with money so you're onto a good investment but don't expect him to spend too much on you. He might go overboard for a special item of jewellery or something for the home but on the whole he is sensible with money and would rather put money into your children's future than send them on the school skiing trip.

Boring at times, he will sometimes want space to himself. Make your stand from the very beginning or you just won't stand a chance. You must also make sure your home is in order when he first comes into it or you won't get past the first date. A messy home to him is a sign of a sure mismatch. (It's OK by him if his home is messy, by the way, so long as it is his mess.)

Treat him mean to keep him keen in the beginning. I know it may sound cruel but, believe me, it's good advice. My middle brother is a Taurus and he has lived with his girlfriend, whom I now call my sister-in-law through embarrassment, for the last ten years. He loves his food and is a fantastic cook. The first two possessions he bought for his home were a settee and a bed, the two most important things to him. As for his wedding, well, it still isn't booked, but he can tell you what tie he will be wearing on the day. My sister-in-law wanted to go on holiday to Thailand but my brother wouldn't even think about venturing so far afield. After postponing her dream for year after year, she finally booked a ticket to go without him. Love won the day as a week later he booked a ticket to go with her. Sometimes you just have to push this stubborn sign hard. It will be worthwhile.

SEXUAL NEEDS

Taurus needs a person who allows them to dominate. Cat and dog fights all the time are no good. A bit of a spark from time to time that gets made up in the bedroom – that's fine. But they don't want to be falling out all the time. It's not healthy for them, nor for their partners come to that. Very few people can fully satisfy this demanding sign. Older Taurus people will probably admit that they have difficult ways; those in their teens and twenties will hotly deny it.

The older Taurus gets (wait for it – this is a good bit)

the better the sex tends to become. They think up new things all the time, whereas some of the other signs of the zodiac (no names mentioned) tend to want the same over and over again. Taurus like it over and over again but they like to experiment too, which for couples in their forties can prove pure bliss. Married or living with a boring Taurus? Then just mention how you'd like to make love on a boat and they will whisk you off sooner than you can say the word pleasuredome. But just don't expect it to be Sydney Bay they take you to. They don't like to go too far from home. You could just end up with toy boats in the bath, but don't worry, there will be plenty of candles around to get you in the perfect mood.

This is a sign that is dominant in lovemaking and those that claim not to be have not discovered the full extent of their sexuality yet. This may be down to something that happened in an early relationship, but whatever the reason, they should try to uncover their true physical needs. They could be missing out on an awful lot of fun if they don't. Don't expect them to tell you that they love you all of the time. This is a sign that speaks through actions and not words. Lovemaking to Taurus is like a work of art and they will be very proud of making you happy, so whatever you do, please don't let them think they've pleased you when they haven't. This is one sexy sign. Sex will not just be about the act itself but it will be about the way they sit, or cross their legs, or even the way they dress. All this can speak volumes about how they feel about you. A Taurus in the first throes of love is a fashion statement to be reckoned with, but a broken-hearted bull is a walking fashion disaster. We are talking tracksuit heaven here.

Now, please don't get me wrong, Taurus doesn't want to be with you all of the time. It's just that you need to be 'thinking' about him or her all the time. So that means the odd little phone call here or a text message on the mobile there.

Slow, long and lingering kisses are a must. If you even think about pulling away your affections then watch out, they will withdraw sexual favours quicker than you can blow them a kiss. There will be no hesitation about venturing out to find someone else to fill the void.

Taurus people are great and masterful lovers and they also know how to treat you when you are feeling down, but their main need is that you return the favour and know when to give them the love and attention they seek. You also have to know when to back off, but they will tell you just by the look in their eye. It is up to you not to push them.

All in all their sexual needs are strong but they are needs that any person with an appetite for love will be willing to give in to and even relish and enjoy for many years to come.

TRUEST NEED AND DESIRE

DOMINANCE

Marriage Partners at a Glance

This is just a taster. For more detail, turn to the chapter called Between the Sheets.

BEST BETS

VIRGO will help the bull keep his or her life in order and will also make sure that dinner is on time, a priority for a food lover like the bull.

CAPRICORN will understand Taurus's needs: when to go out, when to stay in and how to sizzle in the bedroom.

SCORPIO is the bull's polar opposite. These two can fill in the missing blanks in each other's lives and can turn each other on with just a flutter of the eyelashes.

FAIR CHANCE

CANCER is a great friend and lover but can be a little moody at times. Cancer doesn't know when to end an argument so these two often end up in stalemate.

LIBRA will be a little too changeable for Taurus but will brighten up the days and put a skip in the bull's step.

LEO will look good on Taurus's arm and can keep the laughter going for years, but may be a little too social for the bull's liking.

PISCES is fun but dangerous and may take things too far, even for a daredevil like Taurus.

TAURUS and Taurus will understand each other but will also end up with horns locked for months over even the smallest of issues.

HEAVY WEATHER

GEMINI is way too much of a flirt for Taurus, who can turn heads but also knows how far (i.e. not too far) to take the fun, unlike lovable Gemini.

SAGITTARIUS is too far out for the bull and will not supply the security or sense of predictability the bull needs.

AQUARIUS is too busy talking about his or herself to indulge Taurus in the way the bull would like.

ARIES is the worst marriage partner for Taurus: different time clocks and sometimes different planets.

Top Ten Turn-offs

1 Bad breath
2 Liars
3 Houses with no personality
4 People who won't say I love you
5 Bad cooks
6 Small portions of food and bad service in restaurants
7 Partners who work night shifts
8 People who drink too much
9 People who talk too much
10 People with voices louder than Taurus's own

HOW TO SEDUCE TAURUS

The first thing that you will need to do is check up on your restaurants and make sure you pick a good one. A bad eating-place is a great insult to the bull who will expect you to know that the environment and service of any eating establishment is just as important as the clothes and perfume you choose to wear. Don't take Taurus anywhere too crowded either. An intimate setting with good food and wine is far better than any noisy club for a first date. (Don't get me wrong. The bull can party with the best of them. But this is not the occasion.) Since the three most important things to Taurus are food, sex and money, if you can combine the three on the first date it could turn out to be the date of a lifetime.

You must make an effort to tell your Taurus date about your past, even if you don't like talking about it yourself. You see, the bull needs to get a firm picture of what you are like as a family man or woman. A great idea is to go up to a small child when you are out and make a fuss. Taurus just adores home-makers and this will put you miles out in front for very little effort. (Just think of yourself as a politician!)

Taurus likes people who know how to do the simple things in life well. It is not about wearing designer clothes and ordering à la carte, but it is more to do with dressing well and then ordering decent and good-tasting food. This date will expect the best but will also expect you to pay your share, if not pick up the whole bill. The bull wants to see you invest something in him or her, in order to judge whether or not you have serious intentions.

It is not unusual for Taurus to let you know how he or she feels about you rather quickly and this can happen in one of two ways. You'll be invited home if you've made the grade, and the door will slam in your face if you haven't. You see, home is very important to the bull and opening it up to you will show how much respect you have earned.

A word from the wise. Whatever you do, don't even think about taking food from Taurus's plate. No matter how sexy or fun it may seem at the time, the bull will take it as a great insult if you dare to touch his or her food without permission. Only if invited may you venture near your partner's plate. You could find yourself dumped quicker than a pile of hot bricks if you don't obey this rule.

You should find a date with this sign great fun, for Taurus is full of amusing and interesting conversation, and will fill you in on family anecdote until you feel you already know Uncle Bob and Auntie Flora. Taurus is dependable and will not tell you any lies. It will be held against you if you make up any porkies, so better not. The bull will find out and you will end up feeling like a fool.

Use your first date to establish the ground rules. The bull will be confused and unhappy if you change them later, so get them set down at the start. Be prepared, though, to have to put up with your partner flirting with others, and for them to expect you to be an exhibitionist as and when they say, and to be calm when they require that too. But don't worry. Just tune in to this sexy sign and the rest will come naturally.

Tell-tale Signs that Taurus has Fallen

Taurus in love is quite a funny sight. The love-struck bull will spend days if not months walking about with nose up in the air expecting all around to notice the wonderful new glow that surrounds them. He or she also tends to speak in a more sensual voice when in the throes of passion. I am not talking Greta Garbo here but a definite lowering of the voice as if to impart a secret (and that's just to order a drink at the bar).

Taurus does, I'm afraid, tend to eat more when in love and so the first year of a relationship can see the bull putting on a few pounds, usually around the waist and neck. He or she will also go to great lengths to show the loved one how passionate these feelings are. Numerous gifts will be bought, each of them full of significance. You may think it is an insult when you get a new set of pots and pans but to the bull that is just a way of showing commitment and trust for the future.

Expect a little embarrassment at first as the bull likes to show its affection in public and will not mind calling across a crowded store to ask 'cuddlebum' to come over to the counter. After a while you will forget the pet names and start to enjoy instead the kind of attention that only a person born under this sign can give to you.

Now, if you want to talk about sex, then this is the sign to do it with, for they can give off more steam than a kettle. But first you need to make sure that you continue to lavish as much attention on your lover as you did on the first day you met. If your eyes start to wander for even just a second then Taurus will be off flirting with your best friend. You will also have to spend money on your Taurus lover if you are to prove year after year that you are still in love. A Taurus who says at Christmastime 'let's not bother with presents this year' is talking out of . . . well, let's just say that this is unconvincing. Taurus wants every bit of sparkly stuff your eyes can find and if you leave the price tag on so much the better.

One of the things you can be sure of is that you're getting value for money because the bull really does give his or her all to a lover, unlike many of the other signs (mentioning no names). As a dominant sign, Taurus will show his or her true feelings through actions and not words. If you have had an argument and your partner is still willing to make love to you then you can rest assured that it is not a serious tiff. You will still be together next week. It is only when Taurus withholds affection and attention (like their polar opposite, Scorpio) that you must start to worry, for then offence has been taken and it will take some serious creeping and crawling to get back into your lover's heart – and bedroom.

If this is meant to be then nothing will stop you from being together. These marriages can last for ever. Just keep an eye on that growing family – unless it has always been your ambition to start a family football team!

TAURUS PEOPLE IN YOUR LIFE

This section tells you about the people you work, rest and play with.

Taurus in the Workplace

Chances are that the owner or chef of your favourite restaurant or take away is Taurus. The bull loves food so much that more often than not he or she has a brush with the food business at some point in a career. The bull loves cash too, so look in your local bank if you want a Taurus partner to share your days with. To be able to touch money is pure bliss to this lover of the stuff; they will spend hours imagining it's theirs.

Taurus loves to mix with people but prefers to do it on home turf. If Taurus people are in a place where they feel they do not have authority, they can often feel unprofessional or inferior, and this can reflect quite dramatically on the success and drive that those around them witness.

They don't miss a trick and their bark is much worse than their bite. If your boss shouts at you when angry then you are probably getting off lightly. Other signs as bosses will throw things or sack their staff on the spot, but Taurus will just have a good old moan and then carry on as normal hoping that you have learnt your lesson.

Typical Taurus professions are singing and dancing. Taurus is very good with its voice and light on its feet. Bono and Joe Cocker are true-to-form bulls, so too, in a sense, is footballer David Beckham.

The Taurus boss will be a sergeant-major one day and a mate the next, and then a stranger on day three. Colleagues can never anticipate a boss like this and moods can change in seconds. Don't think for a moment that you can get away two hours early just because the boss is smiling at you. The bull is testing you to see if you would dare to cross the wonderful line that has been drawn for you at work.

Bulls command respect, but things have to be done their way or not at all. They do not take kindly to anything done without their approval, regardless of the results. They look upon their staff and workmates as their children. This is the sign that you will see in the washroom with a queue of people revealing their problems. They are brilliant at listening to people's problems. If the Samaritans charged and a Taurus was the boss then they would make a fortune.

Taurus likes to hold the reins and usually does so very well. These people are capable of making a lot of money for those around them but are also tempted from time to time to get greedy and to ask for more than they should. They drive themselves too hard and are not very good at shifting responsibility onto someone else. They want to make sure that they get the job done as they see fit and not as someone else thinks is right.

It is not very easy to work for Taurus but the bull does make it worth your while in the end. Christmas bonuses are nearly always a sure thing, as is the odd gift from time to time. Don't turn down an invitation to a family dinner – this will give great offence.

Taureans are ambitious and expect the same from those around them. However hard they climb, they have always got their sights set higher. Their staff love them one day and hate them the next. They expect people to read their minds as to how things should be done. If they get anything wrong a natural flair for diverting the blame to lie at someone else's feet comes into play. All in all this is a sign that makes life fun if you work with them and unpredictable if you work for them. They will take you to great places, ensure that you never feel blue and always provide a shoulder for you to cry on when the going gets tough.

Love Stars

The Taurus Mother-in-law

I really do love Taurus the bull, but as a mother-in-law, oh dear! She probably even had a hand in the selection of you. She may have been planning the marriage of her child since nursery school. She will, however, have ensured that her child got to go to the best parties so it's not all doom and gloom, even if the child did have to sit down to a square meal before going.

If she says no she means no and there is no changing her mind. If you try to go via one of her close ones to persuade her then you may as well use the front page of the newspaper to declare an out-and-out war.

She will do her best to persuade you to have lots of children because she adores large families. She can really cook, too, so daughter- or son-in-law may have a hard time living up to her standards. Never mind. She will come over and fill up your freezer for you. However, she won't stop going on about it for months. Indeed, she will tell all of her friends what an unfit wife or husband you are, so don't bother with that one unless you really are dire with the domestics.

She may not give you the space you crave so try to establish the right lifestyle from day one. It is no use spending weekend after weekend with her the first year of your marriage only to say you are busy every other weekend the following year. She will take it as a snub and will make your life a misery.

No matter how nice your house, she would much rather have you round to hers, even if it's your party. But don't get too down. Your friends will love her and will probably spend hours in the kitchen (her favourite room) telling her their sexual problems.

She is a little two-faced, I'm afraid. No matter how nice she is to your face she cannot stop herself from making the odd jibe behind your back. It may not even be true – she is a terrific storyteller. Best idea is to get her round at children's bedtime each night. She will tell them wonderful tales and get them all off to sleep for you.

You better had be married, by the way. Don't expect her to approve of living together. She may say she doesn't mind but she is old-fashioned deep down. She would rather be able to introduce you as her son- or daughter-in-law than as 'the person my child is co-habiting with'.

This is not the best choice for a mother-in-law but make her part of your life and you will have a friend who is fun and worthy and will never let you down – unless, that is, you let her child down. Then it's World War Three, for she will go to the ends of the Earth to protect her own. She makes a great grandmother too, and spends hours thinking of how she can make life easier for you.

This earth sign is a mother-in-law whom you will cherish, relish and hate all at the same time, but the moment you're feeling ill you can bet she'll be there with a remedy and a word of encouragement. Don't be too hard on her. She has more love to give than anyone could possibly realize.

Taurus Children

Watch this child for he or she is a bit of a rogue. Be prepared for other children's parents to complain that their child will no longer cross the road for fear of the bogey man, thanks to your child. The little bull knows how to tell a tale and will make up many a tall story to while away the time.

They are very stubborn schoolchildren. If there's a problem, don't just force them into school. They are likely to play truant by hiding out and watching videos all day. Instead you must address the problem as a serious one and treat them as an adult if you want to build a trusting and honest relationship with them.

They like their sweets but watch that they don't end up needing to be in the dentist's chair too often. If they say they have had one bag then you can bet they've had three. They have plenty of friends and do have a tendency to get interested in the opposite sex a little too young. Sex education for this sign is a must as soon as possible – if you want to avoid becoming a grandparent in your prime, that is.

They are terrific at relating to people of all ages and you must not be surprised if they go around with a group a lot older than them. Just make sure that the group is a positive and not a negative influence. These are strong personalities who are not frightened to voice their likes and dislikes, but try not to let them come across as arrogant. What you see is what you get and if they say they are going to be prime minister or president then don't doubt them. They really do mean it. The faith they have in their destiny leads this child to success, but it is not all fun and sunlight with this bundle of joy. You must be prepared that they will treat your house as a hotel and when they want feeding they will not take kindly to any delays. If you say dinner is at six and they come in at two minutes to, they expect to see it on the table on time. They will not back down easily in an argument, which can be embarrassing in public. There is your six-year-old Taurus shouting at you, 'No, mother, I've told you I'm not doing that!'

They will attract admirers far too soon for any parent's liking and will prefer to have friends of the opposite sex than of their own. It is not just the attention that it creates. They really do prefer to have someone of the other gender around them and that is why their partners later in life are usually their best friends too.

They like their social life and will probably like all of the latest soaps as well. It is not unknown for a teenage bull to pass up a date for a crucial episode of a favourite programme.

Don't expect a Taurus child to defer to you all the time. They think they know the best way to get something done, even when they are very young, and they will not walk, talk or potty train until absolutely ready.

They can eat plenty, so lock the cookie cupboard or you could just end up with a very attractive, funny but roly-poly child. Whatever your Taurus child does in life, he or she will bring you great joy.

Taurus Friends

As long as you act like a friend then the bull will treat you like a friend but if you step out of line then the bull will go out of its way to put you back in your place, including reminding you of everything that has ever been done for you. You may even get a bill for all the times you've been paid for over the years, and you'll be expected to pay it too. Although the bull's wrath is not as bad as Scorpio's, it is not far off.

But this isn't what usually happens. The bull is a great friend. If you want someone to tell your problems to then you have found the perfect sign. Taurus, along with Virgo, is the one who will give up an entire evening just to sit and listen to you blow off steam about your lover, your mother-in-law or your boss. The bull may not come up with the best advice but at least the advice will be from the heart.

Your bull friend will, however, flirt with your partner. This is not to get up your nose, it is just the way your friend is. This is a demanding friend, too. You will be expected to give your all to the friendship and if invited to a dinner party you'd better accept. These friendships are, however, usually lifelong ones. Taurus likes to spend time with people he or she shares memories with. Then, just to embarrass you, he or she will talk about sex very openly.

Treat Taurus well and Taurus will treat you better. However, you are not allowed to have as many acquaintances as your Taurus friend. On a night out, make sure you have plenty of money because Taurus can last the distance better than most and will know where all the latest hotspots are. Taurus will have fun on the dance floor, and probably a funny way of dancing too – this is not a subtle sign. I have always imagined John Travolta's character in *Saturday Night Fever* to be Taurus from the way he walks with his head stuck out, strutting his stuff and giving his all on the dance floor. The way this character loved women was also typically

Taurus, flirting with anyone who would cast a glance his way and willing only to work at the things that he enjoyed in life.

This is a friend you can trust but also one who is rather domineering and expects to get a lot back from the friendship. Do not lend Taurus any money. This has broken up many a good relationship with someone born under this sign. Taurus forgets that you lent it quicker than you can remember to ask for it back. However, Taurus can introduce you to the right people and I know many a marriage that Taurus has been responsible for, simply by pushing people together who didn't have the nerve to approach each other.

One last thing to remember. If you arrange to go out with your Taurus friend, you will find him or her completely reliable. You will never be let down. And don't take Taurus for granted or think that this makes for a dull person. Taurus, who likes to experience everything in life, is sure to take you on an exciting journey, attracting many appealing and sometimes very different faces into your life.

Gemini
May 22 to June 21

GENEROUS, RESTLESS, ADAPTABLE, excitable, fickle and two-sided: these are the key words to describe Gemini. The twins illustrate Gemini's instinct to share. In almost every aspect Gemini has a dual personality. This sometimes makes Gemini rather difficult to understand, as I'm sure you can imagine, for these individuals are seldom on an even keel. They are unpredictable: either flat on the floor or up there on cloud nine. However, this is exactly where their magnetism lies, and it ensures them a constant stream of admirers.

To those around them, Gemini people are a mystery. They hold the interest of others very well, but few people know how to handle them. Their versatility keeps those around them on their toes. Being such an attractive character is marvellous, of course, but the very thing that makes them so, their quicksilver nature, is also pretty hard on their constitution. The energy they have in abundance is nervous energy, but they can burn this up. Gemini people frequently suffer from nervous exhaustion. I know that Geminis find it hard to relax but I advise them to try. Their batteries must be recharged or they will never achieve all of the many things they have planned for themselves.

In spite of their somewhat complex characters, Geminis are generally easy to get along with. They make pleasant and interesting company at social gatherings since their own enjoyment is so apparent and so infectious that it works on the entire company. Geminis are warm-hearted with a soft spot for children and old people. They go out of their way to help anyone in need. It is only people who are as strong as they are, or even stronger, whom they find hard to help. The green-eyed monster steps in and on comes a new attitude: 'Let them sort themselves out!'

Ms Gemini loves children but finds looking after her own a bit of a handful. Indeed, all domestic routine is a little irksome to her. Not too organized in this direction, she frequently longs to get away from it all. Mr Gemini also loves children and animals. When he marries he will expect a lot of mothering and looking after. It is not a far-off possibility that neither Mr or Ms Gemini has picked up a vacuum cleaner for at least a month. In fact to have picked up the vacuum cleaner only a month ago would be good form.

Gemini is fond of expensive and good clothes. Buy Gemini a designer jumper and you've got a very happy friend indeed. This is much better than cash, because Geminis like others to spend money on them. They won't spend it on themselves, you see, only on the ones they love. They have a lot of lovely traits. It is just sometimes hard to see them all under that somewhat tough exterior.

Highly intelligent and capable of doing great things, people born under this sign find concentration for any length of time difficult. For this reason they usually prefer to have authority rather than be ruled by it. They have the qualities to succeed well on their own but sometimes take on rather more than they can handle and in this way create trouble for themselves. Grinding away at any one thing for any length of time bores them to distraction. Come to think of it, that includes marriage, or any partnerships for that matter. They need a steadying influence. It is no good for them to go out with or even just be friends with someone who encourages their reckless streak. This will lead them to self-destruction. If you love your Gemini friend or lover and know you are a bad influence, then step away for their sake.

It is not unknown for Gemini to marry twice or even have two lovers. They want to make sure that they are not missing out on anything. My Gemini uncle Leo Petulengro – who funnily enough is one of twins; how truly Gemini can you get? – has displayed some typical traits over the years, such as writing great pieces of work while working in a bar to help out a friend. He lives life as he sees fit and is just as happy talking to a person who doesn't have two pennies to rub together as to a millionaire from Hollywood. I've seen him do both!

Gemini

He has a way of adapting himself to any situation. If you are a Gemini and feel that you cannot do this, then learn. It is part of your personality and you could be neglecting a brilliant talent.

Gemini give off mixed signals. At times it is hard to know if these people really like you or not. And because Gemini likes to move on quickly, it may turn out that just as you fall for one of them as a friend or lover, they have moved onto the next new face, just to be sure they are not missing anything. But I must emphasize that Gemini really is one of the best friends you could have. If you throw a bash of some sort you will notice how it is incomplete without your Gemini friend to throw in a bit of fun and mischief. Just don't expect to have your Gemini friend all to yourself. These people are so adaptable and versatile that they are sure to have many friends. You will not often see all of these friends mixed together, however. There are far too many of them and anyway Gemini's taste for so many different kinds of people means that, put all together in a room, their personalities would soon clash.

Walk into a bar and look for the person who is hosting ten conversations at once. Go and tell this person that you think he or she is a Gemini. You have a very good chance of being right. It's better than playing the lottery – it could just be you who scoops the star prize of this charming person. If they deny it, check their birthday with a friend just to be sure. These people have also been known to say black just because you say white.

Talk about a flirt! Gemini could sweet-talk the coldest of hearts in under sixty seconds and still leave time for Ms Gemini to reapply her lipstick or for Mr Gemini to fix his tie. No one person is ever the centre of a Gemini's world. They don't give anyone 100 per cent of their affection. They don't know how to. But romance tempts them and they start on the road to love sooner than most of us, often going for just the person that most people would warn them against. They love to travel too, and if they can fall in love with someone from far away, so much the better. Pierre had better not think it is just his onions that dear old Jane is after – she has far bigger plans for him than he can imagine.

You will also be able to tell Gemini people from the way their eyes glisten as they talk. Don't confuse this look with the Scorpio gaze. Scorpio will look into your soul through your eyes, while Gemini is not necessarily staring at you. It's just that his or her eyes tend to gleam – the sort that most of us only get after a couple of glasses of wine. Mind you, maybe dear old Gemini has had one or two. With the Gemini social calendar it certainly wouldn't surprise me!

Many Geminis work in the media. They can handle the stress that work of this nature brings with it. Many other signs are not able to ride with the changes in this way. Gemini's ruling planet Mercury is what bestows this ability to handle change so well. Indeed, Mercury dictates change, agitating Gemini constantly to move onto fresher and greener pastures. Prince William is a typical Gemini. He is the perfect prince, but as we saw from his visit to Chile in 2001 he is also at home getting his hands dirty and living without even so much as a lightbulb.

Geminis are among the most generous friends or

lovers you could ever have, who would much rather spend cash on you than on themselves. Don't forget, though, that this is partly dependent on Gemini's remarkable ability to get you to spend your cash on him or her! Who could deny Gemini that outfit on which those misty eyes have gazed so lovingly and longingly, and especially if you've just had dinner bought for you. No matter that the difference in cost is £100 or so.

Treat them well but keep them on their toes. (They hate predictability.) They can be two-faced, but they are not the only ones. They are always looking around for the party that they just know is going on somewhere. Many people with a Gemini in the family end up living by the motto, 'If you can't beat 'em, join 'em', and that is just what I advise you to do if you want to keep this fun, restless and generous sign as a part of your life.

SECRETS OF THE SEXES

So how do the males and females of the species differ then? Let's have a look.

Ms Gemini

This girl really does have a dual personality. You have to be prepared to share everything with her. Your car, your wallet, your friends – but you must not expect her to do the same for you. It simply isn't a two-way street with Ms Gemini. She'd be insulted if you even thought about it. She will go on for hours to friends about how she doesn't get invited out with her partner but if he wanted to join her on a girls' night she'd be absolutely flabbergasted. I mean, what on earth could he be thinking? Doesn't he know that a girls' night out is just for her and her friends? Oh no. She will instruct you to put yourself nicely to bed and tell you she will be in at eleven. She will then go onto get steaming drunk and arrive home at 3 a.m. with ten guys' telephone numbers written in biro on her hand.

Don't get me wrong. She will make a charming companion and a very good wife. Ms Gemini will join in with whatever you do and adapt herself to new situations with ease. Just got a new promotion and want to impress the boss? Go out for dinner and take Ms Gemini. She really could charm the birds from the trees and she will sell your image so well that you'll be looking at a pay rise before the main course arrives. Get the deal signed by dessert, though, or it could be curtains by coffee. She can talk for her nation and she knows just what to say to both delight and rile those around her.

She has little respect for money, though she may get worried when she has none. Hers is not a brain that dwells on issues like mortgages or rents. Don't trust her with managing the money or you will both end up on the street. Look out, though, because she will do a brilliant job of convincing all her friends that it was you who got her thrown out of the house when the bills went unpaid, and her story of the episode will deserve an Oscar. When single, she manages to get by by the skin of her teeth, largely because she can sweet-talk her way in and out of anything.

Gemini

She can be exciting company and will talk to you for hours. She is likely to be extremely pretty. She is a woman you will always be able to forgive, whatever her misdemeanours, because you will know she never meant any harm. Even if she told your best friend that he was the finest-looking man in the world, she will convince you that he was having a bad time and that she did it for you.

She is a bit of a hoarder. Look in her cupboards and you will take a walk down memory lane. She may even have her old school gymslip (if you're lucky). The things she has managed to hoard over the years won't mean much to you, but they will mean the world to her. Whether it is a book of matches or an old pair of socks, it will be the key to a memory sure to bring a big smile to those lovely Gemini lips – and a good tale will be told too.

Kylie Minogue is a classic Gemini, who plays the dual roles of girl and woman very well, has fans of all ages and can dress for any occasion. She has even had an assortment of boyfriends from the wild-at-heart to the homestay type.

Have a heart and Ms Gemini will keep on coming back for more, but if you are mean to her then you will end up in her book of bastards, which is probably rather full by the time she is twenty-one. She needs to have a partner who is willing to listen to as much nonsense as reality, but he can be sure that come next year they could as well be living in Sydney as in Swindon. Oh, and if she phones you up and asks you on a chatshow for a makeover, don't go. Ms Media-lover is the ultimate volunteer for exposé shows, and this is where you could find yourself being dumped on national television, with confessions only the most imaginative could predict she would come clean to!

Mr Gemini

One of the most individual characters that you will ever meet is Mr Gemini. You two are talking and one moment you think he doesn't like you and the next you know that he adores you. When the girlfriend of a Gemini man comes to me it is often to say she doesn't understand his ways and is beginning to think she is going a bit mad. One minute the relationship is going wonderfully and the next they seem to be on the verge of a break-up. And that is even with couples who have been married for twenty years!

You must be prepared to adapt yourself to his moods; otherwise you won't get on well at all. If he likes you he will be most gentle. If he doesn't he can be most rude. If he adores you he can be both! So as you can see this is one confusing man to let into your life.

Why then, you might ask, do people keep on coming back for more? Fun, is the answer. Life with Mr Gemini is never boring. Indeed, life will never be the same again if you let Mr Gemini into your life and your heart.

Gemini man is suave, with a subtle sense of humour. He is even-tempered, a good talker and will charm the pants off your relatives and friends (to use a turn of phrase). He is clothes-conscious. He likes you to have plenty of different clothes and changes in hairstyle; variety in everything is appreciated. You must be a good listener because he loves to explain things to you. He adores children and animals. Don't be fooled if he acts cool towards children. He really loves them.

You will see this man make and lose a fortune twenty times over if you stick with him, and the beautiful thing about it is that he will still be laughing when it happens for the twenty-first time!

You have to put up with him flirting with your friends. He may even have gone out with one of them in years gone by. It's OK, though. He doesn't have secrets and he will tell you all about it. However, it will be as he remembered it and not necessarily exactly as it happened.

He makes plans to rule the world. Even if he doesn't reveal his plans he will have every intention for you to play your part in the scheme. He may spring surprises on you, and you would be well advised to spring a few on him too, even if it is just over what you are having for dinner or where you are going at the weekend. He requires some space, too, though you don't necessarily get to be given any. This is the deal, and much as you will love him, you will probably hate him too. Friends feel the same. At least one of your crowd will have been insulted beyond forgiveness by him and she will ask you time and time again what you are doing with such a liability in your life. And the reason is that when things are fun they are unbelievably good fun. How could you turn down a man who can constantly surprise you, love you and enrage you? At least life with this man keeps you on your toes and keeps your therapist in business. (Only kidding!) Remember, too, that he expects you to be dependable, reliable and unpredictable all at the same time, as well as keeping his meal warm for three hours while he helps a friend out of a crisis (which wasn't a crisis until he got involved). Like many people I know, you really will keep on coming back for more.

SEXUAL NEEDS

You may think after reading so far that you would have to be an acrobat and a lovemaking professional to please Gemini, but that is not true at all. Gemini wants someone willing to invest time getting to know them and their body in order to perfect lovemaking and make it as exciting as possible. It is not so much about nifty technique (though that should not be completely ruled out), but more about the amount of attention that you are prepared to give, from day one right through to the end.

Sex for Geminis can be a way of life. They use sex appeal to get what they want in love, in work and even around their friends. If you fall out, there's charm lavished on you until you gladly forgive. Geminis can wrap anyone around their little fingers. Good grief, they can even flirt with animals. When Gemini walks into a room the new presence brings about a change in the air that not even the least emotional person could fail to notice. They ooze sex, though they don't know they are doing it. At least, I don't think so. I'm still trying to work that one out for myself. But they do know how to get what they want. You will find it hard to remember who did the chatting up. It was just that you clicked immediately. Geminis have been known to attract partners by insulting them, but then they wouldn't be the first sign in history to do that (would they now, Pisces?).

Geminis' direct approach to life means that they are not good at lying. This doesn't mean they won't cheat on their partner. It means they won't cheat very successfully. They might as well wear a sandwich board that proclaims, 'I am sleeping with your best friend.' When they do cheat, it is likely to be with someone you know. You see, they are social animals, and introduce you to so many people, and you do all end up so tied together.

You could not accuse Gemini of being shy or inhibited. This creature is proud of its body. When you walk down a street and glance in someone's window and then quickly glance away (or maybe not) because the person in there was walking about naked, that was a Gemini. And whoever they were you can be sure they didn't care! This trait can be embarrassing if you live with a Gemini and Auntie Prude comes to stay.

The downside here is that Gemini doesn't have to be emotionally involved in order to have sex. Sex is not a sign of absolute commitment for this person. Gemini can turn on and off like a tap and has no time for romantic trimmings. These people like sex (love it, in fact). It is a very important part of a relationship to them and they need to fancy someone a lot, but this isn't the biggest help when you are the one sneaking out of commitment-shy Gemini's bed at 6 a.m. the next morning.

They also like the quiet life and are not afraid of saying that they watch the latest soaps. It's just that they go out to the parties after the soaps have finished. They will also talk about the people in their favourite soap as if they were real and as if the events occurring were true. Don't be taken in by this self-delusion. What you must be with a Gemini is straight. You'll be respected for it, and better off in the long run.

And even if you do go in for a one-night stand (though I know I shouldn't say this), it's sure to be a memorable night. No, let me take that back. I really don't want to encourage you in this way. I am a Scorpio and strongly believe that true love should rule the day. But it's true, lectures aside, that sex with Gemini is sure to be a popular choice with many.

TRUEST NEED AND DESIRE

PHYSICAL ATTRACTION

Marriage Partners at a Glance

This is just a taster. For more detail, turn to the chapter called Between the Sheets.

BEST BETS

ARIES can stimulate the mind and body of the Gemini and these two can become best friends as well as lovers.
GEMINI and Gemini will drive each other to distraction and keep on coming back for more.
LIBRA understands Gemini well and knows what is needed to keep both of them happy and stimulated, mentally and physically.
AQUARIUS is sexy and intelligent and proves to be just what Gemini has been looking for.

Gemini

LEO looks good, which is important, and can mix as well with kings as with paupers just like Gemini. These two will want to rule the world together.

SCORPIO will probably be the one who seduced Gemini. These two will have fun.

SAGITTARIUS makes up the other half as Gemini's polar opposite and playful fights are sure to ensue.

HEAVY WEATHER

TAURUS digs its heels in more than Gemini, and indeed may as well pull out the knives right now because that's the way things usually end up between these two.

CANCER is far too emotional and thinks the digs Gemini makes are for real when Gemini was only trying to have fun.

VIRGO is too organized for fly-by-night Gemini who feels constrained.

CAPRICORN is far too organized and goal-orientated for feel-as-you-go Gemini.

PISCES and Gemini indulge in too much game-playing and double-dealing and after a while the jokes aren't fun any more.

Top Ten Turn-offs

1 Jealousy
2 Nit-pickers
3 Hoarders
4 Guzzleguts

5 People who repeat themselves
6 Meanness
7 People who dance but can't
8 People who wear matching clothes
9 The word 'commitment'
10 Planners

HOW TO SEDUCE GEMINI

If you want to seduce Gemini then you are going to have to take him or her to somewhere new. Go to the local bar or nightclub and so many of Gemini's friends will be around that you won't get a moment alone with the object of your desires. If you can afford it, then take Gemini far away. Gemini will dine out on the tale for many years to come and it should place you firmly as a front runner. Another approach is to take them where you know lots of people – Geminis love to hang out with people who are popular.

Don't play too hard to get. This sign has some patience but not a lot and will move on quicker than most if you do not respond soon enough. A first date can go either way depending on what sort of mood Gemini is in and how dark the humour is that day. I know many a person who has spent an enjoyable evening with Gemini only to discover the next day that everything they were told was a lie. They'd clearly got Gemini on a dark-humoured day.

Use your time wisely. Tell Gemini everything you wouldn't normally dare to talk about on a first date. The chances are high that your date thinks your dreams to become a Hollywood star are perfectly valid and will even lend you the money for a plane ticket to get there (both of you, that is).

Gemini is a tease. Don't expect to arrange a second date quickly. Gemini is more likely to say, 'See you around,' and then turn up on your doorstep the very next morning with croissants and fresh orange juice.

If you want to get Gemini into bed then you stand a pretty good chance of doing so. When Julia Roberts said to Richard Gere in *Pretty Woman* that he didn't have to bother with all the trimmings because he was onto a sure thing, she spoke like a true Gemini. (Not that I am insinuating anything. I'm sure you get my drift.)

None the less Gemini will play it cool, or blow hot and cold, and I advise you to be cool too. Overkeen will scare Gemini off. Gemini likes to do all of the chasing. Talk about the future and not the past. Remember that Gemini doesn't look back or learn from past mistakes – look ahead with Gemini if you want to win this one over. And give your date the benefit of the doubt if you feel put down. Gemini is only trying to be funny.

Above all, don't go to a place with no atmosphere. Even a restaurant has to be full of fun for Gemini to enjoy eating there. And if you get asked if you want to call it a night, be aware that indefatigable Gemini is just testing the water to see if you are as much of a party animal as he or she is. Because you can be sure that Gemini would rather get the train to Paris for breakfast than go home to put on pyjamas and make a mug of cocoa.

Tell-tale Signs that Gemini has Fallen

Do not be surprised when Gemini is all over you like a rash one day and out of sight the next. Gemini can't help being changeable. Your best bet is to play it cool and not to shout and complain. If you do then wicked Gemini might just decide to enjoy the wind-up. If Gemini has fallen in love with you, you will hear about it, from friends, family, and even the local newsagent. All have been told how special you are. They may have been told about your sex life too – with a fair amount of fictional licence, I might add.

Gemini in love is excitable and vivacious. You'll be showered with gifts, but watch out as you may have to share the credit card bill a month later. Gemini isn't good with money and tends to think that when you pay with a card it doesn't really cost anything. Money isn't important to Gemini (the less so the more they are in love), and your lover won't mind whether you have any or not. I must say it would be rather better if you did, because Gemini isn't likely to bring much money into the union, but will do a very good job of spending it none the less.

When Gemini starts to introduce you to all the many different characters in his or her life, this is a sign of trust. The opening up of Gemini's life to you in this way shows that you have been accepted. Gemini in love will be as willing to share the rough times with you as the smooth. They will dress up for you, start being nice to everyone they had no time for before, and take you to places you never even knew about. Just don't expect too much in the kitchen – Gemini will make one or two dishes well but that will be it.

A real giveaway is a bounce or a skip in the walk of smitten Gemini. Nothing that anyone wants will be too much trouble. These are sensitive souls really. All that bluster is just a front, you know. If you ever say anything nasty to them they will never forget it, so think carefully before you speak. Gemini, on the other hand, can be as sharp as they like. It's one rule for them and another for you!

Geminis can stay faithful for ever once they've found the right person but they need to have had a couple of experiences in love before they settle down for good, or they will always wonder what they have been missing.

One last way to see if Gemini is in love with you or not – to try to lead a conversation for more than five minutes. If you can succeed then you know your lover has other thoughts on his or her mind – which for Gemini can only be love, since love's the only thing more important than talking. So that's two for the price of one: Gemini's in love, and you get a chance to get your point across!

GEMINI PEOPLE IN YOUR LIFE

This section tells you about the people you work, rest and play with.

Gemini in the Workplace

Geminis get tagged by their employers as oddballs. Not only do they have a strange way of getting the job done but they also treat their colleagues as if they are best friends one day and arch enemies the next. They have usually made their way up the career ladder more through good luck and force of personality than hard work, which is against their nature. They see the socializing aspect of work as being just as important as the job itself. In fact, they find it hard to believe that a job exists where you cannot have fun and lark about. They are the people who can draw a crowd, which makes them great at selling things. If they can work on commission, then all the better. They like a competitive edge to what they have to achieve.

They need constant pressure and change to bring out the best they can do, and they have great skill at sweet-talking their way out of a jam. Any work linked to travel pleases ruling planet Mercury, and any work requiring social skills is a winner too. Geminis need to be able to talk as often and as freely as they want to. (No librarians here, please!) If they feel verbally hindered in a job then they are likely to get up and walk out over the most trivial of problems, which has grown out of all proportion just because Gemini didn't feel able to speak his or her mind at the right time.

Life is for living and work is something to do to earn a crust when Gemini is not out having fun or relaxing. Probably the best job in the world for Gemini would be gossip columnist: writing about people's lives, hearing all the best scandal and getting paid for it.

Gemini would rather supervise than do the grafting. Thus they are usually at the top of their professions. In the very early days their superiors will have taken note of their ability to take charge and will have placed them as the leader and organiser behind a big desk where they can doodle and play games on the computer when nobody's looking. You can also bet that they will have their private phone book with them at work. After all, why waste your own money when someone else can foot your social phone bill?

Gemini bosses can charm their staff into working overtime without pay. If charm doesn't work they manage to elicit sympathy instead. They promise what they cannot really come up with, but don't think them liars for they really want to believe that they can keep these promises. They want all their staff to think them indispensable. Staff don't necessarily play along, especially when they wise up to the fact that the Gemini boss is presenting their ideas as his or her own. Not that Gemini doesn't have ideas. Gemini can come up with the most ingenious ideas, but they are rather impractical. New staff get thrown in at the deep end, and the motto is 'sink or swim'. Even the least important member of the team is full of bravado if a Gemini. This is the person who tries to convince you that you got your job largely down to him or her, even if only for opening the door to you at your interview.

Most of their hard work is done in the brain. Manual work is unthinkable to Gemini. So long as they put their mind to it, they can make a great success of their lives, and once they start a journey to a goal very little can hold them back. Gossip and intrigue in the office is a hurdle, but although they flirt like there is no tomorrow they rarely go too far. They save the love drama for outside the office. These are men and women who like to have different compartments to their lives.

Working with a husband or wife would not succeed because that would not give Gemini the space this funny and talented sign requires. And when I say talented, I mean it. Anyone with the charm to earn the money they need without even picking up pen and paper or tool is surely a person of talent.

The Gemini Mother-in-law

This woman can outlast you at any family party and will not be afraid of calling her son- or daughter-in-law a lightweight in front of many onlookers. This is a woman who takes great delight in sparring with her close ones and you will not be spared. In fact, you are probably prime bait. She will do her best to rile you and to get you to enter into playful fights with her, which every now and then could go a bit too far.

You will feel as if you have known her all your life and she will convince you that life with her family is just one long party. But don't wear a dress that is too short or too low-cut or to try to outspeak her in company, because she will turn on you. She will remember anything embarrassing you have ever done and bring it up whenever it suits her, even if it is twenty years down the line.

She will not hesitate to drop in uninvited and will even organize Christmas or New Year's Eve parties at your house without letting you know. Your kids' birthdays will be organized from Coco the clown to a barman for the adults. That is, so long as she remembered the birthday in the first place. She won't foot the bill though. That will be given to you in a manner that suggests you agreed with all of this and are delighted at how it all went. She will also make an effort to use every plate in the house and then leave them for you to wash up while she takes your partner out to find some more fun and excitement.

She prefers long-distance holidays to a day trip to Bognor. She takes so much luggage that you think for one happy moment that she is emigrating. Not so, unless you are willing to go too. She likes to keep her loved ones around her.

She doesn't have a nasty side but she can say things that are hurtful. She will have forgotten them by breakfast-time while you continue to stew for the next three weeks. But don't say anything bad to her. She will declare war and that is not a sight that I should like to be around to see. She tells white lies but this is something her children take for granted, so better not argue with your other half about what his or her mother said or promised to do.

Not the best taste in make-up, I'm afraid. Yes, you guessed it. Gemini mother-in-law is still wearing that awful bright blue eyeshadow and that salmon-pink lipstick. All the same, as mothers-in-law go, this is a sexy sign and no amount of bad make-up, or aprons and saucepans, can cast her in a totally unattractive light. She has a certain something that is sure to keep the admirers flocking round well into her eighties. Don't mix her with your friends. She will not purposely set out to seduce them but she has been known to gather male admirers many years younger than herself. So when your friend offers to share the babysitting with your mother-in-law, say no!

She will not frown on any new ideas you have. If any money problems arise she will do her best to help you out of them (though she also won't let you forget it). For every pain there is a pleasure mixed in and she will go to the ends of the earth to make sure that her loved ones are happy. So welcome her with open arms. Just take what she says with a pinch of salt. She is still only a child at heart, no matter how many she may have of her own.

Gemini Children

You will not forget meeting a Gemini child. This child can mix just as easily with adults as with children of like age. Gender is not an obstacle either and this child could well have a best friend of the opposite sex and of quite a different age.

Wherever you take Gemini children they show a keen interest. See a parent and child engaged in an earnest discussion rather than squabbling and bickering and you are probably looking at a Gemini child. Such a child can be a great pillar of strength for the family in times of crisis.

They are not frightened of going to school but they don't like doing any work when they get there. Although Gemini children can get on very well with their parents, even to the extent of being like best friends, that doesn't mean the relationship is automatically an easy one. Indeed, it is likely to be an interesting one, and even a bit of a rollercoaster ride. If you are a Water-sign parent, Cancer, Scorpio or Pisces, then you can bet that this child has brought you to tears at some point – indeed, at birth, at thirty and probably very many times in between too.

A Gemini child will, I'm afraid, tell porkies, especially about where they have been. It is usually only the Fire signs of the zodiac (Aries, Leo and Sagittarius) who are quick enough to catch them out in any lies.

Although I would not mind bringing up a Gemini child, I think I would need some extra help around the house to ensure that the child got to school on time and wasn't getting up to too much mischief behind the bike sheds. But I would know that I had a child who could help me with ideas and give me inspiration. Just like every sign of the zodiac, there is a good side and a bad side. It depends which assets are important to you and what you find intolerable in a personality that will finally dictate whether you could handle this active and forward-thinking child. If you are feeling down the Gemini child will do a great job of cheering you up. If he or she spends money on you you may want to question its source. Perhaps the child sold one of their Christmas gifts to do so.

A Gemini child will not be averse to getting a job while still at school, but it is more likely to be in the local nightclub than the local café. These children will invite plenty of friends round for you to cook for and will probably insist on major birthday parties. A day out with the family will not cut it and that's just when they're seven! Encourage them to stick to the subjects they are good at at school for they have talent but a short attention span. They are not usually overweight because they burn off so much energy with their social activities. Don't be surprised if the teacher rings you up to complain that your child is getting a little too clever with the hockey stick. We are not talking sporting ability here. The downside to Gemini sociability is a bit of a tendency to goad people. They won't cause fights intentionally, however, but coming home with one black eye at some point in their lives is a lucky escape rather than a major disaster.

This is one child who will prove a major hit with your friends and family. Before long you've got aunts and uncles calling you to convince you to let little Gemini go to that rock concert, and isn't it rather mean of you to have said no. And the funny thing is, you were about to give in anyway, because Gemini's charm works just as well on you.

Gemini Friends

A Gemini friend is a good friend to have for as long as they are around. They will do anything to help you out and one of the best aspects of having their friendship is that they are certain to introduce you to some truly gorgeous men and women. Whether they will let you have their affections all to yourself is another matter, of course. When they are feeling in the mood they will ring you up every day. Then you may not hear from them for a month or more while they get involved with whichever experience it is that has taken over their life this time.

A warning. They want to but they cannot keep secrets, so be careful what you tell them. Confide in them and before long the person you have been complaining about knows every detail. Gemini doesn't want to land you in it. But Gemini does want to defend you and fight your corner, and this is all that's happening here.

You can trust them to provide you with fun and never be boring. If you agree to go on holiday, don't let them do the booking, or you'll end up in Antarctica when you'd just thought of going to Amsterdam. And don't forget that they don't really understand the concept of money. If you lend it, they will forget to give it back. If you mention it, you will feel worse than they did for forgetting it.

I used to have a Gemini friend and I can honestly say she was one of the best, funniest and most fascinating friends I have ever had the pleasure of knowing, even though she could madden me too. She was beautiful and funny and could attract men quicker than I could dial a taxi. She was always the first to stick up for me in any kind of an argument, though later she would make fun of my problems. I never knew who I was going to find at her house, and sometimes I would phone her only to find out that she had gone away to another country for a few weeks. Her romantic history was a book all of its own. I used to laugh to myself at her antics for she was to me a prime example of a Gemini.

If you have a Gemini friend, make sure you keep your own life in order even if his or hers isn't. You may not be as good as handling the ups and downs as your friend is, and you could well end up in a mess while Gemini comes out smelling of roses. And keep your man or woman away from them, out of temptation's reach. That aside, I do believe this is a great friend to have who will prove that we really were put on this earth to have fun.

Cancer

June 22 to July 23

CHANGEABLE, PROTECTIVE, LOVING, shrewd and caring: these are the key words to describe Cancer. Cancer people have wonderful qualities and are an asset to anyone's life. Their loyalty, sympathy, understanding, generosity, sincerity and kindness are life-enhancing. No, they are not complete and utter angels, but they are kind-hearted souls who only have people's best interests at heart, even when they're interfering.

They do not mean to but Cancer people are capable of placing a great deal of pressure on those around them. They can convince their loved ones that they have not had any attention for months on end when the truth is that you just popped out for an hour. Emotional blackmail is one of their specialities and it is unlikely that any crab has ever gone through life without a blow-out from time to time over the levels of attention being received. By the time the crab is about nine, he or she has got the fine art of manipulation down to a tee. Like its fellow Water sign Scorpio, the crab can give as good as it gets, although the crab will always deny having had a go at anyone for any reason that was not fully justified. Think of the creature that is called the crab, and you will get the picture. Crabs go backwards and from side to side very happily. But when they want to go forwards they have their claws at the ready, just in case they are going to be attacked. Whoever said that attack is the best form of defence must have been a crab, but what they didn't know was that they were giving away a trade secret.

The crab symbolizes tenacity. This accounts for their legendary devotion to family and loved ones, whose welfare and interests they always consider before their own. A wonderful and admirable quality this is, but it can be taken too far. The crab has determination, and if it sets out to do something worthwhile then no effort is too great. The crab's self-discipline and capacity for work are tremendous and this combined with conscientiousness and attention to detail is a recipe for success. But sometimes the crab allows itself to be held back by overconsiderateness to the people it loves. Strong bonds of love can sometimes prevent Cancer people from attaining what they are capable of.

Cancer people must think carefully whenever opportunities come their way, and not let them slip through their fingers. They are ambitious and skilled. They regard the world as their oyster and the idea of travel attracts them, not just for holidays but also for work. But they mustn't take the world's cares on their shoulders. I have many Cancer friends. Being a Water sign myself I tend to attract them. The thing I know all too well about my Cancer friends is that they are ready to cry before I am over problems that they may not even fully understand. This understanding and sympathy for the feelings and problems of others exerts a gravitational pull. Anyone in trouble goes to a Cancer friend, who, being a believer that a trouble shared is a trouble halved, immediately takes on more than half. Cancer people are great friends, but they mustn't be taken for granted.

Cancer people are sensitive and easily hurt, but they hardly ever bear anyone a grudge. They are far too forgiving by nature. They will call you up an hour after a major falling out and act as if nothing has happened because they have forgiven you already. They don't cope all that well with problems of their own, and if something does not get fixed quickly they can fall into a depression which may take months if not years to get out of.

Give them your time and they will give you their heart. You may find them a little overbearing but they can make you a home so cosy you want to stay there for years. They take on your family (and any children you may have) as their own too. It is in their nature to look after those who are not as strong as they are and they do it very well indeed.

In affairs of the heart Cancer's affection is sincere and love once given is for life. Career and ambition mean that those born under this sign often do not settle down until later in life. Once they do, there are no half measures. Boy, how they settle! They make wonderful marriage partners. Ms Cancer is the perfect wife and home-maker, though Mr Cancer does tend to cling a little to the 'how Mother did it' routine, so you'd better look out for that.

Also bear in mind that Cancer is not as predictable as you may think. Don't expect to come home and find your dinner on the table every night or your bed made every day. Cancer people are tidy but they measure tidiness by their own standards and I know as many slovenly ones as I do meticulous ones. They expect you to clean up after yourself. If you don't there will be shoes left in the middle of the floor or plates left unwashed as a reproach. And woe betide you if you even think about belching in front of your Cancer mate or eating with your mouth full. This is not only disgusting, it is unforgivable.

When Cancer people put their minds to something they can do it, but their emotions are what let them down time and time again. I also have to say – many will disagree but I believe it to be true – that Cancer people really are quite selfish. It is their way or the highway. They are quite capable of going all out for what they want.

Cancer is sexy and not frightened of showing feelings for other people. They will go to the ends of the earth for those they love and I mean the ends. Birthday and Christmas presents will be something to be treasured. Much thought goes into any gift, which is sure to have an original and unusual slant to it.

In business Cancer is shrewd, but doesn't always

manage to pay bills on time. Sometimes the crab is too busy living life to look at things like paperwork and bills. Their polar opposite is Capricorn and both share a stubborn streak, which helps them to get to the top of many an important profession. Cancer people who turn to writing are usually very good at it but prefer to talk into a cassette-recorder than type away at a keyboard. Passion is a Cancer quality, and they are especially passionate about what they want to do with their lives and what they want to achieve. There will be some surprises too. Just when you think you have got them sussed they go and do something shocking, anything from the sublime to the ridiculous. In all senses, George Michael is a typical Cancer: sexy, talented, loving, and capable of surprising us all, diving head-first into every experience that life offers. Pamela Anderson, the *Baywatch* babe, is another typical Cancer: a terrific mother and a sex bomb with it. You may have read reports that she had a swing in her bedroom when she was married to rock man Tommy Lee, and I can believe it. That is just what they're like underneath the sweet exterior.

If you stick by Cancer you will always be loved. Their cunning way with words can get you into places you had never even dared think about. I cannot promise they will keep the same set of friends all their lives. There are bound to be a string of people whom they have at some point upset and who are not willing to forgive them, and these probably include Taurus, Leo and Gemini. And what a shame, not to forgive a sign which is in itself so forgiving.

Cancer can appear arrogant. The crab has learnt

over a long period of time to look after itself. And it can look after others too. Maybe there is arrogance there. But who could cope without the crab?

SECRETS OF THE SEXES

So how do the males and females of the species differ then? Let's have a look.

Ms Cancer

If you are lucky enough to fall for a Cancer girl, be sure to stay true. She likes all the cards on the table, a sensible approach to life and love, and more emotional security than financial.

She is honest and will be as straightforward with you as she can. She will expect the same from you. Don't even think about double-crossing her. Emotional happiness is one of the most important things to her and if you can give her the security she craves then you are halfway there. You have to make her feel loved, needed and wanted all at the same time. She is someone you can trust and is a proper partner in the old-fashioned way. If she truly loves you then she will support your ideas all the way. She'd even put her house up for collateral if you needed it and then write it off to experience if you lost it all. Indeed, Ms Cancer has been known to give up everything she has built up in order to fall in with the man she loves. This is particularly true on her second major relationship. You see, she cannot believe that she could fail again, and so does everything in her power to keep this union as strong as possible.

Ms Cancer will do many thoughtful things for her partner: putting his slippers out, making nice things to eat. She will not remember to make the bed every day, but you can expect to find rose petals scattered over the pillows. It is the emotionally rewarding things she likes to do. And she doesn't mean to be demanding but, let's face it, she is. If you are not there when she wants you to be, you'll get the cold treatment when you eventually do arrive. Even if she is five hours early and you have been slogging away at the office. But once you have her in your life you will not want to let her go. The void she would leave would be impossible to fill. She is affectionate, emotional, sentimental, determined and patient. If you have a problem, she will wait as long as necessary for you to work it out. She would do anything to save you from being hurt. But if you lie to her once you may as well lie to her a hundred times because you will be branded a deceiver from day one. In spite of her sympathetic nature, she can be cold as ice if you upset her.

Like wine she improves with age. It is not unusual to see older Cancer women with younger men. But of course you'd never guess her age, she looks so good. She has terrific stamina, too, and can party with the best of them if she is in the right mood. However, she cannot hold her drink. Even if the drink is not alcoholic but she believes it to be, she'll feel drunk after the first sip. Alcohol affects her both mentally and physically. She can become a bit of a pain, too, and you could end up with her crying on your shoulder over her schooldays. On the other hand, she could become sexy and playful. The gamble is yours.

There is no getting away from the fact that the full moon affects her, as does her time of the month. The two combined can cause a great outpouring of emotion and on-the-spot threats of divorce, all of which are forgotten about later. But she will always be sympathetic to any problems you have. She is the kind of person you could tell all your troubles to. She will keep your secrets and be the perfect confidante. She is also fun to be with and will make life better and more comfortable for whomever she decides to share it with. She likes to be near water, for which she has an affinity, and any time she is getting testy, do her (and yourself) a favour and run her a nice bath with some aromatherapy oils in it. She'll be back to normal in no time.

Ms Cancer loves children and always has a word of advice or reassurance for them. She will take on any children in your life as her own. In many ways, she is a child at heart herself. She understands the way a child's mind reacts and the way its heart feels. No matter how many negative things you can say about this woman – her strange moods, her lack of ability to handle money – you cannot dislike her. She will bring out the best in you, and you can't say fairer than that.

Mr Cancer

The reason so many people fall for Mr Cancer is his brilliant ability to relate to people. If he has grown up with a sister then you might think it is because of this feminine influence in his childhood. But the actual nitty-gritty of it is that he is effeminate, but in the most masculine of ways (trust me, I am not contradicting myself). This is a man you can go shopping with, who doesn't mind looking at women's clothes, and who could probably pick you out an outfit more successfully than you could yourself. What's more, it will look better on you than anything you've ever tried on before. Which is a way of saying that this is a man who can make you feel sexy.

He likes to smell good and he wears lovely aftershave. Before he marries or settles down Mr Cancer has plenty of girlfriends. He understands them so well, you see. He has got a terrific imagination, is very romantic and amusing, and is also terribly persistent. His ways of showing his affections are sometimes strange. He may only take you to a burger joint for dinner but he will take you for a romantic walk along the beach afterwards.

His best friend is often his mother. You may be held in comparison to her. Never mind, he will treat you like a goddess anyway – and expect you to act like one. He will get very hurt if you flirt with other men, but he is not particularly jealous.

He is a hard worker and takes a pride in what he does. You will find him a romantic partner who will go to great lengths to make you happy. There is nothing that he wouldn't do for someone he loves but he will also expect the same from you. He won't really like you going out without him. He wants to be invited even if you both know he cannot come, just so that he feels involved.

As a lover he is both masterful and giving. It's difficult to leave Mr Cancer for this very reason, even if you know he's not really the right one for you. It's just that the sex is so nice. Just like Ms Cancer, he gets moody too, and this is one of his less attractive traits. Some people call him immature because of it. However, a marriage with Mr Cancer should be a happy one, since he tends to do all of his flirting before the wedding rather than after. Marriage is important to him and something he does not embark upon lightly. If he says 'I do' then he means it from the bottom of his heart. If you are nice, he will be nicer. If you are horrible, then he can be an absolute pig.

Beware of his friends trying to lead him into bad ways. This man has a wide and varied circle of friends who would love nothing better than to lead him astray and are often weaker than he is. Make friends of them, not enemies, in the spirit of 'if you want to beat them, join them'. Otherwise you'll create an us and them set-up, peppered with emotion, and you can only lose out.

This is one of the few men in the zodiac you can expect to remember birthdays and anniversaries. (Make sure you don't forget his, unless you want the silent treatment for a week.) He is imaginative and loves to learn things so you can look forward to a good and stimulating life together. As long as those ever-changing spirits of his stay on the up and up, the romance will just keep on getting better and better.

SEXUAL NEEDS

Security always comes first with this sign. You'd better tell your date that you love them if you want them even to begin to think about sleeping with you.

Cancer people would rather have you at their house than go to yours. They feel safer in their own environment. If they do come to yours, you could wake up in the middle of the night to find them sitting drinking coffee with your flatmate and putting his or her love life and problems to rights.

As lovers they are both understanding and responsive. You only have to tell them once what you do and do not like in the bedroom. They will make a mental note of it so that they can please you next time. They like a lot of attention, too, so don't think that you can just lie back – oh no. You have to give just as much in love as you get.

If you appear happy, then your lover will be happy. Cancer people often take the emotional lead from their close ones. If you go to work unhappy then heaven help the people your partner has to work with because Cancer can spread the blues like wildfire. Crabs don't mind telling people that they are in a bad mood (or should I say crabby?), something most of us don't like to admit to. To them it is a completely acceptable occurrence.

Withdraw your emotions from your Cancer lover and you could be in for some problems. Your lover will set out to make your life as miserable as his or her life feels. This could be the full works: Ms Cancer turning up in black with a face veil and hanky in tow at the staff party you are attending, for example. If you hurt the crab or make him or her feel inadequate then this damage could last for a long time. The crab is a fighter, though, and will try to rectify the situation first. Since you can never be completely sure what's going on beneath that gorgeous smile, why not dish out another compliment? It will be worth it in the long run.

Love and sex go together and you will not often find Cancer embarking on a relationship he or she doesn't feel strongly about – unless alcohol is involved. (Mind you, for Cancer that's probably just one glass.) Don't get jealous if your lovely crab mate flirts with your friends. This is a lover you can take seriously and if he or she is flirting with your friend it is probably just as a way of getting to the good bits of someone's life story. In fact, if this sign weren't so passion-orientated, I'd recommend them to the priesthood – in the confessional they'd hear enough secrets to satisfy their curiosity and they wouldn't mind not passing them on.

Remember, give and you shall receive (oops, sounding a little priest-like myself now) but if you are selfish in your lovemaking then you may as well pack your bags. Nothing but oodles of lovemaking will do for Cancer and this sweet crab deserves it too, for all the love and support (and passion, of course) he or she will give back to you in return.

TRUEST NEED AND DESIRE

INNATE PASSION

Marriage Partners at a Glance

This is just a taster. For more detail, turn to the chapter called Between the Sheets.

BEST BETS

CANCER with Cancer will understand each other's important needs and satisfy them too.

VIRGO will help organize Cancer and will give them the straight talk and stability they need (must avoid the temptation to organize them too much, though).

SCORPIO will play out Cancer's every sexual and emotional fantasy.

PISCES will indulge the crab in the dramatics and the fun that they both live life for.

FAIR CHANCE

ARIES with Cancer could work so long as Cancer doesn't try to lead this sexually exciting fire sign.

TAURUS proves an instant attraction to Cancer but both must agree to disagree over certain points. Otherwise, this could be sizzling.

LIBRA will manage to keep Cancer on the straight and narrow and will probably declare love before the crab does too!

SAGITTARIUS will help the crab make their dreams into reality.

CAPRICORN is reliable and steadfast though sometimes a little too cold.

HEAVY WEATHER

GEMINI is just too much of a flirt and a philanderer for emotionally demanding Cancer, who will get fed up with watching the clock waiting for Gemini to return.

LEO is too interested in what's going on around Cancer to give the crab all the attention they want.

AQUARIUS is too unreliable and tells too many fairy tales for Cancer.

Top Ten Turn-offs

1 Liars
2 Slovenliness
3 Beer bellies
4 Swearing
5 People who talk about themselves all the time
6 People who put themselves before others
7 Obviously tarty or cheap clothes
8 People who gargle when they snore
9 Men and women who won't talk about issues
10 Lateness

HOW TO SEDUCE CANCER

OK, lesson number one if you want to seduce Cancer is play it cool. They like people who hold a certain amount of mystery. Glance their way every ten minutes or so with a smile and they'll be over in no time. When they come over, what they will want to know is not a lot to ask. Just your life history right down to how many men or women you have ever slept with. Maybe you don't have to reveal it all at once.

Take your crab on a date near water. Believe me, water works for Water signs. I have seen it happen not once but many times. Somewhere tranquil puts Cancer in the mood for love and if you give your crab a cocktail then you should be well away! Out will tumble a life history and you'll soon know exactly what to expect in the bedroom. (The following day there will be denials that the conversation took place, of course.) The more difficult thing is getting Cancer away from his or her friends. These are popular people who like to spend time in the environments and with the people they already know.

Cancer is a cautious sign. Best friends mean a great deal to Cancer people but it is not easy to work your way up to that spot in the charts. Believe me, I know. I have many friends who are Cancer and it takes some time before you get let into that inner circle. They may let you think you've got there straight away, but that's just so that they can suss out you and your thoughts and desires.

The crab needs to feel itself the centre of attention, so make sure to ask plenty of questions and tease out the information. Let the crab take the lead in love, too, or you'll scare him or her off. After you've gained your green card you'll be free to sweep them off their feet.

Ignore any quiet spells Cancer may have during the course of your date. Water signs are deep and emotional characters who like to be left quiet when they say so and given attention when they demand.

Give plenty of compliments for underneath that confident Cancer style is a lot of insecurity. Cancer will take everything you say far deeper than you may have meant. Good points if you say Cancer looks lovely but top points if you compliment the crab mind. Then you will be way ahead of the game, for Cancer people don't have as much confidence in their mental abilities as you may think. They often regret what they say, even though they are likely to have spent an hour thinking about it before uttering it.

Cancer loves music so a live music venue is a good idea. If you want to introduce your crab to your mum and dad then you would be doing well too; Cancer loves families. Other signs would feel threatened by the connotations of such a meeting, but not Cancer.

That's it! Lots of compliments and somewhere tranquil. Tranquil, but with atmosphere. Sounds crazy, I know, but then these are contrary people. You may want to take out some extra cash too. You never know where you'll end up with this one.

Tell-tale Signs that Cancer has Fallen

When Cancer is in love the whole wide world will know about it. Not because they shout it from the highest rooftops. Oh no. It's just that quiet smugness that anyone in the know will instantly recognize as pure and passionate love. If in any doubt, their routines will temporarily go out of sync too.

One of the problems the crab faces in love is that he or she tries too hard to own the chosen person. All very well if the lover is a submissive sort. But if it is someone who likes to get their own way every now and then, you could be in for trouble.

Cancer in love gets a bit lazy. Things such as work and housework will not seem important next to the wonderful first throes of love. Don't try to tell them off. It won't work. If you want any sense out of them, better wait until the first throes of passion have worn off (even if you are the one they feel passionate about). And if you are the one Cancer is passionate about, well, enjoy. They will spend their money on you, and open up their life to you as if it were a book. Don't be fooled, though. Cancer will never tell you everything. They like to keep you guessing.

Cancer is a giving person and will try to fulfil you by trying new and exciting things in the kitchen (as well as the bedroom). If they have spent ten hours traipsing round the shops for bamboo leaves and exotic herbs they won't want to wash up, mind you. It might be worth remembering that. It's not just about giving, though. If the crab is in your arms the chances are this is no accident and he or she has been planning it for months. If you are a friend of the crab then don't take offence if he or she dumps you for a while. The obsession with the new person has taken hold and all else has gone out of the window. Don't worry. Your friend will soon be back, begging on bended knee for your forgiveness and with a very imaginative excuse too. Cancer's success rate tends to be high. This is a sign whose interest in love is sparked off at a very early age and they soon gather enough good experience in relationships to know what they want and how to get it. They've also chosen the names for their potential children fairly early on in life!

Cancer can scare people away but that is probably just as well. Indeed, if they don't think you are right for them, a fighting look will appear in those lovely eyes and that rounded face. You, meanwhile, will accuse your friends of trying to break you up while the lovely crab grins behind you. It's not all love and harmony with the crab, you know. But the crab does love to be in love and does put heart and soul into making things work. Only if you are not serious will the crab start to get funny with you. With the crab on your side you will feel that you can rule the world. The foot rubs and massages that other people can only dream about will be yours on demand should you fall in love with this lovely sign.

CANCER PEOPLE IN YOUR LIFE

This section tells you about the people you work, rest and play with.

Cancer in the Workplace

O to have a Cancer boss. What a joy! Not only can you emotionally blackmail a Cancer boss into giving you time off work for a pet with a sore throat but you can also talk him or her into letting you do things that other bosses never would. The bad news is that these bosses are not as good with money as they say they are, so you may not always get paid on time. It's unintentional. And you are more likely to end up lending them a fiver than threatening to take legal action.

Just remember, the crab's home life is more important than work. If your boss looks serious about something it is less likely to be about your sloppy work than about little Jimmy's cold. At work, untidiness and smoking will bother Cancer bosses. (They may smoke, but you can't.) So if you are going on a job interview, hide the cigarettes.

Cancer people are hardworking. Your boss has worked day and night to get where he or she is today. And this is a good boss: sympathetic, tolerant and kind. When these bosses see faults in those working for them, they will do their best to help their employees overcome the problems. They will go so far as to invest time and money on you, sending you on training courses. They see their employees more as family members than staff. However, if you let them down they will take it personally, and will tell you so too. The family-style office can be a little intense and suffocating for all concerned.

They are good organizers and know what they want. Staff parties will be the kind of bash you remember for a long time. Don't get your boss drunk though, or you'll hear all kinds of information you'd probably be better off not knowing. Cancer is the confidant of so many people that he or she really does know the score. Ordinarily the crab would be as tight as a clam but with a drink inside all kinds of secrets start to come out. I am sure you would rather continue doing your job without knowing who is and isn't your enemy, since it can serve no purpose other than to infuriate.

Personal cleanliness and grooming are very important in the office led by Mr or Ms Cancer. This boss gives the staff security, friendship and discipline, and rarely fails to get loyalty in return. This is a hard taskmaster, but harder on his or herself. If you are asked to work late, then your boss will do so too. Or rather, the Cancer body clock being what it is, your boss would probably prefer you came in early in the morning rather than worked until midnight. Cancer likes home life too much to give up a warm bath and a good book before bed for work.

Work is none the less important and mixing business with pleasure is not a Cancer policy as a rule. Cancer people adore entertaining and tend to spoil their staff with kindness but they know very well that when they say jump, their staff will jump. Otherwise they wouldn't be there. When it comes to the crunch, however, there's only one person who can do that important job. And that's the crab. No one, except perhaps a fellow Cancer, could put that finishing touch to the job. This could be undermining for you, so be aware of it.

The crab is artistic and knows the best words to use so when the time is right and the crab member of staff wants to quit a job then the letter of resignation will be a screenplay in its own right. And if the boss is Cancer too then the letter will be redolent of all the emotional manipulation that's gone on.

I would love Cancer as a boss. I would know that the job will always get done, even if there are a few tears of both worry and laughter along the way, for their heart is in what they do.

The Cancer Mother-in-law

One thing to learn about your Cancer mother-in-law is never ever to insult her. No matter how trivial or meaningless the remark, she will stew over it for many years. No woman likes to be insulted but for Cancer woman the damage is doubled, for she takes things to heart so. Too much, in fact, but let me take that back, as I wouldn't want to offend her now, would I?

She claims confidence but if her son or daughter does not phone her regularly she's on the doorstep in no time checking that everything is OK. She may have her insecurities but let's look at her good points. She will give her grandchildren more love than you could dream of and will probably not mind looking after them at a moment's notice. She will have plenty of tales to tell them to keep them entertained. She would even call in sick at work to spend time with your children, such is her loyalty towards them and you.

She spends more than she should on them and you at Christmas and birthdays, and puts a lot of thought into her gifts. Be sure to thank her accordingly: that silk scarf is likely to have been ordered from overseas, not just from a local store.

You will be able to talk to her about problems and she will in fact encourage you to do so but this is the Cancer subject who won't keep your problems to herself. Such is her need to help you that she'll bring it up at her weekly women's meeting so that they can all put their heads together and solve it for you.

Although she can tell you where to be and at what time, you must not expect her to conform to your schedule. She has a habit of turning up unannounced, claiming that you invited her to dinner weeks ago but she didn't have time to confirm. She is certainly not a mean woman but she does tend to see things only from her point of view. She has lots of friends of her own but she will expect to be invited to all your parties too. And she won't necessarily invite you to hers. She likes surprises, so if you want to see her eyes light up then give her gifts. Flowers won't go amiss but many Cancer people are allergic to pollen, so check first with your partner to make sure that the gesture doesn't fall flat. She develops a rather strange dress sense as she gets older, and you may find it hard to choose the right gift for her. But make the effort because she really is worth it. You may have to lend her a bob or two from time to time, since handling money is not her number-one talent.

Take time out to get to know her. That's the only way that you will understand her. Her heart is in the right place but it is a demanding place. If you make the time for her she will give back to you much more love and affection than she receives. She has a lot to tell you for she has learnt many lessons over the years. Just don't give her too much to drink at one of your parties, or she will end up crying on the dining-room table over her first love whom she hasn't seen for fifty years.

Interfering, yes, but aren't most mothers-in-law? She will want to make sure that you take care of her little baby, for that is what her son or daughter will always be to her. But she will never undermine the relationship for she understands how important it is to you and to her child, no matter how much she treats your partner like her babe-in-arms.

Cancer Children

Cancer children are an absolute joy and your worst nightmare all in one. They are very needy children who need constant reassurance. It is not unusual for them at some stage of their lives to try to run away. They are testing you to the limit to make sure that they are genuinely loved and part of your life.

This is not a simple child. Cancer children will have got the world pretty much sussed by the age of nine, and that includes a good inkling about sex. As teenagers they tend to enter into physical relationships a little too soon. Keep an eye on them. You may have heard 'Jenny's' but actually that was 'Johnny's' where your crab daughter is staying overnight.

They are creative, can entertain themselves well, and at some stage in their lives are likely to pursue the arts. They have a charitable streak. That black eye is likely to result from sticking up for someone else rather than from fighting for themselves. They hate to see weaker children being picked on. All through life they will gather a vast array of friends both fat and thin, ugly and beautiful, because they don't judge by external appearance alone.

This child is the prime candidate to follow Mum or Dad in the family business. From a very young age he or she will be asking all about what you do and how it works. Given the chance the child will step in and reprimand anyone you complain about at work, so beware of what you say about the boss. It could prove embarrassing if you introduce your child to your boss and the child begins to tell your boss a thing or two!

Don't expect Little Crab not to want the limelight. This child will be sneaking downstairs to join in the conversation around the dinner-party table. Even if you're talking about sex or politics, your son or daughter will think that the points they wish to make are every bit as valid as yours. In this way, Cancer children are never really childlike. Their evident maturity leads their parents to talk to them as equals. They will embark on relationships early and will want you to meet the person they have fallen for. They try to see good in everyone, which as I'm sure you can imagine is a problem as much as an asset in life. Let them have their fun in love but give them good guidance. They need to learn, and they cannot fight against those full-on emotions of theirs. Anyway, they are pretty good at resorting to emotional blackmail or to doing things behind your back, so you may as well give in and have it all out in the open.

Not the most intellectual of children, their calling in life tends to be one of the more unusual ones. This is not really doctor, lawyer, shop-owner or accountant material. Maths is certainly not a strong point, though this is more likely to be because they didn't bond with the maths teacher than because of an innate inability. Treat your Cancer child with respect and you will have a child you can be proud of. Let the child go off and do weird and wonderful things with his or her career. I myself would be very honoured to have the first singing trapeze artist for my child.

Cancer Friends

Your Cancer friend is with you for life – until you hurt him or her. Then the deed is not forgotten and before long news of your perfidy has spread among your friends. And all you did was fail to keep to an arrangement on a Saturday night.

Cancer people work hard and play hard and have a habit of falling in love hard and fast if a compatible sign is around. They have a physical vulnerability which can lead into bad habits with food and drink and if you see Cancer friends developing problems do try to help before the problems get out of hand. The late Princess Diana, born under Cancer, developed an eating disorder when she felt deprived of support and attention. Do not take too harsh an attitude with people of this sign – bolster them up instead.

Your Cancer date may be late, but you'd better not do the same. You'll need to keep your promises, and Cancer doesn't like to be treated as a fool. Mind you, sometimes they do just stand themselves right in the firing line. Your Cancer friends will absorb a lot of your time and energy. But they are fun to be with and can open your eyes to many new and exciting things. Their love life on its own will be enough to pull you away from your favourite soap opera.

It is not always good to tell the crab what is wrong with his or her life. Crabs like to work it out for themselves and then turn to you for support. They can be pretty psychic, even if they don't admit it, so they may be more aware of developing problems, such as a partner's disloyalty, than you think. Just stand by ready to offer help.

Don't be surprised if, no matter how good a friend this is, there's a bit of jealousy over your successes or a little flirting with your partner. This is part of Cancer make-up and is more to be tolerated than to get upset about. They have a way with people and this can be good for you. Want to get to know the person behind that gorgeous face you've just seen? Get your Cancer friend to apply the charm and magnetism that opens the door for you.

You won't regret having Cancer friends, even if they are overpowering. There is no middle ground for them. They are either up or down. They change ten times before they go out because they can't get the clothes to feel right. I have never met the crab who was happy with the first outfit that was tried on, even if he or she goes back to the first outfit after having tried on the other nine. Although Cancer people are often on the short side, they have great style and could look good in a potato sack, and they know it deep down inside. The fussing is just another way to get attention.

I love my Cancer friends. I love the way they can be late but I'm not allowed to. I love the way they can spend a fortune on clothes but my spending gets frowned upon. I love them because every last one has, underneath it all, a pure and loyal heart.

Leo

July 24 to August 23

GENEROUS, WARM-HEARTED, proud, fun-loving and dignified: these are the key words to describe Leo. The lion is someone to be reckoned with. There is nothing wishy-washy about Leo. Born leaders, they are mentally strong and have a magnetic personality, which guarantees a loyal following. Indeed, Leo can intimidate and inspire in equal measure. When Leo holds court – which the lion likes to do – he or she can be sure of an audience.

Leo is also ambitious, emotionally generous, and gives life his or her all. Proud of their loved ones, Leos like to walk around with a good-looking partner on their arm. It is often physical appearance that first attracts Leo. Charming Leo is rarely bad-tempered. You really have to rattle the lion's cage to bring out any ill manners.

Generous with money, Leos will give their last penny to the ones they love, but you'd better not ask for their cold hard cash. You must wait to be given it, or risk causing the lion severe embarrassment. Leo is easily embarrassed, surprisingly. It is those high standards. You need only wear an outfit with shoes that don't match to send a Leo beetroot within minutes from the humiliation of it all.

Elegant, attractive, and with so much magnetism at their disposal, it seems only fair to mention Leo's less delightful qualities. So, let's face it, Leo is inclined to be impatient and intolerant. The lion may take five hours to get ready, but you'd better not take more than five minutes. And in that time you must come out looking like a prince or princess. Leo is also quick-tempered, and more than a little arrogant when it wants to be. But there you are, lucky Leo can get away with it all. The lion's charm knows no bounds.

The warmth of Leo's ardent nature matches the warmth of the planet that governs them, the sun. This radiant person is attractive both physically and mentally, and fatal to the opposite sex. But don't jump to conclusions. You may see Leo deep in conversation with an attractive person but they could just as well be discussing the weather as anything sexual or romantic. It is obvious that Leo is a strong character, but the nature of that character is not obvious in itself.

Candid people, anything underhanded is repugnant to them. If they want to say anything about you they will say it to your face. Sincere in all they do and say, their many friends know they can always rely on Leo's loyalty and affection. They have a sensible approach to the problems of life and are much sought after by people needing advice. They combine attentive listening with genuine sympathy and the logic needed to help you sort out a fix.

They get on well with people younger than them, partly because they are lucky to look more youthful than their years, but also because they think young. No matter what age they are, they are in touch with what is going on. No middle-aged boredom for Leo.

A clever brain and a capacity for deep constructive thinking can carry Leos right to the top of their chosen career. Determination and sheer grit are also hallmarks of the Leo character. Having set their sights on a goal they are relentless in their efforts to achieve it. They aim high, knowing that even if they fall short they will still have done very well, and that the charm they possess will probably make up for the rest anyway.

They are naturally elegant, appreciating quality and refinement. They like to be surrounded by beautiful things and to live in an attractive home. In this home they are gracious hosts, making visitors most welcome. They are talented people, clever with their hands, and often shine in the arts. The high standards they set for themselves make them perfectionists. If you work or live with a Leo you'll know that you are meant to live up to their high standards too.

Partying is definitely on the cards for Leo. They love to have a good time and it is rare that a Leo will turn down an invitation. If you date a Leo you may struggle to keep up with the endless round of parties. Leo will go to any event without hesitation and not hold back once there. When you are out with the king of the jungle, don't be perturbed by the way he or she can talk to strangers. Don't think your friend is disloyal or a flirt. Think of it as your Leo clearing the way for you to make sure you don't end up with any undesirable company. Holidays with Leo will be great fun: a mixture of adventure and relaxation, which I'm sure you will agree is the perfect combination.

Remember Dorothy and her friends in *The Wizard of Oz*? Remember the cowardly lion? Well, this is another side to Leo. Leo the lion does not have as much self-confidence as it appears. You see, the lion is only human after all. Like any Fire sign, Leo does something off-the-cuff then spends hours worrying that it was the wrong thing. When this insecurity takes hold, Leo works against it by getting strength from helping those less fortunate or less able. It is not unusual to see Leo involved with some sort of charity or voluntary work.

Leo is faithful and loving and if Leo marries you then you can rest assured that this is the sort of person who will not easily stray. Leo is too proud for that. Hasn't the lion already made the perfect choice of partner? It would have to be a major problem between you before Leo would be so silly as to be unfaithful.

Like other Fire elements Leo has a quick temper. You may find it hard to understand Leo at times and this is because there are many different layers to this personality. They have a strong layer on top of a weak layer on top of a strong layer and so on and so on, until you really don't know where you are. Leo's strength usually wins the day, however, though money problems are something that can weaken the lion, causing embarrassment and discomfort. Leo hates to be broke (much like us all). So much so, in fact, that Leo will do almost anything to get back on top. It is this determination that can end up making our lion friends very rich.

This is a personality to be treasured, a cause of amusement and bewilderment all at the same time. Treat these people well though, for whether friend, relative or lover they are not as strong as you think and they need support just like the rest of us. One last thing: don't forget to profess love to your Leo every day. Otherwise your lion may just think that your feelings have changed. This stands true even if you are on your honeymoon. Remember this and dignified, fun Leo will love you till the end of time.

SECRETS OF THE SEXES

So how do the males and females of the species differ then? Let's have a look.

Ms Leo

You have got to show Ms Leo that you are the boss from the word go or she will eat you for breakfast. She likes her partner in life to be as near perfect as possible, just as she does with everything. She has terrific pride and can always cover up her mistakes in a nice way. She will entertain your friends beautifully but she will also try to organize your life if you let her. You will need plenty of money to entertain her as she likes to go to the best places. The more expensive and trendy a restaurant is the better she likes it. She's a bit of a snob, you see.

A matchmaker, she will pair off your friends at a rate of knots, but you'd better not look elsewhere or it's off with your head. She may embarrass you but you may not embarrass her. Ms Leo's reputation is far too important for her to allow herself to look silly in front of friends, family or workmates. Don't be embarrassed about Ms Leo's clothing. Why should I be? I hear you say. Well, she is the original Gucci girl who thinks that designer is the only way to go.

If she decides she wants you there is very little you can do to escape. She doesn't normally go for incompatible associations, however, so maybe you just have to trust her judgement. You will be pleased you are being pursued once you see how much pleasure she can bring into your life. She is kind and if you have a problem and need a place to stay then she will welcome you with open arms. For a night, that is. After two or three she is starting to show impatience. This Fire sign needs her home space back after a while and will let you know your time is up in no uncertain terms.

She is a perfectionist. If she does not think you look good, she will set about reinventing you on her style terms. You may be wondering if she thinks she's perfect and the answer to that is yes, she does. She even thinks the lack of confidence she suffers from time to time rounds off her character beautifully. She may choose her mate well but she also has a lot of friends whose role in her life is solely to get her into the right places. She is a bit of a materialist, but I think you've already worked that one out, haven't you? Money is important to her and she is not that fond of people who don't have any. She tends to think they haven't worked hard enough.

In love she may make mistakes but she often knows she is doing so. Her life is a learning process. She goes into war time and time again to learn how to perfect the battle, does our lioness. It is a long time before she gives that up, even if she is constantly butting her head against a brick wall.

Her kind-heartedness will lead her to help her friends out of awkward patches but remember that this is done on her terms. Don't try your luck for too long or you will end up with an enemy instead of a friend. You will rarely have her undivided attention, either, so just don't expect it. She knows how to work a crowd. You'll see her dazzling everyone she passes. It's either her magnetism or her jewellery. She has a cat-like swagger that can turn heads too.

So what happens when she makes a mistake in public? Well, it's your fault, of course! But by the time you two are on your own again she's giving you far too much attention for you to be able to feel angry with her.

Mr Leo

I call him Mr Importance. He usually holds down a good position in work and has plenty of luxury in his life. He's got the leather black sofa in his sitting room, soft lighting and well-stocked drinks cabinet, and whether he is entertaining or has seduction on his mind you know that he is guaranteed success.

He is creative, and works and plays hard. He loves

danger and will frighten you to death in his fast car. His many admirers see him living up to any reputation he cares to make. He has a magnetic personality, and little time for idle people or laziness. He will give you lots of headaches but you will find him a wonderful and constant lover. While young he will woo the prettiest faces and they will all still adore him years down the line. That Leo charm is always at work. But don't think he isn't plain good fun too – he is!

Ruled by the sun he is happy-natured but the sun goes down on all of us and his dark days can be hard for a partner to handle. He seems so up so much of the time that it is hard for others to understand how he can get so down. This up and down quality is in the nature of Fire signs and Leo certainly has it big-time.

He is a snob. There is no denying it. If he doesn't like the name his parents gave him he will change it to something he considers more regal. I wouldn't put it past him to choose the name of a king. (Oddly enough, there are many Leos in the royal family: Queen Elizabeth the Queen Mother, Princess Anne, Princess Margaret, Princess Beatrice of York, Captain Mark Phillips, the Countess of Snowdon and many others. What do you make of that?)

Sexy Leo has such love and enthusiasm for life that he manages to give a wake-up call to the rest of the world. He is a human magnet. If he touches your life for only a moment you can be sure that that moment will be a memory you carry with you for ever. He helps his loved ones get the most of life too.

He enjoys, indeed loves, sex. To him it truly is a beautiful act. Beneath that grand and cool exterior is a man who knows that this contact goes much deeper than merely skin to skin. Making love to Leo can be fireworks. But that's enough stroking of his ego now. Let's take a tally of his faults.

He does tend to forget how important other people are. His loved ones can feel a little left behind. He assumes you'll understand that he will get to you when he has the time. Then he'll opt for the heartfelt speech instead, not realizing that it is all too late.

Yes, if you get involved with Leo you will be playing with Fire, but it could take you to heaven and back, and what a story you'll have to tell when you come back down to earth. If he marries you, he really does love you. Stand by your man and don't let anyone tell you any different because you're on a right royal road to happiness.

SEXUAL NEEDS

No matter how much time you have got to get ready, you must always look good for Leo, and that means having that ready-for-bed look all at the same time. Leo likes a partner – whether that's a partner for ever or for one night – to look after him or herself very well indeed. No slumming it, please. Even Leo when depressed will not lower those famous standards.

Life for Leo is all about love and sex and relationships. That's all three together. Certainly relationships without sex bore the lion very quickly indeed and if his or her persuasion hasn't worked then it is off to the next one. Even young Leos will constantly be pushing the relationship to the next stage, only then to go off in search of new adventure. This is not an insult. No matter how good-looking you are or how nice a person you are, once young Leo has absorbed that lesson in life he or she will be off in pursuit of the next learning experience.

Leos are not afraid to make love in public places. Out is the need for quiet and privacy and in comes fun and adventure in the great outdoors. The lion would rather be outside than inside, so long as the usual high standards can be maintained, that is. No grubby corners for Leo, please.

What about the Leo who has been hurt? It doesn't take much imagination to guess what the wounded lion is like. Resentment, coldness, even using sex as a weapon – oh yes, don't expect to get off lightly. This is where relationships can break down. Don't hurt the lion if you don't want to invite punishment!

The lion is very aware of his or her powers of attraction. The lion heart is a stronghold open only to the honoured so don't think you can escape or even dream of turning the lion down. Don't try to play them at their own sex games, either, or you'll start a war that you cannot finish. This is an exciting relationship so why should you want to turn it down anyway? One minute you are having dinner with your lion at Auntie Mavis's and all on your best behaviour and the next minute you are up to no good among the daffodils in the back garden. And it won't matter to Lord or Lady Leo if it is raining cats and dogs so better take your umbrella.

There will be very few complaints from the bedroom

once you're involved with Leo (or, if not the bedroom, then wherever that nookie corner is). There has to be romance for Leo too, so don't worry, it's not all pure sex. Leo needs to find you attractive and compatible before even thinking about hanky-panky.

Don't ever try a face-off in any argument. Stubborn Leo will push further than most and you could end up in a major break-up over something too petty for either of you even to remember. Instead, be proud of your sexy Leo, as he or she is proud of you. Just remember to chase the lion harder than the lion chases you, even if it takes some doing.

TRUEST NEED AND DESIRE

A SEXY AND BEAUTIFUL PARTNER

Marriage Partners at a Glance

This is just a taster. For more detail, turn to the chapter called Between the Sheets.

BEST BETS

ARIES will provide Leo with both spark and glamour and will not be afraid to give in to the lion's wildest fantasies.
LEO with Leo will drive each other mad with desire and they will either do or die together.
SAGITTARIUS is going to convince Leo that anything is possible, and with Sagittarius it probably is.

FAIR CHANCE

TAURUS is capable of giving Leo the kind of romance Leo needs but may pull the reins in a little too tight.

GEMINI will give Leo all the excitement he or she craves but may take a little too much of the limelight too. Still, Gemini will always hold Leo's interest.

LIBRA is the original romantic and together Leo and Libra can create great families. They can also bicker for their nation!

AQUARIUS provides the laughter that Leo needs to survive.

PISCES is a little too clever and a little too sexy all at the same time for our Leo.

HEAVY WEATHER

CANCER strikes the right seductive note for Leo but otherwise proves too attention-demanding.

VIRGO is too straight-laced for Leo and tries to keep Leo under lock and key. Virgo also knows dear Leo's tricks too well.

SCORPIO is where Leo has met his or her match and their combined egos won't fit in the same house.

CAPRICORN is a stick-in-the-mud just when Leo is getting ready to don the party hat.

Top Ten Turn-offs

1 Bad dress sense
2 Nasal hair
3 Controllers

4 People who burp
5 People who smoke roll-up cigarettes
6 Laziness (in others, of course)
7 Loudmouths
8 People who spend more than they earn
9 People who borrow money from Leo
10 Fake designer wear

HOW TO SEDUCE LEO

If you've read this far, you can probably guess. Yes, you've got to take your Leo date to the right place and you've got to wear the right clothes. This is far more so than with Taurus, to whom you can talk about family and gain all kinds of brownie points, or Capricorn and Libra, who are more interested in seeing that you are reliable. Oh no, Leo wants to see how much cash you've got and what your success quotient is. If you get high ratings in the first five minutes, then you will be through to the finals. But if you get off to a bad start you'll find it very difficult to make up lost ground. Your Leo date will get a headache, leave early and promise you another date which never sees the light of day.

You don't have to have billions in the bank. You just have to have the potential to make billions. If you do then Leo will stick by you through thick and thin and even if you don't make it in the end it won't matter because Leo will know that you could have.

So take Leo somewhere glamorous. Think Dynasty, and you will get the idea. A swanky health club would be a winner. You can sit in the club bar and drink champagne and brandy. No time for exercise of course. We don't want to be all hot and sweaty. Not yet anyway. The lion's tastebuds are set for spicy foods, so a sophisticated eastern restaurant is another option. (Not your local curry house, please.)

Leo likes to wear a heady scent. Beat the lion at its own game and wear a strong scent of seduction, preferably a classic like Chanel if you want to make a real impression. During conversation your date will switch from one topic to another at lightning speed and you'd better interrupt to hold onto the subjects that interest you. This is the man and woman who would take gold if talking was an Olympic sport.

Don't plan on a late night. Leo starts off on a high but can come down quicker than a lead balloon once he or she runs out of puff. If you think of a firework going off you will know what I mean. As quickly as Leo goes up in a blaze of glory, the extinguished lion is falling back down to earth again. But you will have fun. What I love about this sign is that Leo will do its best to give you a good time even if you are the one trying to impress. Leo likes company and is always good to spend time with. Don't worry that the lion is leading you up the garden path. This tasteful person doesn't waste time or money on anyone they don't already like. And the lion knows what it likes.

Tempted by a lion? Want a tip? Keep the evening short and sweet. Leave him or her wanting more and you'll find messages on your answering machine the moment you get back in the door. Oh yes – and don't forget to compliment Leo's hair. The crowning glory is one of Leo's finest assets and, when it comes to flattery, weakest points. So there's your chance to score.

Tell-tale Signs that Leo has Fallen

Leo in love is a sight for sore eyes. Like the victor in a battle displaying the trophy, Leo will preen before one and all with the prize – you – on his or her arm. And it probably was a battle, when you were wooed and won by this glamorous sign.

First they announce it to the world. Unlike some of the Water and Earth signs, they do not try to compartmentalize their lives. Rather they will integrate you into their work, home and social circle so that everyone can see the new spark that has ignited them. There's a little bit of romantic overoptimism that leads to talk of marriage early on which later the lion will regret and deny. Unless of course you take them up on it there and then and fly yourselves to Las Vegas for an instant wedding officiated by Elvis (or someone who looks like him).

The lion, if serious about you, will be pleased at evidence that you have your finances under control. He or she will also want you to get rid of things from your romantic past. All those CDs from your music-loving ex will have to go. A new hairstyle is a reliable sign that Leo has embarked on a new relationship. Either that, or a relationship has just ended.

Your Leo lover will trust you completely. Indeed, a Leo in love is a gullible person. But think about it. Surely it's wonderful to put all of your faith and trust in someone from the beginning? But that comes from a deep and intense Scorpio – you must make up your own mind on this one. More physical signs of a Leo in love are a racing heart that would give a doctor palpitations, and a red glow to match.

I am afraid that Leo's friends can wave goodbye for a while now for there is only so much that this busy lion can fit into a normal diary. Newly in love Leo has other priorities – well, for the next couple of weeks anyway. No, I'm only joking. Expect to see Leo take off with his or her new love to somewhere exotic for the two to explore each other and create memories for both to cherish. Just don't ask where the money for the trip will come from. After all, you did say you were very successful in your work, didn't you?

LEO PEOPLE IN YOUR LIFE

This section tells you about the people you work, rest and play with.

Leo in the Workplace

Let's get one thing straight first of all, shall we? That Leo you have seen working in the office or the shop down the road. You may think they own it, but they probably don't. They just give the impression of being the boss. This can lead to some very embarrassing moments. Indeed, dear reader, this is where the fun begins. No one in power likes to be upstaged. A usurped boss will go all out to bring about the downfall of the lion. The lion in turn will fight back and probably win. So the lion ends up as the boss anyway, winning the entire kingdom and the prince or princess who was waiting on the sidelines. In short, this is a jammy so-and-so who will do well in life through charm and sheer arrogance.

The lion really must be the boss. These people strive for the top from very early on, even to the point of being the first among their friends to get a Saturday job. And when working for others, they treat the business as if it were their own. (With the result I described above!)

Leo's employees know their place; Leo makes sure of that. The dedication and drive of Leo bosses are contagious, even if their strict rules and discipline are not easy for others to comply with. If they say that lunch is at 1 o'clock, they don't mean five past or five to. They get upset when things don't go right and find it difficult to make allowances for workers who are not up to scratch or are having an off-day. Some would say their Leo bosses are control freaks. I have to disagree. In my view they are just born leaders.

Despite the iron will, their legendary charm and warmth are still there. Leos love to be made a fuss of and love to be one of the gang – something their employees rarely feel easy with. The staff's respect for their boss is such that they feel uncomfortable when the boss lets his or her hair down. You can spot the Leo boss at parties from a mile away. There at the big table in the restaurant where you went for a quiet dinner is a Leo boss acting like it is his or her fifth birthday party and the staff are all the lion's little friends. Don't forget that Leo loves surprises, whether it is a birthday cake, or finding out that the staff have reached their target figures mid-week instead of at the end of the week.

Leo bosses help employees to sort out their problems and even offer a shoulder to cry on – so long as it is not in office time, that is. Don't think cruel, think professional. That is what the lion is. The boss will remember your birthday, and understand when you have a personal crisis on. But they won't necessarily give you time off – unless it really is a matter of life or death. You'll get some worthwhile words of wisdom instead, and you'll remember them too.

Partnerships don't work for Leos. They have their own way of doing things and they don't like to share the reins. They are happy to poach staff from other companies and if it's you the lion's eyes are on I advise you to jump at the opportunity for some new and exciting work. In Leo's eyes poaching people is not wrong, it's just business fair and square.

You will find Leo a good and trusting boss, but don't expect a blind eye to be turned to any shortcuts or sloppy work. Pushing and shoving has got your boss where they are today, with a good few fights en route, and the lion won't think much of anyone who's sitting back and not pulling their weight. They got to the top in the end, and they will want you to know that you can too.

If you want to get on Leo's good side, I suggest you work overtime for free. You may think it sounds like a dreadful idea, but when bonus time comes round your name will be on the top of the list.

If you join Leo's team you are on to a winner. Leo will always play it fair and square with you, whatever your position (as long as it's lower than theirs).

Leo Mother-in-law

If she doesn't like you, she will tell you straight away.

What she thinks and feels is written all over her face, not to mention coming out of her mouth. But it would take a very incompatible daughter- or son-in-law not to find some sort of common ground with this sun-worshipping sign.

Leo mothers-in-law are vulnerable. Don't be surprised to learn of a brush with an antidepressant in the past. The lion can suffer from depression and this woman won't have got to the rich and rewarding place she is today without going through a bare patch or two. Don't go saying that you thought a Leo's life was one long party. I did say (oh, yes I did) that the sun can go down on Leo and leave the poor lion in darkness. So a little understanding could be called for.

Your Leo mother-in-law will treat you very well indeed because anyone her precious child chooses can only be good. If her child loves you, she will love you too. Family is important to her and she can often get more satisfaction out of her grandchildren than her own children. Her own children were a learning experience for her, and by the time she has grandchildren she feels she's doing it right.

Don't mess with this woman, though, and, certainly don't cheat on her child. With her well-honed social skills she'll find out exactly what you've been up to, and even if your partner forgives you, she certainly won't. Like any lioness looking out for her cubs, she'll attack ferociously, and her methods can range from obvious to devious. Better watch out what she feeds you next time you visit their house!

It is going to be very hard to satisfy her at Christmas. The Crown jewels won't be good enough.

She won't say anything ungrateful, but her shoulders will hunch up like a tired animal's. Here's a good idea. She suffers from back problems as she gets older, so give or buy her a massage and you're sure to be in her good books for a long time to come.

She will claim to have done everything, been everywhere and got the T-shirt. Don't try to outsmart her. She doesn't like a smart alec. Open doors for her to show her you know your place. Go down on bended knee if you like. She'll find that quite acceptable. She is the queen of all she surveys, after all. But she's fun and your children will love her. She's an ace babysitter – so long as you don't mind coming home to a full-on party with your children dressed up like glamour models. She's a bit inclined to come round when you least expect her, so lock the door if you want privacy. Better bolt it too. This isn't a woman who is easily hindered.

She will be a valued and a valuable part of your family. Your friends will get crushes on her (you'd better let on to them how old she really is). Enjoy her. She is unique.

Leo Children

Leo children can range from idle to overactive – usually they start off idle and then pick up speed until before long you can't catch up with them. They can be uproariously loud or quiet as mice. The girl is a tomboy, and although she will become graceful when older, for now you'd better not waste the party frock.

They can't wait to be big and they have so many

plans that they're likely to wish their childhood away. They would rather hang out with big brother or sister's friends than with friends their own age and this is often where their first relationships begin. Arguments ensue, as you can imagine. No one likes to lose their best friend to a little brother or sister.

They will remain loyal to their family and if a parent becomes unemployed little Leo will be up at five every day doing the paper-round to help out. They won't even mention the money again. Family really is everything to the loyal little lion. But lioncub won't do the housework. The child probably doesn't even like the place the family lives in. And they would really rather pick their own school clothes than wear that uniform. Only if you encourage your lioncubs to treat their rooms as miniature palaces (a palace being their preferred abode, of course) will you see any domestic effort. And designer clothes for school would go down rather well too!

You won't like the kind of people lioncub idolizes. Only the pop star who goes off the rails will arouse little Leo's curiosity. Nobody ordinary and straightforward will do for them. Don't worry too much about where this child is going. Lions always land on their paws, from their very cheek as well as their ability to get things right first time.

Expect your lioncub to appear in a Shakespeare play at some point in their childhood. As much as lions love adventure, so too do they love the arts, and clever, stylish and, for a child, very much out of the ordinary Shakespeare is just right for them.

Lioncubs want to choose their own bedtime. Be clever and tell them an earlier time than is strictly necessary and allow them to negotiate you to a later time, where they will feel that they have won.

You are, I'm afraid, going to have a nightmare with their hair and they will go through more hairstyles than hot dinners in a quest to find the right style. Their hair is their crowning glory, but glory doesn't come easy. Be especially careful with the hair of your little lioness. If she announces one day she wants it all cut off you'd better dissuade her. No matter what she says at the time she is sure to come to regret it. Then she will place the blame anywhere but on her own (shorn) head.

Listen to this wise child. They talk a lot more sense than you may realize. Don't underestimate the child's potential. So if lioncub has an obsession with science then encourage the child and, if you can, get special lessons. One day your lioncub could invent something that makes this world a better – no, a more exciting place – to live.

Leo Friends

You must share your Leo friends with many others. If you don't see them for a month or more you must still greet them like you saw them yesterday. They can't stand moody people and will drop you quicker than a rotten apple if you sulk. When life is fun with them it's terrific but if Leo's got the blues you'll have to listen to all the tales of woe. Just don't bore Leo with yours!

Supposing you go out with a Leo friend. Off you go to a club or a bar. What you'll soon realize is that this isn't a night out with your friend, it's a night out with a whole bunch of people your Leo friend knows. There's one solution, if you really do want some unalloyed Leo company: have yourself a good time with somebody else. After a while Leo realizes you are doing very well without them and pads their way back to you to check up on the scene where you are. You see, lions just can't help looking around, but the more fun you can have without them, the more they'll be tempted back to your side.

Or just give in and go along with the crowd. And if you've got your very good-looking partner with you, keep them under lock and key. Leos think anyone who is good-looking is their property. There's a compliment in there somewhere. Leo wouldn't be friends with you if you weren't as gorgeous as you are!

In the comfort of your crowd, let your Leo friend talk nonstop about life, work, and future plans for world domination. Don't mock them. It might all come true. You'll have to spend a bit of money on the lion, but they'll do the same for you if you need it. The difference here is that the lion expects the money to be repaid the next day. Hence the world of Leo continues. These people really do live in a bit of a bubble. They probably believe they are in some way related to royalty. If not, they will certainly behave as if they are.

Leos stay friends with all their exes. I recently did a show with the American movie actor George Hamilton, who appeared with his ex-wife Alana Hamilton. Well, I would rather die than share airspace with any ex of mine (and believe me, none of them were half bad), so I've always found this side of the Leo rather baffling.

Leos will have the best parties in town with the

prettiest faces. Just don't try to steal a beauty from under the lion's nose! In the lion you have a generous, encouraging, inspiring friend – even if you have to share this regal creature with many others.

Virgo

August 24 to September 23

MODEST, SHY, PRACTICAL, intelligent, overcritical and perfectionist: these are some of the key words to describe Virgo. It is not very often that anyone can put one over on Virgo. These people have an uncanny gift for seeing through others. Their intuition, another of their strong characteristics, seldom leads them astray.

Virgo is very good at telling other people what is wrong with their lives, and the annoying thing is that Virgo is usually right. But Virgos are much less good at sorting out their own lives. They worry too much about how the world views them and they see no recovery from any embarrassment they have suffered. Until of course the storm blows over and they start to do well again, when old embarrassments will finally be forgotten, or simply denied.

Amuse yourself by reading this chapter to Virgo friends

and watching them shake their head and deny almost all of it. You see, Virgo will admit to nothing. You cannot say anything to them that they do not already know and please don't criticize them for they are much better at criticizing themselves than you will ever be. They won't admit to faults, they deny they ever try to organize others and they swear they don't make out their shopping list in aisle order. (If you can't find the washing powder just ask them and they will call back 'aisle fifteen section four' quicker than Dale Winton in *Supermarket Sweep*.) And oddly enough all this is partly why they make such good advisers – for they do. They don't take what you say at face value. They query and probe and ask why you feel this way, and what if X was Y, and what about Z, and in this way help those around them to take many other points into consideration. These reasonable, analytical people are the ones you want to have around in times of trouble. Then they really come into their own, with their enviable characteristics of coolness in a crisis, competence, quick-thinking and compassion. Combined with their methodical, calm and down-to-earth manner, these qualities make them invaluable.

But you don't have to wait until disaster strikes to call upon your Virgo friends. Their sense of humour is wonderful and they have a terrific ability to tell a good story and to take a joke (as long as it does not blacken their character, that is). Their enormous capacity for fun and enjoyment makes them great company. Adaptability, another of the Virgo qualities, ensures that they are at home in any surroundings and with any type of person. They are conscientious, too, with a fine sense of responsibility and a desire always to do the right thing. However, if I had to pick one attribute that really sets them apart, it would be their selflessness. They always put the other fellow first, considering others' feelings before their own at no matter what personal cost.

They are kind-hearted and generous and not too good with money. They'd rather spend it, or give it away, than set it aside for a rainy day. Those that do save have probably experienced a major financial problem that has shocked them into saving instead of spending. It is a pity they are not good with money, really, because in every other way they make excellent partners and home-makers, with a genuine love for the warmth and closeness of the family circle. Although they love social activities and are much in demand, they put their home first every time and do not like to spend too much time away from it.

In business Virgo's quick brain and keen awareness of opportunity makes him or her a competitor to be reckoned with. This is a business person who plays fair and would never pull a dirty trick for his or her own furtherance. Careers that require organizational skills suit Virgo. It is hard for Virgo not to organize people and although this is a good thing for a boss to see in an employee, it can become annoying when your Virgo assistant tells you not to wear that suit to an important meeting because it simply doesn't make the right statement.

The true Virgo is idealistic, sometimes a dreamer, tender-hearted, and often a poet. Virgo life runs in five-year cycles. Every fifth year from the date of birth some significant event occurs in Virgo's life which will determine the shape of things for the next five years. Not such a surprise for a well-organized sign, is it, to see a regular pattern emerging! Virgo is no angel, not all the time, well, only 90 per cent of the time anyway. Or at least they try to be. You see, Virgos believe that the wrongs and rights they do get added up at the end of their life. Virgos believe in accountability.

Virgo people can be shy, but not when you expect it. They will do everything to avoid the person they are attracted to, but if they see a potential hot date for a friend they'll be over there taking down numbers and making plans before you can stop them. And they have some odd habits. A Virgo friend of mine used to collect the complimentary soap and shampoo you get in hotels. Well, that's OK, but was anyone ever allowed to use one? Not me, anyway! Another friend never paid for a drink when we were out but would offer me champagne the moment we stepped into her home. There is no argument about it: Virgo has weird ways, and thinks that everyone else is the same. Listen up, Virgo. They're not! But we'll forgive you, lovely creatures, for these strange traits of yours.

Natural-born counsellors, Virgos always offer advice and help to their friends, colleagues, partner, children, neighbours, newsagent . . . They don't always wait to be asked. They exude confidence even if they are not feeling great inside. They like to wear the earthy colours that represent their sign. They have friends and sometimes partners of different ages and they don't believe you have to be over eighteen to have an opinion. They don't have to live in their own country but can settle easily in a foreign land as long as they are given some space to make their own. They succeed well in life because they expect things to go their way. This is why they feel so downcast when things fail. They just weren't expecting it. And shy or not they will walk into a place as if they own it until someone slights them and then their confidence, of which they were almost unaware, will crumble.

My worry with Virgo people is that they spend too much time on others and their own life suffers as a result. If you tell them you are having a bad week they may just go and plan a parade in your honour and cancel their own plans. They don't expect you to do the same in return, either, but are quite happy to be at your beck and call – whether you want them to or not. They learn from those around them and are not afraid of hard work, which makes them great bosses and marriage partners.

Just be wary of crossing them. They never forget. Twenty years later they will still be hoarding the information about that time when you let them down, or didn't pay them back that fiver. They will pay for you on a night out and not begrudge a penny of it, but ask to borrow money and Virgo turns into Dan the Debt Collector. Fail to pay it back and your reputation will be ruined – in Virgo's eyes.

They have remarkable acting ability, but tend not to consider such a profession. Not unless they want a few roles to hide behind, that is. They'd rather stay single than marry the wrong person. They are not above having affairs but I have rarely seen an affair turn into true love for a Virgo. They like things to be clean and simple if the relationship is to be the beginning of something they can build on.

SECRETS OF THE SEXES

So how do the males and females of the species differ then? Let's have a look.

Ms Virgo

Ms Virgo is a practical girl who earns the respect of her own sex but sometimes attracts jealousy from them too. She believes that if you want something badly enough, you'll get it. She'd prefer to have one partner rather than lots but like us all she has to go through the mill. By the time she is twenty she will have a tale of woe to tell about the lover who had to leave her for a worthy reason. She will fail to tell you that the worthy reason was her best friend. This kind of detail is rarely uncovered unless you are very clever with your questioning. Ms Virgo has her pride. She does get jealous but she is nothing like Ms Scorpio or Ms Cancer. She is perfectly capable of getting her own back on a jilting lover by spreading little rumours about a mysterious genital disease. Even the person she's talking about will believe it and run off to the doctor.

She does not like taking chances. She picks partners and jobs that promise a natural progression towards success. She does not want to join the rat race because she'd rather feel she was onto a sure thing with people who knew her true value.

She will spend much of her time counselling her friends about their problems and is not very good at keeping secrets. It's all for your own good, you know. That personal problem that you've got, well, she'll bring it up at a dinner party because there's someone there she's sure can help you out. You can only blush crimson and wish to disappear under the table. Once a Virgo friend called me to tell me her friend thought I had been terrible on a radio show. Now that information I could have done without at the time and many other friends would never have said it. Many women only like to tell you the good, but Ms Virgo thinks you should have the good, the bad and the ugly and will consider it her personal responsibility to keep you well informed.

She will consult you before making a decision but her mind is already made up. She hears what she wants to hear and anything else goes in one ear and out the other. She makes mistakes in love when young and learns a great deal by them. And boy, can she make mistakes. Her first love is likely to have been the most unsuitable candidate you can imagine but her eyes will still glisten when she remembers him. The sad thing is that when she is young, she is the one likely to have been dumped.

She is a hard worker and will aid and abet you in whatever you set out to do, but if you idle or flag, she can nag. She is neat and tidy and you are likely to find her home spotless – and yours too before long. This is the kind of guest who will help to clean up after a dinner party but while you are serving coffee she's cleaning out the cupboards and showing everyone the dust marks that have built up over the months. And yet she means so well.

She has a habit of dressing to show off her worst features. If big-boned she'll be in horizontal shapes because she read somewhere that horizontal shapes were classic. She turns to reading to find out where she should be going in life and with whom. She has great choice in writers, mind you, so if you like books she's the person to borrow from.

Her downside is the way she interferes, but I can think of worse traits. If you had a woman in your life who cooked, cleaned and listened to your problems, I'm sure you wouldn't complain too much. Not until you hear the request she has made on the radio for a cheer-up song for your sister Jane whose boyfriend has just left her for someone else – but, oh dear, Jane didn't know it yet. She does now! Ride it through. If you give her time she'll come up trumps for you again and again, and being honest has never been a crime to Ms Virgo. Not yet.

Mr Virgo

Let's talk about how to spot Mr Virgo, shall we? Look around the noisy nightclub. He is the one trying to have a conversation over the noise and I mean a real conversation too. And not only will he tell you who he's going to go home with, he'll succeed through his sheer cheek. Mr Virgo has a knack of getting his own way. He is likeable and adaptable and well respected by his fellow men. He has a touch of femininity about him which makes it easy for his mates to tell him their problems. But like Ms Virgo he won't keep your secrets to himself. He just loves having gossip to share with people, and he really does to try to help you out. He's just looking for information for you. Don't tell him off. There's no point. He can't help it.

He is probably a good cook so you're in for a treat here, girls. You can sit back and put your feet up while he does all the hard work. Women adore him, so you will have to be prepared for lots of competition. He does at times find it hard to talk about his feelings and there is a dark side to him which can lead into depression. You will not find out about it from anything he says outright, but you'll find a piece of paper with life's good and bad points jotted down, or some such, and you'll know he's struggling through a crisis of his own.

He is, of course, perfect to have around when you are having a crisis. Calm, rational, dependable, thoughtful and caring, he really is an asset. Lucky, and blessed with good health (though also a hypochondriac), Mr Virgo has a wonderful way of paying you compliments just when you are feeling down. He has a fine, sometimes quirky sense of humour and can make you laugh until your sides hurt. However, if he doesn't find something funny he'll convince you that it is you who is warped, not him.

He will treat you well, though he is inclined to be a little selfish when it comes to falling in with your wishes. Quite good at managing financial matters, you will find his bills in order, if only because his conscience wouldn't allow otherwise. Don't expect to find stacks of money salted away, or piles of shares, mind you. Mr Virgo is likely to have spent the last five years paying off his latest credit card.

He probably collected something in his childhood, something odd which he still has hidden somewhere at home. One friend of mine had a passion for car insignia. He even had the angel from a Rolls-Royce, as well as a Porsche badge or two. Today he's got his own Porsche, but those little stolen baubles from his childhood are still in a box in a kitchen cupboard – though he doesn't know I know they are there. And he'd die if any little Virgo took the badge from his Porsche.

Mr Virgo's intuition will never lead him astray, and his wit will never let him down. You will love this slightly oddball character.

SEXUAL NEEDS

Virgo is not frightened of telling you what he or she wants from love. In fact, it might become just a bit intimidating. It is all very well being told what you are good at in bed, but Virgo will tell you where you are going wrong too. There might even be diagrams cut out and pinned to the wall. Then there's the requirement to act out scenes from Virgo's favourite films (not to mention the odd naughty movie). It's no good being squeamish around Virgo.

So if you want to know what you are letting yourself in for, here are the two most important facts. The first is that Virgo makes some rather strange requests in love so if you like to go for the alternative then you have found your man/woman. The second is that if you have strange tastes then your Virgo mate will call you a freak. Got it? Good. Glad we got that straight.

You'd better be into sex because Virgo does like rather a lot of it and if there's any sign of cooling off you'd better ask Virgo what's troubling him or her. You see, Virgo allows difficulties, whatever they may be, to permeate all aspects of his or her life. This person just isn't good at transcending problems. If your lover is being funny with you it could be because they did not get the pay rise they were expecting at work, rather than anything you've done.

You might think at first meeting that Virgo is, as their sign would suggest, virginal, but that is very far indeed from the truth. That quiet woman in glasses is just dying to unravel her long hair and show you what she has on underneath. But don't get too excited, boys. She is saving the real show for the one she loves and is not into giving her body freely. None the less, still waters run deep, especially where sex and the Virgo is concerned. Singer Shania Twain's seductive look gives more away than perhaps she realizes, and there's more to Harry Connick Junior the crooner's smile than meets the eye. And Virgo Hugh Grant didn't hold back when he met up with prostitute Divine Brown.

Virgo men and women both tend to have some sort of a hang-up about their body: anything from their hips to their nose to their toenails. They will not talk about sex all the time, may not even mention it, but when they do start talking they can make even Scorpio blush with the kind of things they have in mind. They usually have their fair share of literature on sex, since Virgo is a sign that likes to learn from books. And whatever it is they learn from the printed word, something really works. You won't have much to complain about with your Virgo lover. Treat them well and they will treat you better, and you will have a right royal romp every night to boot.

TRUEST NEED AND DESIRE

PERFECT LOVE

Marriage Partners at a Glance

This is just a taster. For more detail, turn to the chapter called Between the Sheets.

BEST BETS

TAURUS and Virgo fulfil each other's wildest fantasies once they've worked up the courage to admit them to each other.

CANCER indulges in the full-on love fest that Virgo needs and also knows how to behave in public (a must for Virgo).

VIRGO with Virgo will lead the perfect life, so long as each knows when to let the other have the spotlight.

CAPRICORN fits in with Virgo like they were made for each other, and they probably were.

PISCES is sex on legs but love and hate come close together and that's just when Pisces and Virgo are married.

FAIR CHANCE

SCORPIO is sexy if a little hard to control.

SAGITTARIUS intrigues but also annoys Virgo, saying the wrong thing at the worst time.

AQUARIUS has all the words needed to talk Virgo into the bedroom and up the aisle, but for how long is the question.

HEAVY WEATHER

ARIES is too much of a loose cannon for Virgo, who likes to exercise some control.

GEMINI is too much of a livewire and threatens not to deliver what Virgo has been promised. Virgo decides Gemini is all talk.

LEO is a show-off and Virgo would rather be the one to hold court.

LIBRA proves irresistible to Virgo, who finds sexy Libra heaven and hell rolled into one.

Top Ten Turn-offs

1 Know-it-alls (Virgo already knows it all)
2 Chewing gum
3 Body odour
4 Unpunctuality
5 Spendthrifts
6 Bad cooks
7 Facial hair
8 People who burp after food
9 Untidiness
10 Organizers (that's Virgo's job)

HOW TO SEDUCE VIRGO

You must remember that your average Virgo is very conscious of detail and will notice your dress and grooming. An untidy hairstyle or a ladder in your stocking could scare them off – and this is just the average Virgo. Heaven forbid that you appear with a hair out of place before an above average Virgo! If your date runs for the phone box claiming an urgent call to make, even with mobile in hand, then they have been put off by the lipstick liner that is outside of your lipline or the Old Spice you borrowed off your dad at the last minute.

Virgos are so kind-hearted, though, that they will

find it hard to be horrible to you on your first date. If they have agreed to go out with you then it is because they have genuine feelings for you and they want your date together to be a success. Ask them which restaurant they would like to go to, and Virgos say, 'I don't mind, you choose.' Don't be deceived. They know exactly where they want to go, and if they should offer up a loose suggestion then act on it for it is likely that the subtext is 'take me here if you want to impress me'.

They will not be afraid to spend money on you and have been known to be a little foolish with their cash where those they love are concerned. Some famous Virgos have spent millions on their spouses. They believe you can show love through material things. There is some materialism in the Virgo. Check out their gear. You'll notice at least one designer label, and it is more likely to be on sunglasses or watch than on clothing. Don't forget to bring a little cash to the occasion yourself. This excellent marriage partner and wonderful home-maker is well worth investing in, and will not let you down or leave you when times get rough.

On the first date, take Virgo to a familiar place. (Do your detective work to find out where it should be.) Virgos are more confident on home ground and more willing to reveal themselves. Not until the second date can you fly them to Paris by Concorde. An earth sign ruled by Mercury, the travel bug hits them hard once they find their confidence.

A restaurant is always good for a first date and Virgos love their food but add to the detective work some enquiries about food allergies or preferences. More Virgos are vegetarians than any other sign of the zodiac.

Virgos are not easy people, and don't give themselves up freely, but you won't have to wait too long for sex if Virgo is getting the right vibes from you. They do follow their famous intuition and are not embarrassed to strip off in front of you if instinct is giving it the nod.

If you really want to get the fires of romance burning hot then get Virgo to cook for you at home. No doubt Virgo has already done the shopping list (in aisle order, naturally) and you can be sure of an array of delights to await you. And who knows where dessert might lead.

Just be careful of talking about your problems too early on or you could well determine your role in Virgo's life as that of a friend to be pitied rather than as a lover. You see, everyone tells Virgo their problems. Be different and ask Virgo about theirs for a change. They might thank you in kind!

Tell-tale signs that Virgo has Fallen

Virgo in love cannot stop talking about the person who has captured his or her heart. The car, home and even designer watch go up for sale to set Virgo and partner up in their new life together. If jealous, Virgo will go all out to destroy the reputation of the third party, accusing them of anything from body odour to an unpaid overdraft. They are by no means the most jealous sign of the zodiac but they do like to be able to call their own their own.

When in love, Virgo doesn't hold back. It's odd to think that this is the so-called virgin of the zodiac. If Virgo seems unwilling to marry you, don't get upset. Virgo doesn't have to marry a person to stay true to them. If you are puzzled by the jealousy quotient, well, you think you know Virgo inside out one day and then the next you find you are living with a stranger. Virgo is complex, and not obvious.

Although idealists, they are not unrealistic, and Virgo judgement is usually good. If Virgo says he or she thinks you could spend your lives together, this will be the result of considered and lengthy thought. Both Mr and Ms Virgo are worriers, though, so don't be surprised if when they tell you they love you they offer you the chance to change your mind a dozen times. This is Virgo's way of finding security. Virgos would rather know sooner than later if your intentions are not the same as theirs. Life is far too short to make mistakes – even if they are moving through it at only five miles an hour.

I have decided to let you in on a secret. Virgo likes to wash after sex. Don't take offence. Virgo is fastidious. They are quite willing to get dirty all over again and very soon, just so long as they can scrub up again to that virginal look they like to assume. There you are. They can't fool you now.

Virgos often get sick when they fall in love. If your Virgo colleague has called in sick and you know he or she has a new lover, don't doubt the truth of the phone call. They are more likely genuinely ill than in bed with their new love. This is a sometimes hypochondriac sign, but not a dishonest one. Passionate emotions can sometimes make a person ill. I once knew a Virgo who sneezed at people he didn't like. He seemed to be allergic to them. And a Virgo bathroom cabinet looks like the overspill for the local Boots the chemist.

Virgo in love will not be able to wallow in bed all day. He or she will be up making breakfast or

163

organizing your sock drawer. Even people with Virgo as their ascendant find themselves organizing things that don't belong to them. That friend who washes the cup you made her tea in as soon as she has finished it is definitely under Virgo influence. When she starts telling you how to reorganize your kitchen you'd better put your foot down.

The best thing about Virgo is how much they enhance your life. If you're in the wrong job they'll talk you into changing it. Car not working? They'll arrange for it to be fixed.

Want to be sure of Virgo's love? If he or she takes your hand in public and kisses you, you are onto a sure thing. If Virgo is confident enough to show the people around that you are a couple, then you can be confident you have Virgo for keeps.

VIRGO PEOPLE IN YOUR LIFE

This section tells you about the people you work, rest and play with.

Virgo in the Workplace

Clever, quick and with a sense of fair play, Virgo is the good guy in the world of business. You won't be able to pull the wool over your Virgo boss's eyes, either. Pull a sickie and Virgo boss will be on the phone offering remedies, and will want to know that you took them and exactly how well they worked when you return to work the following day, for you will be ready to return to work the next day. And don't go malingering in the office either. Virgo boss will be over with a remedy in one hand and your afternoon schedule in the other.

Take a peek at your Virgo colleague's notepad, just for fun. You are sure to find a well-polished lyric or a humorous phrase there. Virgo singer and musician Harry Connick Junior didn't get where he got to by being afraid to put his jazzy riffs down on paper whenever they came to him. Virgo has talents that go beyond the ordinary workplace. However, you do not often see Virgo at the top of the tree. Virgo's talents are often expended making other people money. They are much better at doing the hard slog than at sitting back and taking all the praise, unlike a few other signs I could mention! (But I'll be kind, like a Virgo would, and not mention them.) Virgos are not easy-going in the office. They can't sit still, and as a boss dish out orders at a rate that can annoy new staff who haven't got used to them yet. Don't slate them. The other people in the office, who know Virgo very well, have plenty of reason to defend their boss to you.

Those who do make it to the top do so through sheer hard work with a dose of well-deserved luck rather than through the help of others. Good reliable staff for Virgo are essential. Virgo bosses need to like their staff as people, even though they will not socialize much with them. They are critical, conscientious and expect their staff to match their capacity for work. They are good at delegating. They see no reason why they should have a dog and bark themselves.

They are fair, considerate, loyal and sincere, and expect the same from you. Their businesses succeed because of their good public relations, even if they haven't quite managed to keep up with the latest computer equipment. They don't mix work and pleasure. When it is time for play Virgos want to get as far away as possible from the people they have been telling what to do all year. Some say a Virgo in the workplace is like a policeman on patrol. Everything is Virgo's business and if you are on the phone in tears then your boss will sort your life out, tell you to chuck the boyfriend, advise you on a suitable partner, and expect you to get back on with your work double-quick.

One word of warning if you work for a Virgo. Be punctual with your work. If Virgo wants your work in by a certain day, then make sure you do it, or better still earn a few points by getting it in early. Time counts for everything, and Virgo would rather you got everything in on time and then left the office smartly at close of business than stay late to slog it out because you've taken too long. Expect to be paid for doing overtime, because Virgo doesn't want any favours. Just brilliant, precise work done exactly to time. Get it right for this boss and he or she will not fail to appreciate you.

The Virgo Mother-in-law

You really have landed yourself in it here, haven't you? Virgo mother-in-law will have vetted you completely before you were allowed anywhere near her son or daughter, and will have gone to great lengths to dig up all the dirt on you. She'll need to know that not only are you in love with her child but also that you are fully competent and reliable to take care of her precious one.

Indeed, she'll need to know she can rely on you a bit herself, too, and believe me she's going to be around for a long time. Virgos have endurance. OK, you've obviously passed the first few hurdles if Ms Virgo is now your mother-in-law. So what have you got to look forward to?

The next twenty Christmases are already planned so better forget that skiing holiday or at least get a request in a few years early for a Christmas off. Otherwise, take her along on the ski trip. She likes to be involved. Funny, then, how she is often the loner in the crowd, trying to make herself a part of things but always holding a little back too. She can never completely relax, and will have had every illness going at some point in her life. Not really, of course, but she likes to think she has. She has a medicine cabinet large enough to supply a hospital and if you tell her how you feel she will do a great job of diagnosing what's wrong with you. Here's an odd thing: she has a rumbling stomach that can be heard across the dinner table but she won't like to declare herself as the source of the gurgle.

She will take on the job of grandmother very well, helping you to raise and organize your children and even dressing for the role. She'd rather look the part than be mutton dressed as lamb. She will spend the first four years of your child's life worrying about what school the grandchild should go to. She probably turned up at the christening with a printed list. I can't guarantee that you'll get a whole night out if she's babysitting, mind you. She will be on the phone to the restaurant declaring that your child has chicken pox, though you'll find it's just that he fell asleep on the train set, leaving little indentations on the side of his face.

Don't take her for a fool. She is very clever indeed, if a little overanxious. She is likely to have married for life and can inspire you to work through your difficulties and make your partnership succeed as well as hers has done. Once you start telling her your problems, however, you will have to keep up the bulletins, so make a decision from the beginning and be prepared to stick to it. Once she knows a little she will carry on nagging until she knows it all. She often has a furrowed brow for even if she hasn't had a troubled life she will claim she has. The grandmother in the Tescos advert is probably a Virgo. She knows all the staff by name and expects them to run around after her. She is very picky about her food, reading labels and analysing them and probably went for the organic option long before it was trendy.

She will insist on buying her children underwear long after they have passed the age of knickers up to the waist. Expect a weary look on your partner's face on Christmas mornings. Toss the thermals in the pile along with all the other items that she has deemed a necessity. They'll come in handy when you finally go on that holiday to the Himalayas.

She can flirt when she wants and she can dress to kill, but she is much more likely to dress and act in exactly the right way for the right occasion. You can rely on her and you'll always have her support. But you may have to teach her that when you say no you mean no. Take her away with you on holiday and see her let her hair down. Just remember to put up with the complaints about her digestive system, even though she keeps eating the very foods that caused the complaints in the first place.

Virgo

Virgo Children

A Virgo child is not out every single night, and is more likely to want friends in the family home than to go over to theirs. If you are staying in for a night in front of the television, be warned that little Virgo has already ringed the programmes you are all going to watch and won't go to bed until the clock has tinged on the very hour you have set for bedtime.

This child will be the boss of you from the day he or she is born (believe me, I have a Virgo son). I remember when I first looked into my son's eyes. Even though he couldn't really focus the expression was clearly saying right, let's get organized, shall we? He slept through the night from day one and if anyone woke him he would glare as if to say, don't you know it's bedtime, you fool? We eat when he wants to eat and we play when he wants to play, but I can't complain as he's tailored himself a very nice little schedule. The clever little chap has made sure that my husband and I get enough sleep so that we can both work hard. He's chosen the school, the college and the visits to foreign countries, and he wants to be sure that there is going to be the money to pay for it all.

Impatient would be an understatement. He breast-feeds with an attitude that says come on, come on, time is money, money is time. At least I know that my darling Paris is going to see his Mummy and Daddy very comfortable in years to come for he is a boss already and good at it. Although all of this is true I would be telling only half of it if I didn't also point out that he is a little angel with a sense of humour I never imagined a child could possess. When you have a Virgo child you'll wonder what you ever did without them. I certainly wonder how I coped before Paris came along to sort me out. And I was holding out for Libra so that I could emotionally blackmail him! Now I wouldn't change him for all the tea in China.

These are determined children and you'd better believe them when they announce their plans for when they are grown-up. Involve them in as much as possible of what you do and they'll be happy. They will have friends of both sexes and a wide range of ages. They will learn about sex by talking to older friends long before thinking of doing it themselves. They can be little know-it-alls and will ask the frankest of questions of the grown-ups around them, so watch out for a little embarrassment and maybe think about covering their ears up from time to time! Show them lots and lots of love if you want to make sure you never have trouble on your hands. And how could you fail to love this bossy but endearingly individual child?

Virgo Friends

A Virgo friend really is a friend for life. No, really. More so probably than anybody else. Need some money, a place to sleep, a few words of wisdom? All of these requests Virgo friends can fulfil. Offer your Virgo friend a place to stay and it will be in better shape on departure than it was on his or her arrival. Your Virgo friends may find it hard to be nice to the new faces you introduce them to, however. Their first instinct is to be shy and to back off while they suss out the new individual. After all, if Virgo takes on a friend, it's for life, not just for a year.

If you can, don't work with your Virgo mate. There will be a major bust-up at some point. Virgo doesn't like to mix work with pleasure and finds friendships in the workplace a little irksome. But they will try hard, none the less. They will make sure that you always have someone to talk to but they will often comment on your work too, whether you want it or not.

Your family and friends will love your Virgo chum, and even if Virgo flirts it won't be taken too far. Virgos may not be the trendiest dressers in the zodiac but they are smart and dignified and what's more, if you have a stain on your party dress they will know just how to get it out. However, I'm afraid that Mr or Ms Virgo will not be nice to your partner if they decide the partner isn't right for you. They are also going to be the first to phone you up if your lover has been caught snogging someone else. And they will expect you to be grateful for having been told.

They are more of an asset than a drawback, even if they do make you look at life from a more serious angle. If you decide to go on holiday then leave all the arrangements to Virgo, who'll get the best deal and have the names of all the best bars and restaurants to visit when you get there. Virgos are not frightened to get involved with the party spirit either. Romance is their problem area, and especially when young they are likely to go for the wrong type. Expect to help Virgo out of a few scrapes, and then to be told how you could have done it better.

You'll have to wait for Virgo to finish a good meal

before contemplating going to the club. And they'll insist you get some good food down you too. They'd like to have friends who are biddable but in fact you have to be strong to cope with a Virgo so some colourful relationships often ensue. They hate it when friends and lovers don't mix and if it reaches a critical point then friends lose out as Virgo's chosen partner gets undivided loyalty.

Virgos are not frightened to look their age. They like to reach age milestones publicly. They will look forward to the thirtieth (fortieth, fiftieth) birthday party they have asked you to arrange for them. So long as you get the colour scheme right, of course, so that it matches the new outfit they have bought.

Take their advice. They know what they are talking about. Stand by when they are going through a bad romance, even if they have given you the heave-ho. They will need you again and you will be glad to have such a valuable person back in your life. And if your button comes off or you have a headache then don't worry because your Virgo friend is a walking repair shop and chemist, not to mention counsellor, guide and matchmaker (though not always to your taste). And the best thing of all is that you will never be let down. Not after all the organizational trouble they have gone to on your behalf!

Libra

September 24 to October 23

BALANCE, JUSTICE, HARMONY, partnership. sociability and refinement: these are the key words for lovely Libra. Theirs is something of a conflicting personality and the scales, which are their birth sign, are the keynote. Libra people require balance, but they can go quite a long way in one direction before realizing they need to double-back and balance up the other side of their life. For example, for long periods they will do nothing, then suddenly they become possessed by a fanatical desire to work and no one can stop them. Emotionally they are happy, witty, charming and irresistible – sometimes – and then quiet, withdrawn and a little depressed at other times. There is no happy medium, but in the long run balance is achieved.

These are the best fathers in the zodiac. They always know the right thing to say to a tired or unruly child. Yes, every woman's dream, but does that follow through in the bedroom, I hear you ask. This is the person for whom the bedroom is the most important room in the house and you can find everything in there from beautiful pictures and boxes of chocolates right down to sexy underwear and a tea-maker. They are ready for anything and quite expert when it comes to sex. So there's your answer. Actor Michael Douglas (talking of expertise in the bedroom!) has played plenty of sexy roles in his career but he made the ultimate Libra move by becoming a dad again at an age when most of the other signs are planning their children's weddings.

Libra people learn the arts of seduction quite young. As children they probably had dates for the primary school disco, indeed, more than one at the same time, most likely, since they will have identified several suitable conquests and gone after them all. They also have some fine qualities, among them kindness, tolerance, patience, sensitivity and generosity. They are trusting, too. However, since I have talked about balance, I shall have to warn you about the less endearing facets of their personality, such as obstinacy, moodiness and an inclination towards unreliability. They must curb these tendencies in order to attain real happiness in life. Their genuine sweetness and kindness make them very loving people and it is a shame to have a blot on that particularly beautiful copybook.

They were born to have families and the Libra people I know who have opted out have usually got some compelling planetary conflict in their charts to explain it. On the whole they want nothing more than a happy family life and fun times. They don't handle money difficulties very well so keep an eye on any bank accounts you share. They are not sneaky but they will not want to tell you the bad news that the account is overdrawn and you could find yourself running into unnecessary problems.

People love to be around Libra. Libra shows such interest in what people have to say and can always think of a compliment. Libra is even nice to the people he or she doesn't get on with, for Libra doesn't like to have enemies. Libra is easily hurt, and dreadfully upset to be the cause of hurt to anyone else. It takes something terrible in a Libra childhood to turn Libra nasty. At the extreme edges of this personality you find Libra getting other people to do the dirty work of upsetting the people Libra doesn't like. But that's pretty rare. I needed to warn you that it can happen, that's all.

All Libra subjects are romantic, good-looking charmers. Who can resist them? And here another word of warning. Because they are so utterly attractive to the opposite sex, they can sometimes find their attentions wandering. But take heart, anyone married to Libra, they always return to home base. They cannot help the odd flirtation, but home is where the heart is, and their heart is very much with you if they have committed to you. Libra doesn't marry unless for real, and divorce is unthinkable.

Libra loves children and it is a lucky child who has Libra for a parent. Libra will ensure that a child never goes short of that most basic of human needs – unconditional love. They do tend to have children later rather than sooner and so bring the additional advantage of maturity to the role of parent. Libra will ensure that family life is happy.

With finances they are cautious. Sometimes they

spend days thinking about which decision to make, only to go and make the wrong decision anyway. But they do try hard and while those who are not so well acquainted with Libra may think them a trifle mean, they would be quite wrong. Libra isn't mean, but doesn't like to see money squandered or wasted.

Oddly, in spite of their clear attractiveness to others and the certain knowledge that they are well liked, Libra people are self-conscious. They give an appearance of shyness or off-handedness. Yet, should a challenge present itself, this self-consciousness will be overcome and Libra will lose him or herself in the urgency of the moment. They can do very well for themselves indeed, and it is only by falling for the wrong partner that Libra life can be derailed. Be good to Libra and you will be treated like royalty. Be mean and you could end up with an emotional wreck on your hands.

They certainly have plenty of courage when the occasion demands, and plenty of charm too. Indeed, you could say that they can get away with murder. Artistic and individual, you will find Libra browsing in art galleries and unusual little shops. They dress impeccably and have perfect manners. From baby talk one minute to world affairs the next, they really can mix with all ages and perform well on all social occasions.

Be honest with your Libra lover. They cannot stand dishonesty. They'd rather hear nothing than hear lies. They don't ask for a lot but they do need to feel secure with you and know that you are not going to let them down. And they will flirt with your friends but it is just that well-honed social muscle at work rather than anything you should be concerned about.

They love to socialize and are not afraid of staying to the end of the party – and then to go onto the next one. When you converse with Libra at a party remember that they sometimes play devil's advocate from the sheer enjoyment of debate. An Air sign, they like to talk, and you should be prepared for someone who will convince you they know more about your favourite subjects than you do. But don't think Libra is overbearing. Oh no. Libra will sweet-talk you and compliment you just to make you feel good. Their verbal skills make them good lawyers, and they could get to the bottom of many a mystery just with their wit and their vocabulary.

They can talk but you'll be pleased to learn that they listen too. They are not afraid to tell you if you are wearing the wrong outfit for a date or if your home is a mess, but they have this magical gift of being able to do it in the nicest way. They don't have hundreds of best friends because to have just a few is good enough for them. Don't let them down unless you can bear to be looked at with wounded eyes until you feel about worm-height. Ruled by Venus, the planet of love, Libra knows how to use emotions to get what he or she wants.

The more you get to know Libra the more surprised you will be by the many layers to this personality. But one thing is undeniable. Libra's aim in life is nothing other than to make this world a better place for us all.

SECRETS OF THE SEXES

So how do the males and females of the species differ then? Let's have a look.

Ms Libra

A natural charmer, she is well balanced and knows what she wants out of life. She can be led into things, but not driven. She has a will of her own and it is only by giving into excessive emotions or even to lust that she will go down the wrong path. She is sensitive and tolerant. These girls are usually very attractive too and know exactly how to dress to grab your attention.

Venus rules Ms Libra, and everything takes second place to love. Happy in almost any environment she doesn't necessarily need money (though, as many a girl knows, it does help). She's inclined to be penny-wise and pound-foolish. She will talk for hours about how you can save money on the running of your car but she will then produce a pair of Gucci shoes from the boot of hers. But she's not stubborn. You can always make her see your point of view providing you go the right way about it.

She lets the whole world know when she is in love and treats the object of her affections like the best thing since sliced bread. She does like to play the odd game in love but she can afford to since she has enough admirers to keep her occupied well into her fifties, and that's just the front-runners. She will want to be treated like a character in a romantic novel. A flight on Concorde for lunch in New York or a candlelit dinner on a flower-strewn balcony both fall into the category of acceptable dates for this one. Oysters and champagne also go down well but don't skimp. She can spot a cheap bottle of fizzy from a mile away. She likes the people she mixes with to look as good as she does, so if your phone is no longer ringing off the hook then it could be that dodgy pair of trainers you bought last month! She will lead you a merry dance and won't have a clue that she's being bad. For her it's just fun and games designed to make life joyful and worth living.

If you criticize her she will not like it and if you try to apologize and take it back she will like it even less since somewhere along the line you are being dishonest. She may stretch the truth, but only for the purposes of fun. You, of course, may not.

The kind of person she goes for is not as easy to spot as you may think. It's not just good looks she needs. There's something sexy called for too, and you've got to know how to look after yourself, right down to the scent you wear and the underwear you buy.

If Ms Libra enters your life, do not expect it to stay the same. Ms Libra improves anyone's life and can make any place into a home. Family is important to her and she longs to have her own. Like Mr Libra she is better off waiting until she is older before starting a family, and for one thing getting her need for the high life out of her system first is a very good idea. I once had a client married to a Ms Libra who was fed up with her flirting. It turned out that they'd married at eighteen, and Ms Libra hadn't had any time to get up to high jinks. They split up after a while but eight years later got back together again, and were much stronger and happier than they had been first time round. They still send me Christmas cards, with a photo put in by the husband to show me how happy they look: ever the Taurus standing by his woman. You, too, couldn't go far wrong with Ms Libra.

Mr Libra

Mr Libra is a man of action, always full of life. Pander to his ego if you want to please him. Encourage him for he can do anything with the right partner behind him. He does not care to take decisions on his own; he likes everything to be a partnership. This man needs his other half to feel complete. He needs only to resist the urge to marry too young. He, like Ms Libra, needs a few wild oats first. Once married, he's reliable and loving. And good around the home too.

He is straight in his business dealings but when young he is sometimes a little crooked in his romantic affairs. He is extremely popular with both sexes. He will spend freely on a lover and enjoy doing so. He will romance you very well but don't forget to return the favour. This is a man for whom you can buy flowers, so long as they are not cheap ones, that is. He looks good in a suit and can close power deals with a fluttering of his eyelashes, and gorgeous ones they are too. He is a great ladies' man until he settles down.

He wants someone special who can make their mark in the world, so be honoured if he has chosen you. A strong and masterful lover, if he promises to take you away and make passionate love to you then he means it. He loves to impress you and goes out of his way to make the moment a romantic one. My word of caution: don't be persuaded into talking about your exes or you will face a constant string of inquiries and pleas for reassurance. Far better to say you cannot remember much, or you will end up talking more about sex than doing it.

Mr Libra can end up very successful indeed at work and there is likely to be an artistic quality to what he does. His office is a comfortable place and he treats those that he works with like family. He is naturally good with animals, too, and would even stop his car to help an injured one. However, no matter how good-looking and successful and considerate of others he is, he will always be looking for praise, for underneath that self-aware exterior is an insecure and uncertain little soul. He isn't always comfortable naked, and there may be something about his body that he doesn't like.

His taste in music doesn't suit many. If you find yourself making love to a seventies soundtrack, just coolly turn round and say you prefer something more modern. He loves music, so he's sure to have plenty to choose from. It's just that in his choice of favourite artists he doesn't always keep up with the times.

Don't flirt with anyone else if you are his partner. You will make him angry and jealous. You must have eyes only for him. He may well have married someone older or younger than himself. Given that his music tastes are of an era of their own anyway, he doesn't necessarily have much in common with people of his own age. This is the guy who will celebrate his fiftieth birthday at the trendiest bar in town. Before you start making fun, remember that this man will know, right up until the day he dies, how to dress beautifully. So before you get embarrassed, just clock all those admirers waiting on the sidelines.

SEXUAL NEEDS

What Libra requires sexually is your full attention. Don't glance over a shoulder. And why should you, with a Libra lover? Their perfect understanding of the opposite sex makes them a popular choice in love.

Sex for Libra really does start with a capital S. Everyone is a possible sexual conquest, in business as well as personal arenas. With such flattery and charm they could get themselves a bad reputation. But Libra is more of a tease than out-and-out promiscuous. Libra won't go all the way, whatever he or she says, unless you are someone pretty special. Libra people both give and receive love with real style but their sex appeal, so important to them, was not as easy for them to acquire as you might imagine.

Libra people need to flirt and it is very difficult for them to stop. It becomes a way of life. But I shall say it again, just to convince you: they rarely take it anywhere. If they have committed to you, you will experience love such as you never have before. I hope you are good with your hands! Libra likes hours of massage and stroking and kissing and cuddling. It's not all straight down to business with sensual Libra.

Libra requires you to look good all the time, I'm afraid, so waxed legs and bikini lines and clean toenails are a must – and that's just for the boys. (An old joke but a good one!) Don't be surprised if your Libra lover wants sex in the middle of the day. The time of day doesn't matter to Libra if the atmosphere and the mood is right. Just better make sure you're not in the office at the time. All hot and sweaty by the fax machine may not be advisable.

Tell the truth to your lover or you will repulse him or her with your lies. Keep your promises, even if it is just that back massage you said you'd give. You won't be forgiven for backing out of a promise such as that.

You need to be all your lover's fantasies rolled into

one: adviser, poet, masseur – and good old raunchy
lover, as and when the mood takes hold. Libra needs a
lot of pleasing so expect to have your work cut out for
you. Be assured that you will get back all that you give
and more. There's no happier person in the world than
Libra with a good and loving and trusted partner, and
this Libra will do everything in his or her power to
make you feel on top of the world.

TRUEST NEED AND DESIRE

ROMANCE

Marriage Partners at a Glance

This is just a taster. For more detail, turn to the chapter
called Between the Sheets.

BEST BETS

ARIES is Libra's polar opposite. These two will have
plenty to smile about both in and out of the bedroom.
GEMINI tells Libra what Libra wants to hear, and can
take him or her to the moon and back.
SAGITTARIUS has the nerve to do the things that Libra
has only dreamt about.
AQUARIUS not only tells Libra what Libra wants to hear
but gives it to him or her too.

FAIR CHANCE

TAURUS looks after Libra as Libra desires but at times
comes across as a little staid and boring. Dig deeper,

Libra. There's more to the bull than meets the eye.

CANCER indulges Libra in a world of pure love and seduction.

LEO proves instant attraction for Libra and passion moves faster than Concorde when these two forces collide.

LIBRA with Libra will stroke each other's egos but may get in each other's limelight.

PISCES is a lot for Libra to handle. Emotional blackmail becomes a way of life for them both.

HEAVY WEATHER

VIRGO is not impulsive enough for Libra, who likes to act upon feelings.

SCORPIO proves uncontrollable and Libra bangs its dear head against the wall in the effort to understand the scorpion.

CAPRICORN is too tame for Libra and their pleasures lie in different areas.

Top Ten Turn-offs

1 Spitefulness
2 Dirty fingernails
3 People who pick their feet
4 Flirts (Libra is the only one allowed to do any flirting)
5 Casual clothes worn when out for the evening
6 Dirty jokes in mixed company
7 People who wear night-clothes after 9 in the morning
8 False nails

9   People who can't handle their drink (even though
    Libra can't)
10 Billy Liars

HOW TO SEDUCE LIBRA

As so often, the choice of location is key. And what is
the key? Well, it's no good to artistic and picky Libra if
the food in a restaurant is superb but the place itself has
had a cheap paintjob. Don't suggest dinner at home
either for Libra likes to socialize, so save the candles in
the front room bit for later.

First of all, smile. (I sound like your mother, don't
I?) Libra likes to see a good big genuine smile. Then
make sure that you are groomed right down to your
toes. Libra will notice if your shoes are not cleaned and
will not be afraid to remark upon it. Show your date a
good time and make 'em laugh. Libra loves to laugh
and you will score top points if you can tickle the funny
bone. Don't smirk when Libra sings along to a tune you
think is desperately untrendy. They do tend to get
stuck in a certain era of their life, especially musically.
Don't go denting their pride, now, will you?

Talk about family because Libra will want to know
how your two families will fit together, should things
progress in that way. Let your date talk about him or
herself for a bit, and don't worry because it will be your
turn next and Libra won't stop until every stone has
been unturned and every fact, taste and opinion
revealed. And if any of those opinions is not liberal
you'd better confess it now and save yourselves a lot of

heartache later. Libra doesn't want to discover further down the line that you don't like gays, for example. That's wholly unacceptable to Libra.

Try not to be insensitive about anything Libra expresses. Stroke your date's ego and self-esteem and that will put you high up in the running. Don't judge him or her by the past. Libra learns and grows from experiences and doesn't count any of them a waste of time. I have yet to meet the Libra who didn't spend his or her early years learning some valuable if embarrassing lessons. Better find out what your date wants from the future; that's a much more worthy conversational route. And compliment Libra's appearance. (That works on anyone, I know, but it is especially good for Libra.) The more confidence you can inspire in your date the more intimate you will feel together and the more you will find out about each other.

Go for seduction really slowly, but be prepared for the lightning strike of Libra once he or she has decided to seduce you. Libra can move faster than a cobra! If you want to test the water look deep into Libra's eyes. If you can see that this smile comes all the way from the heart, then you're in, to put it bluntly.

Give of yourself, make your date laugh, don't pass judgement, and experience the joy. In an interesting and artistic setting, the pair of you should have a ball.

Tell-tale signs that Libra has Fallen

All Air signs love to talk and Libra is no exception, especially when he or she has fallen in love. Then it is non-stop talk about this wonderful person, how gorgeous the lover is right down to the colour of his or her eyes and the way those lovely lips always stumble over a certain pronunciation. In fact Libra turns into Shakespeare overnight and it takes a great deal to shut him or her up. And sometimes, I'm sorry to say, in the immature Libra it is all bluster and nothing has really happened at all. They are just trying to look good in front of their friends. But far more often the love is genuine and the story is for real.

Libra in love will spend on you, do right by you and make sure you and your loved ones are all looked after. Libra will support and love you. Libra may well want a bit of action before you are quite ready for sex but it is a very important part of Libra's expression of his or her feelings, especially when the feelings have become this overwhelming. Libra will move house, town or even country if that is what makes you happy. Libra's friends will not fail to notice how radiantly happy he or she is. Without a partner Libra really is just half of what he or she could be.

Libra in love walks as if on wheels and love songs pour out of the stereo. Every one of your friends is welcomed with open arms. (But that doesn't last for ever. When the first throes of passion are over they will soon tell you what they do and do not like about the people you hang out with.) They will integrate you into every niche of their life. Indeed they will parade you in front of a panel of friends whom they trust in order to be able to talk about you later – in the most glowing of terms, of course. Libra in love is a force of nature. Libra may still flirt, but he or she is saving the best for you.

Libra gains confidence with a partner in his or her life and begins to want to explore new places. He or she wants to know your future plans, your past ideas, and every little thought you've ever had in your head. You'll be treated to poetry (not necessarily that good). You will have a loyal, sensual lover. But I advise you to sort out that CD collection first!

LIBRA PEOPLE IN YOUR LIFE

This section tells you about the people you work, rest and play with.

Libra in the Workplace

Libra as a boss looks at first glance like the perfect choice to be in charge, but if you look a little closer you will see that he or she doesn't really have a clue. Whether boss or employee, Libra gets by on a wing and a prayer. The brainwork is there but a great deal of their success is accounted for by the eyelash-fluttering charm, which isn't the most substantial of bases.

They can get away with murder and they usually do. They like things to be run on oiled wheels. They have staff eating out of their hand. They try not to take liberties with those they work with but it is all too easy to do so with the sense of duty their employees feel towards them. After all, Libra boss remembers their birthdays and buys them flowers when they are feeling down, so how could they not give them 100 per cent in return, even if asked to work overtime to cover up for something Libra didn't quite organize properly?

Libra dislikes formality among colleagues and is usually on first-name terms with everyone. Formality comes in when dealing with customers, however. This is the school teacher who doesn't mind being called by his or her first name by the pupils, so long as they revert to title and surname when the head teacher appears. Libra make great teachers, as it happens, but even better story-tellers.

Workers of the opposite sex will nearly always have a soft spot for Libra, or even a little crush. Although not brilliant with money, Libra is fair. Libra boss would never cheat anyone out of a fair day's pay. New business ideas are thoughtfully and carefully planned before being put into operation. Libra relies on good staff but if something is important wants to step in to do the job personally. Libra likes a job that involves travel and doesn't mind paying for it out of his or her own pocket if it is going to further his or her career or reputation in some way.

Not as rounded in their abilities as you may think and it is only by the way Librans handle the people around them that they manage to convince everyone they are at the top of their profession. That important document? Oh, what a story they have to tell about how that got lost. They do not like to work late into the evening because night time is for socializing, not unless their job has a social component to it. Bar staff or club host – these are good roles for garrulous and charming Libra.

One lesson to learn is that work is what you get paid for and it is not all about fun. For some reason this fact escapes Libra from time to time. If Libra is on your staff better go for friends and family discount on your phone bills. And look out for those pretty coloured pens that disappear into Libra's pockets. This artistic employee will make your office look like a home away from home, but be on guard against the gossip they will spread. A lovely colleague but one who must repeatedly be told to pay attention, just as they were at school, as you'll see if you manage to get your hands on an old school report.

The Libra Mother-in-law

She will treat you as one of her own, look after your children (even if they come from a previous relationship) and even take your friends under her protective wing. Watch out for her taste for toy boys though! Her home is a fun and fairly tidy place with many things on the walls that have special memories for her. She does not dress her age but looks smart.

She will take her grandchildren to places that are pleasing to the eye as well as a learning experience for the brain. She is quite capable of donning rollerblades to see what the fuss is all about. She is indecisive, though. That's the scales for you. Always weighing things up. Shopping with her is a nightmare. She doesn't even notice the queue of people building up behind her as she continues to chat to the shopkeeper about all and sundry. She will fork out for some wonderfully funky clothes for your children, however, so send her shopping with them instead.

Around fifty or so she'll start to carry excess weight and it has a lot to do with too much salt in her diet causing bloatedness. She is not the best drinker in the world and has a taste for strange little tipples. Now at least you know what to do with that bottle of cherry brandy in the back of your cupboard.

Don't let on you think she is a child at heart or she'll try to assert control and then you will see her domineering streak. Don't be shy about putting your foot down with her either. She is the mistress of emotional blackmail. She practically wrote the book. She is more than capable of crying crocodile tears, so check out the real reason behind the behaviour and look out for the onion in the pocket before you believe that you've really done her wrong.

She loves company and often keeps pets. If her husband has died her loyalty to him will remain undiminished and she is unlikely to marry again. It's cats for company instead – as well as her wonderful family, of course.

She's prone to putting alcohol in all of her favourite dishes and you may get sloshed without knowing it when you go round for dinner. At least you can be sure of having a good time. In fact, she won't let you go till you do. Don't squirm when she flirts. OK, it is a little bit embarrassing, especially if the man is half her age, but she won't take it too far. There's no guaranteeing, mind you, that the young man won't want to take it further. Move over, Mrs Robinson. This is the sexiest mother-in-law around.

Libra Children

Libra children want you to trust in them and tell them everything and treat them as your equal. They are good at foreign languages and have plenty of friends who range from the predictable to the bizarre. They learn from everybody they meet and don't want all their friends to be the same. They have a low boredom threshold and want to be able to call on any one of a number of different kinds of person for entertainment. There's an old head on young shoulders here, and one indication of this is how well they understand money constraints, long before they are old enough to have any of their own.

If you want to tell them off, do yourself a favour. Don't scream and shout. Sit little Libra down and calmly explain why what they have done is wrong and why it has hurt Mum and Dad. They would no more hurt their parents than they would step on the tail of the neighbour's cat, to whom they have taken a great shine, by the way, following it around all over the place. You will get much further with little Libra by reaching out to them and understanding them than by trying to enforce discipline.

Libra children don't always need company. They can entertain themselves for hours with a few toys, trying to decide which is their favourite. Don't take them to toy shops too often because they will be spoiled for choice. You know the expression, 'like a kid in a sweetshop'? Well, the kid who inspired the phrase was definitely Libra. There are the Libra kids, beside themselves with excitement and perfectly unable to choose.

They need help in order to excel at school. Their best subjects are artistic and practical ones. Reading and writing and maths can be hard for young Libra to grasp, especially if he or she does not like the teacher. With Art as a favourite, Libra children get into the habit of drawing on things they shouldn't, such as on bedroom walls, on the street, or on their desk at school. There will be a few hours of detention if they get caught. If they have got a Libra grandmother she will gladly display their works of art on her walls should you run out of space.

Parents spoil them, especially if they are not the first children. After a boisterous or demanding child, little Libra will seem like an angel sent by special request. But look again and you will see that Libra has got Mummy and Daddy wrapped around a little finger. Water isn't their favourite indulgence so bathing and teeth-cleaning will have to be encouraged.

If you are stuck for an entertainment for your Libra child, think about music lessons. Many a Libra can play at least one instrument. And you'll be doing everyone else a favour later in life if you can encourage Libra to develop a bit of good musical taste while young!

Teenage Libra falls in and out of love very quickly. You may find yourself shuffling one date out of the front door while the next one is already waiting in the kitchen and Libra is upstairs getting changed. Encourage Libra not to grow up too soon. Life goes by fast enough for us all without marrying off your children at sixteen. Better check that when they say they are going to bed they really are – not clambering down the wall to go to a party with the latest heartthrob around town.

Libra Friends

Have a Libra friend and you'll get all the gossip hot off the presses. You'll also get an inkling of a certain two-facedness as they shake the hand of a new acquaintance one minute and then say what a fat bum the next. Mind you, Libra won't be hanging around with you unless you've got at least one flattering attribute on offer, so there's something to feel good about.

No, I'm not saying they are shallow. They will go out of their way to help you and will not mind paying for you if you are running short. They often call their friends their family, and this is what you mean to them. Just don't mind being dropped quicker than a hot brick when some lover starts to play with the heartstrings of your Libra friend. The heart calls and Libra follows and sometimes forgets everyone else. But it won't be for long. They'll get back to you – eventually.

Libra has many different friends to satisfy his or her many different needs. These people like to be invited to all the latest clubs and parties and if you are not suitable for a particular venue then they will go to the friend who is, and then get back to you when something suitable for you comes up. They don't mean to be rude but it can come across that way, especially to those who have been dumped when their image did not fit the bill.

They will flirt with people but are more likely to want to put the life back into a relationship that has become stale than to break it up. They can see when things are not working and they really do want their friends to be happy. They add colour, glitz and glamour to anyone's life and they make you feel loved. If your confidence is in need of a boost, this is the friend to do it. They peak at night-time and like to go out a lot. They have best friends of the opposite sex and although the friends may be looking for something more, Libra probably is not.

It's more luck than good judgement where money is concerned and although I do not like to recommend gambling I would say to Libra have a flutter if you have a strong instinct about something because it will probably pay off. Libra would rather live with someone else than alone and one cause of a falling out is likely to be when he or she forgets to pay the rent on time and spends it instead on a beautiful picture to hang in the front room. Saturdays will be great fun as Libra spends all day primping and preening for the biggest night out of their week. They will offer advice and it will often be good but they don't like the world to see them as a serious advice-giver – that would scare them! – so you might just have to be quiet about the way Libra helped you out. One good thing about their advice is their well-balanced capacity to see the other side of the problem, which can help you out of a rut. They like to think they are spiritual but the candles are more likely to be about romance than religion.

Your Libra friend is a pair of emotional scales who is either up or down and who will change so often that you cannot categorize him or her. Then your friend will look at you with love and you will be unable to stay angry for a moment longer.

Scorpio
October 24 to November 22

INTENSE, DEEP, DETERMINED and jealous: these are the key words to describe Scorpio. I think that this contradictory character, strong and weak all at the same time, is perhaps the most mysterious of all the signs. These people have a wonderful ability to get up off the floor, dust themselves down and start all over again. Like the scorpion itself, they do have a sting, but they only use it when they do not have any alternative.

Difficult to fathom, Scorpio's outward appearance and manner bears little resemblance to the innermost personality. Although they are proud people with great determination, there is a streak of recklessness in them, sometimes suppressed by good common sense but not as often as it should be. They are clever about getting what they want. Ranting and raving is not their style and they do not like confrontation. Fierce determination plus quiet dedication gets them where they want to go. Their minds and their characters are strong and yet they know moments of deep uncertainty and nervousness about which they will reveal very little. Their ups are high up and their downs are way down low. But how could it be any other way with such a dramatic sign as this?

People don't always realize just how straightforward the scorpion is in many ways. Once Scorpio people have given their word, they will never go back on it, and can be relied upon in any circumstances. If they say yes, they mean yes. It is very hard for those around them to sway them once they have made up their minds. Sometimes their forthright manner borders on the sarcastic (who – them? Never) and when they are roused they certainly do have a cutting tongue, but those who love them know that this hazard is compensated for by the reassuring knowledge that they can always rely on dear old Scorpio for a true and honest opinion.

Friends are important but family means most to them. They think of the long-term, not the short-term, and for them blood is thicker than water. If they don't like someone they meet they simply won't bother with them. Mind you, what they were thinking will have been written all over their face. They don't mean to be rude. I just call them honest. This is what makes it good to have them around. After all, far better to know where you stand from day one than to be led down the garden path, don't you think?

They are prone to jealousy, however. A Scorpio can

live happily with a partner for years and then one day something clicks and Scorpio decides to stop the partner going out with a group of friends he or she has known for years. There may have been no indication that this was coming. Whatever it is, Scorpio's sting is in the air when guarding whatever it considers most precious from real or imagined threat. As soon as Scorpio feels secure about people and possessions then you have a person devoid of jealousy and radiant with the inner composure that people often comment upon in this sign.

They are generous by nature and would give their last penny to someone whose need they felt was greater than their own. However, being money-conscious, they very seldom find themselves without it, and yet at the same time they are quite happy with the simple things in life. Luxuries are nice, but sincerity and good friendships are so much more important. They need and appreciate their friends and they return the love they receive many times over. For someone they care for, nothing is too much trouble and no sacrifice is too great. I have a Scorpio friend who loves to spend Christmas at home with her family. When she discovered that a friend had no family and no plans, she quickly turned all her own treasured plans on their head in order to accommodate her friend, although it was a considerable sacrifice for her. Instead of a quiet Christmas at home, she threw a party for lots of people, and gave her friend one of her happiest Christmases in years.

The right partner in life is vital, someone who will give purpose to the scorpion's life and driving power to his or her ambitions. Love is essential, an absolute necessity. Scorpio people are wise and shrewd, emotional and magnetic, in short quite fascinating, but I bet they don't really understand themselves or their emotions.

Julia Roberts is a Scorpio who has tried many times to make a commitment to the one she loved, only to back off time and again. The only time she managed to say I do (and barefoot, I must add, in typical Scorpio fashion) was to fellow Scorpio Lyle Lovett. They jumped in at the deep end as Scorpios so often do and when it was over they remained in constant contact in case one needed the other. No one but a fellow Water sign could know or understand the requirements of a friend or lover better.

If they want something then they want it so badly they can taste it. It becomes an obsession and no amount of lecturing or counselling will change their mind. They will sit and listen to you for hours and you may think that you've managed to change their mind but then they will walk right out and do it anyway. When they want to have a good time then they are the original party animal, but if they decide to have a few early nights then it's out with the slippers and cocoa and you'll think you are living with the Waltons.

No friend will go to greater extremes for you. Other friends will support you and make sacrifices for you but they will have thought first of all about the impact on themselves. Scorpio never stops to think. Caution is thrown to the wind and Scorpio moves heaven and earth to help you.

They work hard when they find a job they have a

passion for. Then you won't find a more dedicated sign in the entire zodiac. But if there's something they don't like, well, there's no changing their mind or convincing them to try it one more time. If the Scorpio child doesn't like bananas, just give up and don't buy them. If a Scorpio husband does not like DIY it's no good buying hammer and nails and leaving them around the house just in case.

They are not hypochondriacs for they genuinely do not like being ill. They just don't have time for it. They have so many ambitions in life to fulfil. They won't be able to tell you them out loud, however. They prefer fate to guide them and they trust that they are on the path to something good, without necessarily knowing what it is. The actresses of this sign, such as Meg Ryan, Demi Moore and Jodie Foster, all knew they were going to be famous from a very young age, though they may not have been able to put their future into words. These actresses are good enough to have earned Oscars, and you can be sure that any Scorpio, actor or not, can entertain his or her friends with enough drama to deserve an Oscar off the screen as well.

When the scorpion goes bad, it goes all the way. Scorpio's two ruling planets, Mars and Pluto, ensure that nothing is done by halves. If Scorpio tries drugs or alcohol it will be to extremes and he or she may require professional help somewhere down the line. This is not to say that every Scorpio who reaches for a drink is automatically a drunk. But it does mean that opposite the angel on every Scorpio's shoulder is a devil whispering, go on, try it, you know you'd like another. When Scorpio decides to get healthy it will be done without half measures too, and less determined friends will be ashamed to stand next to lean and toned Scorpio. It is always the eyes that give a Scorpio away. There's nothing these eyes can hide. One indulgence too many and 'guilty' flashes out like neon. Lies reveal themselves, and love shines out bright and clear.

Love Scorpio and they will love you back as a friend, partner or even mother-in-law. Just don't ever be dishonest; it is the one thing they cannot stand. And make sure you ask them how they are doing from time to time. That confident stance is not as solid as you may think. Lend them your support and together you'll go onto many great things.

SECRETS OF THE SEXES

So how do the males and females of the species differ then? Let's have a look.

Ms Scorpio

When Ms Scorpio stings you, she really can hurt, but she will only do it when betrayed. Treat her well and she will be the best friend or partner you've ever had. She will go to great pains to make you happy. She will only go out with you in the first place if she genuinely likes you, never just to fill in the time. Once you are committed to each other she will stand by you through thick and thin. No matter how large a money problem you have suffered she will support you and help you until you have made a million and climbed back up the social ladder. She does not care what people think of her. She is much more concerned with the reality of what is going on in her life. If she has a problem with you then it is to you that she will want to talk, not Auntie Mavis or Uncle Frank but you and you alone, and anything that anyone else says will not matter a jot. She cares only about sorting out your relationship, and certainly not what onlookers may say.

She will look good for you. Ms Scorpio has a terrific magnetism, which attracts many admirers, and as a marriage partner can be unpredictable, but be warned, she has a built-in lie detector. If you want to lie, don't look her in the eye, or she'll read you like a book. And if you avoid her stare, then you might as well sign the confession anyway. As for her unpredictability, you'll have to learn to ride with it.

She has lots of friends who are important to her for many different reasons. She will find good in all of them but they may be less well inclined towards each other. It probably wouldn't be wise to try to mix them all together at a party.

Not one to mince her words, if she thinks you have a problem with her then she will ask you what it is. If you don't tell her she will make it her mission to find out, going so far as to search through your bank books and clothes to find a clue.

If she works hard and enjoys what she does as a living, then she will have a very nice home indeed, in which the bedroom is likely to be the best decorated place. I have not met a Scorpio yet who did not have a television in their bedroom ('Darling, you've just got to be able to watch your favourite movies in bed!'). If she doesn't like her job and hasn't yet discovered her niche in life, then she is a walking disaster. She'll make everyone's life hell and then drag you down with her. Better ask Ms Scorpio what she wants out of life. If she doesn't know, run a mile, because she is dangerous in this unfocused state. Just remember to tell her before you go that you believe it's in her stars for her to make it big in what she decides to do. She has a great belief in fate, so you could just be giving her the boost she has long been in need of.

Men are not her downfall. If she doesn't like you, she won't give you a chance – unlike charitable Ms Cancer who has been known to sleep with men she feels sorry for. Oh no – Ms Scorpio will have to think you are something special to give herself to you and when she does it will be mind, body and soul.

Don't cheat on her or you will find out years later that the job you didn't get, the car that wouldn't start, the pizzas that kept getting delivered to your door every half an hour were are all her way of getting revenge. (Don't ask how she stopped you getting the job. She has means.) She likes others to learn their lessons as well as she does hers. She doesn't usually marry the wrong man because she has a good nose for danger. A little bit of danger in the bedroom can be acceptable, though! An asset to your life, but not a woman to be taken lightly.

Mr Scorpio

We have a very proud man in Mr Scorpio, who likes to have his achievements known. He goes to great pains to plan out his life and suffers greatly if things don't work out as he wished. He's a perfectionist, and has a great need for security. When he marries, it is for life. If he lives with someone for years and years you'd better ask him some serious questions because it is likely that his heart is not in the relationship. If he felt it was the real thing, he'd have gone down the aisle (or along the beach, or wherever takes his fancy). If his commitment is complete, then he needs to make legally his the woman he loves. Or the man he loves, come to that. There's a much higher than average percentage of Scorpios among the gay men who apply for marriage in America.

A passionate man in everything he does, he is possessive and jealous too. A perfect lover, he is not altogether the perfect husband unless you are very much in love with him. He will shout at you for not putting his socks together in his sock drawer, yet he is the master at leaving wet towels on the bed. He will make you cheese on toast all right, but the mess that he leaves behind will need industrial-strength cleaning. He must watch the drinking and smoking, which can be indulged in to excess. The expression 'a little of what you fancy does you good' has never been heard of by Mr Scorpio. To him, more is better.

He is very serious about his work. Whatever it is, whether he is a multi-million-pound businessman or a cobbler, he will think it important to do the job properly. The only time you will see him late for work is when he is indulging in a hobby that is his passion. Nipping to a bike shop to pick up a spare part for his latest acquisition is a completely plausible reason for getting in late for Mr Scorpio, whether that means late to work or late home. However much he loves you, he will forget from time to time that you or anybody else exists. It must be very nice in his world, since he always knows the answer to everything!

You must let him take the lead. He doesn't like his women to be stronger than he is. So the trick is to let him think he's in control, while all the time you are in the driving seat. Keep him happy and this man can lead you onto great things. Remember that he does not marry for the sake of it. He means it, and you can rely on that. His air of confidence can open doors but you need to realize that a little river of doubt runs inside him. He does, even if it is not apparent, need your support.

Try to say positive things to him. If he asks you a question, answer it directly. If you are not willing to be his friend, confidante or lover, say so, and he will find someone who is. He will make your friends welcome but if they belittle him or his work then you'd better get rid of them quick. His comments will cut through the air faster than any apology can be mustered, and it will be decision-time for you for he will expect you to stand by him no matter what. He is old-fashioned in his values.

Not one for beating around the bush, if he intends to woo you then you will hear about it. He won't take a year to put an invite your way. You'll know of his intentions because he will tell you. He picks sexy partners over 'pretty' ones. This man could be all that you need. Protector, lover and friend all in one, he will not hesitate in travelling to the furthest corners of the world to help you in your quest for success. With his support and love you can grow to be better than you ever dreamed. Life to him is a movie just ready for the making.

SEXUAL NEEDS

Scorpio is one of the more uninhibited signs. It is important to Scorpio to be fulfilled sexually and mentally. A marriage or relationship without sex is not a relationship worth having. Scorpio is intense and if he or she doesn't feel wanted twenty-four seven, niggling insecurities begin to surface. On the other hand, overconfident Scorpio – which can be the case – can be a nightmare in a relationship with his or her cocksure attitude and demanding ways.

One good thing about Scorpio (actually, loads of good things, but this one is a bit of a rarity): these lovers keep their secrets for their partner and don't tell the world what they get up to. Ladylike in public and sluttish in private, you could say. (And that's just the men!) Your Scorpio friend may ask you about your sex life but don't expect to be told anything in return. Or don't believe it if you do! Scorpios sometimes get carried away with ideas of their own grandeur and since they are not going to tell you the truth (that's too private), they might as well tell you a whopper. Weird logic, but it works.

Scorpio relishes new relationships and makes each experience an adventure, even changing lifestyle to accommodate a new mate if so desired. A good-looking face and body are important to Scorpio but although physical appearance may be the initial attraction, love must soon follow before sex is indulged in. The times Scorpio does jump straight into the physical usually end up being regretted.

Massage, candle light, champagne and the like are all a necessary part of the indulgence of sex. Better not forget Valentine's Day, or the date you first kissed, for underneath that quiet first impression is a true romantic who wants nothing less than all of you. And that means that besides the rumpy-pumpy there's quite a lot of lying around in bed talking about life, love and work to do. This is all part of romance to Scorpio. They must be careful not to build everything up so much that they or their partner gets let down. An evening of passion on a warm beach is all very well but once the sun has gone down and the night has turned cold then you just have to call it a day. Sometimes Scorpio just has to learn when to stop!

TRUEST NEED AND DESIRE

HOT, PASSIONATE BUT MEANINGFUL SEX

Marriage Partners at a Glance

This is just a taster. For more detail, turn to the chapter called Between the Sheets.

BEST BETS

TAURUS, Scorpio's polar opposite, fills in the missing blanks. Together their appetite for sex proves insatiable.

CANCER bonds with its fellow water sign beautifully, and after all the tiffs and the emotional blackmail, there will be plenty of passionate making-up.

PISCES with Scorpio makes an intense and unique relationship that is sure to last many years. These two become more and more like each other as time passes.

LEO loves having good-looking Scorpio on his or her arm and they will adore each other truly, madly and deeply.

VIRGO and Scorpio are a strange match that works amazingly well because Virgo, a bit like Taurus, supplies the missing links, such as that Virgo speciality, organization. They will tell the whole world of their love after the first date!

FAIR CHANCE

ARIES shares with Scorpio the ruling planet Mars and these two get on great as friends and then as lovers, but the spark may be put out before they get the chance to build anything lasting.

LIBRA is a great match for Scorpio but can end up becoming a parent figure, especially if older than Scorpio which is quite often the case.

SCORPIO with Scorpio: deep, intense and at times downright dangerous. If you marry you can be pretty sure it will last, but get that ring on his or her finger quick or you'll be left in a spin wondering where that sexy and so unforgettable soulmate has got to.

SAGITTARIUS and Scorpio can be great for a while but to have any longevity sacrifices are needed on both sides.

HEAVY WEATHER

GEMINI cannot ever gain Scorpio's trust. Those white lies Gemini tells could well turn into whoppers.

CAPRICORN can be a little intimidating for Scorpio, turning Scorpio's confidence to bluster. Scorpio should prepare to be ruled.

AQUARIUS talks too much for poor old Scorpio who won't be able to get a word in edgeways.

Top Ten Turn-offs

1 Boring underwear
2 Bad breath
3 Lack of ambition
4 Lies
5 Infidelity
6 Ex-girlfriends or boyfriends of yours
7 People who bite the skin around their nails
8 Lack of money
9 Predictability
10 Cheap shoes

HOW TO SEDUCE SCORPIO

The first lesson in love is that you must try to be yourself. The dramatist in the scorpion's nature doesn't mind a little extension to your original character but essentially Scorpio doesn't like people who pretend to be something they're not.

Take Scorpio somewhere new and exciting that is

full of interesting characters for you to talk about and then proceed to find a cosy table where no one else can see you. Scorpios like to observe without being observed. Try also to find a place that has a bit of mystery and intrigue to it. You don't have to spend a fortune. Scorpio will be as happy with a cheap bar as an expensive one so long as it has the all-important ingredient: atmosphere, darling, atmosphere.

Scorpio will want to hear all about you. If you're keeping any secrets, don't let Scorpio get even a whiff of them or they'll drag the truth out of you (or your friends and neighbours). They won't stop until they have heard it all. I'm not joking!

Water signs have a tremendous affinity with water. (Water is a powerful element in this respect.) Take your Scorpio out near a river or a lake and you increase the chance of passion. Water relaxes Scorpio and makes them more giving of themselves. Keep family stuff for another date. Scorpio won't want to tell you all about his or her family yet.

You may wonder if your Scorpio date is serious or simply playing with you. There they are, carrying on as if you are the only person in the world and wanting to know everything about you down to the name of your primary school teacher. (Scorpios make great detectives.) Don't even think about cutting the night short. A short date tells Scorpio you are not giving your all and you may as well say goodbye for good in that case. Remember that Scorpio is the boss (or so they think).

Don't let Scorpio drink too much unless you want a bag of bones on your hands. Like fellow Water signs Cancer and Pisces, Scorpio cannot handle alcohol too well. And to put it bluntly, if your date is plastered, you have no chance of scoring, do you?

How you look at your companion and how you treat him or her is what counts on the first date. If you were a millionaire and took Scorpio for lunch on your yacht, the champagne would be wasted if you were not looking into each other's eyes as you clinked glasses. The contact 'you' make with Mr or Ms Scorpio is what is important. Money can come into the equation later! Scorpios rarely pick someone who isn't capable of making a bob or two. These people have a way of backing a winner. Maybe you should take them to the racetrack, with their nose for winners. Just look out that with their tendency to excess you don't end up at Monte Carlo as your flutter has turned into a major gambling fest.

The best bet of all could be to get yourself invited into Scorpio's home. It's sure to be a palace of pleasure – and I'm not just talking about the decor either!

Tell-tale signs that Scorpio has Fallen

A Scorpio in love is a very interesting sight indeed: the confident and happy look on Scorpio's face says 'in love' and the smirk says physical satisfaction is part of the picture too. This is a fiery and uninhibited personality to whom success in love is more important than most people realize. Even one put-down or off-hand remark from a partner hurts Scorpio's confidence and can easily cause problems in sexual relationships. Scorpio people have a constant need for reassurance. They cannot make love if they feel their partner's feelings are not as strong as they once were. They are not unfaithful when in love. They feel far too emotional to want to betray their partner or indeed themselves. They, however, are capable of using sex as a weapon of manipulation, and Scorpio is a masterful lover.

Scorpio's moods are infectious, and apparent, not only to their lover but also to all around them. When Scorpio feels like romance or a bit of lovemaking, they only have to look you in the eye and you will know. (And anyone around is likely to guess too!) Scorpios are passionate, affectionate, sensitive and responsive. It is quite easy to see why Bruce Willis fell for Scorpio seductress Demi Moore, who has been a sex siren in her own right both in and out of the movies. Meg Ryan too has set many a heart fluttering. And let's not leave out the boys. Look at Leonardo Di Caprio. Whoever would have thought such a young face could have such a powerful effect on women and men of all ages? You see, Scorpio knows no boundaries. It is not unusual for Scorpio men to be found attractive by other men. It is about the respect and admiration that this sign seems to demand.

Beware of hurting Scorpio in love. The scorpion does not forgive easily. If your house starts to smell strange it will be the old kipper-behind-the-radiator trick, and guess who put that there? Scorpio's ruling planet Mars is the planet of change and unpredictability and this is how they can be in love. If you even think about betraying them you will be lucky if they ever acknowledge you again in private or public. They will do a good job of instantly forgetting your name and they mean it. It is far too hurtful for this sign to harp on a bad thing and they will muster every bit of strength they can find to move on as quickly and painlessly as possible.

However, once in love with you, Scorpio will explore love and sex with you right to the limits. Slowly but surely the real Scorpio is unveiled, the one the rest of the world doesn't get to see. The scorpion shows its true colours only to people it trusts and, believe me, this is a trust worth gaining. Loyalty, magnetism and insight are key words. On the reverse side of the coin is ruthlessness and oversuspicion, evident in the scorpion who feels cornered or betrayed.

When single, Scorpio people are great achievers. When they fall in love their partner's life becomes as important as theirs. Life-long ambitions are dismissed in favour of personal fulfilment with a partner. There won't be recriminations. If Scorpio loves you, he or she will follow your lead. Love will be demonstrated physically, of course, but mentally too for this is the meeting of soulmates – if it were not, Scorpio would not be satisfied.

You will get back everything you put into a relationship with this powerful and loving sign. Watch out for the way that Scorpio goes all quiet on you once the realization hits home that he or she is in love. It's a real treat – and it's also one of the few times you're likely to see the scorpion quiet. Look out for that strange expression on Scorpio's face, but don't worry, it's more likely to be a kiss they want to give you than a right-hander – if your intentions are honourable, that is!

SCORPIO PEOPLE IN YOUR LIFE

This section tells you about the people you work, rest and play with.

Scorpio in the Workplace

Scorpios are a force to be reckoned with. Employees and bosses alike know within the first hour of their company that they will not stand for any nonsense. More people get hired and fired by Scorpios than any other sign. They are very particular. If people don't suit them they won't take the time to train them to their way, like many other signs in the zodiac would. No, the employees get shown the door instead. Scorpio is a hard taskmaster who wants admiration before he or she has even done anything to gain respect.

Everyone else is expected to fit in with Scorpio's ways. Those who remain loyal to Scorpio at work never go unrewarded. Scorpio doesn't mind mistakes being made so long as they don't involve money. Anyone who goes out of their way to do something for Scorpio will not be forgotten. Neither will anyone who goes out of their way to obstruct Scorpio be forgotten.

Scorpio people are not afraid to take chances where business is concerned, whether theirs or yours. Their career has probably been built on gambling and speculation and their ambition is strong. As soon as they have achieved one thing they are looking around for another challenge. The greater the challenge the more they enjoy it. Their employees, colleagues and bosses never find them or their work dull or uninteresting.

They are sure to be the source of much inspiration – and maybe even enjoyment – in the workplace.

Something to beware of. Scorpios think they are the boss, whether they are or not. They also consider themselves transparent. If they want to leave early to see to their own affairs then they will, and will consider it perfectly justified, even if it is only to launder their favourite shirt. Don't go telling tales on them. Their actions are noticeable enough on their own and you don't need to go about spilling the beans. They certainly do not think they have anything to hide.

Most of the time they are great but when they are in a bad mood, run for cover. They will spread their bad moods like the flu. When others are in a bad mood Scorpio will go out of their way to cheer them up, but get Scorpio in a bad mood and no one – quite rightly – dares go near them.

They work hard. If they enjoy their job they make a great success of it. There is many a loyal Scorpio worker behind people achieving big successes. They want fame when it suits them but when they want to go about unrecognized, don't try to spotlight them. They only ever want praise from their loved ones, in truth. All the rest is a bit of an act for them.

Scorpios are best advised to keep work in the workplace and friends outside of it. Make friends with Scorpio at work and before you know it work goes out of the window and you become emotionally dependent on each other as well as being professionally irresponsible. It is not advisable.

Scorpios are good public speakers, unafraid to look powerful people in the eye. They can convince you they know everything and can convince you to buy anything. Loyal workers too but beware that no matter how happy they seem in their job there will come a time when they will want to own the place. With their power and energy they may just succeed. Those close to Scorpio will be proud of what they achieve, and anyone who ever doubted Scorpio will soon be made aware of how powerful, ambitious and successful they really are.

The Scorpio Mother-in-law

Oh dear, where shall I start? She means well, but she is going to want to know everything, and I mean everything, including the contraception you use. She has even been known to talk about your sex life to others too. There are two extremes to this sign: if she talks about sex, she will talk about everything to do with sex; otherwise she will never mention it. She's not prudish. It's just that you cannot guarantee what she will regard as sacrosanct.

She will value her role as mother and will want to play it out properly. Doubts as to whether she raised her kids properly will always plague her. She will never be satisfied that she did everything she could for your spouse. Perhaps it was because she allowed Daisy or Doug to miss out on maths club as a child that he or she did not get that promotion last month – that's how her mind works.

There will be times when she drops herself right in the middle of your life together and eats with you day and night, and there will be times when she steers clear of you for weeks on end. That is because she throws her energies into things 100 per cent, and cannot, no matter how much she tries, do two things at once.

If you don't tell her what is going on in your life, she will guess, and you'll just look silly for being evasive. If you ask her to babysit or housesit for you then you must be prepared that she won't be able to stop herself from taking a peek in your bathroom cabinets and bedside-table drawers. She will not, however, read your diary. She is a woman of principle, though her principles fight with her need to know things. Anyway, she doesn't need to read the words on paper. She's already worked it all out for herself. And then she'll step in to tell you what's needed. She'll put it so beautifully you'll think you sought her advice in the first place and should be grateful for it.

If you're organizing a party or a wedding, make sure you have plenty of money. She'll want all of her close friends to come and she'll insist that they are your friends too, even if you've never met half of them. Don't think her mean. She is not. She'd give you her last penny if you needed it. She may, however, take any such pleas for help as a sign that you can't cope.

She is brilliant with children and will get on with all of your friends too. She is a little slow to bond with her in-laws as she doesn't take kindly to relationships she has not chosen herself or have not been directly chosen by her loved ones. She will never forget her manners, however. She's a dab hand in the kitchen too, and will want to teach you a dish or two to keep her beloved child well fed.

If you expect Scorpio mother-in-law to grow old

gracefully you are in for a disappointment. It is not until she passes forty that she fully realizes that life is for living, and from there it is up all the way. You are more likely to find her going off to Thailand for her holidays than Tenerife. She likes full-on adventure and fun. She will make life exciting and your kids will adore her. You may find she gets on your nerves when she's around but you won't half miss her when she's gone. Make the most of her. She really is a wonderful mother-in-law.

Scorpio Children

The Scorpio child is wise the day he or she is born, and knows exactly what the score is. You won't ever need to teach little scorpions about sex because they will have picked up all they need to know from ear-wigging back in the days when you thought they were snoozing in the pram.

You will enjoy having a child like this around. Scorpio children have a dry sense of humour and are excellent company even when young. They learn to walk sooner than most because they already know they have places to go and people to see. If they do something wrong, be careful about the punishment you deal. They may never forgive you or forget it if they consider it unjustified. Far better to sit them down and discuss the problem. If you tell them they have hurt you they will feel much worse than they could through any telling-off.

They are bound to have a problem with one if not more teachers at school. They act a little arrogant, and want to know the answers to everything. A little annoying for a teacher trying to convey French when Little Lucy asks for the Latin equivalent, for example. If they come home late, they may have been on detention, but more likely they have run into an adventure on the way home, involving any one of a dozen weird and wonderful scenarios.

Even at a tender age they speak their minds. This may invite trouble. Although Scorpio children are quick with their tongues they are not usually big for their age and they may have to eat their words in front of older children. And there are plenty of crocodile tears about with Scorpionette. I know. I was a Scorpio child! I had a very good line in crying and manipulation. Unfortunately now it is a lot harder to play the same tricks. My husband (also Scorpio) just tells me not to bother. Oh well. At least it worked for a while.

Young Scorpios are not afraid of hard work but like to earn the money for it. They will quibble over the rate for their Saturday job, and even over their pocket money. At school they come out tops in subjects such as Drama and English. They love pantomime season and will probably even try for a part one year. You may wonder what is going on when the lead goes off with food poisoning and the Scorpio child steps in with a surprising knowledge of the part. I need say no more.

Watch the relationships they go for in their teens. They don't develop their taste until their twenties and they could make commitments while young that are hard to get out of. After all, it could prove very expensive to bring back your golden child from Australia where they emigrated on just such a youthful love whim.

Life is often fun for these children and they are usually happy-natured with a good sense of humour. This is a child whose company you can enjoy.

Scorpio Friends

With your Scorpio friends it's all or nothing. If you fall out, they might just do their best to turn your friends against you too. If you are friends, then you are best friends. They like to be the ringleader and the centre of attention. If you are having a party, get them involved in the organizing. Before you know it, they've hired a band from the charts to sing for you. Just make sure you don't have to foot the bill, as their tastes don't usually coincide with their budget. They just want everyone to have a good time. If you are feeling down, go out with Scorpio.

They like to keep work and friends separate. They are more interested in having a good time once the job of work is done than discussing the finer points of their day. They may exaggerate what they do for a living. You could walk into their workplace asking to see the boss only to be greeted by Scorpio the secretary instead. It's not lying, exactly, just embroidery.

Scorpios are very psychic, second only to Pisces. They will know if something is troubling you and can help you to uncover things you haven't admitted to yourself yet. This is the kind of friend on whose doorstep you could turn up and find yourself immediately invited to share dinner and a bottle of wine. Scorpio friends won't help you to save money – that is not what they are about – but they can advise you how to make it. But don't go into business with one. You'll be met at the workplace by a completely different person to the one you thought you knew. For Scorpio work and friendships don't mix.

They might be into a bit of manipulation but they would never harm anyone badly. They believe in karma, and that there is a price to pay for any bad that people do. Pluto their co-ruler guards souls in the after-life, and Scorpios get from Pluto a very deep approach to both life and death. Their sense of humour is in a class of its own – not everyone always gets the joke. They are known for having quite distinctive (and sometimes very dirty) laughs. You can sometimes identify Scorpio by that distinctive, slightly smoky voice.

A great friend to have, but a bad enemy. They do not forgive easily and so if you have fallen out it was probably just the once. They attract the opposite sex like a magnet, which is not always a comfortable situation among their friends. There is no arguing, though – this is a sexy sign.

They mix well with a wide range of people and are as happy at the newest club as at bingo down the road. They say things they don't mean when they are drunk. This is the only time you should ignore what they say. In spite of their intense take on life they don't deal with big issues all that well and indeed the whole dying thing really rather miffs them.

Oh, and if you weren't listening before, then listen up now. You can't let them know you have other close friends. They like to think that you are there for them and them alone. They may have other people around them but if you cancel a date you can consider yourself dismissed. And don't argue with them. They are always right, even when they are wrong. I may have made dear old Scorpios sound mean as friends but they're not. They simply like things to be the way they like them, and they know they're good enough fun to warrant it too.

Sagittarius
November 23 to December 21

OPTIMISTIC, FREEDOM-LOVING, philosophical, expansive and honest: these are the key words to describe Sagittarius. Those born under this sign are generally acknowledged to be the luckiest of the zodiac signs. They fall on their feet and are more often than not lucky in their health and their chosen career. The archer is shown with its arrow pointing to the sky, and to aim high is typical of ambitious Sagittarius. The archer usually experiences success in life too, almost always reaching the goal aimed for. The only time you will see archers down is when they do not know what they want, but put a goal in their sight and they will get to it quicker than most of us could even dream. Quick-thinking, and patient only up to a point, they are happiest in jobs with plenty of activity and mental stimulation. They wouldn't think about entering into a job or even a relationship that was not full of twists and turns. Those who do, get bored and restless and eventually react – which can have some dramatic effects on both them and their close ones.

Popular with the opposite sex, and not too attached to the home, they like to spread their wings. There is many a Sagittarius in, say, a ten-year relationship who still keeps only a toothbrush at the partner's house. One foot keeps the door open just in case the archer needs to bolt, even from people the archer truly loves.

Ms Sagittarius is a great girl for fun and getting out and about. Even married, she is not domesticated and her home is unlikely to be beautifully kept, but she'll make you very welcome if you call in. Mr Sagittarius has a tendency to go to his club or out with the boys a little too often and this can often lead to his partner feeling neglected. All Sagittarius people can be a little slow to show their feelings. However, in marriage they are fair, although inclined to jealousy and possessiveness since they, more than most, are aware of the temptations that lie around.

Sound common sense is one of their greatest assets and yet they are born gamblers. Odd, isn't it? They have phases of saving money like mad, really denying themselves, and then suddenly an overwhelming urge to spend comes over them. Their finances are therefore usually in a state of fluctuation.

Sagittarius is a wonderful friend who can be relied upon for sympathetic advice, understanding and help. Those to whom they give their friendship can count themselves lucky indeed, for their affection is worth having. Children and animals instinctively recognize them as friendly, and they are likely to be popular in a social sense with people of all ages. Kind-hearted, they would rather tell a white lie to avoid hurting somebody in spite of their essential honesty and dislike of deceit.

Nothing is too big for them to tackle. They have lots of grit, which combined with their natural ambition, enterprise and courage allows them to take on ventures which lesser mortals envy, though also admire. While others are having second thoughts, Sagittarius dives unhesitatingly into difficult and sometimes dangerous situations.

Sagittarius has the gift of words. This is a wonderful ability, allowing archers to extricate themselves from almost any awkward situation. Everybody likes these people. They are the life and soul of the party, and would never be nasty to anybody. There is no bitchy streak in Sagittarius. Life is too short for this, they reason, and although they are not averse to the odd quip or dry piece of humour they will not dwell on it in a way that makes anyone feel bad.

Naturally we must look at the bad side too. It's true that Sagittarius can let you down, just when you don't need it. If you want Sagittarius to keep a promise you'd better keep a close eye on the situation and make an exaggerated point of letting them know how important this is to you. They do not mean to let you down. They just can't help living for the moment. When you are still waiting for them at 10 o'clock at night, redoing make-up or reapplying aftershave, they are already down the disco with another friend who also asked but at the right time, namely the last minute. However, they are so nice underneath it all that you can't help but forgive them. If they do let you down they will be genuinely sorry for doing so. They are children at heart. Sagittarius is the sign that doesn't really grow up. Here's a useful tip for you. They do give in to emotional blackmail. (But don't let on I said so.)

The thing about Sagittarius is that they are so optimistic and enthusiastic about life that they are just asking for it all to go their way. When they are excited they walk with a bit of a gallop. Their natural confidence sways fate strongly in their direction. They must only beware of relying too much on good luck. Taking too big a gamble with anything in life has been the downfall of many a successful businessperson.

Such free spirits are a great hit on the singles scene. What a triumph, to land the one who has always got away! They love to laugh and have fun, and it can be difficult to get them to sit down and talk about anything of a serious nature. Once caught, they become both lover and best friend, which is, I am sure, most people's dream. Those who cheat do it because they have been dared, or because temptation has just floated their way. To them love is fun. What many of us take seriously is a laughing matter to Sagittarius. (If they start to laugh in bed it is just from high spirits and a sense of fun, so don't get a complex!)

No wonder some of the best comedy actors have been born under this funny sign: the divine Bette Midler, funny girl Pamela Stephenson, and among the men Jim Davidson, Syd Little, Richard Pryor and Woody Allen. All of these people know how to make others laugh, and know how to make money at it too.

Although great people to have in your life, they are not great at keeping secrets. A secret bubbles and boils away inside the archer causing great discomfort until it bursts out at the most inopportune moment. Sagittarius people love to socialize and contrive to have an interesting mix in their social circle. They don't know how to be rude so any cutting comment is made thoughtlessly rather than from any real nastiness. (Which doesn't always make it better, I know.) They are interested in masses of things and always come up with interesting topics of discussion. Their own weakness is a tendency to put too much trust in people. A pretty face does not mean a nice person. This is a lesson both Mr and Ms Sagittarius must learn.

Don't try to pin the archer down, or he or she will gallop away. Offer a guiding hand, and don't let on what it really means when the marriage licence is signed or the belongings are moved into your house. Sagittarius likes to live in a fantasy world and if you indulge this then you can keep everybody happy. You can view your commitments with gravity, while Sagittarius, committed to the same extent, views them with laughter as tremendous fun. Let the archer keep his or her childhood fantasies as a part of everyday life and you are sure to find nothing but enjoyment with this life-loving sign.

SECRETS OF THE SEXES

So how do the males and females of the species differ then? Let's have a look.

Love Stars

Ms Sagittarius

You may think when you first meet her that you understand her straight away, but you would be wrong. It takes at least a year to get to know her. She changes pace so rapidly that each time you think you have got her number she goes and changes again and you are left in bewilderment. She may say she loves to see shows at the theatre but come next month when you want to take her to the show you've booked she'll look at you as though you are crazy because she wants to go rock-climbing instead. The truth is that she probably doesn't remember that she had a thing about shows the other week. She looks to the future, not the past, and no amount of talking to her will convince her that you are right. She has a habit of laughing in people's faces, which can be more than a little annoying at times.

This is a very feminine woman outwardly, hiding a sensible personality inside. She does not take life too seriously, but she is not dumb either. Ms Sagittarius is broad-minded and open. She doesn't like anything underhand. She has a good brain and understands a lot of technical problems. She could probably take a motor car to pieces and put it back together again. She can, however, have a wicked temper, so be sure to keep on the right side of her. She is a gambler, a sucker for a hard-luck story and loves all types of people. Variety is the spice of life to her. She wants to know everything that is going on in your life, not in order to control you, but out of sheer fascination.

I don't think I have yet met a woman born under this sign who did not make some sort of a dramatic change to her life by the time she was thirty. It is usually a change in lover, job or country, or all three at once.

She dates men in her young days as if they are appetizers at a party, moving quickly onto the next in case it is tastier and more exciting then the one before. Sex to her is a bit of a game. She has the ability to make you think you are perhaps not as good as the last person in her life. This is not the case, first because she cannot really remember who the last person was, and secondly because it is not in her nature to be bitchy. It's just that perhaps you don't have her full attention all the time.

She doesn't like arguments and will not go for someone unless pushed to the limit. Then, however, it will be in such a way as to make you think you have done something you will never ever be forgiven for. Don't worry, though. She will not mention it next time she sees you and chances are she really has forgotten all about it.

Don't take this woman too lightly. The way to get into her good books is to go along with her off-the-cuff style at the same time as giving her plenty of support so that she knows if she changes her mind you won't think her a fool. She, in turn, will encourage you to go for your dreams. In addition, she will not hesitate to do a favour for you. Mind you, small and short favours are her speciality. To go for longer than a day with a fixed plan is something of a nightmare for her.

She can flirt with the best of them but she isn't aware of doing it. She thinks that men and women are all the same and has just as many male as female friends in her close circle with no sexual undertones whatsoever. (At least to her!) She is a brilliant mother who acts more like a friend to her children than an authority figure. She will jump up on the monkey bars with the kids rather than stand by watching.

You will find it hard to keep up with her ever-changing style and the way she is always onto the next big project. If she asks you to start an aerobics class with her don't rush out and get a year's membership straight away as by tomorrow it could be yoga she's into. But whatever role she fulfils in your life, you are sure to enjoy yourselves. If you don't have someone to laugh with, in the words of Ms Sagittarius, you're just not living. With Ms Sagittarius you won't be short of life-enhancing fun.

Mr Sagittarius

Mr Sagittarius likes you to play hard to get. He likes shy people. A word of advice, girls: let him do the chasing. He is very masculine and likes everyone to know it. He has a superior air about him, and you must not shoot him down. He will never make a promise to you unless he fully intends to keep it but you must be prepared that circumstances could well change beyond his control, such as that football match he had forgotten about, or the friend who unexpectedly rang up. All plausible excuses to our Mr Sagittarius. For him, life is to be made up as you go along. This man has got a way of putting things over. He can always put himself in the right, and can prove black is white if he wants to too. But he is very lovable, and life with him will not be dull.

If he is talking closely to a friend of yours, don't get jealous. He is more likely to be talking about the love he has for you rather than chatting her up. You see, you will be the last to know how he feels about you. Why should he explain to you? He's with you, isn't he? To this man that is proof enough that his feelings are genuine.

Be careful of getting involved in business with him. He has trouble finishing what he starts and you could find yourself doing the overtime while he goes down the pub. He is an ideas man who requires someone to run with his suggestions and make them into something workable.

Don't think that he is bad, though. He is just a boy through and through. I have met sixty-year-old archers who have still not managed to turn into men. They think they know what life is all about but each week their philosophies change. It is not unusual for them to have changed religion at least once before they are thirty.

Mr Sagittarius loves to travel and foreign countries and foreign love put tingles up his spine. If he is in an environment that is new to him he gets googly-eyed just thinking how many new things there are for him to learn. He doesn't want to stay on the move for ever. It is just that he always wants to know what else there is for him to explore. Even if he stays put he'll still be exploring in some way. The way for you to keep this man is to join him on his quest for learning. It isn't sex and passion that he wants. It's inner fulfilment. However, as I'm sure you can imagine, any man can think his brain is down his trousers and sometimes does explore using that region. Wrong, boys! It is in your head. The best way to find fulfilment, Mr Archer, is to stick to something for more than just a month. Find a partner who can share or at least understand your goals. Sign up for that course you are always wishing you'd done. No one will stare. All you are going to get is admiration. So quit being so edgy and say yes for once.

Well, you want to know if he is a good catch, don't you? The answer is yes, but he is also a very expensive one as he likes to change his style and his home on a regular basis. He has a large circle of friends all wanting to hear the latest joke he has up his sleeve. If you don't laugh when you are around him, then bid him farewell. This is a man who needs to laugh in order to live. You won't be doing either of yourselves a favour if you deny this major part of his make-up.

A cheater? No, but if put in temptation's way he is weaker than most. If he has to go away on business for a month you'd better book a ticket to go and see him, or he will have forgotten what you look like by the time you pick him up again at the airport at home. If you want him to fall in love with you, seduce him with your mind. He loves people with knowledge and will sign up for a lifetime course of devotion if you do.

SEXUAL NEEDS

So what, you want to know, does this sign expect in the bedroom? Well, that would be your first mistake. The bedroom is unlikely to be this Fire sign's favourite. Those of the archer mould like excitement and unpredictability, and a night under the stars would hold more appeal than satin bedsheets. This is a sign that has plenty of energy. When they say they want to stay up with you all night they mean it and they're not all talk either. Before you get slightly the wrong impression, in purely sex terms we are talking more about quality than quantity here. The stamina's good but the archer does fall off the case after a while!

An appealing physical appearance pulls Sagittarius in but their deepest need is for intellect. And Sagittarius wants to fall in love with the person he or she sleeps with, but the insatiable appetite is for experience. This means, I'm afraid, a leaning towards one-night stands. They are not selfish lovers by any means, rather the reverse. Something of a tendency to dish it out to everyone! If you are in love with Sagittarius you are going to have to make it clear that you won't accept anything other than a monogamous relationship. If you don't say, he or she won't know. It's like a child eating every last sweet in the jumbo-size packet and then saying that you never said not to, and by the way now they feel sick which isn't their fault at all.

Sagittarius's ruling planet is Jupiter, the planet of self-expansion, and the archers constantly try to improve themselves and shoot onto bigger and better things. They rarely go back to an ex since they are always looking ahead. Indeed, if they should consider their ex-lovers at all, it will only be with a promise to themselves to raise their standards next time. Onwards and upwards is their motto. At least you needn't feel jealous of your predecessors.

Sagittarius's world is an individual one, and not wholly without inhibitions where sex is concerned. A one-night stand is one thing but for a longer relationship Sagittarius needs to find a lot of trust. Sex is an important part of a relationship to Sagittarius people and they give a lot to the people they love. They are generous and considerate and beneath that brash exterior have an awful lot of self-doubt. Be careful you don't abuse the energy they put into the relationship and neglect them. Trouble can start brewing and once it reaches boiling point . . . Let's just say that when a Fire sign goes pop, you don't want to be around to see the devastation.

If you want the best out of this sign, you need to be romantic. You'll know what your archer wants because he or she will talk freely about sex. There's plenty of stamina, as I hinted at before, and all in all this is a lover you'll struggle to keep up with. Just when you think that things are over you get that look that says 'more'. Torrid lovers by nature, in their souls they want to possess you entirely in the most romantic of senses.

And don't forget the changeability factor. What works sexually for Sagittarius today may not work so well tomorrow. These people need to explore all of their feelings to the full. If they seem discontented, don't be alarmed. They wouldn't be with you if they didn't want to be, but they have a great need continually to analyse and consider what is going on in their life. You must allow this to take place. This is part of the need for exploration and understanding that is in the archer's blood.

Archers can be clumsy too. They need another sign to balance them properly. Give to them and they will give double back but don't play games with sex and use it as a weapon. This does not appeal to them and they will simply pack up and move on. They prefer hot passionate love to long drawn-out liaisons, but this need can be satisfied as much in the later years of a long and happy relationship as in the early days. Sagittarius can always take experimental notions to new heights.

TRUEST NEED AND DESIRE

INSTANT CONNECTIONS

Marriage Partners at a Glance

This is just a taster. For more detail, turn to the chapter called Between the Sheets.

BEST BETS

ARIES and Sagittarius make great sex together but the sparks can fly as quick in arguments as in love. None the less, definitely one to keep the interest going.
LEO not only satisfies Sagittarius sexually but also pleases him or her mentally. Who could ask for more?
LIBRA indulges in all of the suggestions Sagittarius makes. Take care you don't get caught in public, you two!
AQUARIUS is outrageous enough for Sagittarius but they may have problems deciding who's the boss.

FAIR CHANCE

GEMINI is Sagittarius's polar opposite and each makes up for what is missing in the other. That is, if Gemini will let Sagittarius get a word in edgeways.

CANCER and Sagittarius: sexually intriguing. Bursts of flame from these two.

VIRGO proves a real challenge and catches the interest of Sagittarius, but longevity is a problem for these two.

SAGITTARIUS with Sagittarius is great in the beginning but money troubles can bring their perfect union to a sharp and sudden end.

PISCES is very attractive to Sagittarius but they can drive each other to destruction as well as distraction.

HEAVY WEATHER

TAURUS is a little bit too much of a stick-in-the-mud for Sagittarius. Unless they have started out as friends, they don't really give each other the chance to discover one another's full capabilities.

SCORPIO gets great fun from this duo but in the end is too possessive and doesn't get enough commitment from Sagittarius.

CAPRICORN is not adventurous enough for Sagittarius, who wants to be able to act on impulse, not plans.

Top Ten Turn-offs

1 Baby talk
2 People who apologize all the time
3 Envy
4 People who talk more than Sagittarius does
5 Organizers
6 The word 'long-term'
7 Men/women who take hours to get ready
8 Obsessive cleanliness

9   Annoying laughs
10 Penny pinchers

HOW TO SEDUCE SAGITTARIUS

When you approach Sagittarius, you'd better not use any old line. You must be prepared to come up with something witty and original. These people need, no, demand originality. Listen carefully to what they are really saying, too, because most of the time they are asking you questions instead of giving you a chance to find out something about them.

Ask Sagittarius to suggest a place to go. Let him or her be the one to summon up the excitement. You're sure to fire up the archer's imagination if you do. Second thing: no tricks. Sagittarius is the kind of person who wants only the best from you, only to see your utmost potential (more than you've seen it yourself even). Sagittarius only backs winners so if you are out on a date you already know your scorecard looks good. Sagittarius can act a bit superior and give you the feeling that you need to make an impression yourself. This is partly true, but your main concern should be to find out as much as you can about your date. I hear all too often about people who have dated the archer and after a month still not known how to impress or seduce them and this is because they have spent most of the time talking about themselves thanks to all of the questions that Sagittarius likes to ask. Sagittarius people are not private or secretive, as such. It's more about their intense fascination with everyone else. And anyway, Sagittarius has too much going onto be able to sum it all up neatly for the other person.

These are modern men and women, up-to-date with the latest gadgets and goings-on. Better modern art than the Renaissance period (if you are into culture, that is). They work hard and play hard and will not mind meeting you straight from work for a date. In fact, that kind of arrangement (minimum time-wasting) is probably preferred.

So, you've got glammed up and you are ready to go out and impress Sagittarius. On your first date you have got more chances of knocking down his or her defences than you do on the second. If you want any important questions answering, now is the time to ask. Do bear in mind, however, that by the second date the answer could be a different one anyway, depending on the response you gave first time round.

Now they may well tell you that they love you on the first date, but you must not do the same. They can jump in at the deep end, but if you do you'll scare them off. Keep a bit of mystery about you if you want Sagittarius to come back for more. You Water signs of the zodiac (Cancer, Scorpio and Pisces) are less well equipped for this but do try. It could stand you in good stead.

Your Sagittarius date will be honest with you and will not lead you on. If this looks like a mismatch, it will be written all over Sagittarius's face. If it looks good you'll know that too. And beware the legendary persuasion of Sagittarius. Better take your toothbrush with you, just in case. If Sagittarius wants you, you won't be able to say no. If you can manage not to be seduced all the way then so much the better. A whole night of kissing will do you no harm!

Tell-tale signs that Sagittarius has Fallen

When Sagittarius falls in love they find it difficult to talk about anything else and friends will get frustrated and bored. I give my Sagittarius friends a wide berth for a week or two when they fall in love. I wait for the initial 'mad spell' to wear off first. You see, they will talk about the person who has captured their heart with all the fervency of a new devotee. The two 'm's will be freely mentioned – marriage and mortgages. Don't be upset if the archer offers you marriage and then proceeds to stay engaged to you for seven or eight years. The initial commitment has been made but the final furlong can sometimes be quite a while in the covering.

Talking of religion (and I was thinking in religious terms of Sagittarius's devotion), if the new partner is of a different religion Sagittarius will be thinking about converting. Indeed, to Sagittarius someone else's religion and culture is likely to be much more interesting than their own. A lot of archers fall in love on holiday and this is no accident. They really do want to pack up their life and move somewhere new. If you don't speak the same language then so much the better as far as they are concerned.

Don't get me wrong. These are pretty complicated characters to understand. One day they are enthusiastic about love, but the next I'm afraid they appear to have lost interest. Being part-human part-beast isn't that easy, as I'm sure you can appreciate. Plans can be altered before the ink on your deposit for a house together has dried. If they love you they will trust in you so use your power well. You may be in shock but remember that Sagittarius is a child and sometimes just needs a guiding hand. Hang on in there. We all make mistakes, and if you want to be with the archer you will probably need to learn the art of forgiveness.

Sagittarius is not the most practical of signs and doesn't have the best sense of timing. If you get woken up at five in the morning with a rose and breakfast on a tray then smile and accept. If the archer appears to abandon his or her family for you, don't cold-shoulder them yourself. Sagittarius will one day return to where they first found security and you'll be out in the cold. If you've established a relationship with the archer's family and friends, all the better for you. Think of a child who wants a new toy every week only to go back to the one that was first in their heart, for it brings with it the most security. Make yourself part of Sagittarius's security network and you'll be there for keeps.

SAGITTARIUS PEOPLE IN YOUR LIFE

This section tells you about the people you work, rest and play with.

Sagittarius in the Workplace

In a Sagittarius CV you are likely to see not one but many different kinds of job. They get bored easily and if they fancy a change will not mind giving up a good wage to go grape-picking in Spain. They are able workers but they do not always pay enough attention to their own assets. Funny, this lack of self-awareness in a sign with such a philosophical bent, and considering how religious they can become when the mood takes them. But then again they are all about moving on, and of course moving up, though how they get there is a tale all of its own.

The bosses of this sign confuse their staff who do not know whether to love or hate them. It isn't very often that they lose their temper but when they do they don't care who is present. In front of other staff or customers, they will say their piece. Perfectionists and sticklers for discipline, they don't always realize that their staff have wound them around their collective little finger. Flattery and praise makes Sagittarius putty in other people's hands. This can be bad for business and the archer may not be the soundest decision-maker on the team. However, Sagittarian vitality is contagious and these people can fire up the rest with both drive and ambition. Sagittarius promises people the earth and the rest of the team have to rein in the sun and the moon in order to get it. But they will follow the archer's arrow. Sagittarius people are ambitious and born to be successful. They are not afraid to have a go at anything. They could sell ice to the Inuit and sand to the Bedouin. They expect their staff to be as brilliant as they are and the confidence they inspire in their staff can make them just that.

With Fire as their element they start off with a lot of energy but without others to stoke them up they will flicker and die. They are ideas people, excellent at working on more than one project at a time. They get around obstacles with great style and are capable of generating the sort of alternative ideas that can help us all to move into the future, and to do so with style. Just beware of the running out of stamina, or the tendency to get bored.

They work odd hours better than set hours. A rigid routine makes them bored, depressed and unimaginative. They need to express their personality in their work, even down to the swearing they are prone to do at the most inappropriate times. They like to strut and that often athletic-looking figure does make them worthy of attention. A lot of models are born under this sign. Check out that mirror, Sagittarius. You could be missing out on a fun and lucrative future.

For me, Sagittarius is one of the harder signs to spot. However, if I've received an insult and a compliment in the same sentence and am left wondering whether I should kiss this person or hit them, then I might guess I'm with Sagittarius! The most wonderful thing about Sagittarius in the workplace is that they tell you the truth, so that you always know where you stand. They are not prone to double-dealing. And I for one would prefer to know what people are thinking rather than have it said behind my back, wouldn't you?

The Sagittarius Mother-in-law

This is a woman who will always be fair and square with you, and will give you a proper chance to impress her and prove that you are worthy of her child. She loves her children very much, and will love her grandchildren too, but she won't exactly be your conventional mother-in-law. She has her own way of doing things and it is likely that she brought up her own children in many towns and countries rather than just one. She will, I'm afraid, talk about sex in public and her son or daughter was probably one of the first to learn about the birds and the bees, just as they found out pretty quick the truth about Father Christmas. She is forward-thinking, and though she likes fantasy as much as the next person she cannot help but give a straight answer when asked a question, especially by her child. She won't ever fob the child off with anything less than the truth.

When she first meets you, she's likely to say something inappropriate. Supposing she's heard you've been on a diet. She's very likely to say, 'That diet wasn't up to much, was it? Still, you can always try another one.' She doesn't mean this in a nasty way at all. She just says whatever comes first into her head. Give her the benefit of the doubt, and try to think of her blatant honesty as a good point. If she gives a compliment, for example, she means it. I can think of worse characteristics for a mother-in-law than honesty!

Although not quite so cool as Leo, she will fulfil her grandmother role admirably, and your children can look forward to getting all the latest gear. Sagittarius people are children at heart so she'll get on with yours very well. Just remind her about the babysitting she said a month ago she'd do. She lives day by day and so you will have to remind her the week and the day before you want her if you are to get the night out that you've planned.

She ages well and works as hard at sixty as she did at thirty. Indeed, she finds it incredibly hard to give up her work. If widowed or divorced, you won't see her settling down to marriage again. She would rather take it easy and have a few boyfriends. Commitment a second time round is not common in Sagittarian women. Her imagination can work overtime but if she tells you at eighty that she is moving to another country then watch out, she really does mean it. She's certain to make a success of any new beginnings whatever her age, and as for you, you'll have somewhere new to visit on your summer holiday. You'll always know where you stand with her, but don't count on an inheritance for your old age. She's a gambler, don't forget.

Sagittarius Children

These children pretend they don't want to learn but underneath that uninterested mumble is a mind sharper than that of many adults. What I love about Sagittarius children is that they can shock and surprise – in the nicest sense. This is an old mind in a young body, and they can come out with more quips and cutting remarks than many of the more obviously intelligent signs. They don't need twenty-four-hour attention because they can entertain themselves. Don't build things up for them, or they'll be bored and their enthusiasm burnt out by the time whatever it is arrives. Don't promise them, just do.

They love their parents and are fiercely protective of them, and are likely to give anyone a dressing-down who they think has done their family a wrong – whatever the age difference. They probably pick Leos as friends at secondary school because they like fashion and Leo has a good sense of style (better than Sagittarius, in fact) and understands how important labels are. Don't spend your hard-earned money on Sagittarius's fads until you have established at least a hint of longevity. Otherwise they are onto the next thing before you have even got the shopping bags through the front door.

They are usually tidy, largely because they don't hoard things. Don't expect to see the same faces around them throughout their childhood. They get bored and move on and like to explore many friendships. At a party on their own they can end up looking awkward and may make fools of themselves. The truth is that when they are children they look at others around them to find their own identity. You'd never guess this, of course, because they go out of their way to look supercool.

They don't misbehave much. They are too busy having a good time to play up. They are great children, there's no doubt about it. Don't try to make them grow up too fast. They love being children so much they stay that way through much if not all of their adulthood!

Sexually they are slow starters, and have too short an attention span for full-on relationships in their youth. They are more likely to be best friends with the opposite sex than lovers. They are good advice-givers, even for problems they have never experienced themselves, because they listen to what is going on around them and develop great understanding.

The boys of this sign often want to be footballers, and they should persist since top footballers of this sign include Ryan Giggs, Les Ferdinand, Dennis Wise,

Geoff Hurst, Billy Bremner, Paul McGrath, Carlton Palmer and Gary Lineker. The girls want to do jobs typically done by men, and they succeed very well. Sagittarius's comic personality opens many doors, even into the serious professions.

This is your child, best friend and adviser all in one. Best of all he or she will make you laugh – now, next year and for many years to come.

Sagittarius Friends

In any crisis your Sagittarius friends can lighten the atmosphere with their sense of humour. They make life easier to get through. I haven't met a Sagittarius yet who did not have a sense of humour (even if occasionally a little too dark for my liking).

You can make as many arrangements as you like with them but they will always do what they like when they like and no amount of shouting or emotional blackmail is going to make them do differently. I have many Sagittarius friends, but I don't see them that often. When I do see them, it is because they have come to stay with Rob and me (we live in Torquay in Devon and it is like the south of France here in the summer) and they generally stay for a week or two – longer than other friends do. Then we don't see them again until the following year. Maybe it has something to do with the climate here in Torquay, but I stand by my beliefs and say it has much more to do with their star sign. You see, a Fire sign, especially Sagittarius, loves you when it sees you but can't remember your name or address when it doesn't.

These people do well in life and don't mind paying for you if you are short of cash. They can be selfish and self-centred at times but because they do it in a way that is funny you end up laughing at them instead of getting mad at them. If they try to get away with too much and ride their luck too hard then they can fall out with the very people they love as friends, but I have witnessed too many archers talk their way back into their friends' hearts to be much concerned about this.

They like to do two things at once. Don't be offended if you pop round to see them and they are twitching away on the TV controls while you tell them a sob story and ask for advice. Believe me, they will give just as good advice while not looking at you as they will while staring straight into your eyes. If you ask what they think about life they will talk with a very serious tone but if you probe a little further you will soon see that it is really quite impossible for them to be serious about anything.

They love people and can introduce you to many new friends, but whether they will turn up at the party they have invited you to is another matter. Someone could have invited them somewhere else five minutes before you were due to share a cab, and you'll be stuck outside wondering why they're not answering their door.

They will lend you money and share their friends with you, but they will never tolerate a lie. Learn early on that they want the truth, the whole truth and nothing but the truth and you will find yourself on their Christmas card list, every other year at least. Expect them to show you a side to life that you never even thought of looking at before. Above all else, treat them with love. They need lots from everyone so that they may find the confidence they need. With all that love, they can rule the world – and a more benevolent ruler you could not find.

Capricorn
December 22 to January 20

CAUTIOUS, RESERVED, PRUDENT, ambitious, constructive and disciplined: these are the key words to describe Capricorn. The goat symbolizes courage and determination. With their sheer pluck, common sense and capacity for hard work, Capricorn people will tackle anything no matter how impossible it may seem. Any setback is seen as a challenge and gives Capricorn even greater impetus to achieve objectives. Contentment seems to evade them before about their fortieth year. Until this time they generally find it rather difficult to conform to other people's rules and regulations. They deserve to do well for they have all of the necessary qualifications: strong will, independence, conscientiousness, sincerity and stamina. Will-power backed up by a realistic attitude to life and with many talents at their disposal pretty much ensures success.

Though great friends, truthful, trustworthy and loyal, at work they are so ambitious that they are often high up in their chosen profession and they do not always make the nicest or kindest bosses in the zodiac. Nor are they flexible. Capricorn bosses I have known have been brilliant but hard. When they say they want the astrology column they want it yesterday, even if it doesn't go to print for another week.

They are shrewd with money, and spend and invest wisely. They always have something for a rainy day and they enjoy the security this provides. They do have the odd mad moment, however. None the less, serious and purposeful is their approach to life and its problems. They do have an excellent though sometimes bizarre sense of humour, a great asset which is much appreciated by those with whom they come into contact, but they sometimes need reminding to bring it into play. Worriers, their own health concerns and those of their loved ones weigh heavily upon them. They can get stuck in their own problems while pretending to the outside world that nothing is wrong. Capricorn funnyman Jim Carrey seems to be stuck in this cycle as professionally he is a huge hit but privately the story seems to be that of divorce and broken engagements. A successful chart and a man who is meant for great things, he perhaps only needs to learn to trust those he loves.

No half-measures with these guys. They have strong likes and dislikes, with a useful knack of being able to conceal their feelings until it suits them to show their hand. It may come as a surprise to you to find that, despite being essentially sensible, down-to-earth and organized, they have a powerful romantic streak. It is absolutely essential for Capricorn to marry for love. Whoever they marry must be capable of keeping the joy and excitement of the early days alive for as long as they stay together. Jogging along in a humdrum existence is not for them.

If you ask Capricorn a question, be prepared that you may not like the answer. If you reveal your problems, be prepared that Capricorn will not leave you alone until you have made the change they deem so necessary for your happiness. Capricorn people are so ambitious that they want success not only for themselves but for their nearest and dearest as well. This may make them sound modern in their thinking, and in some respects they are, but underneath it all they are traditionalists. They want everything done the right way, straight down the line and by the book. They like to have fun but it has to be at the right time. If you act out of turn, you'll get a look that's half stern, half puzzled. Even the strongest of signs can be made to feel inferior to this bossy Earth sign.

To get on the right side of Capricorn, treat them as you would wish to be treated. Don't try to make a fool of them. You will not easily get them to speak about how they feel. They have a thick skin with a soft layer underneath. You have to get through the armour first. If you do, you are likely to find a person who is loyal and loving, and consistent for many years to come.

At some point in your life you will meet a Capricorn you do not like. These people have a hard side that they will use when they need to. If you do not know them properly this can shock and upset you. They have worked hard for what they have and don't like the thought of anything or anyone they think can jeopardize what they have built up. Common sense may be their middle name but that does not mean they are not prone to a bit of craziness now and then. It will be on their own terms too.

You may have gathered by now that Capricorn people like to be the boss. Indeed, they insist on it. You'll have to quietly lead them round to your way of thinking, and choose your time carefully when you want to tell them of any changes you would like to make. Let them know – or at least think – that they are in charge.

Mostly an asset, but sometimes a hindrance – but then who wants someone who is always the same? Once you let Capricorn into your life you will feel as if you have had them there for ever, and if you should ever lose them you won't forget them. They have such an individual way of doing things that you will find yourself copying their habits, especially ones to do with the home. A not-so-good habit of theirs, however, is overindulgence in food. They enjoy good food but tend to go for the traditional stuff that's high in fat. Encourage them into healthier eating habits if you can.

Capricorns often surprise themselves and other people with the kind of partners they choose. It may look like a mismatch, but what onlookers do not realize is that underneath that cool, calm exterior is a passionate being just dying to live life to the full. Being of the element Earth, they are often attracted to the Water signs, who can nourish their dreams and help them to grow. Cancer, Scorpio and Pisces can often be seen with Capricorn, or perhaps rather 'heard', thanks to the loud and colourful conversations they enjoy. They love their home and are not too obsessed with career to be an indifferent parent. Mel Gibson, now on baby number seven, is a good example of that.

If they seem a little backwards in coming forwards with their friendship this is only because they do not rush into new relationships. They don't really rush into anything. Therefore it is strange how they are always in a hurry! Capricorn in a queue wants everyone in front to move a little quicker but when the goat gets to the counter it takes as long as it likes, even if only to pay for groceries in the local store. (I dread to think what they are like when it comes to buying a house.)

Whatever role Capricorn plays in your life, give them time, and don't try to push them into things. If you try to push them there is the danger they will back out and let you down. If you have upset them they will tell you straight, but they will tell you when you have pleased them too. Don't expect them to reveal all areas of their life to you at once. They take their time in trusting people. Better not to ask questions. After a while they will start to wonder why you haven't asked them anything and will start to inform you of it all, telling you probably more than you had wanted to know in the first place.

Yes, they can be a little distant, even to those they love and trust, but give them the benefit of the doubt and let time answer all of your questions. They wouldn't stay with you if they didn't love you. Life to them is all about planning and if you were not the dream they have long sought you wouldn't be with them as part of the plan. Some say that being chosen by a Capricorn is a bit like being given a Grammy. They must think you're perfect for the part, so be proud, stand tall and don't take the criticism too much to heart. They don't mean any harm. They just know best. Or so they think.

SECRETS OF THE SEXES

So how do the males and females of the species differ then? Let's have a look.

Ms Capricorn

At first glance you might think she does not like you. She approaches everyone she meets with a great deal of caution, looking at you side on rather than straight in your face. She does not take well to criticism so telling her the dress she is wearing is not the best colour for her is not the way to go. Instead, take the polite approach. Shake her by the hand with a smile if you are a woman and kiss her on the cheek if you are a man. The age of chivalry is to her very much still in fashion and this will score you top points in her charm book. Just know how far to take the chivalry though. Past beaus will tell you that she can swing a punch if she feels taken advantage of.

Ms Capricorn needs a lot of understanding. She will have you dangling on a string if you don't watch out. She has a fascination with the unusual and likes to experiment with clothes, food and, oh yes, sex. She is strong-willed, hard-working and sincere. She is obstinate, and an angel one minute and a she-devil the next. Early in life she falls for the wrong men and it is not until much later that she meets the right partner. When she does, it is a match for life. She likes a hard-working man who can give her affection and security. She will go for your personality rather than your looks, so cut down on the aftershave and step up your conversation skills.

She is the kind of woman who knows what she wants. After her early mistakes she develops a built-in lie detector and a sure instinct of what is right and what is wrong for her. She can steer away from trouble very easily. Be careful of upsetting her or you'll make yourself an enemy and a stubborn one at that. Once she has passed judgement you will find it very hard to talk her around.

She's not easy to pick out in a crowd. She doesn't gather a group around her or make an exhibition of herself. She stays on the sidelines taking everything in. She is in no hurry to impress or to get to know new people. She would rather observe and then make up her own mind in her own time. Indeed, none of the Earth signs – Capricorn, Taurus and Virgo – make a big noise in a crowd. It's the Air signs – Gemini, Libra and Aquarius – who gain the attention. But the people who take their time end up making a bigger impact on people's lives. This is one woman who will live life to the full. The difference is she won't be in a rush, like many of us. She usually ends up at the top of her career and gains respect from both sexes in the process. She is not afraid of work, and professionally can succeed very well among men, as well as among women.

It may take her longer than others to achieve success, but that is because she is thinking about her decisions every step of the way. Whether she runs her own small business or a multi-million-pound empire, she will do so with such precision that her successes are likely to be long-lasting, and those with whom she works are likely to be fulfilled in their jobs.

Just before you think you've got Capricorn parcelled up and labelled, let me tell you something else. In spite of their strong personalities and definite characteristics, no two Capricorn women are the same. I have noticed that twins born under this sign could not look or be more different if they tried. The goat appears in many guises. And don't forget that Capricorn woman is sexy. Man oh man is she sexy. But not in your usual way. Capricorn has developed her own style. Capricorn singer Sade, for example, has earthy sex appeal in bucketloads and her steadfast approach to her career is certain to have been behind the successful comeback she made in 2001.

Ms Capricorn will not accept anything but the best so if she chooses you as a partner you can be sure that she thinks you're the tops. What's more, she'll take you to new heights both personally and professionally. Who can say better than that?

Mr Capricorn

Where to start with the lovely Mr Capricorn? He is a man who means business, and business is one of the most important things to him. Without a successful career he cannot feel like a man. He needs to know that he is well respected and that he can walk into a place and hear people whisper about how well he has done. Indeed it quite suits him for you to be in awe of him, if you wouldn't mind.

You will have to accept the fact that no matter how progressive he is in his thinking, he likes his traditional ways. If dinner is not on the table at the right time he can become quite moody. Without some sort of a routine he begins to feel unsafe. Only by having a fixed schedule can he find the security he needs to make his next and no doubt most important move.

In love he is slow to show his affections. He hates to risk your not returning a compliment, or pulling your hand away from his. He prefers to take his time and to let the woman in his life make the first move. Not so traditional there, you may think, and you'd be right. In love, caution rules the day for Mr Capricorn, at least to begin with.

You must be careful not to say anything to him that could be taken as an insult. If you don't have something nice to say then say nothing at all. He on the other hand may make cutting remarks to you. This is only fair because he has more of an insight into people than you or anyone else has, and he is allowed to speak his mind as and when it pleases him. So there!

You won't get lots of affection from him until he is completely sure of you. He likes you to appreciate his conversation and ask his advice. In business he can be quite ruthless, but in romance he's rather helpless and needs guidance from you. He is a perfectionist, however, and once he takes anything on – you included – he must put his whole self into it. You do the groundwork and then he'll take over the organizing. He'll forgive you for things but probably won't forget them. He doesn't like jealous partners and he'll need you to share his interests: be they cars, football, good looks, Jennifer Aniston and/or curry. He doesn't like giggling or gossip.

You'll have plenty of time for enjoyment but he also wants you to know the things that are important to him. You may think him too serious or lacking in fun but he has a very good sense of humour and absolutely loves to laugh. The reason he will not show this side of himself to you straight away is that he does not need to. He isn't going to amuse you into bed. He has a cool, calm way that can get him into the highest rankings but can also trick you into thinking that he is higher up in his profession than he really is. He holds himself very well. And this makes him sexy. But be careful how you tell him so, or he may think you're making fun of him. He will treat you like a princess at some times and like you don't exist at others. His feelings towards you have not changed, he just needs his space.

Many Capricorn people are avid readers of books and if you move in with Mr Capricorn and he suggests going to bed early don't dig out your sexy nightie just yet. He could have more intention of reading his latest novel than getting up to mischief under the covers. There is a time for everything, and once he's finished the book you may find the passionate man you were seeking. Things have to be on his terms, but if you are prepared to fall in with this, then you may just find yourself with a man who comes home on time, does very well in his job and knows how to please you in the bedroom too.

SEXUAL NEEDS

Capricorn likes long-drawn-out lovemaking and that includes all the stuff that goes on before you get anywhere near bed. Love is a serious business. Capricorn people see themselves as worthy, and they do not allow just anyone to knock down their defences and see into their private world.

For Capricorn sex is a very special thing. Some of them use sex as a way of understanding people and working out what makes them tick. However, just one broken heart and they are running back to Mummy and Daddy to marry the beau next door. Don't expect them to be adventurous. If a job is worth doing then it is worth doing well and that doesn't involve trying to do it balanced on top of the washing machine. Not unless you plan it in advance and bring the appropriate protection (I'm talking cushions here).

You may have heard rumours of longevity in the lovemaking department and it is still not certain whether this is fact or fiction but I have heard some evidence of the goat's staying power. What is indisputable is that Capricorn is very good, no, excellent at sex. Everything has room for improvement and they don't mind spending hours making love and perfecting their technique. Nothing's obvious with

Capricorn and at first meeting you may think that sex is something very far from their thoughts. Not so. And they are better at it than you think too.

OK. We've heard all about how serious Capricorn is. But we also know these are people of charm and presence, and if you want to know how things work on the flirting front, well let me tell you that Capricorn, in the right mood, loves to flirt, and does it very well. A consummate flirt, you might say. Indeed, not above sex to get on at work, I'm ashamed to say (including sleeping with the boss if so required), though I'm sure they couldn't be completely hard-hearted and business-like about it. Indeed, Capricorn has an understated desire for variety, and although not a cheater or deceiver by nature, if it is a learning and advancing issue, well . . .

I shouldn't tell you this really, but I will. A number of Capricorn people have told me about dreams in which they are making love to someone and judges are holding up scorecards. Deep in the soul of Capricorn is a need for their performance to be judged – and given top marks. Competitive lovemaking on a bed of money would probably be their number-one fantasy (so long as you didn't crease the money too much).

Capricorn can send out mixed signals. It's all part of making sure they always come out on top. With their gift for meaning two things at once they should probably consider politics as a career. If you don't have similar plans to your Capricorn mate and are not willing to change your plans to fit, then you may as well pack it in now. Gorgeous creatures, Capricorn, but they are very selfish and you do have to go along with what they want. They love their family, mothers in particular, and you'll have to get by the family members in order to reach the goat's heart. They can belittle their family but you'd better not. Arrogant? Yes. Power hungry? Yes. Erotic? Yes. You must make up your own mind whether you are willing to go on the exciting but confusing journey this sign wants to take you on.

TRUEST NEED AND DESIRE

CONTROL

Marriage Partners at a Glance

This is just a taster. For more detail, turn to the chapter called Between the Sheets.

BEST BETS

TAURUS gives Capricorn all the goat wants, plus more. These two may have trouble ever making it out of the bedroom.

VIRGO finds a dream partner in Capricorn. Their joint capacity to plan things is the icing on the cake, and passion places the cherry on top.

FAIR CHANCE

ARIES provides the excitement but can be too hot for Capricorn to handle a lot of the time.

CANCER is a little too emotional for Capricorn, though the lovemaking is sure to be top of the charts.

CAPRICORN and Capricorn's joint stubbornness can get in the way of their undoubted mutual passion.

PISCES has passion for Capricorn and together they manage to keep out of the trouble they would independently find.

HEAVY WEATHER

GEMINI is too wild even for experimental Capricorn. These two end up calling each other's bluff.

LEO loves to wind up Capricorn but doesn't always know when to call time on the games and silly antics.

LIBRA finds Capricorn a real head-turner but conversation is stilted between two signs with such different styles of living.

SCORPIO finds Capricorn a bit too heavy and has trouble giving up the driving seat.

SAGITTARIUS is a little too impulsive for Capricorn, who prefers to have some sort of a gameplan.

AQUARIUS butts heads with Capricorn the goat, and when these two don't get what they want from each other they resort to name-calling.

Top Ten Turn-offs

1 Karaoke singers
2 Too much make-up
3 Sob stories
4 People who wear clothes that are too tight
5 People who talk for the sake of it
6 Weak-willed people
7 Show-offs (even though it's OK for Capricorn to do it)

8 Backseat drivers
9 People who don't stand their ground
10 People who can't handle their drink

HOW TO SEDUCE CAPRICORN

Capricorns are pretty fixed in their views on life so if they tell you they don't fancy Italian then take it that they hate Italian and cross that restaurant off your list. They tend to prefer traditional, rather heavy food, so go to an old-fashioned restaurant with dark wood on the walls and steak-and-kidney pudding on the menu. They work hard so don't take it personally if they tell you they have to go home early because they have to be up with the lark in the morning. At least you know this is someone who will always be able to put bread on the table (along with pies, puddings and ale).

If you have been seeing Capricorn for a while and haven't got past kissing, you probably aren't too disappointed, since the kissing is likely to be worth lingering on. All the same, you will want to move on a stage at some point. Just don't hurry your Capricorn. They are confident in their own opinion and if they are still seeing you then you can guarantee it is because they regard you highly.

They see life as a challenge and enter into dating a bit as if it is a competition. They like to show their skills in the game of life. Expect to have to answer questions about how much money you make, who you know and where you have travelled to. Don't be surprised if your date has an obsession with a famous film star. This is a sign that is a Hollywood icon in its dreams, and likes to fantasize about being filmed in bed making love.

Both security and space are important to Capricorn, even physical space, such as in a concert hall. Don't take them anywhere they will end up feeling cramped. That will dampen their ardour very quickly. Pay for big comfy seats in the cinema instead, where you can snuggle up together.

Don't be upset if your date has opinions on everything and even claims to know more about your job than you do. This is a trait that serves Capricorn well in life and they are not about to change a winning strategy, even in the name of romance and flattery.

I haven't yet told you what you really want to know, have I? Here you are then. To seduce Capricorn on the first date, back off. Act as though you are only mildly interested and you will soon find your arm grabbed and your date begging for you to stay. Capricorn people hate to think that they are not important and will try to prove otherwise to you. Doing all the groundwork and then letting them make (or appear to make) the first move is the key. It might be hard to hold back, though. Capricorn has this laid-back kind of attitude that leads both men and women to want to grab them and kiss them full on the mouth as if to try to get some kind of reaction. Both Mr and Ms Capricorn are angel and devil rolled into one. You need to play it clever, and to seduce them with your mind as well as your body, for they will choose brains over beauty every time.

Capricorns often fall for people who are already attached or who have no desire to be attached at all. I think they really do believe they can change the world. No one will ever live up to the high expectations this sign has of them, so don't get too upset when they look at you wanting more. This is simply Capricorn being Capricorn.

First dates with a sign like this are always nervy. You feel more like you are on a job interview than a romantic evening out. You'd better think up some good answers to that classic question about where you see yourself in ten years' time. My favourite line is, 'I plan to be prime minister.' Try it. You'll have your date dragging you to the bedroom to talk tactics in no time.

Tell-tale signs that Capricorn has Fallen

Capricorn in love suddenly comes up with a whole new gameplan, involving two instead of one. They like to work in a team and so are happy to give up solo plans in favour of joint ones. They love sex and the first few months are sure to be filled with steamy passion. There will come a time when the sexy nightwear is abandoned for the comfortable slippers, but don't pack your bags – this is the best sign yet that Capricorn is well and truly smitten.

They also start to plan joint pensions and other financial necessaries once you have decided that you are meant for one another. They will do anything for you – apart from give up their careers, that is. Without their chosen profession they are not able to feel like a real man or woman. They work harder for reputation than for money. They like to be thought tough in business since it earns them respect. Don't get paranoid if they call you and explain they have to work late in the office – they really do.

This is a man or woman who has everything they need laid out ready the night before, whether it is for a workday or a weekend. Be careful of doing things like squeezing the toothpaste in the middle or drinking milk straight from the bottle. That's a major passion-killer to these people.

They are not in as big a hurry to marry as you may think. Even if the big question gets posed, don't go making up your wedding lists just yet. It could be months if not years before anything gets booked, and even then it may get delayed in order to make every detail as perfect as possible and to make sure that it fits in with career plans.

A wonderful thing happens when the goat falls in love – the brown paper wrapping comes off the sense of humour and suddenly you can see their sense of fun in all its glory. I'm afraid much of the rest of the time the humour stays under wraps, though the goat will never admit to this.

When they love they love completely, and parade the person who has stolen their heart as if a fragile jewel to be looked at but not touched. They like to hold hands but do so in a manner that comes across more in ownership than affection. They can start to become a bit childlike, the more in love they are. Some even adopt a funny way of talking that to friends is just plain bizarre, if not downright irritating. Fortunately this stage is usually short-lived.

If Capricorn is over thirty there's generally a tale to tell of the one that got away in their youth because they waited too long to reveal the extent of their feelings. In spite of their arrogance, they look upon the person they choose to be their partner in life as a protector of sorts, someone to save them from the bad things in life and to pick them up should they fall. Capricorns have a sixth sense that they will live for a long time, and the majority of them do. They know that it is important to find someone who can go through life with them listening to their gripes and groans. A single Capricorn may claim to be happy but deep down inside needs someone special, and knows it.

This sign is at its best when in love, and life no longer feels like a competition. But don't play games or the goat will hit back with a winning hand that leaves you both embarrassed and sorry that you started any rivalry. Give your loyalty and you can expect to receive it back doubled.

CAPRICORN PEOPLE IN YOUR LIFE

This section tells you about the people you work, rest and play with.

Capricorn in the Workplace

It's not very often that Capricorn gets lucky. If in a position of authority it is because they made it there through lots of hard work. They deserve to be admired. Like any goat on top of a mountain, they never got there the easy way.

As bosses, Capricorns don't ask anyone to do

anything they would not do themselves. If there is a rush on at work, they roll up their sleeves and get stuck in. They enjoy being the boss and are fair, sympathetic and honest. They admire these qualities in those who work for them. They won't stand any nonsense and believe in a good day's work for a good day's pay. Quick to spot shirkers they give them fair warning to pull up their socks before taking action. They can't stand sloppiness, excuses and inefficiency. Others may say they take their work too seriously, but they know it is the only way to get results. They keep work and home life separate and I know more than a few Capricorn people who tell their spouses not to phone them at work except in an emergency.

If not the boss, Capricorn people will act as if they are. They believe they are supposed to take control and the truth is that they are very good at it. They are purposeful in their work and won't cut corners nor take too long. If you give them a contract they will read every line of it. They make deals when the time is right and the preliminaries have been seen to. They were born to work and a Capricorn without a position is an unhappy person. Jobless they become moody and irrational, complaining about how they were supposed to be doing this and that and eventually allowing envy to eat away at them. Their appetite for life will always see them get back on their feet, and as soon as they are in a job once again they will start working out how to take over the company.

At job interviews they must be careful not to reveal their true ambitions. If they do, the interviewer will fear for his or her job and send them away. They are excellent in a crisis, want to make money for their company, and have the brains and drive to get to the top of their career. Comfortable in the workplace, their sex drive can see them becoming embroiled in relationships with people they work with. Apart from this weakness, they are essentially well-oiled and efficient machines and expect everyone around them to be the same. They like to have a timetable and to stick to it. These are the kids at school who were able to direct all of their friends to the classes they are meant to be attending. They don't like to work on commission. They like to know exactly what is coming in and when. If promised a rise in three months' time, they will be at the boss's door on the hour demanding it. They have good memories and learn their business well. They want to build up something solid and stay with a company long-term. It is not their desire to flit from job to job.

Capricorn will make it to the top. Professional jealousy is the only obstacle on the way. Before you know it, Capricorn is telling everyone how he or she liked the company so much they bought it. Unlike many of the other signs who blow hot air, Capricorn means what it says.

The Capricorn Mother-in-law

This woman's children will always be her babies no matter what anyone says. She may even have some awful pet names she still calls them by, although you had better not have a pet name for her since as a rule she hates them.

Her door will always be open for her family but anyone else and she'll need to know a bit about them first. If she is still married you will see that she is the boss of the relationship and her husband is sure to have a routine set for him that he must follow. She may go so far as to serve set meals on set nights. She hates to waste money and so likes to plan ahead.

If ever you have a problem or even fall out with her child, you can count on her to counsel you through it. She may not, however, tell you what you want to hear. She will tell you exactly what she thinks. She is dedicated to finding out the truth but is also moralistic. Although she may continue to enjoy her own sex life, you must not talk to her about yours. She will find it distasteful.

She is insecure yet she will come across as the opposite. Her children's schools are likely to have been very carefully chosen. She goes to the supermarket on the same day of each week. Don't get me wrong. She is not boring. Quite the opposite. She cannot possibly sit at home doing nothing all day. She probably still works and if not she is certainly involved in committees and community-organizing. She has plenty of self-respect and others respect her too. If she likes you she will take you under her wing and give you confidence. If she doesn't, you'll be made to feel unwelcome, and might wonder what on earth it is she knows about you.

She can handle herself brilliantly in new company but will not try to change to please anyone. What you see is what you get. She won't mind telling you if she doesn't think you're good enough. It's up to you to prove to her that you are. She's not in a hurry so it can take months or even years for her to call you family.

Allow her to treat her son or daughter as if still her baby, which her child will always be to her. The nicest thing you can do to break down the defences of an Earth sign is to ask her round for dinner. Don't leave it too long or she'll think you don't want to get to know her and will put on a very cold front indeed.

Don't try to charm her. This won't work. Show her your bank balance, tell her your career plans, but don't tell her how young she looks (she already knows). All she is interested in is how well you can take care of her child. She is not overly eager for her children to marry so don't take it as an insult if she tells you both to take your time. She will not approve of you spending a fortune on clothes. You'll score more brownie points telling her how you invested in a really good quality coat because you knew it would last a few winters instead of just one. You will love this woman because you won't have to waste time wooing her. The cold hard facts and possibly a copy of your bank balance is all she'll need to make up her mind, but then what more could any mother-in-law ask for than a secure future for her babies?

Capricorn Children

Here we have the original prototype for the school prefect. The young Capricorn will wake you up if you oversleep to make sure that you have enough time to get them to school. That is, of course, so long as you have chosen a school they deem worthy of their presence. They are none too happy if you are late dishing up dinner either. To say they are the boss of you is an understatement. You'd better brush up your parenting skills to pass muster with these children.

The good news is that they know when to bow down to a greater power so if you draw the lines clearly and show them what's what, and never give in to emotional blackmail, then you stand a good chance of winning their respect. Don't think that when the light is on in their room until all hours that they are playing computer games. Oh no. The young goat is still doing homework. These children want to shine in class. They will want a good education, because they have no plans to be poor when they are older. They are likely to research schools for you.

They like sex but do not rush into things. Kissing is as far as they will go when young so hold back your scolding because they won't forgive you for mis-understanding them. They believe in and demand justice. If you tell them off for something they haven't done they will set up court in the sitting room and plead their case to the relevant parties.

Both friendship and admiration are important to young Capricorn. A little arrogant, it's true, but they are a great source of support to less confident children. They excel fairly early on and develop a pretty good idea of future career prospects. They don't mind hard work but if you want them to wash your car then you must pay for it. It will be a fair price, though, because they will know the going rate for such a job, as well as the average bedtime and the appropriate pocket money per year of age.

They are strong-willed and will not wear something

they don't like, no matter how much you try to talk them round. They will not change their minds on any score once made up. Don't renege on any promises or you'll have them in a major tantrum with full-on body-to-floor contact and arms and legs flailing. A deal is a deal as far as they're concerned.

They love animals and you would do well to buy them a pet for they will look after it most responsibly. They have a great deal of common sense too, or is that business sense? While other kids are sneaking out to concerts, little Mandy or Matthew is selling the tickets at a profit. They can quite easily find employment. They give this air to all around that they can handle themselves, and it is only their temper that can let them down from time to time.

They will try anything once but will not be talked into doing something that is dangerous or embarrassing. They need to keep their pride and dignity. They mix as well with parents' friends as with their own, and sometimes even better. They love the outdoors and benefit from going for walks in the countryside. They don't much like late nights and can get moody after 9 p.m. This is their way of telling you that they need their sleep because they have important work to do. They like to have some sense of order in the day. They will be loyal, and loving, and you will be very proud of them.

Capricorn Friends

At first you'll be warning your friends off the Capricorns around. They are so bossy and so inclined to put people down, and far too cold to have anyone's best interests at heart. But you'd be wrong. The truth is that a Capricorn friend will do anything for the ones he or she loves. Unfortunately this includes telling them where they have gone wrong, who they should be talking to and a whole host of other details. What the outsider does not realize is that this is the natural instinct of the goat who only wants to help loved ones improve their lives and have a better time.

Capricorn friends come across as older than they are. They know what advice to give before you have even got the question out. If the advice were bad then you would have been right to be wary of them. But they really do know what they are doing. And they are capable of being the force behind a sign that doesn't have the get-up-and-go to make it all happen for themselves. Think carefully before you and Capricorn mix business with pleasure, however. Capricorn can be one thing in private but something else altogether at work.

They like routine so don't let them down. They will have planned everything in advance and will not forgive you easily for upsetting the order of things. They have an individual sense of humour, which not everyone finds funny. They can be both plodders and leaders. They move slowly on issues of little importance to them but if there is a chance of making money or improving job prospects you won't see them for dust. Both men and women of this sign depend on a job for their identity.

They are down-to-earth and don't require fancy clothes or trendy bars to have a good time. They would rather sit around the table at home with a good bottle of wine and the latest gossip about friends, family and, of course, career. However long you have known them, you'll still be finding things out that surprise you. Their choice in partners will never cease to amaze, for one. Or else you'll discover months down the line that they were seeing someone in private and you never guessed. A dark horse, but loyal to those they love.

They will keep your secrets, unlike other people, but they will push you to make changes they think are good for you until you have no alternative but to give in. They will be the first of your friends to have a pension and will urge you to get one too. They pick their friends carefully and they don't run with losers. Not all of your friends will like Capricorn, but you know your Capricorn friend better than they do.

Aquarius
January 21 to February 19

INDEPENDENT, INTELLECTUAL, DISTANT and idealistic: these are the key words to describe Aquarius. Aquarius people are highly individual characters with many interesting facets to their personality, one of the most admirable being complete sincerity. They have a well-developed sense of duty which their deep understanding of human nature ensures they never express as a duty but rather as a pleasure. They are dedicated people who know what they want out of life and how to get it. They work relentlessly to achieve their objectives. They are single-minded and self-disciplined, both of which qualities enable them to do something worthwhile with their lives.

Aquarius people tend to have close-knit families to which they are devoted. They also make the most loyal friend. The fortunate person upon whom their friendship has been bestowed can rely come hell or high water upon their unswerving loyalty. Their capacity for fun combined with a natural wit make them a much sought-after companion. They are great exponents of let's-make-the-best-of-it and have the ability to turn the dullest chore into fun. If something onerous has to be done, Aquarius understands that it'll get done quicker and better with a smile than with a long face.

Those born under this sign are keen travellers. Something of the explorer is within them, and almost impossible to shake off. It is unlikely they would keep going to the same place for their annual holiday. They'd rather try something new each year, visiting more and more out-of-the-way places, the more unusual the better. Climate no object! Indeed, they love all kinds of weather. That's probably an Aquarius you see out walking in the rain when the rest of us are running for cover.

They have a gift for getting on well with everyone, especially children and old people. They have a youthful outlook, are fair and rarely draw conclusions before having heard both sides of the story, a characteristic you can imagine that particularly endears them to children. They are good judges of character and not easily fooled by impressions other people create. Natural themselves, they do not tolerate artifice in others. They can spot a veneer from a hundred paces. Although they love to socialize, they are not afraid of hard work. However, they are not as goal-orientated as for example Capricorn, their preceding zodiac sign, because the well-being of friends and loved ones is more important than anything else. Aquarius would not think twice about taking a day off work to look after a close one who was not well. Look out, though, if you are feeling unwell and Aquarius comes to look after you. With the Aquarius tendency to talk non-stop about everything under the sun you could end up with more of a headache than you started with.

Their real charm arises from an ability to come back with a smile and an opportunity to make up no matter how they have been treated. Unlike the Water signs of the zodiac, Cancer, Scorpio and Pisces, who go all out to exact revenge, for Air sign Aquarius life is for the living and the more friends they can pack in the better. And if you are one of those friends, please don't forget birthdays. Aquarius people are like children on birthdays, loving nothing more than to unwrap a mystery present. Everyone around will get caught up in the enthusiasm too because Aquarius is not a self-centred sign, not when there is fun to be shared anyway.

They don't mind working hard but because they also like to have fun they can give mixed signals to both close ones and the boss at work, each of whom expects to be the priority in Aquarius's life. It has to be said that, although willing to work hard, they do tend to be a bit sloppy and to skate over the finer details. It is all very well completing something but they might also try to go back over their work and ensure it is of a uniformly high standard. This is the child who dashes off its homework and then dashes off out to play, and doesn't change its habits much with age.

Air signs love to talk, about themselves, their friends, their workmates, anyone. It isn't mean-spirited gossip. They just want to know what everyone is up to. They have no competitive instinct either. They are simply nosy. There's no malice behind the questions they ask or the statements they make. If you have problems, they will listen, though they are not always on hand to help. If something more interesting comes up they'll be off to lend an ear elsewhere.

Aquarius is in no hurry to put down roots, and prefers to leave things open-ended. An Aquarian home, where it does exist, almost certainly needs work doing to it that its owner has not yet got round to. Aquarius doesn't always need to have a partner, either. Even those who are married feel the need to do a runner from time to time. Whereas some signs have to be half of a whole, Aquarius would rather be a little bit of everything. This doesn't mean Aquarius people don't settle down and marry. Indeed they do, and very successfully too. They love their families, as you already know. They are, however, quite inward-thinking. Partners are likely to feel that no matter how much of a couple they are, they never completely own Aquarius.

They are good at sports, but tend to suffer sprains and minor injuries. They also get cold at the funniest of times, and feel warm when everyone else is shivering. Indeed, Aquarius has a temperature dial all of its own, and this water-carrier is quite likely to turn up in the middle of December with more skin showing than most of us would expose at the height of summer.

Witty and funny, these people talk in riddles, the meaning of which even they do not always know. They would rather have spiritual enlightenment than material gain. Their capacity to forgive can genuinely surprise onlookers. They back down and let loved ones off the hook just when the rest of us would have packed up and left. On the other side of the coin, they cannot commit completely to a partner. They need to have a great many friends. The stimulus of variety and being surrounded by lots of different faces sparks them off. They are independent characters, not afraid of taking chances in life and experiencing new things. Clever and talented, they do tend to see life with flowers around everything and this gullible nature can let them down. They stand out in a crowd, however. They will be dressed well but just that bit differently, maybe even a bit hippy.

Sexually this is a sign that should be interested in alternatives like tantric sex. Or so they say and who am I to argue? But the truth is that they are a little too impatient to spend hours indulging in any one thing, even sex. It is quick passion they like rather than anything long-drawn-out. And anyway it may prove difficult to get Aquarius people on their own for any length of time at all since they love company so much. I know an Aquarius woman who invited her friends along on her honeymoon, much to the dismay of her Scorpio husband who wanted her all to himself.

Aquarius finds it hard to get too upset about anything so this is someone good to have around in a crisis. These people can take your mind off your worries by their sheer joviality. They can spend money like it is water and don't mind buying rounds of drinks for people they have never met before. You don't have to worry about jealousy either; they don't know the meaning of the word. Life is for fun and if things don't work out, well, whatever will be will be.

No one is less obsessed with finding a relationship. They know they will have happiness so long as they keep on that merry journey that is life. This is a person who is kind, courteous and above all else good fun. Who better to make a part of your life?

SECRETS OF THE SEXES

So how do the males and females of the species differ then? Let's have a look.

Ms Aquarius

Don't be misled by Ms Aquarius's apparent helplessness. She is actually very sensible. Not easily impressed by talk, actions speak much louder to her. Outwardly flippant and happy with lots of charm, inside she is self-controlled, honest and would like the right partner to lean on, if the right partner should happen to come along. She will make a great addition to anyone's life but she does need an outlet other than marriage and children. She will never fuss over nothing and she can keep a cool head in a crisis. For all that she seems detached, however, you must keep her in the picture. Have secrets and she will find it hard to trust you again.

She is not afraid of moving on. Life is too short to spend arguing. If you constantly bicker with her you may just come home to find her bag packed and a very polite note wishing you and your family well.

Don't worry that she has many friends of the opposite sex. She loves people and without conversation and laughter there is no point to life, so although you can't impress her with conversation it's no good being the silent type either. She has heard enough in her lifetime to know that it is not what you say that counts but what you do. She can talk as much rubbish as the next person, as well she knows, so she tends to believe almost nothing of what she hears and only half of what she sees.

She may at times come across as being masculine in her attitude and emotions. Where other women get jealous, she does not. She is perfectly happy to mix both sexes together purely as friends. If you don't want her to do something she will not argue with you, but she will go onto do exactly what she had planned in the first place. Her home is unlikely to be a palace, certainly not where tidiness is concerned. She will leave plates and dishes until either you take them out or they walk out. She doesn't pass the buck all the time. It's just that she has a lot she wants to do and she doesn't like to waste her time on matters she deems unimportant. She will never be short of admirers and new ones join her fan club all the time. She doesn't encourage them too much. She knows how to give a nice smile but also how to keep suitors at a proper distance.

She has many dreams for the future and because she talks about them a great deal it may seem that she has a poor handle on reality. However, she is perfectly capable of giving life to her dreams. With her social contacts she may just 'arrive' sooner than even she thinks. What people find most confusing about her is the way she is both forward-thinking and old-fashioned at the same time. If you want to impress her you'll have to show her something she hasn't seen before, and believe me, she's seen most of it by the time she is in her twenties.

Something about her clothing will attract your attention. One part of her outfit will be out of place, slightly zany in relation to the rest of her. She is enigmatic and strange, and does have a bit of a split personality, saying one thing one day and the opposite the following week. Her beauty is that she can spread new ideas and enthusiasm and is brilliant at bringing people together.

I can't help thinking that some of her behaviour is an act. How is it that no matter how many changes she goes through she remains at thirty-six or even sixty-six much like the young girl who emerged at sixteen? She doesn't want to let on about this though, for fear of having to settle down. For you to get her number and have a hold on her is unthinkable. She's got to keep you on your toes.

She can carry ideas but she needs other people to help her see them through. It helps her if she learns this, and learns that she doesn't have to be on the run all the time. Then she may put time and energy into growing one strong link instead of many weak ones, and truly find the happiness that life can bring.

Mr Aquarius

A heartbreaker, and unfortunately he knows it. He has the gift of the gab and can talk his way into, and out of, anything. He is great fun to be with but won't be interested in you unless you attract him mentally as well as physically. He likes to be the boss so you have to be subtle about getting your own way. Better let him think that changes are his ideas not yours. He likes other people to notice you, but he'd prefer it if you did not notice anyone else. Confused? You will be! He is an emotional man who likes to be loved but not possessed. He must feel a sense of freedom in order to be able to give you the honesty you no doubt need.

He will claim to be easy-going and that he can run with the crowd, and to a certain degree this is true, but he also has some very fixed ways that he finds difficult to change and will defend to the death. Air signs like to think they're flexible but Mr Aquarius is a fixed sign too. That makes him a bit more subtle than your average Air sign. He needs a certain amount of routine in his life. He likes to think he's different, and he is, but he doesn't change his character as often as he would like you to believe.

This man climbs up the career ladder on both talent and charisma. The sky is the limit, and he is not phased by people much higher up the ranks than he is. The same goes for love, when he confidently woos someone an outsider would consider out of his league.

He has an open mind. He does not judge anyone too hastily. He gives everyone the chance to prove themselves, and he doesn't bear grudges. He moves on quickly and leaves old loves behind with not so much as a backward glance. He has many friends and is always ready to listen, which can be misinterpreted by the opposite sex. He often has a coterie of women friends who wish they could be more than just friends.

You may have heard the expression 'a loner in a crowd' and this is how I think of Mr Aquarius. Although rarely on his own, he does not always fit in with the faces that surround him. He loves to have relationships and relishes each new person in his life as an adventure ready for the making. But he just isn't cut from quite the same cloth as most people.

He doesn't live in the present. He's always planning ahead and talking about what he is going to do next. This is a bit annoying for his loved ones, who are very much in the present and would like to be noticed. After all, what use is working towards something if you do not take the time to savour the taste of it when you get there?

You can tell him anything, and he will give you good advice. He may not keep it to himself, but as long as you realize this ahead of time, and trust his judgement, then it will be all right. He always finds something good to say about people and is a great confidence booster. Just don't expect him to remember tomorrow what he said to you today. Try to seduce him, mind and body. Find some original ways of doing so and you are sure to keep him coming back.

SEXUAL NEEDS

Look, this may sound odd, but it's true. Aquarius people often go for dark-haired partners. They like someone with an air of mystery about them and blondes can appear outgoing and too easy to read. They don't want to be able to see everything from your face. They want your secrets to slowly reveal themselves. A mask and a darkened room may be taking it a bit too far but then again if you get invited to a fancy-dress party that's your clue as to what to wear to pique the interest of Aquarius.

Typical of Air signs, they know exactly what you want to hear and are pretty good at knowing what not to say too. The danger with Aquarius is being tempted to fall into bed too quickly with them. They will try to get you into bed on the first date but they don't want you to give in easily. It's a test. So don't jump in at the deep end. The problem is that for you the first date, and the ensuing passion, may be the culmination of six months' worth of flattery and flirting and romance. Unfortunately, Aquarius didn't notice he or she was being wooed. Aquarius was simply exhibiting normal Aquarius behaviour, and fairly indiscriminately sharing it with everyone. So on your first date, your companion just thought he or she got you easy. Try talking about sex rather than doing it. That should keep the phone ringing for many days after the date.

This is a self-assured person with strong sex appeal who can find a partner effortlessly. Though old-fashioned where home values are concerned, there is nothing traditional in his or her attitude to sex. Unpredictable, changeable, demonstrative and natural lovers, they will prove their love in many different ways and keep you very happy.

Don't be fake. If you don't really know what you're talking about, don't waste your breath. Once you have entered into a physical relationship with Aquarius, life will

never be the same again. They will give you much love
and are not afraid to talk to you about future plans. Look
out for promises not being fulfilled but remember that it
is because your partner has got carried away with new
ideas, rather than lacked commitment. Think of it this
way. By the time Aquarius people get round to carrying
out their promises, they have moved onto bigger, better
and probably more erotic ideas. So it's worth the wait.
Sexually they need lots of variety and they want you to be
able to talk about your dreams and desires. Be open-
minded. Half the things they talk about really are all talk
– but then just think about that other half!

TRUEST NEED AND DESIRE

PLAYFUL TEASING

Marriage Partners at a Glance

This is just a taster. For more detail, turn to the chapter
called Between the Sheets.

BEST BETS

GEMINI starts Aquarius off with laughter and they don't
stop before they have seen, tasted and experienced the
whole world.

LIBRA ensures that sparks fly at the outset and for many
years to come. Non-stop passion.

SAGITTARIUS gives Aquarius all the fun of the fair where
the ride never stops. Nor does their devotion to one
another.

Love Stars

FAIR CHANCE

AQUARIUS and Aquarius stimulate each other mind, body and soul. Commitment is a problem, however.

ARIES gives Aquarius the excitement Aquarius needs and is able to keep up the social side too. A real star couple, when they get it right.

LEO furnishes Aquarius with fun and beauty, but conversation could see them come a cropper.

VIRGO will catch Aquarius's interest but may not be able to keep it.

HEAVY WEATHER

TAURUS may be too much of a homebody for sociable Aquarius.

CANCER puts too many restrictions on this lively and ever busy sign.

SCORPIO loves the limelight but may not get a look in with this social-hopping and talkative sign. Conversations may not be deep enough for Scorpio either.

PISCES knows how to annoy Aquarius. A battle of wills, and rarely a nice one.

CAPRICORN doesn't understand Aquarius. These two cannot even agree to disagree.

Top Ten Turn-offs

1 People who keep all the good gossip for themselves
2 Party poopers
3 People who don't get a round in
4 Tales of woe

5   Greedy eaters
6   People who use pet names
7   People who try to be too knowledgeable
8   People who flick their hair (that's for Aquarius to do)
9   Nail-biters
10 Bad company

HOW TO SEDUCE AQUARIUS

The first step with an Air sign such as Aquarius is to take your time and not to underestimate the person. The more you hurry, the quicker things will be over. You'll be left wondering how such a beautiful beginning could have such a quick ending.

You could be forgiven for thinking upon first meeting that Aquarius is arrogant but you would be wrong. Nor is Aquarius dumb. Aquarius people are far more intelligent and modest than they sometimes get credit for. Don't make the mistake of spending the first date telling Aquarius all about you and not allowing Aquarius to lift the lid on him- or herself. It's easy to do this, with the amount of questions Aquarius asks. These people simply love to talk about life and to find out about people. The more knowledge they can cram into their brains the happier they are. Spend some time trying to discover your date's past. It's sure to be interesting. It may not be easy to find out, however. Aquarius tends to forget the past. Not because it was bad, just because the future is more engaging.

A cheap tactic, this, but one which could score you a few brownie points on your first date: if you see someone selling flowers for charity, buy one. Aquarius wants to make the world a better place and any token gesture towards improvement of someone else's lot will warm Aquarius's heart. If you get really lucky, you may find a disadvantaged person in need of on-the-spot help that you can offer. How dastardly of me! But it is true. If you can offer genuine assistance to someone in distress, Aquarius's heart will melt. But please don't go setting anything up. You'll never carry it off. And, hey, maybe you should offer help anyway without thinking of your own gain. (I had to add that.)

Don't judge Aquarius by the company he or she keeps. This is someone who enjoys varied and eclectic friendships, and can be as passionate about an acquaintance as about a best friend. This is an inventive mind, which you can impress with science and talk of what may be up in the skies, and a vivid imagination, which friends are sure to make fun of. Aquarius people are romantics though not as obviously so as the Water signs of the zodiac, Cancer, Scorpio and Pisces. You have to seduce Aquarius cleverly and then keep them interested. (This can be a lifetime's undertaking, by the way. But think how fresh your relationship will still be years down the line.)

So where do you go on a first date? Hmm. You see, it is not so much where you take your date as who is around when you get there. Somewhere crowded and you won't get a decent conversation with the object of your affections all night. Aquarius loves people and in a social setting will talk to one and all. You will get more undivided attention in a restaurant where you can talk to one another. At least that way you get the chance to know a little about your date before someone else steals onto the scene. If it's summer, why not try a picnic? Aquarius loves fresh air, and you will be able to see when someone approaches to muscle in on the game, giving you the chance to divert your Aquarius's attention elsewhere.

Don't forget, if you haven't had a chance to get to know your lover or would-be lover properly then he or she probably hasn't had the chance to get to know you well either. Aquarius wants to study you and work you out before placing trust in you, and that can take weeks or even months. The good news is that Aquarius wants a friend as much as a lover, which I am sure is a bonus for anyone. Although sex is important, without the opportunity to laugh with you as well, our friend the water-carrier just wouldn't see the point of taking the relationship any deeper.

You may find it disappointing at the end of the evening when Aquarius says goodnight without asking when you will see each other again. You must not take it to heart. This is the way of Aquarius people. But if they don't like someone a great deal in the first place, they wouldn't have agreed to a date at all. In other words, you are already halfway there.

Tell-tale signs that Aquarius has Fallen

Aquarius in love babbles even more nonsense than usual, most of it about moving countries or changing the world with the new person who has entered his or her heart. Better take these words lightly. This is characteristic Aquarius behaviour. What they promise in the heady early days does not necessarily transpire. They mean well, though.

Aquarius people make a good life for the ones they love, getting by on luck as much as on talent. A strong hand from the partner to keep them on the career ladder may help. As for at home, don't think just because you have become a couple that you'll have a Casanova in the bedroom. If you want full-time attention you will have to hide the remote control and consider a gag to stop the talking.

Aquarius in love with you will examine your career and your life and tell you how you can improve it. He or she is not beyond making rash decisions, so take the advice with a pinch of salt. However much he or she loves you, you may not be able to return the favour. Aquarius doesn't take too kindly to being told what to do by the person who is supposed to be combined lover and best mate (and much less so by anyone whose position of authority should allow them to issue directives).

If you settle down with Aquarius don't expect the first five years to be easy, but equally don't despair because Aquarius wouldn't have gone against all those freedom-loving instincts to settle down at all without really loving the chosen person. Allow a bit of independence. Aquarius, having made the commitment, will almost certainly remain faithful. This is not a sign who actively looks for affairs. The unpredictability factor remains, however. If you have given your heart to Aquarius, don't be surprised when you learn periodically that you are moving town, or even country. Just loyally follow.

Aquarius as part of a couple feels even younger

than ever. In this new frame of mind, anything seems possible. Your relationship may be the same as anyone else's, but Aquarius will consider it unique. The need to be different is strong in this sign, and Aquarius in love with you will be fulfilling, annoying and interesting all at the same time. Family affairs will be fine. Aquarius will want to meet all your family and see all your childhood pictures. If Aquarius wants to be the boss too much you may have to take the classic route of taking decisions behind the scenes while Aquarius thinks he or she is in charge. Rest assured, this person thinks you are special to have made a commitment to you. There is probably a string of broken hearts left behind, and to onlookers it will seem like the eternal bachelor or bachelorette has been won over by a force greater than themselves.

One of the few problems is live-wire Aquarius wanting to move onto the next stage in the relationship without delay, and not wanting to feel confined by notions of what is a proper timetable. Try to set a pace you know will make a base for a lasting relationship. Don't let a wonderful beginning scupper itself. You wouldn't want to let a sign like this out of your life easily.

AQUARIUS PEOPLE IN YOUR LIFE

This section tells you about the people you work, rest and play with.

Aquarius in the Workplace

Many Aquarius people make it to the top in the workplace. As well as being boss, they are also a friend to those who work beneath them. They like people to be happy in their work and believe in treating everyone as equals. They do not insist on references and a clean sheet, but they do expect employees and business contacts alike to understand them and respect their wishes. They can't stand slowness and lack of initiative. They expect their orders to be carried out without question, but they can forget the important things that need to be done. They need a strong right-hand person to remind them now and then of neglected issues, though not someone who makes a fuss.

Moaners and people who are not team players are not welcome. Aquarius bosses like people who achieve results, and they judge them on this basis, and not by appearance. If it's beauty or brains, Aquarius will go for brains every time. They want to make money and they know that brainwork is what counts. Employees can make a mistake, but only once. Twice isn't accepted. Personal problems voiced in the office or allowed to impinge on someone's work are a problem for driven Aquarius bosses, but being the humanitarians they are they do their best to sympathize.

Computers are often a substantial part of Aquarius's work. Aquarius people are capable of bringing the most stone-age of businesses into the twenty-first century. They are brilliant at getting people to work together and can make you feel like doing a job that normally you'd cross the street to avoid. A bit tight-fisted where petty cash and wages are concerned, they are otherwise forward-thinking bosses who are great to work for as long as they believe that you are giving as much to the business as they are.

For the Aquarius employee, problems can begin when someone suggests a change to the way a task is being done. Aquarius barely listens, and certainly doesn't take it on board. It might sink in after a while, but essentially Aquarius likes to do things his or her way. The challenge for a boss is to give the employee a bit of credit – Aquarius can find ways of pushing a business ahead that the boss may not have even thought of.

The more Aquarius people can travel as part of their job the better. Pilot would be a excellent career choice except to the extent that it requires commitment and Aquarius likes to change job as often as possible. Aquarius does not, of course, lack ambition, and expects to reach the top of at least one of the many trees it climbs. An ideal job for Aquarius is business consultant. Travelling from one company to another, from one country to another even, advising businesses on strategy and how to improve the way they work: perfect. As you may have guessed, as both boss and employee Aquarius doesn't suit longevity and needs constant change. A tied-down Aquarius, robbed of an outlet for water-carrier's marvellous sense of humour, is not a happy creature, nor a productive one.

If you want overtime out of your employee, tell Aquarius that what you have asked of him or her is really an act of humanity. In no time the coat is taken off and the pen picked up. No other sign in the zodiac feels quite so responsible for the human race. Aquarius people go out of their way to put back into the community what others may be happy simply taking out.

If you are the boss, one word of caution. Do check that Aquarius has finished his or her work. Aquarius people are terrific at whatever they choose to do but they do tend to have problems finishing things off. They'd rather supply the initial idea and impetus, but then let someone else take it all the way through to the end.

The Aquarius Mother-in-law

She'll be straight over on moving day, helping you throw a party. She'll offer unasked-for opinions on choice of furniture and decor, but you won't mind too much. You know she means well. She's not the jealous type, and if you have the love of her son or daughter, she will almost certainly love you too.

She won't be hard on you either. She will absolutely refuse to get involved in her children's arguments. You can sort out your own domestics. (If she does stick her nose in, try to get a look at her chart. There's something very earthy there for her to get involved in this way.) She's more interested in making small talk about anything and everything than getting involved in disputes. She's modern in her views, and probably likes fringe theatre and modern and alternative art.

Don't be upset if she turns down Christmas lunch with you in favour of mixing with her own friends. Much as she loves her children, she's not particularly clannish, and much prefers her independent life. Mind you, if you make plans that don't involve her, and she finds herself at a loss, she won't be too happy with you.

You probably have to thank her for being the stimulating and encouraging mother she was to your spouse. She will have helped her child to reap knowledge from everywhere possible, and from life itself. The child of an Aquarius mother is wiser than most.

Her best friend is likely to be an Aquarius. She needs an Aquarius woman to run with, one who has her energy and the enthusiasm to keep studying and experiencing life. She probably doesn't chase men, at least not in search of security and flattery, but she does want a good time, and if you stick with her you will probably find it. She is a very clever woman, witty, humane and unshockable. At some point in her life she has probably had a career that she is proud of. Even if she is no longer working, she doesn't feel the best is behind her. Oh no. Tomorrow is always far more exciting than yesterday to this woman.

She shops for deals and is not unwilling to cut out the odd coupon or two. She is an animal lover who will have acquired, or been adopted, by many pets. And contrary to what you might expect from footloose Aquarius, she probably brought up a large family. (She doesn't do things by half.) The oldest child will have helped bring the youngest up. That's Aquarius's delegating skill coming to the fore. But none of them will have stayed in watching the television after school. Mum will have taken them on adventures. OK. I admit it. She took them to the odd pub too, but her heart was in the right place.

If she's coming round to yours for dinner, don't tell her what you are cooking. By the time she arrives she will have spent so much time looking forward to it that she will have become bored with the idea and be grabbing your coat ready to drag you off to the nearest takeaway. In the unlikely event that she doesn't like you, she will resort to craftiness, pretending that she needed a bit of the company of her child and then dragging your partner off to a party. Don't be surprised if she takes on a new religion or faith over the years. She has always had spiritual interests, and besides she likes to do her best to ensure that when her day comes she has a gold card to get in through the right set of pearly gates.

She will every now and then have to be helped out of the odd crisis. Don't be surprised when you find your partner trying to get her phone reconnected. It's not that she couldn't afford the bill. It's just that she spent so long working out the best deal for phone services that she quite forgot to pay for the current one. She's a joy and a delight, and a more offbeat mother-in-law you could not hope to find.

Aquarius Children

Expect wildly contradictory school reports on your Aquarius child, reports which seem to be talking about two different children. How can the child excel so in some areas and fail so in others? It's definitely partly to do with talking too much in class, and missing half of what the teacher says. Then there's that variable attention span of the Aquarius. Does the subject grab the child's imagination or not? If not, then you can guarantee the child will find other amusements. But when a subject does strike the right chords, no one can excel like the little water-carrier.

Aquarius children always have lots of friends. They are not afraid to make friends with the kind of kids others back away from either. Aquarius children don't judge by appearances. They see much deeper than surface values, and they don't reject a child for being overweight or not having nice clothes to wear. This is a trait for any parent to be proud of. Saying that, you will have to buy them some trendy clothes. They are aware of trends and like to keep up with them, more out of excitement for the new than any desire to compete or get one over on anyone. If you can buy them something space-age, even better. The Aquarius child is bound to want to be an astronaut (the ultimate among jobs that involve travel!) for at least part of his or her childhood. Mind you, between their first and last schools, Aquarius child will have talked about at least a dozen careers, all with equal and overwhelming enthusiasm.

Young Aquarius will bring home every stray he or she finds, even the perfectly groomed Persian cat still wearing its name tag. The child is attracted to animals and animals to the child. Friends are also gathered up. Many children will fill the role of best friend over the years. Many a club will be joined and many an after-school activity sampled. Better wait until the first rush of enthusiasm has deepened into something lasting before you go buying expensive equipment.

Aquarius children won't always get their homework in on time, but the excuses will be worth listening to.

They will have had all sorts of new thoughts about the project, though they will have failed to explore most of them. They are ideas people even when they are children, and can always identify a gap for a new business. Watch television with them and they'll tell you how this advertiser has got it wrong and that one got it right, and how that programme-maker missed the mark because really the important thing would have been to . . . and on and on. Beware, the ideas flow freely and the talk sounds convincing, but little Alex Aquarius didn't actually finish that project he got for homework, did he? They do need your support at school. These are children who suffer from exam nerves, and you need to be there on hand making sure their nerviness doesn't get out of all proportion.

They will not, as a rule, have a lot of boyfriends and girlfriends. If they do get involved in a relationship at a relatively young age it is probably a case of a friend who turned into something more, rather than any great desire on the part of Aquarius to explore sex for the sake of it. It is also rare that Aquarius people marry childhood friends. They are far too well aware that there is a whole world out there to explore.

You will often catch the Aquarius child day-dreaming. It's probably the only time he or she isn't bugging you to know why the sky is blue and what makes birds stay up in the air. These questions and a million others you will be obliged to answer. A great present for an Aquarius child is a science kit. It's safer, too, because otherwise the child will be experimenting with goodness knows what and before you know it creating fireworks in the shed.

You have a feeling that you have a remarkable child here, and you do. Just don't put your house on the market to pay for that college course yet. By the time they are on their fifth option, you'll be living in a tent. But always give this unusual and fun child loads of moral support. They are worth it.

Aquarius Friends

Friends are everything to this Air sign. To fall out would be a terrible thing and Aquarius goes to great lengths to keep on-stream everyone they have so carefully gathered. Given how much of their time is spent in cloud-cuckooland thinking about what their next important move is, it is not surprising that this doesn't always work, and that friends get fed up waiting around. None the less, Aquarius, rich in love if poor in money, knows just what it takes to have and to give a good time. Aquarius friends are great at planning special occasions to make you happy. They love to party and have many strange and wonderful friends to party with. Any kind of a function at their house is a kind of a free-for-all attended by many different personalities. The house itself is a mixture of styles from the many places that life has taken them. A truly happy Aquarius would be living in an open-plan space. Confining Aquarius into small rooms with many walls around is likely to make him or her feel trapped and niggly.

Your Aquarius friends will try to force you into doing things with your life that you may not be ready for. This is only their way of trying to help you. To them the future is everything and is where everyone's success lies. I have quite a few Aquarius friends, as it happens, though I don't see them all the time. Each time I do see them, they make quite an impact on my life. If I raise the subject of my career, they can always tell me about exciting new approaches I hadn't thought of before. They are pretty strong personalities and if they are a part of your circle you are going to have to accept the fact that not everyone will like them. Indeed they will have a few enemies here and there. They rarely come to blows, though. Their sense of humour allows them to laugh their way out of many things, and to make their opponent laugh too.

If you want to be a true friend to Aquarius, help them to better their own lives. It is all very well being able to change the world and make other people happy and make a lot of money for your company but unless you are happy with where you are at in your life then you are not living it to the full. For example, it is not unusual for Aquarius to stay with someone they feel a sense of duty to, and you may want to give them a helping hand if you can see they are genuinely unhappy.

They have tons of friends of the opposite sex, which makes it great if you want to meet a whole host of eligible partners. They love talking and, unlike others we won't mention, don't spend all of their time talking about themselves. When they want to they can be quiet and aloof, usually when planning their next big move in life. And believe me, you'll see a lot of this over the course of a long friendship.

Look around at Aquarius's friends and you may

begin to think this person is a bit of a stud. All these people dancing attendance on the water-carrier! Step back for a minute. You'll soon see these really are friends, with no hint of anything else. And this is the way Aquarius likes to keep it, unless the other parties push their luck. The unions which then ensue can be very short though sweet indeed.

Funny and inventive, they can brighten up the darkest of days and would never let you down in a time of crisis. Not intentionally, anyway. The main problem is that they get you all excited planning something and then at the last minute they try to talk you into doing something else, the something new that has popped into their forward-thinking mind. Don't neglect your Aquarius friends, even if they sometimes seem to neglect you. They need you more than you realize.

Pisces
February 20 to March 20

EMOTIONAL, SENSITIVE, MOODY, imaginative, impressionable and changeable: these are the key words to describe Pisces. The Pisces personality is reputed to be one of the most fascinating of all. Sensitive and artistic, they have something of the psychic in them. (Indeed, this is the most psychic sign in the zodiac.) They have an unselfish and generous disposition and although generally hopeless at managing money nevertheless make good marriage partners, for they are intensely loyal and will stand by their chosen one through thick and thin. Erratic by nature, Pisces people do not find concentration easy. Routine jobs bore them. But they are quick-witted and alert, and these assets see them through.

Because of the many conflicting sides to their

character, only those who know them intimately and take a deep interest in them can claim to understand them. To most people Pisces is a mystery, and this is one of the reasons they are so attractive to the opposite sex. Although their moods change with the wind, they rarely get angry with people or bear a grudge. Underneath their complex exterior is a heart of gold. When they allow their personality full rein they win many admirers, arousing some jealousy along the way too.

Highly sensitive, they are aware of the feelings of others and susceptible to others' opinions. They can seem shy on first meeting, but in truth are sociable and blessed with great conversational skills. Look before you leap should be their maxim, but their smooth talking usually gets them out of the trouble they all too easily find. The heart and soul of a person is what matters to Pisces, and they are better equipped than most to see beyond a person's outer layer. Their adaptability can, however, be a drawback. Rather too easily influenced by those around them, they can be swayed by others and neglect to use their own judgement. A shame, since their judgement is so often sound. Bit of a drama queen, they are sometimes arrogant and self-centred. 'That's enough about me, let's talk about you. What do you think of me?' is probably self-aware and funny Pisces' favourite line.

Artistic, imaginative, original, they have a real talent for design, though don't much like putting in the hard work that turns great ideas into reality. Patience and dedication are not among their strong points; these are at variance with their quick-witted, easily distracted cast of mind. Natty Pisces has a happy knack of always appearing well groomed and well dressed, able to transform the most ordinary of garments just by wearing them. Taste only occasionally deserts Pisces. When it does so, they tend to overdress.

In love, Pisces is a devil, and I mean that in the nicest possible way. If these people think they can get a rise out of you, they will. They want to see the emotional you and they like to see how far they can push you. There may come a time when you think they have lost the plot. Think again. These are people who know exactly where the limit is, and that is where they are planning to take you. Blood is thicker than water to Pisces. And if Pisces wants you to be part of the family, you'd better look out, because he or she will do all that's necessary to get you. Once you are caught, give up the struggle. Pisces won't rest until he or she has secured you and found out everything about you.

Try not to hurt Pisces' feelings. These people take things to heart. A flippant comment can cause great pain to such a sensitive creature. Sensitive, yes, but consistent, no. Pisces can change like the wind. If you have planned a nice night in, don't get too comfy too quick. Before you know it your coat is tossed over to you and you are expected to go down the pub for a spur-of-the-moment evening out.

Lousy drinkers, fanatic and picky eaters. Easily addicted, be it to chocolate and shopping or drink and drugs. Obsessive. Moderation not a part of their vocabulary. When you read that Pisces is loyal to the end you'd be forgiven for thinking, 'Well, they'd have to be, wouldn't they? How many people can live with these characteristics?' The truth is that in Pisces you have a friend, partner and family member who will always make life special. Pisces lifts anyone's life out of the humdrum into the realm of the extraordinary.

Think of two fish trying to swim in two directions at once without coming apart. This symbol of Pisces represents the sign's duality very well. These people can look on the bright side of life but they are not afraid to look on the dark reverse too. Death holds something of a fascination for them. They can make jokes about death, but rather than being flippant are just trying to cope with a subject that as well as fascinating them scares them too.

Sexually this is a sign that is hot, hot, hot, and many a stranger lusted after in the street or sending tingles down spines over the radio will turn out to have been Pisces. Face to face, Pisces has a way of gazing at you that will make you come over all weak. In part this is the Pisces intuitive nature at work, knowing just what it takes to connect to you.

Unafraid to show friendship or affection in public, there will also be times when Pisces is as cold as its fishy nature would suggest. Don't be concerned. Impressionable Pisces is more likely to have been made jittery by a bad vibe from elsewhere than to be upset with you. If Pisces is upset with you, you'll know about it.

Pisces can make a beautiful home out of any kind of accommodation, and doesn't need a fortune to do so. However, these are not the tidiest of souls, and that beautifully arranged interior is likely to be marred by piles of ironing. Yes, our sensitive, dreamy Pisces can be a bit of a slob.

These people have a habit of seeking change when

you least expect it. Pisces goes so deeply into things as to bury itself on the spot, but then all of a sudden a major upheaval is announced and a new country of abode is on the cards. Pisces people have enough experience of life to make good decisions, and enough daring to be unafraid. Pisces usually finds success, even if it means turning life upside down to do so, and you can trust their intuition to the nth degree. Pisces people will be bringing artistic and pleasurable changes into all our lives for many years to come.

SECRETS OF THE SEXES

So how do the males and females of the species differ then? Let's have a look.

Ms Pisces

Be careful with this woman. She is very sensitive, and her instincts are razor-sharp. She will know if you are two-timing her. Frankly, she will always be a problem to you, but at the same time she will bring you great joy. She can't resist telling you white lies but she'll never tell you a whopper. She is inclined to overdress. She demands lots of attention, even if it means behaving badly to get it. Her temper is easily roused, and it would be unwise to make her jealous. She loves variety, but this doesn't encompass sports, which bore her. She adores her children. An erratic housekeeper, she none the less finds time for the special touches such as baking cakes.

Her creative nature makes her a pleasure to have around. She has a way of making the world a more beautiful place. Slightly unpredictable with living things, Pisces is either green-fingered, bringing renewed life to every wilting plant, or capable of killing a plant just by looking at it. Odd that she can go to such extremes but as you know by now she is not one to do anything by halves. She is an all-or-nothing kind of woman. When she feels like playing the role of devoted wife and mother she does it very well. When she wants to let her hair down, nothing can get in her way. She needs a partner who lets her get away with a lot but also knows when to say no to her. A partner who dared say no to Ms Pisces would be a very attractive suitor indeed.

She's generous and unselfish with her loved ones. She's not selfless, though. She knows she'll get what she wants too. Such is her confidence in herself, that life generally does turn her way. Strangers wouldn't dare to obstruct her anyhow. Her first approach is always the polite one but if that fails she goes in for the kill. I always use my Pisces friends to complain for me in restaurants or shops. I know then that the matter will be dealt with efficiently. The Pisces style leaves no room for anyone to make a cutting retort. Far too cultured to be nasty, she'll probably impress rather than diminish her hapless victim. Think of your favourite movie star and how you would feel to be in the same room. This is how this woman can make you feel. Trembling and shaking, but impressed none the less.

She more often than not drinks to excess. Either that or she's teetotal. No fence-sitting for Ms Pisces. She has many friends and is capable of working as hard as she plays so long as what she is doing engages her sufficiently. She's ambitious for success, and not afraid to tackle work other people would turn their noses up at. She takes life to the limit, and is rather unafraid of death. Like her fellow Water sign Scorpio, she finds the end of life more of a fascination than a worry. This isn't to say she'll go for death-defying stunts, such as BASE-jumping off skyscrapers (though extreme sports do hold something of an attraction for Pisces). But it does mean she would far rather her friends and family had a party on the day she died than a morbid ceremony. She'd like her passing to the new realm to be celebrated.

She can drive you wild with the way she runs her life. You come home one day to find all of her clothes in bin bags. She isn't leaving you. She's just decided to shed her current image in favour of an entirely new one, and she's going the whole hog. She isn't wasteful. It will all go to the nearest charity shop. And it doesn't matter if she hasn't got a penny. She'll manage somehow. With the way she holds herself, you'd think people bowed down in front of her wherever she went. Maybe they do.

She wants a partner to be her whole world. She'll show you a life full of twists, turns, laughter, tears and unstoppable love.

Mr Pisces

He likes the limelight. He gets bored easily and workwise does not usually settle down early but moves around a lot. He gets on in life since he has a mathematical brain and a big imagination. Best as his own boss, he can't stand being told what to do. He's got a thing about money and usually succeeds in his ventures. Very ambitious indeed! He will fascinate and charm you and he will be quick to spot insincerity on your part. He must have plenty of affection. If he loves you he will go all out to please you.

If he wants a woman he will chase her but in such a way that other people think he is bestowing a favour on her. He can tell instinctively who likes him and who doesn't, and so his success rate is usually high. He is often successful in business, too, and this is down to a special combination of good instinct and willingness to take chances. It's not an easy road, though, and the more successful he is the more likely it is that he has tales to tell of woe experienced en route.

He will give you the impression he is special, because quite simply he is. Fascinating eyes and good shoes, he knows what aftershave to wear, what books to read, and where to take a friend or lover to have fun. His home is probably beautiful, or at least unusual, and is very likely to be near water. If he lives in the city, he has probably managed to give his home a seaside, preferably Mediterranean, feel. He needs to feel a touch of the ocean and a hint of tranquillity to be able to sleep at night and work during the day.

He never means to come across as rude but if he doesn't like you then you will know about it. It's not so much what he says as the way he says it. He has plenty of friends though, and every one of them is sure to be able to tell you what a great guy he is and how much he's helped them out in the past. He doesn't do this for effect. He feels that the world is his kingdom and friends his subjects who rely on him, and yet all along he's looking for a woman to mother him. His own mother is an angel in his eyes. To the outside world his childhood was perfect, whether true or not. He must keep up appearances. If he has no money to go out he'll say he isn't quite in the mood instead.

His tastes can change with the weather and what he loves in you one minute he may hate in you the next. A good actor, he can convince you that you have done him wrong even if it was him flirting at that party. He has a small group of best friends likely to be with him throughout life. Unlike Air signs, Gemini, Libra and Aquarius, who look ahead and change friends as it suits them, Water signs need to have their past with them in order to decide their future. He will try very hard not to forget your birthday because his own is so important to him, so please return the favour.

He attracts partners readily but is not easily satisfied. He needs someone who understands how deeply he views life. He will spin you around and make you dizzy and swoon. Being with him is like drinking champagne. All those bubbles just rush to your head.

This man is unforgettable. It is almost as though he expects to be famous. If you asked him for his autograph he wouldn't be surprised. Once you let him into your life you will find it hard to let him go. He is in control when he wants to be, but the rest of the time it is up to you to make the right decisions. Tell him your dreams and he'll help to make them reality because he understands their importance. Moody at times, yes, but then aren't all dreamers?

SEXUAL NEEDS

Well, you've landed a good one here. This is one of the sexiest signs in the zodiac. These people have a flair for the dramatic and can make the grottiest of settings seem the most mysterious and romantic place on earth. They are not easy, though. You will have to set about capturing this heart very carefully indeed for the fishes don't leap into sexual relationships unless the relationship means something.

Pisces loves to have an effect on people, to flirt and dish out compliments and then sit back and watch the result. This sort of behaviour is very easily misinterpreted and can cause all kinds of awkwardness and embarrassment. This isn't what Pisces wanted, of course, but it happens none the less. It's something to watch out for (for Pisces themselves and those around them).

Sex is a very private thing for Pisces. They will show affection in public for someone they love, but that's a long way down the relationship line. To begin with they like to have an air of mystery about them, and do not lay all of their cards on the table. They don't like familiar behaviour from someone they don't feel they know well enough.

They need to feel plenty of genuine affection before giving themselves sexually. Although they like to put on the dramatics, in reality they are in touch with their feelings and believe in expressing them honestly. This doesn't mean you can second-guess your Pisces lover. Prediction is a difficult game when it comes to Pisces in love. The fishes may plan a wedding but if they didn't feel it was right on the day they wouldn't go through with it.

Be a little old-fashioned and courteous. Pretend you're both in an old black and white movie, the sort the object of your affections is very likely to have grown up on. Don't try to be clever, and don't tell silly jokes. Pisces cares what other people think, and won't want to be associated with you if your opinions diverge, or you act the fool.

Now, I've made it clear that Pisces is hot, hot, hot, but also rather cool. Are you keeping up with me? It's like this: in front of friends and family is one story, but behind closed doors – assuming you've managed to convince him or her of your genuine affections – is another matter altogether. When the lights go off and the candles are lit and the door is locked, this is no cold fish you have on your hands, this is a hot-blooded animal. Repeat a word to friends or out in public and you can kiss the passion goodbye, however. Pisces wants to keep everyone guessing, and that includes you. Ten years down the line Pisces will still be producing tricks from up his or her sleeve, but that can't be bad, can it?

Unfaithfulness is unforgivable. Stray, you won't be able to stay with Pisces. Your deceived lover will make your life a living hell. More than one engagement is not unusual in Pisces' life, nor are short-lived but passionate relationships. Actress Drew Barrymore married a man she had known a matter of weeks, only to divorce him a short while later. Pisces people need lovers who are both sensitive and dominant. You may wonder how you can put the two together. You can, and Pisces is the one to show you how.

Pisces can blow hot and cold in relationships, and this

may not be the most comfortable partnership you've ever found. Pisces can forget there are other people in the world, but the heart is in the right place and this person can take you to highs you've never dreamed of.

TRUEST NEED AND DESIRE

RAW EMOTION

Marriage Partners at a Glance

This is just a taster. For more detail, turn to the chapter called Between the Sheets.

BEST BETS

CANCER gives Pisces all the emotion and the understanding Pisces needs. These two speak the same language: the language of love.

VIRGO falls hard and fast for Pisces though when flirting ends fighting can begin.

SCORPIO and Pisces are true soulmates who end up looking and speaking alike as the years progress.

FAIR CHANCE

PISCES with Pisces enjoy love and hate in equal measure, but they would go to the ends of the earth for each other.

TAURUS enjoys the fun but may have trouble lasting the distance with the extremes to which Pisces likes to experiment.

LEO has the guts to play the Pisces game, but how long Leo will stand for it is another matter.

LIBRA puts too many demands on Pisces and these two end up pulling out their hair in despair and devotion.

SAGITTARIUS proves an instant hit but these two fall out of love as quickly as they fell in, especially if Pisces doesn't listen to Sagittarius's needs and desires.

CAPRICORN offers love but is not impulsive enough for fly-by-night Pisces.

HEAVY WEATHER

GEMINI and Pisces wouldn't trust each other as far as they could throw one another.

ARIES is just too unpredictable for dear old Pisces and these two lead each other into one disaster after another.

AQUARIUS – oh dear. Better get out the boxing gloves. But check them for horseshoes first since these two will not only fight but fight dirty.

Top Ten Turn-offs

1 People who dress too modestly (you've got to flaunt it, darling!)
2 People who talk about sex in public (Pisces likes to save it for private, which is just as well given what Pisces has in mind)
3 People who wear odour-eaters or shoes that aren't designer-made
4 Foul mouths in public

5   Not talking dirty in private
6   People who don't drink
7   No sense of style
8   Other people's children
9   Cheery people in the morning
10 Feet being tickled while asleep

HOW TO SEDUCE PISCES

No matter how keen you are, leave a certain amount of distance in order to create mystery. If you reveal all at once, Pisces doesn't get to appreciate your many strata. Pisces is the sort of person who takes apart a layered cake in order to experience the sensation of each flavour individually.

Take your date somewhere dark and mysterious, like an underground club, or go somewhere connected to the sea, even a seafood restaurant (Pisces likes anything to do with the sea). Don't go for anything educational such as a talk. Pisces people think they know a great deal but they are in fact the most unworldly of all. They prefer to withdraw from reality and take themselves to a dreamland where everything is safe and their own rules apply. They often don't like school for the reason it teaches fact, not fantasy.

Mr and Ms Pisces are likely to have a love of music but do your homework first and find out exactly what sort of music they like. A concert could be excellent if you get it right. If none of these ideas appeals to you, then learn lesson number one: you have to be imaginative if you want to impress Pisces. Predictability does not impress. Pisces people want to learn things and to live life more fully. They are changeable and like surprises. That's your best bet, really. Just don't tell them where you are going and don't go to somewhere you think they could guess. However, I must reassure you that in agreeing to go out with you at all Pisces has pretty strong feelings for you. Pisces people make up their minds very early on about people and their instincts are remarkably accurate. If Pisces thinks you are good for each other, you probably are.

Don't be angry if your date tells you a few white lies as you get to know each other. He or she is trying to impress you. Like all Water signs a faultline of insecurity runs beneath that confident and sometimes cocky shell. A bit of manipulation is possible too, including telling the waiter off for not serving you correctly in order to show you they are concerned for you and demanding of standards.

Buy your date flowers. Even Mr Pisces will melt at the sight of a single red rose and you will be able to read the pleasure in his face. Relax and enjoy the date. Whatever you do, don't challenge Pisces to a drinking game. It isn't big and it isn't clever and the next thing is you've got Pisces on stage with the band grabbing the microphone from the lead singer, or dragging you off to the airport to hijack a plane. You could even find yourself married by morning. Take your time and get to know your Pisces dreamboat well. Just one last thing: Pisces people have sensitive extremities. When you finally get them into bed, don't tickle those feet!

Tell-tale signs that Pisces has Fallen

Pisces people do not show their affections in public in an overt or crude manner, but you will be expected to furnish regular tokens of your devotion, such as gifts of flowers and notes pledging your love. No matter how much you are in love there will be times when you think Pisces is from another planet. Be grateful that you are so different. Life will always be interesting for you both. Pisces understands what is going on in your life, even before you do. These people are just brilliant to have on your side when anything goes wrong, though I'd advise you not to get stuck in an argument with them yourself. They know every game plan and trick in the book. They seem naive but it is all a bit of a con, even if they've conned themselves into the bargain. With Pisces on your side, you can't go wrong.

Pisces, both male and female, want to be boss in the relationship, and evidence of seeking control is a clear indication of Pisces in love. None the less, Pisces will do anything to make you happy, including giving up long-cherished ambitions. If Pisces loves you, you become an extension to them. If you hurt, they hurt; if you need a change, they need a change; and so on until you cannot tell where one of you ends and the other begins.

Artistic doodlers, Pisces will draw hearts and entwine your names on letters, envelopes, notebooks, newspapers, whatever is around. If you have a text phone or email you may well find poetry on its way to you across the ether. When the love bug bites, Pisces' romantic side reveals itself, but it's meant for you, not for anyone else.

If Pisces doesn't like a member of your family, I'm afraid it will show. Fishy faces give away a lot of secrets. Pisces isn't any good at pretending to like people it doesn't. At least you know Pisces isn't pretending to be fond of you.

Pisces in love may try to manipulate you. This may not be obvious at first. Your lover is the one giving up a job, moving home, changing lifestyle for you. Then you start to see that this is an exchange deal where you have to do any one of a number of things in order to show your love. You may not have realized it, but that was the bargain. If you don't keep up your end Pisces will think you've fallen out of love. This is a tough one, and will wear you out. Don't be fooled. Be straight with the facts and the realistic possibilities, and after a while Pisces will smile and behave like a good girl or boy again, and look at you with eyes that speak volumes of emotion. Onlookers will envy the loving partnership you have clearly found.

PISCES PEOPLE IN YOUR LIFE

This section tells you about the people you work, rest and play with.

Pisces in the Workplace

Pisces in the workplace is a poor listener who prefers to hear the sound of his or her own voice. Anyone working for such a boss needs to be mentally strong and ought not take them too seriously. Pisces bosses do show their appreciation, though in the most unusual of ways. In truth, they need looking after. Although their brain never stops they are terribly forgetful. Their impatience causes annoyance and their unorthodox tactics leave their staff bewildered. They believe in being open and are brilliant negotiators. As managers they are lousy, always passing the buck and then smoothing things over. They can talk their way out of a paper bag and make people feel sorry for them even when they were in the wrong. Fortunately, their staff are usually hand-picked. They can't work with just anyone but allowed control over who they do work with they can assemble the oddest selection of people into a team that really hums.

As employee rather than boss, you'll find them daydreaming much of the time. That mental space travel they are doing could just furnish the next exciting plan, be it for their own or their company's benefit. They like to stick up for the underdog and if someone picks on a colleague they will be the first to stand up in his or her defence. They see themselves as the righter of wrongs and if they feel strongly enough they will lead a revolution in the workplace.

Creative professions suit this sign. If dreams always came true then Pisces would find itself in Hollywood playing out fantasies and switching from one brilliant role to another. Hard-nosed business isn't where it's at for Pisces although they know from a long way off whether a deal is good or bad. They are more interested in reputation than money. Fame, not fortune, please for the fish. They want people to admire what they have achieved and if it does include a flash car then they want you to know that they got there through hard work and not luck.

Practical skills are not there in abundance. School was more of a social centre than a place of learning. Pisces earns trust and professional standing through sheer presence though an outsider might just wonder how they got to be in such a position of power, lacking all the fundamental skills in the way they do.

You have by now guessed that the fish does not live in the real world. To get the most from this artistic, perceptive and imaginative sign, try to let them pick their own projects. If their heart is in what they are doing, and they do not feel shaped or controlled from outside, they will do their best work. And when your Pisces employee gives you that funny look, beware, because this secretive sign is planning to take over the company. With the imagination Pisces has and the confidence he or she can muster, this take-over bid is likely to succeed. What's more, with that winning Pisces personality, there will be many supporters cheering on the sidelines.

The Pisces Mother-in-law

Once met, never forgotten. She has more family secrets than any other sign in the zodiac but if you think she's willing to give them up then think again. She can make you feel like an outsider or take you straight into the bosom of the clan. She's the head of the family, both nuclear and extended. Whether you get accepted depends on how you first approach her. If you've got any secrets, she'll winkle them out of you with that special Pisces knowledge-seeking device. Her uncanny way of getting to the truth will have you quaking in your boots if you have anything to hide. The most innocent of questions will have you yielding all manner of private information and she will use it however she chooses. If you want to impress her then be real. She loves characters, but she can't stand people who are fake.

She was not what you would call a conventional mother. She fed her children well but not always at conventional times or in conventional places. She is artistic and will have encouraged the same in her children. Whatever they wanted to do was fine by her, as it is for her grandchildren. She will tell her grandchildren, just as she told her children, that the world is their oyster. She would swim the largest ocean if she thought it would lead her family to a better life.

In marriage this woman is the boss and has probably managed to etch a permanent worried crease on her husband's forehead. Her children will also have the worried look from time to time as they ponder what on earth she may be thinking of doing next. She will love to have grandchildren and will take them to the most unusual and wonderful places.

She loves scandal and gossip. She has great legs and shows them off in the latest shoes. She knows just how to dress and has a terrific sense of style. She will still be turning heads at seventy and eighty. She loves the theatre and thinks that people who dress to excess and talk with their hands are marvellous. She mixes well in all kinds of company and knows just what to say – unless she's been at her secret drinks stash, that is.

When her eyes start rolling, watch out. It's show time and there could be casualties.

Life with her is both mad and exciting. You think you are having an early night with your partner but when the doorbell rings it's your mother-in-law with bottle in hand and an exciting tale to tell you. She won't feel like a mother-in-law but more like a best friend. You can't often fool her. She has got your number. She doesn't take sides in arguments. She knows how fragile feelings can be as she is prone to moodiness herself. She may give you a sore head but you'd rather buy in the headache tablets than give her up.

Pisces Children

These children adore water. Unlike most youngsters, Pisces children love bathtime and will want to stay in the water long after the prune stage has set in. This child will delight you, coming out with wonderful expressions and acute observations. Don't let these impressionable youngsters watch too much TV. Not only will it stultify their imagination, it could also lead to some embarrassing outbursts when guests are around. These children like attention and don't care what it takes to get it.

They do not like conventional toys, and aren't that impressed by crazes. They prefer unusual playthings. These children often have an imaginary friend who can be described right down to taste in clothes and colour of eyes. Don't be concerned. This is the child's artistic and imaginative nature working overtime. Fishes find it hard to give up certain objects from their babyhood so you will have to be clever how you part them and their favourite blanket or cuddly toy. It could prove rather embarrassing sticking out of their backpack on the way to college.

Little fishes talk a lot but not much of it makes any sense. They are great at getting information out of people, including friends of yours, who may get given advice by your Pisces child and what's more would do well to act upon it too.

Many Pisces children long to be actors and an obsession with a favourite movie can drive parents to distraction. It may be just another phase, but don't knock it – many successful actors have been born under this sign: Peter Fonda, Drew Barrymore, Patsy Kensit, Ray Winstone, Rob Lowe, Michael Caine, to name a varied few.

A small circle of friends is preferred over many. They are well respected at school, even though they may look back on their education with horror. Exam time is a nightmare for them and you may need to teach them some relaxing techniques to help them through. By the time they've left school they've got a million and one ideas. They may even go straight into business. They will already have gathered people around them who trust them enough to work for them. Not the best with money, they do at least know how to get hold of it when they need it. You'll remember how as a younger child they often borrowed against next week's pocket money.

There will be many tears with this child and not all of them will be real. There will also be many special times when you feel truly honoured to have such a person in your life. This is a child who talks to its parents rather than shutting them out. The danger is that this small fry wants to become a big fish all too quickly, and wants to experiment with things unsuitable for its young age (or indeed any age). This is an addictive personality, with a tendency to pick up bad habits, and you need to watch over him or her carefully. Never tell these children not to do something. Instead try to talk them out of things by showing them something else instead.

This child will make you laugh more often than cry, and in your later years will be there for you when needed. A Pisces child is truly a blessing.

Pisces Friends

Pisces are true friends. Your battles become their battles. You will have to accept the fact that they flirt with the people you like but it does not usually go beyond flirting. They have to flirt to know they are alive. They are good at giving compliments, too, but only where due, so if they say you look good then you can go out with confidence.

They don't do anything quietly and they like to take people to the edge – and then bungee-jump off it. Silly injuries may force them to give up a sport they like, only to talk about it ever after instead, and in much exaggerated terms. Ask your fishy friend how much they paid for a new top, and then ask them again the following day. The price is sure to have trebled. Pisces people tell tall stories but usually harmlessly.

They may love you as a friend but they will not

listen to any advice you want to give. You may know the person they are seeing is wrong for them, but they like to learn the hard way. Don't feel neglected. They will want you to pick up the pieces when their heart gets shattered. They have such an instinctive nature that they know when something is going to go wrong, but they want to experience it anyway. They have a roving eye, and a fondness for drama. If you get a tear-laden phone call at night it could just as easily be a fight your friend has had over hair colour than anything serious.

Although their taste in love is not always perfect they get it right in the end, and when they do hit bull's-eye they are likely to forget you exist for a few months. When they've got over the initial white heat of the relationship, they will be back round at yours as though nothing has happened and they have not neglected you for ages. It will be up to you to overlook this fault in their personality.

Just when you think you are outgrowing the party lifestyle they will be on at you to renew your membership to the latest club. They thrive on people, parties and gossip, and not to have a new story to tell every week is like not having air to breathe. This is the friend who will arrange a surprise birthday party for you and make sure your partner is treating you right. (Doing the same for them might be seen as interference, however.) They don't like being confined in one place for too long so expect them to nip round to yours on a regular basis. Only get nervous when they arrive with paintbrush in hand to freshen up your old look (even though you moved in just three months ago). They might just be feeling so confined in their own place that they are making big moves on yours.

The reason they make such great friends is that if they have a feeling about something or someone then 99 per cent of the time they are right. Who better to guide you through life than someone who understands you better than you know yourself? If you have a partner, just look your Pisces friend in the eyes and say hands off. If you don't tell them they'll think it's a free-for-all. Be up front with them and you'll have a friend for ever.

Love is What
You Need

IT MAY BE a cliché, but it is a very true one: love is the most important thing in the world. It is the basic need of every creature. Our whole reason for living is to give love and to receive love. Without it nothing is worthwhile.

I think we all have our moments of envy and discontent. Perhaps the Joneses have got a bigger car and the Smiths go on a world cruise every year, while you've still got your old model and can't even afford a week's holiday. This is human nature, but when you boil it all down, what matters is the closeness and well-being of our loved ones and the quality of our friendships. These are the real needs of life. We can do without a car and smart holidays even though we may wish we could have them, but we cannot do without love. There are so many different relationships in love, aren't there? We love our partner, our children, our mother and father and our friends. Make sure you are getting the love you need. In the course of my work I deal with much distress caused by unhappy marriages or bad relationships between family members. Life is too short not to sort out differences and find ways to improve your life.

Marriage is one of the most difficult partnerships in the world. It is the one that needs the most working at if it is to succeed. After all, here we have two complete individuals with separate thoughts and ideas. Even if they are the same element, other parts of their charts can bring in clashes that lead them to fight and disagree with one another. Having to consider someone else, whose ideas and views are not necessarily your own, for all the important moves and changes you make to your life takes a lot of time and hard work and sometimes patience too. You don't ever really know a person until you live with them. You can come up against all sorts of petty aggravations, which can easily grow out of all proportion unless a deep understanding is there in the first place.

Many signs marry for physical attraction alone. Gemini, Leo and Libra, for example, can't help but fall for a pretty face. I would be the last to say that physical attraction is not important – it most certainly is – but there has to be companionship as well. After all, physical beauty can fade. On the other hand, it can be equally dangerous to marry on mental harmony alone, with no other bond. While mental compatibility is necessary there is always the danger that after a while one or the other will meet someone for whom there is an immediate physical attraction. So do yourself a favour, whatever sign you are, and find yourself a partner in life whom you fancy but who can make you laugh as well. Remember that when you live with someone or even marry them, you mustn't just lie back and put your feet up. You must constantly work together as a team to improve your life and make each other happy.

Many of the clients I have given readings to over the years are the last single person among their group of friends and feel that they have been left on the shelf. They come to me, asking me if they should marry the person who has just asked them or whether they should wait for Mr or Ms Right who is just around the corner. They will say of the current 'make-do' person in their life, 'Well, he is very kind' or 'She says she loves me and I'm sure I can grow to feel the same way.' No! Don't accept second best. I've seen it all too often that the moment Ms X marries Mr Not-Quite-Right, the right person comes along. Then you have a real mess on your hands that sometimes leads to losing both people, not just one. Let your heart and mind communicate. Even write a list of the reasons why you should stay with someone and the reasons why you should leave. If the leaving column is longer, then smile and pack your bags and think of the excitement of the unknown that is just ahead of you. Admittedly this can be hard for Virgo and Capricorn but give it a go, you may just find the man or woman of your dreams.

I have also given far more readings than I would like to people who are waiting for their partner to die so that they may be released from the hell they are living. Whether it has always been bad or has only just turned sour, don't wish your life or anyone else's away, but move on. Love can die, we all know that, but usually only if it is killed, not of its own accord. Love is a living thing and like every other living thing it requires care, attention and nourishment, not from just one person but from both. The most common problem I have observed with clients of every sign is lack of communication. Even Air signs Gemini, Libra and Aquarius can find themselves lost for words if their partner is not giving them the attention and devotion they need. I see people in my consulting rooms who cannot discuss the most important and intimate problems with their partner, the one person in the world with whom they should feel completely free. Getting into a rut is common too: seeing each other as a familiar piece of furniture rather than the special people they should be.

MAKING IT WORK

Try to make your home a nice place for yourself and your partner to come home to. Walk in the door with a smile on your face even if you have had a bad day at work. Find out how your partner has been and then tell them about your problems. Water signs Cancer, Scorpio and Pisces need to be able to talk and if they feel their partner is not interested in them they wilt like a plant left in a cold and lonely corner. OK, you Fire signs Aries, Leo and Sagittarius may find it hard to stay quiet for more than a minute but at least make the effort, so that you both get to feel that you are important and listened to, and that what has happened to you really counts. Earth signs Taurus, Virgo and Capricorn can't stand to come home to a messy place even if they themselves are at times slobs, so don't leave last night's dinner sitting on the sofa but tidy up a little and light a candle or two. You never know what effect it could have. Spreading a little comfort can work both ways.

Many of us don't find it easy to talk about money problems and money is an all-too-common problem in many marriages, whether you are an Antonia whose Rupert won't buy you the latest Gucci design or a Gert whose Bert won't pay the overdue bills on the council house. The position is different but the circumstances and result the same, and you cannot argue about money all day long and make love happily at night. Pisces and Scorpios are very good at lying about money matters and more often than not are found with a credit-card bill stuck behind the sofa which they try to convince their loved ones is an old one or one they'd completely forgotten about. So all of you signs lay your cards on the table and not only will you all sleep easier but you'll live longer too. Stress is the number-one killer and yet the most easily solved if you can stop, look and listen to what is going on in your life.

Relationships and marriage are a two-way path. When was the last time you complimented your partner on their appearance and when was the last time you told your loved one how proud you are of them? Think back to the last time you were given a compliment and remember how good it felt. Now do the same for a close one of yours.

Of course there are sometimes cases where one partner is completely dominated by the other. If you have married a sign that is stronger than your own then it is important to find your own area of control so that you don't lose sight of who you are. In short, if the good times outweigh the bad, then stay and work at what you have together. But if the bad times outweigh the good then take it from me, every step you take away from the person who is hurting you is another step closer to the happiness you seeking.

Overcoming the Affair
and Other Problems

TOUGH ONE THIS, I know, and more people than you think have been through it. Every week I get hundreds of letters from clients asking if they should take back a cheating partner and the answer is never easy.

Of course, it all comes down to you, and whether you feel you can live without this person. Some people would rather live with a cheater than not have them at all. What is most important is that you keep your self-respect. Remember that all of us, no matter what stage we are at in our relationship, were individuals before we met that special someone and can be individuals again afterwards.

No matter how much you love someone it is very hard to forget a betrayal. For different star signs different levels of betrayal apply. Some people see lying about money the worst thing in the world, while to others a simple flirtation with no further intentions is unforgivable. The reality is that it is very hard to forgive someone for doing something that they knew would be unacceptable to you.

I once had a client who was a Gemini who just

couldn't stop cheating, although he loved his wife dearly. For the purpose of this book we shall call him Tom. Tom just didn't know what to do for the best. He couldn't help himself, he said, and when he came to see me he was toying with the idea of suicide. Sometimes you just can't see past the end of your nose unless someone else points out the obvious. I had to tell Tom that his problem was an illness of sorts and that he must see a counsellor. You see, dear reader, sometimes I don't know everything – although I do know that even my job has limitations and there are times when I must let someone else work their expertise. Tom went, but only with my persuasion. I keep in touch with Tom to this day and he still goes to counselling, but he is also still married. Any problem in life – be it to do with marriage, business or health – cannot be solved unless you face it. So no matter how bad you think your problem is, whatever your dilemma, bring things out into the open.

Earth and Water signs in particular tend to bottle up their problems and make themselves ill. Look at Cancerian Princess Diana – at how she used to keep things in and how ill it made her. But look at the strength of character she found when she did seek help.

HOW FAITHFUL ARE YOU?

Some of us have a predilection for straying, others would like to but don't, others wouldn't dream of it. What about you?

Overcoming the Affair

ARIES

They can't resist straying if the leash is long enough, and they are inclined to boast which means they get caught out. On the other hand, the Aries betrayed will exact a dreadful revenge.

TAURUS

Not a player, the bull. Taurus's need for someone reliable to come home to is too great.

GEMINI

Very poor at lying and so not very good at maintaining the deceit. Unfortunately, when they do cheat, it is likely to be with someone you know.

CANCER

In an unhappy relationship they will seek fulfilment on the side. If it is Cancer being cheated on, don't ever interfere. You'll get the blame for being the messenger, and the cheater will be forgiven.

LEO

Leo is too proud to stray. Hasn't the lion already made the perfect choice of partner? It would have to be a major problem before Leo would play away.

VIRGO

Not above having affairs, but affairs rarely turn into true love for Virgo. Above all, Virgo hates to put his or her reputation in jeopardy, and can stay faithful for that reason alone.

LIBRA

These romantic, good-looking charmers can find their attentions wandering, but they always return to home base. Once they marry, their commitment is for real, and divorce is unthinkable.

SCORPIO

Serious about marriage, serious about love, Scorpio is never unfaithful – unless they don't feel quite in love enough.

SAGITTARIUS

Put in the position of temptation, Sagittarius is weaker than most. Dare Sagittarius to cheat, and they probably will. Make it clear that you, their partner, won't stand for it, and they probably won't. As simple as that.

CAPRICORN

Unless they are in love, not the most faithful of signs. Imagine opening up a box of chocolates and being told you had to glance and then take just one. However, they are loyal to the end if they feel they can expect the same from you.

AQUARIUS

They need a little bit of independence, and don't like to be told what's what. Their sheer unpredictability undermines their loyalty quotient. Be warned.

PISCES

They hate unfaithfulness in others so don't even think about staying with them if you have strayed; when they find out they will make your life a living hell. They, on the other hand, have often given in to temptation.

THE POWER OF THOUGHT

If you are one of the rare few who are entirely happy with their lot, then read no further, but also be honest with yourself and make your life the best it can be. If, on the other hand, you ever ask yourself, What is it all about? then stick with me a little longer. Very few of us, I think, have not wondered at some time or another what it is all for. Not when everything is going our way, for then we're too busy enjoying life, but in times of stress or when our relationships or businesses are not going well, or when fate seems weighted against us. A great deal has been written about the power of positive thinking and I for one believe strongly in it. Negative thoughts are only destructive. It is within the power of each one of us to reshape the circumstances in which we find ourselves. Much of our life is mapped out for us, is predestined, I believe, but much depends on what you make of it.

We have all read stirring stories of how people have risen to the challenge when faced with seemingly insurmountable problems. Douglas Bader was a famous great air ace, who having lost both his legs in a tragic flying accident at a young age was determined that he would fly again, and not as a passenger either, but on active service. This he did indeed do and he passed with flying colours and was one of the great heroes of the Second World War. Had he not possessed such an unquenchable spirit he could easily have sunk into oblivion, eventually accepting that he must remain immobile for the rest of his life.

There are times when our daily round seems like a daily grind. We get up, go to work, eat and sleep, and each new day seems exactly like the last. Sometimes we long for something new on the horizon. But we can change our lives. It is within our power to make the change, no matter how big, if we are really determined. 'Think that you can and you will, think big and your deeds will grow' is a line I remember every day from a poem called 'It's all in a state of mind'. We must attract happiness to us. You know, another saying I like is, 'Laugh and the world laughs with you, weep and you weep alone.' If we project a dreary image then we are going to draw others of similar ilk. If we can put on a smile, even if we have to work at it sometimes, then we will attract happy people, even attract happiness from those who were not feeling too good.

I have another theory. I believe that you could choose at random any acquaintance and say to them, 'I'm so sorry to hear about your trouble,' and that person would say, 'How did you know?' or 'How kind of you to sympathize.' Each and everyone of us has troubles. Some keep them to themselves better than others so that we never know how much they have suffered, especially Water signs Cancer, Scorpio and Pisces. None of us is singled out for misfortune; we all have our share. And we all need help from time to time, someone to help us see the way: close family, good true friends. Not everyone is so blessed and I have taken the place of the true friend with many of the people who have come to see me, so many of them deep in trouble and not knowing which way to turn. Pouring their hearts out to me takes a burden from them. I am proud and happy to have been able to help so many. I do predict their future, of course, but I also help them to bend it by their own will into something better, happier, fuller and more rewarding. A tip for everyone: try to take time out of your day to ask a friend how he or she is, or to pass on a compliment. You'll be amazed at the chain effect it can have – and how that good effect will come back round to you.

I like to feel that my work is worthwhile. When I am asked for advice I always put myself in my client's place and offer advice that is not too demanding for his or her nature. But I do give the advice that I can see will be the best in the long run, even if it is not what the client wants to hear.

We can change our lot, but the initiative must come from within. Help from others is only effective if we are prepared to help ourselves first. If all is not well in your world, don't accept it. Often it helps to think of the advice you would give someone else in that position, then act on it yourself.

Between
the Sheets

THIS IS IT, your compatibility guide. Find out what you are like with each sign. You can even look up your ex's to see if you were right to let them go.

ARIES AND ARIES

If these two Fire signs can survive the first few years they should have a partnership for life. Life is fun and fast-moving for them and they have a fantastic ability to keep the romance alive, long after other signs would have given up. Their consideration for others can, however, cause problems. What they see as doing a favour for a friend in need their partner may see as an out-and-out flirtation. There the arguments commence and, believe me, they are not a pretty sight.

These two are ambitious in their careers – once they have managed to find out what it is they want to do (which has been known to take thirty years or more). It is more common than not for them to find their calling when they are well into their thirties, and so it is the relationships begun in youth that face the bigger strain, for who knows whether both will like where they are when this searching finally comes to an end.

Aries seems to need to make life more interesting by every now and then upsetting the apple cart just for the sake of it. If these two are in the wrong frame of mind one will claim black is white and the other that white is black. They need to learn to put themselves in their partner's position (though not when they are in the 'black is white' sort of mood) and then perhaps they won't make the sort of mistakes that they are bound to regret later.

One thing is sure: life will never be boring. You need never expect to come home and find the dinner on the table at the same time every evening. And just when you think it's roast beef and Yorkshire pudding, the curry-house menu is on the table and your partner has a look that says, 'Surely you knew we'd be having a takeaway tonight.' And you're both as bad as each other! Neither of you should ever expect the other to turn up on time. Each has a time schedule of his or her own, but each will find it totally unacceptable for the other to be late. Give each other a little room to make mistakes and you should see each other well into old age, but try to keep the reins on each other and you can forget it. You won't see each other for dust.

ARIES AND TAURUS

When these two get together the whole world will hear about it. That is not to say they argue a lot. Rather it is playful banter as Taurus tries to control and arrange Aries and the ram in return springs surprises on the earthy old bull that will leave them both in a complete and utter spin. It is not the best match in the zodiac but funnily enough it is quite a common one. You may even find that the couples of these signs are quite different in age. This is the case with many of my clients of this colourful coupling.

Aries will go at the relationship hammer and tongs to begin with but can often cool off just when Taurus is beginning to find his or her feet. The sensual bull will pull the right punches by bringing his or her sexual wiles into the situation just when Aries is giving up hope or getting bored. In this way each can keep the other interested for years. However, Taurus feels inferior to the too-clever Aries, which can push the bull to do things to test his or her powers of attraction. A tight leash around the bull's neck is called for. Anything one can do the other can do better and life can turn into a bit of a competition, either with each other, or both of them against the world. The ram will always be one step ahead of the bull and will even be able to finish the bull's sentences. This is all very well if Taurus approves of the ending but nine times out of ten Aries has bullied Taurus into the ram's way of thinking. What Aries may not realize is that the bull is standing firm and even if it takes twenty years the bull will finally get round to expressing dislike of the food that the ram has always ordered for them whenever they have gone out for a meal. Aries is also too efficient for Taurus's liking, and the bull would like to plan his or her own agenda once in a while.

A jealous pair and life is heaven and hell in turn. If they do decide to make a go of it then they will have plenty to tell their grandchildren, that is, if Taurus can get a word in edgeways. And grandchildren they are likely to have – they could well procreate abundantly, since sex is the main thing they have in common.

ARIES AND GEMINI

I like these two together. They are like boxers sparring in a ring. Although this is a recommended match, I must point out that Aries is just that little bit too quick for Gemini's liking. Gemini prefers a slower pace in life, and less planning and rushing. Don't get me wrong: the Gemini is indeed a party animal who would not dream of turning down an exciting invitation. It is just that where Aries would decide on a whim to move in with you, Gemini will want to keep all options open. Gemini likes to be in charge of deciding when changes happen. If Gemini is not in the driving seat he or she can begin to feel very shaky, and has been known under such circumstances to flee without so much as a goodbye note. Another problem is that Gemini finds it very hard to let go of the past and will probably still be in touch with at least two exes. All very well until the exes want to have an innocent little chat or a shoulder to cry on when the latest relationship is not going to plan. A right mish-mash of emotions begins to emerge for poor old Aries. Mistrust between the two is rife and to make it worse neither would hesitate to flirt as a means of hurting the other if they wanted to.

Both thrive on affection and this is one of the things that holds them together. Sex between these two is usually very exciting but it can also lead them to go too far. This may well be a twosome who take their exploits to some public places, leading to some very embarrassing situations if caught. They make great parents, raising their children in a modern and understanding way that produces very bright and well-mannered young people. A word of warning though: don't start what you can't finish. If you are thinking of beginning an argument that you don't want to see escalate then leave well alone or you could be in for a long night. Bear in mind that life is not a competition and treat each other as equals. You're sure to have lots of fun together, in public and private.

ARIES AND CANCER

Quite a coupling these two. They have a strong sexual and mental attraction and can stay together far longer than friends and family would expect them to. You can be sure that when these two met, sparks really did fly. They are likely to have a very colourful story about how they first got it together. Aries and Cancer will not be frightened to announce to the whole world the love they have found and how strongly they feel about each other, but they really do need to learn to keep a slower pace before friends and even one another begin to think it's all talk.

I must point out that some of these marriages do not last. It can often be the worst combination for both of them. What one of them sees as unacceptable the other sees as the only way to go in a situation. It can be as if they are talking different languages. They also attract very different sets of friends into their lives and both may have to cut back on their social circle if this is a union they want to last into old age. This I think is a case where your partner in life must be everything to you: lover and best friend. If not, then this is a mixture that doesn't work, especially with all of the hangers-on that Cancer usually has lurking in the background.

Cancer does have a habit of dulling the Aries light and more often than not this is a good fling for them both rather than anything long-lasting. It would take an awful lot of energy to keep the relationship going, but it can and has been done. After having read this, mind you, those determined Aries and Cancer characters are likely to decide to do a very good job of proving me wrong. Stubbornness could well take them into their twilight years, if not into the next lifetime.

ARIES AND LEO

Leo can handle Aries very well indeed. This is an ideal partnership. Leo supplies the organization that Aries needs and Aries provides the excitement and fire that is necessary to keep the relationship alive.

Two Fire signs together is something not all astrologers recommend. When Fire signs fight they really go to town, but oh how passionate that making up can be. Their fault can be that they like to get others involved in their arguments. Very often their friends end up taking sides in things that just don't concern them. If Aries and Leo learn to keep their business private then they stand a better chance.

They don't always realize that they make excellent friends as well as lovers but they really do. Not only do they share the same stamina but Aries' ruling planet Mars keeps the unpredictability going in the relationship and keeps Leo's interest in there too, while Leo's ruling planet the Sun brings laughter into any dispute and ensures that neither party stays mad for long. A problem for them, however, is that neither will ever give in or say they were wrong in an argument. These two are like a dog with a bone. At least it gives the other a reason to stick around, even if it's just to prove a point over another minor issue.

ARIES AND VIRGO

These two don't mix at all well, I'm afraid. Aries makes Virgo uptight over most things and Virgo gives Aries much cause to reach screaming pitch with frustration. They will find it hard to agree on any important matters. The ram is also a little too outgoing for the earthy nature of the Virgo and when Virgo wants a romantic night in curled up together in front of the television Aries wants to be out painting the town red. When one starts to feel tired and sleepy the other just starts to wake up.

One of the ways you could add staying power to this union would be to agree to disagree and to live as two separate personalities who want to be together. But this is something I have rarely seen from a Virgo. A Virgo believes that a partner should give up the past and engage fully in the relationship. The many cronies or should I say friends that a Virgo tends to gather could also be a problem for an Aries who, in love, likes it to be just the two of you. Aries will call in at a moment's notice for a rendezvous and expect Virgo to cancel everything he or she was doing with friends. Virgo, the great friend to all, finds this unacceptable.

A good way to keep this fire burning bright would be to plan days to be together but then leave an open diary for certain days too, so that you can have both freedom and security. Dear old Virgo gets their planned agenda but Aries can add spontaneity by picking a surprise place sometimes too. Just remember what I said, though, Aries – you may well find a dozen of Virgo's friends waiting for you when you get there!

ARIES AND LIBRA

This is a combination I seem to see a lot of during the summer for some reason. And it really is a fine combination while it lasts. But Aries finds it very hard to stay loyal or faithful and lack of understanding between the two grows almost unnoticeably over a period of time. They are likely to have some fine old arguments in public, but each will claim it is the other who started it. However, this is a pairing that I have predicted success for and many successful marriages and couplings have occurred between these two signs.

One of the things that keeps them together is the

love and loyalty that Libra shows to Aries, who is bound to have caused a few hiccups in the early days. The ram longs to be tamed and will see how far it can push Libra, who nine times out of ten succumbs to any sort of emotional blackmail, but is also capable of giving as much as he or she gets. Do not be mistaken into thinking that Libra is a fool. Libra people know exactly what they are doing from day one, and if Libra intends to seduce the ram then the chances of success are very high. Libra will know just what to say and do to turn Aries to jelly and will only play the fool when necessary to achieve the desired result.

The fiery temper of Aries can often hurt our gentle Libra, who may think that he or she is not loved, but don't be fooled, Libra, the ram wouldn't be with you if it didn't think this was a winning combination. These two need to take time to consider how each other is feeling. Otherwise they can spend much of their lives together wondering if each really knew or understood what the other was going through. So, you see, you really are more alike than you thought. Just five minutes out of each day to ask how your partner is and you should see each other grow old. And most gracefully too, I might add.

ARIES AND SCORPIO

The initial attraction between these two is no doubt because they share the same ruling planet, Mars. I have seen many such partnerships last, but the problem with this duo is that both are hot-headed and ambitious but their ambitions all too often lie in different directions. What one finds it acceptable to spend all of his or her money on, the other does not. Jealousy is more often than not a problem and is the cause of most break-ups. These two may claim they ended up feeling more like brother and sister but they can never have just a friendship because their animal sexual attraction is always bubbling away underneath the surface. More likely they start off as friends and end up as lovers.

With Mars ruling them both they like to try to outwit each other and can often end up with horns locked, daring each other to see how far they will go. If one can drink ten pints the other can drink eleven. And even though each is secretly dying for the other to give in they will see things through to the death just to keep their reputations intact, both to each other and of course to any onlookers since both are exhibitionists. Aries has a wonderful tendency of saying the wrong thing at the wrong moment, which can prove embarrassing, especially among new friends, and Scorpio will never let Aries forget it. If these two want to last into the twilight years they both need to stop making life a competition and start living it as a team. After all, if you can share Mars surely you can share other things in life, such as money, a home and friends. Well, maybe not, but give it a go – life will always be fun. You both enjoy family life and any children you have are sure to be very happy ones. A word of advice, though: you don't have to buy them every toy you see. Spend time and energy on your kids rather than money. You have the talent to do so. Why not use it?

ARIES AND SAGITTARIUS

This can be a great partnership and socially these two will get on like a house on fire, but when it comes down to the nasties in life like money and domestic affairs they just can't agree. You see, both have their own ways of dealing with things and as they are Fire signs they are quick off the mark to put life right – which can result in expensive and painful mistakes for them both. Compromises are more often than not a way of life for these two. But this is a relationship which astrologers recommend and that is because these two are willing to adjust to each other and to go the extra mile for each other. The sex is great, fantastic in fact, but they ought to learn to go for quality rather than quantity – they'll save each other a lot of energy that way. These two may more often be a one-night stand than a long-term affair but if they do decide to set up house they will find that they begin to become very much alike. After a period of time people will even say that they look alike. Birthdays and Christmases are sure to be fun since these two like to celebrate.

My advice to you: do not try to change each other. Have your little idiosyncrasies and allow your partner his or hers. Sagittarius will try to push Aries into things the archer is not even sure it wants itself, and what began as a dare could end up as a fifty-year marriage down the line. Just be sure that it is what you want first. As long as Sagittarius asks Aries at the right time, Sagittarius will get everything he or she wants – and more.

ARIES AND CAPRICORN

There is a lot to be said for these two when they get it together. Fire and Earth is an odd union. They become so intertwined that they can lose sight of who they were before they met. Don't think for a second that Capricorn can curb the wild ways of Aries. Oh no, the ram will continue to do what it wants when it wants and if necessary behind Capricorn's back. The goat needs to learn to live life a little more and not to plan everything so much. Capricorn's career can get in the way of all the fun that the ram likes to have and the ram can accuse Capricorn of being a bore or a stick-in-the-mud.

The Aries sense of humour may be the initial spark of attraction and these two are likely to have flirted for quite some time before the real fun began. Capricorn will enjoy the fresh air that Aries can breathe into his or her life but the goat may find the ram a little too much to handle at times. Capricorn can expect to come home for a quiet night in and find a dozen or more of Aries' friends settled in, one of them in the goat's favourite armchair. And if you are one of the friends, unless you want to see these two fall out badly and never speak to each other again, you had better not interfere. Do not get involved when they argue, however good your intentions are. It is only when others take notice of the bickering that these two may realize that their futures do not lie together after all, and neither will hesitate to blame a third party for the split. But that said, this is a union that is safe, all in all.

ARIES AND AQUARIUS

These two create sparks together. They love each other so much they could kill each other and that's only on the first date. Don't be fooled into thinking that they didn't know what they were getting into five years down the line. These are two very clued-up signs of the zodiac. They play dumb just to divert the blame for any mistakes they have made elsewhere. The big problems start when their two families mix and secrets from their colourful pasts start to creep out of the woodwork.

They both have a tendency to look to the past for answers and they need to learn that they will only ever find them by moving forwards and looking ahead. Both Aries and Aquarius say things to each other that they don't mean. If they started off as friends and then became lovers they will willingly admit that they fancied each other for years but each will blame the other for not having made the sparks fly sooner. But my only real worry with this couple is what they will do when life returns to normality after the honeymoon period. Perhaps they will play games for the next fifty years. Maybe they will pretend each night that they have only just met. They are not short of imagination, but my advice is this: one of you should stop expecting so much, and then the other can do so as well, and you can appreciate what you have instead of what you don't. Learn to enjoy today together. You don't need to play games all the time when there is so much fun to be had with reality.

As you can imagine, Fire and Air can create quite a show and when these two get together they are sure to set plenty of tongues wagging. A good match on which the planets are sure to shower their approval.

ARIES AND PISCES

If they said they hated each other they would be lying for this pair can't help but adore each other. But by the same token they will watch and listen and not hesitate to take each other's bait. Both are hot-headed and this can lead to some hot passion. They will love but not necessarily like each other. You see, each wants the other to be more like him or herself and each wants to be given in to. As time goes by, each can think the other is more and more in the wrong. They will never say this to each other's face but they will instead tell their friends, your friends and anyone else who is willing to listen. They have even been caught telling the pets!

Pisces loves the dramatic and Aries will give them the attitude but not the control. It is a battle of wills and a case of who dares wins. They can go on and on like this. Eventually one will tire of the other's inability to give in and turn on their heels quickly and unexpectedly. They probably didn't even know they were going to do it. They'd just had enough one day. Either that or they decide to jump in at the deep end and go for marriage. If they do, they may well last the distance. When they've made the decision and the commitment they will stick to it, and surprise everyone by making a very good job of working things out.

They both, like good wine, improve with age and in time will not allow anyone to say a bad word about the other. Why not start as you mean to go on? Bear in mind that you shouldn't play the game with the other if you are not deadly serious. Also remember to give each other a bit of a break sometimes. The rewards if you do are likely to be wonderful.

TAURUS AND TAURUS

On the first date these two will probably be talking about how big their family is going to be. Their love of families should hold them together for many years and outside influences such as in-laws won't bother them much. The real danger in this union is misinterpretation of each other's actions. It doesn't happen often but it is dangerous when it does. They are both so stubborn, you see, that neither will want to give in or forget what the other has done.

Natural home-makers, there will be no problem giving up the high life they may have enjoyed before meeting each other. In fact, they are probably doing each other a favour if they stop the partying they've been indulging in seven days a week, although I am sure they would never admit it. They love to flirt and they are not too picky either. The butcher, the baker, the candlestick-maker – any of them will do. The good news is that it is very rare that they take it any further than flirtation – unless, of course, they start to play games and see how far they can push each other. Then we are off into some very dangerous territory. I have had clients of this pairing where one has had an affair and both have ended up entirely blaming the lover. Don't tangle with these two!

It is a problem deciding who is going to take the lead in love. These are two dominant personalities who will want to take the initiative. As a couple they can come across as moody. This is their sulking act. Each is trying to get the other to give in. You won't be able to guess their next action either. They will pull many aces out of their sleeves and they've both got degrees in emotional blackmail. With such even matching in the battle for power neither will ever win completely. Just make sure it doesn't turn into a war of attrition. Learn to give some space, and now and then to let love do the talking. Sex is sizzling and will be just as special at seventy as it was at seventeen.

TAURUS AND GEMINI

This is a pairing that is sure to divide friends, for they will never be able to tell whether these two love or hate each other, with the way they talk and behave. Taurus will usually win hands down in any arguments with Gemini, even when in the wrong. You see, Gemini is a very good talker, but Taurus has longevity and won't give in until Gemini has come round. Every sign – apart from Capricorn – will in the end give into Taurus.

The bull has great difficulty adapting to Gemini's moods. What Gemini wants one day is something he or she has always hated the next. Just as the bull has its sweets and snacks out and is curled up on the sofa, Gemini is ready to take off somewhere. These two should never try to plan a surprise for each other, for neither will like it, and it will be treated as something done to be mean not to be nice. Gemini hates Taurus's dominant attitude and brings out in Taurus a sensitive and possessive streak. The bull may well accuse Gemini of cheating, which if the bull has not kept up the excitement that caused the initial attraction Gemini may well be doing. The partnerships that have lasted between these two signs are usually due to their good sex life. An argument can often be ended with some passionate making up.

Just remember, you two, that you don't have to try to outwit each other all the time. Take it easy and enjoy the pace that life sets for you. From the outside, you see, it really does look as if Gemini is on fast forward while Taurus has forgotten to release the pause button. Try dancing lessons – at least then you can move to the same beat instead of dancing to such different tunes all the time.

TAURUS AND CANCER

This is a very touchy couple to talk about – it can go either way. When it is good it is very very good and when it is bad it is horrid. These two really do make or break each other. Cancer has the stamina, if he or she really tries, to cope with Taurus's strength of mind and stubbornness. Cancer can even put up with the selfish streak that Taurus exhibits from time to time – since Cancer understands what it is like to want your own way – and on the whole it is a great partnership. Many astrologers find that they are too much for each other and will eventually become sick of the relationship, in the way that you can eat too many sweets and start to feel queasy. However, I prefer to think of them as the delicacy in the sweetshop of couplings.

Over the years these two become more and more like each other and will get into a fine routine. It is as if they melt into one another and become one. A problem they can face is that Cancer wants to involve his or her family in their life together, whereas Taurus is more concerned with creating their own – especially the making of it! They can learn to live with each other but may not find it so easy to live with the baggage that each brings to the relationship.

It is not so lucky a union if they meet each other later in life. If one makes a mistake, the other will think it has carte blanche to do anything it likes – which, as you can imagine, often has dreadful consequences. A word of warning to the two of you: life, no matter how exciting it may be, is not a race to the finish.

TAURUS AND LEO

The stable and very earthy Taurus will not like the flash Leo being in the front line. Leo has to be number one at all times while Taurus simply cannot understand why anyone would try to equal, let alone better, the bull. Their joint need to be leader could be the destruction of them both unless, of course, one is willing to back down. But the bull is too stubborn for this, and Mr or Ms Leo the Limelight won't let go either. Leo doesn't like to be nagged by Taurus, and gets his or her revenge by making jokes to friends behind Taurus's back. If Taurus finds out he or she will go to great lengths to re-establish the untarnished reputation.

This is a chancy match and one which could see as much fight as fusion. Socially, this couple is the envy of many others, but what you see out in public is unlikely to be what goes on behind closed doors. They are great at organizing events and parties and perhaps would be better as work partners than lovers. Earthy Taurus tries to pull the reins in on Leo, while Leo is interested in how much it can tug and how much the bull will take. It may sound like a nightmare, but these two can go on and on like this for years. Just when you finally lose patience and tell them to stop arguing, they will politely inform you that they were not arguing at all. Leave well alone. They are a force to be reckoned with. Don't choose sides either, because neither will forgive you. With these two it's like a jazz band and a classical orchestra playing at the same time and trying to drown each other out. Friends and family will give you their own versions of what is going on, according to which of the two has furnished the details. Just remember that both are equally capable of telling tall stories.

TAURUS AND VIRGO

You could not put more stubborn people together if you tried, except perhaps by adding Capricorn to the mixture. Virgo and Taurus are both capable of getting their own way – clash! What do you do with two signs who are as good as each other at winning an argument? My advice is back off before they turn on you. However, these two can be good together. Each can fill in the other's blanks, and they can gel together very well indeed so long as there are no major issues they think differently about. In fact, it may be worth discussing the important points on the first date to save time and bother later on. If they sort out differences at the off, they can find their way to the happiness they both seek. Financially, however, these two have a problem. As quickly as Virgo accumulates, Taurus speculates – another clash.

The happy side to this partnership is that they can stay together for ever provided they don't try to search for things that aren't there. Each has a tendency to think the grass is greener on the other side. They must not be frightened to talk about whatever they are thinking about – they will often find their preoccupations are the same. Great for raising families, these two will bring up children with sound moral values.

Be careful. As time goes by, you must both learn that you have to practise what you preach. Neither of you can truly tell the other what to do. However, for a nice bonus, an experimental side to both your natures could see an extremely interesting sex life.

TAURUS AND LIBRA

Earth and Air is a funny old union and not one that astrologers recommend. However, these two could turn out to be the biggest love affair of each other's life. If they have the nerve to enter into marriage, the chances are they will be as in love at eighty as they were at eighteen. It is the jump into commitment that may be one of their initial problems, for each takes love very seriously. While some couples move in with each other with abandon, and then out again just as easily, these two hesitate long and hard to take such a major step.

Taurus is a little too deep at times for Airy Libra, and can rub him or her up the wrong way. A timing and co-ordination problem means that one wants to go skiing for a holiday while the other dreams of sunny beaches. Each has a fierce temper when roused and says unfortunate things, which do not get forgotten by the other half.

The bull wants to take the lead in love and with the determination he or she can wield probably succeeds. A shame though, for Libra would pull some nice surprises if given the chance. Taurus susses out early on that Libra is a sucker for emotional blackmail and so poor old Libra can end up being dominated and, if sufficiently in love, giving up dreams and ambitions to make Taurus happy. Libra can get his or her own back too, mind you. Libra knows a few tricks to rile the bull, and sexual persuasion is not beneath this lovable sign.

Both are ruled by Venus, the planet of love, which is probably the source of their initial attraction to each other. Each likes to flirt with others, but rarely takes it further. A pairing that is sure to have many onlookers, even if they are under cover for safety.

TAURUS AND SCORPIO

Wow, what a great combination. Not only are they polar opposites, which means instant animal attraction, they also know exactly what the other wants out of life. No long courtship needed here. They can argue as well as they can flirt, and very often they do both together. Whether they give each other what they know each other wants and needs depends on how generous they are feeling, for these two signs can be nice but they can be nasty too. They are easily influenced by each other, and yet when they disagree each is too proud to back down. They will go to great lengths to prove a point – any point. None the less, they succeed as lovers and are friends too. They always have something to talk about and the passion to make it worthwhile solving problems. With a quick temper and a frank tongue on each side, fights flare up but tenderness is genuinely meant and compliments only uttered if heartfelt.

Sexually these two are wonderfully compatible. All in all, a match more than likely to last and one I recommend, not just for the physical but for the mental aspects too.

TAURUS AND SAGITTARIUS

Fire and Earth are not always the greatest but these two have a better chance than most, whether for marriage or a business partnership. This is a successful couple which gets what it wants out of life. However, Sagittarius's superior attitude can bother Taurus, who likes things a little bit more low-key. While Sagittarius wants bright light and excitement, Taurus wants soft lights and predictability. Now don't get me wrong, the bull knows how to party, but the archer will initiate the idea far more often than the bull. If it came down to it, Taurus would outlast Sagittarius, partying way past the time the archer was ready to go home. However, the bull doesn't really want to. Taurus prefers one-on-one meetings to group get-togethers.

These two don't trust each other much. This leads to misunderstandings, sometimes very public ones. But it is a passionate relationship, and one which many others would envy.

The first few months will see its fair share of arguments and a great deal of splitting up and being reconciled. Sagittarius's temper can dent the confidence of the bull. After a while the bull doesn't feel good enough even to think about leaving such a fortunate coupling. As long as they can learn to allow each other's differences, and concentrate on each other's good points, they will work things out.

Here's my advice to you two. You have a tendency to bring up each other's pasts, wanting each other to pay the price for relationships long gone. Your life together started from the moment you met. Look to the future, not to what went before, if you want to survive.

TAURUS AND CAPRICORN

I just love these two together and some of my favourite married friends are this very coupling.

You know this pair. They walk around hand in hand with not a care in the world. They declare from the highest mountaintops the love they have found for each other. They stick by each other through thick and thin, have eyes for no one else, and believe themselves each to have found their soulmate. To friends and family they seem older than their years. They settle early on into a routine that others could take sixty years to develop. As two Earth signs they genuinely enjoy the prospect of setting up home together, and have been known to do so within a week of meeting – so long as they can decide whose house to settle in.

But that's not the whole story. There are a few other details you should know too. Though brilliant together they can also become bored of each other because they are so much alike. And talk about stubborn. Their silent treatments can go on for days if not weeks, though luckily they both tend to decide to move on at about the same time. About once a year they have a stonking argument that could bring the walls down.

Each needs to be satisfied in his or her career to ensure the continuing success of their love lives. Failure in one area can affect the other. I strongly urge each of you to make a conscious effort not to change for the other, but to keep some sense of your individuality. After all, it was the individual who attracted you in the first place. None the less, I strongly recommend this pairing, although as friends of mine have proved in the past, it can end up in matching tracksuits – you have been warned!

TAURUS AND AQUARIUS

Talk about annoying each other! These two will flirt and tease and neither will bore of doing it for years. Taurus is turned on by Aquarius, and together they can get into trouble. The story of how these two met is likely to be a quirky one. Indeed, it is possible that they first met when each was seeing or even married to someone else. This, as you can imagine, is not a good basis for future trust over the ensuing years. Each will want to know exactly where the other is at all times.

Aquarius is far more sociable than Taurus. Taurus prefers a night of cuddling up indoors while Aquarius wants to go out and show off the lover to the whole world. Don't get me wrong. The bull likes parties, it is just that he or she prefers the party to be at home, with the bull at its heart.

When they do have problems, Aquarius will be more willing to talk. Taurus is slower to offload deep dark secrets. Taurus likes home comforts a little too much for Aquarius, who is ready to pack up at a moment's notice should the right offer come their way. Just when Aquarius is getting ready for the pair of them to move onto greener pastures, Taurus is picking out new carpets and wallpaper for the existing home. This is not the best match in history but one which, with time and commitment from both parties, could prove to be very rewarding. The good point is that Taurus can soon make any place into a home for them both, no matter how far away from friends and family. And after all, home is where the heart is, especially when these two fall in love.

TAURUS AND PISCES

A most interesting mix. Strangely enough these two can make each other very happy. Not only will they love each other to bits, they will also hate each other a little too. Taurus is really too boring for Pisces, and Pisces is too outlandish for Taurus. Pisces knows exactly what to say to wind the bull up, and this pairing will annoy as much as it pleases. Taurus likes good food and Pisces likes, or should I say loves, a good drink. Only by making a whole night of it and indulging each other's fantasies can they find an understanding of any sort – and how long can they keep that up?

Taurus tries to ground Pisces a little too much. Pisces always has a new destination in mind to explore, while the bull wants thrills closer to home. The bull wants to invest in the long-term, not the short-term. Taurus is likely to come home to find that Pisces has rearranged all the furniture, upsetting the familiarity the bull so wants and needs. Dinnertime is tricky too. Pisces is unpredictable and loves to surprise with exotic foods, while Earth signs like the same meals on a regular basis.

Earth and Water can mix and sustain each other but this is not the most compatible match. They need to adapt to each other's needs, making a plan for when to stay in and when to go out. Then again, Pisces changes the plan just as Taurus has got comfortable with it.

A fun and different life awaits these two if they ever admit the true extent of their deep feelings for each other. Friends of the bull will not recognize him or her once the fish has worked its Watery magic, loosening those roots that the bull loves to put down. Once these two fall in love they can do anything. The sky is the limit.

GEMINI AND GEMINI

Broke but happy is the best way to describe these two. Not the best influence on each other's careers, they will encourage each other to keep trying new things rather than stick to the same project for any length of time. At home they are either very orderly or completely the reverse, hardly ever a happy medium. Each blames the other for his or her own shortcomings. Neither has a lot of ambition and although they are gifted, they lack the push that would get them real success. They will flirt to the ends of the earth with each other, but are also completely understanding when one of them flutters his or her eyelashes at another. These two should not push marriage on each other, for they are of a sign that can feel trapped. Each needs to let the other think the door is open, and then each will want to stay a little more.

With two such unpredictable and unreliable people, neither should count on the other turning up on time. In fact, they shouldn't bother booking restaurants, but rather go out to places that don't take reservations. Their gossipy nature makes it hard for them not to criticize each other, but each will fight tooth and nail to stop the other leaving if a real threat arises. Not the easiest of relationships, but a popular choice. And once the twins hit it off for real, life does get better and better.

My advice to you? Watch out for petty mind games. Be aware that each of you can give as good as you get, so don't start what you can't finish. And finally, never put down your partner's family. Your partner won't forgive you, and may just end up telling your in-laws every word you said.

GEMINI AND CANCER

This is a tough one. The crab never really knows if it can trust Gemini's flirting, which borders on the unacceptable more often than the crab likes. These two get along fine – if they don't conform to type, that is, which is not very often. Cancer is too considerate, and too soft and sensitive for Gemini. Gemini is hard and thoughtless in Cancer's eyes. Gemini gives Cancer money worries and Cancer gives Gemini a pain in the neck.

Gemini runs away from commitment whereas Cancer bounds towards it. The crab finds it difficult to understand why Gemini would want to have anyone else in his or her life apart from the crab and so tries to stop outings with friends. This is the worst thing possible – constrain Gemini and he or she runs. All you'll see is a pair of fleeing heels. If Cancer can feel secure enough to realize that Gemini is not going anywhere, then these two may start to have some fun. Very often, however, Gemini's flirting and teasing drives Cancer up the wall and then you see a side of the crab that is rather unattractive.

Don't be fooled by Cancer's tears. The crab is good at emotional blackmail. Only if both parties bring their skeletons out of the closet will they start to see each other for what they really are, and find the happiness they both seek. The positive side to this union is that they can teach each other new things. Will they want to use this new knowledge to build a future together? That is the real question.

GEMINI AND LEO

These two know exactly how to have a good time, which is just what they do when they get together. The big question is whether they can ride the storms as well. Gemini's pace of life is not always quick enough for Leo, so boredom can set in. Gemini can do without life's trimmings, but these are essential to Leo. The pettiness of Leo doesn't get a kindly response from Gemini, and the lion needs a firmer hand than Gemini can supply. Both love to have fun, but it is hard to say which one will take the lead in times of stress. The answer could well be neither. If allowed to, the lion will do whatever he or she wants. Don't get me wrong. Lions don't think they're spoilt, they know they're spoilt. They really do believe they are royalty and should be treated accordingly.

None the less, this is a match I would give my blessing to, for life will prove colourful for this combination. They are both strong and are sure to encourage each other to go to the limit on both personal and professional levels. You may think when you see them together that they are about to hit each other. But look again. They are really about to kiss each other. They will drive each other to a frenzy, to the extent that it can interfere with friends who feel left out of this exciting drama. Just remember: one of you has to take the wheel, or you'll crash.

GEMINI AND VIRGO

What a poor combination this can turn out to be, with each ending up feeling neglected and self-pitying. Gemini doesn't like the criticism and sarcasm that Virgo dishes out and Virgo cannot make allowances for Gemini's turns of mood. Gemini talks too much for Virgo, and Virgo tries to organize Gemini's life. Virgo gives advice but is not very good at taking it. Gemini has too many alternative friends for Virgo, who often picks friends to satisfy his or her agony-aunt complex. These two not only speak different languages, they also come from different countries with radically different cultures. If they make a go of it they are likely to have as many bad days as good – and that's if they are lucky.

The combination of Air and Earth makes for storms, not only for them but also for friends and family who get drawn in whether they want to or not. Is it all bad news? Actually not. These two can have conversations that last until the early hours, and during this time will put the world to rights. It's a shame they cannot put their life together to rights too. The choice is yours but I must advise you that you may well feel you are taking two steps forward and two steps back. Then again, the two-step can be fun to dance.

GEMINI AND LIBRA

These two Air signs will whip up a load of mischief together and won't care who knows about it either. Life together is full of surprises, which suits Gemini very well indeed, while Libra is perfectly adept at riding the changes. These two can make a go of it. It takes a lot for one to ruffle the other's feathers, and they rarely disagree over anything important. They have a lot of tolerance for each other. They flirt to make each other jealous, which can prove confusing for the rest of us.

They don't really know the word 'limit', and financial problems are likely to beset them. Libra spends money on Gemini, who appreciates the gifts but usually wants something else too. They egg each other onto buy all kinds of nice things, and get a shock when the statements come in. Then they flutter their eyelashes at each other, and go onto the next unsuitable purchase.

One of Gemini's weaknesses is a tendency to look around and see what everyone else is up to and what Gemini is missing. Libra only has to have his or her heart broken once. They never quite recover. It is up to Gemini not to play with Libra's feelings.

Both of you must share the spotlight. Take it in turns on the pedestal. You have the chance to make each other truly happy.

GEMINI AND SCORPIO

You may want to set up the boxing ring now. These two just can't wait to get at each other, in every sense of the word. Scorpio has the drive but can't drive Gemini far enough. Gemini resents Scorpio's pushiness. Each tries to change the other into a replica of itself. They can battle for days, months, or even years.

These two don't have much in common but they do often make best friends. They encourage each other into bad ways, getting involved in things untoward and egging each other on into infidelities. For them to be lovers, however, needs a lot of self-control. The more mature one nags the other to change his or her ways. An odd but common characteristic of this pairing is that Gemini is often the older but behaves like the younger. If they do break up, they can remain friends. But they have too much fun to give up on the partnership that easily. It's not the most mature relationship in the world. They lead each other down some very dodgy paths. They make each other feel young, but unfortunately none of us can bypass growing up for ever.

If you are part of this union, try to adopt a slower pace. If not, you'll reach your ten-year anniversary at a hundred-mile-an-hour pace and then wonder what on earth you did to get there. Savour what you have. You may just enjoy it, if the chemistry between the two of you is anything to go by.

GEMINI AND SAGITTARIUS

What starts off as game-playing ends up as a serious relationship. A strong attraction is at work between these two, but there's more against this relationship than for it. Unless, that is, both are willing to work at it seven days a week. Gemini can two-time if so desired, or so he or she believes, thanks to the faith Sagittarius has in their union. Sagittarius, therefore, carries the burden of not giving them chance or cause. The archer should remember: give Gemini an inch and the twins take a yard. Mind you, Sagittarius can give Gemini a rough time too. Only true love will see this pair making it through.

The mix of Fire and Air will see some colourful arguments and some passionate making-up. Together they enjoy a great social life. Gemini has more social stamina and can last the distance better. That's Sagittarius snoring over the final glass of wine or beer. Gemini flirts but Sagittarius can handle this trait most of the time – in itself a rarity. Sagittarius does not, however, tolerate open and obvious flirting. Gemini: know your limit and don't rub the archer's nose in it or you will be the one who ends up with egg on your face.

Sagittarius can open up many new horizons for Gemini, who thought he or she led a full life before discovering the fun Sagittarius could offer. These two are able to uncover talents in each other neither knew were there. Not the best match, but an interesting one, and one that is helped along as the Age of Aquarius makes us more relaxed.

GEMINI AND CAPRICORN

Not a match made in heaven, and not something your friends would recommend. Gemini is too untamed for dear Capricorn, who likes to feel in control of his or her mate. If Capricorn suggests you go out for dinner on Thursday night, he or she doesn't want to come home and find all your friends sprawled in the front room. Good old Gemini may, however, enjoy the battle. For

Gemini, it is a game. But Capricorn is deadly serious in the fight to own you. Don't even think about going out with friends, Gemini, without telling Capricorn first.

Capricorn has good points and many of them. Capricorn can help Gemini make the most out of life, and cultivate skills Gemini barely knows it has. One of the biggest attractions for these two is the feeling of tasting forbidden fruit. You can be certain that friends were whispering that it would be short-lived, giving stubborn Capricorn every reason to make the relationship last. My advice to you both: don't try to change a leopard's spots. Live with each other for who you are and not for who you want each other to be, and Capricorn, lighten up on those schedules!

GEMINI AND AQUARIUS

Talk about love at first sight, these two really know how to make a go of things. This is a lovely match, a match of hearts and minds. These two stimulate each other mentally as much as physically. They could talk away into the morning hours, friends and lovers both. They flirt and arouse each other with talk of what they will do to each other. It's not all roses, of course. Gemini can spread the flirting around elsewhere, which Aquarius is not always so keen on. Then again, in the right frame of mind Aquarius can do some pretty smooth talking too.

These two don't go to bed on an argument. They make up before things get out of hand. Aquarius's career may require moving from one town or even country to another, and the gypsy side of Gemini will go along quite happily, so long as Gemini is convinced the grass is greener on the new side. Aquarius, you may have to play games here, if Gemini doesn't want to up sticks. Let Gemini think you don't want him or her to come, and then you are guaranteed to be joined in your new venture by your beloved partner. Confused? Yes, you will be, but happy too.

Just make sure you don't spend more time talking about what you want to do than actually doing it. Keep up to speed with what's going on around you, and know when to put your plans into action.

GEMINI AND PISCES

It's heaven and hell at the same time with two such strong characters. Gemini is dominant in a crowd and Pisces dominant in one-to-one situations. Put the two together and you have a battle.

Friends will tell these two how good they'd be together way before they have even thought of it. As soon as they do get together, you can guarantee an intense relationship. They can argue over the silliest of things, and need to learn the meaning of give and take. Without creating a bit of leeway, they won't ever progress to what should be an interesting union. Pisces usually wins the battle for power in a set-up such as this, not through being more clever but through being more determined. Gemini can find other things to focus on in life, but Pisces gets what it is doing between its teeth and doesn't let go until it has won. Each uses seductive powers to show the other what he or she would miss should things ever go awry.

It takes more energy than average to keep this relationship going. These two need to keep working at things for years to come. Pisces must also be prepared that, while the fish keeps problems close to its scaly chest, Gemini tells them all to the world. A few ground rules are definitely needed before these two take on the serious commitment of marriage.

CANCER AND CANCER

Two Water signs together are a powerful combination, even more so when both are of the same sign as well as the same element. Both romantic and generous in spirit, this union can last for years. The only problem is how to decide who loves the other more.

Both worry over trivialities and have a problem with each other ever having had a past. Many Cancer couples get together in childhood and stay that way just to prevent anyone else ever getting a look in. They have been known to marry too soon, but even these unions usually last. These two get nowhere fast and are known for being late arriving anywhere. A tendency to cling holds them together. Overemotional, they often don't expect things to go their way. Instead, they are just waiting for things to go wrong. Never leave a message for Cancer asking to be called back, with no explanation why you rang. By the time you speak to each other, Cancer will have thought of a thousand disasters that could have befallen you. Financial issues are of a different complexion. Shrewd business moves usually ensure the absence of money worries, though these two do like to lavish money on each other as proof of love.

OK, you two, so long as you don't let your imagination or your intimations of doom run away with you then you should find your union lasting well into old age. Physically, you won't have any complaints. With time sex just gets better and better. I haven't yet seen two people of this sign who have not been content to spend their lives together, so you have my and I'm sure many other people's approval. Please put the hankies away now.

CANCER AND LEO

Not the perfect match – a doubtful relationship this one. They will stick together and stick up for each other, but both are vulnerable to other more compatible signs. They can't thrash out their problems together without both ending up feeling hurt. They ask themselves if it is worth the pain. Only they can decide, but they really do have a tendency to rub each other up the wrong way. Although there are many good points to this union, there are many bad points too. It takes two strong-willed people to battle against the stars, and that is what these two are doing. Of course, we all have different qualities. As long as these two can respect each other's differences, they could be on the right track.

So what got them together in the first place? Well, there's Cancer's sexiness and Leo's smooth talking. Both know how to look and act, and this is more likely to have proved the turn-on than the subject of their conversations. They need to beware of listening to friends who might try to split them up. If they work together and not apart they can beat the odds, but they must remember to allow each other to retain individuality. There are a lot of reasons for these two to work things out but it requires patience and dedication, which neither has in abundance.

CANCER AND VIRGO

I like these two together, though they are inclined to push each other a little too far. Virgo needles Cancer with criticism, and Cancer's generosity annoys Virgo. Virgo's advice to Cancer is usually right, which does nothing but get up Cancer's nose. Cancer's sentimentality is too much for Virgo, and Virgo is not romantic enough for Cancer.

This relationship can work if these two make an effort to understand what each other needs. Instead of trying to mould each other into something more familiar and manageable, they need to appreciate each other's uniqueness. Virgo needs to lay off the criticism, especially of things in Cancer's past. Tactlessness can knock emotional Cancer's confidence for six. But these two can build each other up if they only try. Let them work things out for themselves, and they will surely perform miracles.

CANCER AND LIBRA

Not that common a combination. They find each other cocky. Cancer antagonizes Libra and Libra is not demonstrative or thoughtful enough for Cancer. But Libra does have a calming effect on the uptight crab. Mind you, Libra makes the crab uptight too. These two have a fair chance of making it. Not the best chance, but a fair one. They must also be careful of the emotions they can stir up in each other. All may be fair in love and war but I think these two are prepared to pull some pretty low punches.

Don't think for one minute that these two don't love each other. The problem is that they are pitted against the rest of the world, a world that doesn't think they are right for each other and is sticking its oar in. A large part of what determines success for them is outside influences, particularly in-laws. Not that they cannot cause each other problems as well. Libra has a tendency to flirt, which Cancer finds unforgivable (even though it rarely goes beyond flirting). Both love children and families but should not rely on them to find the happiness they should be discovering in each other.

I wouldn't condemn this relationship but I wouldn't encourage it either. These two will end up emotional wrecks if they go to war on each other. Remember that you are both in this together, and go forwards instead of backwards. Don't take everything to heart your partner says. Trust in each other and you could be on the right track.

CANCER AND SCORPIO

Yes, this is a good match, but not everyone agrees. Tissue manufacturers like these two because, happy or sad, they spend much of their time in tears. They drive each other mad but they make a good team all the same. The scorpion is quick to lose its temper, which upsets the sensitive crab, and the crab tries to do too much for the scorpion, who likes to make its own plans. None the less, they will love each other to the end of their days, and even if the relationship ends the two partners will sigh a wistful thought for many years to come over what might have been.

They make a good marriage. Each needs to create a base, and does so much better than most. There's no real question about the nature of this relationship because these two will have understood each other from the start. They don't have to find it all out as they go along. That doesn't mean it's perfect. Cancer has a tendency to accuse Scorpio of unacceptable behaviour, but Cancer should beware because Scorpio will strike out if pushed into a corner. Scorpio needs to say to Cancer the magic words 'I love you' a little more often than it does. It doesn't matter how strong your love is, the crab still needs telling several times a day.

Don't give up your careers for each other. Both of you are capable of making your mark on the world, all the more so if you support each other. And if you decide to have children, don't neglect their emotional welfare because you are so tied up with your own.

CANCER AND SAGITTARIUS

Life is not easy for these two. They claim to know what they want but then they go in the opposite direction to that in which they said they'd go. These two have their fair share of problems. Sagittarius makes plans and leaves Cancer behind for fear of having his or her wings clipped. Cancer gets told at the last minute about what is a fait accompli. The emotional crab feels the archer has let him or her down. The crab wants the archer there twenty-four seven but the archer feels that constant demonstration of commitment is not what's needed. Think again, Sagittarius. It is a rule with Cancer that if you love them you are supposed to be able to read their minds. Sometimes it is OK for you to go off with your friends, but at other times it is not. If you loved the crab, you'd know.

The beginning of these relationships is always exciting and it is not unusual for this duo to rush a little too quickly into marriage. Keep a slow pace to begin with. It will take a year, not a day, for you two to even begin to understand each other. And it will be ten years before you've got the full measure of each other.

I am afraid the crab could be a little too serious for the talk-its-way-out-of-a-paper-bag archer. This union will be short and sweet unless both agree to give the other the distance each needs to be the individual who caused sparks to fly in the first place. A lot of effort is required for this union, but then again, don't all the best relationships require a bit of hard work?

CANCER AND CAPRICORN

This is a great match. So many people wish they could have this kind of union that these two should thank their lucky stars. The main reason I give my approval so readily to these two is that each ends up being the anchor the other needs. Capricorn finds it hard to get in touch with his or her emotions while Cancer gets overemotional. By joining together these two become the perfect foil for each other. Cancer keeps Capricorn afloat and Capricorn keeps Cancer grounded.

This duo also works well in business. One supplies the structure and the other the style. I won't say which is which. I'll let you work it out for yourself. Cancer can be lazy. Bills get written out but not sent off for weeks. Capricorn can prove a little too critical for the emotional crab. But it's pretty much plain sailing apart from the odd little wave.

Friends don't usually approve of this mix. This couple mustn't expect automatic support from those around them. Friends may even feel jealous because when these two get together they forget that anybody else exists. They spend much of their time talking and putting the world to rights and discussing the many possibilities of their own relationship. Neither pushes the other into mischief. They may seek forbidden fruit to add spice to the mixture, but each is far more likely to windowshop than buy. A match I feel confident will last, whatever the outside influences.

CANCER AND AQUARIUS

A strange pairing indeed and in business the downfall of many a company.

On first meeting, Aquarius is insensitive to Cancer, and each finds the other intensely irritating. Cancer believes Aquarius thinks he or she knows everything. Aquarius finds Cancer far too serious for his or her own good. Then all of a sudden circumstances drive them together and, good heavens, they love each other so intensely that they cannot speak about any past in which each other has not figured.

It's not an easy ride. Aquarius finds the crab demanding. The crab thinks its demands are all very fair and just. Arguments begin and go on for days. Aquarius shouts and Cancer sulks.

Both of you have got to do an awful lot of changing if you want to make your partnership work. You have to remember not to accuse without proof. Otherwise the other one might just commit the crime for which they have been punished. Bear in mind that even if you don't like to discuss past loves, you don't have to involve present friends in the union. It takes two to make a relationship, so stop chewing your friends' ears off and start living what could be a fun life together. The first five years are the test. Once you've gone beyond this, you should find a lasting and satisfying union.

CANCER AND PISCES

I love these two together, and love really is the key word. These two love to love each other. They love to hate each other a little bit too. And if they were not involved in a relationship they would still find their way into each other's lives. They cannot bear to be apart. At times Cancer can be a little weak-willed for Pisces, who needs someone to keep him or her on the straight and narrow. But mostly they will love and protect each other deep into old age, looking through the skin and bones and deep into the soul of one another. Looks may have attracted these two but brains keep them together.

Don't think them boring. These two can get into no end of mischief. They are quite likely to end up in a distant country committed to a strange job or lifestyle and wondering how they got there. I'll tell you how. Curiosity took Pisces there and faithfulness sent Cancer along too. A great couple to bring up children, the only problem is timing. Cancer is likely to want them long before Pisces' parental instincts have kicked in. I'd recommend this match time and time again. Their love will never die. They create a beautiful feeling in life and are able to make the best out of any situation they find themselves in. Anything is possible when these two get together.

LEO AND LEO

Fight Fire with Fire and what do you get? Actually, a great combination. Their intellectual interests give these two much in common, and life is full of energy and fun for them. They make each other happy. Sex is very important to both of them and they have an exciting physical relationship. They are not afraid to take life and love to new heights and they bring out a wild streak in each other. These two will not be leaving much to the imagination, believe me.

The problems kick in when they realize they are each other's equal. You see, the lion always likes to feel he or she is superior. Excesses of pride can make them put each other down in public. They also have a tendency to disrespect each other's possessions. One is asking where his or her favourite item of clothing is while the other is out cleaning the car with it.

They may flirt to wind each other up, but they flirt best of all with each other. If they flirt outside the relationship, major game-playing soon ensues. Then the fights come along. These two enjoy a good head-to-head. If this relationship is more than six months old, they will already have done enough fighting to be pretty well practised at it. There's a dangerous tendency to deny lovemaking as a way to punish the other half, but this can only end in disaster. Keep arguments out in the open where they belong, you two. Don't go taking them into the bedroom. You'll only be hurting yourself, you know – and that goes for both of you.

LEO AND VIRGO

Fire and Earth are a funny old combination. Neither can really get the other going. They try hard but never manage to give each other what each other needs. This relationship brings difficulties and doubts to both signs. Virgo is not with it enough for Leo. Virgo finds Leo's inquisitiveness annoying. Virgo finds Leo difficult to handle, not good for a sign which likes to be in control, even when it is quite plainly not capable of it. Leo flirts too much for Virgo, and tries to initiate the sexual relationship sooner than Virgo would like. Virgo doesn't understand why Leo insists on spending so much money on things which are not needed.

On they go, winding each other up. But this union can work, given time and understanding. Virgo is a planner, and Leo is a leader. The key is for Virgo to do the planning, and to let Leo think it is in charge. Virgo needs to let Leo claim the glory, and Virgo can do this if in the right mood. You can see that this is on pretty shaky ground. So what got these two together in the first place? It's about how different they are, and how they show each other things from a new perspective. Five years is make-or-break time. By this stage they know if they can go the distance. And it wouldn't hurt for Leo to learn to give in occasionally. It could reap great romantic rewards for the two of them.

LEO AND LIBRA

These two can really buzz. Some terrific one-liner will have got them together in the first place, and it's fun pretty much from the word go. They can last well into old age together, and will share much good humour and some great memories.

They've got a few problems to get through, though. This team is good, but money mars the fun. Leo is too possessive at times for Libra, who likes a lot of rope. Libra needs time to think about changes, whereas Leo corners at speed, changing direction at the drop of a hat. Leo gets frustrated because Libra loves to talk about ideas but keeps Leo waiting for ages before putting them into practice.

Responsible and loving Libra makes a great parent and Leo adds the excitement factor that children need, so they are sure to raise a stable and happy family. The only trouble is that as soon as they settle into a home, Leo gets itchy feet and wants to move onto another adventure. Just as well that Libra can make each place look like home again, no matter where. Before I forget: sex gets better between these two with every year that passes, but then if you are part of this duo, you already know that. Just watch money matters, the only real downfall in a well-starred relationship.

LEO AND SCORPIO

These two can argue, and oh how they love it. There's a smile beneath the frown and they enjoy the sparring. Something is always on the boil here. Evenly matched, they try to outwit each other but rarely succeed. Their playful arguments liven up their time together. Dangers lie in Scorpio's quick and hurtful tongue, and Leo's tendency to retreat into his or her shell. Scorpio apologizes but both know when what was said was really meant.

Scorpio loves the way Leo looks, and Leo loves the sexual power Scorpio gives off. The worry here is that these two can take things too far. Neither grounds the other enough. Together they could spend for their country in the shopping Olympics. The difference being that Scorpio snips off price tags and Leo sticks them on. Scorpio can't remember how much something cost (or so he or she claims), while Leo triples the price to impress you. If they both have money, this is fine. If they are living on a shoestring, they are probably heading for the dogs.

Careerwise, both are set for success, and can even work well together. Leo comes up with the ideas and Scorpio sells them. Not a perfect match, but an energetic one in which each has the willingness to work things out. If you are on the sidelines, you'll be driven to distraction if you try to referee their many matches, so chuck the whistle away, I advise you.

LEO AND SAGITTARIUS

Two Fire signs often hit it off, especially in their twenties. They meet late at night, have one drink too many and say how much they fancy each other. They often stay together for months. But years? Well, this is not a bad match, I must say. I have seen many successful marriages between these two Fire signs. The animal magnetism does not fade. It only takes a glance from another person and both will warn the interloper away. They guard their love like an animal guards its young. They can fight well and neither likes to give in. Woe betide anyone who tries to split them up, and that includes family and friends. Children do not usually come immediately but when they do they come thick and fast, and twins are not unusual to this combination.

The excitement does burn away as they get older. Each is able to guess what the other will do next. Fire signs thrive on unpredictability, but two Fire signs just aren't unpredictable enough for each other. However, they help each other develop new interests and rarely stray far from each other.

My tip? Don't try to fix what is not broken. Do not look for problems where there are none. A good argument is fine, but bickering will wear you both out. Relax and enjoy all the many things you have in common. Show your emotions through actions and not words.

LEO AND CAPRICORN

These two are making many compromises. This is not an easy mix. They pull in different directions. Leo is living life in the fast lane, while Capricorn is at home making careful and finely detailed plans. Leo is an exhibitionist, while Capricorn defends his or her privacy. It's not a disaster, these two together. But it is challenging, and both need to consider carefully what they are getting into.

Capricorn needs to know what is around the corner. Success comes to the goat from planning. It's no good Capricorn loosening up when planning is what the goat does best. Capricorn's career is usually taking off when Leo's is coming down. However, in these circumstances these two can support each other. And that's my advice to you. Work as a team. Merge your futures and you could end up heading in the same successful direction.

Watch out, Capricorn, for Leo's quick temper. Take what the lion says with a pinch of salt, but listen to the good bits: those the lion really does mean. Leo, you too watch out for Capricorn's harsh tongue. Tell the goat not to communicate his or her needs in such a brusque way. Try to take it easy, both of you, and trust each other a little more.

LEO AND AQUARIUS

These two follow a zig-zag path through life, neither of them sure where they are going, but drunk on love for each other. They hit it off straight away. Each tantalizes the other. Leo loves to listen to Aquarius talk and in doing so finds his or her inquisitive mind perfectly satisfied. When these two first get together you are sure to hear about it. They will display their love and affection to all around, to the point of embarrassment. They set out to rule the world, but they aim to make it a better-looking place too.

There are, as in any relationship, some problems. The lion finds it hard to keep up with Aquarius, who has more energy. But Leo has the ideas in the first place. Aquarius needs to watch out for the lion's temper and ability to spend money like it's water. The lion wants constant change whereas Aquarius wants to work on and improve the situation they are in. This is a great union, but these two need keeping on a short lease or they'll get each other into trouble, both financially and romantically. They may end up setting a pace for each other that even Casanova couldn't keep up with.

Go for gold, if you are this pairing, but be prepared that life will have one or two lessons to teach you on the way.

LEO AND PISCES

These two are like cat and dog. They are fascinated by each other, but just too different to stay friends. Love soon turns into hate. Pisces gets fed up with out-and-out exhibitionist Leo, and Leo hates the way Pisces tries to steal the limelight. Each thinks itself more classy than the other. Leo tries but never succeeds in ruling Pisces. The power struggle between these two can go on for ever.

Physically, not a bad match. Each has high expectations of the other, including that the other be the pleasure-giver. Neither is prepared to give that much of him- or herself. Life is about sharing, which Leo in particular does not find easy. Crossed wires, confused signals and mixed feelings abound.

Lay your cards on the table. It's the only way. Try every day to work things out. If strategies don't work, review them. If you have the energy, go for it, but you really will need it. Pisces, stop trying to change Leo and to dampen the lion's spirits. Leo, stop getting jealous of Pisces. OK, now let the romance begin.

VIRGO AND VIRGO

Two peas in a pod. A lovely pair, a fine match, but a little given to worrying. What will happen tomorrow?

Will we last? Will I make the shops? The problems are endless that these two find in life. When they first get together, it's like they are looking in a mirror. They understand each other perfectly. They feel the same about the serious issues in life and together they want to right the world. They spend many a night sorting out the world's problems.

The problem is that Virgo is very good at looking at other people's lives and working out what's wrong, but no good at doing the same for his or her own life. So when these two soulmates get together, they start giving each other advice. It's painfully accurate advice, too, and it can be just too hard to take.

They both work hard (as a rule) and make a very comfortable home. If each has a home at the time they meet, it will take a long time before one gives up his or her pad to move in with the other. When they commit, they usually stay together. One break-up in life is enough for this perfectionist but loving sign. If they do part, it will be permanent, with no looking back.

One thing is for sure. They make the world a better place. They bring out each other's kindness, in itself a quality worth fighting for. This is a good match. One that will bring these two much happiness and many discussions, for years and years to come.

VIRGO AND LIBRA

These two have probably found each other by accident. They are not afraid to say how different they are. Virgo doesn't take Libra seriously enough and doesn't listen to all that Libra has to say, which is usually a lot. Libra thinks Virgo is not easy-going enough and can get fed up with the constant criticism. The physical attraction has to be very strong for this partnership to survive, and luckily it usually is.

The problems get serious when Libra's eye starts to roam. Libra finds it very hard not to flirt, and the temptation increases when Virgo is giving advice about how Libra should look and act. Virgo should not worry about Libra's infidelity, however. Libra could never get it past Virgo. Virgo is likely to have considered the possibility of Libra with someone else, dismissed it as a bad option, challenged Libra with it – and all before Libra has even noticed the person.

If these two are going to work things out, something has got to give. And that could be a shame. The very qualities that make Libra so charming are what Virgo tries to change. The very things Virgo is good at doing are what Libra finds interfering and obtrusive. Overlook the comments, turn the other way when the flirting is going on, and you two may find peace. But then each of you is too forthright not to speak your mind. A loud and colourful battle for love and power is always on the cards.

VIRGO AND SCORPIO

These two annoy the hell out of each other but keep coming back for more. The more time they spend together the more they like each other. However, if they have to part company for a short time, the magic takes some rekindling, and each wonders if the other has changed his or her mind.

These two are taking a chance on life and pushing things to extremes. Scorpio's extremely emotional nature upsets Virgo and Virgo's methodical ways work Scorpio up to screaming pitch. Both are suspicious and interpret the actions of the other wrongly. These two should not accuse each other of having an affair. They are likely to be wrong, but then Scorpio will go and do it just to spite Virgo.

They do love each other. And they have that rare quality: respect for each other. They don't flatter each other face to face, but word gets round from friends, repeating the praise each has said in the other's honour. They like to look good as a couple, and give each other sartorial advice. And a chilled-out pair of perfectionists they can be too. But it is a complicated match. Both want to lead and neither to follow. Virgo doesn't let Scorpio have the freedom Scorpio needs. Scorpio begins to feel suffocated. You have no chance of this relationship working if you both stay the same as you were at the outset. None the less, I give you my blessing. You can have real fun together.

VIRGO AND SAGITTARIUS

This is rather like meeting someone you like the look of but who is from another country. You just know there are going to be complications. Virgo doesn't always understand unpredictable Sagittarius, and wires get easily crossed. Sagittarius means what he or she says and this angers Virgo who only likes to hear from a partner what he or she wants to hear.

The best aspect of this coupling is that they stimulate each other. Sagittarius pulls the rug out from under Virgo, who's busy asking where they are going, when, what they will do when they get there and what time they will come home again. Organization is not one of Sagittarius's best skills, so even if they wanted to tell the whole story they couldn't. They've changed the restaurant booking at the last minute anyway.

Often Sagittarius is the older of the two. Virgo finds it hard to change the archer, especially an older archer, but doesn't give in until just before breaking point. What saves these two is the wonderful dry sense of humour they both have. Laughter is sure to be a large part of this unconventional relationship. This is not a union that I would say can work every time but it has great potential and if nothing else these two will come away having learnt a great deal and with a new and fresh outlook on life. If they decide to stay together they must remember that a mistake is a mistake, and give each other a little more understanding, wherever the weaknesses lie.

VIRGO AND CAPRICORN

These two Earth signs will happily while away the hours in each other's arms, never needing to seek solace elsewhere. Virgo tells Capricorn how to live life and Capricorn picks up on the most relevant bits of advice and uses them to his or her advantage. Problems can be talked through, and bonds are strong. These two are perfect for marriage.

Neither could get away with flirting. There would be a big price to pay for that. After these two have pledged love to one another, there's no going back. Physically they should feel very secure but both long to be more adventurous. They only need to find the courage to admit it. Neither is one for affairs. Virgo cannot hide his or her emotions and doesn't believe in doing so anyway. The game-playing that so many go in for is not on their list of priorities at all. Both crave commitment. Sharing the same element, they are likely to have the same goals, and to want to take the same path to reach them. They will not be disappointed when they join forces.

VIRGO AND AQUARIUS

A bit of a strange match, these two. I am not sure who would have done the seducing. If it were a quick romance that got them together then it would have been Aquarius who did all the talking. If it was a slow seduction, Virgo is the one likely to have pulled the strings. This is a pair that likes to play games and doesn't mind who knows its business. Mostly it is better to keep your private life private, but these two will wash their dirty linen in public, I'm afraid to say.

Virgo proves too conventional for impulsive Aquarius much of the time, but at least curious Virgo is mentally stimulated. I cannot give these two my wholehearted approval, but I do completely understand how they managed to fall into each other's arms. What they will find difficult is to build up anything solid. These two have different ways and certainly have different ideas about bringing up a family. Better allocate each other your own departments of power. Aquarius talks a little too much hot air for Virgo, who likes facts and figures laid out on the table, unless of course they are Virgo's own when they may be guarded a little more secretively. Virgo also finds it hard to tolerate Aquarius's terrible time-keeping. Only by organizing things from the start will you both avoid getting a shock further down the line.

Remember, you two, you are not alike, and should not expect to be. Allow yourselves to be the individuals you are if you want a long-term relationship and not just a short-term romance.

VIRGO AND PISCES

I give these two my complete and utter approval. When they get together, you will hear all about it. You will see an announcement in the paper or a card will come through your door explaining all. These two bring out an exhibitionist streak in each other. They will set out to make the world theirs and there is no mountain high enough to get in their way. These two are unbeatable. They bring out new talents in each other and give each other the inspiration they both need to make their lives the best they can be.

Problems only develop if Pisces loses interest. Virgo invests everything in this union, but Pisces takes a little bit longer to commit. Pisces likes to make sure this really is the right match. Nine times out of ten when they get together they stay together, and they last for ever. They even improve with age. What a combo!

A word of advice for Virgo. If it is the early days, and Pisces' interest is waning, play it cool. Pisces doesn't like to be knowingly chased. The fish likes to do the seducing. And, Pisces, if you feel strongly about Virgo, take the nagging as constructive advice. Virgo wouldn't be with you if he or she didn't adore you. Earth and Water together create an environment of great nurture. They can create fantastic families together, and have a lot of fun over the making of them too – but I won't go into that right now!

LIBRA AND LIBRA

This is the joining of two great hearts. They both feel they have met the person they were looking for. A good match, but just remember that too much of anything sweet can make you sick.

Ruled by the planet Venus, the goddess of love, they can't really go wrong. They usually rush into marriage but take everything else at a slower pace. They get on well and share a sense of humour. Children are important but rarely take priority. They have them when they feel ready. They love to talk and can spend much time in discussion of trivia. They can tell you exactly what happened in the soap opera that evening or what price your favourite bottle of wine is that week. Both appreciate beautiful clothes and things in the home and their domain is likely to be a lovely one. Alternative but tasteful artwork will adorn the walls.

They need to be careful of living in a rut, which can occur if they give up too much for one another. They should not lose sight of who they were before they met. Neither should they be afraid of the odd argument. A bit of conflict can be healthy. Both love proudly and are not afraid to show their affection in public. Their love for one another could keep them together for ever. Only substantial difficulties will split them up. Emotional blackmail, however, is the name of the pit into which these two clever and romantic Air signs can fall. They can give in to things with each other that neither would dream of giving up for anyone else.

A wonderful thing about these two is how much they go out of their way to plan surprises for each other: a romantic meal, little presents, tickets for a concert. And all this long after they have married each other. A match of pure love. Just remember that real love is all about supporting each other, and each other's dreams and desires, and not just your own. Make your lives the best they can be and don't take the easy options.

LIBRA AND SCORPIO

Some of my best friends have been of these signs, but when they get together they can bring each other down. They feel so strongly for each other they want to change the way they think, dress and act for each other. Scorpio tries to change quicker than Libra, who first waits to see how far Scorpio is willing to go. What a pair! They attract and repel each other at the same time.

Friends don't like to see this. They begin to say how nice you are individually but how your pairing doesn't work. And you do bring out the worst in each other. Libra doesn't stick to the rules that Scorpio makes. Scorpio flares up. Scorpio hates it that Libra would rather be silent and sullen than have a good row. Scorpio ends up winning because he or she knows what buttons to press to get Libra to do the right thing. A word of warning, Scorpio. Libra will take this treatment only for so long. It could be a year, it could be ten, but one day Libra will get up and walk out of your life. Treat Libra well if you want to keep this person in your life and your heart. It is one thing to love someone but quite another to manipulate him or her, which is what Scorpio often does.

But this relationship is special. These two will go to any lengths to please each other, even giving up a career. Libra needs more self-confidence. He or she can end up feeling lucky just to have landed a Scorpio. Believe me, we all have our faults and Scorpio is no different. Let the scorpion know it is lucky to have you, Libra. If they don't, plenty of others will!

LIBRA AND SAGITTARIUS

These two hit it off but you can be certain that friends, if asked, would never have put them together. The main attraction is the visions they bring out in one another. They will not be afraid to tell each other their fantasies and dreams in life. This is a union that can and usually does work, though they can be too easy-going, not getting things done and still talking instead of doing years down the line. It helps if Libra is a few years older and wiser.

Sagittarius sometimes resents flirty Libra and Libra can't see why Sagittarius can't take a joke. Sagittarius will be pretty good at getting Libra to do what the archer wants eventually, and this is mainly through good old emotional blackmail. Money problems more often than not are the thing responsible for breaking this duo up. I give these two the thumbs-up, but I also recommend that you be aware of the pitfalls so that you can try to improve on your weak points from the very beginning.

Mind you, there is no point giving advice to these two. They already think they have things down to a tee. Be careful – what starts as a minor irritation now could turn into a major one in five years' time when it is too late to bring up your side of the story and both of you are getting set in your ways. Discuss worries at the outset, and you should make it to your golden anniversary. Libra loves the way that Sagittarius can constantly surprise and this adds to the mystery and keeps the fire well lit. This match should provide both partners with much happiness for many years to come.

LIBRA AND CAPRICORN

Many couples of this pairing have been to see me individually, neither letting onto the other. They usually ask why the other doesn't understand their needs, but they never bother to tell each other what those needs are. This is not the easiest match in the world. Capricorn can often dull Libra's light and take away the very thing that others find attractive. Libra finds it hard to be him- or herself around Capricorn, and spends a lot of time thinking before speaking, not an easy thing for an Air sign to do. However, they can look after each other, even mother each other. Libra requires something else though, so Capricorn is going to have to be both mother and lover to this romantic Air sign. Libra must try to give Capricorn more commitment. Libra doesn't mind asking for commitment but isn't so good at giving it to poor old goat.

What attracts these two to each other is a sense of mystery. Capricorn looks powerful to Libra, something Libra finds irresistible. However, to make this relationship work, they have to stop communicating from different levels and start seeing each other as equals. Then and only then will this duo begin to work out their love affair and make it something permanent. Capricorn's element is Earth, which can hold a great attraction to the Airy Libra, who dreams of building up a secure home and family (once they've had their fill of parties and excitement, of course). A piece of advice: speak to each other about your problems, not to other people. You could save yourself a lot of time, and you may even find the harmony that for two signs like you is such a priority.

LIBRA AND AQUARIUS

A great pair these two. Their relationship is based on laughter. They can get over any problem life presents so long as they have each other. They attract a lot of friends, for they hold court like the true entertainers they are. The matching of two Air signs is the meeting of two great minds. Sometimes they find it hard to agree with each other but mostly they lead a fulfilling and exciting life. Neither is frightened to experiment and both love to talk to people and discover new places and tastes. It is like finding out your best friend wants to be your lover, with the added bonus that you fancy each other like mad.

Watch out you don't get fat, you two. Your passionate natures make you passionate about foods when you get together and those pounds (or kilos, for the modern) have a tendency to pile on. Some people eat when they are brokenhearted, but cannot eat when they are in love. These two eat when they are in love. And they can eat equally as well as they can love.

For some reason Libra has difficulty trusting Aquarius. The seed of doubt is easily sown in Libra's mind. Aquarius does not keep secrets very well. Things Libra thought were private end up being public property. But there's no doubt that these two create magic. A lot of elements would love to create the sorcery that two Air signs can. They will fight for each other and never give up, creating a firm base that can withstand the greatest of storms. The only question is who is the boss. I don't think you'll ever find out. What one lacks the other makes up for, and balance is what life and love is all about. One to watch and learn by. Even on their bad days they will end up laughing with each other.

LIBRA AND PISCES

These two can have success but it is not guaranteed. Watching these two argue is like seeing masters at work. Both like to see how far they can push the other. They always back down in the end, and the making-up can be romantic, so much so that they can even begin arguments for fun.

They both want their independence and they both want to be together. This partnership is a strange one. The beautiful thing about it is that these two really want their relationship to work. And so it can, as long as fate doesn't intervene. They usually get together later in life. Libra has very often had a long-term relationship before ending up in the arms of beloved Pisces. Not an issue for Libra, who feels he or she has lived life to the full, is missing nothing and is able to give Pisces the commitment the fish craves. Pisces is a great romantic, and Libra is the king or queen of romance, so they can dance their nights away and talk sweet talk for years and years.

Pisces likes to be in control. Libra lets Pisces assume control, apart from in the bedroom, that is, where Libra likes to take the initiative as and when it suits. When you see these two together you may wonder what is going on. Does he really love her? Why was Libra flirting? Don't be deceived. Pitfalls – there are some, but only when one loses faith in the other, and that doesn't happen easily. This relationship isn't big enough for more than two and that includes in-laws. If these two want a future they must be prepared to give up the past. Not a pairing many astrologers recommend but it can and has worked.

SCORPIO AND SCORPIO

At first glance you'd think these two were crazy to be together. At second glance you'd notice just how very well suited they were. They both love to be looked after but they also long to dominate, so they give each other a bit of everything – a must for Scorpio, who hates to feel he or she has missed out on anything. No one knows who wears the trousers in the relationship. That's because one is in charge in some areas and the other is in charge in others. Simple really. Well, no, but they seem to manage it. An interesting combination, full of love one minute and hate the next, but they usually make it. They understand each other very well and stick together through thick and thin. Once they decide to commit to marriage they make it work, not just because of the love they feel for each other, but also because they hate the thought of failing.

Jealousy is a big problem. Each finds it acceptable to have friends who fancy them, while each finds it unacceptable for the partner to do the same. It's one rule for one, and another for the other. Never mind. They rarely keep to the rules anyway, and their sense of humour can help them out of most dilemmas.

They like to push things to the limit. They ought to be careful how they let off steam when they need to – they could end up in a police cell with their capacity for extreme behaviour. When they stay together they keep each other balanced. When good they are very good and when they want to be bad, they will fight and argue with the best of them.

Generous, masterful lovers, age improves them. This couple will still be kissing in public at eighty, and talking over the dinner table at home just like they did when they first met.

SCORPIO AND SAGITTARIUS

Scorpio quashes dear old Sagittarius's plans. It takes a strong Fire sign not to be extinguished by Water. A lot of compromising is necessary to make this one stick. Sagittarius must make allowances for Scorpio's quick temper and Scorpio must not get at Sagittarius for not always carrying out promises. They can, however, keep each other interested for years and years.

Scorpio has a tendency to belittle Sagittarius, but only because he or she is frightened of Sagittarius leaving. Scorpio remembers things that Sagittarius said in fun and brings them up in disputes. Scorpio dredges up past lovers of Sagittarius's to taunt the archer with.

Love comes thick and fast when these two meet but it can I'm afraid vanish in just as dramatic a fashion and they rarely stay friends afterwards. Sagittarius finds Scorpio sexy and Scorpio finds Sagittarius enigmatic. One of the biggest favours these two can do for each another is to learn to love each other for what each other is, and forget about checking that this and that promise was carried out or debt paid off. Does it matter? Start enjoying today. Be friends before you become lovers. Then let the love that you both really want have a chance to blossom.

SCORPIO AND CAPRICORN

A colourful couple, in every sense of the word: including their divergent taste in clothing. Scorpio is a little outlandish for conservative Capricorn, who secretly loves it but doesn't admit to it. These two don't quite know what to make of each other. They are likely to have fancied each other long before they did anything about it. Capricorn usually makes the first move: a quick one-liner and the rest is, as they say, history.

This is one relationship you can be sure will not be forgotten by either of them. It may not last for ever, but they have a significant effect on one another. Scorpio finds it difficult to take the lead. Capricorn believes he or she knows what is best for both of them. Scorpio doesn't mind being dominated, though might prefer it to be more covert. A slower pace would suit them both, before they lose themselves in the relationship and forget who they are as individuals.

Capricorn may not be exciting enough for Scorpio, who likes to live life close to the edge. Capricorn prefers a bit more predictability. They can work things out but each must stand his or her ground. Passion is good. In that respect this couple leaves nothing to be desired, and the bedroom is probably their favourite place to spend time together.

SCORPIO AND AQUARIUS

A difficult one this. They want to be together but are better friends than lovers. At first Scorpio sees Aquarius as a dizzy fool who talks rubbish. After a while Aquarius starts to work its allure. Once smitten, the scorpion strikes. Soon Scorpio has Aquarius just where he or she wants.

Scorpio lives out his or her dreams, where Aquarius prefers just to talk about them. This can be a good match, but it is not ideal. They know how to rub each other up the wrong way. Scorpio says things which Aquarius finds hard to forget, however they were meant. Quite a romantic duo but once the dust has settled they may find it hard to discover any real common ground. This is where all the hard work begins. These two have been known to have children in an attempt to make the relationship more stable – rarely a good idea. This relationship can work if both parties are willing to get over the hurdles and not to bring up problems time and time again, a habit both has. Love can win through. Think positive. Remember to listen when the other talks and you'll be halfway there. The best point about this duo is that they will always have something to talk about – and argue about too!

SCORPIO AND PISCES

These two know how to have fun. The more time they spend in each other's company the deeper the laughter gets. They talk about things most of us wouldn't even dare think about. This Watery partnership can work very well.

They need to progress with their union at the same

speed, avoiding the guessing games that are such a temptation. The main danger with two Water signs is that they have a tendency to jump in at the deep end. They need to try to savour the whole experience of being together, not just the dramatic parts. If these two decide to marry they will feel like they are still courting in twenty years' time, and not always for the best reasons. They do have a tendency to test each other. They fall out over little things, not big things. In the bad times they stick together like glue. Any doubt over faithfulness, however, and the betrayed partner is off in a flash.

They don't really understand each other that well. They have to learn to make allowances for each other's idiosyncrasies. Pisces gets upset at Scorpio's indecision and Scorpio gets annoyed at Pisces' wastefulness. Scorpio finds the smallest decisions hardest, such as what to make for dinner. Scorpio talks about making one dish and then serves up another. Pisces doesn't want to eat it.

Given a little faith and dedication, and the ability to ignore niggles, these two have enough common ground to be able to surmount problems. Their love tends to grow with each year that passes.

SAGITTARIUS AND SAGITTARIUS

When these two fall in love they don't know where one ends and the other begins. Life is not easy though. Money problems beset these two. They spend and spend hoping the other will say when it is time to stop, which of course he or she never does. They come up with great ideas but are not very good at taking them and running with them. Sometimes Fire needs the help of another element to make its ideas work.

These two have a harmonious relationship. They stay in love and can survive the troubles of life once they make the commitment, which they tend to make either extremely quickly or extremely slowly. They enjoy a good argument and don't take it too much to heart. They stay together through things that would split other people up. They love to get involved in what each other is doing, but together have trouble finishing what they started. Although not as common a union as you might think, they do have staying power. Difficulties are overcome together. They have the energy to satisfy each other physically and spend many a night content in each other's arms. They can gossip the night away too, about how they are going to do this and that with their lives.

A fun combination, but be careful that you don't become so similar that you get bored with each other's company. Keep going forwards and don't let your ideas and ambitions become stale. Make sure you both do what you say – don't let it be all talk.

SAGITTARIUS AND CAPRICORN

This relationship is often ignited in the workplace, and can be between a boss and an employee. What develops over time is trust, but just how much of a match are they? Well, these two can do just as good a job of annoying each other as they can of getting along. They need to be careful that the very things they love about each other do not become the things they hate too. Sagittarius will spend a lot of time trying to seduce Capricorn, who gets very high-minded about it all, wanting proof that this person is worthy before things get so personal. (That's why a lot of these unions are begun at work. The mutual respect is established first.) Unless, of course, Sagittarius is stunning and then Capricorn may make an exception.

Sagittarius has a wonderful ability to make his or her partner feel like there is nobody else in the world. The difficulty is that Sagittarius never believes that anyone could be as serious about the archer as the archer would like. Capricorn claims that Sagittarius cannot make room in his or her life for the demanding goat personality. If both parties would start talking to each other instead of to everyone else, the problems would be quickly solved.

Capricorn could do with relaxing a little. Who knows, the goat may just find itself having fun once it realizes the archer is its equal. These two must tell each other what they want and how they feel. Then they will find the love and trust that they both seek.

SAGITTARIUS AND AQUARIUS

These two make a lovely match, and don't take the word lovely to mean tame. These two are wild, and they know how to turn heads. They do not dress alike but each shows much style and grace and together they look stunning. They are not afraid of a good party, but are equally capable of creating a loving home and base. They get the best of both worlds when they join forces.

A hard couple to work out. They get very close to each other and then back away. This duo takes two steps forward and one step back. But they shouldn't give up. This is an interesting and worthy match. Aquarius loves to help Sagittarius and can carry the archer's dreams and desires to fruition. Sagittarius may get a little fed up with the hot air that Aquarius tends to blow from time to time, but sees enough action to make it worthwhile. They get on great, like a house on fire, apart from when they are fighting when they really will seem to be on fire.

One thing is for sure. If they listen to each other's advice and not that of friends, they can last the distance. If they involve others in their arguments they will soon be history. Pride will not let either one of these two back down when anyone else is watching. They should remember not to say things they don't mean. A fun and compatible pair for whom romance is likely to last well into old age, when they will still complement each other with their looks and dress sense.

SAGITTARIUS AND PISCES

These two can cause each other as much misery as happiness. They tend to carry on exactly as they started. If manners are thrown out of the window at the beginning, then their pet names for each other will be unspeakable in public. If they started off courteously, the sky is the limit and onlookers will envy the loving image they portray.

Fire and Water is a strange mix. Only when they are really in love will you see these two together. They don't toy with others for they know the consequences could be hard to handle. Pisces can be too dramatic and overbearing for Sagittarius, who doesn't mind having fun but doesn't share the longevity of Pisces. They get on great in the bedroom but the timing isn't always right.

Sagittarius has plenty of fun to offer Pisces and is sure to prove a worthy partner. But can they go the distance? If they can get past the rubbish they both talk and tell it like it is, then yes, but keep telling fairy tales and they will only have themselves to blame for the mess. The main appeal can be defiance. Family and friends don't expect these two to last and don't offer support, thereby creating a challenge.

Give it time and prove them wrong. You two know you can be good for each other. Just watch your finances. They can go up and down to the most dramatic levels.

CAPRICORN AND CAPRICORN

These two Earth signs are like two pigs in heaven. They bring out each other's best but they also make each other lazy. They set up home together, let down those Capricorn defences and wallow in love and comfort. They give each other the security that Earth signs crave. Marriages last for life and each is all the other needs.

These two get on brilliantly. However, rather more goat than pig in fact, they can butt heads. They banter rather than argue but can fall out over the smallest things. Both are stubborn. Petty disputes last for weeks, gaining an importance they do not deserve. They go through intense stages, and occasionally go in for dramatics, but the reality is that they are very much at home with one another. Call in unexpectedly and you won't find the smart Capricorn couple you know and love, but two overgrown kids. They may say they don't trust each other but they wouldn't be together if they didn't. Life and love are both too important for these two even to think about playing games. Both are career-orientated and so long as they have found their calling in life are likely to be truly happy. They help each other make full use of their abilities.

Love is on the cards for these two, and as long as they are together they will always have a good time.

CAPRICORN AND AQUARIUS

Not that common a combo. Only when they have known each other for a long time are they likely to become an item. Either that or it is an instant attraction. They need to know their feelings for each other are strong, and the only way to determine this is either to find out over a very long period of time, or else to experience fireworks on first meeting. Getting to know each other for a month or so and then deciding to go out is just too tame.

I'm afraid there's a bit of game-playing and a bit of pulling in opposing directions with these two. They want to stay together but every move they make tells the other it's not working. Opposites attract, and these two will end up in each other's arms if they want to. Airy Aquarius smoothtalks its way into Capricorn's heart. Capricorn thinks Aquarius is special, and readily invites him or her in. However, they delight in telling anyone who wants to listen what the other's bad points are. Don't lose faith too quickly. They like to shock us, whether by getting together or by moving apart.

Beware of getting into a rut, I advise you. Learn how to live with each other and celebrate your differences. After all, that's what love is all about.

CAPRICORN AND PISCES

These two are the envy of many. They know just how to be in love. I won't go into all of the details. Let's just say they both have every important relationship area covered. Differences? Well, there are a few. They can argue, both about money and about values. They need to get over their differences early on. If they don't see eye to eye after a year they ought to call it quits, and save both themselves and their friends and close ones a lot of earache.

Both like to work hard and play hard. They are more than capable of creating a successful personal and professional life together. They really can be the talk of the town. Everyone will want to know how clever Capricorn managed to tame wild Pisces and how Pisces managed to loosen up and seduce the very particular Capricorn. Passion for these two is constant. Neither hesitates in showing affection to the other, even when the whole world is looking on.

Work hard and you will stay together. Stop believing and you may as well throw in the towel. What this union requires is faith, from both of you. And remember to be honest with each other about money.

AQUARIUS AND AQUARIUS

This is a fairly public relationship. When they get together, everyone is informed, including the exes. They are not always the best influence on each other, but they have great fun. They can make the best of any bad situation. Each has found their equal.

Perhaps they are of too similar a character to get anything really constructive done with their lives. These two would rather spend their Sundays in bed than get up and do anything. This is all very well until it comes time to get important things in life done. That phone bill you were supposed to pay, did you? What about the shopping for tonight's dinner?

Listen up, you two. Your love can last for years but with the time you waste years are what you need. Then again, what better to waste your time on. The choice is yours. Don't expect to win any arguments. Each of you will go to any length to prove that you were right.

As for sex, I totally understand why neither of you wants to get out of bed on Sunday. You'll have plenty of friends and a great social life, and no need for jealousy. You have the capacity to be very happy indeed.

AQUARIUS AND PISCES

The attraction between these two is likely to have been instant and hot, sizzling in fact. They will have wanted to know everything about each other. But how did they fare after the first date? There is great excitement here but after a time one of them is going to have to give in and allow the other to be the leader. This, I'm afraid, is going to be a struggle.

They are strong characters and intelligent too. They both love the high life and have a great social time together. They don't mind wasting time so long as it is on fun things. It is hard to condemn such a union but the fact is that they don't give each other a lot of support, and each may have to look outside the relationship for stability. As much as these two can help each other, they can hinder each other too. Sex is great but the power struggle comes into play in the bedroom as well. Neither likes to relinquish control. If they can get through the first two years, there is great hope for this couple. Just keep out of their way for those first two years! They each have an addictive personality and may find their relationship becomes more of a habit than a choice.

Make the effort to communicate and to give each other support, and you could keep the flame alight.

PISCES AND PISCES

This union could imitate that of two movie stars. The twists and turns will be dramatic. These two could lead each other into bad ways, but they could lead each other into good ways too. I must give them their due and say go for it. They will have fun and, who knows, they may even find lasting romance. The stars are in their favour.

It may take these two a while to find each other but when they do they will find that they share many of the same types of friend and probably even have the same favourite restaurants. Longevity is not always a sure thing, however. There is such intensity here that these two probably jumped straight in at the deep end with not a thought for those they left behind. You've guessed it: they could have been living with someone or even married before they met but once the thunderbolt strikes there is no ignoring it. These two just have to give in to what their stars are telling them to do.

Sex is brilliant for these two and will keep them both coming back for more. Conversation is more than stimulating too and if not lovers these two can always be friends. They have a great base to build on and who knows where it could take them, given the right mood and setting.

Don't lead each other into much mischief. Think constructive and life will be constructive. Think mischief and you'll find it before you can blink. Remember: keep focused on the good life and it will be yours, but give in to your whims and who knows where your heavenly union will end up.

The Saturn Return

THERE COME TIMES in our lives when we need a change, perhaps to establish roots, get married, have children, or perhaps to leave the partner we no longer feel we are meant to grow old with. You may have thought that this was just life and the changes it throws upon us by chance, but it is in fact the work of the planets, particularly Saturn, known as the Prince of Time.

Just as animals know when to hibernate and flowers know when to bud, so we know – thanks to the invisible prompting of the planets – when we should move onto the next important stage of our life. Between the ages of twenty-eight and thirty, fifty-eight and sixty, and again, if we're lucky enough to reach our late eighties, the ages of eighty-six to eighty-eight, we experience what is called in astrological terms our Saturn Return. These are the times when our self-development takes a great leap forward, though the process is not always an easy one. You may already know that this planet is most commonly called the Great Teacher. I have had many a person walk into my boutique for a reading with 'Saturn Return' written all over his or her face. The poor old souls have no idea at all why they have reached a critical point; why she has finally tired of the man who has been hitting her, or why he has decided to stop letting his woman take him for a ride with his money while seeing his best friend behind his back. Oh yes, Saturn Return people give me far more of a story than any *Jerry Springer Show* could. Women who are going through this experience often change their hair colour or style dramatically. If you look around you at people in their thirties, you will see that they are usually living out the decisions they made between the ages of twenty-eight and thirty. This is when they got married, had their children, or decided to go independent in business.

The first Saturn Return, between the ages of twenty-eight and thirty, is the most dramatic. This is when we leave youth behind and enter adulthood. The things we can do both shock and please us but also bring us into the reality of life. Before this age you are likely only ever to have talked about what you are going to do, but your Saturn Return brings the movies right into your living room. This can be quite a daunting experience as you make decisions that are sure to surprise those around you, but these decisions can be of great benefit to your future.

The second Saturn Return, between the ages of fifty-eight and sixty, is when we leave behind the preoccupations of the adult world to become mature senior men and women. Once again we make decisions that benefit our current situation, and perhaps even go for a change of image with our hair or clothes. You know when you look at someone and think that they don't look young any more but instead look like a really responsible mature older person? They've probably just gone through their second Saturn Return, so congratulate them.

The third Saturn Return between the ages of eighty-six and eighty-eight is when we become very wise old souls indeed, and is when other people start to turn to us for advice and guidance rather than covering their ears when we speak.

MY FIRST TIME ROUND

My experience of a Saturn Return is a prime example indeed. I had been travelling along happily with a nice life and a nice husband and a few nice bits of work but as soon as my Saturn Return hit I had this incredible urge to have children. My life suddenly no longer had meaning without a son or daughter to share it with. Spotting an advantageous time in my chart I convinced my husband Rob that we should start trying immediately. To our surprise two weeks later I fell pregnant with our son Paris. As if that wasn't enough I went from writing for a magazine and a few regionals to writing for two national daily newspapers, the *Express* and the *Star*, *OK!* magazine, *Company* magazine, over seventy regionals, and then proceeded to write another book: this one! And I felt I had to tell people through my writing the importance of astrology and relationships. My appetite for life was insatiable and all of the things I have a passion for – my home, my family, my career – became my focus. I didn't care about going out, I was more interested in making our home perfect. We knocked through our bedroom to make one big room and it was so good that *House Beautiful* came to photograph it. Our son is perfect and the joy of our life. I sadly hear about people getting postnatal depression but I was lucky enough not to have any such problem. My Saturn Return saw me cementing the things I already had and building up other important things on them. However, I could just as easily have given up the marriage and career I had if they were not right for me.

My calling in life was already there and my Saturn Return helped me to go even further with it. I am looking forward to a little bit of a rest now until the second Saturn Return, and to enjoying the pleasures the first Return has placed in my life.

GOOD OR BAD?

Saturn is the second largest planet in our solar system; Jupiter is the biggest. Saturn has three main rings but hundreds and maybe even thousands of smaller ones made up of ice and rock that swirl around the planet. It also has twelve moons, the largest of which is Titan. Many astrologers say that Saturn is bad news but I can't agree with that. Like the planet Mars, Saturn was once an agricultural god. He presided over Saturnalia, a great feast and public holiday which was later adopted by the Christians and renamed Christmas. So there must be a good side to him, don't you think? Even a bad planet can lead us to do good things. Saturn makes major events occur in our careers and our relationships, which bring about a change in our attitudes and cause us to take new directions that can change the entire shape of our lives.

Although Saturn can make us cold, aloof and selfish, it can also help us with perseverance and determination, without which we could not achieve many of our goals or make the changes we desire. It helps us practically and spiritually to prepare for the end of an important cycle in our life and to start a new one. For some this could mean a new addition to the family, for others the ending of a relationship. It could be the beginning of a new career or even a proposal to the person we realize we want to stay with. Women, in particular, are prone to do some pretty crazy things, such as dye their hair new colours. My husband, Rob, owns a hair salon and I get him to check the ages of the women who come in asking for dramatic changes to their appearance. It's never a surprise to find that many of them are in their first, second or even third Saturn Returns.

Let's take a look at some famous examples.

Saturn Calling

Jesus Christ found his calling at twenty-eight and although this example is a rather showy one of me to use, it is a good one and a just one.

Saturn Career Changes

Taurus Prime Minister Tony Blair was elected MP for Sedgefield on 9 June 1983 at the age of thirty and his

Saturn Return eventually took him right to the door of Downing Street.

Cancer George Michael really did make a life-changing decision as this extract from the *Independent* proves:

> People told him he would be wasting his time, but singer George Michael called the meeting anyway. At 10.30 a.m. on 26th October 1992, the 28-year-old pop star rode the lift to the 43rd floor of the Sony headquarters in Manhattan and walked into a room for the biggest confrontation of his career. He shook hands with the three Sony executives in the office – Paul Russell, chairman of Sony Music Entertainment UK, Michael Schulhof, head of Sony's operations in the United States, and Norio Ohga, Sony's world president. Then he began to speak. He wanted a divorce from his record company. He explained that he would provide Sony with no more albums, despite being contracted to record six in the next 10 years. He told them he had no confidence in the ability of the Japanese company to understand the creative process. He felt he had been transformed from someone who was viewed as a long-term artist to 'little more than software'.

There he was, twenty-eight years old, one of the most successful and wealthy pop singers in the world, telling Sony that they were ruining his career.

Leo singer and actress Jennifer Lopez left her long-time boyfriend, Singer Puff Daddy, when she was thirty. She learnt that they were destined to be friends, and this was also the time that she launched her solo singing career and found success in the charts on both sides of the Atlantic. She had found her true calling. A few years ago her public had only ever seen her as an actress, and a very good one, but Jennifer claims that singing had always been her true dream and she followed it, pushed on by her Saturn Return.

Saturn Babies

Cancer Pamela Anderson had her baby at twenty-eight and if you have seen any footage of her as a mum you will see that she adores her children. This was a meaningful and important turning point in her life.

Libra Catherine Zeta Jones had her first child and married her husband of the same sign, Michael Douglas, at thirty.

Scorpio Luciana Morad became pregnant by Rolling Stone Mick Jagger at twenty-nine and had his love child.

Taurus Patsy Palmer became pregnant twice during her Saturn Return.

Cancer Emma Noble had her first child at twenty-eight.

Pisces Patsy Kensit had baby Lennon at age twenty-eight and then left her husband, Oasis singer Liam Gallagher.

Wherever or however your Saturn Return affects you, enjoy it. Remember that it will help your life, not hinder it, and if sometimes that means throwing out the old and getting on with the new then so be it. Go along with Saturn and the journey it wants to take you on. Be optimistic. Your destination is worth reaching.

COMPATIBILITY CHARTS

SUN SIGN MATCHES

Table One: Harmony

Person 2

	Aries	Taurus	Gemini	Cancer	Leo	Virgo	Libra	Scorpio	Sagittarius	Capricorn	Aquarius	Pisces
Pisces	3	9	3	10	3	8	5	9	2	9	4	10
Aquarius	5	3	9	2	7	5	10	3	7	4	10	
Capricorn	4	9	4	10	3	10	4	10	2	10		
Sagittarius	7	3	8	2	10	3	8	4	9			
Scorpio	7	9	4	8	4	9	4	9				
Libra	8	4	10	3	8	5	10					
Virgo	2	9	4	9	4	10						
Leo	10	3	9	2	10							
Cancer	3	8	2	9								
Gemini	6	2	10									
Taurus	3	9										
Aries	9											

Person 1

SUN SIGN MATCHES

Table Two: Loyalty

Person 2

Person 1	Aries	Taurus	Gemini	Cancer	Leo	Virgo	Libra	Scorpio	Sagittarius	Capricorn	Aquarius	Pisces
Pisces	3	6	2	10	3	7	3	10	4	2	3	10
Aquarius	4	3	9	4	6	4	10	4	6	3	10	
Capricorn	3	10	4	7	2	10	5	9	4	10		
Sagittarius	10	4	5	3	10	5	7	2	10			
Scorpio	5	8	3	10	4	9	3	10				
Libra	6	4	10	4	7	4	10					
Virgo	5	10	3	7	2	10						
Leo	9	2	3	2	10							
Cancer	3	7	2	10								
Gemini	2	2	10									
Taurus	3	10										
Aries	5											

SUN SIGN MATCHES

Table Three: Home Life

	Aries	Taurus	Gemini	Cancer	Leo	Virgo	Libra	Scorpio	Sagittarius	Capricorn	Aquarius	Pisces
Pisces	6	6	7	10	5	6	6	9	6	6	5	9
Aquarius	7	3	10	3	3	5	10	3	6	4	10	
Capricorn	2	9	4	5	3	10	5	6	4	10		
Sagittarius	10	4	6	1	10	3	3	4	10			
Scorpio	8	9	6	10	8	3	5	9				
Libra	8	5	10	5	4	3	10					
Virgo	4	10	4	5	4	8						
Leo	9	4	6	3	8							
Cancer	4	3	2	9								
Gemini	7	3	10									
Taurus	2	10										
Aries	9											

Person 1

Person 2

SUN SIGN MATCHES

Table Four: Excitement

Person 2

	Aries	Taurus	Gemini	Cancer	Leo	Virgo	Libra	Scorpio	Sagittarius	Capricorn	Aquarius	Pisces
Pisces	4	7	8	10	7	6	5	10	3	3	4	10
Aquarius	2	3	10	3	5	7	10	5	8	2	9	
Capricorn	3	9	4	7	4	9	3	3	10	8		
Sagittarius	10	4	7	5	10	2	7	2	10			
Scorpio	9	9	7	10	4	6	5	10				
Libra	5	8	10	3	6	4	9					
Virgo	3	9	2	6	4	10						
Leo	9	6	7	3	9							
Cancer	4	2	2	7								
Gemini	9	3	10									
Taurus	2	7										
Aries	10											

Person 1

SUN SIGN MATCHES

Table Five: Overall Compatibility scores for sun signs

Person 2

	Aries	Taurus	Gemini	Cancer	Leo	Virgo	Libra	Scorpio	Sagittarius	Capricorn	Aquarius	Pisces
Pisces	4	7	5	10	5	7	5	10	4	5	4	10
Aquarius	5	3	10	3	5	5	10	4	7	3	7	
Capricorn	3	9	4	7	3	10	4	7	5	10		
Sagittarius	9	4	7	3	10	3	6	3	10			
Scorpio	7	9	5	10	5	7	4	10				
Libra	7	5	10	4	6	4	10					
Virgo	4	10	3	7	4	10						
Leo	9	4	6	3	9							
Cancer	4	5	2	9								
Gemini	6	3	10									
Taurus	3	9										
Aries	8											

Person 1

MOON SIGN MATCHES

Table One: Harmony

Person 2

Person 1	Aries	Taurus	Gemini	Cancer	Leo	Virgo	Libra	Scorpio	Sagittarius	Capricorn	Aquarius	Pisces
Pisces	10	5	10	10	8	10	9	10	8	8	8	10
Aquarius	10	9	10	9	8	9	10	6	10	4	10	
Capricorn	9	10	4	8	10	4	5	10	9	5		
Sagittarius	9	5	9	4	10	6	10	10	10			
Scorpio	7	10	10	10	7	7	5	10				
Libra	8	4	10	5	6	4	8					
Virgo	10	10	6	4	10	8						
Leo	4	6	7	7	10							
Cancer	4	6	10	10								
Gemini	8	8	10									
Taurus	6	8										
Aries	10											

MOON SIGN MATCHES

Table Two: Loyalty

Person 2

	Aries	Taurus	Gemini	Cancer	Leo	Virgo	Libra	Scorpio	Sagittarius	Capricorn	Aquarius	Pisces
Pisces	5	8	4	10	5	9	5	10	6	4	5	10
Aquarius	6	5	10	6	8	6	10	6	8	5	10	
Capricorn	5	10	6	9	4	10	7	10	6	10		
Sagittarius	10	6	7	5	10	7	9	4	10			
Scorpio	7	10	5	10	6	10	5	10				
Libra	8	6	10	6	9	6	10					
Virgo	7	10	5	9	4	10						
Leo	10	4	5	4	10							
Cancer	5	9	4	10								
Gemini	4	4	10									
Taurus	5	10										
Aries	7											

Person 1

MOON SIGN MATCHES

Table Three: Home Life

	Aries	Taurus	Gemini	Cancer	Leo	Virgo	Libra	Scorpio	Sagittarius	Capricorn	Aquarius	Pisces
Pisces	8	8	9	10	7	8	8	10	8	8	7	10
Aquarius	9	5	10	5	5	7	10	5	8	6	10	
Capricorn	4	10	6	7	5	10	7	8	6	10		
Sagittarius	10	6	8	3	10	5	5	6	10			
Scorpio	10	10	8	10	10	5	7	10				
Libra	10	7	10	7	6	5	10					
Virgo	6	10	6	7	6	10						
Leo	10	6	8	5	10							
Cancer	6	5	4	10								
Gemini	9	5	10									
Taurus	4	10										
Aries	10											

Person 1

Person 2

MOON SIGN MATCHES

Table Four: Excitement

Person 2

Person 1	Aries	Taurus	Gemini	Cancer	Leo	Virgo	Libra	Scorpio	Sagittarius	Capricorn	Aquarius	Pisces
Pisces	6	9	8	10	9	8	7	10	5	5	6	10
Aquarius	4	5	10	5	7	9	10	7	10	4	10	
Capricorn	5	10	6	9	6	10	5	5	10	10		
Sagittarius	10	6	9	7	10	4	9	4	10			
Scorpio	10	10	9	10	6	8	7	10				
Libra	7	10	10	5	8	6	10					
Virgo	5	10	4	8	6	10						
Leo	10	8	9	5	10							
Cancer	6	4	4	9								
Gemini	10	5	10									
Taurus	4	9										
Aries	10											

Person 1

MOON SIGN MATCHES

Table Five: Overall Compatibility scores for moon signs

	Aries	Taurus	Gemini	Cancer	Leo	Virgo	Libra	Scorpio	Sagittarius	Capricorn	Aquarius	Pisces
Pisces	7	8	8	10	7	9	7	10	7	6	7	10
Aquarius	7	6	10	6	7	8	10	6	9	5	10	
Capricorn	6	10	6	8	6	9	6	8	8	9		
Sagittarius	10	6	8	5	10	6	8	6	10			
Scorpio	9	10	8	10	7	8	6	10				
Libra	8	7	10	6	7	5	10					
Virgo	7	10	5	7	7	10						
Leo	9	6	7	5	10							
Cancer	5	6	6	10								
Gemini	8	6	10									
Taurus	5	9										
Aries	9											

Person 1 (columns) / Person 2 (rows)

Sun Sign and
Moon Sign Tables

IF YOUR BIRTHDAY falls on the cusp – or 'changeover' date between two signs – then you will need to use the Sun Sign Tables that follow starting on page 435 to check exactly when the signs changed over in the year of your birth, to find out your dominant sign.

If you find no listing for your date of birth, the entry relating to the nearest date before yours applies.

Earlier in the book I discussed moon signs – the sign the moon is in at the time of your birth, which can dictate certain dominant traits in your personality and your health. To find out your moon sign simply look up the year and month of your birth in the Moon Sign Tables starting on page 443. If you find no listing for your actual date of birth, then the sign the moon is in on the date shown in the list preceding your birthday prevails.

These tables are based on Greenwich Mean Time and take into account British Summer Time year by year where appropriate. They are based on the Geocentric Tropical Zodiac. If you were born else-where, work out the British equivalent to your time of birth by adding or subtracting the appropriate number of hours for a rough indication of your moon sign, or indeed your sun sign if you were born on the cusp. However, the positioning of the stars does vary according to geographical location, so you would be best advised to consult a full ephemeris with information relevant to your birthplace for more accurate information, or to consult an astrologer personally. There are several ephemerides and astrological advice sites on the internet: www.msp-online.com will be able to tailor a chart for you.

1920–31

Aqu	21 Jan 1920	Aqu	21 Jan 1924	Aqu	21 Jan 1928
Pis	19 Feb 1920	Pis	19 Feb 1924	Pis	19 Feb 1928
Ari	20 Mar 1920	Ari	20 Mar 1924	Ari	20 Mar 1928
Tau	20 Apr 1920	Tau	20 Apr 1924	Tau	20 Apr 1928
Gem	21 May 1920	Gem	21 May 1924	Gem	21 May 1928
Can	21 Jun 1920	Can	21 Jun 1924	Can	21 Jun 1928
Leo	23 Jul 1920	Leo	23 Jul 1924	Leo	23 Jul 1928
Vir	23 Aug 1920	Vir	23 Aug 1924	Vir	23 Aug 1928
Lib	23 Sep 1920	Lib	23 Sep 1924	Lib	23 Sep 1928
Sco	23 Oct 1920	Sco	23 Oct 1924	Sco	23 Oct 1928
Sag	22 Nov 1920	Sag	22 Nov 1924	Sag	22 Nov 1928
Cap	22 Dec 1920	Cap	22 Dec 1924	Cap	22 Dec 1928
Aqu	20 Jan 1921	Aqu	20 Jan 1925	Aqu	20 Jan 1929
Pis	19 Feb 1921	Pis	19 Feb 1925	Pis	19 Feb 1929
Ari	21 Mar 1921	Ari	21 Mar 1925	Ari	21 Mar 1929
Tau	20 Apr 1921	Tau	20 Apr 1925	Tau	20 Apr 1929
Gem	21 May 1921	Gem	21 May 1925	Gem	21 May 1929
Can	21 Jun 1921	Can	21 Jun 1925	Can	21 Jun 1929
Leo	23 Jul 1921	Leo	23 Jul 1925	Leo	23 Jul 1929
Vir	23 Aug 1921	Vir	23 Aug 1925	Vir	23 Aug 1929
Lib	23 Sep 1921	Lib	23 Sep 1925	Lib	23 Sep 1929
Sco	23 Oct 1921	Sco	23 Oct 1925	Sco	23 Oct 1929
Sag	22 Nov 1921	Sag	22 Nov 1925	Sag	22 Nov 1929
Cap	22 Dec 1921	Cap	22 Dec 1925	Cap	22 Dec 1929
Aqu	20 Jan 1922	Aqu	20 Jan 1926	Aqu	20 Jan 1930
Pis	19 Feb 1922	Pis	19 Feb 1926	Pis	19 Feb 1930
Ari	21 Mar 1922	Ari	21 Mar 1926	Ari	21 Mar 1930
Tau	20 Apr 1922	Tau	20 Apr 1926	Tau	20 Apr 1930
Gem	21 May 1922	Gem	21 May 1926	Gem	21 May 1930
Can	22 Jun 1922	Can	22 Jun 1926	Can	22 Jun 1930
Leo	23 Jul 1922	Leo	23 Jul 1926	Leo	23 Jul 1930
Vir	23 Aug 1922	Vir	23 Aug 1926	Vir	23 Aug 1930
Lib	23 Sep 1922	Lib	23 Sep 1926	Lib	23 Sep 1930
Sco	24 Oct 1922	Sco	24 Oct 1926	Sco	24 Oct 1930
Sag	23 Nov 1922	Sag	23 Nov 1926	Sag	23 Nov 1930
Cap	22 Dec 1922	Cap	22 Dec 1926	Cap	22 Dec 1930
Aqu	21 Jan 1923	Aqu	21 Jan 1927	Aqu	21 Jan 1931
Pis	19 Feb 1923	Pis	19 Feb 1927	Pis	19 Feb 1931
Ari	21 Mar 1923	Ari	21 Mar 1927	Ari	21 Mar 1931
Tau	21 Apr 1923	Tau	21 Apr 1927	Tau	21 Apr 1931
Gem	22 May 1923	Gem	22 May 1927	Gem	22 May 1931
Can	22 Jun 1923	Can	22 Jun 1927	Can	22 Jun 1931
Leo	23 Jul 1923	Leo	23 Jul 1927	Leo	23 Jul 1931
Vir	24 Aug 1923	Vir	24 Aug 1927	Vir	24 Aug 1931
Lib	24 Sep 1923	Lib	24 Sep 1927	Lib	24 Sep 1931
Sco	24 Oct 1923	Sco	24 Oct 1927	Sco	24 Oct 1931
Sag	23 Nov 1923	Sag	23 Nov 1927	Sag	23 Nov 1931
Cap	22 Dec 1923	Cap	22 Dec 1927	Cap	22 Dec 1931

1932–43

Aqu	21 Jan 1932	Aqu	21 Jan 1936	Aqu	21 Jan 1940
Pis	19 Feb 1932	Pis	19 Feb 1936	Pis	19 Feb 1940
Ari	20 Mar 1932	Ari	20 Mar 1936	Ari	20 Mar 1940
Tau	20 Apr 1932	Tau	20 Apr 1936	Tau	20 Apr 1940
Gem	21 May 1932	Gem	21 May 1936	Gem	21 May 1940
Can	21 Jun 1932	Can	21 Jun 1936	Can	21 Jun 1940
Leo	23 Jul 1932	Leo	23 Jul 1936	Leo	23 Jul 1940
Vir	23 Aug 1932	Vir	23 Aug 1936	Vir	23 Aug 1940
Lib	23 Sep 1932	Lib	23 Sep 1936	Lib	23 Sep 1940
Sco	23 Oct 1932	Sco	23 Oct 1936	Sco	23 Oct 1940
Sag	22 Nov 1932	Sag	22 Nov 1936	Sag	22 Nov 1940
Cap	22 Dec 1932	Cap	22 Dec 1936	Cap	21 Dec 1940
Aqu	20 Jan 1933	Aqu	20 Jan 1937	Aqu	20 Jan 1941
Pis	19 Feb 1933	Pis	19 Feb 1937	Pis	19 Feb 1941
Ari	21 Mar 1933	Ari	21 Mar 1937	Ari	21 Mar 1941
Tau	20 Apr 1933	Tau	20 Apr 1937	Tau	20 Apr 1941
Gem	21 May 1933	Gem	21 May 1937	Gem	21 May 1941
Can	21 Jun 1933	Can	21 Jun 1937	Can	21 Jun 1941
Leo	23 Jul 1933	Leo	23 Jul 1937	Leo	23 Jul 1941
Vir	23 Aug 1933	Vir	23 Aug 1937	Vir	23 Aug 1941
Lib	23 Sep 1933	Lib	23 Sep 1937	Lib	23 Sep 1941
Sco	23 Oct 1933	Sco	23 Oct 1937	Sco	23 Oct 1941
Sag	22 Nov 1933	Sag	22 Nov 1937	Sag	22 Nov 1941
Cap	22 Dec 1933	Cap	22 Dec 1937	Cap	22 Dec 1941
Aqu	20 Jan 1934	Aqu	20 Jan 1938	Aqu	20 Jan 1942
Pis	19 Feb 1934	Pis	19 Feb 1938	Pis	19 Feb 1942
Ari	21 Mar 1934	Ari	21 Mar 1938	Ari	21 Mar 1942
Tau	20 Apr 1934	Tau	20 Apr 1938	Tau	20 Apr 1942
Gem	21 May 1934	Gem	21 May 1938	Gem	21 May 1942
Can	22 Jun 1934	Can	22 Jun 1938	Can	22 Jun 1942
Leo	23 Jul 1934	Leo	23 Jul 1938	Leo	23 Jul 1942
Vir	23 Aug 1934	Vir	23 Aug 1938	Vir	23 Aug 1942
Lib	23 Sep 1934	Lib	23 Sep 1938	Lib	23 Sep 1942
Sco	24 Oct 1934	Sco	24 Oct 1938	Sco	24 Oct 1942
Sag	22 Nov 1934	Sag	22 Nov 1938	Sag	22 Nov 1942
Cap	22 Dec 1934	Cap	22 Dec 1938	Cap	22 Dec 1942
Aqu	20 Jan 1935	Aqu	20 Jan 1939	Aqu	20 Jan 1943
Pis	19 Feb 1935	Pis	19 Feb 1939	Pis	19 Feb 1943
Ari	21 Mar 1935	Ari	21 Mar 1939	Ari	21 Mar 1943
Tau	21 Apr 1935	Tau	21 Apr 1939	Tau	20 Apr 1943
Gem	22 May 1935	Gem	21 May 1939	Gem	21 May 1943
Can	22 Jun 1935	Can	22 Jun 1939	Can	22 Jun 1943
Leo	23 Jul 1935	Leo	23 Jul 1939	Leo	23 Jul 1943
Vir	24 Aug 1935	Vir	24 Aug 1939	Vir	24 Aug 1943
Lib	23 Sep 1935	Lib	23 Sep 1939	Lib	23 Sep 1943
Sco	24 Oct 1935	Sco	24 Oct 1939	Sco	24 Oct 1943
Sag	23 Nov 1935	Sag	23 Nov 1939	Sag	23 Nov 1943
Cap	22 Dec 1935	Cap	22 Dec 1939	Cap	22 Dec 1943

1944–55

Aqu	21 Jan 1944	Aqu	21 Jan 1948	Aqu	21 Jan 1952
Pis	19 Feb 1944	Pis	19 Feb 1948	Pis	19 Feb 1952
Ari	20 Mar 1944	Ari	20 Mar 1948	Ari	20 Mar 1952
Tau	20 Apr 1944	Tau	20 Apr 1948	Tau	20 Apr 1952
Gem	21 May 1944	Gem	21 May 1948	Gem	21 May 1952
Can	21 Jun 1944	Can	21 Jun 1948	Can	21 Jun 1952
Leo	22 Jul 1944	Leo	22 Jul 1948	Leo	22 Jul 1952
Vir	23 Aug 1944	Vir	23 Aug 1948	Vir	23 Aug 1952
Lib	23 Sep 1944	Lib	23 Sep 1948	Lib	23 Sep 1952
Sco	23 Oct 1944	Sco	23 Oct 1948	Sco	23 Oct 1952
Sag	22 Nov 1944	Sag	22 Nov 1948	Sag	22 Nov 1952
Cap	21 Dec 1944	Cap	21 Dec 1948	Cap	21 Dec 1952
Aqu	20 Jan 1945	Aqu	20 Jan 1949	Aqu	20 Jan 1953
Pis	19 Feb 1945	Pis	18 Feb 1949	Pis	18 Feb 1953
Ari	20 Mar 1945	Ari	20 Mar 1949	Ari	20 Mar 1953
Tau	20 Apr 1945	Tau	20 Apr 1949	Tau	20 Apr 1953
Gem	21 May 1945	Gem	21 May 1949	Gem	21 May 1953
Can	21 Jun 1945	Can	21 Jun 1949	Can	21 Jun 1953
Leo	23 Jul 1945	Leo	23 Jul 1949	Leo	23 Jul 1953
Vir	23 Aug 1945	Vir	23 Aug 1949	Vir	23 Aug 1953
Lib	23 Sep 1945	Lib	23 Sep 1949	Lib	23 Sep 1953
Sco	23 Oct 1945	Sco	23 Oct 1949	Sco	23 Oct 1953
Sag	22 Nov 1945	Sag	22 Nov 1949	Sag	22 Nov 1953
Cap	22 Dec 1945	Cap	22 Dec 1949	Cap	22 Dec 1953
Aqu	20 Jan 1946	Aqu	20 Jan 1950	Aqu	20 Jan 1954
Pis	19 Feb 1946	Pis	19 Feb 1950	Pis	19 Feb 1954
Ari	21 Mar 1946	Ari	21 Mar 1950	Ari	21 Mar 1954
Tau	20 Apr 1946	Tau	20 Apr 1950	Tau	20 Apr 1954
Gem	21 May 1946	Gem	21 May 1950	Gem	21 May 1954
Can	22 Jun 1946	Can	21 Jun 1950	Can	21 Jun 1954
Leo	23 Jul 1946	Leo	23 Jul 1950	Leo	23 Jul 1954
Vir	23 Aug 1946	Vir	23 Aug 1950	Vir	23 Aug 1954
Lib	23 Sep 1946	Lib	23 Sep 1950	Lib	23 Sep 1954
Sco	24 Oct 1946	Sco	23 Oct 1950	Sco	23 Oct 1954
Sag	22 Nov 1946	Sag	22 Nov 1950	Sag	22 Nov 1954
Cap	22 Dec 1946	Cap	22 Dec 1950	Cap	22 Dec 1954
Aqu	20 Jan 1947	Aqu	20 Jan 1951	Aqu	20 Jan 1955
Pis	19 Feb 1947	Pis	19 Feb 1951	Pis	19 Feb 1955
Ari	21 Mar 1947	Ari	21 Mar 1951	Ari	21 Mar 1955
Tau	20 Apr 1947	Tau	20 Apr 1951	Tau	20 Apr 1955
Gem	21 May 1947	Gem	21 May 1951	Gem	21 May 1955
Can	22 Jun 1947	Can	22 Jun 1951	Can	22 Jun 1955
Leo	23 Jul 1947	Leo	23 Jul 1951	Leo	23 Jul 1955
Vir	24 Aug 1947	Vir	23 Aug 1951	Vir	23 Aug 1955
Lib	23 Sep 1947	Lib	23 Sep 1951	Lib	23 Sep 1955
Sco	24 Oct 1947	Sco	24 Oct 1951	Sco	24 Oct 1955
Sag	23 Nov 1947	Sag	23 Nov 1951	Sag	23 Nov 1955
Cap	22 Dec 1947	Cap	22 Dec 1951	Cap	22 Dec 1955

1956–67

Aqu	21 Jan 1956	Aqu	21 Jan 1960	Aqu	21 Jan 1964
Pis	19 Feb 1956	Pis	19 Feb 1960	Pis	19 Feb 1964
Ari	20 Mar 1956	Ari	20 Mar 1960	Ari	20 Mar 1964
Tau	20 Apr 1956	Tau	20 Apr 1960	Tau	20 Apr 1964
Gem	21 May 1956	Gem	21 May 1960	Gem	21 May 1964
Can	21 Jun 1956	Can	21 Jun 1960	Can	21 Jun 1964
Leo	22 Jul 1956	Leo	22 Jul 1960	Leo	22 Jul 1964
Vir	23 Aug 1956	Vir	23 Aug 1960	Vir	23 Aug 1964
Lib	23 Sep 1956	Lib	23 Sep 1960	Lib	23 Sep 1964
Sco	23 Oct 1956	Sco	23 Oct 1960	Sco	23 Oct 1964
Sag	22 Nov 1956	Sag	22 Nov 1960	Sag	22 Nov 1964
Cap	21 Dec 1956	Cap	21 Dec 1960	Cap	21 Dec 1964
Aqu	20 Jan 1957	Aqu	20 Jan 1961	Aqu	20 Jan 1965
Pis	18 Feb 1957	Pis	18 Feb 1961	Pis	18 Feb 1965
Ari	20 Mar 1957	Ari	20 Mar 1961	Ari	20 Mar 1965
Tau	20 Apr 1957	Tau	20 Apr 1961	Tau	20 Apr 1965
Gem	21 May 1957	Gem	21 May 1961	Gem	21 May 1965
Can	21 Jun 1957	Can	21 Jun 1961	Can	21 Jun 1965
Leo	23 Jul 1957	Leo	23 Jul 1961	Leo	23 Jul 1965
Vir	23 Aug 1957	Vir	23 Aug 1961	Vir	23 Aug 1965
Lib	23 Sep 1957	Lib	23 Sep 1961	Lib	23 Sep 1965
Sco	23 Oct 1957	Sco	23 Oct 1961	Sco	23 Oct 1965
Sag	22 Nov 1957	Sag	22 Nov 1961	Sag	22 Nov 1965
Cap	22 Dec 1957	Cap	22 Dec 1961	Cap	22 Dec 1965
Aqu	20 Jan 1958	Aqu	20 Jan 1962	Aqu	20 Jan 1966
Pis	19 Feb 1958	Pis	19 Feb 1962	Pis	19 Feb 1966
Ari	21 Mar 1958	Ari	21 Mar 1962	Ari	21 Mar 1966
Tau	20 Apr 1958	Tau	20 Apr 1962	Tau	20 Apr 1966
Gem	21 May 1958	Gem	21 May 1962	Gem	21 May 1966
Can	21 Jun 1958	Can	21 Jun 1962	Can	21 Jun 1966
Leo	23 Jul 1958	Leo	23 Jul 1962	Leo	23 Jul 1966
Vir	23 Aug 1958	Vir	23 Aug 1962	Vir	23 Aug 1966
Lib	23 Sep 1958	Lib	23 Sep 1962	Lib	23 Sep 1966
Sco	23 Oct 1958	Sco	23 Oct 1962	Sco	23 Oct 1966
Sag	22 Nov 1958	Sag	22 Nov 1962	Sag	22 Nov 1966
Cap	22 Dec 1958	Cap	22 Dec 1962	Cap	22 Dec 1966
Aqu	20 Jan 1959	Aqu	20 Jan 1963	Aqu	20 Jan 1967
Pis	19 Feb 1959	Pis	19 Feb 1963	Pis	19 Feb 1967
Ari	21 Mar 1959	Ari	21 Mar 1963	Ari	21 Mar 1967
Tau	20 Apr 1959	Tau	20 Apr 1963	Tau	20 Apr 1967
Gem	21 May 1959	Gem	21 May 1963	Gem	21 May 1967
Can	22 Jun 1959	Can	22 Jun 1963	Can	22 Jun 1967
Leo	23 Jul 1959	Leo	23 Jul 1963	Leo	23 Jul 1967
Vir	23 Aug 1959	Vir	23 Aug 1963	Vir	23 Aug 1967
Lib	23 Sep 1959	Lib	23 Sep 1963	Lib	23 Sep 1967
Sco	24 Oct 1959	Sco	24 Oct 1963	Sco	24 Oct 1967
Sag	23 Nov 1959	Sag	23 Nov 1963	Sag	22 Nov 1967
Cap	22 Dec 1959	Cap	22 Dec 1963	Cap	22 Dec 1967

1968–79

Aqu	20 Jan 1968	Aqu	20 Jan 1972	Aqu	20 Jan 1976
Pis	19 Feb 1968	Pis	19 Feb 1972	Pis	19 Feb 1976
Ari	20 Mar 1968	Ari	20 Mar 1972	Ari	20 Mar 1976
Tau	20 Apr 1968	Tau	19 Apr 1972	Tau	19 Apr 1976
Gem	21 May 1968	Gem	20 May 1972	Gem	20 May 1976
Can	21 Jun 1968	Can	21 Jun 1972	Can	21 Jun 1976
Leo	22 Jul 1968	Leo	22 Jul 1972	Leo	22 Jul 1976
Vir	23 Aug 1968	Vir	23 Aug 1972	Vir	23 Aug 1976
Lib	22 Sep 1968	Lib	22 Sep 1972	Lib	22 Sep 1976
Sco	23 Oct 1968	Sco	23 Oct 1972	Sco	23 Oct 1976
Sag	22 Nov 1968	Sag	22 Nov 1972	Sag	22 Nov 1976
Cap	21 Dec 1968	Cap	21 Dec 1972	Cap	21 Dec 1976
Aqu	20 Jan 1969	Aqu	20 Jan 1973	Aqu	20 Jan 1977
Pis	18 Feb 1969	Pis	18 Feb 1973	Pis	18 Feb 1977
Ari	20 Mar 1969	Ari	20 Mar 1973	Ari	20 Mar 1977
Tau	20 Apr 1969	Tau	20 Apr 1973	Tau	20 Apr 1977
Gem	21 May 1969	Gem	21 May 1973	Gem	21 May 1977
Can	21 Jun 1969	Can	21 Jun 1973	Can	21 Jun 1977
Leo	23 Jul 1969	Leo	22 Jul 1973	Leo	22 Jul 1977
Vir	23 Aug 1969	Vir	23 Aug 1973	Vir	23 Aug 1977
Lib	23 Sep 1969	Lib	23 Sep 1973	Lib	23 Sep 1977
Sco	23 Oct 1969	Sco	23 Oct 1973	Sco	23 Oct 1977
Sag	22 Nov 1969	Sag	22 Nov 1973	Sag	22 Nov 1977
Cap	22 Dec 1969	Cap	22 Dec 1973	Cap	21 Dec 1977
Aqu	20 Jan 1970	Aqu	20 Jan 1974	Aqu	20 Jan 1978
Pis	19 Feb 1970	Pis	19 Feb 1974	Pis	19 Feb 1978
Ari	21 Mar 1970	Ari	21 Mar 1974	Ari	20 Mar 1978
Tau	20 Apr 1970	Tau	20 Apr 1974	Tau	20 Apr 1978
Gem	21 May 1970	Gem	21 May 1974	Gem	21 May 1978
Can	21 Jun 1970	Can	21 Jun 1974	Can	21 Jun 1978
Leo	23 Jul 1970	Leo	23 Jul 1974	Leo	23 Jul 1978
Vir	23 Aug 1970	Vir	23 Aug 1974	Vir	23 Aug 1978
Lib	23 Sep 1970	Lib	23 Sep 1974	Lib	23 Sep 1978
Sco	23 Oct 1970	Sco	23 Oct 1974	Sco	23 Oct 1978
Sag	22 Nov 1970	Sag	22 Nov 1974	Sag	22 Nov 1978
Cap	22 Dec 1970	Cap	22 Dec 1974	Cap	22 Dec 1978
Aqu	20 Jan 1971	Aqu	20 Jan 1975	Aqu	20 Jan 1979
Pis	19 Feb 1971	Pis	19 Feb 1975	Pis	19 Feb 1979
Ari	21 Mar 1971	Ari	21 Mar 1975	Ari	21 Mar 1979
Tau	20 Apr 1971	Tau	20 Apr 1975	Tau	20 Apr 1979
Gem	21 May 1971	Gem	21 May 1975	Gem	21 May 1979
Can	22 Jun 1971	Can	22 Jun 1975	Can	21 Jun 1979
Leo	23 Jul 1971	Leo	23 Jul 1975	Leo	23 Jul 1979
Vir	23 Aug 1971	Vir	23 Aug 1975	Vir	23 Aug 1979
Lib	23 Sep 1971	Lib	23 Sep 1975	Lib	23 Sep 1979
Sco	24 Oct 1971	Sco	24 Oct 1975	Sco	24 Oct 1979
Sag	22 Nov 1971	Sag	22 Nov 1975	Sag	22 Nov 1979
Cap	22 Dec 1971	Cap	22 Dec 1975	Cap	22 Dec 1979

1980–91

Aqu	20 Jan 1980	Aqu	20 Jan 1984	Aqu	20 Jan 1988
Pis	19 Feb 1980	Pis	19 Feb 1984	Pis	19 Feb 1988
Ari	20 Mar 1980	Ari	20 Mar 1984	Ari	20 Mar 1988
Tau	19 Apr 1980	Tau	19 Apr 1984	Tau	19 Apr 1988
Gem	20 May 1980	Gem	20 May 1984	Gem	20 May 1988
Can	21 Jun 1980	Can	21 Jun 1984	Can	21 Jun 1988
Leo	22 Jul 1980	Leo	22 Jul 1984	Leo	22 Jul 1988
Vir	22 Aug 1980	Vir	22 Aug 1984	Vir	22 Aug 1988
Lib	22 Sep 1980	Lib	22 Sep 1984	Lib	22 Sep 1988
Sco	23 Oct 1980	Sco	23 Oct 1984	Sco	23 Oct 1988
Sag	22 Nov 1980	Sag	22 Nov 1984	Sag	22 Nov 1988
Cap	21 Dec 1980	Cap	21 Dec 1984	Cap	21 Dec 1988
Aqu	20 Jan 1981	Aqu	20 Jan 1985	Aqu	20 Jan 1989
Pis	18 Feb 1981	Pis	18 Feb 1985	Pis	18 Feb 1989
Ari	20 Mar 1981	Ari	20 Mar 1985	Ari	20 Mar 1989
Tau	20 Apr 1981	Tau	20 Apr 1985	Tau	20 Apr 1989
Gem	21 May 1981	Gem	21 May 1985	Gem	21 May 1989
Can	21 Jun 1981	Can	21 Jun 1985	Can	21 Jun 1989
Leo	22 Jul 1981	Leo	22 Jul 1985	Leo	22 Jul 1989
Vir	23 Aug 1981	Vir	23 Aug 1985	Vir	23 Aug 1989
Lib	23 Sep 1981	Lib	23 Sep 1985	Lib	23 Sep 1989
Sco	23 Oct 1981	Sco	23 Oct 1985	Sco	23 Oct 1989
Sag	22 Nov 1981	Sag	22 Nov 1985	Sag	22 Nov 1989
Cap	21 Dec 1981	Cap	21 Dec 1985	Cap	21 Dec 1989
Aqu	20 Jan 1982	Aqu	20 Jan 1986	Aqu	20 Jan 1990
Pis	18 Feb 1982	Pis	18 Feb 1986	Pis	18 Feb 1990
Ari	20 Mar 1982	Ari	20 Mar 1986	Ari	20 Mar 1990
Tau	20 Apr 1982	Tau	20 Apr 1986	Tau	20 Apr 1990
Gem	21 May 1982	Gem	21 May 1986	Gem	21 May 1990
Can	21 Jun 1982	Can	21 Jun 1986	Can	21 Jun 1990
Leo	23 Jul 1982	Leo	23 Jul 1986	Leo	23 Jul 1990
Vir	23 Aug 1982	Vir	23 Aug 1986	Vir	23 Aug 1990
Lib	23 Sep 1982	Lib	23 Sep 1986	Lib	23 Sep 1990
Sco	23 Oct 1982	Sco	23 Oct 1986	Sco	23 Oct 1990
Sag	22 Nov 1982	Sag	22 Nov 1986	Sag	22 Nov 1990
Cap	22 Dec 1982	Cap	22 Dec 1986	Cap	22 Dec 1990
Aqu	20 Jan 1983	Aqu	20 Jan 1987	Aqu	20 Jan 1991
Pis	19 Feb 1983	Pis	19 Feb 1987	Pis	19 Feb 1991
Ari	21 Mar 1983	Ari	21 Mar 1987	Ari	21 Mar 1991
Tau	20 Apr 1983	Tau	20 Apr 1987	Tau	20 Apr 1991
Gem	21 May 1983	Gem	21 May 1987	Gem	21 May 1991
Can	21 Jun 1983	Can	21 Jun 1987	Can	21 Jun 1991
Leo	23 Jul 1983	Leo	23 Jul 1987	Leo	23 Jul 1991
Vir	23 Aug 1983	Vir	23 Aug 1987	Vir	23 Aug 1991
Lib	23 Sep 1983	Lib	23 Sep 1987	Lib	23 Sep 1991
Sco	23 Oct 1983	Sco	23 Oct 1987	Sco	23 Oct 1991
Sag	22 Nov 1983	Sag	22 Nov 1987	Sag	22 Nov 1991
Cap	22 Dec 1983	Cap	22 Dec 1987	Cap	22 Dec 1991

1992–2000

Aqu	20 Jan 1992	Aqu	20 Jan 1995	Aqu	20 Jan 1998
Pis	19 Feb 1992	Pis	19 Feb 1995	Pis	18 Feb 1998
Ari	20 Mar 1992	Ari	21 Mar 1995	Ari	20 Mar 1998
Tau	19 Apr 1992	Tau	20 Apr 1995	Tau	20 Apr 1998
Gem	20 May 1992	Gem	21 May 1995	Gem	21 May 1998
Can	21 Jun 1992	Can	21 Jun 1995	Can	21 Jun 1998
Leo	22 Jul 1992	Leo	23 Jul 1995	Leo	23 Jul 1998
Vir	22 Aug 1992	Vir	23 Aug 1995	Vir	23 Aug 1998
Lib	22 Sep 1992	Lib	23 Sep 1995	Lib	23 Sep 1998
Sco	23 Oct 1992	Sco	23 Oct 1995	Sco	23 Oct 1998
Sag	22 Nov 1992	Sag	22 Nov 1995	Sag	22 Nov 1998
Cap	21 Dec 1992	Cap	22 Dec 1995	Cap	22 Dec 1998
Aqu	20 Jan 1993	Aqu	20 Jan 1996	Aqu	20 Jan 1999
Pis	18 Feb 1993	Pis	19 Feb 1996	Pis	19 Feb 1999
Ari	20 Mar 1993	Ari	20 Mar 1996	Ari	21 Mar 1999
Tau	20 Apr 1993	Tau	19 Apr 1996	Tau	20 Apr 1999
Gem	21 May 1993	Gem	20 May 1996	Gem	21 May 1999
Can	21 Jun 1993	Can	21 Jun 1996	Can	21 Jun 1999
Leo	22 Jul 1993	Leo	22 Jul 1996	Leo	23 Jul 1999
Vir	23 Aug 1993	Vir	22 Aug 1996	Vir	23 Aug 1999
Lib	23 Sep 1993	Lib	22 Sep 1996	Lib	23 Sep 1999
Sco	23 Oct 1993	Sco	23 Oct 1996	Sco	23 Oct 1999
Sag	22 Nov 1993	Sag	22 Nov 1996	Sag	22 Nov 1999
Cap	21 Dec 1993	Cap	21 Dec 1996	Cap	22 Dec 1999
Aqu	20 Jan 1994	Aqu	20 Jan 1997	Aqu	20 Jan 2000
Pis	18 Feb 1994	Pis	18 Feb 1997	Pis	19 Feb 2000
Ari	20 Mar 1994	Ari	20 Mar 1997	Ari	20 Mar 2000
Tau	20 Apr 1994	Tau	20 Apr 1997	Tau	19 Apr 2000
Gem	21 May 1994	Gem	21 May 1997	Gem	20 May 2000
Can	21 Jun 1994	Can	21 Jun 1997	Can	21 Jun 2000
Leo	23 Jul 1994	Leo	22 Jul 1997	Leo	22 Jul 2000
Vir	23 Aug 1994	Vir	23 Aug 1997	Vir	22 Aug 2000
Lib	23 Sep 1994	Lib	22 Sep 1997	Lib	22 Sep 2000
Sco	23 Oct 1994	Sco	23 Oct 1997	Sco	23 Oct 2000
Sag	22 Nov 1994	Sag	22 Nov 1997	Sag	22 Nov 2000
Cap	22 Dec 1994	Cap	21 Dec 1997	Cap	21 Dec 2000

Sun Signs

2001–10

Aqu	20 Jan 2001	Aqu	20 Jan 2005	Aqu	19 Jan 2009
Pis	18 Feb 2001	Pis	18 Feb 2005	Pis	18 Feb 2009
Ari	20 Mar 2001	Ari	20 Mar 2005	Ari	20 Mar 2009
Tau	20 Apr 2001	Tau	20 Apr 2005	Tau	19 Apr 2009
Gem	21 May 2001	Gem	20 May 2005	Gem	20 May 2009
Can	21 Jun 2001	Can	21 Jun 2005	Can	21 Jun 2009
Leo	22 Jul 2001	Leo	22 Jul 2005	Leo	22 Jul 2009
Vir	23 Aug 2001	Vir	23 Aug 2005	Vir	23 Aug 2009
Lib	22 Sep 2001	Lib	22 Sep 2005	Lib	22 Sep 2009
Sco	23 Oct 2001	Sco	23 Oct 2005	Sco	23 Oct 2009
Sag	22 Nov 2001	Sag	22 Nov 2005	Sag	22 Nov 2009
Cap	21 Dec 2001	Cap	21 Dec 2005	Cap	21 Dec 2009
Aqu	20 Jan 2002	Aqu	20 Jan 2006	Aqu	20 Jan 2010
Pis	18 Feb 2002	Pis	18 Feb 2006	Pis	18 Feb 2010
Ari	20 Mar 2002	Ari	20 Mar 2006	Ari	20 Mar 2010
Tau	20 Apr 2002	Tau	20 Apr 2006	Tau	20 Apr 2010
Gem	21 May 2002	Gem	21 May 2006	Gem	21 May 2010
Can	21 Jun 2002	Can	21 Jun 2006	Can	21 Jun 2010
Leo	23 Jul 2002	Leo	23 Jul 2006	Leo	22 Jul 2010
Vir	23 Aug 2002	Vir	23 Aug 2006	Vir	23 Aug 2010
Lib	23 Sep 2002	Lib	23 Sep 2006	Lib	23 Sep 2010
Sco	23 Oct 2002	Sco	23 Oct 2006	Sco	23 Oct 2010
Sag	22 Nov 2002	Sag	22 Nov 2006	Sag	22 Nov 2010
Cap	22 Dec 2002	Cap	22 Dec 2006	Cap	22 Dec 2010
Aqu	20 Jan 2003	Aqu	20 Jan 2007		
Pis	19 Feb 2003	Pis	19 Feb 2007		
Ari	21 Mar 2003	Ari	21 Mar 2007		
Tau	20 Apr 2003	Tau	20 Apr 2007		
Gem	21 May 2003	Gem	21 May 2007		
Can	21 Jun 2003	Can	21 Jun 2007		
Leo	23 Jul 2003	Leo	23 Jul 2007		
Vir	23 Aug 2003	Vir	23 Aug 2007		
Lib	23 Sep 2003	Lib	23 Sep 2007		
Sco	23 Oct 2003	Sco	23 Oct 2007		
Sag	22 Nov 2003	Sag	22 Nov 2007		
Cap	22 Dec 2003	Cap	22 Dec 2007		
Aqu	20 Jan 2004	Aqu	20 Jan 2008		
Pis	19 Feb 2004	Pis	19 Feb 2008		
Ari	20 Mar 2004	Ari	20 Mar 2008		
Tau	19 Apr 2004	Tau	19 Apr 2008		
Gem	20 May 2004	Gem	20 May 2008		
Can	21 Jun 2004	Can	21 Jun 2008		
Leo	22 Jul 2004	Leo	22 Jul 2008		
Vir	22 Aug 2004	Vir	22 Aug 2008		
Lib	22 Sep 2004	Lib	22 Sep 2008		
Sco	23 Oct 2004	Sco	23 Oct 2008		
Sag	22 Nov 2004	Sag	21 Nov 2008		
Cap	21 Dec 2004	Cap	21 Dec 2008		

MOON SIGNS

1920

Gem	2 Jan 1920	22:12	Sco	2 May 1920	01:38	Tau	2 Sep 1920	16:19
Can	4 Jan 1920	22:19	Sag	4 May 1920	12:59	Gem	4 Sep 1920	20:57
Leo	6 Jan 1920	22:31	Cap	7 May 1920	01:39	Can	7 Sep 1920	00:03
Vir	9 Jan 1920	00:47	Aqu	9 May 1920	14:08	Leo	9 Sep 1920	02:02
Lib	11 Jan 1920	06:48	Pis	12 May 1920	00:31	Vir	11 Sep 1920	03:55
Sco	13 Jan 1920	16:58	Ari	14 May 1920	07:23	Lib	13 Sep 1920	07:11
Sag	16 Jan 1920	05:44	Tau	16 May 1920	10:34	Sco	15 Sep 1920	13:20
Cap	18 Jan 1920	18:34	Gem	18 May 1920	11:13	Sag	17 Sep 1920	22:59
Aqu	21 Jan 1920	05:40	Can	20 May 1920	11:01	Cap	20 Sep 1920	11:09
Pis	23 Jan 1920	14:34	Leo	22 May 1920	11:50	Aqu	22 Sep 1920	23:32
Ari	25 Jan 1920	21:32	Vir	24 May 1920	15:11	Pis	25 Sep 1920	09:57
Tau	28 Jan 1920	02:43	Lib	26 May 1920	21:51	Ari	27 Sep 1920	17:34
Gem	30 Jan 1920	06:05	Sco	29 May 1920	07:33	Tau	29 Sep 1920	22:48
			Sag	31 May 1920	19:20			
Can	1 Feb 1920	07:54	Cap	3 Jun 1920	08:04	Gem	2 Oct 1920	02:32
Leo	3 Feb 1920	09:06	Aqu	5 Jun 1920	20:38	Can	4 Oct 1920	05:29
Vir	5 Feb 1920	11:19	Pis	8 Jun 1920	07:42	Leo	6 Oct 1920	08:14
Lib	7 Feb 1920	16:20	Ari	10 Jun 1920	15:56	Vir	8 Oct 1920	11:23
Sco	10 Feb 1920	01:15	Tau	12 Jun 1920	20:34	Lib	10 Oct 1920	15:45
Sag	12 Feb 1920	13:21	Gem	14 Jun 1920	21:56	Sco	12 Oct 1920	22:14
Cap	15 Feb 1920	02:13	Can	16 Jun 1920	21:26	Sag	15 Oct 1920	07:31
Aqu	17 Feb 1920	13:19	Leo	18 Jun 1920	21:02	Cap	17 Oct 1920	19:16
Pis	19 Feb 1920	21:38	Vir	20 Jun 1920	22:46	Aqu	20 Oct 1920	07:52
Ari	22 Feb 1920	03:36	Lib	23 Jun 1920	04:06	Pis	22 Oct 1920	18:56
Tau	24 Feb 1920	08:05	Sco	25 Jun 1920	13:20	Ari	25 Oct 1920	02:51
Gem	26 Feb 1920	11:42	Sag	28 Jun 1920	01:15	Tau	27 Oct 1920	07:33
Can	28 Feb 1920	14:40	Cap	30 Jun 1920	14:06	Gem	29 Oct 1920	09:59
						Can	31 Oct 1920	11:35
Leo	1 Mar 1920	17:23	Aqu	3 Jul 1920	02:30	Leo	2 Nov 1920	13:38
Vir	3 Mar 1920	20:41	Pis	5 Jul 1920	13:36	Vir	4 Nov 1920	17:03
Lib	6 Mar 1920	01:54	Ari	7 Jul 1920	22:37	Lib	6 Nov 1920	22:24
Sco	8 Mar 1920	10:11	Tau	10 Jul 1920	04:45	Sco	9 Nov 1920	05:49
Sag	10 Mar 1920	21:36	Gem	12 Jul 1920	07:40	Sag	11 Nov 1920	15:27
Cap	13 Mar 1920	10:25	Can	14 Jul 1920	08:03	Cap	14 Nov 1920	03:03
Aqu	15 Mar 1920	21:57	Leo	16 Jul 1920	07:32	Aqu	16 Nov 1920	15:44
Pis	18 Mar 1920	06:24	Vir	18 Jul 1920	08:13	Pis	19 Nov 1920	03:39
Ari	20 Mar 1920	11:42	Lib	20 Jul 1920	12:04	Ari	21 Nov 1920	12:44
Tau	22 Mar 1920	14:58	Sco	22 Jul 1920	20:03	Tau	23 Nov 1920	18:02
Gem	24 Mar 1920	17:25	Sag	25 Jul 1920	07:31	Gem	25 Nov 1920	19:59
Can	26 Mar 1920	20:02	Cap	27 Jul 1920	20:22	Can	27 Nov 1920	20:12
Leo	28 Mar 1920	23:21	Aqu	30 Jul 1920	08:36	Leo	29 Nov 1920	20:33
Vir	31 Mar 1920	03:48						
Lib	2 Apr 1920	10:00	Pis	1 Aug 1920	19:18	Vir	1 Dec 1920	22:46
Sco	4 Apr 1920	18:34	Ari	4 Aug 1920	04:09	Lib	4 Dec 1920	03:50
Sag	7 Apr 1920	05:42	Tau	6 Aug 1920	10:55	Sco	6 Dec 1920	11:52
Cap	9 Apr 1920	18:25	Gem	8 Aug 1920	15:14	Sag	8 Dec 1920	22:10
Aqu	12 Apr 1920	06:31	Can	10 Aug 1920	17:11	Cap	11 Dec 1920	09:59
Pis	14 Apr 1920	15:49	Leo	12 Aug 1920	17:41	Aqu	13 Dec 1920	22:38
Ari	16 Apr 1920	21:28	Vir	14 Aug 1920	18:27	Pis	16 Dec 1920	11:02
Tau	19 Apr 1920	00:07	Lib	16 Aug 1920	21:29	Ari	18 Dec 1920	21:28
Gem	21 Apr 1920	01:14	Sco	19 Aug 1920	04:13	Tau	21 Dec 1920	04:21
Can	23 Apr 1920	02:23	Sag	21 Aug 1920	14:45	Gem	23 Dec 1920	07:14
Leo	25 Apr 1920	04:49	Cap	24 Aug 1920	03:22	Can	25 Dec 1920	07:13
Vir	27 Apr 1920	09:22	Aqu	26 Aug 1920	15:36	Leo	27 Dec 1920	06:16
Lib	29 Apr 1920	16:19	Pis	29 Aug 1920	01:54	Vir	29 Dec 1920	06:37
			Ari	31 Aug 1920	10:02	Lib	31 Dec 1920	10:07

1921

Sco	2 Jan 1921	17:27	Pis	1 May 1921	21:45	Vir	1 Sep 1921	13:06
Sag	5 Jan 1921	03:58	Ari	4 May 1921	08:12	Lib	3 Sep 1921	13:06
Cap	7 Jan 1921	16:10	Tau	6 May 1921	15:31	Sco	5 Sep 1921	15:24
Aqu	10 Jan 1921	04:49	Gem	8 May 1921	19:50	Sag	7 Sep 1921	21:21
Pis	12 Jan 1921	17:10	Can	10 May 1921	22:18	Cap	10 Sep 1921	06:58
Ari	15 Jan 1921	04:14	Leo	13 May 1921	00:16	Aqu	12 Sep 1921	19:00
Tau	17 Jan 1921	12:39	Vir	15 May 1921	02:52	Pis	15 Sep 1921	07:39
Gem	19 Jan 1921	17:23	Lib	17 May 1921	06:46	Ari	17 Sep 1921	19:28
Can	21 Jan 1921	18:35	Sco	19 May 1921	12:22	Tau	20 Sep 1921	05:41
Leo	23 Jan 1921	17:45	Sag	21 May 1921	19:53	Gem	22 Sep 1921	13:40
Vir	25 Jan 1921	17:04	Cap	24 May 1921	05:34	Can	24 Sep 1921	19:05
Lib	27 Jan 1921	18:46	Aqu	26 May 1921	17:17	Leo	26 Sep 1921	21:56
Sco	30 Jan 1921	00:26	Pis	29 May 1921	05:50	Vir	28 Sep 1921	23:01
			Ari	31 May 1921	17:04	Lib	30 Sep 1921	23:41
Sag	1 Feb 1921	10:04	Tau	3 Jun 1921	01:02	Sco	3 Oct 1921	01:37
Cap	3 Feb 1921	22:14	Gem	5 Jun 1921	05:17	Sag	5 Oct 1921	06:22
Aqu	6 Feb 1921	10:59	Can	7 Jun 1921	06:46	Cap	7 Oct 1921	14:46
Pis	8 Feb 1921	23:03	Leo	9 Jun 1921	07:18	Aqu	10 Oct 1921	02:12
Ari	11 Feb 1921	09:51	Vir	11 Jun 1921	08:41	Pis	12 Oct 1921	14:50
Tau	13 Feb 1921	18:44	Lib	13 Jun 1921	12:10	Ari	15 Oct 1921	02:33
Gem	16 Feb 1921	00:53	Sco	15 Jun 1921	18:10	Tau	17 Oct 1921	12:07
Can	18 Feb 1921	03:57	Sag	18 Jun 1921	02:28	Gem	19 Oct 1921	19:20
Leo	20 Feb 1921	04:33	Cap	20 Jun 1921	12:39	Can	22 Oct 1921	00:31
Vir	22 Feb 1921	04:20	Aqu	23 Jun 1921	00:24	Leo	24 Oct 1921	04:07
Lib	24 Feb 1921	05:21	Pis	25 Jun 1921	13:03	Vir	26 Oct 1921	06:39
Sco	26 Feb 1921	09:29	Ari	28 Jun 1921	01:01	Lib	28 Oct 1921	08:48
Sag	28 Feb 1921	17:37	Tau	30 Jun 1921	10:12	Sco	30 Oct 1921	11:34
Cap	3 Mar 1921	05:03	Gem	2 Jul 1921	15:22	Sag	1 Nov 1921	16:08
Aqu	5 Mar 1921	17:45	Can	4 Jul 1921	16:55	Cap	3 Nov 1921	23:38
Pis	8 Mar 1921	05:43	Leo	6 Jul 1921	16:33	Aqu	6 Nov 1921	10:18
Ari	10 Mar 1921	15:58	Vir	8 Jul 1921	16:26	Pis	8 Nov 1921	22:50
Tau	13 Mar 1921	00:14	Lib	10 Jul 1921	18:28	Ari	11 Nov 1921	10:51
Gem	15 Mar 1921	06:28	Sco	12 Jul 1921	23:43	Tau	13 Nov 1921	20:18
Can	17 Mar 1921	10:35	Sag	15 Jul 1921	08:05	Gem	16 Nov 1921	02:39
Leo	19 Mar 1921	12:51	Cap	17 Jul 1921	18:43	Can	18 Nov 1921	06:40
Vir	21 Mar 1921	14:08	Aqu	20 Jul 1921	06:43	Leo	20 Nov 1921	09:32
Lib	23 Mar 1921	15:50	Pis	22 Jul 1921	19:23	Vir	22 Nov 1921	12:17
Sco	25 Mar 1921	19:34	Ari	25 Jul 1921	07:41	Lib	24 Nov 1921	15:31
Sag	28 Mar 1921	02:35	Tau	27 Jul 1921	17:58	Sco	26 Nov 1921	19:37
Cap	30 Mar 1921	12:58	Gem	30 Jul 1921	00:35	Sag	29 Nov 1921	01:03
Aqu	2 Apr 1921	01:21	Can	1 Aug 1921	03:17	Cap	1 Dec 1921	08:32
Pis	4 Apr 1921	13:27	Leo	3 Aug 1921	03:10	Aqu	3 Dec 1921	18:41
Ari	6 Apr 1921	23:30	Vir	5 Aug 1921	02:19	Pis	6 Dec 1921	07:03
Tau	9 Apr 1921	06:59	Lib	7 Aug 1921	02:52	Ari	8 Dec 1921	19:36
Gem	11 Apr 1921	12:15	Sco	9 Aug 1921	06:33	Tau	11 Dec 1921	05:45
Can	13 Apr 1921	15:58	Sag	11 Aug 1921	14:00	Gem	13 Dec 1921	12:06
Leo	15 Apr 1921	18:47	Cap	14 Aug 1921	00:30	Can	15 Dec 1921	15:11
Vir	17 Apr 1921	21:21	Aqu	16 Aug 1921	12:42	Leo	17 Dec 1921	16:34
Lib	20 Apr 1921	00:25	Pis	19 Aug 1921	01:20	Vir	19 Dec 1921	18:02
Sco	22 Apr 1921	04:54	Ari	21 Aug 1921	13:29	Lib	21 Dec 1921	20:52
Sag	24 Apr 1921	11:46	Tau	24 Aug 1921	00:06	Sco	24 Dec 1921	01:33
Cap	26 Apr 1921	21:28	Gem	26 Aug 1921	07:57	Sag	26 Dec 1921	08:01
Aqu	29 Apr 1921	09:25	Can	28 Aug 1921	12:16	Cap	28 Dec 1921	16:16
			Leo	30 Aug 1921	13:29	Aqu	31 Dec 1921	02:32

Moon Signs

1922

Pis	2 Jan 1922	14:44	Can	1 May 1922	09:11	Aqu	2 Sep 1922	18:12
Ari	5 Jan 1922	03:41	Leo	3 May 1922	14:04	Pis	5 Sep 1922	05:41
Tau	7 Jan 1922	14:57	Vir	5 May 1922	17:18	Ari	7 Sep 1922	18:29
Gem	9 Jan 1922	22:25	Lib	7 May 1922	19:21	Tau	10 Sep 1922	07:23
Can	12 Jan 1922	01:46	Sco	9 May 1922	21:00	Gem	12 Sep 1922	18:50
Leo	14 Jan 1922	02:20	Sag	11 May 1922	23:32	Can	15 Sep 1922	03:11
Vir	16 Jan 1922	02:13	Cap	14 May 1922	04:25	Leo	17 Sep 1922	07:47
Lib	18 Jan 1922	03:21	Aqu	16 May 1922	12:46	Vir	19 Sep 1922	09:07
Sco	20 Jan 1922	07:02	Pis	19 May 1922	00:20	Lib	21 Sep 1922	08:43
Sag	22 Jan 1922	13:33	Ari	21 May 1922	13:12	Sco	23 Sep 1922	08:27
Cap	24 Jan 1922	22:28	Tau	24 May 1922	00:44	Sag	25 Sep 1922	10:11
Aqu	27 Jan 1922	09:16	Gem	26 May 1922	09:28	Cap	27 Sep 1922	15:16
Pis	29 Jan 1922	21:33	Can	28 May 1922	15:25	Aqu	30 Sep 1922	00:03
			Leo	30 May 1922	19:33			
Ari	1 Feb 1922	10:35	Vir	1 Jun 1922	22:47	Pis	2 Oct 1922	11:40
Tau	3 Feb 1922	22:39	Lib	4 Jun 1922	01:43	Ari	5 Oct 1922	00:35
Gem	6 Feb 1922	07:41	Sco	6 Jun 1922	04:42	Tau	7 Oct 1922	13:19
Can	8 Feb 1922	12:28	Sag	8 Jun 1922	08:18	Gem	10 Oct 1922	00:43
Leo	10 Feb 1922	13:38	Cap	10 Jun 1922	13:31	Can	12 Oct 1922	09:51
Vir	12 Feb 1922	12:58	Aqu	12 Jun 1922	21:25	Leo	14 Oct 1922	16:00
Lib	14 Feb 1922	12:35	Pis	15 Jun 1922	08:24	Vir	16 Oct 1922	19:03
Sco	16 Feb 1922	14:23	Ari	17 Jun 1922	21:12	Lib	18 Oct 1922	19:42
Sag	18 Feb 1922	19:32	Tau	20 Jun 1922	09:08	Sco	20 Oct 1922	19:26
Cap	21 Feb 1922	04:05	Gem	22 Jun 1922	18:02	Sag	22 Oct 1922	20:06
Aqu	23 Feb 1922	15:12	Can	24 Jun 1922	23:26	Cap	24 Oct 1922	23:34
Pis	26 Feb 1922	03:44	Leo	27 Jun 1922	02:27	Aqu	27 Oct 1922	07:00
Ari	28 Feb 1922	16:41	Vir	29 Jun 1922	04:36	Pis	29 Oct 1922	18:06
Tau	3 Mar 1922	04:51	Lib	1 Jul 1922	07:04	Ari	1 Nov 1922	07:03
Gem	5 Mar 1922	14:47	Sco	3 Jul 1922	10:29	Tau	3 Nov 1922	19:39
Can	7 Mar 1922	21:17	Sag	5 Jul 1922	15:05	Gem	6 Nov 1922	06:33
Leo	10 Mar 1922	00:08	Cap	7 Jul 1922	21:12	Can	8 Nov 1922	15:22
Vir	12 Mar 1922	00:21	Aqu	10 Jul 1922	05:27	Leo	10 Nov 1922	22:04
Lib	13 Mar 1922	23:44	Pis	12 Jul 1922	16:16	Vir	13 Nov 1922	02:35
Sco	16 Mar 1922	00:14	Ari	15 Jul 1922	04:59	Lib	15 Nov 1922	05:00
Sag	18 Mar 1922	03:34	Tau	17 Jul 1922	17:27	Sco	17 Nov 1922	05:58
Cap	20 Mar 1922	10:42	Gem	20 Jul 1922	03:09	Sag	19 Nov 1922	06:52
Aqu	22 Mar 1922	21:18	Can	22 Jul 1922	08:55	Cap	21 Nov 1922	09:32
Pis	25 Mar 1922	09:55	Leo	24 Jul 1922	11:25	Aqu	23 Nov 1922	15:36
Ari	27 Mar 1922	22:48	Vir	26 Jul 1922	12:21	Pis	26 Nov 1922	01:39
Tau	30 Mar 1922	10:37	Lib	28 Jul 1922	13:26	Ari	28 Nov 1922	14:20
			Sco	30 Jul 1922	15:59			
Gem	1 Apr 1922	20:28	Sag	1 Aug 1922	20:35	Tau	1 Dec 1922	02:59
Can	4 Apr 1922	03:45	Cap	4 Aug 1922	03:22	Gem	3 Dec 1922	13:32
Leo	6 Apr 1922	08:12	Aqu	6 Aug 1922	12:19	Can	5 Dec 1922	21:32
Vir	8 Apr 1922	10:08	Pis	8 Aug 1922	23:23	Leo	8 Dec 1922	03:32
Lib	10 Apr 1922	10:36	Ari	11 Aug 1922	12:05	Vir	10 Dec 1922	08:08
Sco	12 Apr 1922	11:07	Tau	14 Aug 1922	00:56	Lib	12 Dec 1922	11:38
Sag	14 Apr 1922	13:26	Gem	16 Aug 1922	11:41	Sco	14 Dec 1922	14:13
Cap	16 Apr 1922	19:01	Can	18 Aug 1922	18:39	Sag	16 Dec 1922	16:27
Aqu	19 Apr 1922	04:28	Leo	20 Aug 1922	21:44	Cap	18 Dec 1922	19:34
Pis	21 Apr 1922	16:43	Vir	22 Aug 1922	22:15	Aqu	21 Dec 1922	01:09
Ari	24 Apr 1922	05:37	Lib	24 Aug 1922	22:05	Pis	23 Dec 1922	10:14
Tau	26 Apr 1922	17:07	Sco	26 Aug 1922	23:02	Ari	25 Dec 1922	22:22
Gem	29 Apr 1922	02:18	Sag	29 Aug 1922	02:27	Tau	28 Dec 1922	11:11
			Cap	31 Aug 1922	08:54	Gem	30 Dec 1922	22:01

1923

Can	2 Jan 1923	05:39	Sag	2 May 1923	05:58	Gem	2 Sep 1923	16:50
Leo	4 Jan 1923	10:33	Cap	4 May 1923	07:14	Can	5 Sep 1923	03:58
Vir	6 Jan 1923	13:59	Aqu	6 May 1923	12:06	Leo	7 Sep 1923	11:52
Lib	8 Jan 1923	16:58	Pis	8 May 1923	21:07	Vir	9 Sep 1923	16:15
Sco	10 Jan 1923	20:04	Ari	11 May 1923	09:12	Lib	11 Sep 1923	18:02
Sag	12 Jan 1923	23:33	Tau	13 May 1923	22:13	Sco	13 Sep 1923	18:46
Cap	15 Jan 1923	03:56	Gem	16 May 1923	10:26	Sag	15 Sep 1923	20:05
Aqu	17 Jan 1923	10:06	Can	18 May 1923	21:02	Cap	17 Sep 1923	23:14
Pis	19 Jan 1923	18:57	Leo	21 May 1923	05:40	Aqu	20 Sep 1923	04:52
Ari	22 Jan 1923	06:36	Vir	23 May 1923	11:52	Pis	22 Sep 1923	13:03
Tau	24 Jan 1923	19:33	Lib	25 May 1923	15:24	Ari	24 Sep 1923	23:23
Gem	27 Jan 1923	07:07	Sco	27 May 1923	16:34	Tau	27 Sep 1923	11:22
Can	29 Jan 1923	15:18	Sag	29 May 1923	16:37	Gem	30 Sep 1923	00:05
Leo	31 Jan 1923	19:56	Cap	31 May 1923	17:27			
Vir	2 Feb 1923	22:11	Aqu	2 Jun 1923	21:04	Can	2 Oct 1923	11:59
Lib	4 Feb 1923	23:38	Pis	5 Jun 1923	04:43	Leo	4 Oct 1923	21:13
Sco	7 Feb 1923	01:37	Ari	7 Jun 1923	16:02	Vir	7 Oct 1923	02:39
Sag	9 Feb 1923	04:58	Tau	10 Jun 1923	04:56	Lib	9 Oct 1923	04:34
Cap	11 Feb 1923	10:08	Gem	12 Jun 1923	17:02	Sco	11 Oct 1923	04:24
Aqu	13 Feb 1923	17:18	Can	15 Jun 1923	03:09	Sag	13 Oct 1923	04:08
Pis	16 Feb 1923	02:43	Leo	17 Jun 1923	11:11	Cap	15 Oct 1923	05:42
Ari	18 Feb 1923	14:20	Vir	19 Jun 1923	17:22	Aqu	17 Oct 1923	10:30
Tau	21 Feb 1923	03:14	Lib	21 Jun 1923	21:43	Pis	19 Oct 1923	18:42
Gem	23 Feb 1923	15:30	Sco	24 Jun 1923	00:19	Ari	22 Oct 1923	05:32
Can	26 Feb 1923	00:55	Sag	26 Jun 1923	01:46	Tau	24 Oct 1923	17:47
Leo	28 Feb 1923	06:30	Cap	28 Jun 1923	03:20	Gem	27 Oct 1923	06:28
			Aqu	30 Jun 1923	06:43	Can	29 Oct 1923	18:38
Vir	2 Mar 1923	08:40	Pis	2 Jul 1923	13:28	Leo	1 Nov 1923	04:59
Lib	4 Mar 1923	09:00	Ari	4 Jul 1923	23:51	Vir	3 Nov 1923	12:05
Sco	6 Mar 1923	09:16	Tau	7 Jul 1923	12:24	Lib	5 Nov 1923	15:22
Sag	8 Mar 1923	11:06	Gem	10 Jul 1923	00:35	Sco	7 Nov 1923	15:36
Cap	10 Mar 1923	15:34	Can	12 Jul 1923	10:32	Sag	9 Nov 1923	14:37
Aqu	12 Mar 1923	23:02	Leo	14 Jul 1923	17:53	Cap	11 Nov 1923	14:38
Pis	15 Mar 1923	09:07	Vir	16 Jul 1923	23:09	Aqu	13 Nov 1923	17:39
Ari	17 Mar 1923	21:05	Lib	19 Jul 1923	03:05	Pis	16 Nov 1923	00:47
Tau	20 Mar 1923	09:59	Sco	21 Jul 1923	06:08	Ari	18 Nov 1923	11:25
Gem	22 Mar 1923	22:31	Sag	23 Jul 1923	08:43	Tau	20 Nov 1923	23:52
Can	25 Mar 1923	09:04	Cap	25 Jul 1923	11:33	Gem	23 Nov 1923	12:31
Leo	27 Mar 1923	16:12	Aqu	27 Jul 1923	15:42	Can	26 Nov 1923	00:27
Vir	29 Mar 1923	19:35	Pis	29 Jul 1923	22:23	Leo	28 Nov 1923	11:00
Lib	31 Mar 1923	20:06				Vir	30 Nov 1923	19:18
Sco	2 Apr 1923	19:25	Ari	1 Aug 1923	08:11	Lib	3 Dec 1923	00:22
Sag	4 Apr 1923	19:33	Tau	3 Aug 1923	20:21	Sco	5 Dec 1923	02:13
Cap	6 Apr 1923	22:20	Gem	6 Aug 1923	08:46	Sag	7 Dec 1923	01:56
Aqu	9 Apr 1923	04:48	Can	8 Aug 1923	19:07	Cap	9 Dec 1923	01:31
Pis	11 Apr 1923	14:51	Leo	11 Aug 1923	02:18	Aqu	11 Dec 1923	03:10
Ari	14 Apr 1923	03:08	Vir	13 Aug 1923	06:43	Pis	13 Dec 1923	08:35
Tau	16 Apr 1923	16:06	Lib	15 Aug 1923	09:26	Ari	15 Dec 1923	18:07
Gem	19 Apr 1923	04:32	Sco	17 Aug 1923	11:38	Tau	18 Dec 1923	06:20
Can	21 Apr 1923	15:27	Sag	19 Aug 1923	14:12	Gem	20 Dec 1923	19:02
Leo	23 Apr 1923	23:49	Cap	21 Aug 1923	17:49	Can	23 Dec 1923	06:39
Vir	26 Apr 1923	04:55	Aqu	23 Aug 1923	23:03	Leo	25 Dec 1923	16:39
Lib	28 Apr 1923	06:47	Pis	26 Aug 1923	06:25	Vir	28 Dec 1923	00:50
Sco	30 Apr 1923	06:32	Ari	28 Aug 1923	16:15	Lib	30 Dec 1923	06:50
			Tau	31 Aug 1923	04:11			

1924

Sco	1 Jan 1924	10:21	Tau	2 May 1924	20:36	Lib	1 Sep 1924	02:36
Sag	3 Jan 1924	11:47	Gem	5 May 1924	08:47	Sco	3 Sep 1924	06:53
Cap	5 Jan 1924	12:21	Can	7 May 1924	21:30	Sag	5 Sep 1924	09:59
Aqu	7 Jan 1924	13:54	Leo	10 May 1924	09:29	Cap	7 Sep 1924	12:40
Pis	9 Jan 1924	18:13	Vir	12 May 1924	18:55	Aqu	9 Sep 1924	15:32
Ari	12 Jan 1924	02:22	Lib	15 May 1924	00:26	Pis	11 Sep 1924	19:16
Tau	14 Jan 1924	13:48	Sco	17 May 1924	02:09	Ari	14 Sep 1924	00:42
Gem	17 Jan 1924	02:27	Sag	19 May 1924	01:33	Tau	16 Sep 1924	08:39
Can	19 Jan 1924	14:04	Cap	21 May 1924	00:49	Gem	18 Sep 1924	19:23
Leo	21 Jan 1924	23:32	Aqu	23 May 1924	02:05	Can	21 Sep 1924	07:54
Vir	24 Jan 1924	06:48	Pis	25 May 1924	06:49	Leo	23 Sep 1924	19:51
Lib	26 Jan 1924	12:13	Ari	27 May 1924	15:16	Vir	26 Sep 1924	05:05
Sco	28 Jan 1924	16:08	Tau	30 May 1924	02:22	Lib	28 Sep 1924	10:51
Sag	30 Jan 1924	18:52				Sco	30 Sep 1924	13:58
Cap	1 Feb 1924	21:02	Gem	1 Jun 1924	14:47	Sag	2 Oct 1924	15:53
Aqu	3 Feb 1924	23:43	Can	4 Jun 1924	03:26	Cap	4 Oct 1924	18:02
Pis	6 Feb 1924	04:12	Leo	6 Jun 1924	15:28	Aqu	6 Oct 1924	21:19
Ari	8 Feb 1924	11:37	Vir	9 Jun 1924	01:39	Pis	9 Oct 1924	02:06
Tau	10 Feb 1924	22:09	Lib	11 Jun 1924	08:39	Ari	11 Oct 1924	08:30
Gem	13 Feb 1924	10:34	Sco	13 Jun 1924	11:55	Tau	13 Oct 1924	16:49
Can	15 Feb 1924	22:32	Sag	15 Jun 1924	12:15	Gem	16 Oct 1924	03:22
Leo	18 Feb 1924	08:08	Cap	17 Jun 1924	11:28	Can	18 Oct 1924	15:47
Vir	20 Feb 1924	14:44	Aqu	19 Jun 1924	11:43	Leo	21 Oct 1924	04:20
Lib	22 Feb 1924	18:56	Pis	21 Jun 1924	14:52	Vir	23 Oct 1924	14:31
Sco	24 Feb 1924	21:46	Ari	23 Jun 1924	21:56	Lib	25 Oct 1924	20:47
Sag	27 Feb 1924	00:16	Tau	26 Jun 1924	08:27	Sco	27 Oct 1924	23:25
Cap	29 Feb 1924	03:12	Gem	28 Jun 1924	20:50	Sag	30 Oct 1924	00:02
Aqu	2 Mar 1924	07:11	Can	1 Jul 1924	09:27	Cap	1 Nov 1924	00:39
Pis	4 Mar 1924	12:44	Leo	3 Jul 1924	21:10	Aqu	3 Nov 1924	02:53
Ari	6 Mar 1924	20:26	Vir	6 Jul 1924	07:14	Pis	5 Nov 1924	07:34
Tau	9 Mar 1924	06:35	Lib	8 Jul 1924	14:53	Ari	7 Nov 1924	14:39
Gem	11 Mar 1924	18:43	Sco	10 Jul 1924	19:35	Tau	9 Nov 1924	23:43
Can	14 Mar 1924	07:07	Sag	12 Jul 1924	21:30	Gem	12 Nov 1924	10:34
Leo	16 Mar 1924	17:30	Cap	14 Jul 1924	21:48	Can	14 Nov 1924	22:56
Vir	19 Mar 1924	00:25	Aqu	16 Jul 1924	22:11	Leo	17 Nov 1924	11:49
Lib	21 Mar 1924	03:59	Pis	19 Jul 1924	00:31	Vir	19 Nov 1924	23:09
Sco	23 Mar 1924	05:26	Ari	21 Jul 1924	06:11	Lib	22 Nov 1924	06:50
Sag	25 Mar 1924	06:28	Tau	23 Jul 1924	15:36	Sco	24 Nov 1924	10:15
Cap	27 Mar 1924	08:37	Gem	26 Jul 1924	03:36	Sag	26 Nov 1924	10:37
Aqu	29 Mar 1924	12:47	Can	28 Jul 1924	16:10	Cap	28 Nov 1924	09:57
Pis	31 Mar 1924	19:12	Leo	31 Jul 1924	03:37	Aqu	30 Nov 1924	10:26
Ari	3 Apr 1924	03:45	Vir	2 Aug 1924	13:04	Pis	2 Dec 1924	13:39
Tau	5 Apr 1924	14:11	Lib	4 Aug 1924	20:19	Ari	4 Dec 1924	20:10
Gem	8 Apr 1924	02:12	Sco	7 Aug 1924	01:22	Tau	7 Dec 1924	05:32
Can	10 Apr 1924	14:52	Sag	9 Aug 1924	04:31	Gem	9 Dec 1924	16:51
Leo	13 Apr 1924	02:13	Cap	11 Aug 1924	06:20	Can	12 Dec 1924	05:20
Vir	15 Apr 1924	10:19	Aqu	13 Aug 1924	07:51	Leo	14 Dec 1924	18:12
Lib	17 Apr 1924	14:25	Pis	15 Aug 1924	10:28	Vir	17 Dec 1924	06:06
Sco	19 Apr 1924	15:23	Ari	17 Aug 1924	15:32	Lib	19 Dec 1924	15:13
Sag	21 Apr 1924	15:04	Tau	19 Aug 1924	23:54	Sco	21 Dec 1924	20:24
Cap	23 Apr 1924	15:33	Gem	22 Aug 1924	11:14	Sag	23 Dec 1924	21:54
Aqu	25 Apr 1924	18:29	Can	24 Aug 1924	23:47	Cap	25 Dec 1924	21:17
Pis	28 Apr 1924	00:39	Leo	27 Aug 1924	11:17	Aqu	27 Dec 1924	20:41
Ari	30 Apr 1924	09:39	Vir	29 Aug 1924	20:17	Pis	29 Dec 1924	22:06

1925

Ari	1 Jan 1925	02:57	Vir	2 May 1925	18:37	Pis	2 Sep 1925	04:02
Tau	3 Jan 1925	11:31	Lib	5 May 1925	03:24	Ari	4 Sep 1925	05:01
Gem	5 Jan 1925	22:52	Sco	7 May 1925	08:20	Tau	6 Sep 1925	08:27
Can	8 Jan 1925	11:31	Sag	9 May 1925	10:26	Gem	8 Sep 1925	15:39
Leo	11 Jan 1925	00:13	Cap	11 May 1925	11:30	Can	11 Sep 1925	02:34
Vir	13 Jan 1925	11:53	Aqu	13 May 1925	13:08	Leo	13 Sep 1925	15:29
Lib	15 Jan 1925	21:31	Pis	15 May 1925	16:23	Vir	16 Sep 1925	03:55
Sco	18 Jan 1925	04:10	Ari	17 May 1925	21:34	Lib	18 Sep 1925	14:16
Sag	20 Jan 1925	07:32	Tau	20 May 1925	04:40	Sco	20 Sep 1925	22:16
Cap	22 Jan 1925	08:21	Gem	22 May 1925	13:50	Sag	23 Sep 1925	04:16
Aqu	24 Jan 1925	08:08	Can	25 May 1925	01:07	Cap	25 Sep 1925	08:35
Pis	26 Jan 1925	08:45	Leo	27 May 1925	13:58	Aqu	27 Sep 1925	11:28
Ari	28 Jan 1925	12:00	Vir	30 May 1925	02:34	Pis	29 Sep 1925	13:18
Tau	30 Jan 1925	18:57						
Gem	2 Feb 1925	05:31	Lib	1 Jun 1925	12:28	Ari	1 Oct 1925	15:05
Can	4 Feb 1925	18:10	Sco	3 Jun 1925	18:21	Tau	3 Oct 1925	18:19
Leo	7 Feb 1925	06:49	Sag	5 Jun 1925	20:32	Gem	6 Oct 1925	00:35
Vir	9 Feb 1925	18:00	Cap	7 Jun 1925	20:44	Can	8 Oct 1925	10:33
Lib	12 Feb 1925	03:05	Aqu	9 Jun 1925	20:53	Leo	10 Oct 1925	23:08
Sco	14 Feb 1925	09:53	Pis	11 Jun 1925	22:40	Vir	13 Oct 1925	11:42
Sag	16 Feb 1925	14:26	Ari	14 Jun 1925	03:03	Lib	15 Oct 1925	21:56
Cap	18 Feb 1925	17:01	Tau	16 Jun 1925	10:15	Sco	18 Oct 1925	05:11
Aqu	20 Feb 1925	18:20	Gem	18 Jun 1925	19:56	Sag	20 Oct 1925	10:10
Pis	22 Feb 1925	19:36	Can	21 Jun 1925	07:35	Cap	22 Oct 1925	13:56
Ari	24 Feb 1925	22:21	Leo	23 Jun 1925	20:29	Aqu	24 Oct 1925	17:11
Tau	27 Feb 1925	04:03	Vir	26 Jun 1925	09:20	Pis	26 Oct 1925	20:13
			Lib	28 Jun 1925	20:13	Ari	28 Oct 1925	23:23
						Tau	31 Oct 1925	03:29
Gem	1 Mar 1925	13:26	Sco	1 Jul 1925	03:31	Gem	2 Nov 1925	09:44
Can	4 Mar 1925	01:37	Sag	3 Jul 1925	06:54	Can	4 Nov 1925	19:05
Leo	6 Mar 1925	14:21	Cap	5 Jul 1925	07:23	Leo	7 Nov 1925	07:15
Vir	9 Mar 1925	01:22	Aqu	7 Jul 1925	06:48	Vir	9 Nov 1925	20:05
Lib	11 Mar 1925	09:42	Pis	9 Jul 1925	07:06	Lib	12 Nov 1925	06:51
Sco	13 Mar 1925	15:36	Ari	11 Jul 1925	09:53	Sco	14 Nov 1925	14:03
Sag	15 Mar 1925	19:50	Tau	13 Jul 1925	16:05	Sag	16 Nov 1925	18:12
Cap	17 Mar 1925	23:06	Gem	16 Jul 1925	01:37	Cap	18 Nov 1925	20:37
Aqu	20 Mar 1925	01:50	Can	18 Jul 1925	13:32	Aqu	20 Nov 1925	22:47
Pis	22 Mar 1925	04:33	Leo	21 Jul 1925	02:31	Pis	23 Nov 1925	01:37
Ari	24 Mar 1925	08:04	Vir	23 Jul 1925	15:16	Ari	25 Nov 1925	05:31
Tau	26 Mar 1925	13:34	Lib	26 Jul 1925	02:28	Tau	27 Nov 1925	10:46
Gem	28 Mar 1925	22:08	Sco	28 Jul 1925	10:54	Gem	29 Nov 1925	17:49
Can	31 Mar 1925	09:42	Sag	30 Jul 1925	15:54			
Leo	2 Apr 1925	22:31	Cap	1 Aug 1925	17:45	Can	2 Dec 1925	03:18
Vir	5 Apr 1925	09:53	Aqu	3 Aug 1925	17:40	Leo	4 Dec 1925	15:12
Lib	7 Apr 1925	18:04	Pis	5 Aug 1925	17:22	Vir	7 Dec 1925	04:12
Sco	9 Apr 1925	23:02	Ari	7 Aug 1925	18:45	Lib	9 Dec 1925	15:51
Sag	12 Apr 1925	02:04	Tau	9 Aug 1925	23:25	Sco	12 Dec 1925	00:01
Cap	14 Apr 1925	04:31	Gem	12 Aug 1925	07:56	Sag	14 Dec 1925	04:22
Aqu	16 Apr 1925	07:22	Can	14 Aug 1925	19:38	Cap	16 Dec 1925	05:58
Pis	18 Apr 1925	11:02	Leo	17 Aug 1925	08:40	Aqu	18 Dec 1925	06:35
Ari	20 Apr 1925	15:44	Vir	19 Aug 1925	21:12	Pis	20 Dec 1925	07:51
Tau	22 Apr 1925	21:59	Lib	22 Aug 1925	08:04	Ari	22 Dec 1925	10:57
Gem	25 Apr 1925	06:32	Sco	24 Aug 1925	16:43	Tau	24 Dec 1925	16:25
Can	27 Apr 1925	17:44	Sag	26 Aug 1925	22:48	Gem	27 Dec 1925	00:18
Leo	30 Apr 1925	06:36	Cap	29 Aug 1925	02:17	Can	29 Dec 1925	10:26
			Aqu	31 Aug 1925	03:40	Leo	31 Dec 1925	22:26

Moon Signs

1926

Vir	3 Jan 1926	11:25	Cap	1 May 1926	23:31	Can	1 Sep 1926	01:48
Lib	5 Jan 1926	23:42	Aqu	4 May 1926	03:30	Leo	3 Sep 1926	13:01
Sco	8 Jan 1926	09:17	Pis	6 May 1926	06:31	Vir	6 Sep 1926	01:39
Sag	10 Jan 1926	15:00	Ari	8 May 1926	08:54	Lib	8 Sep 1926	14:22
Cap	12 Jan 1926	17:08	Tau	10 May 1926	11:33	Sco	11 Sep 1926	02:14
Aqu	14 Jan 1926	17:06	Gem	12 May 1926	15:46	Sag	13 Sep 1926	12:20
Pis	16 Jan 1926	16:47	Can	14 May 1926	22:53	Cap	15 Sep 1926	19:35
Ari	18 Jan 1926	18:02	Leo	17 May 1926	09:20	Aqu	17 Sep 1926	23:21
Tau	20 Jan 1926	22:16	Vir	19 May 1926	21:53	Pis	20 Sep 1926	00:05
Gem	23 Jan 1926	05:54	Lib	22 May 1926	10:02	Ari	21 Sep 1926	23:20
Can	25 Jan 1926	16:29	Sco	24 May 1926	19:40	Tau	23 Sep 1926	23:12
Leo	28 Jan 1926	04:51	Sag	27 May 1926	02:12	Gem	26 Sep 1926	01:51
Vir	30 Jan 1926	17:48	Cap	29 May 1926	06:23	Can	28 Sep 1926	08:35
			Aqu	31 May 1926	09:18	Leo	30 Sep 1926	19:09
Lib	2 Feb 1926	06:10	Pis	2 Jun 1926	11:52	Vir	3 Oct 1926	07:48
Sco	4 Feb 1926	16:38	Ari	4 Jun 1926	14:45	Lib	5 Oct 1926	20:27
Sag	7 Feb 1926	00:00	Tau	6 Jun 1926	18:27	Sco	8 Oct 1926	07:57
Cap	9 Feb 1926	03:48	Gem	8 Jun 1926	23:42	Sag	10 Oct 1926	17:53
Aqu	11 Feb 1926	04:36	Can	11 Jun 1926	07:14	Cap	13 Oct 1926	01:45
Pis	13 Feb 1926	03:56	Leo	13 Jun 1926	17:28	Aqu	15 Oct 1926	07:01
Ari	15 Feb 1926	03:47	Vir	16 Jun 1926	05:48	Pis	17 Oct 1926	09:28
Tau	17 Feb 1926	06:08	Lib	18 Jun 1926	18:18	Ari	19 Oct 1926	09:55
Gem	19 Feb 1926	12:22	Sco	21 Jun 1926	04:39	Tau	21 Oct 1926	10:01
Can	21 Feb 1926	22:28	Sag	23 Jun 1926	11:33	Gem	23 Oct 1926	11:50
Leo	24 Feb 1926	10:59	Cap	25 Jun 1926	15:16	Can	25 Oct 1926	17:07
Vir	26 Feb 1926	23:58	Aqu	27 Jun 1926	17:00	Leo	28 Oct 1926	02:30
			Pis	29 Jun 1926	18:12	Vir	30 Oct 1926	14:42
Lib	1 Mar 1926	12:02	Ari	1 Jul 1926	20:13	Lib	2 Nov 1926	03:21
Sco	3 Mar 1926	22:26	Tau	3 Jul 1926	23:59	Sco	4 Nov 1926	14:36
Sag	6 Mar 1926	06:39	Gem	6 Jul 1926	05:56	Sag	6 Nov 1926	23:50
Cap	8 Mar 1926	12:05	Can	8 Jul 1926	14:16	Cap	9 Nov 1926	07:10
Aqu	10 Mar 1926	14:38	Leo	11 Jul 1926	00:50	Aqu	11 Nov 1926	12:40
Pis	12 Mar 1926	15:02	Vir	13 Jul 1926	13:07	Pis	13 Nov 1926	16:21
Ari	14 Mar 1926	14:51	Lib	16 Jul 1926	01:51	Ari	15 Nov 1926	18:27
Tau	16 Mar 1926	16:06	Sco	18 Jul 1926	13:06	Tau	17 Nov 1926	19:53
Gem	18 Mar 1926	20:42	Sag	20 Jul 1926	21:08	Gem	19 Nov 1926	22:10
Can	21 Mar 1926	05:29	Cap	23 Jul 1926	01:26	Can	22 Nov 1926	02:54
Leo	23 Mar 1926	17:35	Aqu	25 Jul 1926	02:47	Leo	24 Nov 1926	11:10
Vir	26 Mar 1926	06:35	Pis	27 Jul 1926	02:45	Vir	26 Nov 1926	22:35
Lib	28 Mar 1926	18:26	Ari	29 Jul 1926	03:13	Lib	29 Nov 1926	11:12
Sco	31 Mar 1926	04:16	Tau	31 Jul 1926	05:46			
Sag	2 Apr 1926	12:06	Gem	2 Aug 1926	11:25	Sco	1 Dec 1926	22:37
Cap	4 Apr 1926	18:03	Can	4 Aug 1926	20:07	Sag	4 Dec 1926	07:31
Aqu	6 Apr 1926	21:59	Leo	7 Aug 1926	07:12	Cap	6 Dec 1926	13:51
Pis	9 Apr 1926	00:02	Vir	9 Aug 1926	19:38	Aqu	8 Dec 1926	18:21
Ari	11 Apr 1926	01:02	Lib	12 Aug 1926	08:25	Pis	10 Dec 1926	21:43
Tau	13 Apr 1926	02:31	Sco	14 Aug 1926	20:16	Ari	13 Dec 1926	00:32
Gem	15 Apr 1926	06:20	Sag	17 Aug 1926	05:38	Tau	15 Dec 1926	03:22
Can	17 Apr 1926	13:55	Cap	19 Aug 1926	11:21	Gem	17 Dec 1926	06:59
Leo	20 Apr 1926	01:07	Aqu	21 Aug 1926	13:29	Can	19 Dec 1926	12:20
Vir	22 Apr 1926	13:57	Pis	23 Aug 1926	13:13	Leo	21 Dec 1926	20:16
Lib	25 Apr 1926	01:50	Ari	25 Aug 1926	12:30	Vir	24 Dec 1926	07:01
Sco	27 Apr 1926	11:17	Tau	27 Aug 1926	13:25	Lib	26 Dec 1926	19:30
Sag	29 Apr 1926	18:18	Gem	29 Aug 1926	17:38	Sco	29 Dec 1926	07:27
						Sag	31 Dec 1926	16:49

1927

Cap	2 Jan 1927	22:49	Gem	2 May 1927	20:52	Sco	1 Sep 1927	00:35
Aqu	5 Jan 1927	02:09	Can	4 May 1927	23:52	Sag	3 Sep 1927	13:08
Pis	7 Jan 1927	04:05	Leo	7 May 1927	06:38	Cap	5 Sep 1927	23:26
Ari	9 Jan 1927	05:59	Vir	9 May 1927	17:02	Aqu	8 Sep 1927	05:48
Tau	11 Jan 1927	08:55	Lib	12 May 1927	05:26	Pis	10 Sep 1927	08:14
Gem	13 Jan 1927	13:30	Sco	14 May 1927	17:50	Ari	12 Sep 1927	08:17
Can	15 Jan 1927	19:58	Sag	17 May 1927	04:56	Tau	14 Sep 1927	08:02
Leo	18 Jan 1927	04:30	Cap	19 May 1927	14:09	Gem	16 Sep 1927	09:28
Vir	20 Jan 1927	15:09	Aqu	21 May 1927	21:14	Can	18 Sep 1927	13:49
Lib	23 Jan 1927	03:26	Pis	24 May 1927	02:00	Leo	20 Sep 1927	21:13
Sco	25 Jan 1927	15:53	Ari	26 May 1927	04:36	Vir	23 Sep 1927	07:00
Sag	28 Jan 1927	02:19	Tau	28 May 1927	05:49	Lib	25 Sep 1927	18:29
Cap	30 Jan 1927	09:10	Gem	30 May 1927	07:01	Sco	28 Sep 1927	07:04
						Sag	30 Sep 1927	19:52
Aqu	1 Feb 1927	12:20	Can	1 Jun 1927	09:50	Cap	3 Oct 1927	07:11
Pis	3 Feb 1927	13:05	Leo	3 Jun 1927	15:37	Aqu	5 Oct 1927	15:05
Ari	5 Feb 1927	13:19	Vir	6 Jun 1927	00:55	Pis	7 Oct 1927	18:49
Tau	7 Feb 1927	14:50	Lib	8 Jun 1927	12:48	Ari	9 Oct 1927	19:13
Gem	9 Feb 1927	18:54	Sco	11 Jun 1927	01:14	Tau	11 Oct 1927	18:17
Can	12 Feb 1927	01:50	Sag	13 Jun 1927	12:14	Gem	13 Oct 1927	18:11
Leo	14 Feb 1927	11:11	Cap	15 Jun 1927	20:50	Can	15 Oct 1927	20:50
Vir	16 Feb 1927	22:15	Aqu	18 Jun 1927	03:03	Leo	18 Oct 1927	03:07
Lib	19 Feb 1927	10:30	Pis	20 Jun 1927	07:24	Vir	20 Oct 1927	12:43
Sco	21 Feb 1927	23:07	Ari	22 Jun 1927	10:28	Lib	23 Oct 1927	00:27
Sag	24 Feb 1927	10:33	Tau	24 Jun 1927	12:53	Sco	25 Oct 1927	13:07
Cap	26 Feb 1927	18:54	Gem	26 Jun 1927	15:25	Sag	28 Oct 1927	01:47
Aqu	28 Feb 1927	23:12	Can	28 Jun 1927	19:02	Cap	30 Oct 1927	13:20
Pis	3 Mar 1927	00:04	Leo	1 Jul 1927	00:48	Aqu	1 Nov 1927	22:24
Ari	4 Mar 1927	23:18	Vir	3 Jul 1927	09:26	Pis	4 Nov 1927	03:54
Tau	6 Mar 1927	23:07	Lib	5 Jul 1927	20:46	Ari	6 Nov 1927	05:52
Gem	9 Mar 1927	01:29	Sco	8 Jul 1927	09:16	Tau	8 Nov 1927	05:36
Can	11 Mar 1927	07:29	Sag	10 Jul 1927	20:35	Gem	10 Nov 1927	05:02
Leo	13 Mar 1927	16:51	Cap	13 Jul 1927	05:05	Can	12 Nov 1927	06:14
Vir	16 Mar 1927	04:21	Aqu	15 Jul 1927	10:29	Leo	14 Nov 1927	10:49
Lib	18 Mar 1927	16:47	Pis	17 Jul 1927	13:41	Vir	16 Nov 1927	19:13
Sco	21 Mar 1927	05:20	Ari	19 Jul 1927	15:57	Lib	19 Nov 1927	06:40
Sag	23 Mar 1927	17:05	Tau	21 Jul 1927	18:23	Sco	21 Nov 1927	19:25
Cap	26 Mar 1927	02:37	Gem	23 Jul 1927	21:45	Sag	24 Nov 1927	07:52
Aqu	28 Mar 1927	08:37	Can	26 Jul 1927	02:30	Cap	26 Nov 1927	18:59
Pis	30 Mar 1927	10:51	Leo	28 Jul 1927	09:00	Aqu	29 Nov 1927	04:05
			Vir	30 Jul 1927	17:41			
Ari	1 Apr 1927	10:29	Lib	2 Aug 1927	04:43	Pis	1 Dec 1927	10:35
Tau	3 Apr 1927	09:36	Sco	4 Aug 1927	17:15	Ari	3 Dec 1927	14:18
Gem	5 Apr 1927	10:25	Sag	7 Aug 1927	05:13	Tau	5 Dec 1927	15:45
Can	7 Apr 1927	14:42	Cap	9 Aug 1927	14:21	Gem	7 Dec 1927	16:09
Leo	9 Apr 1927	23:00	Aqu	11 Aug 1927	19:44	Can	9 Dec 1927	17:10
Vir	12 Apr 1927	10:18	Pis	13 Aug 1927	22:03	Leo	11 Dec 1927	20:31
Lib	14 Apr 1927	22:52	Ari	15 Aug 1927	22:56	Vir	14 Dec 1927	03:25
Sco	17 Apr 1927	11:18	Tau	18 Aug 1927	00:12	Lib	16 Dec 1927	13:54
Sag	19 Apr 1927	22:47	Gem	20 Aug 1927	03:08	Sco	19 Dec 1927	02:30
Cap	22 Apr 1927	08:34	Can	22 Aug 1927	08:18	Sag	21 Dec 1927	14:57
Aqu	24 Apr 1927	15:41	Leo	24 Aug 1927	15:38	Cap	24 Dec 1927	01:36
Pis	26 Apr 1927	19:36	Vir	27 Aug 1927	00:55	Aqu	26 Dec 1927	09:53
Ari	28 Apr 1927	20:42	Lib	29 Aug 1927	12:02	Pis	28 Dec 1927	15:59
Tau	30 Apr 1927	20:28				Ari	30 Dec 1927	20:17

1928

Tau	1 Jan 1928	23:13	Lib	1 May 1928	03:35	Ari	1 Sep 1928	17:25
Gem	4 Jan 1928	01:19	Sco	3 May 1928	15:37	Tau	3 Sep 1928	20:06
Can	6 Jan 1928	03:27	Sag	6 May 1928	04:31	Gem	5 Sep 1928	22:42
Leo	8 Jan 1928	06:51	Cap	8 May 1928	17:07	Can	8 Sep 1928	01:51
Vir	10 Jan 1928	12:53	Aqu	11 May 1928	03:56	Leo	10 Sep 1928	05:48
Lib	12 Jan 1928	22:17	Pis	13 May 1928	11:32	Vir	12 Sep 1928	11:01
Sco	15 Jan 1928	10:26	Ari	15 May 1928	15:28	Lib	14 Sep 1928	18:11
Sag	17 Jan 1928	23:05	Tau	17 May 1928	16:24	Sco	17 Sep 1928	04:04
Cap	20 Jan 1928	09:47	Gem	19 May 1928	15:55	Sag	19 Sep 1928	16:22
Aqu	22 Jan 1928	17:26	Can	21 May 1928	15:57	Cap	22 Sep 1928	05:15
Pis	24 Jan 1928	22:23	Leo	23 May 1928	18:16	Aqu	24 Sep 1928	16:00
Ari	27 Jan 1928	01:47	Vir	26 May 1928	00:07	Pis	26 Sep 1928	22:59
Tau	29 Jan 1928	04:41	Lib	28 May 1928	09:36	Ari	29 Sep 1928	02:29
Gem	31 Jan 1928	07:46	Sco	30 May 1928	21:39			
Can	2 Feb 1928	11:21	Sag	2 Jun 1928	10:37	Tau	1 Oct 1928	03:58
Leo	4 Feb 1928	15:52	Cap	4 Jun 1928	22:58	Gem	3 Oct 1928	05:08
Vir	6 Feb 1928	22:09	Aqu	7 Jun 1928	09:39	Can	5 Oct 1928	07:20
Lib	9 Feb 1928	07:03	Pis	9 Jun 1928	17:53	Leo	7 Oct 1928	11:18
Sco	11 Feb 1928	18:40	Ari	11 Jun 1928	23:11	Vir	9 Oct 1928	17:13
Sag	14 Feb 1928	07:31	Tau	14 Jun 1928	01:44	Lib	12 Oct 1928	01:14
Cap	16 Feb 1928	18:52	Gem	16 Jun 1928	02:23	Sco	14 Oct 1928	11:28
Aqu	19 Feb 1928	02:45	Can	18 Jun 1928	02:34	Sag	16 Oct 1928	23:43
Pis	21 Feb 1928	07:04	Leo	20 Jun 1928	04:02	Cap	19 Oct 1928	12:49
Ari	23 Feb 1928	09:08	Vir	22 Jun 1928	08:27	Aqu	22 Oct 1928	00:31
Tau	25 Feb 1928	10:41	Lib	24 Jun 1928	16:42	Pis	24 Oct 1928	08:48
Gem	27 Feb 1928	13:07	Sco	27 Jun 1928	04:16	Ari	26 Oct 1928	13:02
Can	29 Feb 1928	17:04	Sag	29 Jun 1928	17:12	Tau	28 Oct 1928	14:15
						Gem	30 Oct 1928	14:10
Leo	2 Mar 1928	22:38	Cap	2 Jul 1928	05:22	Can	1 Nov 1928	14:40
Vir	5 Mar 1928	05:50	Aqu	4 Jul 1928	15:30	Leo	3 Nov 1928	17:13
Lib	7 Mar 1928	15:04	Pis	6 Jul 1928	23:21	Vir	5 Nov 1928	22:41
Sco	10 Mar 1928	02:30	Ari	9 Jul 1928	05:03	Lib	8 Nov 1928	07:04
Sag	12 Mar 1928	15:23	Tau	11 Jul 1928	08:48	Sco	10 Nov 1928	17:52
Cap	15 Mar 1928	03:32	Gem	13 Jul 1928	10:58	Sag	13 Nov 1928	06:19
Aqu	17 Mar 1928	12:28	Can	15 Jul 1928	12:19	Cap	15 Nov 1928	19:24
Pis	19 Mar 1928	17:19	Leo	17 Jul 1928	14:05	Aqu	18 Nov 1928	07:38
Ari	21 Mar 1928	18:53	Vir	19 Jul 1928	17:52	Pis	20 Nov 1928	17:18
Tau	23 Mar 1928	19:05	Lib	22 Jul 1928	01:02	Ari	22 Nov 1928	23:12
Gem	25 Mar 1928	19:53	Sco	24 Jul 1928	11:47	Tau	25 Nov 1928	01:29
Can	27 Mar 1928	22:41	Sag	27 Jul 1928	00:33	Gem	27 Nov 1928	01:22
Leo	30 Mar 1928	04:04	Cap	29 Jul 1928	12:45	Can	29 Nov 1928	00:43
			Aqu	31 Jul 1928	22:31			
Vir	1 Apr 1928	11:53	Pis	3 Aug 1928	05:33	Leo	1 Dec 1928	01:29
Lib	3 Apr 1928	21:46	Ari	5 Aug 1928	10:32	Vir	3 Dec 1928	05:16
Sco	6 Apr 1928	09:27	Tau	7 Aug 1928	14:17	Lib	5 Dec 1928	12:53
Sag	8 Apr 1928	22:19	Gem	9 Aug 1928	17:21	Sco	7 Dec 1928	23:46
Cap	11 Apr 1928	10:54	Can	11 Aug 1928	20:02	Sag	10 Dec 1928	12:28
Aqu	13 Apr 1928	21:04	Leo	13 Aug 1928	22:56	Cap	13 Dec 1928	01:28
Pis	16 Apr 1928	03:17	Vir	16 Aug 1928	03:07	Aqu	15 Dec 1928	13:34
Ari	18 Apr 1928	05:39	Lib	18 Aug 1928	09:53	Pis	17 Dec 1928	23:47
Tau	20 Apr 1928	05:35	Sco	20 Aug 1928	19:56	Ari	20 Dec 1928	07:14
Gem	22 Apr 1928	05:08	Sag	23 Aug 1928	08:28	Tau	22 Dec 1928	11:23
Can	24 Apr 1928	06:13	Cap	25 Aug 1928	20:57	Gem	24 Dec 1928	12:38
Leo	26 Apr 1928	10:12	Aqu	28 Aug 1928	06:56	Can	26 Dec 1928	12:16
Vir	28 Apr 1928	17:27	Pis	30 Aug 1928	13:29	Leo	28 Dec 1928	12:07
						Vir	30 Dec 1928	14:13

1929

Lib	1 Jan 1929	20:08	Aqu	1 May 1929	03:17	Vir	2 Sep 1929	18:26
Sco	4 Jan 1929	06:09	Pis	3 May 1929	13:49	Lib	4 Sep 1929	20:51
Sag	6 Jan 1929	18:49	Ari	5 May 1929	20:49	Sco	7 Sep 1929	02:21
Cap	9 Jan 1929	07:50	Tau	8 May 1929	00:16	Sag	9 Sep 1929	11:39
Aqu	11 Jan 1929	19:32	Gem	10 May 1929	01:21	Cap	11 Sep 1929	23:44
Pis	14 Jan 1929	05:20	Can	12 May 1929	01:44	Aqu	14 Sep 1929	12:15
Ari	16 Jan 1929	13:05	Leo	14 May 1929	03:03	Pis	16 Sep 1929	23:05
Tau	18 Jan 1929	18:36	Vir	16 May 1929	06:33	Ari	19 Sep 1929	07:29
Gem	20 Jan 1929	21:42	Lib	18 May 1929	12:52	Tau	21 Sep 1929	13:44
Can	22 Jan 1929	22:51	Sco	20 May 1929	21:53	Gem	23 Sep 1929	18:24
Leo	24 Jan 1929	23:16	Sag	23 May 1929	09:03	Can	25 Sep 1929	21:51
Vir	27 Jan 1929	00:48	Cap	25 May 1929	21:33	Leo	28 Sep 1929	00:27
Lib	29 Jan 1929	05:18	Aqu	28 May 1929	10:16	Vir	30 Sep 1929	02:51
Sco	31 Jan 1929	13:57	Pis	30 May 1929	21:35			
Sag	3 Feb 1929	01:59	Ari	2 Jun 1929	05:57	Lib	2 Oct 1929	06:09
Cap	5 Feb 1929	14:59	Tau	4 Jun 1929	10:32	Sco	4 Oct 1929	11:40
Aqu	8 Feb 1929	02:33	Gem	6 Jun 1929	11:55	Sag	6 Oct 1929	20:18
Pis	10 Feb 1929	11:41	Can	8 Jun 1929	11:34	Cap	9 Oct 1929	07:49
Ari	12 Feb 1929	18:40	Leo	10 Jun 1929	11:25	Aqu	11 Oct 1929	20:24
Tau	15 Feb 1929	00:01	Vir	12 Jun 1929	13:20	Pis	14 Oct 1929	07:39
Gem	17 Feb 1929	04:00	Lib	14 Jun 1929	18:38	Ari	16 Oct 1929	16:01
Can	19 Feb 1929	06:44	Sco	17 Jun 1929	03:32	Tau	18 Oct 1929	21:27
Leo	21 Feb 1929	08:40	Sag	19 Jun 1929	15:02	Gem	21 Oct 1929	00:53
Vir	23 Feb 1929	10:58	Cap	22 Jun 1929	03:44	Can	23 Oct 1929	03:23
Lib	25 Feb 1929	15:15	Aqu	24 Jun 1929	16:23	Leo	25 Oct 1929	05:54
Sco	27 Feb 1929	22:54	Pis	27 Jun 1929	03:58	Vir	27 Oct 1929	09:08
			Ari	29 Jun 1929	13:19	Lib	29 Oct 1929	13:39
						Sco	31 Oct 1929	20:01
Sag	2 Mar 1929	10:03	Tau	1 Jul 1929	19:30	Sag	3 Nov 1929	04:46
Cap	4 Mar 1929	22:54	Gem	3 Jul 1929	22:12	Cap	5 Nov 1929	15:56
Aqu	7 Mar 1929	10:42	Can	5 Jul 1929	22:19	Aqu	8 Nov 1929	04:32
Pis	9 Mar 1929	19:42	Leo	7 Jul 1929	21:36	Pis	10 Nov 1929	16:29
Ari	12 Mar 1929	01:50	Vir	9 Jul 1929	22:10	Ari	13 Nov 1929	01:41
Tau	14 Mar 1929	06:04	Lib	12 Jul 1929	01:54	Tau	15 Nov 1929	07:17
Gem	16 Mar 1929	09:22	Sco	14 Jul 1929	09:44	Gem	17 Nov 1929	09:52
Can	18 Mar 1929	12:23	Sag	16 Jul 1929	20:59	Can	19 Nov 1929	10:52
Leo	20 Mar 1929	15:26	Cap	19 Jul 1929	09:47	Leo	21 Nov 1929	11:58
Vir	22 Mar 1929	19:04	Aqu	21 Jul 1929	22:19	Vir	23 Nov 1929	14:31
Lib	25 Mar 1929	00:12	Pis	24 Jul 1929	09:38	Lib	25 Nov 1929	19:22
Sco	27 Mar 1929	07:49	Ari	26 Jul 1929	19:12	Sco	28 Nov 1929	02:40
Sag	29 Mar 1929	18:25	Tau	29 Jul 1929	02:23	Sag	30 Nov 1929	12:07
			Gem	31 Jul 1929	06:42			
Cap	1 Apr 1929	07:02	Can	2 Aug 1929	08:14	Cap	2 Dec 1929	23:25
Aqu	3 Apr 1929	19:16	Leo	4 Aug 1929	08:10	Aqu	5 Dec 1929	11:56
Pis	6 Apr 1929	04:51	Vir	6 Aug 1929	08:22	Pis	8 Dec 1929	00:26
Ari	8 Apr 1929	10:56	Lib	8 Aug 1929	10:56	Ari	10 Dec 1929	10:55
Tau	10 Apr 1929	14:15	Sco	10 Aug 1929	17:21	Tau	12 Dec 1929	17:49
Gem	12 Apr 1929	16:12	Sag	13 Aug 1929	03:44	Gem	14 Dec 1929	20:47
Can	14 Apr 1929	18:03	Cap	15 Aug 1929	16:20	Can	16 Dec 1929	21:04
Leo	16 Apr 1929	20:50	Aqu	18 Aug 1929	04:49	Leo	18 Dec 1929	20:34
Vir	19 Apr 1929	01:05	Pis	20 Aug 1929	15:44	Vir	20 Dec 1929	21:22
Lib	21 Apr 1929	07:13	Ari	23 Aug 1929	00:45	Lib	23 Dec 1929	01:03
Sco	23 Apr 1929	15:34	Tau	25 Aug 1929	07:54	Sco	25 Dec 1929	08:11
Sag	26 Apr 1929	02:15	Gem	27 Aug 1929	13:01	Sag	27 Dec 1929	18:11
Cap	28 Apr 1929	14:42	Can	29 Aug 1929	16:02	Cap	30 Dec 1929	05:55
			Leo	31 Aug 1929	17:26			

Moon Signs

1930

Aqu	1 Jan 1930	18:28	Can	2 May 1930	13:53	Cap	1 Sep 1930	20:35
Pis	4 Jan 1930	07:03	Leo	4 May 1930	16:31	Aqu	4 Sep 1930	08:27
Ari	6 Jan 1930	18:26	Vir	6 May 1930	19:10	Pis	6 Sep 1930	21:05
Tau	9 Jan 1930	02:57	Lib	8 May 1930	22:30	Ari	9 Sep 1930	09:20
Gem	11 Jan 1930	07:33	Sco	11 May 1930	03:06	Tau	11 Sep 1930	20:17
Can	13 Jan 1930	08:33	Sag	13 May 1930	09:39	Gem	14 Sep 1930	05:00
Leo	15 Jan 1930	07:36	Cap	15 May 1930	18:39	Can	16 Sep 1930	10:40
Vir	17 Jan 1930	06:56	Aqu	18 May 1930	06:03	Leo	18 Sep 1930	13:16
Lib	19 Jan 1930	08:44	Pis	20 May 1930	18:33	Vir	20 Sep 1930	13:44
Sco	21 Jan 1930	14:25	Ari	23 May 1930	05:54	Lib	22 Sep 1930	13:43
Sag	23 Jan 1930	23:56	Tau	25 May 1930	14:13	Sco	24 Sep 1930	15:07
Cap	26 Jan 1930	11:53	Gem	27 May 1930	19:06	Sag	26 Sep 1930	19:34
Aqu	29 Jan 1930	00:34	Can	29 May 1930	21:24	Cap	29 Sep 1930	03:48
Pis	31 Jan 1930	12:58	Leo	31 May 1930	22:44			
Ari	3 Feb 1930	00:21	Vir	3 Jun 1930	00:37	Aqu	1 Oct 1930	15:09
Tau	5 Feb 1930	09:47	Lib	5 Jun 1930	04:03	Pis	4 Oct 1930	03:47
Gem	7 Feb 1930	16:07	Sco	7 Jun 1930	09:30	Ari	6 Oct 1930	15:51
Can	9 Feb 1930	18:54	Sag	9 Jun 1930	16:55	Tau	9 Oct 1930	02:13
Leo	11 Feb 1930	18:59	Cap	12 Jun 1930	02:20	Gem	11 Oct 1930	10:28
Vir	13 Feb 1930	18:13	Aqu	14 Jun 1930	13:38	Can	13 Oct 1930	16:28
Lib	15 Feb 1930	18:50	Pis	17 Jun 1930	02:11	Leo	15 Oct 1930	20:18
Sco	17 Feb 1930	22:45	Ari	19 Jun 1930	14:13	Vir	17 Oct 1930	22:24
Sag	20 Feb 1930	06:48	Tau	21 Jun 1930	23:33	Lib	19 Oct 1930	23:43
Cap	22 Feb 1930	18:12	Gem	24 Jun 1930	04:59	Sco	22 Oct 1930	01:32
Aqu	25 Feb 1930	06:56	Can	26 Jun 1930	06:56	Sag	24 Oct 1930	05:23
Pis	27 Feb 1930	19:12	Leo	28 Jun 1930	07:05	Cap	26 Oct 1930	12:27
			Vir	30 Jun 1930	07:28	Aqu	28 Oct 1930	22:53
						Pis	31 Oct 1930	11:22
Ari	2 Mar 1930	06:08	Lib	2 Jul 1930	09:47	Ari	2 Nov 1930	23:33
Tau	4 Mar 1930	15:17	Sco	4 Jul 1930	14:56	Tau	5 Nov 1930	09:36
Gem	6 Mar 1930	22:14	Sag	6 Jul 1930	22:49	Gem	7 Nov 1930	16:57
Can	9 Mar 1930	02:33	Cap	9 Jul 1930	08:49	Can	9 Nov 1930	22:03
Leo	11 Mar 1930	04:24	Aqu	11 Jul 1930	20:22	Leo	12 Nov 1930	01:44
Vir	13 Mar 1930	04:53	Pis	14 Jul 1930	08:56	Vir	14 Nov 1930	04:41
Lib	15 Mar 1930	05:42	Ari	16 Jul 1930	21:25	Lib	16 Nov 1930	07:26
Sco	17 Mar 1930	08:46	Tau	19 Jul 1930	07:53	Sco	18 Nov 1930	10:36
Sag	19 Mar 1930	15:24	Gem	21 Jul 1930	14:37	Sag	20 Nov 1930	15:00
Cap	22 Mar 1930	01:40	Can	23 Jul 1930	17:21	Cap	22 Nov 1930	21:42
Aqu	24 Mar 1930	14:04	Leo	25 Jul 1930	17:18	Aqu	25 Nov 1930	07:22
Pis	27 Mar 1930	02:22	Vir	27 Jul 1930	16:34	Pis	27 Nov 1930	19:32
Ari	29 Mar 1930	12:58	Lib	29 Jul 1930	17:17	Ari	30 Nov 1930	08:05
Tau	31 Mar 1930	21:22	Sco	31 Jul 1930	21:05			
Gem	3 Apr 1930	03:41	Sag	3 Aug 1930	04:24	Tau	2 Dec 1930	18:31
Can	5 Apr 1930	08:10	Cap	5 Aug 1930	14:34	Gem	5 Dec 1930	01:30
Leo	7 Apr 1930	11:07	Aqu	8 Aug 1930	02:26	Can	7 Dec 1930	05:30
Vir	9 Apr 1930	13:10	Pis	10 Aug 1930	15:02	Leo	9 Dec 1930	07:52
Lib	11 Apr 1930	15:16	Ari	13 Aug 1930	03:31	Vir	11 Dec 1930	10:04
Sco	13 Apr 1930	18:44	Tau	15 Aug 1930	14:36	Lib	13 Dec 1930	13:05
Sag	16 Apr 1930	00:50	Gem	17 Aug 1930	22:44	Sco	15 Dec 1930	17:18
Cap	18 Apr 1930	10:07	Can	20 Aug 1930	03:00	Sag	17 Dec 1930	22:54
Aqu	20 Apr 1930	21:58	Leo	22 Aug 1930	03:56	Cap	20 Dec 1930	06:11
Pis	23 Apr 1930	10:22	Vir	24 Aug 1930	03:13	Aqu	22 Dec 1930	15:43
Ari	25 Apr 1930	21:08	Lib	26 Aug 1930	02:58	Pis	25 Dec 1930	03:35
Tau	28 Apr 1930	05:07	Sco	28 Aug 1930	05:10	Ari	27 Dec 1930	16:28
Gem	30 Apr 1930	10:24	Sag	30 Aug 1930	11:05	Tau	30 Dec 1930	03:50

1931

Gem	1 Jan 1931	11:32	Sco	1 May 1931	11:26	Tau	1 Sep 1931	20:58
Can	3 Jan 1931	15:19	Sag	3 May 1931	13:14	Gem	4 Sep 1931	08:42
Leo	5 Jan 1931	16:31	Cap	5 May 1931	17:35	Can	6 Sep 1931	17:14
Vir	7 Jan 1931	17:05	Aqu	8 May 1931	01:37	Leo	8 Sep 1931	21:45
Lib	9 Jan 1931	18:48	Pis	10 May 1931	13:01	Vir	10 Sep 1931	23:02
Sco	11 Jan 1931	22:40	Ari	13 May 1931	01:55	Lib	12 Sep 1931	22:42
Sag	14 Jan 1931	04:50	Tau	15 May 1931	13:53	Sco	14 Sep 1931	22:40
Cap	16 Jan 1931	13:01	Gem	17 May 1931	23:25	Sag	17 Sep 1931	00:40
Aqu	18 Jan 1931	23:04	Can	20 May 1931	06:25	Cap	19 Sep 1931	05:47
Pis	21 Jan 1931	10:54	Leo	22 May 1931	11:26	Aqu	21 Sep 1931	14:18
Ari	23 Jan 1931	23:54	Vir	24 May 1931	15:06	Pis	24 Sep 1931	01:28
Tau	26 Jan 1931	12:08	Lib	26 May 1931	17:50	Ari	26 Sep 1931	14:09
Gem	28 Jan 1931	21:16	Sco	28 May 1931	20:07	Tau	29 Sep 1931	03:06
Can	31 Jan 1931	02:07	Sag	30 May 1931	22:48			
Leo	2 Feb 1931	03:23	Cap	2 Jun 1931	03:07	Gem	1 Oct 1931	15:02
Vir	4 Feb 1931	02:56	Aqu	4 Jun 1931	10:23	Can	4 Oct 1931	00:36
Lib	6 Feb 1931	02:54	Pis	6 Jun 1931	21:00	Leo	6 Oct 1931	06:48
Sco	8 Feb 1931	05:04	Ari	9 Jun 1931	09:43	Vir	8 Oct 1931	09:33
Sag	10 Feb 1931	10:22	Tau	11 Jun 1931	21:53	Lib	10 Oct 1931	09:49
Cap	12 Feb 1931	18:38	Gem	14 Jun 1931	07:20	Sco	12 Oct 1931	09:17
Aqu	15 Feb 1931	05:14	Can	16 Jun 1931	13:36	Sag	14 Oct 1931	09:51
Pis	17 Feb 1931	17:22	Leo	18 Jun 1931	17:35	Cap	16 Oct 1931	13:19
Ari	20 Feb 1931	06:20	Vir	20 Jun 1931	20:32	Aqu	18 Oct 1931	20:39
Tau	22 Feb 1931	18:53	Lib	22 Jun 1931	23:22	Pis	21 Oct 1931	07:32
Gem	25 Feb 1931	05:12	Sco	25 Jun 1931	02:34	Ari	23 Oct 1931	20:20
Can	27 Feb 1931	11:45	Sag	27 Jun 1931	06:26	Tau	26 Oct 1931	09:11
			Cap	29 Jun 1931	11:35	Gem	28 Oct 1931	20:46
						Can	31 Oct 1931	06:26
Leo	1 Mar 1931	14:23	Aqu	1 Jul 1931	18:56	Leo	2 Nov 1931	13:38
Vir	3 Mar 1931	14:19	Pis	4 Jul 1931	05:09	Vir	4 Nov 1931	18:07
Lib	5 Mar 1931	13:32	Ari	6 Jul 1931	17:39	Lib	6 Nov 1931	20:02
Sco	7 Mar 1931	14:03	Tau	9 Jul 1931	06:13	Sco	8 Nov 1931	20:20
Sag	9 Mar 1931	17:30	Gem	11 Jul 1931	16:13	Sag	10 Nov 1931	20:39
Cap	12 Mar 1931	00:39	Can	13 Jul 1931	22:28	Cap	12 Nov 1931	22:53
Aqu	14 Mar 1931	11:03	Leo	16 Jul 1931	01:40	Aqu	15 Nov 1931	04:40
Pis	16 Mar 1931	23:26	Vir	18 Jul 1931	03:21	Pis	17 Nov 1931	14:33
Ari	19 Mar 1931	12:23	Lib	20 Jul 1931	05:05	Ari	20 Nov 1931	03:08
Tau	22 Mar 1931	00:43	Sco	22 Jul 1931	07:56	Tau	22 Nov 1931	15:59
Gem	24 Mar 1931	11:17	Sag	24 Jul 1931	12:18	Gem	25 Nov 1931	03:10
Can	26 Mar 1931	19:03	Cap	26 Jul 1931	18:22	Can	27 Nov 1931	12:08
Leo	28 Mar 1931	23:27	Aqu	29 Jul 1931	02:24	Leo	29 Nov 1931	19:05
Vir	31 Mar 1931	00:56	Pis	31 Jul 1931	12:46			
Lib	2 Apr 1931	00:48	Ari	3 Aug 1931	01:10	Vir	2 Dec 1931	00:15
Sco	4 Apr 1931	00:50	Tau	5 Aug 1931	14:04	Lib	4 Dec 1931	03:43
Sag	6 Apr 1931	02:52	Gem	8 Aug 1931	00:59	Sco	6 Dec 1931	05:43
Cap	8 Apr 1931	08:20	Can	10 Aug 1931	08:09	Sag	8 Dec 1931	07:04
Aqu	10 Apr 1931	17:39	Leo	12 Aug 1931	11:29	Cap	10 Dec 1931	09:18
Pis	13 Apr 1931	05:48	Vir	14 Aug 1931	12:24	Aqu	12 Dec 1931	14:10
Ari	15 Apr 1931	18:47	Lib	16 Aug 1931	12:45	Pis	14 Dec 1931	22:51
Tau	18 Apr 1931	06:49	Sco	18 Aug 1931	14:10	Ari	17 Dec 1931	10:49
Gem	20 Apr 1931	16:55	Sag	20 Aug 1931	17:46	Tau	19 Dec 1931	23:44
Can	23 Apr 1931	00:41	Cap	22 Aug 1931	23:59	Gem	22 Dec 1931	10:58
Leo	25 Apr 1931	06:03	Aqu	25 Aug 1931	08:38	Can	24 Dec 1931	19:21
Vir	27 Apr 1931	09:08	Pis	27 Aug 1931	19:27	Leo	27 Dec 1931	01:15
Lib	29 Apr 1931	10:34	Ari	30 Aug 1931	07:56	Vir	29 Dec 1931	05:40
						Lib	31 Dec 1931	09:17

Moon Signs

1932

Sco	2 Jan 1932	12:23		Ari	1 May 1932	22:46		Lib	2 Sep 1932	08:31
Sag	4 Jan 1932	15:15		Tau	4 May 1932	11:45		Sco	4 Sep 1932	10:06
Cap	6 Jan 1932	18:37		Gem	7 May 1932	00:19		Sag	6 Sep 1932	12:00
Aqu	8 Jan 1932	23:44		Can	9 May 1932	11:33		Cap	8 Sep 1932	15:11
Pis	11 Jan 1932	07:49		Leo	11 May 1932	20:45		Aqu	10 Sep 1932	20:16
Ari	13 Jan 1932	19:07		Vir	14 May 1932	03:12		Pis	13 Sep 1932	03:31
Tau	16 Jan 1932	08:02		Lib	16 May 1932	06:32		Ari	15 Sep 1932	13:01
Gem	18 Jan 1932	19:46		Sco	18 May 1932	07:14		Tau	18 Sep 1932	00:34
Can	21 Jan 1932	04:21		Sag	20 May 1932	06:47		Gem	20 Sep 1932	13:13
Leo	23 Jan 1932	09:38		Cap	22 May 1932	07:12		Can	23 Sep 1932	01:12
Vir	25 Jan 1932	12:46		Aqu	24 May 1932	10:32		Leo	25 Sep 1932	10:30
Lib	27 Jan 1932	15:07		Pis	26 May 1932	17:57		Vir	27 Sep 1932	16:05
Sco	29 Jan 1932	17:43		Ari	29 May 1932	05:08		Lib	29 Sep 1932	18:21
Sag	31 Jan 1932	21:06		Tau	31 May 1932	18:04				
Cap	3 Feb 1932	01:39		Gem	3 Jun 1932	06:31		Sco	1 Oct 1932	18:43
Aqu	5 Feb 1932	07:48		Can	5 Jun 1932	17:20		Sag	3 Oct 1932	19:02
Pis	7 Feb 1932	16:15		Leo	8 Jun 1932	02:13		Cap	5 Oct 1932	21:00
Ari	10 Feb 1932	03:17		Vir	10 Jun 1932	09:05		Aqu	8 Oct 1932	01:44
Tau	12 Feb 1932	16:04		Lib	12 Jun 1932	13:40		Pis	10 Oct 1932	09:27
Gem	15 Feb 1932	04:27		Sco	14 Jun 1932	15:59		Ari	12 Oct 1932	19:35
Can	17 Feb 1932	14:01		Sag	16 Jun 1932	16:45		Tau	15 Oct 1932	07:23
Leo	19 Feb 1932	19:48		Cap	18 Jun 1932	17:31		Gem	17 Oct 1932	20:02
Vir	21 Feb 1932	22:23		Aqu	20 Jun 1932	20:12		Can	20 Oct 1932	08:25
Lib	23 Feb 1932	23:21		Pis	23 Jun 1932	02:26		Leo	22 Oct 1932	18:56
Sco	26 Feb 1932	00:20		Ari	25 Jun 1932	12:34		Vir	25 Oct 1932	02:01
Sag	28 Feb 1932	02:39		Tau	28 Jun 1932	01:07		Lib	27 Oct 1932	05:15
				Gem	30 Jun 1932	13:34		Sco	29 Oct 1932	05:30
								Sag	31 Oct 1932	04:40
Cap	1 Mar 1932	07:06		Can	3 Jul 1932	00:05		Cap	2 Nov 1932	04:54
Aqu	3 Mar 1932	14:00		Leo	5 Jul 1932	08:18		Aqu	4 Nov 1932	08:06
Pis	5 Mar 1932	23:15		Vir	7 Jul 1932	14:32		Pis	6 Nov 1932	15:07
Ari	8 Mar 1932	10:35		Lib	9 Jul 1932	19:12		Ari	9 Nov 1932	01:25
Tau	10 Mar 1932	23:19		Sco	11 Jul 1932	22:27		Tau	11 Nov 1932	13:33
Gem	13 Mar 1932	12:01		Sag	14 Jul 1932	00:37		Gem	14 Nov 1932	02:13
Can	15 Mar 1932	22:44		Cap	16 Jul 1932	02:36		Can	16 Nov 1932	14:31
Leo	18 Mar 1932	05:55		Aqu	18 Jul 1932	05:44		Leo	19 Nov 1932	01:34
Vir	20 Mar 1932	09:17		Pis	20 Jul 1932	11:35		Vir	21 Nov 1932	10:07
Lib	22 Mar 1932	09:55		Ari	22 Jul 1932	20:52		Lib	23 Nov 1932	15:07
Sco	24 Mar 1932	09:35		Tau	25 Jul 1932	08:54		Sco	25 Nov 1932	16:37
Sag	26 Mar 1932	10:07		Gem	27 Jul 1932	21:25		Sag	27 Nov 1932	15:58
Cap	28 Mar 1932	13:09		Can	30 Jul 1932	08:06		Cap	29 Nov 1932	15:16
Aqu	30 Mar 1932	19:30								
Pis	2 Apr 1932	05:04		Leo	1 Aug 1932	15:56		Aqu	1 Dec 1932	16:46
Ari	4 Apr 1932	16:53		Vir	3 Aug 1932	21:14		Pis	3 Dec 1932	22:09
Tau	7 Apr 1932	05:43		Lib	6 Aug 1932	00:55		Ari	6 Dec 1932	07:35
Gem	9 Apr 1932	18:26		Sco	8 Aug 1932	03:49		Tau	8 Dec 1932	19:41
Can	12 Apr 1932	05:46		Sag	10 Aug 1932	06:31		Gem	11 Dec 1932	08:25
Leo	14 Apr 1932	14:20		Cap	12 Aug 1932	09:38		Can	13 Dec 1932	20:27
Vir	16 Apr 1932	19:20		Aqu	14 Aug 1932	13:54		Leo	16 Dec 1932	07:12
Lib	18 Apr 1932	20:58		Pis	16 Aug 1932	20:14		Vir	18 Dec 1932	16:08
Sco	20 Apr 1932	20:33		Ari	19 Aug 1932	05:18		Lib	20 Dec 1932	22:30
Sag	22 Apr 1932	19:57		Tau	21 Aug 1932	16:55		Sco	23 Dec 1932	01:51
Cap	24 Apr 1932	21:15		Gem	24 Aug 1932	05:33		Sag	25 Dec 1932	02:41
Aqu	27 Apr 1932	02:05		Can	26 Aug 1932	16:49		Cap	27 Dec 1932	02:31
Pis	29 Apr 1932	10:56		Leo	29 Aug 1932	01:01		Aqu	29 Dec 1932	03:23
				Vir	31 Aug 1932	05:58		Pis	31 Dec 1932	07:16

461

1933

Ari	2 Jan 1933	15:14	Leo	1 May 1933	23:05	Aqu	1 Sep 1933	06:59
Tau	5 Jan 1933	02:36	Vir	4 May 1933	08:39	Pis	3 Sep 1933	09:44
Gem	7 Jan 1933	15:19	Lib	6 May 1933	14:15	Ari	5 Sep 1933	14:15
Can	10 Jan 1933	03:16	Sco	8 May 1933	16:06	Tau	7 Sep 1933	21:35
Leo	12 Jan 1933	13:26	Sag	10 May 1933	15:42	Gem	10 Sep 1933	08:01
Vir	14 Jan 1933	21:41	Cap	12 May 1933	15:15	Can	12 Sep 1933	20:25
Lib	17 Jan 1933	04:02	Aqu	14 May 1933	16:46	Leo	15 Sep 1933	08:30
Sco	19 Jan 1933	08:24	Pis	16 May 1933	21:34	Vir	17 Sep 1933	18:13
Sag	21 Jan 1933	10:53	Ari	19 May 1933	05:45	Lib	20 Sep 1933	00:50
Cap	23 Jan 1933	12:17	Tau	21 May 1933	16:26	Sco	22 Sep 1933	04:59
Aqu	25 Jan 1933	13:57	Gem	24 May 1933	04:31	Sag	24 Sep 1933	07:48
Pis	27 Jan 1933	17:31	Can	26 May 1933	17:11	Cap	26 Sep 1933	10:23
Ari	30 Jan 1933	00:22	Leo	29 May 1933	05:33	Aqu	28 Sep 1933	13:27
			Vir	31 May 1933	16:05	Pis	30 Sep 1933	17:27
Tau	1 Feb 1933	10:40	Lib	2 Jun 1933	23:13	Ari	2 Oct 1933	22:51
Gem	3 Feb 1933	23:04	Sco	5 Jun 1933	02:23	Tau	5 Oct 1933	06:17
Can	6 Feb 1933	11:12	Sag	7 Jun 1933	02:31	Gem	7 Oct 1933	16:18
Leo	8 Feb 1933	21:15	Cap	9 Jun 1933	01:33	Can	10 Oct 1933	04:29
Vir	11 Feb 1933	04:42	Aqu	11 Jun 1933	01:42	Leo	12 Oct 1933	17:01
Lib	13 Feb 1933	09:58	Pis	13 Jun 1933	04:50	Vir	15 Oct 1933	03:23
Sco	15 Feb 1933	13:45	Ari	15 Jun 1933	11:51	Lib	17 Oct 1933	10:06
Sag	17 Feb 1933	16:42	Tau	17 Jun 1933	22:12	Sco	19 Oct 1933	13:26
Cap	19 Feb 1933	19:22	Gem	20 Jun 1933	10:25	Sag	21 Oct 1933	14:54
Aqu	21 Feb 1933	22:29	Can	22 Jun 1933	23:06	Cap	23 Oct 1933	16:13
Pis	24 Feb 1933	02:56	Leo	25 Jun 1933	11:16	Aqu	25 Oct 1933	18:48
Ari	26 Feb 1933	09:43	Vir	27 Jun 1933	22:00	Pis	27 Oct 1933	23:18
Tau	28 Feb 1933	19:20	Lib	30 Jun 1933	06:10	Ari	30 Oct 1933	05:40
Gem	3 Mar 1933	07:17	Sco	2 Jul 1933	10:55	Tau	1 Nov 1933	13:53
Can	5 Mar 1933	19:42	Sag	4 Jul 1933	12:30	Gem	4 Nov 1933	00:02
Leo	8 Mar 1933	06:17	Cap	6 Jul 1933	12:15	Can	6 Nov 1933	12:05
Vir	10 Mar 1933	13:40	Aqu	8 Jul 1933	12:06	Leo	9 Nov 1933	00:57
Lib	12 Mar 1933	18:02	Pis	10 Jul 1933	14:02	Vir	11 Nov 1933	12:22
Sco	14 Mar 1933	20:27	Ari	12 Jul 1933	19:31	Lib	13 Nov 1933	20:11
Sag	16 Mar 1933	22:18	Tau	15 Jul 1933	04:49	Sco	15 Nov 1933	23:50
Cap	19 Mar 1933	00:47	Gem	17 Jul 1933	16:44	Sag	18 Nov 1933	00:34
Aqu	21 Mar 1933	04:39	Can	20 Jul 1933	05:24	Cap	20 Nov 1933	00:24
Pis	23 Mar 1933	10:16	Leo	22 Jul 1933	17:18	Aqu	22 Nov 1933	01:21
Ari	25 Mar 1933	17:49	Vir	25 Jul 1933	03:35	Pis	24 Nov 1933	04:50
Tau	28 Mar 1933	03:32	Lib	27 Jul 1933	11:43	Ari	26 Nov 1933	11:13
Gem	30 Mar 1933	15:13	Sco	29 Jul 1933	17:21	Tau	28 Nov 1933	20:03
			Sag	31 Jul 1933	20:26			
Can	2 Apr 1933	03:49	Cap	2 Aug 1933	21:40	Gem	1 Dec 1933	06:44
Leo	4 Apr 1933	15:15	Aqu	4 Aug 1933	22:22	Can	3 Dec 1933	18:52
Vir	6 Apr 1933	23:31	Pis	7 Aug 1933	00:11	Leo	6 Dec 1933	07:48
Lib	9 Apr 1933	03:59	Ari	9 Aug 1933	04:41	Vir	8 Dec 1933	19:59
Sco	11 Apr 1933	05:31	Tau	11 Aug 1933	12:45	Lib	11 Dec 1933	05:18
Sag	13 Apr 1933	05:51	Gem	13 Aug 1933	23:57	Sco	13 Dec 1933	10:25
Cap	15 Apr 1933	06:53	Can	16 Aug 1933	12:32	Sag	15 Dec 1933	11:47
Aqu	17 Apr 1933	10:03	Leo	19 Aug 1933	00:22	Cap	17 Dec 1933	11:08
Pis	19 Apr 1933	15:54	Vir	21 Aug 1933	10:07	Aqu	19 Dec 1933	10:38
Ari	22 Apr 1933	00:14	Lib	23 Aug 1933	17:29	Pis	21 Dec 1933	12:16
Tau	24 Apr 1933	10:31	Sco	25 Aug 1933	22:44	Ari	23 Dec 1933	17:15
Gem	26 Apr 1933	22:18	Sag	28 Aug 1933	02:20	Tau	26 Dec 1933	01:43
Can	29 Apr 1933	10:58	Cap	30 Aug 1933	04:51	Gem	28 Dec 1933	12:43
						Can	31 Dec 1933	01:06

1934

Leo	2 Jan 1934	13:56	Sag	1 May 1934	01:01	Can	2 Sep 1934	15:41
Vir	5 Jan 1934	02:08	Cap	3 May 1934	02:53	Leo	5 Sep 1934	04:32
Lib	7 Jan 1934	12:19	Aqu	5 May 1934	05:06	Vir	7 Sep 1934	17:16
Sco	9 Jan 1934	19:10	Pis	7 May 1934	08:26	Lib	10 Sep 1934	04:22
Sag	11 Jan 1934	22:16	Ari	9 May 1934	13:09	Sco	12 Sep 1934	13:19
Cap	13 Jan 1934	22:36	Tau	11 May 1934	19:24	Sag	14 Sep 1934	20:03
Aqu	15 Jan 1934	21:56	Gem	14 May 1934	03:38	Cap	17 Sep 1934	00:35
Pis	17 Jan 1934	22:18	Can	16 May 1934	14:17	Aqu	19 Sep 1934	03:06
Ari	20 Jan 1934	01:29	Leo	19 May 1934	02:55	Pis	21 Sep 1934	04:13
Tau	22 Jan 1934	08:27	Vir	21 May 1934	15:35	Ari	23 Sep 1934	05:13
Gem	24 Jan 1934	18:54	Lib	24 May 1934	01:42	Tau	25 Sep 1934	07:47
Can	27 Jan 1934	07:24	Sco	26 May 1934	07:51	Gem	27 Sep 1934	13:34
Leo	29 Jan 1934	20:11	Sag	28 May 1934	10:28	Can	29 Sep 1934	23:15
			Cap	30 May 1934	11:12			
Vir	1 Feb 1934	08:00	Aqu	1 Jun 1934	11:55	Leo	2 Oct 1934	11:44
Lib	3 Feb 1934	17:59	Pis	3 Jun 1934	14:07	Vir	5 Oct 1934	00:30
Sco	6 Feb 1934	01:30	Ari	5 Jun 1934	18:31	Lib	7 Oct 1934	11:19
Sag	8 Feb 1934	06:14	Tau	8 Jun 1934	01:17	Sco	9 Oct 1934	19:31
Cap	10 Feb 1934	08:22	Gem	10 Jun 1934	10:14	Sag	12 Oct 1934	01:31
Aqu	12 Feb 1934	08:57	Can	12 Jun 1934	21:14	Cap	14 Oct 1934	06:04
Pis	14 Feb 1934	09:28	Leo	15 Jun 1934	09:52	Aqu	16 Oct 1934	09:31
Ari	16 Feb 1934	11:40	Vir	17 Jun 1934	22:51	Pis	18 Oct 1934	12:09
Tau	18 Feb 1934	17:03	Lib	20 Jun 1934	09:58	Ari	20 Oct 1934	14:28
Gem	21 Feb 1934	02:17	Sco	22 Jun 1934	17:24	Tau	22 Oct 1934	17:34
Can	23 Feb 1934	14:22	Sag	24 Jun 1934	20:48	Gem	24 Oct 1934	22:59
Leo	26 Feb 1934	03:13	Cap	26 Jun 1934	21:24	Can	27 Oct 1934	07:46
Vir	28 Feb 1934	14:45	Aqu	28 Jun 1934	21:02	Leo	29 Oct 1934	19:42
			Pis	30 Jun 1934	21:39			
Lib	3 Mar 1934	00:01	Ari	3 Jul 1934	00:40	Vir	1 Nov 1934	08:35
Sco	5 Mar 1934	06:58	Tau	5 Jul 1934	06:47	Lib	3 Nov 1934	19:40
Sag	7 Mar 1934	11:57	Gem	7 Jul 1934	15:56	Sco	6 Nov 1934	03:31
Cap	9 Mar 1934	15:21	Can	10 Jul 1934	03:21	Sag	8 Nov 1934	08:32
Aqu	11 Mar 1934	17:36	Leo	12 Jul 1934	16:07	Cap	10 Nov 1934	11:56
Pis	13 Mar 1934	19:25	Vir	15 Jul 1934	05:07	Aqu	12 Nov 1934	14:52
Ari	15 Mar 1934	22:01	Lib	17 Jul 1934	16:47	Pis	14 Nov 1934	17:56
Tau	18 Mar 1934	02:47	Sco	20 Jul 1934	01:29	Ari	16 Nov 1934	21:26
Gem	20 Mar 1934	10:52	Sag	22 Jul 1934	06:27	Tau	19 Nov 1934	01:47
Can	22 Mar 1934	22:13	Cap	24 Jul 1934	08:03	Gem	21 Nov 1934	07:47
Leo	25 Mar 1934	11:02	Aqu	26 Jul 1934	07:43	Can	23 Nov 1934	16:25
Vir	27 Mar 1934	22:43	Pis	28 Jul 1934	07:20	Leo	26 Nov 1934	03:54
Lib	30 Mar 1934	07:36	Ari	30 Jul 1934	08:46	Vir	28 Nov 1934	16:52
Sco	1 Apr 1934	13:34	Tau	1 Aug 1934	13:26	Lib	1 Dec 1934	04:38
Sag	3 Apr 1934	17:36	Gem	3 Aug 1934	21:49	Sco	3 Dec 1934	13:04
Cap	5 Apr 1934	20:45	Can	6 Aug 1934	09:13	Sag	5 Dec 1934	17:52
Aqu	7 Apr 1934	23:42	Leo	8 Aug 1934	22:08	Cap	7 Dec 1934	20:08
Pis	10 Apr 1934	02:52	Vir	11 Aug 1934	10:58	Aqu	9 Dec 1934	21:34
Ari	12 Apr 1934	06:40	Lib	13 Aug 1934	22:32	Pis	11 Dec 1934	23:31
Tau	14 Apr 1934	11:56	Sco	16 Aug 1934	07:50	Ari	14 Dec 1934	02:51
Gem	16 Apr 1934	19:41	Sag	18 Aug 1934	14:10	Tau	16 Dec 1934	07:57
Can	19 Apr 1934	06:26	Cap	20 Aug 1934	17:27	Gem	18 Dec 1934	14:59
Leo	21 Apr 1934	19:10	Aqu	22 Aug 1934	18:18	Can	21 Dec 1934	00:11
Vir	24 Apr 1934	07:19	Pis	24 Aug 1934	18:08	Leo	23 Dec 1934	11:38
Lib	26 Apr 1934	16:31	Ari	26 Aug 1934	18:44	Vir	26 Dec 1934	00:32
Sco	28 Apr 1934	22:06	Tau	28 Aug 1934	21:56	Lib	28 Dec 1934	12:58
			Gem	31 Aug 1934	04:55	Sco	30 Dec 1934	22:40

Moon Signs

1935

Sag	2 Jan 1935	04:26	Tau	2 May 1935	02:10	Sco	2 Sep 1935	16:22
Cap	4 Jan 1935	06:43	Gem	4 May 1935	05:26	Sag	5 Sep 1935	02:47
Aqu	6 Jan 1935	07:04	Can	6 May 1935	11:51	Cap	7 Sep 1935	10:06
Pis	8 Jan 1935	07:18	Leo	8 May 1935	21:55	Aqu	9 Sep 1935	13:43
Ari	10 Jan 1935	09:03	Vir	11 May 1935	10:26	Pis	11 Sep 1935	14:14
Tau	12 Jan 1935	13:25	Lib	13 May 1935	22:47	Ari	13 Sep 1935	13:21
Gem	14 Jan 1935	20:43	Sco	16 May 1935	08:53	Tau	15 Sep 1935	13:11
Can	17 Jan 1935	06:37	Sag	18 May 1935	16:12	Gem	17 Sep 1935	15:49
Leo	19 Jan 1935	18:27	Cap	20 May 1935	21:20	Can	19 Sep 1935	22:28
Vir	22 Jan 1935	07:19	Aqu	23 May 1935	01:08	Leo	22 Sep 1935	08:50
Lib	24 Jan 1935	19:59	Pis	25 May 1935	04:13	Vir	24 Sep 1935	21:19
Sco	27 Jan 1935	06:46	Ari	27 May 1935	06:59	Lib	27 Sep 1935	10:05
Sag	29 Jan 1935	14:09	Tau	29 May 1935	09:59	Sco	29 Sep 1935	22:05
Cap	31 Jan 1935	17:47	Gem	31 May 1935	14:12			
Aqu	2 Feb 1935	18:26	Can	2 Jun 1935	20:44	Sag	2 Oct 1935	08:40
Pis	4 Feb 1935	17:47	Leo	5 Jun 1935	06:19	Cap	4 Oct 1935	17:02
Ari	6 Feb 1935	17:49	Vir	7 Jun 1935	18:26	Aqu	6 Oct 1935	22:19
Tau	8 Feb 1935	20:23	Lib	10 Jun 1935	06:59	Pis	9 Oct 1935	00:25
Gem	11 Feb 1935	02:36	Sco	12 Jun 1935	17:35	Ari	11 Oct 1935	00:20
Can	13 Feb 1935	12:25	Sag	15 Jun 1935	00:56	Tau	12 Oct 1935	23:54
Leo	16 Feb 1935	00:35	Cap	17 Jun 1935	05:21	Gem	15 Oct 1935	01:19
Vir	18 Feb 1935	13:33	Aqu	19 Jun 1935	07:55	Can	17 Oct 1935	06:21
Lib	21 Feb 1935	02:02	Pis	21 Jun 1935	09:56	Leo	19 Oct 1935	15:36
Sco	23 Feb 1935	13:03	Ari	23 Jun 1935	12:21	Vir	22 Oct 1935	03:44
Sag	25 Feb 1935	21:39	Tau	25 Jun 1935	15:54	Lib	24 Oct 1935	16:31
Cap	28 Feb 1935	03:04	Gem	27 Jun 1935	21:07	Sco	27 Oct 1935	04:14
			Can	30 Jun 1935	04:26	Sag	29 Oct 1935	14:17
						Cap	31 Oct 1935	22:30
Pis	4 Mar 1935	05:13	Leo	2 Jul 1935	14:13	Aqu	3 Nov 1935	04:38
Ari	6 Mar 1935	04:41	Vir	5 Jul 1935	02:09	Pis	5 Nov 1935	08:19
Tau	8 Mar 1935	05:43	Lib	7 Jul 1935	14:52	Ari	7 Nov 1935	09:53
Gem	10 Mar 1935	10:13	Sco	10 Jul 1935	02:14	Tau	9 Nov 1935	10:29
Can	12 Mar 1935	18:52	Sag	12 Jul 1935	10:26	Gem	11 Nov 1935	11:53
Leo	15 Mar 1935	06:48	Cap	14 Jul 1935	15:02	Can	13 Nov 1935	15:57
Vir	17 Mar 1935	19:51	Aqu	16 Jul 1935	16:53	Leo	15 Nov 1935	23:52
Lib	20 Mar 1935	08:08	Pis	18 Jul 1935	17:30	Vir	18 Nov 1935	11:10
Sco	22 Mar 1935	18:44	Ari	20 Jul 1935	18:33	Lib	20 Nov 1935	23:52
Sag	25 Mar 1935	03:23	Tau	22 Jul 1935	21:21	Sco	23 Nov 1935	11:35
Cap	27 Mar 1935	09:48	Gem	25 Jul 1935	02:42	Sag	25 Nov 1935	21:08
Aqu	29 Mar 1935	13:41	Can	27 Jul 1935	10:44	Cap	28 Nov 1935	04:28
Pis	31 Mar 1935	15:14	Leo	29 Jul 1935	21:04	Aqu	30 Nov 1935	09:59
Ari	2 Apr 1935	15:31	Vir	1 Aug 1935	09:07	Pis	2 Dec 1935	14:02
Tau	4 Apr 1935	16:19	Lib	3 Aug 1935	21:54	Ari	4 Dec 1935	16:52
Gem	6 Apr 1935	19:36	Sco	6 Aug 1935	09:56	Tau	6 Dec 1935	19:03
Can	9 Apr 1935	02:50	Sag	8 Aug 1935	19:24	Gem	8 Dec 1935	21:37
Leo	11 Apr 1935	13:53	Cap	11 Aug 1935	01:08	Can	11 Dec 1935	01:55
Vir	14 Apr 1935	02:46	Aqu	13 Aug 1935	03:21	Leo	13 Dec 1935	09:07
Lib	16 Apr 1935	15:00	Pis	15 Aug 1935	03:19	Vir	15 Dec 1935	19:33
Sco	19 Apr 1935	01:09	Ari	17 Aug 1935	02:55	Lib	18 Dec 1935	07:58
Sag	21 Apr 1935	09:05	Tau	19 Aug 1935	04:08	Sco	20 Dec 1935	20:02
Cap	23 Apr 1935	15:13	Gem	21 Aug 1935	08:26	Sag	23 Dec 1935	05:44
Aqu	25 Apr 1935	19:43	Can	23 Aug 1935	16:17	Cap	25 Dec 1935	12:26
Pis	27 Apr 1935	22:39	Leo	26 Aug 1935	03:01	Aqu	27 Dec 1935	16:45
Ari	30 Apr 1935	00:26	Vir	28 Aug 1935	15:21	Pis	29 Dec 1935	19:42
			Lib	31 Aug 1935	04:08	Ari	31 Dec 1935	22:15

Moon Signs

1936

Tau	3 Jan 1936	01:11	Lib	2 May 1936	18:43	Ari	2 Sep 1936	22:43
Gem	5 Jan 1936	05:04	Sco	5 May 1936	07:16	Tau	4 Sep 1936	23:05
Can	7 Jan 1936	10:29	Sag	7 May 1936	18:54	Gem	7 Sep 1936	00:55
Leo	9 Jan 1936	18:02	Cap	10 May 1936	04:56	Can	9 Sep 1936	05:16
Vir	12 Jan 1936	04:05	Aqu	12 May 1936	12:46	Leo	11 Sep 1936	12:14
Lib	14 Jan 1936	16:11	Pis	14 May 1936	17:52	Vir	13 Sep 1936	21:20
Sco	17 Jan 1936	04:38	Ari	16 May 1936	20:13	Lib	16 Sep 1936	08:13
Sag	19 Jan 1936	15:10	Tau	18 May 1936	20:47	Sco	18 Sep 1936	20:32
Cap	21 Jan 1936	22:17	Gem	20 May 1936	21:12	Sag	21 Sep 1936	09:24
Aqu	24 Jan 1936	02:01	Can	22 May 1936	23:21	Cap	23 Sep 1936	20:52
Pis	26 Jan 1936	03:34	Leo	25 May 1936	04:42	Aqu	26 Sep 1936	04:52
Ari	28 Jan 1936	04:36	Vir	27 May 1936	13:48	Pis	28 Sep 1936	08:38
Tau	30 Jan 1936	06:37	Lib	30 May 1936	01:38	Ari	30 Sep 1936	09:09
Gem	1 Feb 1936	10:39	Sco	1 Jun 1936	14:11	Tau	2 Oct 1936	08:26
Can	3 Feb 1936	16:58	Sag	4 Jun 1936	01:36	Gem	4 Oct 1936	08:37
Leo	6 Feb 1936	01:26	Cap	6 Jun 1936	11:02	Can	6 Oct 1936	11:30
Vir	8 Feb 1936	11:49	Aqu	8 Jun 1936	18:17	Leo	8 Oct 1936	17:45
Lib	10 Feb 1936	23:46	Pis	10 Jun 1936	23:26	Vir	11 Oct 1936	03:02
Sco	13 Feb 1936	12:24	Ari	13 Jun 1936	02:46	Lib	13 Oct 1936	14:19
Sag	15 Feb 1936	23:55	Tau	15 Jun 1936	04:48	Sco	16 Oct 1936	02:47
Cap	18 Feb 1936	08:20	Gem	17 Jun 1936	06:30	Sag	18 Oct 1936	15:37
Aqu	20 Feb 1936	12:45	Can	19 Jun 1936	09:09	Cap	21 Oct 1936	03:37
Pis	22 Feb 1936	13:55	Leo	21 Jun 1936	14:07	Aqu	23 Oct 1936	12:58
Ari	24 Feb 1936	13:35	Vir	23 Jun 1936	22:16	Pis	25 Oct 1936	18:27
Tau	26 Feb 1936	13:52	Lib	26 Jun 1936	09:24	Ari	27 Oct 1936	20:09
Gem	28 Feb 1936	16:30	Sco	28 Jun 1936	21:52	Tau	29 Oct 1936	19:34
							Gem	31 Oct 1936	18:49
Can	1 Mar 1936	22:26	Sag	1 Jul 1936	09:26	Can	2 Nov 1936	20:01
Leo	4 Mar 1936	07:20	Cap	3 Jul 1936	18:34	Leo	5 Nov 1936	00:38
Vir	6 Mar 1936	18:18	Aqu	6 Jul 1936	00:55	Vir	7 Nov 1936	09:01
Lib	9 Mar 1936	06:26	Pis	8 Jul 1936	05:10	Lib	9 Nov 1936	20:15
Sco	11 Mar 1936	19:03	Ari	10 Jul 1936	08:10	Sco	12 Nov 1936	08:52
Sag	14 Mar 1936	07:05	Tau	12 Jul 1936	10:46	Sag	14 Nov 1936	21:33
Cap	16 Mar 1936	16:51	Gem	14 Jul 1936	13:39	Cap	17 Nov 1936	09:20
Aqu	18 Mar 1936	22:51	Can	16 Jul 1936	17:28	Aqu	19 Nov 1936	19:10
Pis	21 Mar 1936	00:58	Leo	18 Jul 1936	22:58	Pis	22 Nov 1936	02:03
Ari	23 Mar 1936	00:31	Vir	21 Jul 1936	06:54	Ari	24 Nov 1936	05:36
Tau	24 Mar 1936	23:38	Lib	23 Jul 1936	17:31	Tau	26 Nov 1936	06:28
Gem	27 Mar 1936	00:33	Sco	26 Jul 1936	05:54	Gem	28 Nov 1936	06:11
Can	29 Mar 1936	04:52	Sag	28 Jul 1936	17:56	Can	30 Nov 1936	06:40
Leo	31 Mar 1936	13:04	Cap	31 Jul 1936	03:23			
Vir	3 Apr 1936	00:08	Aqu	2 Aug 1936	09:24	Leo	2 Dec 1936	09:44
Lib	5 Apr 1936	12:31	Pis	4 Aug 1936	12:35	Vir	4 Dec 1936	16:31
Sco	8 Apr 1936	01:05	Ari	6 Aug 1936	14:21	Lib	7 Dec 1936	02:56
Sag	10 Apr 1936	13:02	Tau	8 Aug 1936	16:12	Sco	9 Dec 1936	15:28
Cap	12 Apr 1936	23:22	Gem	10 Aug 1936	19:12	Sag	12 Dec 1936	04:07
Aqu	15 Apr 1936	06:49	Can	12 Aug 1936	23:52	Cap	14 Dec 1936	15:25
Pis	17 Apr 1936	10:36	Leo	15 Aug 1936	06:20	Aqu	17 Dec 1936	00:41
Ari	19 Apr 1936	11:20	Vir	17 Aug 1936	14:45	Pis	19 Dec 1936	07:43
Tau	21 Apr 1936	10:37	Lib	20 Aug 1936	01:18	Ari	21 Dec 1936	12:25
Gem	23 Apr 1936	10:38	Sco	22 Aug 1936	13:36	Tau	23 Dec 1936	15:05
Can	25 Apr 1936	13:24	Sag	25 Aug 1936	02:09	Gem	25 Dec 1936	16:24
Leo	27 Apr 1936	20:04	Cap	27 Aug 1936	12:34	Can	27 Dec 1936	17:36
Vir	30 Apr 1936	06:22	Aqu	29 Aug 1936	19:12	Leo	29 Dec 1936	20:14
			Pis	31 Aug 1936	22:05			

1937

Vir	1 Jan 1937	01:46	Aqu	2 May 1937	18:08	Leo	1 Sep 1937	21:21
Lib	3 Jan 1937	10:56	Pis	5 May 1937	01:55	Vir	4 Sep 1937	01:35
Sco	5 Jan 1937	22:58	Ari	7 May 1937	05:47	Lib	6 Sep 1937	07:49
Sag	8 Jan 1937	11:42	Tau	9 May 1937	06:31	Sco	8 Sep 1937	17:00
Cap	10 Jan 1937	22:52	Gem	11 May 1937	05:56	Sag	11 Sep 1937	04:59
Aqu	13 Jan 1937	07:24	Can	13 May 1937	06:00	Cap	13 Sep 1937	17:51
Pis	15 Jan 1937	13:28	Leo	15 May 1937	08:28	Aqu	16 Sep 1937	04:51
Ari	17 Jan 1937	17:48	Vir	17 May 1937	14:20	Pis	18 Sep 1937	12:18
Tau	19 Jan 1937	21:07	Lib	19 May 1937	23:35	Ari	20 Sep 1937	16:30
Gem	21 Jan 1937	23:53	Sco	22 May 1937	11:18	Tau	22 Sep 1937	18:49
Can	24 Jan 1937	02:38	Sag	25 May 1937	00:10	Gem	24 Sep 1937	20:46
Leo	26 Jan 1937	06:08	Cap	27 May 1937	12:53	Can	26 Sep 1937	23:25
Vir	28 Jan 1937	11:31	Aqu	30 May 1937	00:12	Leo	29 Sep 1937	03:14
Lib	30 Jan 1937	19:50						
Sco	2 Feb 1937	07:11	Pis	1 Jun 1937	08:56	Vir	1 Oct 1937	08:29
Sag	4 Feb 1937	19:59	Ari	3 Jun 1937	14:21	Lib	3 Oct 1937	15:32
Cap	7 Feb 1937	07:33	Tau	5 Jun 1937	16:36	Sco	6 Oct 1937	00:56
Aqu	9 Feb 1937	15:59	Gem	7 Jun 1937	16:45	Sag	8 Oct 1937	12:44
Pis	11 Feb 1937	21:09	Can	9 Jun 1937	16:31	Cap	11 Oct 1937	01:46
Ari	14 Feb 1937	00:12	Leo	11 Jun 1937	17:44	Aqu	13 Oct 1937	13:36
Tau	16 Feb 1937	02:35	Vir	13 Jun 1937	22:02	Pis	15 Oct 1937	22:02
Gem	18 Feb 1937	05:22	Lib	16 Jun 1937	06:08	Ari	18 Oct 1937	02:31
Can	20 Feb 1937	09:04	Sco	18 Jun 1937	17:31	Tau	20 Oct 1937	04:09
Leo	22 Feb 1937	13:51	Sag	21 Jun 1937	06:25	Gem	22 Oct 1937	04:40
Vir	24 Feb 1937	20:05	Cap	23 Jun 1937	18:58	Can	24 Oct 1937	05:46
Lib	27 Feb 1937	04:27	Aqu	26 Jun 1937	05:54	Leo	26 Oct 1937	08:43
			Pis	28 Jun 1937	14:36	Vir	28 Oct 1937	14:02
			Ari	30 Jun 1937	20:49	Lib	30 Oct 1937	21:47
Sco	1 Mar 1937	15:23	Tau	3 Jul 1937	00:33	Sco	2 Nov 1937	07:48
Sag	4 Mar 1937	04:08	Gem	5 Jul 1937	02:15	Sag	4 Nov 1937	19:46
Cap	6 Mar 1937	16:22	Can	7 Jul 1937	02:53	Cap	7 Nov 1937	08:50
Aqu	9 Mar 1937	01:34	Leo	9 Jul 1937	03:59	Aqu	9 Nov 1937	21:18
Pis	11 Mar 1937	06:49	Vir	11 Jul 1937	07:16	Pis	12 Nov 1937	07:07
Ari	13 Mar 1937	08:59	Lib	13 Jul 1937	14:05	Ari	14 Nov 1937	12:58
Tau	15 Mar 1937	09:54	Sco	16 Jul 1937	00:37	Tau	16 Nov 1937	15:11
Gem	17 Mar 1937	11:19	Sag	18 Jul 1937	13:20	Gem	18 Nov 1937	15:10
Can	19 Mar 1937	14:26	Cap	21 Jul 1937	01:50	Can	20 Nov 1937	14:48
Leo	21 Mar 1937	19:36	Aqu	23 Jul 1937	12:19	Leo	22 Nov 1937	15:55
Vir	24 Mar 1937	02:44	Pis	25 Jul 1937	20:20	Vir	24 Nov 1937	19:56
Lib	26 Mar 1937	11:48	Ari	28 Jul 1937	02:14	Lib	27 Nov 1937	03:22
Sco	28 Mar 1937	22:51	Tau	30 Jul 1937	06:31	Sco	29 Nov 1937	13:47
Sag	31 Mar 1937	11:32						
Cap	3 Apr 1937	00:16	Gem	1 Aug 1937	09:29	Sag	2 Dec 1937	02:05
Aqu	5 Apr 1937	10:37	Can	3 Aug 1937	11:34	Cap	4 Dec 1937	15:07
Pis	7 Apr 1937	16:59	Leo	5 Aug 1937	13:36	Aqu	7 Dec 1937	03:40
Ari	9 Apr 1937	19:28	Vir	7 Aug 1937	16:54	Pis	9 Dec 1937	14:20
Tau	11 Apr 1937	19:39	Lib	9 Aug 1937	22:59	Ari	11 Dec 1937	21:53
Gem	13 Apr 1937	19:34	Sco	12 Aug 1937	08:37	Tau	14 Dec 1937	01:48
Can	15 Apr 1937	21:03	Sag	14 Aug 1937	20:59	Gem	16 Dec 1937	02:42
Leo	18 Apr 1937	01:12	Cap	17 Aug 1937	09:37	Can	18 Dec 1937	02:03
Vir	20 Apr 1937	08:16	Aqu	19 Aug 1937	20:04	Leo	20 Dec 1937	01:49
Lib	22 Apr 1937	17:51	Pis	22 Aug 1937	03:27	Vir	22 Dec 1937	03:58
Sco	25 Apr 1937	05:21	Ari	24 Aug 1937	08:23	Lib	24 Dec 1937	09:54
Sag	27 Apr 1937	18:05	Tau	26 Aug 1937	11:56	Sco	26 Dec 1937	19:45
Cap	30 Apr 1937	06:56	Gem	28 Aug 1937	15:01	Sag	29 Dec 1937	08:12
			Can	30 Aug 1937	18:03	Cap	31 Dec 1937	21:17

Moon Signs

1938

Aqu	3 Jan 1938	09:31	Gem	1 May 1938	15:44	Sag	1 Sep 1938	00:29
Pis	5 Jan 1938	20:06	Can	3 May 1938	16:50	Cap	3 Sep 1938	12:30
Ari	8 Jan 1938	04:28	Leo	5 May 1938	18:42	Aqu	6 Sep 1938	01:10
Tau	10 Jan 1938	10:05	Vir	7 May 1938	22:17	Pis	8 Sep 1938	12:28
Gem	12 Jan 1938	12:49	Lib	10 May 1938	04:06	Ari	10 Sep 1938	21:40
Can	14 Jan 1938	13:21	Sco	12 May 1938	12:16	Tau	13 Sep 1938	04:54
Leo	16 Jan 1938	13:09	Sag	14 May 1938	22:41	Gem	15 Sep 1938	10:22
Vir	18 Jan 1938	14:13	Cap	17 May 1938	10:51	Can	17 Sep 1938	14:08
Lib	20 Jan 1938	18:27	Aqu	19 May 1938	23:37	Leo	19 Sep 1938	16:26
Sco	23 Jan 1938	02:56	Pis	22 May 1938	11:07	Vir	21 Sep 1938	18:01
Sag	25 Jan 1938	14:52	Ari	24 May 1938	19:34	Lib	23 Sep 1938	20:19
Cap	28 Jan 1938	03:58	Tau	27 May 1938	00:15	Sco	26 Sep 1938	00:58
Aqu	30 Jan 1938	16:00	Gem	29 May 1938	01:51	Sag	28 Sep 1938	09:03
			Can	31 May 1938	01:52	Cap	30 Sep 1938	20:20
Pis	2 Feb 1938	01:58	Leo	2 Jun 1938	02:09	Aqu	3 Oct 1938	08:57
Ari	4 Feb 1938	09:54	Vir	4 Jun 1938	04:21	Pis	5 Oct 1938	20:26
Tau	6 Feb 1938	15:58	Lib	6 Jun 1938	09:36	Ari	8 Oct 1938	05:22
Gem	8 Feb 1938	20:07	Sco	8 Jun 1938	18:01	Tau	10 Oct 1938	11:42
Can	10 Feb 1938	22:25	Sag	11 Jun 1938	04:57	Gem	12 Oct 1938	16:10
Leo	12 Feb 1938	23:33	Cap	13 Jun 1938	17:21	Can	14 Oct 1938	19:31
Vir	15 Feb 1938	00:58	Aqu	16 Jun 1938	06:07	Leo	16 Oct 1938	22:19
Lib	17 Feb 1938	04:28	Pis	18 Jun 1938	18:02	Vir	19 Oct 1938	01:09
Sco	19 Feb 1938	11:38	Ari	21 Jun 1938	03:39	Lib	21 Oct 1938	04:43
Sag	21 Feb 1938	22:34	Tau	23 Jun 1938	09:48	Sco	23 Oct 1938	10:00
Cap	24 Feb 1938	11:28	Gem	25 Jun 1938	12:24	Sag	25 Oct 1938	17:54
Aqu	26 Feb 1938	23:35	Can	27 Jun 1938	12:27	Cap	28 Oct 1938	04:39
			Leo	29 Jun 1938	11:46	Aqu	30 Oct 1938	17:08
Pis	1 Mar 1938	09:13	Vir	2 Jul 1938	12:25	Pis	2 Nov 1938	05:09
Ari	3 Mar 1938	16:16	Lib	3 Jul 1938	16:09	Ari	4 Nov 1938	14:34
Tau	5 Mar 1938	21:29	Sco	5 Jul 1938	23:50	Tau	6 Nov 1938	20:40
Gem	8 Mar 1938	01:33	Sag	8 Jul 1938	10:46	Gem	9 Nov 1938	00:02
Can	10 Mar 1938	04:46	Cap	10 Jul 1938	23:22	Can	11 Nov 1938	01:59
Leo	12 Mar 1938	07:23	Aqu	13 Jul 1938	12:05	Leo	13 Nov 1938	03:50
Vir	14 Mar 1938	10:06	Pis	15 Jul 1938	23:55	Vir	15 Nov 1938	06:38
Lib	16 Mar 1938	14:09	Ari	18 Jul 1938	10:02	Lib	17 Nov 1938	11:04
Sco	18 Mar 1938	20:54	Tau	20 Jul 1938	17:31	Sco	19 Nov 1938	17:25
Sag	21 Mar 1938	07:01	Gem	22 Jul 1938	21:42	Sag	22 Nov 1938	01:57
Cap	23 Mar 1938	19:32	Can	24 Jul 1938	22:53	Cap	24 Nov 1938	12:38
Aqu	26 Mar 1938	07:55	Leo	26 Jul 1938	22:26	Aqu	27 Nov 1938	00:58
Pis	28 Mar 1938	17:51	Vir	28 Jul 1938	22:18	Pis	29 Nov 1938	13:29
Ari	31 Mar 1938	00:32	Lib	31 Jul 1938	00:36			
Tau	2 Apr 1938	04:42	Sco	2 Aug 1938	06:50	Ari	2 Dec 1938	00:01
Gem	4 Apr 1938	07:33	Sag	4 Aug 1938	17:02	Tau	4 Dec 1938	07:00
Can	6 Apr 1938	10:07	Cap	7 Aug 1938	05:33	Gem	6 Dec 1938	10:17
Leo	8 Apr 1938	13:04	Aqu	9 Aug 1938	18:15	Can	8 Dec 1938	11:07
Vir	10 Apr 1938	16:51	Pis	12 Aug 1938	05:45	Leo	10 Dec 1938	11:18
Lib	12 Apr 1938	22:03	Ari	14 Aug 1938	15:34	Vir	12 Dec 1938	12:38
Sco	15 Apr 1938	05:21	Tau	16 Aug 1938	23:24	Lib	14 Dec 1938	16:27
Sag	17 Apr 1938	15:20	Gem	19 Aug 1938	04:51	Sco	16 Dec 1938	23:14
Cap	20 Apr 1938	03:31	Can	21 Aug 1938	07:39	Sag	19 Dec 1938	08:31
Aqu	22 Apr 1938	16:10	Leo	23 Aug 1938	08:26	Cap	21 Dec 1938	19:39
Pis	25 Apr 1938	02:52	Vir	25 Aug 1938	08:43	Aqu	24 Dec 1938	07:59
Ari	27 Apr 1938	10:07	Lib	27 Aug 1938	10:27	Pis	26 Dec 1938	20:40
Tau	29 Apr 1938	14:01	Sco	29 Aug 1938	15:27	Ari	29 Dec 1938	08:13
						Tau	31 Dec 1938	16:47

Moon Signs

1939

Gem	2 Jan 1939	21:18	Sco	2 May 1939	17:36	Tau	3 Sep 1939	10:46
Can	4 Jan 1939	22:19	Sag	4 May 1939	23:11	Gem	5 Sep 1939	20:01
Leo	6 Jan 1939	21:32	Cap	7 May 1939	07:33	Can	8 Sep 1939	01:50
Vir	8 Jan 1939	21:09	Aqu	9 May 1939	18:40	Leo	10 Sep 1939	04:10
Lib	10 Jan 1939	23:12	Pis	12 May 1939	07:09	Vir	12 Sep 1939	04:08
Sco	13 Jan 1939	04:54	Ari	14 May 1939	18:40	Lib	14 Sep 1939	03:38
Sag	15 Jan 1939	14:10	Tau	17 May 1939	03:27	Sco	16 Sep 1939	04:43
Cap	18 Jan 1939	01:44	Gem	19 May 1939	09:05	Sag	18 Sep 1939	09:03
Aqu	20 Jan 1939	14:15	Can	21 May 1939	12:22	Cap	20 Sep 1939	17:11
Pis	23 Jan 1939	02:51	Leo	23 May 1939	14:33	Aqu	23 Sep 1939	04:24
Ari	25 Jan 1939	14:41	Vir	25 May 1939	16:50	Pis	25 Sep 1939	16:59
Tau	28 Jan 1939	00:27	Lib	27 May 1939	20:06	Ari	28 Sep 1939	05:22
Gem	30 Jan 1939	06:50	Sco	30 May 1939	00:47	Tau	30 Sep 1939	16:28
Can	1 Feb 1939	09:21	Sag	1 Jun 1939	07:15	Gem	3 Oct 1939	01:37
Leo	3 Feb 1939	09:05	Cap	3 Jun 1939	15:50	Can	5 Oct 1939	08:15
Vir	5 Feb 1939	08:02	Aqu	6 Jun 1939	02:40	Leo	7 Oct 1939	12:08
Lib	7 Feb 1939	08:30	Pis	8 Jun 1939	15:04	Vir	9 Oct 1939	13:45
Sco	9 Feb 1939	12:23	Ari	11 Jun 1939	03:09	Lib	11 Oct 1939	14:15
Sag	11 Feb 1939	20:24	Tau	13 Jun 1939	12:41	Sco	13 Oct 1939	15:18
Cap	14 Feb 1939	07:41	Gem	15 Jun 1939	18:32	Sag	15 Oct 1939	18:36
Aqu	16 Feb 1939	20:22	Can	17 Jun 1939	21:05	Cap	18 Oct 1939	01:23
Pis	19 Feb 1939	08:51	Leo	19 Jun 1939	21:57	Aqu	20 Oct 1939	11:40
Ari	21 Feb 1939	20:23	Vir	21 Jun 1939	22:56	Pis	23 Oct 1939	00:05
Tau	24 Feb 1939	06:18	Lib	24 Jun 1939	01:31	Ari	25 Oct 1939	12:27
Gem	26 Feb 1939	13:46	Sco	26 Jun 1939	06:25	Tau	27 Oct 1939	23:08
Can	28 Feb 1939	18:06	Sag	28 Jun 1939	13:39	Gem	30 Oct 1939	07:30
			Cap	30 Jun 1939	22:54			
Leo	2 Mar 1939	19:29	Aqu	3 Jul 1939	09:54	Can	1 Nov 1939	13:40
Vir	4 Mar 1939	19:16	Pis	5 Jul 1939	22:17	Leo	3 Nov 1939	18:01
Lib	6 Mar 1939	19:26	Ari	8 Jul 1939	10:49	Vir	5 Nov 1939	20:56
Sco	8 Mar 1939	22:01	Tau	10 Jul 1939	21:25	Lib	7 Nov 1939	23:03
Sag	11 Mar 1939	04:23	Gem	13 Jul 1939	04:19	Sco	10 Nov 1939	01:14
Cap	13 Mar 1939	14:36	Can	15 Jul 1939	07:15	Sag	12 Nov 1939	04:41
Aqu	16 Mar 1939	03:01	Leo	17 Jul 1939	07:30	Cap	14 Nov 1939	10:43
Pis	18 Mar 1939	15:31	Vir	19 Jul 1939	07:07	Aqu	16 Nov 1939	20:00
Ari	21 Mar 1939	02:40	Lib	21 Jul 1939	08:10	Pis	19 Nov 1939	08:00
Tau	23 Mar 1939	11:57	Sco	23 Jul 1939	12:05	Ari	21 Nov 1939	20:35
Gem	25 Mar 1939	19:14	Sag	25 Jul 1939	19:10	Tau	24 Nov 1939	07:22
Can	28 Mar 1939	00:18	Cap	28 Jul 1939	04:50	Gem	26 Nov 1939	15:08
Leo	30 Mar 1939	03:14	Aqu	30 Jul 1939	16:15	Can	28 Nov 1939	20:10
						Leo	30 Nov 1939	23:33
Vir	1 Apr 1939	04:38	Pis	2 Aug 1939	04:41	Vir	3 Dec 1939	02:23
Lib	3 Apr 1939	05:48	Ari	4 Aug 1939	17:22	Lib	5 Dec 1939	05:22
Sco	5 Apr 1939	08:22	Tau	7 Aug 1939	04:46	Sco	7 Dec 1939	08:57
Sag	7 Apr 1939	13:48	Gem	9 Aug 1939	13:04	Sag	9 Dec 1939	13:32
Cap	9 Apr 1939	22:47	Can	11 Aug 1939	17:20	Cap	11 Dec 1939	19:51
Aqu	12 Apr 1939	10:33	Leo	13 Aug 1939	18:09	Aqu	14 Dec 1939	04:42
Pis	14 Apr 1939	23:03	Vir	15 Aug 1939	17:19	Pis	16 Dec 1939	16:14
Ari	17 Apr 1939	10:12	Lib	17 Aug 1939	17:03	Ari	19 Dec 1939	05:02
Tau	19 Apr 1939	18:56	Sco	19 Aug 1939	19:20	Tau	21 Dec 1939	16:31
Gem	22 Apr 1939	01:15	Sag	22 Aug 1939	01:15	Gem	24 Dec 1939	00:35
Can	24 Apr 1939	05:43	Cap	24 Aug 1939	10:34	Can	26 Dec 1939	05:02
Leo	26 Apr 1939	08:54	Aqu	26 Aug 1939	22:09	Leo	28 Dec 1939	07:04
Vir	28 Apr 1939	11:26	Pis	29 Aug 1939	10:42	Vir	30 Dec 1939	08:29
Lib	30 Apr 1939	14:02	Ari	31 Aug 1939	23:14			

1940

Lib	1 Jan 1940	10:44	Pis	1 May 1940	01:56	Vir	1 Sep 1940	12:55
Sco	3 Jan 1940	14:36	Ari	3 May 1940	14:51	Lib	3 Sep 1940	12:54
Sag	5 Jan 1940	20:12	Tau	6 May 1940	03:11	Sco	5 Sep 1940	13:17
Cap	8 Jan 1940	03:30	Gem	8 May 1940	13:32	Sag	7 Sep 1940	15:36
Aqu	10 Jan 1940	12:42	Can	10 May 1940	21:32	Cap	9 Sep 1940	20:46
Pis	13 Jan 1940	00:03	Leo	13 May 1940	03:22	Aqu	12 Sep 1940	04:51
Ari	15 Jan 1940	12:55	Vir	15 May 1940	07:17	Pis	14 Sep 1940	15:25
Tau	18 Jan 1940	01:14	Lib	17 May 1940	09:40	Ari	17 Sep 1940	03:43
Gem	20 Jan 1940	10:30	Sco	19 May 1940	11:11	Tau	19 Sep 1940	16:45
Can	22 Jan 1940	15:34	Sag	21 May 1940	13:00	Gem	22 Sep 1940	05:05
Leo	24 Jan 1940	17:10	Cap	23 May 1940	16:34	Can	24 Sep 1940	14:56
Vir	26 Jan 1940	17:12	Aqu	25 May 1940	23:19	Leo	26 Sep 1940	21:07
Lib	28 Jan 1940	17:43	Pis	28 May 1940	09:39	Vir	28 Sep 1940	23:40
Sco	30 Jan 1940	20:18	Ari	30 May 1940	22:18	Lib	30 Sep 1940	23:46
Sag	2 Feb 1940	01:36	Tau	2 Jun 1940	10:42	Sco	2 Oct 1940	23:12
Cap	4 Feb 1940	09:27	Gem	4 Jun 1940	20:48	Sag	4 Oct 1940	23:55
Aqu	6 Feb 1940	19:21	Can	7 Jun 1940	04:01	Cap	7 Oct 1940	03:29
Pis	9 Feb 1940	06:58	Leo	9 Jun 1940	09:00	Aqu	9 Oct 1940	10:45
Ari	11 Feb 1940	19:49	Vir	11 Jun 1940	12:40	Pis	11 Oct 1940	21:18
Tau	14 Feb 1940	08:35	Lib	13 Jun 1940	15:43	Ari	14 Oct 1940	09:50
Gem	16 Feb 1940	19:09	Sco	15 Jun 1940	18:31	Tau	16 Oct 1940	22:48
Can	19 Feb 1940	01:45	Sag	17 Jun 1940	21:34	Gem	19 Oct 1940	10:58
Leo	21 Feb 1940	04:18	Cap	20 Jun 1940	01:45	Can	21 Oct 1940	21:17
Vir	23 Feb 1940	04:11	Aqu	22 Jun 1940	08:15	Leo	24 Oct 1940	04:50
Lib	25 Feb 1940	03:29	Pis	24 Jun 1940	17:55	Vir	26 Oct 1940	09:08
Sco	27 Feb 1940	04:14	Ari	27 Jun 1940	06:12	Lib	28 Oct 1940	10:35
Sag	29 Feb 1940	07:55	Tau	29 Jun 1940	18:52	Sco	30 Oct 1940	10:24
Cap	2 Mar 1940	15:03	Gem	2 Jul 1940	05:14	Sag	1 Nov 1940	10:21
Aqu	5 Mar 1940	01:08	Can	4 Jul 1940	12:09	Cap	3 Nov 1940	12:23
Pis	7 Mar 1940	13:07	Leo	6 Jul 1940	16:11	Aqu	5 Nov 1940	18:03
Ari	10 Mar 1940	02:00	Vir	8 Jul 1940	18:44	Pis	8 Nov 1940	03:46
Tau	12 Mar 1940	14:43	Lib	10 Jul 1940	21:06	Ari	10 Nov 1940	16:13
Gem	15 Mar 1940	01:51	Sco	13 Jul 1940	00:07	Tau	13 Nov 1940	05:12
Can	17 Mar 1940	09:55	Sag	15 Jul 1940	04:04	Gem	15 Nov 1940	17:00
Leo	19 Mar 1940	14:13	Cap	17 Jul 1940	09:18	Can	18 Nov 1940	02:51
Vir	21 Mar 1940	15:19	Aqu	19 Jul 1940	16:22	Leo	20 Nov 1940	10:37
Lib	23 Mar 1940	14:47	Pis	22 Jul 1940	01:59	Vir	22 Nov 1940	16:10
Sco	25 Mar 1940	14:33	Ari	24 Jul 1940	14:01	Lib	24 Nov 1940	19:24
Sag	27 Mar 1940	16:31	Tau	27 Jul 1940	02:55	Sco	26 Nov 1940	20:44
Cap	29 Mar 1940	22:00	Gem	29 Jul 1940	14:02	Sag	28 Nov 1940	21:18
			Can	31 Jul 1940	21:31	Cap	30 Nov 1940	22:51
Aqu	1 Apr 1940	07:13	Leo	3 Aug 1940	01:19	Aqu	3 Dec 1940	03:13
Pis	3 Apr 1940	19:11	Vir	5 Aug 1940	02:50	Pis	5 Dec 1940	11:36
Ari	6 Apr 1940	08:09	Lib	7 Aug 1940	03:49	Ari	7 Dec 1940	23:26
Tau	8 Apr 1940	20:38	Sco	9 Aug 1940	05:45	Tau	10 Dec 1940	12:26
Gem	11 Apr 1940	07:31	Sag	11 Aug 1940	09:29	Gem	13 Dec 1940	00:06
Can	13 Apr 1940	16:03	Cap	13 Aug 1940	15:15	Can	15 Dec 1940	09:19
Leo	15 Apr 1940	21:42	Aqu	15 Aug 1940	23:08	Leo	17 Dec 1940	16:15
Vir	18 Apr 1940	00:33	Pis	18 Aug 1940	09:10	Vir	19 Dec 1940	21:34
Lib	20 Apr 1940	01:22	Ari	20 Aug 1940	21:14	Lib	22 Dec 1940	01:36
Sco	22 Apr 1940	01:33	Tau	23 Aug 1940	10:16	Sco	24 Dec 1940	04:29
Sag	24 Apr 1940	02:48	Gem	25 Aug 1940	22:12	Sag	26 Dec 1940	06:36
Cap	26 Apr 1940	06:49	Can	28 Aug 1940	06:53	Cap	28 Dec 1940	08:58
Aqu	28 Apr 1940	14:39	Leo	30 Aug 1940	11:29	Aqu	30 Dec 1940	13:09

1941

Pis	1 Jan 1941	20:35	Can	1 May 1941	01:55	Aqu	2 Sep 1941	11:39
Ari	4 Jan 1941	07:34	Leo	3 May 1941	11:32	Pis	4 Sep 1941	17:51
Tau	6 Jan 1941	20:27	Vir	5 May 1941	18:05	Ari	7 Sep 1941	02:29
Gem	9 Jan 1941	08:26	Lib	7 May 1941	21:10	Tau	9 Sep 1941	13:32
Can	11 Jan 1941	17:33	Sco	9 May 1941	21:32	Gem	12 Sep 1941	02:05
Leo	13 Jan 1941	23:38	Sag	11 May 1941	20:49	Can	14 Sep 1941	14:08
Vir	16 Jan 1941	03:45	Cap	13 May 1941	21:04	Leo	16 Sep 1941	23:34
Lib	18 Jan 1941	06:59	Aqu	16 May 1941	00:16	Vir	19 Sep 1941	05:28
Sco	20 Jan 1941	10:03	Pis	18 May 1941	07:34	Lib	21 Sep 1941	08:16
Sag	22 Jan 1941	13:16	Ari	20 May 1941	18:34	Sco	23 Sep 1941	09:23
Cap	24 Jan 1941	17:01	Tau	23 May 1941	07:26	Sag	25 Sep 1941	10:24
Aqu	26 Jan 1941	22:06	Gem	25 May 1941	20:09	Cap	27 Sep 1941	12:45
Pis	29 Jan 1941	05:34	Can	28 May 1941	07:36	Aqu	29 Sep 1941	17:16
Ari	31 Jan 1941	16:02	Leo	30 May 1941	17:15			
Tau	3 Feb 1941	04:40	Vir	2 Jun 1941	00:37	Pis	2 Oct 1941	00:18
Gem	5 Feb 1941	17:09	Lib	4 Jun 1941	05:16	Ari	4 Oct 1941	09:37
Can	8 Feb 1941	02:56	Sco	6 Jun 1941	07:13	Tau	6 Oct 1941	20:51
Leo	10 Feb 1941	09:06	Sag	8 Jun 1941	07:23	Gem	9 Oct 1941	09:22
Vir	12 Feb 1941	12:20	Cap	10 Jun 1941	07:31	Can	11 Oct 1941	21:52
Lib	14 Feb 1941	14:07	Aqu	12 Jun 1941	09:42	Leo	14 Oct 1941	08:28
Sco	16 Feb 1941	15:52	Pis	14 Jun 1941	15:34	Vir	16 Oct 1941	15:34
Sag	18 Feb 1941	18:36	Ari	17 Jun 1941	01:30	Lib	18 Oct 1941	18:53
Cap	20 Feb 1941	22:54	Tau	19 Jun 1941	14:02	Sco	20 Oct 1941	19:25
Aqu	23 Feb 1941	05:01	Gem	22 Jun 1941	02:43	Sag	22 Oct 1941	19:00
Pis	25 Feb 1941	13:18	Can	24 Jun 1941	13:50	Cap	24 Oct 1941	19:40
Ari	27 Feb 1941	23:54	Leo	26 Jun 1941	22:54	Aqu	26 Oct 1941	23:03
			Vir	29 Jun 1941	06:02	Pis	29 Oct 1941	05:50
						Ari	31 Oct 1941	15:38
Tau	2 Mar 1941	12:23	Lib	1 Jul 1941	11:16	Tau	3 Nov 1941	03:18
Gem	5 Mar 1941	01:11	Sco	3 Jul 1941	14:33	Gem	5 Nov 1941	15:51
Can	7 Mar 1941	12:02	Sag	5 Jul 1941	16:13	Can	8 Nov 1941	04:25
Leo	9 Mar 1941	19:18	Cap	7 Jul 1941	17:20	Leo	10 Nov 1941	15:48
Vir	11 Mar 1941	22:50	Aqu	9 Jul 1941	19:36	Vir	13 Nov 1941	00:27
Lib	13 Mar 1941	23:50	Pis	12 Jul 1941	00:43	Lib	15 Nov 1941	05:21
Sco	16 Mar 1941	00:03	Ari	14 Jul 1941	09:35	Sco	17 Nov 1941	06:39
Sag	18 Mar 1941	01:08	Tau	16 Jul 1941	21:29	Sag	19 Nov 1941	05:53
Cap	20 Mar 1941	04:25	Gem	19 Jul 1941	10:09	Cap	21 Nov 1941	05:11
Aqu	22 Mar 1941	10:34	Can	21 Jul 1941	21:14	Aqu	23 Nov 1941	06:46
Pis	24 Mar 1941	19:30	Leo	24 Jul 1941	05:47	Pis	25 Nov 1941	12:09
Ari	27 Mar 1941	06:39	Vir	26 Jul 1941	12:02	Ari	27 Nov 1941	21:26
Tau	29 Mar 1941	19:13	Lib	28 Jul 1941	16:40	Tau	30 Nov 1941	09:18
			Sco	30 Jul 1941	20:08			
Gem	1 Apr 1941	08:06	Sag	1 Aug 1941	22:49	Gem	2 Dec 1941	21:59
Can	3 Apr 1941	19:42	Cap	4 Aug 1941	01:17	Can	5 Dec 1941	10:21
Leo	6 Apr 1941	04:24	Aqu	6 Aug 1941	04:32	Leo	7 Dec 1941	21:42
Vir	8 Apr 1941	09:19	Pis	8 Aug 1941	09:51	Vir	10 Dec 1941	07:11
Lib	10 Apr 1941	10:53	Ari	10 Aug 1941	18:12	Lib	12 Dec 1941	13:44
Sco	12 Apr 1941	10:31	Tau	13 Aug 1941	05:31	Sco	14 Dec 1941	16:50
Sag	14 Apr 1941	10:08	Gem	15 Aug 1941	18:09	Sag	16 Dec 1941	17:09
Cap	16 Apr 1941	11:39	Can	18 Aug 1941	05:37	Cap	18 Dec 1941	16:26
Aqu	18 Apr 1941	16:31	Leo	20 Aug 1941	14:14	Aqu	20 Dec 1941	16:53
Pis	21 Apr 1941	01:07	Vir	22 Aug 1941	19:52	Pis	22 Dec 1941	20:33
Ari	23 Apr 1941	12:34	Lib	24 Aug 1941	23:20	Ari	25 Dec 1941	04:24
Tau	26 Apr 1941	01:22	Sco	27 Aug 1941	01:48	Tau	27 Dec 1941	15:43
Gem	28 Apr 1941	14:10	Sag	29 Aug 1941	04:12	Gem	30 Dec 1941	04:26
			Cap	31 Aug 1941	07:17			

Moon Signs

1942

Can	1 Jan 1942	16:41	Sag	2 May 1942	06:02	Gem	1 Sep 1942	20:40
Leo	4 Jan 1942	03:32	Cap	4 May 1942	06:04	Can	4 Sep 1942	08:59
Vir	6 Jan 1942	12:41	Aqu	6 May 1942	07:56	Leo	6 Sep 1942	21:14
Lib	8 Jan 1942	19:47	Pis	8 May 1942	12:44	Vir	9 Sep 1942	07:30
Sco	11 Jan 1942	00:22	Ari	10 May 1942	20:31	Lib	11 Sep 1942	15:03
Sag	13 Jan 1942	02:30	Tau	13 May 1942	06:36	Sco	13 Sep 1942	20:17
Cap	15 Jan 1942	03:06	Gem	15 May 1942	18:14	Sag	15 Sep 1942	23:57
Aqu	17 Jan 1942	03:52	Can	18 May 1942	06:48	Cap	18 Sep 1942	02:47
Pis	19 Jan 1942	06:43	Leo	20 May 1942	19:20	Aqu	20 Sep 1942	05:26
Ari	21 Jan 1942	13:09	Vir	23 May 1942	06:06	Pis	22 Sep 1942	08:33
Tau	23 Jan 1942	23:18	Lib	25 May 1942	13:20	Ari	24 Sep 1942	12:57
Gem	26 Jan 1942	11:43	Sco	27 May 1942	16:30	Tau	26 Sep 1942	19:34
Can	29 Jan 1942	00:02	Sag	29 May 1942	16:38	Gem	29 Sep 1942	05:04
Leo	31 Jan 1942	10:36	Cap	31 May 1942	15:43			
Vir	2 Feb 1942	18:57	Aqu	2 Jun 1942	15:59	Can	1 Oct 1942	17:02
Lib	5 Feb 1942	01:17	Pis	4 Jun 1942	19:14	Leo	4 Oct 1942	05:34
Sco	7 Feb 1942	05:55	Ari	7 Jun 1942	02:11	Vir	6 Oct 1942	16:12
Sag	9 Feb 1942	09:05	Tau	9 Jun 1942	12:15	Lib	8 Oct 1942	23:30
Cap	11 Feb 1942	11:18	Gem	12 Jun 1942	00:11	Sco	11 Oct 1942	03:45
Aqu	13 Feb 1942	13:27	Can	14 Jun 1942	12:49	Sag	13 Oct 1942	06:09
Pis	15 Feb 1942	16:50	Leo	17 Jun 1942	01:18	Cap	15 Oct 1942	08:13
Ari	17 Feb 1942	22:47	Vir	19 Jun 1942	12:32	Aqu	17 Oct 1942	11:01
Tau	20 Feb 1942	07:57	Lib	21 Jun 1942	21:02	Pis	19 Oct 1942	15:05
Gem	22 Feb 1942	19:46	Sco	24 Jun 1942	01:48	Ari	21 Oct 1942	20:36
Can	25 Feb 1942	08:14	Sag	26 Jun 1942	03:07	Tau	24 Oct 1942	03:51
Leo	27 Feb 1942	19:05	Cap	28 Jun 1942	02:29	Gem	26 Oct 1942	13:18
			Aqu	30 Jun 1942	02:01	Can	29 Oct 1942	00:59
						Leo	31 Oct 1942	13:47
Vir	2 Mar 1942	03:04	Pis	2 Jul 1942	03:46	Vir	3 Nov 1942	01:17
Lib	4 Mar 1942	08:22	Ari	4 Jul 1942	09:11	Lib	5 Nov 1942	09:19
Sco	6 Mar 1942	11:49	Tau	6 Jul 1942	18:22	Sco	7 Nov 1942	13:25
Sag	8 Mar 1942	14:27	Gem	9 Jul 1942	06:09	Sag	9 Nov 1942	14:46
Cap	10 Mar 1942	17:08	Can	11 Jul 1942	18:51	Cap	11 Nov 1942	15:17
Aqu	12 Mar 1942	20:30	Leo	14 Jul 1942	07:07	Aqu	13 Nov 1942	16:48
Pis	15 Mar 1942	01:09	Vir	16 Jul 1942	18:08	Pis	15 Nov 1942	20:27
Ari	17 Mar 1942	07:40	Lib	19 Jul 1942	03:00	Ari	18 Nov 1942	02:30
Tau	19 Mar 1942	16:38	Sco	21 Jul 1942	09:00	Tau	20 Nov 1942	10:37
Gem	22 Mar 1942	04:00	Sag	23 Jul 1942	11:56	Gem	22 Nov 1942	20:34
Can	24 Mar 1942	16:32	Cap	25 Jul 1942	12:37	Can	25 Nov 1942	08:16
Leo	27 Mar 1942	04:03	Aqu	27 Jul 1942	12:37	Leo	27 Nov 1942	21:08
Vir	29 Mar 1942	12:35	Pis	29 Jul 1942	13:49	Vir	30 Nov 1942	09:28
Lib	31 Mar 1942	17:36	Ari	31 Jul 1942	17:54			
Sco	2 Apr 1942	19:53	Tau	3 Aug 1942	01:48	Lib	2 Dec 1942	18:54
Sag	4 Apr 1942	21:04	Gem	5 Aug 1942	12:54	Sco	5 Dec 1942	00:04
Cap	6 Apr 1942	22:42	Can	8 Aug 1942	01:29	Sag	7 Dec 1942	01:32
Aqu	9 Apr 1942	01:56	Leo	10 Aug 1942	13:38	Cap	9 Dec 1942	01:06
Pis	11 Apr 1942	07:19	Vir	13 Aug 1942	00:08	Aqu	11 Dec 1942	00:57
Ari	13 Apr 1942	14:49	Lib	15 Aug 1942	08:30	Pis	13 Dec 1942	02:56
Tau	16 Apr 1942	00:17	Sco	17 Aug 1942	14:36	Ari	15 Dec 1942	08:04
Gem	18 Apr 1942	11:36	Sag	19 Aug 1942	18:34	Tau	17 Dec 1942	16:16
Can	21 Apr 1942	00:09	Cap	21 Aug 1942	20:45	Gem	20 Dec 1942	02:45
Leo	23 Apr 1942	12:20	Aqu	23 Aug 1942	22:07	Can	22 Dec 1942	14:45
Vir	25 Apr 1942	22:00	Pis	25 Aug 1942	23:55	Leo	25 Dec 1942	03:34
Lib	28 Apr 1942	03:48	Ari	28 Aug 1942	03:39	Vir	27 Dec 1942	16:09
Sco	30 Apr 1942	05:58	Tau	30 Aug 1942	10:29	Lib	30 Dec 1942	02:43

1943

Sco	1 Jan 1943	09:38	Ari	1 May 1943	04:38	Lib	1 Sep 1943	18:32
Sag	3 Jan 1943	12:31	Tau	3 May 1943	09:57	Sco	4 Sep 1943	04:19
Cap	5 Jan 1943	12:33	Gem	5 May 1943	17:15	Sag	6 Sep 1943	11:37
Aqu	7 Jan 1943	11:42	Can	8 May 1943	03:16	Cap	8 Sep 1943	16:12
Pis	9 Jan 1943	12:03	Leo	10 May 1943	15:38	Aqu	10 Sep 1943	18:17
Ari	11 Jan 1943	15:21	Vir	13 May 1943	04:20	Pis	12 Sep 1943	18:45
Tau	13 Jan 1943	22:22	Lib	15 May 1943	14:42	Ari	14 Sep 1943	19:08
Gem	16 Jan 1943	08:38	Sco	17 May 1943	21:17	Tau	16 Sep 1943	21:14
Can	18 Jan 1943	20:53	Sag	20 May 1943	00:31	Gem	19 Sep 1943	02:42
Leo	21 Jan 1943	09:43	Cap	22 May 1943	01:59	Can	21 Sep 1943	12:10
Vir	23 Jan 1943	22:02	Aqu	24 May 1943	03:23	Leo	24 Sep 1943	00:33
Lib	26 Jan 1943	08:46	Pis	26 May 1943	05:57	Vir	26 Sep 1943	13:29
Sco	28 Jan 1943	16:49	Ari	28 May 1943	10:16	Lib	29 Sep 1943	00:55
Sag	30 Jan 1943	21:32	Tau	30 May 1943	16:24			
Cap	1 Feb 1943	23:13	Gem	2 Jun 1943	00:29	Sco	1 Oct 1943	10:03
Aqu	3 Feb 1943	23:09	Can	4 Jun 1943	10:45	Sag	3 Oct 1943	17:02
Pis	5 Feb 1943	23:08	Leo	6 Jun 1943	23:02	Cap	5 Oct 1943	22:09
Ari	8 Feb 1943	01:01	Vir	9 Jun 1943	12:02	Aqu	8 Oct 1943	01:38
Tau	10 Feb 1943	06:16	Lib	11 Jun 1943	23:20	Pis	10 Oct 1943	03:43
Gem	12 Feb 1943	15:25	Sco	14 Jun 1943	06:57	Ari	12 Oct 1943	05:11
Can	15 Feb 1943	03:24	Sag	16 Jun 1943	10:34	Tau	14 Oct 1943	07:25
Leo	17 Feb 1943	16:17	Cap	18 Jun 1943	11:29	Gem	16 Oct 1943	12:07
Vir	20 Feb 1943	04:19	Aqu	20 Jun 1943	11:33	Can	18 Oct 1943	20:27
Lib	22 Feb 1943	14:28	Pis	22 Jun 1943	12:36	Leo	21 Oct 1943	08:11
Sco	24 Feb 1943	22:23	Ari	24 Jun 1943	15:52	Vir	23 Oct 1943	21:08
Sag	27 Feb 1943	03:58	Tau	26 Jun 1943	21:52	Lib	26 Oct 1943	08:36
			Gem	29 Jun 1943	06:26	Sco	28 Oct 1943	17:13
						Sag	30 Oct 1943	23:13
Cap	1 Mar 1943	07:18	Can	1 Jul 1943	17:12	Cap	2 Nov 1943	03:35
Aqu	3 Mar 1943	08:55	Leo	4 Jul 1943	05:38	Aqu	4 Nov 1943	07:09
Pis	5 Mar 1943	09:54	Vir	6 Jul 1943	18:44	Pis	6 Nov 1943	10:15
Ari	7 Mar 1943	11:41	Lib	9 Jul 1943	06:43	Ari	8 Nov 1943	13:10
Tau	9 Mar 1943	15:53	Sco	11 Jul 1943	15:39	Tau	10 Nov 1943	16:32
Gem	11 Mar 1943	23:39	Sag	13 Jul 1943	20:35	Gem	12 Nov 1943	21:31
Can	14 Mar 1943	10:50	Cap	15 Jul 1943	22:05	Can	15 Nov 1943	05:22
Leo	16 Mar 1943	23:40	Aqu	17 Jul 1943	21:45	Leo	17 Nov 1943	16:27
Vir	19 Mar 1943	11:41	Pis	19 Jul 1943	21:30	Vir	20 Nov 1943	05:20
Lib	21 Mar 1943	21:19	Ari	21 Jul 1943	23:09	Lib	22 Nov 1943	17:17
Sco	24 Mar 1943	04:21	Tau	24 Jul 1943	03:52	Sco	25 Nov 1943	02:07
Sag	26 Mar 1943	09:22	Gem	26 Jul 1943	12:04	Sag	27 Nov 1943	07:33
Cap	28 Mar 1943	13:04	Can	28 Jul 1943	23:03	Cap	29 Nov 1943	10:41
Aqu	30 Mar 1943	15:56	Leo	31 Jul 1943	11:42			
Pis	1 Apr 1943	18:26	Vir	3 Aug 1943	00:44	Aqu	1 Dec 1943	13:00
Ari	3 Apr 1943	21:17	Lib	5 Aug 1943	12:50	Pis	3 Dec 1943	15:35
Tau	6 Apr 1943	01:38	Sco	7 Aug 1943	22:38	Ari	5 Dec 1943	18:59
Gem	8 Apr 1943	08:41	Sag	10 Aug 1943	05:07	Tau	7 Dec 1943	23:30
Can	10 Apr 1943	19:02	Cap	12 Aug 1943	08:08	Gem	10 Dec 1943	05:31
Leo	13 Apr 1943	07:39	Aqu	14 Aug 1943	08:35	Can	12 Dec 1943	13:46
Vir	15 Apr 1943	19:58	Pis	16 Aug 1943	08:06	Leo	15 Dec 1943	00:36
Lib	18 Apr 1943	05:40	Ari	18 Aug 1943	08:32	Vir	17 Dec 1943	13:21
Sco	20 Apr 1943	12:02	Tau	20 Aug 1943	11:40	Lib	20 Dec 1943	01:54
Sag	22 Apr 1943	15:55	Gem	22 Aug 1943	18:33	Sco	22 Dec 1943	11:44
Cap	24 Apr 1943	18:39	Can	25 Aug 1943	05:06	Sag	24 Dec 1943	17:43
Aqu	26 Apr 1943	21:20	Leo	27 Aug 1943	17:48	Cap	26 Dec 1943	20:23
Pis	29 Apr 1943	00:35	Vir	30 Aug 1943	06:46	Aqu	28 Dec 1943	21:20
						Pis	30 Dec 1943	22:17

Moon Signs

1944

Ari	2 Jan 1944	00:34	Vir	1 May 1944	23:03	Pis	2 Sep 1944	04:13
Tau	4 Jan 1944	04:57	Lib	4 May 1944	11:38	Ari	4 Sep 1944	03:27
Gem	6 Jan 1944	11:44	Sco	6 May 1944	22:16	Tau	6 Sep 1944	03:28
Can	8 Jan 1944	20:47	Sag	9 May 1944	06:26	Gem	8 Sep 1944	06:13
Leo	11 Jan 1944	07:57	Cap	11 May 1944	12:31	Can	10 Sep 1944	12:47
Vir	13 Jan 1944	20:37	Aqu	13 May 1944	17:09	Leo	12 Sep 1944	22:50
Lib	16 Jan 1944	09:28	Pis	15 May 1944	20:34	Vir	15 Sep 1944	11:00
Sco	18 Jan 1944	20:26	Ari	17 May 1944	23:02	Lib	17 Sep 1944	23:47
Sag	21 Jan 1944	03:52	Tau	20 May 1944	01:15	Sco	20 Sep 1944	12:10
Cap	23 Jan 1944	07:25	Gem	22 May 1944	04:26	Sag	22 Sep 1944	23:14
Aqu	25 Jan 1944	08:08	Can	24 May 1944	10:04	Cap	25 Sep 1944	07:54
Pis	27 Jan 1944	07:47	Leo	26 May 1944	19:04	Aqu	27 Sep 1944	13:08
Ari	29 Jan 1944	08:14	Vir	29 May 1944	06:58	Pis	29 Sep 1944	14:56
Tau	31 Jan 1944	11:07	Lib	31 May 1944	19:36			
Gem	2 Feb 1944	17:16	Sco	3 Jun 1944	06:31	Ari	1 Oct 1944	14:29
Can	5 Feb 1944	02:39	Sag	5 Jun 1944	14:26	Tau	3 Oct 1944	13:46
Leo	7 Feb 1944	14:19	Cap	7 Jun 1944	19:40	Gem	5 Oct 1944	14:59
Vir	10 Feb 1944	03:07	Aqu	9 Jun 1944	23:11	Can	7 Oct 1944	19:56
Lib	12 Feb 1944	15:53	Pis	12 Jun 1944	01:57	Leo	10 Oct 1944	05:02
Sco	15 Feb 1944	03:23	Ari	14 Jun 1944	04:40	Vir	12 Oct 1944	17:04
Sag	17 Feb 1944	12:13	Tau	16 Jun 1944	07:51	Lib	15 Oct 1944	05:54
Cap	19 Feb 1944	17:32	Gem	18 Jun 1944	12:11	Sco	17 Oct 1944	18:02
Aqu	21 Feb 1944	19:26	Can	20 Jun 1944	18:27	Sag	20 Oct 1944	04:49
Pis	23 Feb 1944	19:08	Leo	23 Jun 1944	03:25	Cap	22 Oct 1944	13:47
Ari	25 Feb 1944	18:30	Vir	25 Jun 1944	14:57	Aqu	24 Oct 1944	20:17
Tau	27 Feb 1944	19:36	Lib	28 Jun 1944	03:39	Pis	26 Oct 1944	23:51
			Sco	30 Jun 1944	15:09	Ari	29 Oct 1944	00:52
						Tau	31 Oct 1944	00:45
Gem	1 Mar 1944	00:06	Sag	2 Jul 1944	23:36	Gem	2 Nov 1944	01:28
Can	3 Mar 1944	08:38	Cap	5 Jul 1944	04:40	Can	4 Nov 1944	05:03
Leo	5 Mar 1944	20:19	Aqu	7 Jul 1944	07:13	Leo	6 Nov 1944	12:44
Vir	8 Mar 1944	09:17	Pis	9 Jul 1944	08:38	Vir	8 Nov 1944	23:58
Lib	10 Mar 1944	21:54	Ari	11 Jul 1944	10:18	Lib	11 Nov 1944	12:43
Sco	13 Mar 1944	09:11	Tau	13 Jul 1944	13:16	Sco	14 Nov 1944	00:46
Sag	15 Mar 1944	18:30	Gem	15 Jul 1944	18:10	Sag	16 Nov 1944	11:00
Cap	18 Mar 1944	01:11	Can	18 Jul 1944	01:21	Cap	18 Nov 1944	19:19
Aqu	20 Mar 1944	04:54	Leo	20 Jul 1944	10:50	Aqu	21 Nov 1944	01:45
Pis	22 Mar 1944	05:58	Vir	22 Jul 1944	22:24	Pis	23 Nov 1944	06:17
Ari	24 Mar 1944	05:41	Lib	25 Jul 1944	11:07	Ari	25 Nov 1944	08:55
Tau	26 Mar 1944	06:00	Sco	27 Jul 1944	23:15	Tau	27 Nov 1944	10:21
Gem	28 Mar 1944	08:58	Sag	30 Jul 1944	08:48	Gem	29 Nov 1944	11:55
Can	30 Mar 1944	15:59						
Leo	2 Apr 1944	02:54	Cap	1 Aug 1944	14:40	Can	1 Dec 1944	15:16
Vir	4 Apr 1944	15:48	Aqu	3 Aug 1944	17:09	Leo	3 Dec 1944	21:53
Lib	7 Apr 1944	04:21	Pis	5 Aug 1944	17:34	Vir	6 Dec 1944	08:03
Sco	9 Apr 1944	15:10	Ari	7 Aug 1944	17:42	Lib	8 Dec 1944	20:27
Sag	12 Apr 1944	00:01	Tau	9 Aug 1944	19:19	Sco	11 Dec 1944	08:40
Cap	14 Apr 1944	06:55	Gem	11 Aug 1944	23:38	Sag	13 Dec 1944	18:49
Aqu	16 Apr 1944	11:44	Can	14 Aug 1944	07:03	Cap	16 Dec 1944	02:20
Pis	18 Apr 1944	14:27	Leo	16 Aug 1944	17:07	Aqu	18 Dec 1944	07:43
Ari	20 Apr 1944	15:35	Vir	19 Aug 1944	05:00	Pis	20 Dec 1944	11:38
Tau	22 Apr 1944	16:28	Lib	21 Aug 1944	17:44	Ari	22 Dec 1944	14:41
Gem	24 Apr 1944	18:58	Sco	24 Aug 1944	06:12	Tau	24 Dec 1944	17:23
Can	27 Apr 1944	00:49	Sag	26 Aug 1944	16:50	Gem	26 Dec 1944	20:25
Leo	29 Apr 1944	10:36	Cap	29 Aug 1944	00:10	Can	29 Dec 1944	00:44
			Aqu	31 Aug 1944	03:42	Leo	31 Dec 1944	07:18

1945

Vir	2 Jan 1945	16:48	Cap	1 May 1945	19:38	Leo	3 Sep 1945	03:19
Lib	5 Jan 1945	04:43	Aqu	4 May 1945	04:04	Vir	5 Sep 1945	11:36
Sco	7 Jan 1945	17:12	Pis	6 May 1945	09:19	Lib	7 Sep 1945	21:48
Sag	10 Jan 1945	03:54	Ari	8 May 1945	11:23	Sco	10 Sep 1945	09:47
Cap	12 Jan 1945	11:26	Tau	10 May 1945	11:23	Sag	12 Sep 1945	22:36
Aqu	14 Jan 1945	15:55	Gem	12 May 1945	11:12	Cap	15 Sep 1945	10:09
Pis	16 Jan 1945	18:26	Can	14 May 1945	12:51	Aqu	17 Sep 1945	18:18
Ari	18 Jan 1945	20:20	Leo	16 May 1945	17:56	Pis	19 Sep 1945	22:16
Tau	20 Jan 1945	22:47	Vir	19 May 1945	02:55	Ari	21 Sep 1945	23:09
Gem	23 Jan 1945	02:34	Lib	21 May 1945	14:42	Tau	23 Sep 1945	22:53
Can	25 Jan 1945	08:04	Sco	24 May 1945	03:19	Gem	25 Sep 1945	23:31
Leo	27 Jan 1945	15:32	Sag	26 May 1945	15:10	Can	28 Sep 1945	02:38
Vir	30 Jan 1945	01:08	Cap	29 May 1945	01:23	Leo	30 Sep 1945	08:46
			Aqu	31 May 1945	09:33			
Lib	1 Feb 1945	12:45	Pis	2 Jun 1945	15:24	Vir	2 Oct 1945	17:33
Sco	4 Feb 1945	01:21	Ari	4 Jun 1945	18:49	Lib	5 Oct 1945	04:16
Sag	6 Feb 1945	12:56	Tau	6 Jun 1945	20:22	Sco	7 Oct 1945	16:23
Cap	8 Feb 1945	21:27	Gem	8 Jun 1945	21:14	Sag	10 Oct 1945	05:16
Aqu	11 Feb 1945	02:10	Can	10 Jun 1945	23:02	Cap	12 Oct 1945	17:31
Pis	13 Feb 1945	03:51	Leo	13 Jun 1945	03:20	Aqu	15 Oct 1945	03:04
Ari	15 Feb 1945	04:11	Vir	15 Jun 1945	11:07	Pis	17 Oct 1945	08:32
Tau	17 Feb 1945	05:04	Lib	17 Jun 1945	22:05	Ari	19 Oct 1945	10:07
Gem	19 Feb 1945	08:01	Sco	20 Jun 1945	10:35	Tau	21 Oct 1945	09:29
Can	21 Feb 1945	13:42	Sag	22 Jun 1945	22:25	Gem	23 Oct 1945	08:49
Leo	23 Feb 1945	21:58	Cap	25 Jun 1945	08:13	Can	25 Oct 1945	10:11
Vir	26 Feb 1945	08:13	Aqu	27 Jun 1945	15:35	Leo	27 Oct 1945	14:55
Lib	28 Feb 1945	19:56	Pis	29 Jun 1945	20:50	Vir	29 Oct 1945	23:12
Sco	3 Mar 1945	08:32	Ari	2 Jul 1945	00:28	Lib	1 Nov 1945	10:07
Sag	5 Mar 1945	20:43	Tau	4 Jul 1945	03:03	Sco	3 Nov 1945	22:28
Cap	8 Mar 1945	06:36	Gem	6 Jul 1945	05:19	Sag	6 Nov 1945	11:17
Aqu	10 Mar 1945	12:38	Can	8 Jul 1945	08:10	Cap	8 Nov 1945	23:33
Pis	12 Mar 1945	14:48	Leo	10 Jul 1945	12:43	Aqu	11 Nov 1945	09:57
Ari	14 Mar 1945	14:31	Vir	12 Jul 1945	19:57	Pis	13 Nov 1945	17:03
Tau	16 Mar 1945	13:54	Lib	15 Jul 1945	06:12	Ari	15 Nov 1945	20:22
Gem	18 Mar 1945	15:04	Sco	17 Jul 1945	18:28	Tau	17 Nov 1945	20:46
Can	20 Mar 1945	19:31	Sag	20 Jul 1945	06:35	Gem	19 Nov 1945	20:02
Leo	23 Mar 1945	03:31	Cap	22 Jul 1945	16:27	Can	21 Nov 1945	20:13
Vir	25 Mar 1945	14:10	Aqu	24 Jul 1945	23:14	Leo	23 Nov 1945	23:12
Lib	28 Mar 1945	02:14	Pis	27 Jul 1945	03:25	Vir	26 Nov 1945	05:58
Sco	30 Mar 1945	14:49	Ari	29 Jul 1945	06:06	Lib	28 Nov 1945	16:18
			Tau	31 Jul 1945	08:28			
Sag	2 Apr 1945	03:06	Gem	2 Aug 1945	11:22	Sco	1 Dec 1945	04:42
Cap	4 Apr 1945	13:49	Can	4 Aug 1945	15:22	Sag	3 Dec 1945	17:29
Aqu	6 Apr 1945	21:26	Leo	6 Aug 1945	20:52	Cap	6 Dec 1945	05:22
Pis	9 Apr 1945	01:08	Vir	9 Aug 1945	04:23	Aqu	8 Dec 1945	15:33
Ari	11 Apr 1945	01:36	Lib	11 Aug 1945	14:21	Pis	10 Dec 1945	23:18
Tau	13 Apr 1945	00:39	Sco	14 Aug 1945	02:24	Ari	13 Dec 1945	04:13
Gem	15 Apr 1945	00:31	Sag	16 Aug 1945	14:55	Tau	15 Dec 1945	06:28
Can	17 Apr 1945	03:14	Cap	19 Aug 1945	01:28	Gem	17 Dec 1945	07:01
Leo	19 Apr 1945	09:52	Aqu	21 Aug 1945	08:30	Can	19 Dec 1945	07:26
Vir	21 Apr 1945	20:02	Pis	23 Aug 1945	12:03	Leo	21 Dec 1945	09:30
Lib	24 Apr 1945	08:14	Ari	25 Aug 1945	13:29	Vir	23 Dec 1945	14:43
Sco	26 Apr 1945	20:51	Tau	27 Aug 1945	14:33	Lib	25 Dec 1945	23:45
Sag	29 Apr 1945	08:55	Gem	29 Aug 1945	16:46	Sco	28 Dec 1945	11:42
			Can	31 Aug 1945	20:59	Sag	31 Dec 1945	00:31

Moon Signs

1946

Cap	2 Jan 1946	12:09	Gem	2 May 1946	20:03	Sag	2 Sep 1946	17:30
Aqu	4 Jan 1946	21:36	Can	4 May 1946	20:22	Cap	5 Sep 1946	06:23
Pis	7 Jan 1946	04:46	Leo	6 May 1946	23:05	Aqu	7 Sep 1946	17:40
Ari	9 Jan 1946	09:54	Vir	9 May 1946	04:56	Pis	10 Sep 1946	01:44
Tau	11 Jan 1946	13:24	Lib	11 May 1946	13:53	Ari	12 Sep 1946	06:48
Gem	13 Jan 1946	15:41	Sco	14 May 1946	01:08	Tau	14 Sep 1946	10:02
Can	15 Jan 1946	17:31	Sag	16 May 1946	13:45	Gem	16 Sep 1946	12:45
Leo	17 Jan 1946	20:03	Cap	19 May 1946	02:40	Can	18 Sep 1946	15:41
Vir	20 Jan 1946	00:40	Aqu	21 May 1946	14:29	Leo	20 Sep 1946	19:12
Lib	22 Jan 1946	08:31	Pis	23 May 1946	23:36	Vir	22 Sep 1946	23:37
Sco	24 Jan 1946	19:39	Ari	26 May 1946	05:03	Lib	25 Sep 1946	05:39
Sag	27 Jan 1946	08:26	Tau	28 May 1946	07:02	Sco	27 Sep 1946	14:12
Cap	29 Jan 1946	20:16	Gem	30 May 1946	06:53	Sag	30 Sep 1946	01:32
Aqu	1 Feb 1946	05:22	Can	1 Jun 1946	06:28	Cap	2 Oct 1946	14:28
Pis	3 Feb 1946	11:31	Leo	3 Jun 1946	07:39	Aqu	5 Oct 1946	02:25
Ari	5 Feb 1946	15:37	Vir	5 Jun 1946	11:57	Pis	7 Oct 1946	11:07
Tau	7 Feb 1946	18:46	Lib	7 Jun 1946	19:56	Ari	9 Oct 1946	16:03
Gem	9 Feb 1946	21:44	Sco	10 Jun 1946	07:04	Tau	11 Oct 1946	18:19
Can	12 Feb 1946	00:58	Sag	12 Jun 1946	19:49	Gem	13 Oct 1946	19:36
Leo	14 Feb 1946	04:49	Cap	15 Jun 1946	08:38	Can	15 Oct 1946	21:22
Vir	16 Feb 1946	10:03	Aqu	17 Jun 1946	20:14	Leo	18 Oct 1946	00:35
Lib	18 Feb 1946	17:35	Pis	20 Jun 1946	05:42	Vir	20 Oct 1946	05:34
Sco	21 Feb 1946	04:04	Ari	22 Jun 1946	12:17	Lib	22 Oct 1946	12:33
Sag	23 Feb 1946	16:40	Tau	24 Jun 1946	15:54	Sco	24 Oct 1946	21:40
Cap	26 Feb 1946	05:00	Gem	26 Jun 1946	17:06	Sag	27 Oct 1946	09:02
Aqu	28 Feb 1946	14:32	Can	28 Jun 1946	17:09	Cap	29 Oct 1946	21:58
			Leo	30 Jun 1946	17:46			
Pis	2 Mar 1946	20:23	Vir	2 Jul 1946	20:45	Aqu	1 Nov 1946	10:34
Ari	4 Mar 1946	23:22	Lib	5 Jul 1946	03:21	Pis	3 Nov 1946	20:30
Tau	7 Mar 1946	01:07	Sco	7 Jul 1946	13:41	Ari	6 Nov 1946	02:26
Gem	9 Mar 1946	03:11	Sag	10 Jul 1946	02:19	Tau	8 Nov 1946	04:48
Can	11 Mar 1946	06:28	Cap	12 Jul 1946	15:04	Gem	10 Nov 1946	05:06
Leo	13 Mar 1946	11:14	Aqu	15 Jul 1946	02:15	Can	12 Nov 1946	05:15
Vir	15 Mar 1946	17:31	Pis	17 Jul 1946	11:13	Leo	14 Nov 1946	06:52
Lib	18 Mar 1946	01:40	Ari	19 Jul 1946	17:58	Vir	16 Nov 1946	11:05
Sco	20 Mar 1946	12:04	Tau	21 Jul 1946	22:33	Lib	18 Nov 1946	18:11
Sag	23 Mar 1946	00:30	Gem	24 Jul 1946	01:17	Sco	21 Nov 1946	03:57
Cap	25 Mar 1946	13:16	Can	26 Jul 1946	02:43	Sag	23 Nov 1946	15:43
Aqu	27 Mar 1946	23:48	Leo	28 Jul 1946	03:56	Cap	26 Nov 1946	04:38
Pis	30 Mar 1946	06:25	Vir	30 Jul 1946	06:32	Aqu	28 Nov 1946	17:28
Ari	1 Apr 1946	09:15	Lib	1 Aug 1946	12:05	Pis	1 Dec 1946	04:28
Tau	3 Apr 1946	09:55	Sco	3 Aug 1946	21:22	Ari	3 Dec 1946	12:03
Gem	5 Apr 1946	10:25	Sag	6 Aug 1946	09:35	Tau	5 Dec 1946	15:47
Can	7 Apr 1946	12:21	Cap	8 Aug 1946	22:22	Gem	7 Dec 1946	16:29
Leo	9 Apr 1946	16:36	Aqu	11 Aug 1946	09:22	Can	9 Dec 1946	15:49
Vir	11 Apr 1946	23:20	Pis	13 Aug 1946	17:40	Leo	11 Dec 1946	15:46
Lib	14 Apr 1946	08:13	Ari	15 Aug 1946	23:35	Vir	13 Dec 1946	18:08
Sco	16 Apr 1946	19:02	Tau	18 Aug 1946	03:58	Lib	16 Dec 1946	00:08
Sag	19 Apr 1946	07:29	Gem	20 Aug 1946	07:21	Sco	18 Dec 1946	09:43
Cap	21 Apr 1946	20:27	Can	22 Aug 1946	10:05	Sag	20 Dec 1946	21:48
Aqu	24 Apr 1946	07:55	Leo	24 Aug 1946	12:37	Cap	23 Dec 1946	10:49
Pis	26 Apr 1946	15:52	Vir	26 Aug 1946	15:53	Aqu	25 Dec 1946	23:28
Ari	28 Apr 1946	19:44	Lib	28 Aug 1946	21:15	Pis	28 Dec 1946	10:42
Tau	30 Apr 1946	20:30	Sco	31 Aug 1946	05:48	Ari	30 Dec 1946	19:29

Moon Signs

1947

Tau	2 Jan 1947	01:04	Lib	1 May 1947	19:23	Ari	2 Sep 1947	12:01
Gem	4 Jan 1947	03:24	Sco	4 May 1947	02:35	Tau	4 Sep 1947	20:09
Can	6 Jan 1947	03:26	Sag	6 May 1947	12:09	Gem	7 Sep 1947	02:16
Leo	8 Jan 1947	02:52	Cap	8 May 1947	23:54	Can	9 Sep 1947	06:11
Vir	10 Jan 1947	03:44	Aqu	11 May 1947	12:39	Leo	11 Sep 1947	08:02
Lib	12 Jan 1947	07:54	Pis	14 May 1947	00:18	Vir	13 Sep 1947	08:50
Sco	14 Jan 1947	16:15	Ari	16 May 1947	08:54	Lib	15 Sep 1947	10:16
Sag	17 Jan 1947	04:02	Tau	18 May 1947	13:49	Sco	17 Sep 1947	14:11
Cap	19 Jan 1947	17:10	Gem	20 May 1947	15:50	Sag	19 Sep 1947	21:50
Aqu	22 Jan 1947	05:36	Can	22 May 1947	16:26	Cap	22 Sep 1947	08:57
Pis	24 Jan 1947	16:22	Leo	24 May 1947	17:17	Aqu	24 Sep 1947	21:36
Ari	27 Jan 1947	01:09	Vir	26 May 1947	19:49	Pis	27 Sep 1947	09:23
Tau	29 Jan 1947	07:44	Lib	29 May 1947	00:54	Ari	29 Sep 1947	18:57
Gem	31 Jan 1947	11:50	Sco	31 May 1947	08:42			
Can	2 Feb 1947	13:37	Sag	2 Jun 1947	18:53	Tau	2 Oct 1947	02:14
Leo	4 Feb 1947	14:00	Cap	5 Jun 1947	06:51	Gem	4 Oct 1947	07:42
Vir	6 Feb 1947	14:41	Aqu	7 Jun 1947	19:37	Can	6 Oct 1947	11:46
Lib	8 Feb 1947	17:38	Pis	10 Jun 1947	07:46	Leo	8 Oct 1947	14:40
Sco	11 Feb 1947	00:28	Ari	12 Jun 1947	17:33	Vir	10 Oct 1947	16:56
Sag	13 Feb 1947	11:15	Tau	14 Jun 1947	23:43	Lib	12 Oct 1947	19:31
Cap	16 Feb 1947	00:11	Gem	17 Jun 1947	02:20	Sco	14 Oct 1947	23:46
Aqu	18 Feb 1947	12:37	Can	19 Jun 1947	02:31	Sag	17 Oct 1947	06:52
Pis	20 Feb 1947	22:56	Leo	21 Jun 1947	02:06	Cap	19 Oct 1947	17:13
Ari	23 Feb 1947	06:56	Vir	23 Jun 1947	03:01	Aqu	22 Oct 1947	05:38
Tau	25 Feb 1947	13:06	Lib	25 Jun 1947	06:50	Pis	24 Oct 1947	17:45
Gem	27 Feb 1947	17:46	Sco	27 Jun 1947	14:17	Ari	27 Oct 1947	03:29
			Sag	30 Jun 1947	00:46	Tau	29 Oct 1947	10:14
						Gem	31 Oct 1947	14:34
Can	1 Mar 1947	20:57	Cap	2 Jul 1947	13:02	Can	2 Nov 1947	17:31
Leo	3 Mar 1947	22:59	Aqu	5 Jul 1947	01:48	Leo	4 Nov 1947	20:03
Vir	6 Mar 1947	00:46	Pis	7 Jul 1947	14:01	Vir	6 Nov 1947	22:54
Lib	8 Mar 1947	03:50	Ari	10 Jul 1947	00:32	Lib	9 Nov 1947	02:42
Sco	10 Mar 1947	09:51	Tau	12 Jul 1947	08:10	Sco	11 Nov 1947	08:02
Sag	12 Mar 1947	19:33	Gem	14 Jul 1947	12:14	Sag	13 Nov 1947	15:33
Cap	15 Mar 1947	07:59	Can	16 Jul 1947	13:13	Cap	16 Nov 1947	01:37
Aqu	17 Mar 1947	20:34	Leo	18 Jul 1947	12:33	Aqu	18 Nov 1947	13:44
Pis	20 Mar 1947	06:56	Vir	20 Jul 1947	12:19	Pis	21 Nov 1947	02:15
Ari	22 Mar 1947	14:21	Lib	22 Jul 1947	14:33	Ari	23 Nov 1947	12:51
Tau	24 Mar 1947	19:28	Sco	24 Jul 1947	20:41	Tau	25 Nov 1947	20:04
Gem	26 Mar 1947	23:14	Sag	27 Jul 1947	06:39	Gem	27 Nov 1947	23:53
Can	29 Mar 1947	02:25	Cap	29 Jul 1947	19:01	Can	30 Nov 1947	01:30
Leo	31 Mar 1947	05:21						
Vir	2 Apr 1947	08:30	Aqu	1 Aug 1947	07:49	Leo	2 Dec 1947	02:30
Lib	4 Apr 1947	12:39	Pis	3 Aug 1947	19:48	Vir	4 Dec 1947	04:23
Sco	6 Apr 1947	18:56	Ari	6 Aug 1947	06:19	Lib	6 Dec 1947	08:13
Sag	9 Apr 1947	04:12	Tau	8 Aug 1947	14:41	Sco	8 Dec 1947	14:24
Cap	11 Apr 1947	16:08	Gem	10 Aug 1947	20:16	Sag	10 Dec 1947	22:49
Aqu	14 Apr 1947	04:50	Can	12 Aug 1947	22:48	Cap	13 Dec 1947	09:13
Pis	16 Apr 1947	15:45	Leo	14 Aug 1947	23:05	Aqu	15 Dec 1947	21:15
Ari	18 Apr 1947	23:23	Vir	16 Aug 1947	22:48	Pis	18 Dec 1947	09:58
Tau	21 Apr 1947	03:54	Lib	18 Aug 1947	00:04	Ari	20 Dec 1947	21:35
Gem	23 Apr 1947	06:26	Sco	21 Aug 1947	04:44	Tau	23 Dec 1947	06:10
Can	25 Apr 1947	08:21	Sag	23 Aug 1947	13:34	Gem	25 Dec 1947	10:45
Leo	27 Apr 1947	10:43	Cap	26 Aug 1947	01:30	Can	27 Dec 1947	12:01
Vir	29 Apr 1947	14:15	Aqu	28 Aug 1947	14:17	Leo	29 Dec 1947	11:41
			Pis	31 Aug 1947	02:02	Vir	31 Dec 1947	11:47

1948

Lib	2 Jan 1948	14:10	Pis	2 May 1948	19:43	Vir	2 Sep 1948	18:19
Sco	4 Jan 1948	19:51	Ari	5 May 1948	07:27	Lib	4 Sep 1948	17:35
Sag	7 Jan 1948	04:40	Tau	7 May 1948	16:47	Sco	6 Sep 1948	18:33
Cap	9 Jan 1948	15:40	Gem	9 May 1948	23:18	Sag	8 Sep 1948	22:52
Aqu	12 Jan 1948	03:53	Can	12 May 1948	03:37	Cap	11 Sep 1948	06:56
Pis	14 Jan 1948	16:34	Leo	14 May 1948	06:38	Aqu	13 Sep 1948	17:58
Ari	17 Jan 1948	04:42	Vir	16 May 1948	09:13	Pis	16 Sep 1948	06:26
Tau	19 Jan 1948	14:40	Lib	18 May 1948	12:06	Ari	18 Sep 1948	19:01
Gem	21 Jan 1948	20:59	Sco	20 May 1948	15:55	Tau	21 Sep 1948	06:44
Can	23 Jan 1948	23:21	Sag	22 May 1948	21:22	Gem	23 Sep 1948	16:39
Leo	25 Jan 1948	22:58	Cap	25 May 1948	05:07	Can	25 Sep 1948	23:44
Vir	27 Jan 1948	21:56	Aqu	27 May 1948	15:30	Leo	28 Sep 1948	03:33
Lib	29 Jan 1948	22:30	Pis	30 May 1948	03:45	Vir	30 Sep 1948	04:39
Sco	1 Feb 1948	02:28	Ari	1 Jun 1948	15:53	Lib	2 Oct 1948	04:29
Sag	3 Feb 1948	10:26	Tau	4 Jun 1948	01:41	Sco	4 Oct 1948	04:58
Cap	5 Feb 1948	21:29	Gem	6 Jun 1948	08:05	Sag	6 Oct 1948	07:55
Aqu	8 Feb 1948	09:58	Can	8 Jun 1948	11:27	Cap	8 Oct 1948	14:31
Pis	10 Feb 1948	22:36	Leo	10 Jun 1948	13:10	Aqu	11 Oct 1948	00:42
Ari	13 Feb 1948	10:36	Vir	12 Jun 1948	14:48	Pis	13 Oct 1948	13:02
Tau	15 Feb 1948	21:06	Lib	14 Jun 1948	17:32	Ari	16 Oct 1948	01:35
Gem	18 Feb 1948	04:54	Sco	16 Jun 1948	22:03	Tau	18 Oct 1948	12:52
Can	20 Feb 1948	09:07	Sag	19 Jun 1948	04:28	Gem	20 Oct 1948	22:13
Leo	22 Feb 1948	10:05	Cap	21 Jun 1948	12:50	Can	23 Oct 1948	05:20
Vir	24 Feb 1948	09:21	Aqu	23 Jun 1948	23:15	Leo	25 Oct 1948	10:08
Lib	26 Feb 1948	09:05	Pis	26 Jun 1948	11:22	Vir	27 Oct 1948	12:52
Sco	28 Feb 1948	11:24	Ari	28 Jun 1948	23:54	Lib	29 Oct 1948	14:15
						Sco	31 Oct 1948	15:31
Sag	1 Mar 1948	17:41	Tau	1 Jul 1948	10:38	Sag	2 Nov 1948	18:10
Cap	4 Mar 1948	03:50	Gem	3 Jul 1948	17:47	Cap	4 Nov 1948	23:40
Aqu	6 Mar 1948	16:13	Can	5 Jul 1948	21:05	Aqu	7 Nov 1948	08:41
Pis	9 Mar 1948	04:52	Leo	7 Jul 1948	21:52	Pis	9 Nov 1948	20:33
Ari	11 Mar 1948	16:32	Vir	9 Jul 1948	22:03	Ari	12 Nov 1948	09:11
Tau	14 Mar 1948	02:39	Lib	11 Jul 1948	23:31	Tau	14 Nov 1948	20:23
Gem	16 Mar 1948	10:43	Sco	14 Jul 1948	03:28	Gem	17 Nov 1948	05:01
Can	18 Mar 1948	16:12	Sag	16 Jul 1948	10:11	Can	19 Nov 1948	11:09
Leo	20 Mar 1948	18:57	Cap	18 Jul 1948	19:13	Leo	21 Nov 1948	15:31
Vir	22 Mar 1948	19:41	Aqu	21 Jul 1948	06:02	Vir	23 Nov 1948	18:47
Lib	24 Mar 1948	20:01	Pis	23 Jul 1948	18:12	Lib	25 Nov 1948	21:32
Sco	26 Mar 1948	21:50	Ari	26 Jul 1948	06:56	Sco	28 Nov 1948	00:18
Sag	29 Mar 1948	02:47	Tau	28 Jul 1948	18:33	Sag	30 Nov 1948	03:51
Cap	31 Mar 1948	11:34	Gem	31 Jul 1948	02:59			
Aqu	2 Apr 1948	23:18	Can	2 Aug 1948	07:19	Cap	2 Dec 1948	09:16
Pis	5 Apr 1948	11:55	Leo	4 Aug 1948	08:12	Aqu	4 Dec 1948	17:31
Ari	7 Apr 1948	23:26	Vir	6 Aug 1948	07:32	Pis	7 Dec 1948	04:45
Tau	10 Apr 1948	08:57	Lib	8 Aug 1948	07:29	Ari	9 Dec 1948	17:29
Gem	12 Apr 1948	16:19	Sco	10 Aug 1948	09:57	Tau	12 Dec 1948	05:07
Can	14 Apr 1948	21:40	Sag	12 Aug 1948	15:49	Gem	14 Dec 1948	13:42
Leo	17 Apr 1948	01:14	Cap	15 Aug 1948	00:51	Can	16 Dec 1948	19:00
Vir	19 Apr 1948	03:29	Aqu	17 Aug 1948	12:02	Leo	18 Dec 1948	22:02
Lib	21 Apr 1948	05:15	Pis	20 Aug 1948	00:22	Vir	21 Dec 1948	00:18
Sco	23 Apr 1948	07:49	Ari	22 Aug 1948	13:04	Lib	23 Dec 1948	02:59
Sag	25 Apr 1948	12:31	Tau	25 Aug 1948	01:02	Sco	25 Dec 1948	06:38
Cap	27 Apr 1948	20:21	Gem	27 Aug 1948	10:38	Sag	27 Dec 1948	11:28
Aqu	30 Apr 1948	07:15	Can	29 Aug 1948	16:32	Cap	29 Dec 1948	17:46
			Leo	31 Aug 1948	18:40			

Moon Signs

1949

Aqu	1 Jan 1949	02:07	Can	2 May 1949	12:41	Cap	1 Sep 1949	12:05
Pis	3 Jan 1949	12:58	Leo	4 May 1949	19:10	Aqu	3 Sep 1949	19:37
Ari	6 Jan 1949	01:40	Vir	6 May 1949	23:10	Pis	6 Sep 1949	05:26
Tau	8 Jan 1949	14:01	Lib	9 May 1949	01:05	Ari	8 Sep 1949	17:13
Gem	10 Jan 1949	23:28	Sco	11 May 1949	01:53	Tau	11 Sep 1949	06:11
Can	13 Jan 1949	04:55	Sag	13 May 1949	02:57	Gem	13 Sep 1949	18:46
Leo	15 Jan 1949	07:06	Cap	15 May 1949	05:56	Can	16 Sep 1949	04:50
Vir	17 Jan 1949	07:51	Aqu	17 May 1949	12:19	Leo	18 Sep 1949	11:02
Lib	19 Jan 1949	09:03	Pis	19 May 1949	22:26	Vir	20 Sep 1949	13:32
Sco	21 Jan 1949	11:59	Ari	22 May 1949	11:01	Lib	22 Sep 1949	13:41
Sag	23 Jan 1949	17:08	Tau	24 May 1949	23:40	Sco	24 Sep 1949	13:20
Cap	26 Jan 1949	00:21	Gem	27 May 1949	10:25	Sag	26 Sep 1949	14:21
Aqu	28 Jan 1949	09:26	Can	29 May 1949	18:38	Cap	28 Sep 1949	18:06
Pis	30 Jan 1949	20:26						
Ari	2 Feb 1949	09:03	Leo	1 Jun 1949	00:35	Aqu	1 Oct 1949	01:14
Tau	4 Feb 1949	21:56	Vir	3 Jun 1949	04:52	Pis	3 Oct 1949	11:20
Gem	7 Feb 1949	08:38	Lib	5 Jun 1949	07:56	Ari	5 Oct 1949	23:27
Can	9 Feb 1949	15:21	Sco	7 Jun 1949	10:12	Tau	8 Oct 1949	12:26
Leo	11 Feb 1949	18:00	Sag	9 Jun 1949	12:23	Gem	11 Oct 1949	01:01
Vir	13 Feb 1949	18:04	Cap	11 Jun 1949	15:39	Can	13 Oct 1949	11:49
Lib	15 Feb 1949	17:43	Aqu	13 Jun 1949	21:26	Leo	15 Oct 1949	19:34
Sco	17 Feb 1949	18:52	Pis	16 Jun 1949	06:38	Vir	17 Oct 1949	23:40
Sag	19 Feb 1949	22:50	Ari	18 Jun 1949	18:44	Lib	20 Oct 1949	00:46
Cap	22 Feb 1949	05:49	Tau	21 Jun 1949	07:29	Sco	22 Oct 1949	00:18
Aqu	24 Feb 1949	15:25	Gem	23 Jun 1949	18:19	Sag	24 Oct 1949	00:08
Pis	27 Feb 1949	02:53	Can	26 Jun 1949	02:00	Cap	26 Oct 1949	02:11
			Leo	28 Jun 1949	07:00	Aqu	28 Oct 1949	07:50
			Vir	30 Jun 1949	10:26	Pis	30 Oct 1949	17:21
Ari	1 Mar 1949	15:35	Lib	2 Jul 1949	13:21	Ari	2 Nov 1949	05:34
Tau	4 Mar 1949	04:32	Sco	4 Jul 1949	16:21	Tau	4 Nov 1949	18:36
Gem	6 Mar 1949	16:04	Sag	6 Jul 1949	19:44	Gem	7 Nov 1949	06:54
Can	9 Mar 1949	00:19	Cap	9 Jul 1949	00:02	Can	9 Nov 1949	17:34
Leo	11 Mar 1949	04:32	Aqu	11 Jul 1949	06:08	Leo	12 Nov 1949	01:59
Vir	13 Mar 1949	05:23	Pis	13 Jul 1949	15:01	Vir	14 Nov 1949	07:41
Lib	15 Mar 1949	04:39	Ari	16 Jul 1949	02:42	Lib	16 Nov 1949	10:34
Sco	17 Mar 1949	04:25	Tau	18 Jul 1949	15:35	Sco	18 Nov 1949	11:18
Sag	19 Mar 1949	06:30	Gem	21 Jul 1949	02:56	Sag	20 Nov 1949	11:15
Cap	21 Mar 1949	12:05	Can	23 Jul 1949	10:50	Cap	22 Nov 1949	12:20
Aqu	23 Mar 1949	21:10	Leo	25 Jul 1949	15:17	Aqu	24 Nov 1949	16:24
Pis	26 Mar 1949	08:49	Vir	27 Jul 1949	17:35	Pis	27 Nov 1949	00:36
Ari	28 Mar 1949	21:40	Lib	29 Jul 1949	19:19	Ari	29 Nov 1949	12:18
Tau	31 Mar 1949	10:28	Sco	31 Jul 1949	21:44			
Gem	2 Apr 1949	22:01	Sag	3 Aug 1949	01:25	Tau	2 Dec 1949	01:21
Can	5 Apr 1949	07:09	Cap	5 Aug 1949	06:35	Gem	4 Dec 1949	13:27
Leo	7 Apr 1949	12:57	Aqu	7 Aug 1949	13:34	Can	6 Dec 1949	23:30
Vir	9 Apr 1949	15:30	Pis	9 Aug 1949	22:46	Leo	9 Dec 1949	07:27
Lib	11 Apr 1949	15:46	Ari	12 Aug 1949	10:20	Vir	11 Dec 1949	13:30
Sco	13 Apr 1949	15:27	Tau	14 Aug 1949	23:17	Lib	13 Dec 1949	17:44
Sag	15 Apr 1949	16:23	Gem	17 Aug 1949	11:21	Sco	15 Dec 1949	20:12
Cap	17 Apr 1949	20:16	Can	19 Aug 1949	20:13	Sag	17 Dec 1949	21:31
Aqu	20 Apr 1949	03:59	Leo	22 Aug 1949	01:06	Cap	19 Dec 1949	23:00
Pis	22 Apr 1949	15:07	Vir	24 Aug 1949	02:54	Aqu	22 Dec 1949	02:25
Ari	25 Apr 1949	04:00	Lib	26 Aug 1949	03:23	Pis	24 Dec 1949	09:20
Tau	27 Apr 1949	16:40	Sco	28 Aug 1949	04:19	Ari	26 Dec 1949	20:04
Gem	30 Apr 1949	03:46	Sag	30 Aug 1949	07:00	Tau	29 Dec 1949	08:57
						Gem	31 Dec 1949	21:12

Moon Signs

1950

Can	3 Jan 1950	06:55	Sco	1 May 1950	11:36	Tau	1 Sep 1950	02:19
Leo	5 Jan 1950	13:56	Sag	3 May 1950	10:50	Gem	3 Sep 1950	14:45
Vir	7 Jan 1950	19:05	Cap	5 May 1950	11:09	Can	6 Sep 1950	02:53
Lib	9 Jan 1950	23:07	Aqu	7 May 1950	14:23	Leo	8 Sep 1950	12:32
Sco	12 Jan 1950	02:27	Pis	9 May 1950	21:34	Vir	10 Sep 1950	18:54
Sag	14 Jan 1950	05:15	Ari	12 May 1950	08:18	Lib	12 Sep 1950	22:26
Cap	16 Jan 1950	08:06	Tau	14 May 1950	20:58	Sco	15 Sep 1950	00:26
Aqu	18 Jan 1950	12:07	Gem	17 May 1950	09:51	Sag	17 Sep 1950	02:12
Pis	20 Jan 1950	18:41	Can	19 May 1950	21:49	Cap	19 Sep 1950	04:48
Ari	23 Jan 1950	04:37	Leo	22 May 1950	08:05	Aqu	21 Sep 1950	09:00
Tau	25 Jan 1950	17:07	Vir	24 May 1950	15:49	Pis	23 Sep 1950	15:09
Gem	28 Jan 1950	05:42	Lib	26 May 1950	20:25	Ari	25 Sep 1950	23:32
Can	30 Jan 1950	15:49	Sco	28 May 1950	21:59	Tau	28 Sep 1950	10:08
			Sag	30 May 1950	21:43	Gem	30 Sep 1950	22:26
Leo	1 Feb 1950	22:32	Cap	1 Jun 1950	21:27	Can	3 Oct 1950	10:58
Vir	4 Feb 1950	02:35	Aqu	3 Jun 1950	23:19	Leo	5 Oct 1950	21:38
Lib	6 Feb 1950	05:18	Pis	6 Jun 1950	04:57	Vir	8 Oct 1950	04:52
Sco	8 Feb 1950	07:50	Ari	8 Jun 1950	14:44	Lib	10 Oct 1950	08:27
Sag	10 Feb 1950	10:51	Tau	11 Jun 1950	03:12	Sco	12 Oct 1950	09:30
Cap	12 Feb 1950	14:44	Gem	13 Jun 1950	16:04	Sag	14 Oct 1950	09:44
Aqu	14 Feb 1950	19:57	Can	16 Jun 1950	03:44	Cap	16 Oct 1950	10:55
Pis	17 Feb 1950	03:11	Leo	18 Jun 1950	13:36	Aqu	18 Oct 1950	14:27
Ari	19 Feb 1950	13:01	Vir	20 Jun 1950	21:30	Pis	20 Oct 1950	20:53
Tau	22 Feb 1950	01:11	Lib	23 Jun 1950	03:08	Ari	23 Oct 1950	05:58
Gem	24 Feb 1950	14:02	Sco	25 Jun 1950	06:18	Tau	25 Oct 1950	17:02
Can	27 Feb 1950	01:01	Sag	27 Jun 1950	07:25	Gem	28 Oct 1950	05:22
			Cap	29 Jun 1950	07:48	Can	30 Oct 1950	18:03
Leo	1 Mar 1950	08:29	Aqu	1 Jul 1950	09:20	Leo	2 Nov 1950	05:37
Vir	3 Mar 1950	12:23	Pis	3 Jul 1950	13:52	Vir	4 Nov 1950	14:19
Lib	5 Mar 1950	13:59	Ari	5 Jul 1950	22:25	Lib	6 Nov 1950	19:09
Sco	7 Mar 1950	14:55	Tau	8 Jul 1950	10:13	Sco	8 Nov 1950	20:28
Sag	9 Mar 1950	16:37	Gem	10 Jul 1950	23:01	Sag	10 Nov 1950	19:51
Cap	11 Mar 1950	20:07	Can	13 Jul 1950	10:32	Cap	12 Nov 1950	19:25
Aqu	14 Mar 1950	01:52	Leo	15 Jul 1950	19:52	Aqu	14 Nov 1950	21:15
Pis	16 Mar 1950	09:59	Vir	18 Jul 1950	03:05	Pis	17 Nov 1950	02:39
Ari	18 Mar 1950	20:21	Lib	20 Jul 1950	08:33	Ari	19 Nov 1950	11:40
Tau	21 Mar 1950	08:31	Sco	22 Jul 1950	12:26	Tau	21 Nov 1950	23:07
Gem	23 Mar 1950	21:27	Sag	24 Jul 1950	14:54	Gem	24 Nov 1950	11:38
Can	26 Mar 1950	09:15	Cap	26 Jul 1950	16:39	Can	27 Nov 1950	00:12
Leo	28 Mar 1950	18:04	Aqu	28 Jul 1950	18:55	Leo	29 Nov 1950	12:01
Vir	30 Mar 1950	22:59	Pis	30 Jul 1950	23:19			
Lib	2 Apr 1950	00:39	Ari	2 Aug 1950	07:03	Vir	1 Dec 1950	21:52
Sco	4 Apr 1950	00:35	Tau	4 Aug 1950	18:05	Lib	4 Dec 1950	04:28
Sag	6 Apr 1950	00:37	Gem	7 Aug 1950	06:43	Sco	6 Dec 1950	07:18
Cap	8 Apr 1950	02:30	Can	9 Aug 1950	18:26	Sag	8 Dec 1950	07:16
Aqu	10 Apr 1950	07:24	Leo	12 Aug 1950	03:35	Cap	10 Dec 1950	06:16
Pis	12 Apr 1950	15:38	Vir	14 Aug 1950	10:02	Aqu	12 Dec 1950	06:34
Ari	15 Apr 1950	02:31	Lib	16 Aug 1950	14:30	Pis	14 Dec 1950	10:11
Tau	17 Apr 1950	14:59	Sco	18 Aug 1950	17:48	Ari	16 Dec 1950	17:58
Gem	20 Apr 1950	03:53	Sag	20 Aug 1950	20:35	Tau	19 Dec 1950	05:09
Can	22 Apr 1950	16:01	Cap	22 Aug 1950	23:23	Gem	21 Dec 1950	17:49
Leo	25 Apr 1950	01:55	Aqu	25 Aug 1950	02:53	Can	24 Dec 1950	06:17
Vir	27 Apr 1950	08:28	Pis	27 Aug 1950	08:02	Leo	26 Dec 1950	17:45
Lib	29 Apr 1950	11:23	Ari	29 Aug 1950	15:45	Vir	29 Dec 1950	03:40
						Lib	31 Dec 1950	11:18

Moon Signs

1951

Sign	Date	Time	Sign	Date	Time	Sign	Date	Time
Sco	2 Jan 1951	15:57	Ari	2 May 1951	11:26	Lib	3 Sep 1951	05:32
Sag	4 Jan 1951	17:37	Tau	4 May 1951	20:46	Sco	5 Sep 1951	11:48
Cap	6 Jan 1951	17:31	Gem	7 May 1951	07:50	Sag	7 Sep 1951	16:10
Aqu	8 Jan 1951	17:35	Can	9 May 1951	20:12	Cap	9 Sep 1951	19:06
Pis	10 Jan 1951	19:56	Leo	12 May 1951	08:49	Aqu	11 Sep 1951	21:11
Ari	13 Jan 1951	02:06	Vir	14 May 1951	19:43	Pis	13 Sep 1951	23:22
Tau	15 Jan 1951	12:11	Lib	17 May 1951	03:03	Ari	16 Sep 1951	02:48
Gem	18 Jan 1951	00:35	Sco	19 May 1951	06:22	Tau	18 Sep 1951	08:42
Can	20 Jan 1951	13:05	Sag	21 May 1951	06:43	Gem	20 Sep 1951	17:46
Leo	23 Jan 1951	00:11	Cap	23 May 1951	06:07	Can	23 Sep 1951	05:34
Vir	25 Jan 1951	09:25	Aqu	25 May 1951	06:41	Leo	25 Sep 1951	18:07
Lib	27 Jan 1951	16:45	Pis	27 May 1951	10:06	Vir	28 Sep 1951	05:05
Sco	29 Jan 1951	22:03	Ari	29 May 1951	16:53	Lib	30 Sep 1951	13:07
Sag	1 Feb 1951	01:15	Tau	1 Jun 1951	02:33	Sco	2 Oct 1951	18:23
Cap	3 Feb 1951	02:52	Gem	3 Jun 1951	14:03	Sag	4 Oct 1951	21:47
Aqu	5 Feb 1951	04:04	Can	6 Jun 1951	02:31	Cap	7 Oct 1951	00:30
Pis	7 Feb 1951	06:29	Leo	8 Jun 1951	15:11	Aqu	9 Oct 1951	03:19
Ari	9 Feb 1951	11:44	Vir	11 Jun 1951	02:45	Pis	11 Oct 1951	06:46
Tau	11 Feb 1951	20:33	Lib	13 Jun 1951	11:29	Ari	13 Oct 1951	11:20
Gem	14 Feb 1951	08:18	Sco	15 Jun 1951	16:16	Tau	15 Oct 1951	17:37
Can	16 Feb 1951	20:51	Sag	17 Jun 1951	17:25	Gem	18 Oct 1951	02:22
Leo	19 Feb 1951	08:00	Cap	19 Jun 1951	16:37	Can	20 Oct 1951	13:42
Vir	21 Feb 1951	16:42	Aqu	21 Jun 1951	16:04	Leo	23 Oct 1951	02:24
Lib	23 Feb 1951	23:00	Pis	23 Jun 1951	17:49	Vir	25 Oct 1951	14:00
Sco	26 Feb 1951	03:30	Ari	25 Jun 1951	23:14	Lib	27 Oct 1951	22:23
Sag	28 Feb 1951	06:49	Tau	28 Jun 1951	08:17	Sco	30 Oct 1951	03:08
			Gem	30 Jun 1951	19:51			
Cap	2 Mar 1951	09:29	Can	3 Jul 1951	08:27	Sag	1 Nov 1951	05:19
Aqu	4 Mar 1951	12:11	Leo	5 Jul 1951	21:00	Cap	3 Nov 1951	06:39
Pis	6 Mar 1951	15:46	Vir	8 Jul 1951	08:35	Aqu	5 Nov 1951	08:43
Ari	8 Mar 1951	21:16	Lib	10 Jul 1951	18:04	Pis	7 Nov 1951	12:23
Tau	11 Mar 1951	05:32	Sco	13 Jul 1951	00:17	Ari	9 Nov 1951	17:52
Gem	13 Mar 1951	16:36	Sag	15 Jul 1951	03:02	Tau	12 Nov 1951	01:07
Can	16 Mar 1951	05:06	Cap	17 Jul 1951	03:13	Gem	14 Nov 1951	10:15
Leo	18 Mar 1951	16:44	Aqu	19 Jul 1951	02:41	Can	16 Nov 1951	21:27
Vir	21 Mar 1951	01:37	Pis	21 Jul 1951	03:29	Leo	19 Nov 1951	10:11
Lib	23 Mar 1951	07:20	Ari	23 Jul 1951	07:22	Vir	21 Nov 1951	22:34
Sco	25 Mar 1951	10:34	Tau	25 Jul 1951	15:07	Lib	24 Nov 1951	08:07
Sag	27 Mar 1951	12:40	Gem	28 Jul 1951	02:08	Sco	26 Nov 1951	13:30
Cap	29 Mar 1951	14:51	Can	30 Jul 1951	14:42	Sag	28 Nov 1951	15:19
Aqu	31 Mar 1951	18:02				Cap	30 Nov 1951	15:22
Pis	2 Apr 1951	22:45	Leo	2 Aug 1951	03:07	Aqu	2 Dec 1951	15:45
Ari	5 Apr 1951	05:15	Vir	4 Aug 1951	14:17	Pis	4 Dec 1951	18:07
Tau	7 Apr 1951	13:52	Lib	6 Aug 1951	23:33	Ari	6 Dec 1951	23:18
Gem	10 Apr 1951	00:41	Sco	9 Aug 1951	06:23	Tau	9 Dec 1951	07:04
Can	12 Apr 1951	13:04	Sag	11 Aug 1951	10:30	Gem	11 Dec 1951	16:54
Leo	15 Apr 1951	01:17	Cap	13 Aug 1951	12:17	Can	14 Dec 1951	04:22
Vir	17 Apr 1951	11:05	Aqu	15 Aug 1951	12:53	Leo	16 Dec 1951	17:04
Lib	19 Apr 1951	17:13	Pis	17 Aug 1951	13:53	Vir	19 Dec 1951	05:52
Sco	21 Apr 1951	19:54	Ari	19 Aug 1951	16:58	Lib	21 Dec 1951	16:40
Sag	23 Apr 1951	20:39	Tau	21 Aug 1951	23:28	Sco	23 Dec 1951	23:37
Cap	25 Apr 1951	21:20	Gem	24 Aug 1951	09:27	Sag	26 Dec 1951	02:25
Aqu	27 Apr 1951	23:33	Can	26 Aug 1951	21:44	Cap	28 Dec 1951	02:23
Pis	30 Apr 1951	04:13	Leo	29 Aug 1951	10:09	Aqu	30 Dec 1951	01:36
			Vir	31 Aug 1951	20:59			

Moon Signs

1952

Pis	1 Jan 1952	02:11	Leo	1 May 1952	04:12	Aqu	1 Sep 1952	09:02
Ari	3 Jan 1952	05:41	Vir	3 May 1952	16:57	Pis	3 Sep 1952	09:00
Tau	5 Jan 1952	12:44	Lib	6 May 1952	03:38	Ari	5 Sep 1952	08:57
Gem	7 Jan 1952	22:42	Sco	8 May 1952	10:47	Tau	7 Sep 1952	10:49
Can	10 Jan 1952	10:34	Sag	10 May 1952	14:49	Gem	9 Sep 1952	16:07
Leo	12 Jan 1952	23:19	Cap	12 May 1952	17:08	Can	12 Sep 1952	01:25
Vir	15 Jan 1952	12:00	Aqu	14 May 1952	19:14	Leo	14 Sep 1952	13:38
Lib	17 Jan 1952	23:18	Pis	16 May 1952	22:06	Vir	17 Sep 1952	02:41
Sco	20 Jan 1952	07:43	Ari	19 May 1952	02:07	Lib	19 Sep 1952	14:41
Sag	22 Jan 1952	12:20	Tau	21 May 1952	07:29	Sco	22 Sep 1952	00:42
Cap	24 Jan 1952	13:38	Gem	23 May 1952	14:37	Sag	24 Sep 1952	08:32
Aqu	26 Jan 1952	13:06	Can	26 May 1952	00:06	Cap	26 Sep 1952	14:05
Pis	28 Jan 1952	12:46	Leo	28 May 1952	11:59	Aqu	28 Sep 1952	17:24
Ari	30 Jan 1952	14:33	Vir	31 May 1952	00:56	Pis	30 Sep 1952	18:52
Tau	1 Feb 1952	19:51	Lib	2 Jun 1952	12:24	Ari	2 Oct 1952	19:34
Gem	4 Feb 1952	04:55	Sco	4 Jun 1952	20:18	Tau	4 Oct 1952	21:06
Can	6 Feb 1952	16:44	Sag	7 Jun 1952	00:19	Gem	7 Oct 1952	01:16
Leo	9 Feb 1952	05:36	Cap	9 Jun 1952	01:46	Can	9 Oct 1952	09:17
Vir	11 Feb 1952	18:01	Aqu	11 Jun 1952	02:27	Leo	11 Oct 1952	20:50
Lib	14 Feb 1952	05:00	Pis	13 Jun 1952	04:01	Vir	14 Oct 1952	09:50
Sco	16 Feb 1952	13:44	Ari	15 Jun 1952	07:29	Lib	16 Oct 1952	21:43
Sag	18 Feb 1952	19:41	Tau	17 Jun 1952	13:11	Sco	19 Oct 1952	07:09
Cap	20 Feb 1952	22:48	Gem	19 Jun 1952	21:04	Sag	21 Oct 1952	14:11
Aqu	22 Feb 1952	23:48	Can	22 Jun 1952	07:04	Cap	23 Oct 1952	19:28
Pis	25 Feb 1952	00:01	Leo	24 Jun 1952	19:02	Aqu	25 Oct 1952	23:27
Ari	27 Feb 1952	01:12	Vir	27 Jun 1952	08:06	Pis	28 Oct 1952	02:22
Tau	29 Feb 1952	05:02	Lib	29 Jun 1952	20:17	Ari	30 Oct 1952	04:34
Gem	2 Mar 1952	12:37	Sco	2 Jul 1952	05:25	Tau	1 Nov 1952	06:58
Can	4 Mar 1952	23:41	Sag	4 Jul 1952	10:25	Gem	3 Nov 1952	11:03
Leo	7 Mar 1952	12:30	Cap	6 Jul 1952	12:01	Can	5 Nov 1952	18:12
Vir	10 Mar 1952	00:50	Aqu	8 Jul 1952	11:54	Leo	8 Nov 1952	04:56
Lib	12 Mar 1952	11:15	Pis	10 Jul 1952	12:00	Vir	10 Nov 1952	17:47
Sco	14 Mar 1952	19:20	Ari	12 Jul 1952	13:57	Lib	13 Nov 1952	05:57
Sag	17 Mar 1952	01:14	Tau	14 Jul 1952	18:45	Sco	15 Nov 1952	15:17
Cap	19 Mar 1952	05:19	Gem	17 Jul 1952	02:38	Sag	17 Nov 1952	21:32
Aqu	21 Mar 1952	07:54	Can	19 Jul 1952	13:05	Cap	20 Nov 1952	01:39
Pis	23 Mar 1952	09:39	Leo	22 Jul 1952	01:20	Aqu	22 Nov 1952	04:51
Ari	25 Mar 1952	11:35	Vir	24 Jul 1952	14:24	Pis	24 Nov 1952	07:55
Tau	27 Mar 1952	15:06	Lib	27 Jul 1952	02:53	Ari	26 Nov 1952	11:09
Gem	29 Mar 1952	21:36	Sco	29 Jul 1952	13:03	Tau	28 Nov 1952	14:54
			Sag	31 Jul 1952	19:36	Gem	30 Nov 1952	19:53
Can	1 Apr 1952	07:39	Cap	2 Aug 1952	22:26	Can	3 Dec 1952	03:09
Leo	3 Apr 1952	20:09	Aqu	4 Aug 1952	22:40	Leo	5 Dec 1952	13:23
Vir	6 Apr 1952	08:39	Pis	6 Aug 1952	22:05	Vir	8 Dec 1952	01:57
Lib	8 Apr 1952	18:55	Ari	8 Aug 1952	22:34	Lib	10 Dec 1952	14:34
Sco	11 Apr 1952	02:12	Tau	11 Aug 1952	01:47	Sco	13 Dec 1952	00:37
Sag	13 Apr 1952	07:07	Gem	13 Aug 1952	08:37	Sag	15 Dec 1952	06:59
Cap	15 Apr 1952	10:41	Can	15 Aug 1952	18:52	Cap	17 Dec 1952	10:16
Aqu	17 Apr 1952	13:43	Leo	18 Aug 1952	07:19	Aqu	19 Dec 1952	12:02
Pis	19 Apr 1952	16:40	Vir	20 Aug 1952	20:22	Pis	21 Dec 1952	13:46
Ari	21 Apr 1952	19:56	Lib	23 Aug 1952	08:41	Ari	23 Dec 1952	16:30
Tau	24 Apr 1952	00:15	Sco	25 Aug 1952	19:10	Tau	25 Dec 1952	20:46
Gem	26 Apr 1952	06:40	Sag	28 Aug 1952	02:52	Gem	28 Dec 1952	02:48
Can	28 Apr 1952	16:06	Cap	30 Aug 1952	07:23	Can	30 Dec 1952	10:54

Moon Signs

1953

Leo	1 Jan 1953	21:17	Cap	3 May 1953	03:54	Can	2 Sep 1953	03:30
Vir	4 Jan 1953	09:41	Aqu	5 May 1953	09:12	Leo	4 Sep 1953	13:05
Lib	6 Jan 1953	22:36	Pis	7 May 1953	12:46	Vir	7 Sep 1953	00:47
Sco	9 Jan 1953	09:43	Ari	9 May 1953	14:49	Lib	9 Sep 1953	13:27
Sag	11 Jan 1953	17:14	Tau	11 May 1953	16:12	Sco	12 Sep 1953	02:05
Cap	13 Jan 1953	20:54	Gem	13 May 1953	18:27	Sag	14 Sep 1953	13:31
Aqu	15 Jan 1953	21:57	Can	15 May 1953	23:17	Cap	16 Sep 1953	22:19
Pis	17 Jan 1953	22:07	Leo	18 May 1953	07:47	Aqu	19 Sep 1953	03:29
Ari	19 Jan 1953	23:09	Vir	20 May 1953	19:31	Pis	21 Sep 1953	05:06
Tau	22 Jan 1953	02:21	Lib	23 May 1953	08:16	Ari	23 Sep 1953	04:30
Gem	24 Jan 1953	08:21	Sco	25 May 1953	19:32	Tau	25 Sep 1953	03:45
Can	26 Jan 1953	17:07	Sag	28 May 1953	04:08	Gem	27 Sep 1953	05:01
Leo	29 Jan 1953	04:06	Cap	30 May 1953	10:16	Can	29 Sep 1953	09:58
Vir	31 Jan 1953	16:35						
Lib	3 Feb 1953	05:31	Aqu	1 Jun 1953	14:45	Leo	1 Oct 1953	18:54
Sco	5 Feb 1953	17:20	Pis	3 Jun 1953	18:12	Vir	4 Oct 1953	06:40
Sag	8 Feb 1953	02:19	Ari	5 Jun 1953	21:01	Lib	6 Oct 1953	19:28
Cap	10 Feb 1953	07:31	Tau	7 Jun 1953	23:41	Sco	9 Oct 1953	07:56
Aqu	12 Feb 1953	09:16	Gem	10 Jun 1953	03:03	Sag	11 Oct 1953	19:19
Pis	14 Feb 1953	08:58	Can	12 Jun 1953	08:18	Cap	14 Oct 1953	04:51
Ari	16 Feb 1953	08:31	Leo	14 Jun 1953	16:27	Aqu	16 Oct 1953	11:33
Tau	18 Feb 1953	09:52	Vir	17 Jun 1953	03:37	Pis	18 Oct 1953	14:54
Gem	20 Feb 1953	14:28	Lib	19 Jun 1953	16:16	Ari	20 Oct 1953	15:26
Can	22 Feb 1953	22:48	Sco	22 Jun 1953	03:57	Tau	22 Oct 1953	14:47
Leo	25 Feb 1953	10:06	Sag	24 Jun 1953	12:46	Gem	24 Oct 1953	15:05
Vir	27 Feb 1953	22:51	Cap	26 Jun 1953	18:29	Can	26 Oct 1953	18:24
			Aqu	28 Jun 1953	21:51	Leo	29 Oct 1953	01:56
						Vir	31 Oct 1953	13:05
Lib	2 Mar 1953	11:41	Pis	1 Jul 1953	00:08	Lib	3 Nov 1953	01:51
Sco	4 Mar 1953	23:30	Ari	3 Jul 1953	02:24	Sco	5 Nov 1953	14:11
Sag	7 Mar 1953	09:19	Tau	5 Jul 1953	05:23	Sag	8 Nov 1953	01:06
Cap	9 Mar 1953	16:09	Gem	7 Jul 1953	09:43	Cap	10 Nov 1953	10:18
Aqu	11 Mar 1953	19:37	Can	9 Jul 1953	15:54	Aqu	12 Nov 1953	17:30
Pis	13 Mar 1953	20:16	Leo	12 Jul 1953	00:29	Pis	14 Nov 1953	22:16
Ari	15 Mar 1953	19:39	Vir	14 Jul 1953	11:29	Ari	17 Nov 1953	00:34
Tau	17 Mar 1953	19:45	Lib	17 Jul 1953	00:04	Tau	19 Nov 1953	01:15
Gem	19 Mar 1953	22:36	Sco	19 Jul 1953	12:16	Gem	21 Nov 1953	01:55
Can	22 Mar 1953	05:29	Sag	21 Jul 1953	21:58	Can	23 Nov 1953	04:32
Leo	24 Mar 1953	16:14	Cap	24 Jul 1953	04:06	Leo	25 Nov 1953	10:42
Vir	27 Mar 1953	05:04	Aqu	26 Jul 1953	07:02	Vir	27 Nov 1953	20:41
Lib	29 Mar 1953	17:51	Pis	28 Jul 1953	08:07	Lib	30 Nov 1953	09:05
			Ari	30 Jul 1953	08:56			
Sco	1 Apr 1953	05:19	Tau	1 Aug 1953	10:58	Sco	2 Dec 1953	21:30
Sag	3 Apr 1953	14:58	Gem	3 Aug 1953	15:11	Sag	5 Dec 1953	08:08
Cap	5 Apr 1953	22:28	Can	5 Aug 1953	22:00	Cap	7 Dec 1953	16:32
Aqu	8 Apr 1953	03:27	Leo	8 Aug 1953	07:16	Aqu	9 Dec 1953	22:58
Pis	10 Apr 1953	05:49	Vir	10 Aug 1953	18:33	Pis	12 Dec 1953	03:46
Ari	12 Apr 1953	06:19	Lib	13 Aug 1953	07:08	Ari	14 Dec 1953	07:06
Tau	14 Apr 1953	06:31	Sco	15 Aug 1953	19:43	Tau	16 Dec 1953	09:22
Gem	16 Apr 1953	08:28	Sag	18 Aug 1953	06:30	Gem	18 Dec 1953	11:28
Can	18 Apr 1953	13:54	Cap	20 Aug 1953	13:51	Can	20 Dec 1953	14:40
Leo	20 Apr 1953	23:28	Aqu	22 Aug 1953	17:28	Leo	22 Dec 1953	20:23
Vir	23 Apr 1953	11:53	Pis	24 Aug 1953	18:12	Vir	25 Dec 1953	05:24
Lib	26 Apr 1953	00:40	Ari	26 Aug 1953	17:46	Lib	27 Dec 1953	17:11
Sco	28 Apr 1953	11:51	Tau	28 Aug 1953	18:10	Sco	30 Dec 1953	05:43
Sag	30 Apr 1953	20:52	Gem	30 Aug 1953	21:07			

Moon Signs

1954

Sag	1 Jan 1954	16:39	Tau	2 May 1954	01:42	Sco	1 Sep 1954	22:49
Cap	4 Jan 1954	00:44	Gem	4 May 1954	01:07	Sag	4 Sep 1954	11:32
Aqu	6 Jan 1954	06:09	Can	6 May 1954	02:31	Cap	6 Sep 1954	23:09
Pis	8 Jan 1954	09:43	Leo	8 May 1954	07:29	Aqu	9 Sep 1954	07:30
Ari	10 Jan 1954	12:27	Vir	10 May 1954	16:23	Pis	11 Sep 1954	11:54
Tau	12 Jan 1954	15:10	Lib	13 May 1954	04:03	Ari	13 Sep 1954	13:22
Gem	14 Jan 1954	18:29	Sco	15 May 1954	16:42	Tau	15 Sep 1954	13:44
Can	16 Jan 1954	23:01	Sag	18 May 1954	04:53	Gem	17 Sep 1954	14:55
Leo	19 Jan 1954	05:24	Cap	20 May 1954	15:49	Can	19 Sep 1954	18:13
Vir	21 Jan 1954	14:14	Aqu	23 May 1954	00:47	Leo	22 Sep 1954	00:04
Lib	24 Jan 1954	01:30	Pis	25 May 1954	07:08	Vir	24 Sep 1954	08:11
Sco	26 Jan 1954	14:03	Ari	27 May 1954	10:31	Lib	26 Sep 1954	18:11
Sag	29 Jan 1954	01:42	Tau	29 May 1954	11:33	Sco	29 Sep 1954	05:52
Cap	31 Jan 1954	10:25	Gem	31 May 1954	11:41			
Aqu	2 Feb 1954	15:37	Can	2 Jun 1954	12:47	Sag	1 Oct 1954	18:41
Pis	4 Feb 1954	18:03	Leo	4 Jun 1954	16:35	Cap	4 Oct 1954	07:04
Ari	6 Feb 1954	19:14	Vir	7 Jun 1954	00:07	Aqu	6 Oct 1954	16:45
Tau	8 Feb 1954	20:48	Lib	9 Jun 1954	10:59	Pis	8 Oct 1954	22:15
Gem	10 Feb 1954	23:55	Sco	11 Jun 1954	23:29	Ari	10 Oct 1954	23:57
Can	13 Feb 1954	05:10	Sag	14 Jun 1954	11:37	Tau	12 Oct 1954	23:32
Leo	15 Feb 1954	12:36	Cap	16 Jun 1954	22:04	Gem	14 Oct 1954	23:11
Vir	17 Feb 1954	22:01	Aqu	19 Jun 1954	06:26	Can	17 Oct 1954	00:51
Lib	20 Feb 1954	09:15	Pis	21 Jun 1954	12:36	Leo	19 Oct 1954	05:41
Sco	22 Feb 1954	21:43	Ari	23 Jun 1954	16:43	Vir	21 Oct 1954	13:45
Sag	25 Feb 1954	10:00	Tau	25 Jun 1954	19:09	Lib	24 Oct 1954	00:12
Cap	27 Feb 1954	19:57	Gem	27 Jun 1954	20:42	Sco	26 Oct 1954	12:11
			Can	29 Jun 1954	22:36	Sag	29 Oct 1954	00:58
						Cap	31 Oct 1954	13:35
Aqu	2 Mar 1954	02:06	Leo	2 Jul 1954	02:17	Aqu	3 Nov 1954	00:21
Pis	4 Mar 1954	04:32	Vir	4 Jul 1954	08:57	Pis	5 Nov 1954	07:33
Ari	6 Mar 1954	04:40	Lib	6 Jul 1954	18:53	Ari	7 Nov 1954	10:41
Tau	8 Mar 1954	04:33	Sco	9 Jul 1954	07:04	Tau	9 Nov 1954	10:48
Gem	10 Mar 1954	06:06	Sag	11 Jul 1954	19:18	Gem	11 Nov 1954	09:51
Can	12 Mar 1954	10:38	Cap	14 Jul 1954	05:40	Can	13 Nov 1954	10:00
Leo	14 Mar 1954	18:17	Aqu	16 Jul 1954	13:18	Leo	15 Nov 1954	13:04
Vir	17 Mar 1954	04:21	Pis	18 Jul 1954	18:32	Vir	17 Nov 1954	19:53
Lib	19 Mar 1954	15:58	Ari	20 Jul 1954	22:07	Lib	20 Nov 1954	06:02
Sco	22 Mar 1954	04:26	Tau	23 Jul 1954	00:52	Sco	22 Nov 1954	18:13
Sag	24 Mar 1954	16:56	Gem	25 Jul 1954	03:30	Sag	25 Nov 1954	07:01
Cap	27 Mar 1954	03:54	Can	27 Jul 1954	06:41	Cap	27 Nov 1954	19:24
Aqu	29 Mar 1954	11:36	Leo	29 Jul 1954	11:11	Aqu	30 Nov 1954	06:19
Pis	31 Mar 1954	15:16	Vir	31 Jul 1954	17:50			
Ari	2 Apr 1954	15:40	Lib	3 Aug 1954	03:15	Pis	2 Dec 1954	14:37
Tau	4 Apr 1954	14:43	Sco	5 Aug 1954	15:03	Ari	4 Dec 1954	19:34
Gem	6 Apr 1954	14:41	Sag	8 Aug 1954	03:32	Tau	6 Dec 1954	21:22
Can	8 Apr 1954	17:29	Cap	10 Aug 1954	14:19	Gem	8 Dec 1954	21:16
Leo	11 Apr 1954	00:07	Aqu	12 Aug 1954	21:53	Can	10 Dec 1954	21:07
Vir	13 Apr 1954	10:03	Pis	15 Aug 1954	02:16	Leo	12 Dec 1954	22:49
Lib	15 Apr 1954	21:58	Ari	17 Aug 1954	04:37	Vir	15 Dec 1954	03:54
Sco	18 Apr 1954	10:32	Tau	19 Aug 1954	06:26	Lib	17 Dec 1954	12:52
Sag	20 Apr 1954	22:55	Gem	21 Aug 1954	08:56	Sco	20 Dec 1954	00:44
Cap	23 Apr 1954	10:10	Can	23 Aug 1954	12:50	Sag	22 Dec 1954	13:35
Aqu	25 Apr 1954	19:02	Leo	25 Aug 1954	18:22	Cap	25 Dec 1954	01:40
Pis	28 Apr 1954	00:20	Vir	28 Aug 1954	01:44	Aqu	27 Dec 1954	12:00
Ari	30 Apr 1954	02:08	Lib	30 Aug 1954	11:13	Pis	29 Dec 1954	20:09

Moon Signs

1955

Ari	1 Jan 1955	01:55	Lib	3 May 1955	04:26	Pis	1 Sep 1955	15:22
Tau	3 Jan 1955	05:24	Sco	5 May 1955	15:04	Ari	3 Sep 1955	21:23
Gem	5 Jan 1955	07:04	Sag	8 May 1955	03:19	Tau	6 Sep 1955	01:36
Can	7 Jan 1955	08:00	Cap	10 May 1955	16:18	Gem	8 Sep 1955	04:58
Leo	9 Jan 1955	09:42	Aqu	13 May 1955	04:29	Can	10 Sep 1955	08:01
Vir	11 Jan 1955	13:44	Pis	15 May 1955	13:52	Leo	12 Sep 1955	11:02
Lib	13 Jan 1955	21:16	Ari	17 May 1955	19:20	Vir	14 Sep 1955	14:33
Sco	16 Jan 1955	08:15	Tau	19 May 1955	21:11	Lib	16 Sep 1955	19:35
Sag	18 Jan 1955	21:01	Gem	21 May 1955	20:56	Sco	19 Sep 1955	03:19
Cap	21 Jan 1955	09:09	Can	23 May 1955	20:33	Sag	21 Sep 1955	14:12
Aqu	23 Jan 1955	18:58	Leo	25 May 1955	21:54	Cap	24 Sep 1955	03:01
Pis	26 Jan 1955	02:10	Vir	28 May 1955	02:17	Aqu	26 Sep 1955	15:07
Ari	28 Jan 1955	07:19	Lib	30 May 1955	10:08	Pis	29 Sep 1955	00:11
Tau	30 Jan 1955	11:06						
Gem	1 Feb 1955	14:02	Sco	1 Jun 1955	20:54	Ari	1 Oct 1955	05:46
Can	3 Feb 1955	16:36	Sag	4 Jun 1955	09:24	Tau	3 Oct 1955	08:51
Leo	5 Feb 1955	19:29	Cap	6 Jun 1955	22:20	Gem	5 Oct 1955	10:59
Vir	7 Feb 1955	23:44	Aqu	9 Jun 1955	10:29	Can	7 Oct 1955	13:23
Lib	10 Feb 1955	06:33	Pis	11 Jun 1955	20:31	Leo	9 Oct 1955	16:41
Sco	12 Feb 1955	16:39	Ari	14 Jun 1955	03:23	Vir	11 Oct 1955	21:12
Sag	15 Feb 1955	05:07	Tau	16 Jun 1955	06:50	Lib	14 Oct 1955	03:14
Cap	17 Feb 1955	17:34	Gem	18 Jun 1955	07:36	Sco	16 Oct 1955	11:24
Aqu	20 Feb 1955	03:32	Can	20 Jun 1955	07:15	Sag	18 Oct 1955	22:08
Pis	22 Feb 1955	10:08	Leo	22 Jun 1955	07:37	Cap	21 Oct 1955	10:51
Ari	24 Feb 1955	14:05	Vir	24 Jun 1955	10:27	Aqu	23 Oct 1955	23:32
Tau	26 Feb 1955	16:46	Lib	26 Jun 1955	16:56	Pis	26 Oct 1955	09:36
Gem	28 Feb 1955	19:24	Sco	29 Jun 1955	03:05	Ari	28 Oct 1955	15:45
						Tau	30 Oct 1955	18:30
Can	2 Mar 1955	22:40	Sag	1 Jul 1955	15:34	Gem	1 Nov 1955	19:23
Leo	5 Mar 1955	02:49	Cap	4 Jul 1955	04:29	Can	3 Nov 1955	20:11
Vir	7 Mar 1955	08:09	Aqu	6 Jul 1955	16:18	Leo	5 Nov 1955	22:21
Lib	9 Mar 1955	15:20	Pis	9 Jul 1955	02:08	Vir	8 Nov 1955	02:37
Sco	12 Mar 1955	01:05	Ari	11 Jul 1955	09:32	Lib	10 Nov 1955	09:16
Sag	14 Mar 1955	13:13	Tau	13 Jul 1955	14:19	Sco	12 Nov 1955	18:12
Cap	17 Mar 1955	02:01	Gem	15 Jul 1955	16:43	Sag	15 Nov 1955	05:17
Aqu	19 Mar 1955	12:45	Can	17 Jul 1955	17:30	Cap	17 Nov 1955	17:59
Pis	21 Mar 1955	19:44	Leo	19 Jul 1955	18:03	Aqu	20 Nov 1955	06:58
Ari	23 Mar 1955	23:08	Vir	21 Jul 1955	20:07	Pis	22 Nov 1955	18:10
Tau	26 Mar 1955	00:31	Lib	24 Jul 1955	01:17	Ari	25 Nov 1955	01:46
Gem	28 Mar 1955	01:42	Sco	26 Jul 1955	10:19	Tau	27 Nov 1955	05:27
Can	30 Mar 1955	04:05	Sag	28 Jul 1955	22:24	Gem	29 Nov 1955	06:11
			Cap	31 Jul 1955	11:18			
Leo	1 Apr 1955	08:21	Aqu	2 Aug 1955	22:51	Can	1 Dec 1955	05:46
Vir	3 Apr 1955	14:31	Pis	5 Aug 1955	08:03	Leo	3 Dec 1955	06:07
Lib	5 Apr 1955	22:34	Ari	7 Aug 1955	14:59	Vir	5 Dec 1955	08:51
Sco	8 Apr 1955	08:38	Tau	9 Aug 1955	20:03	Lib	7 Dec 1955	14:49
Sag	10 Apr 1955	20:42	Gem	11 Aug 1955	23:33	Sco	10 Dec 1955	00:00
Cap	13 Apr 1955	09:40	Can	14 Aug 1955	01:50	Sag	12 Dec 1955	11:34
Aqu	15 Apr 1955	21:19	Leo	16 Aug 1955	03:34	Cap	15 Dec 1955	00:23
Pis	18 Apr 1955	05:28	Vir	18 Aug 1955	05:57	Aqu	17 Dec 1955	13:19
Ari	20 Apr 1955	09:28	Lib	20 Aug 1955	10:35	Pis	20 Dec 1955	01:01
Tau	22 Apr 1955	10:29	Sco	22 Aug 1955	18:37	Ari	22 Dec 1955	10:04
Gem	24 Apr 1955	10:24	Sag	25 Aug 1955	06:03	Tau	24 Dec 1955	15:32
Can	26 Apr 1955	11:10	Cap	27 Aug 1955	18:56	Gem	26 Dec 1955	17:33
Leo	28 Apr 1955	14:09	Aqu	30 Aug 1955	06:35	Can	28 Dec 1955	17:17
Vir	30 Apr 1955	19:58				Leo	30 Dec 1955	16:36

Moon Signs

1956

Vir	1 Jan 1956	17:31	Aqu	2 May 1956	01:27	Leo	1 Sep 1956	23:13
Lib	3 Jan 1956	21:45	Pis	4 May 1956	13:14	Vir	3 Sep 1956	23:20
Sco	6 Jan 1956	06:00	Ari	6 May 1956	22:04	Lib	6 Sep 1956	00:05
Sag	8 Jan 1956	17:33	Tau	9 May 1956	03:23	Sco	8 Sep 1956	03:27
Cap	11 Jan 1956	06:34	Gem	11 May 1956	06:00	Sag	10 Sep 1956	10:47
Aqu	13 Jan 1956	19:19	Can	13 May 1956	07:21	Cap	12 Sep 1956	21:46
Pis	16 Jan 1956	06:47	Leo	15 May 1956	08:52	Aqu	15 Sep 1956	10:28
Ari	18 Jan 1956	16:17	Vir	17 May 1956	11:40	Pis	17 Sep 1956	22:33
Tau	20 Jan 1956	23:10	Lib	19 May 1956	16:26	Ari	20 Sep 1956	08:47
Gem	23 Jan 1956	03:05	Sco	21 May 1956	23:27	Tau	22 Sep 1956	17:01
Can	25 Jan 1956	04:19	Sag	24 May 1956	08:47	Gem	24 Sep 1956	23:24
Leo	27 Jan 1956	04:06	Cap	26 May 1956	20:11	Can	27 Sep 1956	03:59
Vir	29 Jan 1956	04:18	Aqu	29 May 1956	08:51	Leo	29 Sep 1956	06:48
Lib	31 Jan 1956	06:56	Pis	31 May 1956	21:09			
Sco	2 Feb 1956	13:34	Ari	3 Jun 1956	07:04	Vir	1 Oct 1956	08:24
Sag	5 Feb 1956	00:14	Tau	5 Jun 1956	13:20	Lib	3 Oct 1956	10:02
Cap	7 Feb 1956	13:08	Gem	7 Jun 1956	16:09	Sco	5 Oct 1956	13:20
Aqu	10 Feb 1956	01:52	Can	9 Jun 1956	16:42	Sag	7 Oct 1956	19:46
Pis	12 Feb 1956	12:51	Leo	11 Jun 1956	16:45	Cap	10 Oct 1956	05:48
Ari	14 Feb 1956	21:48	Vir	13 Jun 1956	18:03	Aqu	12 Oct 1956	18:09
Tau	17 Feb 1956	04:48	Lib	15 Jun 1956	21:59	Pis	15 Oct 1956	06:24
Gem	19 Feb 1956	09:50	Sco	18 Jun 1956	05:03	Ari	17 Oct 1956	16:35
Can	21 Feb 1956	12:49	Sag	20 Jun 1956	14:56	Tau	20 Oct 1956	00:06
Leo	23 Feb 1956	14:10	Cap	23 Jun 1956	02:43	Gem	22 Oct 1956	05:28
Vir	25 Feb 1956	15:05	Aqu	25 Jun 1956	15:25	Can	24 Oct 1956	09:23
Lib	27 Feb 1956	17:21	Pis	28 Jun 1956	03:54	Leo	26 Oct 1956	12:27
Sco	29 Feb 1956	22:46	Ari	30 Jun 1956	14:42	Vir	28 Oct 1956	15:09
						Lib	30 Oct 1956	18:10
Sag	3 Mar 1956	08:10	Tau	2 Jul 1956	22:24	Sco	1 Nov 1956	22:25
Cap	5 Mar 1956	20:33	Gem	5 Jul 1956	02:25	Sag	4 Nov 1956	04:56
Aqu	8 Mar 1956	09:19	Can	7 Jul 1956	03:19	Cap	6 Nov 1956	14:25
Pis	10 Mar 1956	20:11	Leo	9 Jul 1956	02:42	Aqu	9 Nov 1956	02:19
Ari	13 Mar 1956	04:26	Vir	11 Jul 1956	02:35	Pis	11 Nov 1956	14:50
Tau	15 Mar 1956	10:32	Lib	13 Jul 1956	04:54	Ari	14 Nov 1956	01:35
Gem	17 Mar 1956	15:11	Sco	15 Jul 1956	10:58	Tau	16 Nov 1956	09:11
Can	19 Mar 1956	18:47	Sag	17 Jul 1956	20:38	Gem	18 Nov 1956	13:44
Leo	21 Mar 1956	21:31	Cap	20 Jul 1956	08:41	Can	20 Nov 1956	16:17
Vir	23 Mar 1956	23:53	Aqu	22 Jul 1956	21:28	Leo	22 Nov 1956	18:10
Lib	26 Mar 1956	03:00	Pis	25 Jul 1956	09:50	Vir	24 Nov 1956	20:32
Sco	28 Mar 1956	08:19	Ari	27 Jul 1956	20:53	Lib	27 Nov 1956	00:11
Sag	30 Mar 1956	16:56	Tau	30 Jul 1956	05:40	Sco	29 Nov 1956	05:34
Cap	2 Apr 1956	04:38	Gem	1 Aug 1956	11:15	Sag	1 Dec 1956	12:59
Aqu	4 Apr 1956	17:24	Can	3 Aug 1956	13:31	Cap	3 Dec 1956	22:37
Pis	7 Apr 1956	04:37	Leo	5 Aug 1956	13:26	Aqu	6 Dec 1956	10:16
Ari	9 Apr 1956	12:45	Vir	7 Aug 1956	12:50	Pis	8 Dec 1956	22:56
Tau	11 Apr 1956	18:03	Lib	9 Aug 1956	13:52	Ari	11 Dec 1956	10:36
Gem	13 Apr 1956	21:30	Sco	11 Aug 1956	18:20	Tau	13 Dec 1956	19:15
Can	16 Apr 1956	00:15	Sag	14 Aug 1956	03:01	Gem	16 Dec 1956	00:05
Leo	18 Apr 1956	03:00	Cap	16 Aug 1956	14:48	Can	18 Dec 1956	01:51
Vir	20 Apr 1956	06:17	Aqu	19 Aug 1956	03:37	Leo	20 Dec 1956	02:11
Lib	22 Apr 1956	10:37	Pis	21 Aug 1956	15:47	Vir	22 Dec 1956	02:56
Sco	24 Apr 1956	16:45	Ari	24 Aug 1956	02:29	Lib	24 Dec 1956	05:39
Sag	27 Apr 1956	01:26	Tau	26 Aug 1956	11:23	Sco	26 Dec 1956	11:09
Cap	29 Apr 1956	12:45	Gem	28 Aug 1956	17:59	Sag	28 Dec 1956	19:20
			Can	30 Aug 1956	21:50	Cap	31 Dec 1956	05:37

Moon Signs

1957

Aqu	2 Jan 1957	17:25	Gem	1 May 1957	13:46	Cap	2 Sep 1957	21:06
Pis	5 Jan 1957	06:04	Can	3 May 1957	19:08	Aqu	5 Sep 1957	07:50
Ari	7 Jan 1957	18:22	Leo	5 May 1957	22:53	Pis	7 Sep 1957	20:04
Tau	10 Jan 1957	04:26	Vir	8 May 1957	01:36	Ari	10 Sep 1957	08:44
Gem	12 Jan 1957	10:42	Lib	10 May 1957	03:57	Tau	12 Sep 1957	20:57
Can	14 Jan 1957	13:04	Sco	12 May 1957	06:48	Gem	15 Sep 1957	07:25
Leo	16 Jan 1957	12:50	Sag	14 May 1957	11:14	Can	17 Sep 1957	14:48
Vir	18 Jan 1957	12:04	Cap	16 May 1957	18:13	Leo	19 Sep 1957	18:30
Lib	20 Jan 1957	12:56	Aqu	19 May 1957	04:12	Vir	21 Sep 1957	19:11
Sco	22 Jan 1957	17:03	Pis	21 May 1957	16:20	Lib	23 Sep 1957	18:32
Sag	25 Jan 1957	00:53	Ari	24 May 1957	04:33	Sco	25 Sep 1957	18:40
Cap	27 Jan 1957	11:33	Tau	26 May 1957	14:42	Sag	27 Sep 1957	21:28
Aqu	29 Jan 1957	23:42	Gem	28 May 1957	21:46	Cap	30 Sep 1957	04:00
			Can	31 May 1957	02:05			
Pis	1 Feb 1957	12:20	Leo	2 Jun 1957	04:45	Aqu	2 Oct 1957	14:04
Ari	4 Feb 1957	00:41	Vir	4 Jun 1957	06:59	Pis	5 Oct 1957	02:14
Tau	6 Feb 1957	11:36	Lib	6 Jun 1957	09:46	Ari	7 Oct 1957	14:56
Gem	8 Feb 1957	19:34	Sco	8 Jun 1957	13:41	Tau	10 Oct 1957	02:47
Can	10 Feb 1957	23:37	Sag	10 Jun 1957	19:09	Gem	12 Oct 1957	13:00
Leo	13 Feb 1957	00:17	Cap	13 Jun 1957	02:37	Can	14 Oct 1957	20:53
Vir	14 Feb 1957	23:17	Aqu	15 Jun 1957	12:24	Leo	17 Oct 1957	01:58
Lib	16 Feb 1957	22:51	Pis	18 Jun 1957	00:15	Vir	19 Oct 1957	04:23
Sco	19 Feb 1957	01:07	Ari	20 Jun 1957	12:45	Lib	21 Oct 1957	05:03
Sag	21 Feb 1957	07:23	Tau	22 Jun 1957	23:37	Sco	23 Oct 1957	05:31
Cap	23 Feb 1957	17:27	Gem	25 Jun 1957	07:06	Sag	25 Oct 1957	07:33
Aqu	26 Feb 1957	05:43	Can	27 Jun 1957	11:00	Cap	27 Oct 1957	12:42
Pis	28 Feb 1957	18:25	Leo	29 Jun 1957	12:30	Aqu	29 Oct 1957	21:33
Ari	3 Mar 1957	06:30	Vir	1 Jul 1957	13:24	Pis	1 Nov 1957	09:18
Tau	5 Mar 1957	17:20	Lib	3 Jul 1957	15:16	Ari	3 Nov 1957	21:59
Gem	8 Mar 1957	02:02	Sco	5 Jul 1957	19:10	Tau	6 Nov 1957	09:37
Can	10 Mar 1957	07:44	Sag	8 Jul 1957	01:21	Gem	8 Nov 1957	19:08
Leo	12 Mar 1957	10:10	Cap	10 Jul 1957	09:35	Can	11 Nov 1957	02:23
Vir	14 Mar 1957	10:19	Aqu	12 Jul 1957	19:43	Leo	13 Nov 1957	07:36
Lib	16 Mar 1957	09:59	Pis	15 Jul 1957	07:32	Vir	15 Nov 1957	11:06
Sco	18 Mar 1957	11:16	Ari	17 Jul 1957	20:14	Lib	17 Nov 1957	13:25
Sag	20 Mar 1957	15:54	Tau	20 Jul 1957	07:57	Sco	19 Nov 1957	15:17
Cap	23 Mar 1957	00:35	Gem	22 Jul 1957	16:33	Sag	21 Nov 1957	17:51
Aqu	25 Mar 1957	12:17	Can	24 Jul 1957	21:04	Cap	23 Nov 1957	22:30
Pis	28 Mar 1957	00:59	Leo	26 Jul 1957	22:16	Aqu	26 Nov 1957	06:16
Ari	30 Mar 1957	12:54	Vir	28 Jul 1957	21:59	Pis	28 Nov 1957	17:16
			Lib	30 Jul 1957	22:21			
Tau	1 Apr 1957	23:10	Sco	2 Aug 1957	01:01	Ari	1 Dec 1957	05:56
Gem	4 Apr 1957	07:30	Sag	4 Aug 1957	06:47	Tau	3 Dec 1957	17:47
Can	6 Apr 1957	13:36	Cap	6 Aug 1957	15:23	Gem	6 Dec 1957	02:59
Leo	8 Apr 1957	17:24	Aqu	9 Aug 1957	02:02	Can	8 Dec 1957	09:15
Vir	10 Apr 1957	19:13	Pis	11 Aug 1957	14:02	Leo	10 Dec 1957	13:22
Lib	12 Apr 1957	20:08	Ari	14 Aug 1957	02:46	Vir	12 Dec 1957	16:28
Sco	14 Apr 1957	21:46	Tau	16 Aug 1957	15:00	Lib	14 Dec 1957	19:22
Sag	17 Apr 1957	01:44	Gem	19 Aug 1957	00:50	Sco	16 Dec 1957	22:35
Cap	19 Apr 1957	09:09	Can	21 Aug 1957	06:48	Sag	19 Dec 1957	02:31
Aqu	21 Apr 1957	19:53	Leo	23 Aug 1957	08:50	Cap	21 Dec 1957	07:47
Pis	24 Apr 1957	08:22	Vir	25 Aug 1957	08:25	Aqu	23 Dec 1957	15:19
Ari	26 Apr 1957	20:21	Lib	27 Aug 1957	07:42	Pis	26 Dec 1957	01:41
Tau	29 Apr 1957	06:17	Sco	29 Aug 1957	08:46	Ari	28 Dec 1957	14:12
			Sag	31 Aug 1957	13:08	Tau	31 Dec 1957	02:36

Moon Signs

1958

Gem	2 Jan 1958	12:20	Sco	2 May 1958	16:14	Tau	2 Sep 1958	19:23
Can	4 Jan 1958	18:21	Sag	4 May 1958	16:43	Gem	5 Sep 1958	08:06
Leo	6 Jan 1958	21:21	Cap	6 May 1958	19:21	Can	7 Sep 1958	18:22
Vir	8 Jan 1958	22:59	Aqu	9 May 1958	01:30	Leo	10 Sep 1958	00:40
Lib	11 Jan 1958	00:52	Pis	11 May 1958	11:27	Vir	12 Sep 1958	03:18
Sco	13 Jan 1958	04:02	Ari	13 May 1958	23:57	Lib	14 Sep 1958	03:44
Sag	15 Jan 1958	08:50	Tau	16 May 1958	12:49	Sco	16 Sep 1958	03:49
Cap	17 Jan 1958	15:13	Gem	19 May 1958	00:13	Sag	18 Sep 1958	05:16
Aqu	19 Jan 1958	23:23	Can	21 May 1958	09:22	Cap	20 Sep 1958	09:13
Pis	22 Jan 1958	09:42	Leo	23 May 1958	16:14	Aqu	22 Sep 1958	16:03
Ari	24 Jan 1958	22:03	Vir	25 May 1958	20:59	Pis	25 Sep 1958	01:33
Tau	27 Jan 1958	10:56	Lib	27 May 1958	23:54	Ari	27 Sep 1958	13:07
Gem	29 Jan 1958	21:46	Sco	30 May 1958	01:33	Tau	30 Sep 1958	01:58
Can	1 Feb 1958	04:40	Sag	1 Jun 1958	02:53	Gem	2 Oct 1958	14:50
Leo	3 Feb 1958	07:37	Cap	3 Jun 1958	05:22	Can	5 Oct 1958	01:59
Vir	5 Feb 1958	08:10	Aqu	5 Jun 1958	10:34	Leo	7 Oct 1958	09:49
Lib	7 Feb 1958	08:23	Pis	7 Jun 1958	19:23	Vir	9 Oct 1958	13:48
Sco	9 Feb 1958	10:04	Ari	10 Jun 1958	07:20	Lib	11 Oct 1958	14:43
Sag	11 Feb 1958	14:12	Tau	12 Jun 1958	20:12	Sco	13 Oct 1958	14:11
Cap	13 Feb 1958	20:55	Gem	15 Jun 1958	07:30	Sag	15 Oct 1958	14:09
Aqu	16 Feb 1958	05:51	Can	17 Jun 1958	16:03	Cap	17 Oct 1958	16:23
Pis	18 Feb 1958	16:39	Leo	19 Jun 1958	22:03	Aqu	19 Oct 1958	22:05
Ari	21 Feb 1958	05:01	Vir	22 Jun 1958	02:21	Pis	22 Oct 1958	07:20
Tau	23 Feb 1958	18:04	Lib	24 Jun 1958	05:42	Ari	24 Oct 1958	19:10
Gem	26 Feb 1958	05:52	Sco	26 Jun 1958	08:30	Tau	27 Oct 1958	08:07
Can	28 Feb 1958	14:15	Sag	28 Jun 1958	11:11	Gem	29 Oct 1958	20:49
			Cap	30 Jun 1958	14:32			
Leo	2 Mar 1958	18:26	Aqu	2 Jul 1958	19:45	Can	1 Nov 1958	08:08
Vir	4 Mar 1958	19:14	Pis	5 Jul 1958	03:57	Leo	3 Nov 1958	17:02
Lib	6 Mar 1958	18:35	Ari	7 Jul 1958	15:18	Vir	5 Nov 1958	22:44
Sco	8 Mar 1958	18:34	Tau	10 Jul 1958	04:09	Lib	8 Nov 1958	01:15
Sag	10 Mar 1958	20:57	Gem	12 Jul 1958	15:46	Sco	10 Nov 1958	01:29
Cap	13 Mar 1958	02:37	Can	15 Jul 1958	00:14	Sag	12 Nov 1958	01:03
Aqu	15 Mar 1958	11:28	Leo	17 Jul 1958	05:30	Cap	14 Nov 1958	01:55
Pis	17 Mar 1958	22:41	Vir	19 Jul 1958	08:41	Aqu	16 Nov 1958	05:52
Ari	20 Mar 1958	11:17	Lib	21 Jul 1958	11:11	Pis	18 Nov 1958	13:57
Tau	23 Mar 1958	00:15	Sco	23 Jul 1958	13:57	Ari	21 Nov 1958	01:28
Gem	25 Mar 1958	12:18	Sag	25 Jul 1958	17:25	Tau	23 Nov 1958	14:30
Can	27 Mar 1958	21:51	Cap	27 Jul 1958	21:53	Gem	26 Nov 1958	03:00
Leo	30 Mar 1958	03:44	Aqu	30 Jul 1958	03:52	Can	28 Nov 1958	13:50
						Leo	30 Nov 1958	22:40
Vir	1 Apr 1958	06:01	Pis	1 Aug 1958	12:12	Vir	3 Dec 1958	05:17
Lib	3 Apr 1958	05:53	Ari	3 Aug 1958	23:14	Lib	5 Dec 1958	09:30
Sco	5 Apr 1958	05:16	Tau	6 Aug 1958	12:04	Sco	7 Dec 1958	11:27
Sag	7 Apr 1958	06:06	Gem	9 Aug 1958	00:15	Sag	9 Dec 1958	12:01
Cap	9 Apr 1958	10:01	Can	11 Aug 1958	09:24	Cap	11 Dec 1958	12:47
Aqu	11 Apr 1958	17:41	Leo	13 Aug 1958	14:42	Aqu	13 Dec 1958	15:38
Pis	14 Apr 1958	04:38	Vir	15 Aug 1958	17:06	Pis	15 Dec 1958	22:13
Ari	16 Apr 1958	17:22	Lib	17 Aug 1958	18:16	Ari	18 Dec 1958	08:45
Tau	19 Apr 1958	06:16	Sco	19 Aug 1958	19:49	Tau	20 Dec 1958	21:37
Gem	21 Apr 1958	18:03	Sag	21 Aug 1958	22:48	Gem	23 Dec 1958	10:08
Can	24 Apr 1958	03:45	Cap	24 Aug 1958	03:38	Can	25 Dec 1958	20:32
Leo	26 Apr 1958	10:42	Aqu	26 Aug 1958	10:28	Leo	28 Dec 1958	04:33
Vir	28 Apr 1958	14:39	Pis	28 Aug 1958	19:25	Vir	30 Dec 1958	10:40
Lib	30 Apr 1958	16:06	Ari	31 Aug 1958	06:35			

1959

Lib	1 Jan 1959	15:20	Pis	1 May 1959	11:59	Vir	2 Sep 1959	08:30		
Sco	3 Jan 1959	18:41	Ari	3 May 1959	22:19	Lib	4 Sep 1959	12:55		
Sag	5 Jan 1959	20:55	Tau	6 May 1959	10:39	Sco	6 Sep 1959	15:52		
Cap	7 Jan 1959	22:50	Gem	8 May 1959	23:34	Sag	8 Sep 1959	18:20		
Aqu	10 Jan 1959	01:52	Can	11 May 1959	11:56	Cap	10 Sep 1959	21:04		
Pis	12 Jan 1959	07:40	Leo	13 May 1959	22:39	Aqu	13 Sep 1959	00:43		
Ari	14 Jan 1959	17:09	Vir	16 May 1959	06:37	Pis	15 Sep 1959	05:54		
Tau	17 Jan 1959	05:32	Lib	18 May 1959	11:05	Ari	17 Sep 1959	13:16		
Gem	19 Jan 1959	18:15	Sco	20 May 1959	12:23	Tau	19 Sep 1959	23:13		
Can	22 Jan 1959	04:46	Sag	22 May 1959	11:50	Gem	22 Sep 1959	11:16		
Leo	24 Jan 1959	12:12	Cap	24 May 1959	11:24	Can	24 Sep 1959	23:48		
Vir	26 Jan 1959	17:13	Aqu	26 May 1959	13:10	Leo	27 Sep 1959	10:35		
Lib	28 Jan 1959	20:53	Pis	28 May 1959	18:42	Vir	29 Sep 1959	18:03		
Sco	31 Jan 1959	00:05	Ari	31 May 1959	04:18					
Sag	2 Feb 1959	03:10	Tau	2 Jun 1959	16:37	Lib	1 Oct 1959	22:07		
Cap	4 Feb 1959	06:28	Gem	5 Jun 1959	05:35	Sco	3 Oct 1959	23:53		
Aqu	6 Feb 1959	10:41	Can	7 Jun 1959	17:43	Sag	6 Oct 1959	00:54		
Pis	8 Feb 1959	16:50	Leo	10 Jun 1959	04:18	Cap	8 Oct 1959	02:39		
Ari	11 Feb 1959	01:55	Vir	12 Jun 1959	12:49	Aqu	10 Oct 1959	06:12		
Tau	13 Feb 1959	13:47	Lib	14 Jun 1959	18:41	Pis	12 Oct 1959	12:06		
Gem	16 Feb 1959	02:39	Sco	16 Jun 1959	21:37	Ari	14 Oct 1959	20:20		
Can	18 Feb 1959	13:49	Sag	18 Jun 1959	22:13	Tau	17 Oct 1959	06:39		
Leo	20 Feb 1959	21:36	Cap	20 Jun 1959	22:01	Gem	19 Oct 1959	18:39		
Vir	23 Feb 1959	02:05	Aqu	22 Jun 1959	23:01	Can	22 Oct 1959	07:22		
Lib	25 Feb 1959	04:28	Pis	25 Jun 1959	03:10	Leo	24 Oct 1959	19:03		
Sco	27 Feb 1959	06:14	Ari	27 Jun 1959	11:28	Vir	27 Oct 1959	03:47		
			Tau	29 Jun 1959	23:11	Lib	29 Oct 1959	08:40		
						Sco	31 Oct 1959	10:13		
Sag	1 Mar 1959	08:33	Gem	2 Jul 1959	12:05	Sag	2 Nov 1959	10:01		
Cap	3 Mar 1959	12:06	Can	5 Jul 1959	00:02	Cap	4 Nov 1959	10:05		
Aqu	5 Mar 1959	17:16	Leo	7 Jul 1959	10:07	Aqu	6 Nov 1959	12:14		
Pis	8 Mar 1959	00:26	Vir	9 Jul 1959	18:15	Pis	8 Nov 1959	17:35		
Ari	10 Mar 1959	09:54	Lib	12 Jul 1959	00:25	Ari	11 Nov 1959	02:10		
Tau	12 Mar 1959	21:37	Sco	14 Jul 1959	04:32	Tau	13 Nov 1959	13:04		
Gem	15 Mar 1959	10:30	Sag	16 Jul 1959	06:41	Gem	16 Nov 1959	01:16		
Can	17 Mar 1959	22:26	Cap	18 Jul 1959	07:41	Can	18 Nov 1959	13:56		
Leo	20 Mar 1959	07:22	Aqu	20 Jul 1959	09:05	Leo	21 Nov 1959	02:03		
Vir	22 Mar 1959	12:26	Pis	22 Jul 1959	12:42	Vir	23 Nov 1959	12:06		
Lib	24 Mar 1959	14:26	Ari	24 Jul 1959	19:54	Lib	25 Nov 1959	18:40		
Sco	26 Mar 1959	14:53	Tau	27 Jul 1959	06:43	Sco	27 Nov 1959	21:20		
Sag	28 Mar 1959	15:31	Gem	29 Jul 1959	19:23	Sag	29 Nov 1959	21:11		
Cap	30 Mar 1959	17:48								
Aqu	1 Apr 1959	22:42	Can	1 Aug 1959	07:23	Cap	1 Dec 1959	20:11		
Pis	4 Apr 1959	06:23	Leo	3 Aug 1959	17:09	Aqu	3 Dec 1959	20:35		
Ari	6 Apr 1959	16:32	Vir	6 Aug 1959	00:29	Pis	6 Dec 1959	00:17		
Tau	9 Apr 1959	04:31	Lib	8 Aug 1959	05:56	Ari	8 Dec 1959	07:59		
Gem	11 Apr 1959	17:24	Sco	10 Aug 1959	09:59	Tau	10 Dec 1959	18:55		
Can	14 Apr 1959	05:47	Sag	12 Aug 1959	12:57	Gem	13 Dec 1959	07:23		
Leo	16 Apr 1959	15:54	Cap	14 Aug 1959	15:18	Can	15 Dec 1959	20:00		
Vir	18 Apr 1959	22:26	Aqu	16 Aug 1959	17:53	Leo	18 Dec 1959	07:57		
Lib	21 Apr 1959	01:17	Pis	18 Aug 1959	22:00	Vir	20 Dec 1959	18:29		
Sco	23 Apr 1959	01:33	Ari	21 Aug 1959	04:52	Lib	23 Dec 1959	02:27		
Sag	25 Apr 1959	00:59	Tau	23 Aug 1959	14:58	Sco	25 Dec 1959	07:00		
Cap	27 Apr 1959	01:33	Gem	26 Aug 1959	03:18	Sag	27 Dec 1959	08:14		
Aqu	29 Apr 1959	04:55	Can	28 Aug 1959	15:33	Cap	29 Dec 1959	07:37		
			Leo	31 Aug 1959	01:32	Aqu	31 Dec 1959	07:15		

Moon Signs

1960

Pis	2 Jan 1960	09:19	Leo	2 May 1960	21:58	Aqu	2 Sep 1960	12:34
Ari	4 Jan 1960	15:22	Vir	5 May 1960	08:57	Pis	4 Sep 1960	13:51
Tau	7 Jan 1960	01:22	Lib	7 May 1960	16:29	Ari	6 Sep 1960	16:26
Gem	9 Jan 1960	13:44	Sco	9 May 1960	20:05	Tau	8 Sep 1960	21:45
Can	12 Jan 1960	02:22	Sag	11 May 1960	20:54	Gem	11 Sep 1960	06:30
Leo	14 Jan 1960	13:58	Cap	13 May 1960	20:50	Can	13 Sep 1960	18:10
Vir	17 Jan 1960	00:02	Aqu	15 May 1960	21:51	Leo	16 Sep 1960	06:46
Lib	19 Jan 1960	08:13	Pis	18 May 1960	01:24	Vir	18 Sep 1960	18:06
Sco	21 Jan 1960	13:58	Ari	20 May 1960	07:55	Lib	21 Sep 1960	02:57
Sag	23 Jan 1960	17:02	Tau	22 May 1960	16:59	Sco	23 Sep 1960	09:16
Cap	25 Jan 1960	17:59	Gem	25 May 1960	03:54	Sag	25 Sep 1960	13:41
Aqu	27 Jan 1960	18:18	Can	27 May 1960	16:06	Cap	27 Sep 1960	16:53
Pis	29 Jan 1960	19:57	Leo	30 May 1960	04:50	Aqu	29 Sep 1960	19:32
Ari	1 Feb 1960	00:40	Vir	1 Jun 1960	16:37	Pis	1 Oct 1960	22:14
Tau	3 Feb 1960	09:16	Lib	4 Jun 1960	01:29	Ari	4 Oct 1960	01:46
Gem	5 Feb 1960	20:58	Sco	6 Jun 1960	06:19	Tau	6 Oct 1960	07:08
Can	8 Feb 1960	09:36	Sag	8 Jun 1960	07:30	Gem	8 Oct 1960	15:16
Leo	10 Feb 1960	21:07	Cap	10 Jun 1960	06:47	Can	11 Oct 1960	02:18
Vir	13 Feb 1960	06:34	Aqu	12 Jun 1960	06:22	Leo	13 Oct 1960	14:54
Lib	15 Feb 1960	13:54	Pis	14 Jun 1960	08:18	Vir	16 Oct 1960	02:39
Sco	17 Feb 1960	19:23	Ari	16 Jun 1960	13:43	Lib	18 Oct 1960	11:30
Sag	19 Feb 1960	23:10	Tau	18 Jun 1960	22:33	Sco	20 Oct 1960	17:05
Cap	22 Feb 1960	01:38	Gem	21 Jun 1960	09:46	Sag	22 Oct 1960	20:15
Aqu	24 Feb 1960	03:32	Can	23 Jun 1960	22:09	Cap	24 Oct 1960	22:28
Pis	26 Feb 1960	06:03	Leo	26 Jun 1960	10:51	Aqu	27 Oct 1960	00:57
Ari	28 Feb 1960	10:38	Vir	28 Jun 1960	22:51	Pis	29 Oct 1960	04:26
						Ari	31 Oct 1960	09:11
Tau	1 Mar 1960	18:18	Lib	1 Jul 1960	08:45	Tau	2 Nov 1960	15:27
Gem	4 Mar 1960	05:07	Sco	3 Jul 1960	15:07	Gem	4 Nov 1960	23:44
Can	6 Mar 1960	17:36	Sag	5 Jul 1960	17:42	Can	7 Nov 1960	10:26
Leo	9 Mar 1960	05:24	Cap	7 Jul 1960	17:33	Leo	9 Nov 1960	22:59
Vir	11 Mar 1960	14:46	Aqu	9 Jul 1960	16:43	Vir	12 Nov 1960	11:22
Lib	13 Mar 1960	21:18	Pis	11 Jul 1960	17:19	Lib	14 Nov 1960	21:06
Sco	16 Mar 1960	01:36	Ari	13 Jul 1960	21:08	Sco	17 Nov 1960	02:51
Sag	18 Mar 1960	04:37	Tau	16 Jul 1960	04:48	Sag	19 Nov 1960	05:16
Cap	20 Mar 1960	07:14	Gem	18 Jul 1960	15:40	Cap	21 Nov 1960	06:01
Aqu	22 Mar 1960	10:10	Can	21 Jul 1960	04:08	Aqu	23 Nov 1960	07:04
Pis	24 Mar 1960	14:02	Leo	23 Jul 1960	16:45	Pis	25 Nov 1960	09:49
Ari	26 Mar 1960	19:29	Vir	26 Jul 1960	04:31	Ari	27 Nov 1960	14:51
Tau	29 Mar 1960	03:13	Lib	28 Jul 1960	14:32	Tau	29 Nov 1960	21:59
Gem	31 Mar 1960	13:32	Sco	30 Jul 1960	21:53			
Can	3 Apr 1960	01:45	Sag	2 Aug 1960	02:02	Gem	2 Dec 1960	07:00
Leo	5 Apr 1960	14:00	Cap	4 Aug 1960	03:24	Can	4 Dec 1960	17:51
Vir	8 Apr 1960	00:00	Aqu	6 Aug 1960	03:20	Leo	7 Dec 1960	06:20
Lib	10 Apr 1960	06:35	Pis	8 Aug 1960	03:42	Vir	9 Dec 1960	19:12
Sco	12 Apr 1960	10:00	Ari	10 Aug 1960	06:21	Lib	12 Dec 1960	06:09
Sag	14 Apr 1960	11:37	Tau	12 Aug 1960	12:36	Sco	14 Dec 1960	13:11
Cap	16 Apr 1960	13:01	Gem	14 Aug 1960	22:29	Sag	16 Dec 1960	16:05
Aqu	18 Apr 1960	15:32	Can	17 Aug 1960	10:42	Cap	18 Dec 1960	16:15
Pis	20 Apr 1960	19:55	Leo	19 Aug 1960	23:17	Aqu	20 Dec 1960	15:48
Ari	23 Apr 1960	02:23	Vir	22 Aug 1960	10:40	Pis	22 Dec 1960	16:47
Tau	25 Apr 1960	10:50	Lib	24 Aug 1960	20:08	Ari	24 Dec 1960	20:34
Gem	27 Apr 1960	21:16	Sco	27 Aug 1960	03:22	Tau	27 Dec 1960	03:30
Can	30 Apr 1960	09:22	Sag	29 Aug 1960	08:18	Gem	29 Dec 1960	13:01
			Cap	31 Aug 1960	11:07			

Moon Signs

1961

Can	1 Jan 1961	00:21	Sag	2 May 1961	05:24	Gem	1 Sep 1961	05:52
Leo	3 Jan 1961	12:53	Cap	4 May 1961	08:39	Can	3 Sep 1961	15:00
Vir	6 Jan 1961	01:47	Aqu	6 May 1961	11:23	Leo	6 Sep 1961	03:00
Lib	8 Jan 1961	13:29	Pis	8 May 1961	14:22	Vir	8 Sep 1961	16:04
Sco	10 Jan 1961	22:07	Ari	10 May 1961	17:55	Lib	11 Sep 1961	04:32
Sag	13 Jan 1961	02:38	Tau	12 May 1961	22:25	Sco	13 Sep 1961	15:21
Cap	15 Jan 1961	03:40	Gem	15 May 1961	04:34	Sag	15 Sep 1961	23:53
Aqu	17 Jan 1961	02:55	Can	17 May 1961	13:17	Cap	18 Sep 1961	05:41
Pis	19 Jan 1961	02:32	Leo	20 May 1961	00:44	Aqu	20 Sep 1961	08:42
Ari	21 Jan 1961	04:26	Vir	22 May 1961	13:37	Pis	22 Sep 1961	09:35
Tau	23 Jan 1961	09:52	Lib	25 May 1961	01:16	Ari	24 Sep 1961	09:39
Gem	25 Jan 1961	18:49	Sco	27 May 1961	09:33	Tau	26 Sep 1961	10:42
Can	28 Jan 1961	06:21	Sag	29 May 1961	14:09	Gem	28 Sep 1961	14:32
Leo	30 Jan 1961	19:04	Cap	31 May 1961	16:19	Can	30 Sep 1961	22:19
Vir	2 Feb 1961	07:47	Aqu	2 Jun 1961	17:44	Leo	3 Oct 1961	09:43
Lib	4 Feb 1961	19:26	Pis	4 Jun 1961	19:50	Vir	5 Oct 1961	22:44
Sco	7 Feb 1961	04:50	Ari	6 Jun 1961	23:23	Lib	8 Oct 1961	11:02
Sag	9 Feb 1961	10:59	Tau	9 Jun 1961	04:37	Sco	10 Oct 1961	21:18
Cap	11 Feb 1961	13:49	Gem	11 Jun 1961	11:40	Sag	13 Oct 1961	05:20
Aqu	13 Feb 1961	14:13	Can	13 Jun 1961	20:49	Cap	15 Oct 1961	11:22
Pis	15 Feb 1961	13:52	Leo	16 Jun 1961	08:15	Aqu	17 Oct 1961	15:36
Ari	17 Feb 1961	14:41	Vir	18 Jun 1961	21:11	Pis	19 Oct 1961	18:09
Tau	19 Feb 1961	18:20	Lib	21 Jun 1961	09:30	Ari	21 Oct 1961	19:35
Gem	22 Feb 1961	01:52	Sco	23 Jun 1961	18:50	Tau	23 Oct 1961	21:06
Can	24 Feb 1961	12:48	Sag	26 Jun 1961	00:03	Gem	26 Oct 1961	00:25
Leo	27 Feb 1961	01:34	Cap	28 Jun 1961	01:58	Can	28 Oct 1961	07:02
			Aqu	30 Jun 1961	02:17	Leo	30 Oct 1961	17:29
Vir	1 Mar 1961	14:11	Pis	2 Jul 1961	02:52	Vir	2 Nov 1961	06:16
Lib	4 Mar 1961	01:20	Ari	4 Jul 1961	05:11	Lib	4 Nov 1961	18:41
Sco	6 Mar 1961	10:22	Tau	6 Jul 1961	10:01	Sco	7 Nov 1961	04:39
Sag	8 Mar 1961	17:03	Gem	8 Jul 1961	17:26	Sag	9 Nov 1961	11:49
Cap	10 Mar 1961	21:17	Can	11 Jul 1961	03:13	Cap	11 Nov 1961	16:58
Aqu	12 Mar 1961	23:28	Leo	13 Jul 1961	14:56	Aqu	13 Nov 1961	20:58
Pis	15 Mar 1961	00:25	Vir	16 Jul 1961	03:54	Pis	16 Nov 1961	00:17
Ari	17 Mar 1961	01:32	Lib	18 Jul 1961	16:37	Ari	18 Nov 1961	03:09
Tau	19 Mar 1961	04:25	Sco	21 Jul 1961	03:03	Tau	20 Nov 1961	06:02
Gem	21 Mar 1961	10:32	Sag	23 Jul 1961	09:40	Gem	22 Nov 1961	09:59
Can	23 Mar 1961	20:22	Cap	25 Jul 1961	12:27	Can	24 Nov 1961	16:20
Leo	26 Mar 1961	08:48	Aqu	27 Jul 1961	12:40	Leo	27 Nov 1961	02:01
Vir	28 Mar 1961	21:28	Pis	29 Jul 1961	12:13	Vir	29 Nov 1961	14:24
Lib	31 Mar 1961	08:20	Ari	31 Jul 1961	12:56			
Sco	2 Apr 1961	16:35	Tau	2 Aug 1961	16:19	Lib	2 Dec 1961	03:06
Sag	4 Apr 1961	22:32	Gem	4 Aug 1961	23:04	Sco	4 Dec 1961	13:28
Cap	7 Apr 1961	02:51	Can	7 Aug 1961	08:56	Sag	6 Dec 1961	20:23
Aqu	9 Apr 1961	06:02	Leo	9 Aug 1961	20:59	Cap	9 Dec 1961	00:29
Pis	11 Apr 1961	08:31	Vir	12 Aug 1961	09:59	Aqu	11 Dec 1961	03:10
Ari	13 Apr 1961	10:55	Lib	14 Aug 1961	22:42	Pis	13 Dec 1961	05:41
Tau	15 Apr 1961	14:17	Sco	17 Aug 1961	09:43	Ari	15 Dec 1961	08:43
Gem	17 Apr 1961	19:55	Sag	19 Aug 1961	17:43	Tau	17 Dec 1961	12:38
Can	20 Apr 1961	04:49	Cap	21 Aug 1961	22:05	Gem	19 Dec 1961	17:47
Leo	22 Apr 1961	16:42	Aqu	23 Aug 1961	23:24	Can	22 Dec 1961	00:50
Vir	25 Apr 1961	05:30	Pis	25 Aug 1961	23:02	Leo	24 Dec 1961	10:25
Lib	27 Apr 1961	16:33	Ari	27 Aug 1961	22:49	Vir	26 Dec 1961	22:29
Sco	30 Apr 1961	00:25	Tau	30 Aug 1961	00:37	Lib	29 Dec 1961	11:25
						Sco	31 Dec 1961	22:40

Moon Signs

1962

Sag	3 Jan 1962	06:22	Ari	1 May 1962	06:11	Lib	1 Sep 1962	03:00
Cap	5 Jan 1962	10:22	Tau	3 May 1962	06:48	Sco	3 Sep 1962	15:45
Aqu	7 Jan 1962	11:59	Gem	5 May 1962	08:16	Sag	6 Sep 1962	03:24
Pis	9 Jan 1962	12:53	Can	7 May 1962	12:28	Cap	8 Sep 1962	12:17
Ari	11 Jan 1962	14:34	Leo	9 May 1962	20:35	Aqu	10 Sep 1962	17:25
Tau	13 Jan 1962	18:00	Vir	12 May 1962	08:10	Pis	12 Sep 1962	19:01
Gem	15 Jan 1962	23:42	Lib	14 May 1962	21:01	Ari	14 Sep 1962	18:32
Can	18 Jan 1962	07:39	Sco	17 May 1962	08:41	Tau	16 Sep 1962	18:00
Leo	20 Jan 1962	17:49	Sag	19 May 1962	18:02	Gem	18 Sep 1962	19:28
Vir	23 Jan 1962	05:53	Cap	22 May 1962	01:07	Can	21 Sep 1962	00:26
Lib	25 Jan 1962	18:51	Aqu	24 May 1962	06:30	Leo	23 Sep 1962	09:07
Sco	28 Jan 1962	06:53	Pis	26 May 1962	10:28	Vir	25 Sep 1962	20:30
Sag	30 Jan 1962	15:58	Ari	28 May 1962	13:14	Lib	28 Sep 1962	09:07
			Tau	30 May 1962	15:16	Sco	30 Sep 1962	21:47
Cap	1 Feb 1962	21:08	Gem	1 Jun 1962	17:40	Sag	3 Oct 1962	09:38
Aqu	3 Feb 1962	22:55	Can	3 Jun 1962	21:57	Cap	5 Oct 1962	19:33
Pis	5 Feb 1962	22:52	Leo	6 Jun 1962	05:22	Aqu	8 Oct 1962	02:19
Ari	7 Feb 1962	22:50	Vir	8 Jun 1962	16:11	Pis	10 Oct 1962	05:28
Tau	10 Feb 1962	00:35	Lib	11 Jun 1962	04:50	Ari	12 Oct 1962	05:40
Gem	12 Feb 1962	05:18	Sco	13 Jun 1962	16:44	Tau	14 Oct 1962	04:43
Can	14 Feb 1962	13:20	Sag	16 Jun 1962	02:02	Gem	16 Oct 1962	04:50
Leo	17 Feb 1962	00:03	Cap	18 Jun 1962	08:28	Can	18 Oct 1962	08:04
Vir	19 Feb 1962	12:26	Aqu	20 Jun 1962	12:48	Leo	20 Oct 1962	15:30
Lib	22 Feb 1962	01:21	Pis	22 Jun 1962	15:58	Vir	23 Oct 1962	02:30
Sco	24 Feb 1962	13:35	Ari	24 Jun 1962	18:42	Lib	25 Oct 1962	15:13
Sag	26 Feb 1962	23:44	Tau	26 Jun 1962	21:34	Sco	28 Oct 1962	03:47
			Gem	29 Jun 1962	01:09	Sag	30 Oct 1962	15:18
Cap	1 Mar 1962	06:37	Can	1 Jul 1962	06:18	Cap	2 Nov 1962	01:16
Aqu	3 Mar 1962	09:50	Leo	3 Jul 1962	13:55	Aqu	4 Nov 1962	09:00
Pis	5 Mar 1962	10:15	Vir	6 Jul 1962	00:22	Pis	6 Nov 1962	13:50
Ari	7 Mar 1962	09:31	Lib	8 Jul 1962	12:47	Ari	8 Nov 1962	15:44
Tau	9 Mar 1962	09:40	Sco	11 Jul 1962	01:04	Tau	10 Nov 1962	15:44
Gem	11 Mar 1962	12:36	Sag	13 Jul 1962	10:58	Gem	12 Nov 1962	15:43
Can	13 Mar 1962	19:25	Cap	15 Jul 1962	17:31	Can	14 Nov 1962	17:48
Leo	16 Mar 1962	05:55	Aqu	17 Jul 1962	21:06	Leo	16 Nov 1962	23:40
Vir	18 Mar 1962	18:32	Pis	19 Jul 1962	22:59	Vir	19 Nov 1962	09:33
Lib	21 Mar 1962	07:27	Ari	22 Jul 1962	00:33	Lib	21 Nov 1962	21:57
Sco	23 Mar 1962	19:27	Tau	24 Jul 1962	02:56	Sco	24 Nov 1962	10:32
Sag	26 Mar 1962	05:48	Gem	26 Jul 1962	06:56	Sag	26 Nov 1962	21:42
Cap	28 Mar 1962	13:44	Can	28 Jul 1962	13:00	Cap	29 Nov 1962	06:59
Aqu	30 Mar 1962	18:42	Leo	30 Jul 1962	21:20			
Pis	1 Apr 1962	20:41	Vir	2 Aug 1962	07:57	Aqu	1 Dec 1962	14:24
Ari	3 Apr 1962	20:40	Lib	4 Aug 1962	20:17	Pis	3 Dec 1962	19:52
Tau	5 Apr 1962	20:25	Sco	7 Aug 1962	08:54	Ari	5 Dec 1962	23:15
Gem	7 Apr 1962	22:00	Sag	9 Aug 1962	19:47	Tau	8 Dec 1962	00:58
Can	10 Apr 1962	03:12	Cap	12 Aug 1962	03:16	Gem	10 Dec 1962	02:07
Leo	12 Apr 1962	12:36	Aqu	14 Aug 1962	07:06	Can	12 Dec 1962	04:21
Vir	15 Apr 1962	00:56	Pis	16 Aug 1962	08:16	Leo	14 Dec 1962	09:20
Lib	17 Apr 1962	13:52	Ari	18 Aug 1962	08:25	Vir	16 Dec 1962	17:58
Sco	20 Apr 1962	01:35	Tau	20 Aug 1962	09:20	Lib	19 Dec 1962	05:40
Sag	22 Apr 1962	11:25	Gem	22 Aug 1962	12:28	Sco	21 Dec 1962	18:17
Cap	24 Apr 1962	19:19	Can	24 Aug 1962	18:33	Sag	24 Dec 1962	05:31
Aqu	27 Apr 1962	01:06	Leo	27 Aug 1962	03:29	Cap	26 Dec 1962	14:17
Pis	29 Apr 1962	04:39	Vir	29 Aug 1962	14:35	Aqu	28 Dec 1962	20:41
						Pis	31 Dec 1962	01:19

Moon Signs

1963

Ari	2 Jan 1963	04:47	Vir	2 May 1963	06:12	Pis	3 Sep 1963	01:35
Tau	4 Jan 1963	07:32	Lib	4 May 1963	17:41	Ari	5 Sep 1963	03:51
Gem	6 Jan 1963	10:13	Sco	7 May 1963	06:15	Tau	7 Sep 1963	05:01
Can	8 Jan 1963	13:41	Sag	9 May 1963	18:41	Gem	9 Sep 1963	06:45
Leo	10 Jan 1963	19:00	Cap	12 May 1963	06:12	Can	11 Sep 1963	10:07
Vir	13 Jan 1963	03:07	Aqu	14 May 1963	15:50	Leo	13 Sep 1963	15:29
Lib	15 Jan 1963	14:04	Pis	16 May 1963	22:30	Vir	15 Sep 1963	22:47
Sco	18 Jan 1963	02:34	Ari	19 May 1963	01:46	Lib	18 Sep 1963	07:59
Sag	20 Jan 1963	14:19	Tau	21 May 1963	02:20	Sco	20 Sep 1963	19:10
Cap	22 Jan 1963	23:21	Gem	23 May 1963	01:53	Sag	23 Sep 1963	07:49
Aqu	25 Jan 1963	05:13	Can	25 May 1963	02:29	Cap	25 Sep 1963	20:14
Pis	27 Jan 1963	08:34	Leo	27 May 1963	05:58	Aqu	28 Sep 1963	06:02
Ari	29 Jan 1963	10:43	Vir	29 May 1963	13:22	Pis	30 Sep 1963	11:44
Tau	31 Jan 1963	12:54						
			Lib	1 Jun 1963	00:08	Ari	2 Oct 1963	13:46
Gem	2 Feb 1963	16:02	Sco	3 Jun 1963	12:37	Tau	4 Oct 1963	13:49
Can	4 Feb 1963	20:40	Sag	6 Jun 1963	00:59	Gem	6 Oct 1963	13:58
Leo	7 Feb 1963	03:05	Cap	8 Jun 1963	12:05	Can	8 Oct 1963	16:00
Vir	9 Feb 1963	11:36	Aqu	10 Jun 1963	21:20	Leo	10 Oct 1963	20:54
Lib	11 Feb 1963	22:18	Pis	13 Jun 1963	04:19	Vir	13 Oct 1963	04:33
Sco	14 Feb 1963	10:38	Ari	15 Jun 1963	08:45	Lib	15 Oct 1963	14:23
Sag	16 Feb 1963	22:55	Tau	17 Jun 1963	10:53	Sco	18 Oct 1963	01:52
Cap	19 Feb 1963	08:58	Gem	19 Jun 1963	11:43	Sag	20 Oct 1963	14:31
Aqu	21 Feb 1963	15:22	Can	21 Jun 1963	12:46	Cap	23 Oct 1963	03:19
Pis	23 Feb 1963	18:16	Leo	23 Jun 1963	15:44	Aqu	25 Oct 1963	14:18
Ari	25 Feb 1963	19:04	Vir	25 Jun 1963	21:56	Pis	27 Oct 1963	21:34
Tau	27 Feb 1963	19:38	Lib	28 Jun 1963	07:40	Ari	30 Oct 1963	00:38
			Sco	30 Jun 1963	19:47			
Gem	1 Mar 1963	21:39	Sag	3 Jul 1963	08:10	Tau	1 Nov 1963	00:41
Can	4 Mar 1963	02:08	Cap	5 Jul 1963	19:02	Gem	2 Nov 1963	23:48
Leo	6 Mar 1963	09:14	Aqu	8 Jul 1963	03:35	Can	5 Nov 1963	00:08
Vir	8 Mar 1963	18:33	Pis	10 Jul 1963	09:51	Leo	7 Nov 1963	03:24
Lib	11 Mar 1963	05:34	Ari	12 Jul 1963	14:15	Vir	9 Nov 1963	10:14
Sco	13 Mar 1963	17:50	Tau	14 Jul 1963	17:14	Lib	11 Nov 1963	20:07
Sag	16 Mar 1963	06:26	Gem	16 Jul 1963	19:26	Sco	14 Nov 1963	07:56
Cap	18 Mar 1963	17:33	Can	18 Jul 1963	21:44	Sag	16 Nov 1963	20:38
Aqu	21 Mar 1963	01:19	Leo	21 Jul 1963	01:15	Cap	19 Nov 1963	09:21
Pis	23 Mar 1963	05:03	Vir	23 Jul 1963	07:06	Aqu	21 Nov 1963	20:49
Ari	25 Mar 1963	05:36	Lib	25 Jul 1963	16:02	Pis	24 Nov 1963	05:31
Tau	27 Mar 1963	04:56	Sco	28 Jul 1963	03:37	Ari	26 Nov 1963	10:23
Gem	29 Mar 1963	05:12	Sag	30 Jul 1963	16:07	Tau	28 Nov 1963	11:47
Can	31 Mar 1963	08:13				Gem	30 Nov 1963	11:14
Leo	2 Apr 1963	14:45	Cap	2 Aug 1963	03:11	Can	2 Dec 1963	10:45
Vir	5 Apr 1963	00:20	Aqu	4 Aug 1963	11:23	Leo	4 Dec 1963	12:20
Lib	7 Apr 1963	11:49	Pis	6 Aug 1963	16:44	Vir	6 Dec 1963	17:25
Sco	10 Apr 1963	00:13	Ari	8 Aug 1963	20:05	Lib	9 Dec 1963	02:21
Sag	12 Apr 1963	12:47	Tau	10 Aug 1963	22:37	Sco	11 Dec 1963	14:03
Cap	15 Apr 1963	00:25	Gem	13 Aug 1963	01:15	Sag	14 Dec 1963	02:52
Aqu	17 Apr 1963	09:32	Can	15 Aug 1963	04:38	Cap	16 Dec 1963	15:20
Pis	19 Apr 1963	14:51	Leo	17 Aug 1963	09:16	Aqu	19 Dec 1963	02:27
Ari	21 Apr 1963	16:28	Vir	19 Aug 1963	15:40	Pis	21 Dec 1963	11:26
Tau	23 Apr 1963	15:50	Lib	22 Aug 1963	00:25	Ari	23 Dec 1963	17:40
Gem	25 Apr 1963	15:06	Sco	24 Aug 1963	11:38	Tau	25 Dec 1963	20:56
Can	27 Apr 1963	16:27	Sag	27 Aug 1963	00:14	Gem	27 Dec 1963	21:57
Leo	29 Apr 1963	21:25	Cap	29 Aug 1963	11:55	Can	29 Dec 1963	22:06
			Aqu	31 Aug 1963	20:35	Leo	31 Dec 1963	23:09

Moon Signs

1964

Vir	3 Jan 1964	02:48	Cap	1 May 1964	05:41	Can	1 Sep 1964	00:12
Lib	5 Jan 1964	10:10	Aqu	3 May 1964	18:05	Leo	3 Sep 1964	02:35
Sco	7 Jan 1964	21:03	Pis	6 May 1964	03:41	Vir	5 Sep 1964	05:11
Sag	10 Jan 1964	09:48	Ari	8 May 1964	09:13	Lib	7 Sep 1964	09:19
Cap	12 Jan 1964	22:12	Tau	10 May 1964	11:07	Sco	9 Sep 1964	16:19
Aqu	15 Jan 1964	08:46	Gem	12 May 1964	11:00	Sag	12 Sep 1964	02:47
Pis	17 Jan 1964	17:03	Can	14 May 1964	10:53	Cap	14 Sep 1964	15:29
Ari	19 Jan 1964	23:09	Leo	16 May 1964	12:31	Aqu	17 Sep 1964	03:46
Tau	22 Jan 1964	03:22	Vir	18 May 1964	17:02	Pis	19 Sep 1964	13:20
Gem	24 Jan 1964	06:04	Lib	21 May 1964	00:41	Ari	21 Sep 1964	19:42
Can	26 Jan 1964	07:50	Sco	23 May 1964	10:57	Tau	23 Sep 1964	23:44
Leo	28 Jan 1964	09:45	Sag	25 May 1964	23:02	Gem	26 Sep 1964	02:45
Vir	30 Jan 1964	13:09	Cap	28 May 1964	11:59	Can	28 Sep 1964	05:38
			Aqu	31 May 1964	00:31	Leo	30 Sep 1964	08:52
Lib	1 Feb 1964	19:24	Pis	2 Jun 1964	10:59	Vir	2 Oct 1964	12:42
Sco	4 Feb 1964	05:12	Ari	4 Jun 1964	18:02	Lib	4 Oct 1964	17:43
Sag	6 Feb 1964	17:34	Tau	6 Jun 1964	21:18	Sco	7 Oct 1964	00:57
Cap	9 Feb 1964	06:10	Gem	8 Jun 1964	21:48	Sag	9 Oct 1964	11:02
Aqu	11 Feb 1964	16:38	Can	10 Jun 1964	21:16	Cap	11 Oct 1964	23:31
Pis	14 Feb 1964	00:07	Leo	12 Jun 1964	21:35	Aqu	14 Oct 1964	12:14
Ari	16 Feb 1964	05:09	Vir	15 Jun 1964	00:28	Pis	16 Oct 1964	22:30
Tau	18 Feb 1964	08:44	Lib	17 Jun 1964	06:53	Ari	19 Oct 1964	05:03
Gem	20 Feb 1964	11:47	Sco	19 Jun 1964	16:48	Tau	21 Oct 1964	08:23
Can	22 Feb 1964	14:48	Sag	22 Jun 1964	05:02	Gem	23 Oct 1964	10:02
Leo	24 Feb 1964	18:10	Cap	24 Jun 1964	18:01	Can	25 Oct 1964	11:37
Vir	26 Feb 1964	22:30	Aqu	27 Jun 1964	06:20	Leo	27 Oct 1964	14:13
Lib	29 Feb 1964	04:45	Pis	29 Jun 1964	16:55	Vir	29 Oct 1964	18:24
Sco	2 Mar 1964	13:54	Ari	2 Jul 1964	00:50	Lib	1 Nov 1964	00:24
Sag	5 Mar 1964	01:46	Tau	4 Jul 1964	05:41	Sco	3 Nov 1964	08:24
Cap	7 Mar 1964	14:34	Gem	6 Jul 1964	07:41	Sag	5 Nov 1964	18:42
Aqu	10 Mar 1964	01:33	Can	8 Jul 1964	07:56	Cap	8 Nov 1964	07:04
Pis	12 Mar 1964	09:03	Leo	10 Jul 1964	08:00	Aqu	10 Nov 1964	20:07
Ari	14 Mar 1964	13:13	Vir	12 Jul 1964	09:44	Pis	13 Nov 1964	07:27
Tau	16 Mar 1964	15:29	Lib	14 Jul 1964	14:41	Ari	15 Nov 1964	15:08
Gem	18 Mar 1964	17:25	Sco	16 Jul 1964	23:32	Tau	17 Nov 1964	18:56
Can	20 Mar 1964	20:11	Sag	19 Jul 1964	11:27	Gem	19 Nov 1964	19:57
Leo	23 Mar 1964	00:14	Cap	22 Jul 1964	00:25	Can	21 Nov 1964	20:03
Vir	25 Mar 1964	05:41	Aqu	24 Jul 1964	12:29	Leo	23 Nov 1964	20:58
Lib	27 Mar 1964	12:47	Pis	26 Jul 1964	22:34	Vir	26 Nov 1964	00:03
Sco	29 Mar 1964	22:03	Ari	29 Jul 1964	06:24	Lib	28 Nov 1964	05:53
			Tau	31 Jul 1964	11:59	Sco	30 Nov 1964	14:30
Sag	1 Apr 1964	09:40	Gem	2 Aug 1964	15:27	Sag	3 Dec 1964	01:23
Cap	3 Apr 1964	22:35	Can	4 Aug 1964	17:12	Cap	5 Dec 1964	13:52
Aqu	6 Apr 1964	10:22	Leo	6 Aug 1964	18:10	Aqu	8 Dec 1964	02:56
Pis	8 Apr 1964	18:45	Vir	8 Aug 1964	19:49	Pis	10 Dec 1964	14:58
Ari	10 Apr 1964	23:06	Lib	10 Aug 1964	23:52	Ari	13 Dec 1964	00:10
Tau	13 Apr 1964	00:35	Sco	13 Aug 1964	07:31	Tau	15 Dec 1964	05:31
Gem	15 Apr 1964	01:05	Sag	15 Aug 1964	18:43	Gem	17 Dec 1964	07:20
Can	17 Apr 1964	02:23	Cap	18 Aug 1964	07:37	Can	19 Dec 1964	07:01
Leo	19 Apr 1964	05:39	Aqu	20 Aug 1964	19:38	Leo	21 Dec 1964	06:30
Vir	21 Apr 1964	11:17	Pis	23 Aug 1964	05:12	Vir	23 Dec 1964	07:41
Lib	23 Apr 1964	19:07	Ari	25 Aug 1964	12:13	Lib	25 Dec 1964	12:05
Sco	26 Apr 1964	05:00	Tau	27 Aug 1964	17:22	Sco	27 Dec 1964	20:11
Sag	28 Apr 1964	16:45	Gem	29 Aug 1964	21:15	Sag	30 Dec 1964	07:20

Moon Signs

1965

Cap	1 Jan 1965	20:05	Gem	2 May 1965	20:25	Sag	2 Sep 1965	00:00
Aqu	4 Jan 1965	09:03	Can	4 May 1965	22:38	Cap	4 Sep 1965	10:51
Pis	6 Jan 1965	21:05	Leo	7 May 1965	00:49	Aqu	6 Sep 1965	23:32
Ari	9 Jan 1965	07:07	Vir	9 May 1965	03:46	Pis	9 Sep 1965	11:55
Tau	11 Jan 1965	14:08	Lib	11 May 1965	08:04	Ari	11 Sep 1965	22:48
Gem	13 Jan 1965	17:47	Sco	13 May 1965	14:09	Tau	14 Sep 1965	07:55
Can	15 Jan 1965	18:34	Sag	15 May 1965	22:31	Gem	16 Sep 1965	15:05
Leo	17 Jan 1965	17:56	Cap	18 May 1965	09:19	Can	18 Sep 1965	19:59
Vir	19 Jan 1965	17:54	Aqu	20 May 1965	21:49	Leo	20 Sep 1965	22:33
Lib	21 Jan 1965	20:28	Pis	23 May 1965	10:13	Vir	22 Sep 1965	23:29
Sco	24 Jan 1965	03:01	Ari	25 May 1965	20:17	Lib	25 Sep 1965	00:15
Sag	26 Jan 1965	13:32	Tau	28 May 1965	02:46	Sco	27 Sep 1965	02:47
Cap	29 Jan 1965	02:20	Gem	30 May 1965	05:58	Sag	29 Sep 1965	08:42
Aqu	31 Jan 1965	15:16						
Pis	3 Feb 1965	02:54	Can	1 Jun 1965	07:04	Cap	1 Oct 1965	18:28
Ari	5 Feb 1965	12:42	Leo	3 Jun 1965	07:46	Aqu	4 Oct 1965	06:47
Tau	7 Feb 1965	20:22	Vir	5 Jun 1965	09:33	Pis	6 Oct 1965	19:13
Gem	10 Feb 1965	01:34	Lib	7 Jun 1965	13:29	Ari	9 Oct 1965	05:53
Can	12 Feb 1965	04:12	Sco	9 Jun 1965	20:03	Tau	11 Oct 1965	14:15
Leo	14 Feb 1965	04:53	Sag	12 Jun 1965	05:09	Gem	13 Oct 1965	20:38
Vir	16 Feb 1965	05:04	Cap	14 Jun 1965	16:20	Can	16 Oct 1965	01:25
Lib	18 Feb 1965	06:44	Aqu	17 Jun 1965	04:50	Leo	18 Oct 1965	04:50
Sco	20 Feb 1965	11:46	Pis	19 Jun 1965	17:28	Vir	20 Oct 1965	07:12
Sag	22 Feb 1965	20:57	Ari	22 Jun 1965	04:28	Lib	22 Oct 1965	09:20
Cap	25 Feb 1965	09:16	Tau	24 Jun 1965	12:14	Sco	24 Oct 1965	12:31
Aqu	27 Feb 1965	22:13	Gem	26 Jun 1965	16:17	Sag	26 Oct 1965	18:08
			Can	28 Jun 1965	17:19	Cap	29 Oct 1965	03:05
			Leo	30 Jun 1965	16:58	Aqu	31 Oct 1965	14:49
Pis	2 Mar 1965	09:37	Vir	2 Jul 1965	17:10	Pis	3 Nov 1965	03:21
Ari	4 Mar 1965	18:44	Lib	4 Jul 1965	19:42	Ari	5 Nov 1965	14:20
Tau	7 Mar 1965	01:48	Sco	7 Jul 1965	01:38	Tau	7 Nov 1965	22:28
Gem	9 Mar 1965	07:13	Sag	9 Jul 1965	10:53	Gem	10 Nov 1965	03:53
Can	11 Mar 1965	11:01	Cap	11 Jul 1965	22:28	Can	12 Nov 1965	07:28
Leo	13 Mar 1965	13:22	Aqu	14 Jul 1965	11:07	Leo	14 Nov 1965	10:13
Vir	15 Mar 1965	14:55	Pis	16 Jul 1965	23:43	Vir	16 Nov 1965	12:54
Lib	17 Mar 1965	17:03	Ari	19 Jul 1965	11:11	Lib	18 Nov 1965	16:09
Sco	19 Mar 1965	21:32	Tau	21 Jul 1965	20:12	Sco	20 Nov 1965	20:36
Sag	22 Mar 1965	05:36	Gem	24 Jul 1965	01:46	Sag	23 Nov 1965	02:56
Cap	24 Mar 1965	17:06	Can	26 Jul 1965	03:51	Cap	25 Nov 1965	11:45
Aqu	27 Mar 1965	05:58	Leo	28 Jul 1965	03:36	Aqu	27 Nov 1965	23:03
Pis	29 Mar 1965	17:31	Vir	30 Jul 1965	02:54	Pis	30 Nov 1965	11:38
Ari	1 Apr 1965	02:17	Lib	1 Aug 1965	03:54	Ari	2 Dec 1965	23:21
Tau	3 Apr 1965	08:27	Sco	3 Aug 1965	08:20	Tau	5 Dec 1965	08:09
Gem	5 Apr 1965	12:53	Sag	5 Aug 1965	16:48	Gem	7 Dec 1965	13:25
Can	7 Apr 1965	16:23	Cap	8 Aug 1965	04:21	Can	9 Dec 1965	15:56
Leo	9 Apr 1965	19:22	Aqu	10 Aug 1965	17:08	Leo	11 Dec 1965	17:07
Vir	11 Apr 1965	22:14	Pis	13 Aug 1965	05:36	Vir	13 Dec 1965	18:35
Lib	14 Apr 1965	01:38	Ari	15 Aug 1965	16:56	Lib	15 Dec 1965	21:33
Sco	16 Apr 1965	06:41	Tau	18 Aug 1965	02:26	Sco	18 Dec 1965	02:40
Sag	18 Apr 1965	14:31	Gem	20 Aug 1965	09:19	Sag	20 Dec 1965	10:01
Cap	21 Apr 1965	01:23	Can	22 Aug 1965	13:02	Cap	22 Dec 1965	19:26
Aqu	23 Apr 1965	14:03	Leo	24 Aug 1965	14:00	Aqu	25 Dec 1965	06:43
Pis	26 Apr 1965	02:00	Vir	26 Aug 1965	13:35	Pis	27 Dec 1965	19:16
Ari	28 Apr 1965	11:10	Lib	28 Aug 1965	13:52	Ari	30 Dec 1965	07:38
Tau	30 Apr 1965	17:02	Sco	30 Aug 1965	16:53			

Moon Signs

1966

Tau	1 Jan 1966	17:45	Lib	1 May 1966	19:30	Ari	1 Sep 1966	22:26
Gem	4 Jan 1966	00:04	Sco	3 May 1966	21:23	Tau	4 Sep 1966	10:58
Can	6 Jan 1966	02:38	Sag	6 May 1966	00:52	Gem	6 Sep 1966	21:50
Leo	8 Jan 1966	02:49	Cap	8 May 1966	07:12	Can	9 Sep 1966	05:25
Vir	10 Jan 1966	02:34	Aqu	10 May 1966	16:51	Leo	11 Sep 1966	08:59
Lib	12 Jan 1966	03:53	Pis	13 May 1966	04:54	Vir	13 Sep 1966	09:24
Sco	14 Jan 1966	08:08	Ari	15 May 1966	17:14	Lib	15 Sep 1966	08:32
Sag	16 Jan 1966	15:39	Tau	18 May 1966	03:47	Sco	17 Sep 1966	08:34
Cap	19 Jan 1966	01:44	Gem	20 May 1966	11:38	Sag	19 Sep 1966	11:22
Aqu	21 Jan 1966	13:25	Can	22 May 1966	16:59	Cap	21 Sep 1966	17:52
Pis	24 Jan 1966	01:57	Leo	24 May 1966	20:36	Aqu	24 Sep 1966	03:47
Ari	26 Jan 1966	14:32	Vir	26 May 1966	23:21	Pis	26 Sep 1966	15:48
Tau	29 Jan 1966	01:41	Lib	29 May 1966	01:59	Ari	29 Sep 1966	04:28
Gem	31 Jan 1966	09:41	Sco	31 May 1966	05:10			
Can	2 Feb 1966	13:39	Sag	2 Jun 1966	09:38	Tau	1 Oct 1966	16:46
Leo	4 Feb 1966	14:12	Cap	4 Jun 1966	16:09	Gem	4 Oct 1966	03:42
Vir	6 Feb 1966	13:11	Aqu	7 Jun 1966	01:20	Can	6 Oct 1966	12:10
Lib	8 Feb 1966	12:51	Pis	9 Jun 1966	12:56	Leo	8 Oct 1966	17:23
Sco	10 Feb 1966	15:15	Ari	12 Jun 1966	01:25	Vir	10 Oct 1966	19:25
Sag	12 Feb 1966	21:33	Tau	14 Jun 1966	12:27	Lib	12 Oct 1966	19:28
Cap	15 Feb 1966	07:25	Gem	16 Jun 1966	20:24	Sco	14 Oct 1966	19:20
Aqu	17 Feb 1966	19:25	Can	19 Jun 1966	01:03	Sag	16 Oct 1966	20:59
Pis	20 Feb 1966	08:04	Leo	21 Jun 1966	03:28	Cap	19 Oct 1966	01:56
Ari	22 Feb 1966	20:29	Vir	23 Jun 1966	05:07	Aqu	21 Oct 1966	10:41
Tau	25 Feb 1966	07:52	Lib	25 Jun 1966	07:22	Pis	23 Oct 1966	22:20
Gem	27 Feb 1966	17:01	Sco	27 Jun 1966	11:03	Ari	26 Oct 1966	11:02
			Sag	29 Jun 1966	16:30	Tau	28 Oct 1966	23:04
						Gem	31 Oct 1966	09:26
Can	1 Mar 1966	22:46	Cap	1 Jul 1966	23:51	Can	2 Nov 1966	17:42
Leo	4 Mar 1966	00:54	Aqu	4 Jul 1966	09:14	Leo	4 Nov 1966	23:34
Vir	6 Mar 1966	00:35	Pis	6 Jul 1966	20:39	Vir	7 Nov 1966	03:08
Lib	7 Mar 1966	23:48	Ari	9 Jul 1966	09:15	Lib	9 Nov 1966	04:53
Sco	10 Mar 1966	00:47	Tau	11 Jul 1966	21:02	Sco	11 Nov 1966	05:52
Sag	12 Mar 1966	05:18	Gem	14 Jul 1966	05:50	Sag	13 Nov 1966	07:35
Cap	14 Mar 1966	13:55	Can	16 Jul 1966	10:42	Cap	15 Nov 1966	11:37
Aqu	17 Mar 1966	01:34	Leo	18 Jul 1966	12:26	Aqu	17 Nov 1966	19:03
Pis	19 Mar 1966	14:17	Vir	20 Jul 1966	12:46	Pis	20 Nov 1966	05:52
Ari	22 Mar 1966	02:32	Lib	22 Jul 1966	13:38	Ari	22 Nov 1966	18:30
Tau	24 Mar 1966	13:30	Sco	24 Jul 1966	16:31	Tau	25 Nov 1966	06:36
Gem	26 Mar 1966	22:40	Sag	26 Jul 1966	22:04	Gem	27 Nov 1966	16:29
Can	29 Mar 1966	05:22	Cap	29 Jul 1966	06:03	Can	29 Nov 1966	23:48
Leo	31 Mar 1966	09:10	Aqu	31 Jul 1966	16:01			
Vir	2 Apr 1966	10:29	Pis	3 Aug 1966	03:35	Leo	2 Dec 1966	05:00
Lib	4 Apr 1966	10:39	Ari	5 Aug 1966	16:14	Vir	4 Dec 1966	08:47
Sco	6 Apr 1966	11:30	Tau	8 Aug 1966	04:36	Lib	6 Dec 1966	11:42
Sag	8 Apr 1966	14:54	Gem	10 Aug 1966	14:36	Sco	8 Dec 1966	14:17
Cap	10 Apr 1966	22:02	Can	12 Aug 1966	20:39	Sag	10 Dec 1966	17:12
Aqu	13 Apr 1966	08:41	Leo	14 Aug 1966	22:48	Cap	12 Dec 1966	21:30
Pis	15 Apr 1966	21:12	Vir	16 Aug 1966	22:34	Aqu	15 Dec 1966	04:19
Ari	18 Apr 1966	09:25	Lib	18 Aug 1966	22:05	Pis	17 Dec 1966	14:17
Tau	20 Apr 1966	19:59	Sco	20 Aug 1966	23:24	Ari	20 Dec 1966	02:38
Gem	23 Apr 1966	04:26	Sag	23 Aug 1966	03:51	Tau	22 Dec 1966	15:06
Can	25 Apr 1966	10:46	Cap	25 Aug 1966	11:37	Gem	25 Dec 1966	01:12
Leo	27 Apr 1966	15:08	Aqu	27 Aug 1966	21:55	Can	27 Dec 1966	07:57
Vir	29 Apr 1966	17:48	Pis	30 Aug 1966	09:47	Leo	29 Dec 1966	11:56
						Vir	31 Dec 1966	14:32

Moon Signs

1967

Lib	2 Jan 1967	17:03	Pis	3 May 1967	00:47	Leo	1 Sep 1967	14:06
Sco	4 Jan 1967	20:15	Ari	5 May 1967	13:09	Vir	3 Sep 1967	17:06
Sag	7 Jan 1967	00:27	Tau	8 May 1967	02:08	Lib	5 Sep 1967	18:02
Cap	9 Jan 1967	05:52	Gem	10 May 1967	14:07	Sco	7 Sep 1967	18:43
Aqu	11 Jan 1967	13:05	Can	13 May 1967	00:09	Sag	9 Sep 1967	20:39
Pis	13 Jan 1967	22:44	Leo	15 May 1967	07:47	Cap	12 Sep 1967	00:43
Ari	16 Jan 1967	10:47	Vir	17 May 1967	12:50	Aqu	14 Sep 1967	07:08
Tau	18 Jan 1967	23:38	Lib	19 May 1967	15:29	Pis	16 Sep 1967	15:53
Gem	21 Jan 1967	10:36	Sco	21 May 1967	16:29	Ari	19 Sep 1967	02:46
Can	23 Jan 1967	17:50	Sag	23 May 1967	17:05	Tau	21 Sep 1967	15:20
Leo	25 Jan 1967	21:19	Cap	25 May 1967	18:57	Gem	24 Sep 1967	04:20
Vir	27 Jan 1967	22:35	Aqu	27 May 1967	23:44	Can	26 Sep 1967	15:44
Lib	29 Jan 1967	23:32	Pis	30 May 1967	08:18	Leo	28 Sep 1967	23:39
Sco	1 Feb 1967	01:44	Ari	1 Jun 1967	20:06	Vir	1 Oct 1967	03:37
Sag	3 Feb 1967	05:55	Tau	4 Jun 1967	09:03	Lib	3 Oct 1967	04:33
Cap	5 Feb 1967	12:10	Gem	6 Jun 1967	20:50	Sco	5 Oct 1967	04:13
Aqu	7 Feb 1967	20:16	Can	9 Jun 1967	06:17	Sag	7 Oct 1967	04:31
Pis	10 Feb 1967	06:18	Leo	11 Jun 1967	13:17	Cap	9 Oct 1967	07:03
Ari	12 Feb 1967	18:16	Vir	13 Jun 1967	18:23	Aqu	11 Oct 1967	12:46
Tau	15 Feb 1967	07:18	Lib	15 Jun 1967	21:57	Pis	13 Oct 1967	21:38
Gem	17 Feb 1967	19:14	Sco	18 Jun 1967	00:24	Ari	16 Oct 1967	08:57
Can	20 Feb 1967	03:46	Sag	20 Jun 1967	02:19	Tau	18 Oct 1967	21:40
Leo	22 Feb 1967	08:03	Cap	22 Jun 1967	04:46	Gem	21 Oct 1967	10:37
Vir	24 Feb 1967	09:03	Aqu	24 Jun 1967	09:11	Can	23 Oct 1967	22:25
Lib	26 Feb 1967	08:44	Pis	26 Jun 1967	16:49	Leo	26 Oct 1967	07:39
Sco	28 Feb 1967	09:09	Ari	29 Jun 1967	03:52	Vir	28 Oct 1967	13:17
						Lib	30 Oct 1967	15:30
Sag	2 Mar 1967	11:53	Tau	1 Jul 1967	16:42	Sco	1 Nov 1967	15:25
Cap	4 Mar 1967	17:34	Gem	4 Jul 1967	04:37	Sag	3 Nov 1967	14:51
Aqu	7 Mar 1967	02:03	Can	6 Jul 1967	13:46	Cap	5 Nov 1967	15:44
Pis	9 Mar 1967	12:41	Leo	8 Jul 1967	19:57	Aqu	7 Nov 1967	19:45
Ari	12 Mar 1967	00:52	Vir	11 Jul 1967	00:06	Pis	10 Nov 1967	03:42
Tau	14 Mar 1967	13:53	Lib	13 Jul 1967	03:19	Ari	12 Nov 1967	14:58
Gem	17 Mar 1967	02:17	Sco	15 Jul 1967	06:17	Tau	15 Nov 1967	03:51
Can	19 Mar 1967	12:07	Sag	17 Jul 1967	09:21	Gem	17 Nov 1967	16:39
Leo	21 Mar 1967	18:03	Cap	19 Jul 1967	12:59	Can	20 Nov 1967	04:12
Vir	23 Mar 1967	20:07	Aqu	21 Jul 1967	17:59	Leo	22 Nov 1967	13:45
Lib	25 Mar 1967	19:49	Pis	24 Jul 1967	01:28	Vir	24 Nov 1967	20:44
Sco	27 Mar 1967	19:10	Ari	26 Jul 1967	12:00	Lib	27 Nov 1967	00:46
Sag	29 Mar 1967	20:08	Tau	29 Jul 1967	00:39	Sco	29 Nov 1967	02:12
			Gem	31 Jul 1967	12:59			
Cap	1 Apr 1967	00:11	Can	2 Aug 1967	22:30	Sag	1 Dec 1967	02:09
Aqu	3 Apr 1967	07:48	Leo	5 Aug 1967	04:25	Cap	3 Dec 1967	02:25
Pis	5 Apr 1967	18:28	Vir	7 Aug 1967	07:35	Aqu	5 Dec 1967	04:56
Ari	8 Apr 1967	06:56	Lib	9 Aug 1967	09:34	Pis	7 Dec 1967	11:20
Tau	10 Apr 1967	19:55	Sco	11 Aug 1967	11:43	Ari	9 Dec 1967	21:43
Gem	13 Apr 1967	08:13	Sag	13 Aug 1967	14:52	Tau	12 Dec 1967	10:31
Can	15 Apr 1967	18:35	Cap	15 Aug 1967	19:17	Gem	14 Dec 1967	23:17
Leo	18 Apr 1967	01:52	Aqu	18 Aug 1967	01:17	Can	17 Dec 1967	10:21
Vir	20 Apr 1967	05:41	Pis	20 Aug 1967	09:18	Leo	19 Dec 1967	19:20
Lib	22 Apr 1967	06:40	Ari	22 Aug 1967	19:47	Vir	22 Dec 1967	02:20
Sco	24 Apr 1967	06:18	Tau	25 Aug 1967	08:20	Lib	24 Dec 1967	07:26
Sag	26 Apr 1967	06:26	Gem	27 Aug 1967	21:07	Sco	26 Dec 1967	10:35
Cap	28 Apr 1967	08:54	Can	30 Aug 1967	07:33	Sag	28 Dec 1967	12:08
Aqu	30 Apr 1967	14:57				Cap	30 Dec 1967	13:11

Moon Signs

1968

Aqu	1 Jan 1968	15:24	Can	2 May 1968	01:48	Cap	1 Sep 1968	13:21
Pis	3 Jan 1968	20:36	Leo	4 May 1968	12:52	Aqu	3 Sep 1968	16:19
Ari	6 Jan 1968	05:45	Vir	6 May 1968	20:56	Pis	5 Sep 1968	20:27
Tau	8 Jan 1968	18:02	Lib	9 May 1968	01:19	Ari	8 Sep 1968	02:49
Gem	11 Jan 1968	06:53	Sco	11 May 1968	02:28	Tau	10 Sep 1968	12:06
Can	13 Jan 1968	17:53	Sag	13 May 1968	01:53	Gem	12 Sep 1968	23:54
Leo	16 Jan 1968	02:08	Cap	15 May 1968	01:31	Can	15 Sep 1968	12:27
Vir	18 Jan 1968	08:10	Aqu	17 May 1968	03:22	Leo	17 Sep 1968	23:24
Lib	20 Jan 1968	12:46	Pis	19 May 1968	08:53	Vir	20 Sep 1968	07:14
Sco	22 Jan 1968	16:27	Ari	21 May 1968	18:14	Lib	22 Sep 1968	11:58
Sag	24 Jan 1968	19:23	Tau	24 May 1968	06:15	Sco	24 Sep 1968	14:38
Cap	26 Jan 1968	21:56	Gem	26 May 1968	19:11	Sag	26 Sep 1968	16:30
Aqu	29 Jan 1968	01:06	Can	29 May 1968	07:42	Cap	28 Sep 1968	18:44
Pis	31 Jan 1968	06:15	Leo	31 May 1968	18:52	Aqu	30 Sep 1968	22:11
Ari	2 Feb 1968	14:40	Vir	3 Jun 1968	03:51	Pis	3 Oct 1968	03:21
Tau	5 Feb 1968	02:15	Lib	5 Jun 1968	09:47	Ari	5 Oct 1968	10:35
Gem	7 Feb 1968	15:08	Sco	7 Jun 1968	12:28	Tau	7 Oct 1968	20:06
Can	10 Feb 1968	02:33	Sag	9 Jun 1968	12:41	Gem	10 Oct 1968	07:43
Leo	12 Feb 1968	10:48	Cap	11 Jun 1968	12:05	Can	12 Oct 1968	20:23
Vir	14 Feb 1968	16:01	Aqu	13 Jun 1968	12:47	Leo	15 Oct 1968	08:07
Lib	16 Feb 1968	19:20	Pis	15 Jun 1968	16:42	Vir	17 Oct 1968	16:57
Sco	18 Feb 1968	21:59	Ari	18 Jun 1968	00:50	Lib	19 Oct 1968	22:03
Sag	21 Feb 1968	00:47	Tau	20 Jun 1968	12:25	Sco	22 Oct 1968	00:04
Cap	23 Feb 1968	04:11	Gem	23 Jun 1968	01:21	Sag	24 Oct 1968	00:32
Aqu	25 Feb 1968	08:36	Can	25 Jun 1968	13:42	Cap	26 Oct 1968	01:14
Pis	27 Feb 1968	14:42	Leo	28 Jun 1968	00:29	Aqu	28 Oct 1968	03:43
Ari	29 Feb 1968	23:15	Vir	30 Jun 1968	09:25	Pis	30 Oct 1968	08:54
Tau	3 Mar 1968	10:27	Lib	2 Jul 1968	16:09	Ari	1 Nov 1968	16:50
Gem	5 Mar 1968	23:16	Sco	4 Jul 1968	20:19	Tau	4 Nov 1968	03:01
Can	8 Mar 1968	11:20	Sag	6 Jul 1968	22:03	Gem	6 Nov 1968	14:47
Leo	10 Mar 1968	20:26	Cap	8 Jul 1968	22:23	Can	9 Nov 1968	03:26
Vir	13 Mar 1968	01:50	Aqu	10 Jul 1968	23:04	Leo	11 Nov 1968	15:44
Lib	15 Mar 1968	04:22	Pis	13 Jul 1968	02:04	Vir	14 Nov 1968	01:53
Sco	17 Mar 1968	05:32	Ari	15 Jul 1968	08:52	Lib	16 Nov 1968	08:25
Sag	19 Mar 1968	06:53	Tau	17 Jul 1968	19:30	Sco	18 Nov 1968	11:04
Cap	21 Mar 1968	09:34	Gem	20 Jul 1968	08:12	Sag	20 Nov 1968	11:03
Aqu	23 Mar 1968	14:16	Can	22 Jul 1968	20:30	Cap	22 Nov 1968	10:20
Pis	25 Mar 1968	21:15	Leo	25 Jul 1968	06:54	Aqu	24 Nov 1968	11:03
Ari	28 Mar 1968	06:31	Vir	27 Jul 1968	15:09	Pis	26 Nov 1968	14:53
Tau	30 Mar 1968	17:54	Lib	29 Jul 1968	21:31	Ari	28 Nov 1968	22:26
Gem	2 Apr 1968	06:39	Sco	1 Aug 1968	02:10	Tau	1 Dec 1968	08:57
Can	4 Apr 1968	19:12	Sag	3 Aug 1968	05:10	Gem	3 Dec 1968	21:05
Leo	7 Apr 1968	05:27	Cap	5 Aug 1968	06:57	Can	6 Dec 1968	09:43
Vir	9 Apr 1968	12:02	Aqu	7 Aug 1968	08:37	Leo	8 Dec 1968	22:02
Lib	11 Apr 1968	14:59	Pis	9 Aug 1968	11:46	Vir	11 Dec 1968	08:58
Sco	13 Apr 1968	15:31	Ari	11 Aug 1968	17:53	Lib	13 Dec 1968	17:08
Sag	15 Apr 1968	15:23	Tau	14 Aug 1968	03:36	Sco	15 Dec 1968	21:30
Cap	17 Apr 1968	16:22	Gem	16 Aug 1968	15:50	Sag	17 Dec 1968	22:26
Aqu	19 Apr 1968	19:57	Can	19 Aug 1968	04:14	Cap	19 Dec 1968	21:32
Pis	22 Apr 1968	02:46	Leo	21 Aug 1968	14:39	Aqu	21 Dec 1968	21:00
Ari	24 Apr 1968	12:32	Vir	23 Aug 1968	22:20	Pis	23 Dec 1968	23:02
Tau	27 Apr 1968	00:22	Lib	26 Aug 1968	03:44	Ari	26 Dec 1968	05:02
Gem	29 Apr 1968	13:10	Sco	28 Aug 1968	07:37	Tau	28 Dec 1968	14:57
			Sag	30 Aug 1968	10:40	Gem	31 Dec 1968	03:10

Moon Signs

1969

Can	2 Jan 1969	15:52	Sco	1 May 1969	09:48	Gem	2 Sep 1969	19:23
Leo	5 Jan 1969	03:54	Sag	3 May 1969	11:18	Can	5 Sep 1969	06:56
Vir	7 Jan 1969	14:41	Cap	5 May 1969	11:56	Leo	7 Sep 1969	19:35
Lib	9 Jan 1969	23:31	Aqu	7 May 1969	13:28	Vir	10 Sep 1969	07:20
Sco	12 Jan 1969	05:31	Pis	9 May 1969	17:04	Lib	12 Sep 1969	17:01
Sag	14 Jan 1969	08:17	Ari	11 May 1969	23:09	Sco	15 Sep 1969	00:24
Cap	16 Jan 1969	08:38	Tau	14 May 1969	07:28	Sag	17 Sep 1969	05:41
Aqu	18 Jan 1969	08:16	Gem	16 May 1969	17:41	Cap	19 Sep 1969	09:13
Pis	20 Jan 1969	09:21	Can	19 May 1969	05:30	Aqu	21 Sep 1969	11:30
Ari	22 Jan 1969	13:44	Leo	21 May 1969	18:12	Pis	23 Sep 1969	13:22
Tau	24 Jan 1969	22:13	Vir	24 May 1969	06:06	Ari	25 Sep 1969	15:55
Gem	27 Jan 1969	09:53	Lib	26 May 1969	15:06	Tau	27 Sep 1969	20:29
Can	29 Jan 1969	22:35	Sco	28 May 1969	20:04	Gem	30 Sep 1969	04:06
			Sag	30 May 1969	21:29			
Leo	1 Feb 1969	10:28	Cap	1 Jun 1969	21:06	Can	2 Oct 1969	14:52
Vir	3 Feb 1969	20:40	Aqu	3 Jun 1969	21:04	Leo	5 Oct 1969	03:24
Lib	6 Feb 1969	04:59	Pis	5 Jun 1969	23:14	Vir	7 Oct 1969	15:20
Sco	8 Feb 1969	11:17	Ari	8 Jun 1969	04:37	Lib	10 Oct 1969	00:47
Sag	10 Feb 1969	15:22	Tau	10 Jun 1969	13:06	Sco	12 Oct 1969	07:18
Cap	12 Feb 1969	17:28	Gem	12 Jun 1969	23:48	Sag	14 Oct 1969	11:32
Aqu	14 Feb 1969	18:30	Can	15 Jun 1969	11:52	Cap	16 Oct 1969	14:35
Pis	16 Feb 1969	20:03	Leo	18 Jun 1969	00:34	Aqu	18 Oct 1969	17:20
Ari	18 Feb 1969	23:49	Vir	20 Jun 1969	12:52	Pis	20 Oct 1969	20:25
Tau	21 Feb 1969	07:02	Lib	22 Jun 1969	23:02	Ari	23 Oct 1969	00:17
Gem	23 Feb 1969	17:41	Sco	25 Jun 1969	05:30	Tau	25 Oct 1969	05:32
Can	26 Feb 1969	06:11	Sag	27 Jun 1969	07:59	Gem	27 Oct 1969	13:01
Leo	28 Feb 1969	18:11	Cap	29 Jun 1969	07:44	Can	29 Oct 1969	23:13
Vir	3 Mar 1969	04:06	Aqu	1 Jul 1969	06:49	Leo	1 Nov 1969	11:34
Lib	5 Mar 1969	11:32	Pis	3 Jul 1969	07:26	Vir	3 Nov 1969	23:59
Sco	7 Mar 1969	16:55	Ari	5 Jul 1969	11:17	Lib	6 Nov 1969	09:57
Sag	9 Mar 1969	20:47	Tau	7 Jul 1969	18:53	Sco	8 Nov 1969	16:16
Cap	11 Mar 1969	23:39	Gem	10 Jul 1969	05:31	Sag	10 Nov 1969	19:29
Aqu	14 Mar 1969	02:09	Can	12 Jul 1969	17:47	Cap	12 Nov 1969	21:08
Pis	16 Mar 1969	05:03	Leo	15 Jul 1969	06:28	Aqu	14 Nov 1969	22:53
Ari	18 Mar 1969	09:27	Vir	17 Jul 1969	18:41	Pis	17 Nov 1969	01:52
Tau	20 Mar 1969	16:20	Lib	20 Jul 1969	05:19	Ari	19 Nov 1969	06:31
Gem	23 Mar 1969	02:12	Sco	22 Jul 1969	13:02	Tau	21 Nov 1969	12:52
Can	25 Mar 1969	14:18	Sag	24 Jul 1969	17:10	Gem	23 Nov 1969	20:59
Leo	28 Mar 1969	02:36	Cap	26 Jul 1969	18:09	Can	26 Nov 1969	07:10
Vir	30 Mar 1969	12:52	Aqu	28 Jul 1969	17:34	Leo	28 Nov 1969	19:21
			Pis	30 Jul 1969	17:30			
Lib	1 Apr 1969	20:02	Ari	1 Aug 1969	19:55	Vir	1 Dec 1969	08:13
Sco	4 Apr 1969	00:21	Tau	4 Aug 1969	02:03	Lib	3 Dec 1969	19:16
Sag	6 Apr 1969	02:56	Gem	6 Aug 1969	11:50	Sco	6 Dec 1969	02:28
Cap	8 Apr 1969	05:04	Can	8 Aug 1969	23:57	Sag	8 Dec 1969	05:42
Aqu	10 Apr 1969	07:46	Leo	11 Aug 1969	12:38	Cap	10 Dec 1969	06:20
Pis	12 Apr 1969	11:41	Vir	14 Aug 1969	00:32	Aqu	12 Dec 1969	06:27
Ari	14 Apr 1969	17:13	Lib	16 Aug 1969	10:50	Pis	14 Dec 1969	07:56
Tau	17 Apr 1969	00:43	Sco	18 Aug 1969	18:53	Ari	16 Dec 1969	11:56
Gem	19 Apr 1969	10:28	Sag	21 Aug 1969	00:10	Tau	18 Dec 1969	18:35
Can	21 Apr 1969	22:17	Cap	23 Aug 1969	02:47	Gem	21 Dec 1969	03:28
Leo	24 Apr 1969	10:50	Aqu	25 Aug 1969	03:35	Can	23 Dec 1969	14:08
Vir	26 Apr 1969	21:55	Pis	27 Aug 1969	04:03	Leo	26 Dec 1969	02:21
Lib	29 Apr 1969	05:43	Ari	29 Aug 1969	05:57	Vir	28 Dec 1969	15:19
			Tau	31 Aug 1969	10:51	Lib	31 Dec 1969	03:17

1970

Sco	2 Jan 1970	12:01	Ari	2 May 1970	09:32	Lib	2 Sep 1970	18:25
Sag	4 Jan 1970	16:32	Tau	4 May 1970	13:05	Sco	5 Sep 1970	05:54
Cap	6 Jan 1970	17:29	Gem	6 May 1970	18:17	Sag	7 Sep 1970	14:57
Aqu	8 Jan 1970	16:47	Can	9 May 1970	02:17	Cap	9 Sep 1970	20:50
Pis	10 Jan 1970	16:36	Leo	11 May 1970	13:22	Aqu	11 Sep 1970	23:32
Ari	12 Jan 1970	18:48	Vir	14 May 1970	02:10	Pis	13 Sep 1970	23:56
Tau	15 Jan 1970	00:21	Lib	16 May 1970	14:01	Ari	15 Sep 1970	23:35
Gem	17 Jan 1970	09:07	Sco	18 May 1970	22:48	Tau	18 Sep 1970	00:22
Can	19 Jan 1970	20:13	Sag	21 May 1970	04:10	Gem	20 Sep 1970	04:02
Leo	22 Jan 1970	08:40	Cap	23 May 1970	07:12	Can	22 Sep 1970	11:42
Vir	24 Jan 1970	21:32	Aqu	25 May 1970	09:25	Leo	24 Sep 1970	22:55
Lib	27 Jan 1970	09:41	Pis	27 May 1970	11:59	Vir	27 Sep 1970	11:53
Sco	29 Jan 1970	19:33	Ari	29 May 1970	15:27	Lib	30 Sep 1970	00:32
			Tau	31 May 1970	20:03			
Sag	1 Feb 1970	01:48	Gem	3 Jun 1970	02:10	Sco	2 Oct 1970	11:34
Cap	3 Feb 1970	04:20	Can	5 Jun 1970	10:26	Sag	4 Oct 1970	20:30
Aqu	5 Feb 1970	04:19	Leo	7 Jun 1970	21:17	Cap	7 Oct 1970	03:09
Pis	7 Feb 1970	03:37	Vir	10 Jun 1970	10:02	Aqu	9 Oct 1970	07:25
Ari	9 Feb 1970	04:17	Lib	12 Jun 1970	22:27	Pis	11 Oct 1970	09:29
Tau	11 Feb 1970	07:59	Sco	15 Jun 1970	08:00	Ari	13 Oct 1970	10:12
Gem	13 Feb 1970	15:29	Sag	17 Jun 1970	13:37	Tau	15 Oct 1970	11:00
Can	16 Feb 1970	02:17	Cap	19 Jun 1970	16:04	Gem	17 Oct 1970	13:44
Leo	18 Feb 1970	14:53	Aqu	21 Jun 1970	17:00	Can	19 Oct 1970	19:59
Vir	21 Feb 1970	03:41	Pis	23 Jun 1970	18:11	Leo	22 Oct 1970	06:12
Lib	23 Feb 1970	15:29	Ari	25 Jun 1970	20:52	Vir	24 Oct 1970	18:57
Sco	26 Feb 1970	01:22	Tau	28 Jun 1970	01:35	Lib	27 Oct 1970	07:36
Sag	28 Feb 1970	08:37	Gem	30 Jun 1970	08:24	Sco	29 Oct 1970	18:14
Cap	2 Mar 1970	12:53	Can	2 Jul 1970	17:21	Sag	1 Nov 1970	02:23
Aqu	4 Mar 1970	14:33	Leo	5 Jul 1970	04:26	Cap	3 Nov 1970	08:32
Pis	6 Mar 1970	14:48	Vir	7 Jul 1970	17:11	Aqu	5 Nov 1970	13:10
Ari	8 Mar 1970	15:16	Lib	10 Jul 1970	06:02	Pis	7 Nov 1970	16:32
Tau	10 Mar 1970	17:43	Sco	12 Jul 1970	16:40	Ari	9 Nov 1970	18:51
Gem	12 Mar 1970	23:38	Sag	14 Jul 1970	23:24	Tau	11 Nov 1970	20:50
Can	15 Mar 1970	09:19	Cap	17 Jul 1970	02:18	Gem	13 Nov 1970	23:49
Leo	17 Mar 1970	21:39	Aqu	19 Jul 1970	02:44	Can	16 Nov 1970	05:23
Vir	20 Mar 1970	10:29	Pis	21 Jul 1970	02:37	Leo	18 Nov 1970	14:36
Lib	22 Mar 1970	21:56	Ari	23 Jul 1970	03:43	Vir	21 Nov 1970	02:50
Sco	25 Mar 1970	07:09	Tau	25 Jul 1970	07:18	Lib	23 Nov 1970	15:38
Sag	27 Mar 1970	14:05	Gem	27 Jul 1970	13:53	Sco	26 Nov 1970	02:23
Cap	29 Mar 1970	18:59	Can	29 Jul 1970	23:14	Sag	28 Nov 1970	10:01
Aqu	31 Mar 1970	22:07				Cap	30 Nov 1970	15:05
Pis	3 Apr 1970	00:00	Leo	1 Aug 1970	10:44	Aqu	2 Dec 1970	18:44
Ari	5 Apr 1970	01:32	Vir	3 Aug 1970	23:34	Pis	4 Dec 1970	21:55
Tau	7 Apr 1970	04:02	Lib	6 Aug 1970	12:32	Ari	7 Dec 1970	01:03
Gem	9 Apr 1970	09:02	Sco	8 Aug 1970	23:55	Tau	9 Dec 1970	04:24
Can	11 Apr 1970	17:33	Sag	11 Aug 1970	08:06	Gem	11 Dec 1970	08:33
Leo	14 Apr 1970	05:15	Cap	13 Aug 1970	12:23	Can	13 Dec 1970	14:33
Vir	16 Apr 1970	18:06	Aqu	15 Aug 1970	13:30	Leo	15 Dec 1970	23:22
Lib	19 Apr 1970	05:34	Pis	17 Aug 1970	13:01	Vir	18 Dec 1970	11:05
Sco	21 Apr 1970	14:14	Ari	19 Aug 1970	12:51	Lib	21 Dec 1970	00:00
Sag	23 Apr 1970	20:14	Tau	21 Aug 1970	14:47	Sco	23 Dec 1970	11:25
Cap	26 Apr 1970	00:25	Gem	23 Aug 1970	20:04	Sag	25 Dec 1970	19:27
Aqu	28 Apr 1970	03:42	Can	26 Aug 1970	04:58	Cap	28 Dec 1970	00:00
Pis	30 Apr 1970	06:37	Leo	28 Aug 1970	16:38	Aqu	30 Dec 1970	02:23
			Vir	31 Aug 1970	05:36			

Moon Signs

1971

Pis	1 Jan 1971	04:08	Leo	1 May 1971	09:35	Aqu	2 Sep 1971	07:03
Ari	3 Jan 1971	06:26	Vir	3 May 1971	21:03	Pis	4 Sep 1971	08:50
Tau	5 Jan 1971	10:00	Lib	6 May 1971	09:59	Ari	6 Sep 1971	08:43
Gem	7 Jan 1971	15:09	Sco	8 May 1971	22:02	Tau	8 Sep 1971	08:38
Can	9 Jan 1971	22:09	Sag	11 May 1971	08:07	Gem	10 Sep 1971	10:26
Leo	12 Jan 1971	07:24	Cap	13 May 1971	16:08	Can	12 Sep 1971	15:22
Vir	14 Jan 1971	18:57	Aqu	15 May 1971	22:19	Leo	14 Sep 1971	23:38
Lib	17 Jan 1971	07:53	Pis	18 May 1971	02:39	Vir	17 Sep 1971	10:29
Sco	19 Jan 1971	20:03	Ari	20 May 1971	05:11	Lib	19 Sep 1971	22:47
Sag	22 Jan 1971	05:15	Tau	22 May 1971	06:31	Sco	22 Sep 1971	11:32
Cap	24 Jan 1971	10:31	Gem	24 May 1971	08:01	Sag	24 Sep 1971	23:42
Aqu	26 Jan 1971	12:35	Can	26 May 1971	11:27	Cap	27 Sep 1971	09:51
Pis	28 Jan 1971	13:01	Leo	28 May 1971	18:16	Aqu	29 Sep 1971	16:38
Ari	30 Jan 1971	13:36	Vir	31 May 1971	04:48			
						Pis	1 Oct 1971	19:36
Tau	1 Feb 1971	15:49	Lib	2 Jun 1971	17:26	Ari	3 Oct 1971	19:40
Gem	3 Feb 1971	20:35	Sco	5 Jun 1971	05:36	Tau	5 Oct 1971	18:42
Can	6 Feb 1971	04:07	Sag	7 Jun 1971	15:27	Gem	7 Oct 1971	18:53
Leo	8 Feb 1971	14:06	Cap	9 Jun 1971	22:44	Can	9 Oct 1971	22:12
Vir	11 Feb 1971	01:58	Aqu	12 Jun 1971	04:02	Leo	12 Oct 1971	05:31
Lib	13 Feb 1971	14:50	Pis	14 Jun 1971	08:01	Vir	14 Oct 1971	16:16
Sco	16 Feb 1971	03:21	Ari	16 Jun 1971	11:05	Lib	17 Oct 1971	04:47
Sag	18 Feb 1971	13:44	Tau	18 Jun 1971	13:39	Sco	19 Oct 1971	17:30
Cap	20 Feb 1971	20:36	Gem	20 Jun 1971	16:24	Sag	22 Oct 1971	05:31
Aqu	22 Feb 1971	23:41	Can	22 Jun 1971	20:30	Cap	24 Oct 1971	16:04
Pis	25 Feb 1971	00:04	Leo	25 Jun 1971	03:13	Aqu	27 Oct 1971	00:10
Ari	26 Feb 1971	23:30	Vir	27 Jun 1971	13:07	Pis	29 Oct 1971	04:56
Tau	28 Feb 1971	23:55	Lib	30 Jun 1971	01:22	Ari	31 Oct 1971	06:26
						Tau	2 Nov 1971	05:55
Gem	3 Mar 1971	03:02	Sco	2 Jul 1971	13:45	Gem	4 Nov 1971	05:27
Can	5 Mar 1971	09:48	Sag	4 Jul 1971	23:58	Can	6 Nov 1971	07:15
Leo	7 Mar 1971	19:55	Cap	7 Jul 1971	07:03	Leo	8 Nov 1971	12:58
Vir	10 Mar 1971	08:10	Aqu	9 Jul 1971	11:26	Vir	10 Nov 1971	22:45
Lib	12 Mar 1971	21:05	Pis	11 Jul 1971	14:14	Lib	13 Nov 1971	11:05
Sco	15 Mar 1971	09:30	Ari	13 Jul 1971	16:32	Sco	15 Nov 1971	23:49
Sag	17 Mar 1971	20:22	Tau	15 Jul 1971	19:10	Sag	18 Nov 1971	11:29
Cap	20 Mar 1971	04:36	Gem	17 Jul 1971	22:47	Cap	20 Nov 1971	21:36
Aqu	22 Mar 1971	09:27	Can	20 Jul 1971	03:57	Aqu	23 Nov 1971	05:52
Pis	24 Mar 1971	11:06	Leo	22 Jul 1971	11:17	Pis	25 Nov 1971	11:46
Ari	26 Mar 1971	10:45	Vir	24 Jul 1971	21:10	Ari	27 Nov 1971	15:03
Tau	28 Mar 1971	10:16	Lib	27 Jul 1971	09:12	Tau	29 Nov 1971	16:08
Gem	30 Mar 1971	11:45	Sco	29 Jul 1971	21:50			
						Gem	1 Dec 1971	16:25
Can	1 Apr 1971	16:51	Sag	1 Aug 1971	08:49	Can	3 Dec 1971	17:51
Leo	4 Apr 1971	02:06	Cap	3 Aug 1971	16:31	Leo	5 Dec 1971	22:18
Vir	6 Apr 1971	14:16	Aqu	5 Aug 1971	20:46	Vir	8 Dec 1971	06:41
Lib	9 Apr 1971	03:16	Pis	7 Aug 1971	22:34	Lib	10 Dec 1971	18:19
Sco	11 Apr 1971	15:27	Ari	9 Aug 1971	23:27	Sco	13 Dec 1971	07:01
Sag	14 Apr 1971	02:02	Tau	12 Aug 1971	00:56	Sag	15 Dec 1971	18:37
Cap	16 Apr 1971	10:37	Gem	14 Aug 1971	04:11	Cap	18 Dec 1971	04:07
Aqu	18 Apr 1971	16:45	Can	16 Aug 1971	09:50	Aqu	20 Dec 1971	11:32
Pis	20 Apr 1971	20:07	Leo	18 Aug 1971	17:57	Pis	22 Dec 1971	17:10
Ari	22 Apr 1971	21:08	Vir	21 Aug 1971	04:19	Ari	24 Dec 1971	21:09
Tau	24 Apr 1971	21:07	Lib	23 Aug 1971	16:23	Tau	26 Dec 1971	23:44
Gem	26 Apr 1971	21:59	Sco	26 Aug 1971	05:09	Gem	29 Dec 1971	01:38
Can	29 Apr 1971	01:45	Sag	28 Aug 1971	16:56	Can	31 Dec 1971	04:02
			Cap	31 Aug 1971	01:53			

Moon Signs

1972

Leo	2 Jan 1972	08:22	Cap	2 May 1972	20:28	Can	2 Sep 1972	02:12
Vir	4 Jan 1972	15:51	Aqu	5 May 1972	06:35	Leo	4 Sep 1972	06:54
Lib	7 Jan 1972	02:33	Pis	7 May 1972	13:26	Vir	6 Sep 1972	13:16
Sco	9 Jan 1972	15:03	Ari	9 May 1972	16:34	Lib	8 Sep 1972	21:37
Sag	12 Jan 1972	02:57	Tau	11 May 1972	16:47	Sco	11 Sep 1972	08:16
Cap	14 Jan 1972	12:25	Gem	13 May 1972	15:57	Sag	13 Sep 1972	20:42
Aqu	16 Jan 1972	19:03	Can	15 May 1972	16:16	Cap	16 Sep 1972	09:07
Pis	18 Jan 1972	23:27	Leo	17 May 1972	19:38	Aqu	18 Sep 1972	19:04
Ari	21 Jan 1972	02:35	Vir	20 May 1972	02:57	Pis	21 Sep 1972	01:07
Tau	23 Jan 1972	05:17	Lib	22 May 1972	13:37	Ari	23 Sep 1972	03:44
Gem	25 Jan 1972	08:14	Sco	25 May 1972	02:01	Tau	25 Sep 1972	04:27
Can	27 Jan 1972	12:02	Sag	27 May 1972	14:33	Gem	27 Sep 1972	05:14
Leo	29 Jan 1972	17:21	Cap	30 May 1972	02:12	Can	29 Sep 1972	07:39
Vir	1 Feb 1972	00:56	Aqu	1 Jun 1972	12:14	Leo	1 Oct 1972	12:26
Lib	3 Feb 1972	11:07	Pis	3 Jun 1972	19:51	Vir	3 Oct 1972	19:31
Sco	5 Feb 1972	23:18	Ari	6 Jun 1972	00:26	Lib	6 Oct 1972	04:35
Sag	8 Feb 1972	11:37	Tau	8 Jun 1972	02:14	Sco	8 Oct 1972	15:27
Cap	10 Feb 1972	21:49	Gem	10 Jun 1972	02:24	Sag	11 Oct 1972	03:52
Aqu	13 Feb 1972	04:36	Can	12 Jun 1972	02:45	Cap	13 Oct 1972	16:43
Pis	15 Feb 1972	08:10	Leo	14 Jun 1972	05:10	Aqu	16 Oct 1972	03:50
Ari	17 Feb 1972	09:50	Vir	16 Jun 1972	11:04	Pis	18 Oct 1972	11:11
Tau	19 Feb 1972	11:12	Lib	18 Jun 1972	20:39	Ari	20 Oct 1972	14:21
Gem	21 Feb 1972	13:36	Sco	21 Jun 1972	08:43	Tau	22 Oct 1972	14:37
Can	23 Feb 1972	17:52	Sag	23 Jun 1972	21:14	Gem	24 Oct 1972	14:03
Leo	26 Feb 1972	00:15	Cap	26 Jun 1972	08:36	Can	26 Oct 1972	14:45
Vir	28 Feb 1972	08:39	Aqu	28 Jun 1972	18:02	Leo	28 Oct 1972	18:14
						Vir	31 Oct 1972	01:00
Lib	1 Mar 1972	19:00	Pis	1 Jul 1972	01:18	Lib	2 Nov 1972	10:27
Sco	4 Mar 1972	07:00	Ari	3 Jul 1972	06:22	Sco	4 Nov 1972	21:46
Sag	6 Mar 1972	19:36	Tau	5 Jul 1972	09:24	Sag	7 Nov 1972	10:16
Cap	9 Mar 1972	06:49	Gem	7 Jul 1972	11:04	Cap	9 Nov 1972	23:10
Aqu	11 Mar 1972	14:41	Can	9 Jul 1972	12:30	Aqu	12 Nov 1972	11:01
Pis	13 Mar 1972	18:39	Leo	11 Jul 1972	15:06	Pis	14 Nov 1972	19:55
Ari	15 Mar 1972	19:37	Vir	13 Jul 1972	20:17	Ari	17 Nov 1972	00:42
Tau	17 Mar 1972	19:28	Lib	16 Jul 1972	04:49	Tau	19 Nov 1972	01:52
Gem	19 Mar 1972	20:13	Sco	18 Jul 1972	16:15	Gem	21 Nov 1972	01:05
Can	21 Mar 1972	23:27	Sag	21 Jul 1972	04:46	Can	23 Nov 1972	00:32
Leo	24 Mar 1972	05:46	Cap	23 Jul 1972	16:10	Leo	25 Nov 1972	02:13
Vir	26 Mar 1972	14:48	Aqu	26 Jul 1972	01:06	Vir	27 Nov 1972	07:25
Lib	29 Mar 1972	01:42	Pis	28 Jul 1972	07:28	Lib	29 Nov 1972	16:15
Sco	31 Mar 1972	13:49	Ari	30 Jul 1972	11:50			
Sag	3 Apr 1972	02:27	Tau	1 Aug 1972	14:57	Sco	2 Dec 1972	03:42
Cap	5 Apr 1972	14:20	Gem	3 Aug 1972	17:33	Sag	4 Dec 1972	16:22
Aqu	7 Apr 1972	23:36	Can	5 Aug 1972	20:18	Cap	7 Dec 1972	05:06
Pis	10 Apr 1972	04:57	Leo	7 Aug 1972	23:57	Aqu	9 Dec 1972	16:53
Ari	12 Apr 1972	06:32	Vir	10 Aug 1972	05:23	Pis	12 Dec 1972	02:31
Tau	14 Apr 1972	05:54	Lib	12 Aug 1972	13:28	Ari	14 Dec 1972	08:58
Gem	16 Apr 1972	05:17	Sco	15 Aug 1972	00:20	Tau	16 Dec 1972	11:58
Can	18 Apr 1972	06:46	Sag	17 Aug 1972	12:49	Gem	18 Dec 1972	12:24
Leo	20 Apr 1972	11:48	Cap	20 Aug 1972	00:37	Can	20 Dec 1972	11:57
Vir	22 Apr 1972	20:25	Aqu	22 Aug 1972	09:42	Leo	22 Dec 1972	12:35
Lib	25 Apr 1972	07:34	Pis	24 Aug 1972	15:28	Vir	24 Dec 1972	16:03
Sco	27 Apr 1972	19:56	Ari	26 Aug 1972	18:40	Lib	26 Dec 1972	23:23
Sag	30 Apr 1972	08:30	Tau	28 Aug 1972	20:43	Sco	29 Dec 1972	10:11
			Gem	30 Aug 1972	22:56	Sag	31 Dec 1972	22:51

1973

Sign	Date	Time	Sign	Date	Time	Sign	Date	Time
Cap	3 Jan 1973	11:30	Tau	2 May 1973	01:01	Sco	1 Sep 1973	05:18
Aqu	5 Jan 1973	22:46	Gem	4 May 1973	01:16	Sag	3 Sep 1973	15:25
Pis	8 Jan 1973	08:02	Can	6 May 1973	01:35	Cap	6 Sep 1973	04:01
Ari	10 Jan 1973	14:57	Leo	8 May 1973	03:37	Aqu	8 Sep 1973	16:30
Tau	12 Jan 1973	19:24	Vir	10 May 1973	08:13	Pis	11 Sep 1973	02:39
Gem	14 Jan 1973	21:40	Lib	12 May 1973	15:31	Ari	13 Sep 1973	09:55
Can	16 Jan 1973	22:38	Sco	15 May 1973	01:10	Tau	15 Sep 1973	14:58
Leo	18 Jan 1973	23:41	Sag	17 May 1973	12:42	Gem	17 Sep 1973	18:48
Vir	21 Jan 1973	02:24	Cap	20 May 1973	01:30	Can	19 Sep 1973	22:01
Lib	23 Jan 1973	08:17	Aqu	22 May 1973	14:17	Leo	22 Sep 1973	00:56
Sco	25 Jan 1973	17:52	Pis	25 May 1973	01:04	Vir	24 Sep 1973	03:59
Sag	28 Jan 1973	06:10	Ari	27 May 1973	08:13	Lib	26 Sep 1973	08:01
Cap	30 Jan 1973	18:54	Tau	29 May 1973	11:26	Sco	28 Sep 1973	14:19
			Gem	31 May 1973	11:52	Sag	30 Sep 1973	23:48
Aqu	2 Feb 1973	05:55	Can	2 Jun 1973	11:21	Cap	3 Oct 1973	12:02
Pis	4 Feb 1973	14:21	Leo	4 Jun 1973	11:50	Aqu	6 Oct 1973	00:48
Ari	6 Feb 1973	20:28	Vir	6 Jun 1973	14:52	Pis	8 Oct 1973	11:22
Tau	9 Feb 1973	00:53	Lib	8 Jun 1973	21:16	Ari	10 Oct 1973	18:29
Gem	11 Feb 1973	04:10	Sco	11 Jun 1973	06:52	Tau	12 Oct 1973	22:35
Can	13 Feb 1973	06:44	Sag	13 Jun 1973	18:43	Gem	15 Oct 1973	01:08
Leo	15 Feb 1973	09:12	Cap	16 Jun 1973	07:37	Can	17 Oct 1973	03:29
Vir	17 Feb 1973	12:32	Aqu	18 Jun 1973	20:18	Leo	19 Oct 1973	06:25
Lib	19 Feb 1973	17:58	Pis	21 Jun 1973	07:28	Vir	21 Oct 1973	10:19
Sco	22 Feb 1973	02:36	Ari	23 Jun 1973	15:48	Lib	23 Oct 1973	15:28
Sag	24 Feb 1973	14:15	Tau	25 Jun 1973	20:36	Sco	25 Oct 1973	22:28
Cap	27 Feb 1973	03:03	Gem	27 Jun 1973	22:17	Sag	28 Oct 1973	07:58
			Can	29 Jun 1973	22:08	Cap	30 Oct 1973	19:57
Aqu	1 Mar 1973	14:21	Leo	1 Jul 1973	21:56	Aqu	2 Nov 1973	08:58
Pis	3 Mar 1973	22:30	Vir	3 Jul 1973	23:32	Pis	4 Nov 1973	20:25
Ari	6 Mar 1973	03:36	Lib	6 Jul 1973	04:24	Ari	7 Nov 1973	04:18
Tau	8 Mar 1973	06:50	Sco	8 Jul 1973	13:06	Tau	9 Nov 1973	08:25
Gem	10 Mar 1973	09:31	Sag	11 Jul 1973	00:48	Gem	11 Nov 1973	09:59
Can	12 Mar 1973	12:29	Cap	13 Jul 1973	13:45	Can	13 Nov 1973	10:47
Leo	14 Mar 1973	16:08	Aqu	16 Jul 1973	02:14	Leo	15 Nov 1973	12:21
Vir	16 Mar 1973	20:42	Pis	18 Jul 1973	13:06	Vir	17 Nov 1973	15:41
Lib	19 Mar 1973	02:49	Ari	20 Jul 1973	21:43	Lib	19 Nov 1973	21:16
Sco	21 Mar 1973	11:16	Tau	23 Jul 1973	03:40	Sco	22 Nov 1973	05:07
Sag	23 Mar 1973	22:27	Gem	25 Jul 1973	06:58	Sag	24 Nov 1973	15:11
Cap	26 Mar 1973	11:15	Can	27 Jul 1973	08:10	Cap	27 Nov 1973	03:13
Aqu	28 Mar 1973	23:11	Leo	29 Jul 1973	08:29	Aqu	29 Nov 1973	16:17
Pis	31 Mar 1973	07:54	Vir	31 Jul 1973	09:35			
Ari	2 Apr 1973	12:47	Lib	2 Aug 1973	13:14	Pis	2 Dec 1973	04:31
Tau	4 Apr 1973	14:58	Sco	4 Aug 1973	20:36	Ari	4 Dec 1973	13:49
Gem	6 Apr 1973	16:12	Sag	7 Aug 1973	07:37	Tau	6 Dec 1973	19:08
Can	8 Apr 1973	18:04	Cap	9 Aug 1973	20:29	Gem	8 Dec 1973	20:57
Leo	10 Apr 1973	21:32	Aqu	12 Aug 1973	08:52	Can	10 Dec 1973	20:52
Vir	13 Apr 1973	02:47	Pis	14 Aug 1973	19:14	Leo	12 Dec 1973	20:45
Lib	15 Apr 1973	09:50	Ari	17 Aug 1973	03:15	Vir	14 Dec 1973	22:22
Sco	17 Apr 1973	18:51	Tau	19 Aug 1973	09:13	Lib	17 Dec 1973	02:54
Sag	20 Apr 1973	06:02	Gem	21 Aug 1973	13:26	Sco	19 Dec 1973	10:45
Cap	22 Apr 1973	18:49	Can	23 Aug 1973	16:07	Sag	21 Dec 1973	21:20
Aqu	25 Apr 1973	07:20	Leo	25 Aug 1973	17:49	Cap	24 Dec 1973	09:41
Pis	27 Apr 1973	17:09	Vir	27 Aug 1973	19:33	Aqu	26 Dec 1973	22:43
Ari	29 Apr 1973	22:52	Lib	29 Aug 1973	22:53	Pis	29 Dec 1973	11:09
						Ari	31 Dec 1973	21:33

1974

Tau	3 Jan 1974	04:37	Lib	2 May 1974	23:39	Pis	1 Sep 1974	01:29
Gem	5 Jan 1974	07:59	Sco	5 May 1974	04:43	Ari	3 Sep 1974	12:57
Can	7 Jan 1974	08:28	Sag	7 May 1974	12:06	Tau	5 Sep 1974	22:50
Leo	9 Jan 1974	07:42	Cap	9 May 1974	22:15	Gem	8 Sep 1974	06:36
Vir	11 Jan 1974	07:42	Aqu	12 May 1974	10:34	Can	10 Sep 1974	11:38
Lib	13 Jan 1974	10:23	Pis	14 May 1974	23:02	Leo	12 Sep 1974	13:53
Sco	15 Jan 1974	16:54	Ari	17 May 1974	09:18	Vir	14 Sep 1974	14:12
Sag	18 Jan 1974	03:13	Tau	19 May 1974	16:09	Lib	16 Sep 1974	14:17
Cap	20 Jan 1974	15:48	Gem	21 May 1974	19:53	Sco	18 Sep 1974	16:14
Aqu	23 Jan 1974	04:50	Can	23 May 1974	21:45	Sag	20 Sep 1974	21:48
Pis	25 Jan 1974	17:00	Leo	25 May 1974	23:12	Cap	23 Sep 1974	07:22
Ari	28 Jan 1974	03:31	Vir	28 May 1974	01:26	Aqu	25 Sep 1974	19:38
Tau	30 Jan 1974	11:40	Lib	30 May 1974	05:16	Pis	28 Sep 1974	08:14
						Ari	30 Sep 1974	19:25
Gem	1 Feb 1974	16:53	Sco	1 Jun 1974	11:11	Tau	3 Oct 1974	04:39
Can	3 Feb 1974	19:05	Sag	3 Jun 1974	19:22	Gem	5 Oct 1974	12:00
Leo	5 Feb 1974	19:11	Cap	6 Jun 1974	05:48	Can	7 Oct 1974	17:30
Vir	7 Feb 1974	18:52	Aqu	8 Jun 1974	18:02	Leo	9 Oct 1974	21:02
Lib	9 Feb 1974	20:11	Pis	11 Jun 1974	06:43	Vir	11 Oct 1974	22:55
Sco	12 Feb 1974	00:59	Ari	13 Jun 1974	17:52	Lib	14 Oct 1974	00:11
Sag	14 Feb 1974	10:02	Tau	16 Jun 1974	01:45	Sco	16 Oct 1974	02:24
Cap	16 Feb 1974	22:16	Gem	18 Jun 1974	05:59	Sag	18 Oct 1974	07:15
Aqu	19 Feb 1974	11:21	Can	20 Jun 1974	07:21	Cap	20 Oct 1974	15:45
Pis	21 Feb 1974	23:15	Leo	22 Jun 1974	07:30	Aqu	23 Oct 1974	03:20
Ari	24 Feb 1974	09:12	Vir	24 Jun 1974	08:11	Pis	25 Oct 1974	15:56
Tau	26 Feb 1974	17:11	Lib	26 Jun 1974	10:58	Ari	28 Oct 1974	03:13
Gem	28 Feb 1974	23:09	Sco	28 Jun 1974	16:40	Tau	30 Oct 1974	11:59
Can	3 Mar 1974	02:59	Sag	1 Jul 1974	01:21	Gem	1 Nov 1974	18:23
Leo	5 Mar 1974	04:49	Cap	3 Jul 1974	12:19	Can	3 Nov 1974	23:00
Vir	7 Mar 1974	05:33	Aqu	6 Jul 1974	00:41	Leo	6 Nov 1974	02:30
Lib	9 Mar 1974	06:52	Pis	8 Jul 1974	13:25	Vir	8 Nov 1974	05:18
Sco	11 Mar 1974	10:41	Ari	11 Jul 1974	01:10	Lib	10 Nov 1974	07:59
Sag	13 Mar 1974	18:20	Tau	13 Jul 1974	10:20	Sco	12 Nov 1974	11:24
Cap	16 Mar 1974	05:41	Gem	15 Jul 1974	15:53	Sag	14 Nov 1974	16:39
Aqu	18 Mar 1974	18:38	Can	17 Jul 1974	17:56	Cap	17 Nov 1974	00:43
Pis	21 Mar 1974	06:33	Leo	19 Jul 1974	17:43	Aqu	19 Nov 1974	11:39
Ari	23 Mar 1974	16:02	Vir	21 Jul 1974	17:10	Pis	22 Nov 1974	00:11
Tau	25 Mar 1974	23:09	Lib	23 Jul 1974	18:19	Ari	24 Nov 1974	11:58
Gem	28 Mar 1974	04:33	Sco	25 Jul 1974	22:47	Tau	26 Nov 1974	21:04
Can	30 Mar 1974	08:39	Sag	28 Jul 1974	07:00	Gem	29 Nov 1974	02:57
			Cap	30 Jul 1974	18:11			
Leo	1 Apr 1974	11:40	Aqu	2 Aug 1974	06:46	Can	1 Dec 1974	06:21
Vir	3 Apr 1974	13:56	Pis	4 Aug 1974	19:26	Leo	3 Dec 1974	08:31
Lib	5 Apr 1974	16:23	Ari	7 Aug 1974	07:15	Vir	5 Dec 1974	10:40
Sco	7 Apr 1974	20:26	Tau	9 Aug 1974	17:12	Lib	7 Dec 1974	13:43
Sag	10 Apr 1974	03:28	Gem	12 Aug 1974	00:13	Sco	9 Dec 1974	18:13
Cap	12 Apr 1974	13:57	Can	14 Aug 1974	03:48	Sag	12 Dec 1974	00:35
Aqu	15 Apr 1974	02:34	Leo	16 Aug 1974	04:26	Cap	14 Dec 1974	09:04
Pis	17 Apr 1974	14:43	Vir	18 Aug 1974	03:42	Aqu	16 Dec 1974	19:48
Ari	20 Apr 1974	00:19	Lib	20 Aug 1974	03:45	Pis	19 Dec 1974	08:12
Tau	22 Apr 1974	06:53	Sco	22 Aug 1974	06:37	Ari	21 Dec 1974	20:35
Gem	24 Apr 1974	11:10	Sag	24 Aug 1974	13:35	Tau	24 Dec 1974	06:44
Can	26 Apr 1974	14:17	Cap	27 Aug 1974	00:15	Gem	26 Dec 1974	13:14
Leo	28 Apr 1974	17:03	Aqu	29 Aug 1974	12:52	Can	28 Dec 1974	16:15
Vir	30 Apr 1974	20:00				Leo	30 Dec 1974	17:05

Moon Signs

1975

Vir	1 Jan 1975	17:33	Aqu	2 May 1975	05:33	Leo	2 Sep 1975	23:06
Lib	3 Jan 1975	19:22	Pis	4 May 1975	17:34	Vir	4 Sep 1975	23:28
Sco	5 Jan 1975	23:40	Ari	7 May 1975	06:02	Lib	6 Sep 1975	22:38
Sag	8 Jan 1975	06:39	Tau	9 May 1975	17:03	Sco	8 Sep 1975	22:46
Cap	10 Jan 1975	15:58	Gem	12 May 1975	01:43	Sag	11 Sep 1975	01:42
Aqu	13 Jan 1975	03:03	Can	14 May 1975	08:07	Cap	13 Sep 1975	08:12
Pis	15 Jan 1975	15:23	Leo	16 May 1975	12:38	Aqu	15 Sep 1975	17:51
Ari	18 Jan 1975	04:03	Vir	18 May 1975	15:45	Pis	18 Sep 1975	05:32
Tau	20 Jan 1975	15:20	Lib	20 May 1975	18:05	Ari	20 Sep 1975	18:07
Gem	22 Jan 1975	23:21	Sco	22 May 1975	20:26	Tau	23 Sep 1975	06:43
Can	25 Jan 1975	03:19	Sag	24 May 1975	23:52	Gem	25 Sep 1975	18:13
Leo	27 Jan 1975	04:00	Cap	27 May 1975	05:31	Can	28 Sep 1975	03:06
Vir	29 Jan 1975	03:14	Aqu	29 May 1975	14:10	Leo	30 Sep 1975	08:19
Lib	31 Jan 1975	03:14						
			Pis	1 Jun 1975	01:32	Vir	2 Oct 1975	10:02
Sco	2 Feb 1975	05:53	Ari	3 Jun 1975	14:01	Lib	4 Oct 1975	09:38
Sag	4 Feb 1975	12:11	Tau	6 Jun 1975	01:17	Sco	6 Oct 1975	09:09
Cap	6 Feb 1975	21:43	Gem	8 Jun 1975	09:48	Sag	8 Oct 1975	10:36
Aqu	9 Feb 1975	09:17	Can	10 Jun 1975	15:21	Cap	10 Oct 1975	15:30
Pis	11 Feb 1975	21:45	Leo	12 Jun 1975	18:45	Aqu	13 Oct 1975	00:10
Ari	14 Feb 1975	10:22	Vir	14 Jun 1975	21:10	Pis	15 Oct 1975	11:40
Tau	16 Feb 1975	22:08	Lib	16 Jun 1975	23:41	Ari	18 Oct 1975	00:20
Gem	19 Feb 1975	07:34	Sco	19 Jun 1975	02:59	Tau	20 Oct 1975	12:43
Can	21 Feb 1975	13:17	Sag	21 Jun 1975	07:35	Gem	22 Oct 1975	23:50
Leo	23 Feb 1975	15:12	Cap	23 Jun 1975	13:56	Can	25 Oct 1975	08:56
Vir	25 Feb 1975	14:36	Aqu	25 Jun 1975	22:33	Leo	27 Oct 1975	15:19
Lib	27 Feb 1975	13:39	Pis	28 Jun 1975	09:33	Vir	29 Oct 1975	18:46
			Ari	30 Jun 1975	22:02	Lib	31 Oct 1975	19:55
Sco	1 Mar 1975	14:35	Tau	3 Jul 1975	09:53	Sco	2 Nov 1975	20:07
Sag	3 Mar 1975	19:06	Gem	5 Jul 1975	18:58	Sag	4 Nov 1975	21:10
Cap	6 Mar 1975	03:40	Can	8 Jul 1975	00:22	Cap	7 Nov 1975	00:46
Aqu	8 Mar 1975	15:10	Leo	10 Jul 1975	02:49	Aqu	9 Nov 1975	08:00
Pis	11 Mar 1975	03:49	Vir	12 Jul 1975	03:55	Pis	11 Nov 1975	18:42
Ari	13 Mar 1975	16:18	Lib	14 Jul 1975	05:21	Ari	14 Nov 1975	07:17
Tau	16 Mar 1975	03:52	Sco	16 Jul 1975	08:23	Tau	16 Nov 1975	19:37
Gem	18 Mar 1975	13:42	Sag	18 Jul 1975	13:32	Gem	19 Nov 1975	06:14
Can	20 Mar 1975	20:47	Cap	20 Jul 1975	20:46	Can	21 Nov 1975	14:35
Leo	23 Mar 1975	00:30	Aqu	23 Jul 1975	05:56	Leo	23 Nov 1975	20:47
Vir	25 Mar 1975	01:20	Pis	25 Jul 1975	16:58	Vir	26 Nov 1975	01:04
Lib	27 Mar 1975	00:51	Ari	28 Jul 1975	05:27	Lib	28 Nov 1975	03:47
Sco	29 Mar 1975	01:09	Tau	30 Jul 1975	17:53	Sco	30 Nov 1975	05:36
Sag	31 Mar 1975	04:10						
			Gem	2 Aug 1975	04:01	Sag	2 Dec 1975	07:33
Cap	2 Apr 1975	11:09	Can	4 Aug 1975	10:15	Cap	4 Dec 1975	10:59
Aqu	4 Apr 1975	21:45	Leo	6 Aug 1975	12:42	Aqu	6 Dec 1975	17:12
Pis	7 Apr 1975	10:17	Vir	8 Aug 1975	12:53	Pis	9 Dec 1975	02:52
Ari	9 Apr 1975	22:43	Lib	10 Aug 1975	12:51	Ari	11 Dec 1975	15:06
Tau	12 Apr 1975	09:53	Sco	12 Aug 1975	14:30	Tau	14 Dec 1975	03:38
Gem	14 Apr 1975	19:14	Sag	14 Aug 1975	18:59	Gem	16 Dec 1975	14:11
Can	17 Apr 1975	02:26	Cap	17 Aug 1975	02:25	Can	18 Dec 1975	21:48
Leo	19 Apr 1975	07:14	Aqu	19 Aug 1975	12:09	Leo	21 Dec 1975	02:53
Vir	21 Apr 1975	09:42	Pis	21 Aug 1975	23:32	Vir	23 Dec 1975	06:27
Lib	23 Apr 1975	10:41	Ari	24 Aug 1975	12:02	Lib	25 Dec 1975	09:27
Sco	25 Apr 1975	11:40	Tau	27 Aug 1975	00:44	Sco	27 Dec 1975	12:28
Sag	27 Apr 1975	14:21	Gem	29 Aug 1975	11:52	Sag	29 Dec 1975	15:53
Cap	29 Apr 1975	20:09	Can	31 Aug 1975	19:34	Cap	31 Dec 1975	20:17

1976

Aqu	3 Jan 1976	02:33	Gem	1 May 1976	04:04	Cap	2 Sep 1976	16:29
Pis	5 Jan 1976	11:36	Can	3 May 1976	14:52	Aqu	4 Sep 1976	22:20
Ari	7 Jan 1976	23:21	Leo	5 May 1976	23:08	Pis	7 Sep 1976	06:11
Tau	10 Jan 1976	12:09	Vir	8 May 1976	04:20	Ari	9 Sep 1976	16:18
Gem	12 Jan 1976	23:18	Lib	10 May 1976	06:39	Tau	12 Sep 1976	04:30
Can	15 Jan 1976	07:00	Sco	12 May 1976	07:02	Gem	14 Sep 1976	17:32
Leo	17 Jan 1976	11:14	Sag	14 May 1976	07:04	Can	17 Sep 1976	05:06
Vir	19 Jan 1976	13:25	Cap	16 May 1976	08:32	Leo	19 Sep 1976	13:09
Lib	21 Jan 1976	15:11	Aqu	18 May 1976	13:03	Vir	21 Sep 1976	17:15
Sco	23 Jan 1976	17:48	Pis	20 May 1976	21:27	Lib	23 Sep 1976	18:27
Sag	25 Jan 1976	21:51	Ari	23 May 1976	09:07	Sco	25 Sep 1976	18:33
Cap	28 Jan 1976	03:24	Tau	25 May 1976	22:06	Sag	27 Sep 1976	19:21
Aqu	30 Jan 1976	10:34	Gem	28 May 1976	10:21	Cap	29 Sep 1976	22:14
			Can	30 May 1976	20:38			
Pis	1 Feb 1976	19:47	Leo	2 Jun 1976	04:37	Aqu	2 Oct 1976	03:50
Ari	4 Feb 1976	07:17	Vir	4 Jun 1976	10:20	Pis	4 Oct 1976	12:10
Tau	6 Feb 1976	20:13	Lib	6 Jun 1976	13:59	Ari	6 Oct 1976	22:50
Gem	9 Feb 1976	08:15	Sco	8 Jun 1976	15:58	Tau	9 Oct 1976	11:11
Can	11 Feb 1976	16:58	Sag	10 Jun 1976	17:06	Gem	12 Oct 1976	00:14
Leo	13 Feb 1976	21:31	Cap	12 Jun 1976	18:45	Can	14 Oct 1976	12:23
Vir	15 Feb 1976	22:58	Aqu	14 Jun 1976	22:32	Leo	16 Oct 1976	21:48
Lib	17 Feb 1976	23:14	Pis	17 Jun 1976	05:43	Vir	19 Oct 1976	03:23
Sco	20 Feb 1976	00:14	Ari	19 Jun 1976	16:32	Lib	21 Oct 1976	05:26
Sag	22 Feb 1976	03:19	Tau	22 Jun 1976	05:21	Sco	23 Oct 1976	05:16
Cap	24 Feb 1976	08:54	Gem	24 Jun 1976	17:36	Sag	25 Oct 1976	04:49
Aqu	26 Feb 1976	16:48	Can	27 Jun 1976	03:28	Cap	27 Oct 1976	05:55
Pis	29 Feb 1976	02:42	Leo	29 Jun 1976	10:39	Aqu	29 Oct 1976	10:06
						Pis	31 Oct 1976	17:53
Ari	2 Mar 1976	14:22	Vir	1 Jul 1976	15:46	Ari	3 Nov 1976	04:46
Tau	5 Mar 1976	03:18	Lib	3 Jul 1976	19:34	Tau	5 Nov 1976	17:23
Gem	7 Mar 1976	15:55	Sco	5 Jul 1976	22:33	Gem	8 Nov 1976	06:21
Can	10 Mar 1976	01:57	Sag	8 Jul 1976	01:05	Can	10 Nov 1976	18:27
Leo	12 Mar 1976	07:54	Cap	10 Jul 1976	03:49	Leo	13 Nov 1976	04:36
Vir	14 Mar 1976	09:57	Aqu	12 Jul 1976	07:53	Vir	15 Nov 1976	11:45
Lib	16 Mar 1976	09:44	Pis	14 Jul 1976	14:37	Lib	17 Nov 1976	15:33
Sco	18 Mar 1976	09:18	Ari	17 Jul 1976	00:40	Sco	19 Nov 1976	16:31
Sag	20 Mar 1976	10:35	Tau	19 Jul 1976	13:11	Sag	21 Nov 1976	16:03
Cap	22 Mar 1976	14:49	Gem	22 Jul 1976	01:40	Cap	23 Nov 1976	16:04
Aqu	24 Mar 1976	22:20	Can	24 Jul 1976	11:38	Aqu	25 Nov 1976	18:30
Pis	27 Mar 1976	08:34	Leo	26 Jul 1976	18:18	Pis	28 Nov 1976	00:48
Ari	29 Mar 1976	20:37	Vir	28 Jul 1976	22:23	Ari	30 Nov 1976	11:02
			Lib	31 Jul 1976	01:13			
Tau	1 Apr 1976	09:33	Sco	2 Aug 1976	03:55	Tau	2 Dec 1976	23:41
Gem	3 Apr 1976	22:15	Sag	4 Aug 1976	07:03	Gem	5 Dec 1976	12:38
Can	6 Apr 1976	09:05	Cap	6 Aug 1976	10:55	Can	8 Dec 1976	00:20
Leo	8 Apr 1976	16:36	Aqu	8 Aug 1976	15:57	Leo	10 Dec 1976	10:11
Vir	10 Apr 1976	20:15	Pis	10 Aug 1976	23:01	Vir	12 Dec 1976	17:55
Lib	12 Apr 1976	20:53	Ari	13 Aug 1976	08:49	Lib	14 Dec 1976	23:12
Sco	14 Apr 1976	20:14	Tau	15 Aug 1976	21:05	Sco	17 Dec 1976	02:00
Sag	16 Apr 1976	20:15	Gem	18 Aug 1976	09:53	Sag	19 Dec 1976	02:53
Cap	18 Apr 1976	22:44	Can	20 Aug 1976	20:33	Cap	21 Dec 1976	03:12
Aqu	21 Apr 1976	04:48	Leo	23 Aug 1976	03:30	Aqu	23 Dec 1976	04:48
Pis	23 Apr 1976	14:28	Vir	25 Aug 1976	07:03	Pis	25 Dec 1976	09:37
Ari	26 Apr 1976	02:37	Lib	27 Aug 1976	08:41	Ari	27 Dec 1976	18:32
Tau	28 Apr 1976	15:37	Sco	29 Aug 1976	10:05	Tau	30 Dec 1976	06:43
			Sag	31 Aug 1976	12:29			

Moon Signs

1977

Gem	1 Jan 1977	19:42	Sco	2 May 1977	16:23	Tau	2 Sep 1977	00:52
Can	4 Jan 1977	07:12	Sag	4 May 1977	15:58	Gem	4 Sep 1977	12:27
Leo	6 Jan 1977	16:20	Cap	6 May 1977	15:54	Can	7 Sep 1977	01:02
Vir	8 Jan 1977	23:22	Aqu	8 May 1977	17:59	Leo	9 Sep 1977	12:12
Lib	11 Jan 1977	04:47	Pis	10 May 1977	23:30	Vir	11 Sep 1977	20:33
Sco	13 Jan 1977	08:44	Ari	13 May 1977	08:30	Lib	14 Sep 1977	02:06
Sag	15 Jan 1977	11:17	Tau	15 May 1977	20:04	Sco	16 Sep 1977	05:45
Cap	17 Jan 1977	13:02	Gem	18 May 1977	08:50	Sag	18 Sep 1977	08:28
Aqu	19 Jan 1977	15:12	Can	20 May 1977	21:35	Cap	20 Sep 1977	11:04
Pis	21 Jan 1977	19:30	Leo	23 May 1977	09:12	Aqu	22 Sep 1977	14:12
Ari	24 Jan 1977	03:20	Vir	25 May 1977	18:30	Pis	24 Sep 1977	18:30
Tau	26 Jan 1977	14:41	Lib	28 May 1977	00:27	Ari	27 Sep 1977	00:41
Gem	29 Jan 1977	03:37	Sco	30 May 1977	02:55	Tau	29 Sep 1977	09:22
Can	31 Jan 1977	15:19						
Leo	3 Feb 1977	00:10	Sag	1 Jun 1977	02:53	Gem	1 Oct 1977	20:33
Vir	5 Feb 1977	06:17	Cap	3 Jun 1977	02:07	Can	4 Oct 1977	09:08
Lib	7 Feb 1977	10:35	Aqu	5 Jun 1977	02:44	Leo	6 Oct 1977	20:57
Sco	9 Feb 1977	14:04	Pis	7 Jun 1977	06:35	Vir	9 Oct 1977	05:58
Sag	11 Feb 1977	17:11	Ari	9 Jun 1977	14:35	Lib	11 Oct 1977	11:28
Cap	13 Feb 1977	20:14	Tau	12 Jun 1977	01:57	Sco	13 Oct 1977	14:10
Aqu	15 Feb 1977	23:45	Gem	14 Jun 1977	14:49	Sag	15 Oct 1977	15:27
Pis	18 Feb 1977	04:45	Can	17 Jun 1977	03:28	Cap	17 Oct 1977	16:50
Ari	20 Feb 1977	12:23	Leo	19 Jun 1977	14:53	Aqu	19 Oct 1977	19:36
Tau	22 Feb 1977	23:07	Vir	22 Jun 1977	00:28	Pis	22 Oct 1977	00:27
Gem	25 Feb 1977	11:50	Lib	24 Jun 1977	07:34	Ari	24 Oct 1977	07:34
Can	28 Feb 1977	00:01	Sco	26 Jun 1977	11:40	Tau	26 Oct 1977	16:53
			Sag	28 Jun 1977	13:01	Gem	29 Oct 1977	04:08
			Cap	30 Jun 1977	12:48	Can	31 Oct 1977	16:40
Leo	2 Mar 1977	09:24	Aqu	2 Jul 1977	12:57	Leo	3 Nov 1977	05:03
Vir	4 Mar 1977	15:18	Pis	4 Jul 1977	15:32	Vir	5 Nov 1977	15:15
Lib	6 Mar 1977	18:34	Ari	6 Jul 1977	22:04	Lib	7 Nov 1977	21:49
Sco	8 Mar 1977	20:36	Tau	9 Jul 1977	08:33	Sco	10 Nov 1977	00:40
Sag	10 Mar 1977	22:42	Gem	11 Jul 1977	21:15	Sag	12 Nov 1977	01:03
Cap	13 Mar 1977	01:40	Can	14 Jul 1977	09:49	Cap	14 Nov 1977	00:51
Aqu	15 Mar 1977	05:59	Leo	16 Jul 1977	20:51	Aqu	16 Nov 1977	02:00
Pis	17 Mar 1977	12:06	Vir	19 Jul 1977	05:58	Pis	18 Nov 1977	05:58
Ari	19 Mar 1977	20:23	Lib	21 Jul 1977	13:08	Ari	20 Nov 1977	13:13
Tau	22 Mar 1977	07:05	Sco	23 Jul 1977	18:13	Tau	22 Nov 1977	23:09
Gem	24 Mar 1977	19:38	Sag	25 Jul 1977	21:03	Gem	25 Nov 1977	10:48
Can	27 Mar 1977	08:16	Cap	27 Jul 1977	22:14	Can	27 Nov 1977	23:20
Leo	29 Mar 1977	18:40	Aqu	29 Jul 1977	23:05	Leo	30 Nov 1977	11:52
Vir	1 Apr 1977	01:23	Pis	1 Aug 1977	01:24	Vir	2 Dec 1977	23:04
Lib	3 Apr 1977	04:38	Ari	3 Aug 1977	06:54	Lib	5 Dec 1977	07:17
Sco	5 Apr 1977	05:39	Tau	5 Aug 1977	16:18	Sco	7 Dec 1977	11:31
Sag	7 Apr 1977	06:08	Gem	8 Aug 1977	04:29	Sag	9 Dec 1977	12:20
Cap	9 Apr 1977	07:40	Can	10 Aug 1977	17:04	Cap	11 Dec 1977	11:26
Aqu	11 Apr 1977	11:24	Leo	13 Aug 1977	03:56	Aqu	13 Dec 1977	11:00
Pis	13 Apr 1977	17:49	Vir	15 Aug 1977	12:25	Pis	15 Dec 1977	13:10
Ari	16 Apr 1977	02:52	Lib	17 Aug 1977	18:48	Ari	17 Dec 1977	19:11
Tau	18 Apr 1977	14:02	Sco	19 Aug 1977	23:34	Tau	20 Dec 1977	04:54
Gem	21 Apr 1977	02:37	Sag	22 Aug 1977	03:02	Gem	22 Dec 1977	16:51
Can	23 Apr 1977	15:24	Cap	24 Aug 1977	05:30	Can	25 Dec 1977	05:29
Leo	26 Apr 1977	02:42	Aqu	26 Aug 1977	07:41	Leo	27 Dec 1977	17:51
Vir	28 Apr 1977	10:50	Pis	28 Aug 1977	10:47	Vir	30 Dec 1977	05:13
Lib	30 Apr 1977	15:11	Ari	30 Aug 1977	16:12			

1978

Lib	1 Jan 1978	14:30	Pis	1 May 1978	09:00	Vir	1 Sep 1978	20:45
Sco	3 Jan 1978	20:34	Ari	3 May 1978	14:27	Lib	4 Sep 1978	07:15
Sag	5 Jan 1978	23:02	Tau	5 May 1978	21:52	Sco	6 Sep 1978	15:37
Cap	7 Jan 1978	22:54	Gem	8 May 1978	07:18	Sag	8 Sep 1978	21:38
Aqu	9 Jan 1978	22:05	Can	10 May 1978	18:41	Cap	11 Sep 1978	01:18
Pis	11 Jan 1978	22:51	Leo	13 May 1978	07:16	Aqu	13 Sep 1978	03:08
Ari	14 Jan 1978	03:05	Vir	15 May 1978	19:14	Pis	15 Sep 1978	04:09
Tau	16 Jan 1978	11:31	Lib	18 May 1978	04:23	Ari	17 Sep 1978	05:49
Gem	18 Jan 1978	23:06	Sco	20 May 1978	09:37	Tau	19 Sep 1978	09:43
Can	21 Jan 1978	11:50	Sag	22 May 1978	11:30	Gem	21 Sep 1978	16:56
Leo	24 Jan 1978	00:01	Cap	24 May 1978	11:41	Can	24 Sep 1978	03:31
Vir	26 Jan 1978	10:55	Aqu	26 May 1978	12:10	Leo	26 Sep 1978	16:01
Lib	28 Jan 1978	20:07	Pis	28 May 1978	14:37	Vir	29 Sep 1978	04:10
Sco	31 Jan 1978	03:02	Ari	30 May 1978	19:52			
Sag	2 Feb 1978	07:13	Tau	2 Jun 1978	03:50	Lib	1 Oct 1978	14:15
Cap	4 Feb 1978	08:49	Gem	4 Jun 1978	13:53	Sco	3 Oct 1978	21:47
Aqu	6 Feb 1978	09:04	Can	7 Jun 1978	01:30	Sag	6 Oct 1978	03:05
Pis	8 Feb 1978	09:48	Leo	9 Jun 1978	14:07	Cap	8 Oct 1978	06:52
Ari	10 Feb 1978	12:57	Vir	12 Jun 1978	02:34	Aqu	10 Oct 1978	09:42
Tau	12 Feb 1978	19:51	Lib	14 Jun 1978	12:54	Pis	12 Oct 1978	12:12
Gem	15 Feb 1978	06:24	Sco	16 Jun 1978	19:27	Ari	14 Oct 1978	15:06
Can	17 Feb 1978	18:55	Sag	18 Jun 1978	21:59	Tau	16 Oct 1978	19:22
Leo	20 Feb 1978	07:09	Cap	20 Jun 1978	21:51	Gem	19 Oct 1978	02:06
Vir	22 Feb 1978	17:39	Aqu	22 Jun 1978	21:08	Can	21 Oct 1978	11:53
Lib	25 Feb 1978	02:02	Pis	24 Jun 1978	21:57	Leo	24 Oct 1978	00:03
Sco	27 Feb 1978	08:27	Ari	27 Jun 1978	01:54	Vir	26 Oct 1978	12:30
			Tau	29 Jun 1978	09:21	Lib	28 Oct 1978	22:49
						Sco	31 Oct 1978	05:52
Sag	1 Mar 1978	13:01	Gem	1 Jul 1978	19:37	Sag	2 Nov 1978	10:02
Cap	3 Mar 1978	15:57	Can	4 Jul 1978	07:33	Cap	4 Nov 1978	12:40
Aqu	5 Mar 1978	17:50	Leo	6 Jul 1978	20:12	Aqu	6 Nov 1978	15:03
Pis	7 Mar 1978	19:46	Vir	9 Jul 1978	08:44	Pis	8 Nov 1978	18:05
Ari	9 Mar 1978	23:09	Lib	11 Jul 1978	19:47	Ari	10 Nov 1978	22:11
Tau	12 Mar 1978	05:18	Sco	14 Jul 1978	03:45	Tau	13 Nov 1978	03:35
Gem	14 Mar 1978	14:48	Sag	16 Jul 1978	07:48	Gem	15 Nov 1978	10:45
Can	17 Mar 1978	02:49	Cap	18 Jul 1978	08:32	Can	17 Nov 1978	20:16
Leo	19 Mar 1978	15:11	Aqu	20 Jul 1978	07:41	Leo	20 Nov 1978	08:08
Vir	22 Mar 1978	01:48	Pis	22 Jul 1978	07:26	Vir	22 Nov 1978	20:56
Lib	24 Mar 1978	09:40	Ari	24 Jul 1978	09:47	Lib	25 Nov 1978	08:06
Sco	26 Mar 1978	15:00	Tau	26 Jul 1978	15:51	Sco	27 Nov 1978	15:37
Sag	28 Mar 1978	18:37	Gem	29 Jul 1978	01:31	Sag	29 Nov 1978	19:22
Cap	30 Mar 1978	21:23	Can	31 Jul 1978	13:28			
Aqu	2 Apr 1978	00:05	Leo	3 Aug 1978	02:10	Cap	1 Dec 1978	20:43
Pis	4 Apr 1978	03:20	Vir	5 Aug 1978	14:28	Aqu	3 Dec 1978	21:35
Ari	6 Apr 1978	07:51	Lib	8 Aug 1978	01:29	Pis	5 Dec 1978	23:36
Tau	8 Apr 1978	14:22	Sco	10 Aug 1978	10:10	Ari	8 Dec 1978	03:39
Gem	10 Apr 1978	23:28	Sag	12 Aug 1978	15:41	Tau	10 Dec 1978	09:50
Can	13 Apr 1978	10:59	Cap	14 Aug 1978	18:02	Gem	12 Dec 1978	17:54
Leo	15 Apr 1978	23:30	Aqu	16 Aug 1978	18:14	Can	15 Dec 1978	03:49
Vir	18 Apr 1978	10:42	Pis	18 Aug 1978	18:04	Leo	17 Dec 1978	15:37
Lib	20 Apr 1978	18:52	Ari	20 Aug 1978	19:29	Vir	20 Dec 1978	04:33
Sco	22 Apr 1978	23:37	Tau	23 Aug 1978	00:07	Lib	22 Dec 1978	16:39
Sag	25 Apr 1978	01:59	Gem	25 Aug 1978	08:31	Sco	25 Dec 1978	01:30
Cap	27 Apr 1978	03:27	Can	27 Aug 1978	19:59	Sag	27 Dec 1978	06:07
Aqu	29 Apr 1978	05:27	Leo	30 Aug 1978	08:39	Cap	29 Dec 1978	07:15
						Aqu	31 Dec 1978	06:52

1979

Pis	2 Jan 1979	07:07	Leo	3 May 1979	01:56	Cap	1 Sep 1979	11:31
Ari	4 Jan 1979	09:41	Vir	5 May 1979	14:40	Aqu	3 Sep 1979	13:57
Tau	6 Jan 1979	15:17	Lib	8 May 1979	02:46	Pis	5 Sep 1979	14:02
Gem	8 Jan 1979	23:42	Sco	10 May 1979	12:08	Ari	7 Sep 1979	13:29
Can	11 Jan 1979	10:14	Sag	12 May 1979	18:24	Tau	9 Sep 1979	14:13
Leo	13 Jan 1979	22:16	Cap	14 May 1979	22:24	Gem	11 Sep 1979	17:53
Vir	16 Jan 1979	11:09	Aqu	17 May 1979	01:25	Can	14 Sep 1979	01:27
Lib	18 Jan 1979	23:39	Pis	19 May 1979	04:18	Leo	16 Sep 1979	12:25
Sco	21 Jan 1979	09:49	Ari	21 May 1979	07:29	Vir	19 Sep 1979	01:15
Sag	23 Jan 1979	16:06	Tau	23 May 1979	11:20	Lib	21 Sep 1979	14:10
Cap	25 Jan 1979	18:27	Gem	25 May 1979	16:27	Sco	24 Sep 1979	01:53
Aqu	27 Jan 1979	18:11	Can	27 May 1979	23:51	Sag	26 Sep 1979	11:34
Pis	29 Jan 1979	17:25	Leo	30 May 1979	10:08	Cap	28 Sep 1979	18:39
Ari	31 Jan 1979	18:11				Aqu	30 Sep 1979	22:47
Tau	2 Feb 1979	22:03	Vir	1 Jun 1979	22:40	Pis	3 Oct 1979	00:22
Gem	5 Feb 1979	05:32	Lib	4 Jun 1979	11:10	Ari	5 Oct 1979	00:27
Can	7 Feb 1979	16:05	Sco	6 Jun 1979	21:03	Tau	7 Oct 1979	00:45
Leo	10 Feb 1979	04:25	Sag	9 Jun 1979	03:13	Gem	9 Oct 1979	03:07
Vir	12 Feb 1979	17:17	Cap	11 Jun 1979	06:23	Can	11 Oct 1979	09:09
Lib	15 Feb 1979	05:36	Aqu	13 Jun 1979	08:05	Leo	13 Oct 1979	19:11
Sco	17 Feb 1979	16:11	Pis	15 Jun 1979	09:56	Vir	16 Oct 1979	07:50
Sag	19 Feb 1979	23:49	Ari	17 Jun 1979	12:52	Lib	18 Oct 1979	20:43
Cap	22 Feb 1979	03:59	Tau	19 Jun 1979	17:17	Sco	21 Oct 1979	08:01
Aqu	24 Feb 1979	05:11	Gem	21 Jun 1979	23:22	Sag	23 Oct 1979	17:08
Pis	26 Feb 1979	04:51	Can	24 Jun 1979	07:24	Cap	26 Oct 1979	00:10
Ari	28 Feb 1979	04:54	Leo	26 Jun 1979	17:46	Aqu	28 Oct 1979	05:16
			Vir	29 Jun 1979	06:13	Pis	30 Oct 1979	08:28
Tau	2 Mar 1979	07:09	Lib	1 Jul 1979	19:07	Ari	1 Nov 1979	10:08
Gem	4 Mar 1979	12:59	Sco	4 Jul 1979	05:57	Tau	3 Nov 1979	11:16
Can	6 Mar 1979	22:34	Sag	6 Jul 1979	12:54	Gem	5 Nov 1979	13:26
Leo	9 Mar 1979	10:47	Cap	8 Jul 1979	16:06	Can	7 Nov 1979	18:23
Vir	11 Mar 1979	23:41	Aqu	10 Jul 1979	16:58	Leo	10 Nov 1979	03:14
Lib	14 Mar 1979	11:40	Pis	12 Jul 1979	17:22	Vir	12 Nov 1979	15:20
Sco	16 Mar 1979	21:48	Ari	14 Jul 1979	18:57	Lib	15 Nov 1979	04:15
Sag	19 Mar 1979	05:37	Tau	16 Jul 1979	22:43	Sco	17 Nov 1979	15:28
Cap	21 Mar 1979	10:55	Gem	19 Jul 1979	04:59	Sag	19 Nov 1979	23:55
Aqu	23 Mar 1979	13:50	Can	21 Jul 1979	13:40	Cap	22 Nov 1979	06:01
Pis	25 Mar 1979	15:04	Leo	24 Jul 1979	00:30	Aqu	24 Nov 1979	10:35
Ari	27 Mar 1979	15:47	Vir	26 Jul 1979	13:01	Pis	26 Nov 1979	14:16
Tau	29 Mar 1979	17:36	Lib	29 Jul 1979	02:05	Ari	28 Nov 1979	17:16
Gem	31 Mar 1979	22:09	Sco	31 Jul 1979	13:45	Tau	30 Nov 1979	19:54
Can	3 Apr 1979	06:23	Sag	2 Aug 1979	22:04	Gem	2 Dec 1979	23:02
Leo	5 Apr 1979	17:57	Cap	5 Aug 1979	02:21	Can	5 Dec 1979	04:01
Vir	8 Apr 1979	06:51	Aqu	7 Aug 1979	03:27	Leo	7 Dec 1979	12:09
Lib	10 Apr 1979	18:44	Pis	9 Aug 1979	03:05	Vir	9 Dec 1979	23:32
Sco	13 Apr 1979	04:14	Ari	11 Aug 1979	03:10	Lib	12 Dec 1979	12:28
Sag	15 Apr 1979	11:16	Tau	13 Aug 1979	05:21	Sco	15 Dec 1979	00:06
Cap	17 Apr 1979	16:22	Gem	15 Aug 1979	10:42	Sag	17 Dec 1979	08:35
Aqu	19 Apr 1979	20:01	Can	17 Aug 1979	19:17	Cap	19 Dec 1979	13:53
Pis	21 Apr 1979	22:40	Leo	20 Aug 1979	06:28	Aqu	21 Dec 1979	17:12
Ari	24 Apr 1979	00:51	Vir	22 Aug 1979	19:11	Pis	23 Dec 1979	19:49
Tau	26 Apr 1979	03:27	Lib	25 Aug 1979	08:13	Ari	25 Dec 1979	22:40
Gem	28 Apr 1979	07:48	Sco	27 Aug 1979	20:11	Tau	28 Dec 1979	02:07
Can	30 Apr 1979	15:11	Sag	30 Aug 1979	05:38	Gem	30 Dec 1979	06:31

1980

Can	1 Jan 1980	12:29	Sag	1 May 1980	22:20	Gem	1 Sep 1980	01:50
Leo	3 Jan 1980	20:47	Cap	4 May 1980	07:13	Can	3 Sep 1980	06:39
Vir	6 Jan 1980	07:48	Aqu	6 May 1980	14:02	Leo	5 Sep 1980	14:22
Lib	8 Jan 1980	20:37	Pis	8 May 1980	18:33	Vir	8 Sep 1980	00:30
Sco	11 Jan 1980	08:54	Ari	10 May 1980	20:43	Lib	10 Sep 1980	12:22
Sag	13 Jan 1980	18:16	Tau	12 May 1980	21:23	Sco	13 Sep 1980	01:05
Cap	15 Jan 1980	23:49	Gem	14 May 1980	22:08	Sag	15 Sep 1980	13:26
Aqu	18 Jan 1980	02:23	Can	17 May 1980	00:53	Cap	17 Sep 1980	23:43
Pis	20 Jan 1980	03:32	Leo	19 May 1980	07:14	Aqu	20 Sep 1980	06:29
Ari	22 Jan 1980	04:51	Vir	21 May 1980	17:32	Pis	22 Sep 1980	09:25
Tau	24 Jan 1980	07:31	Lib	24 May 1980	06:10	Ari	24 Sep 1980	09:36
Gem	26 Jan 1980	12:11	Sco	26 May 1980	18:36	Tau	26 Sep 1980	08:53
Can	28 Jan 1980	19:02	Sag	29 May 1980	05:04	Gem	28 Sep 1980	09:21
Leo	31 Jan 1980	04:08	Cap	31 May 1980	13:13	Can	30 Sep 1980	12:47
Vir	2 Feb 1980	15:21	Aqu	2 Jun 1980	19:28	Leo	2 Oct 1980	19:57
Lib	5 Feb 1980	04:04	Pis	5 Jun 1980	00:08	Vir	5 Oct 1980	06:18
Sco	7 Feb 1980	16:45	Ari	7 Jun 1980	03:22	Lib	7 Oct 1980	18:29
Sag	10 Feb 1980	03:18	Tau	9 Jun 1980	05:29	Sco	10 Oct 1980	07:14
Cap	12 Feb 1980	10:10	Gem	11 Jun 1980	07:22	Sag	12 Oct 1980	19:36
Aqu	14 Feb 1980	13:18	Can	13 Jun 1980	10:30	Cap	15 Oct 1980	06:36
Pis	16 Feb 1980	13:53	Leo	15 Jun 1980	16:22	Aqu	17 Oct 1980	14:51
Ari	18 Feb 1980	13:42	Vir	18 Jun 1980	01:47	Pis	19 Oct 1980	19:30
Tau	20 Feb 1980	14:35	Lib	20 Jun 1980	13:55	Ari	21 Oct 1980	20:41
Gem	22 Feb 1980	17:57	Sco	23 Jun 1980	02:25	Tau	23 Oct 1980	19:55
Can	25 Feb 1980	00:35	Sag	25 Jun 1980	13:00	Gem	25 Oct 1980	19:16
Leo	27 Feb 1980	10:10	Cap	27 Jun 1980	20:45	Can	27 Oct 1980	21:00
Vir	29 Feb 1980	21:53	Aqu	30 Jun 1980	02:02	Leo	30 Oct 1980	02:39
Lib	3 Mar 1980	10:39	Pis	2 Jul 1980	05:48	Vir	1 Nov 1980	12:19
Sco	5 Mar 1980	23:21	Ari	4 Jul 1980	08:45	Lib	4 Nov 1980	00:31
Sag	8 Mar 1980	10:37	Tau	6 Jul 1980	11:30	Sco	6 Nov 1980	13:18
Cap	10 Mar 1980	19:01	Gem	8 Jul 1980	14:33	Sag	9 Nov 1980	01:24
Aqu	12 Mar 1980	23:43	Can	10 Jul 1980	18:44	Cap	11 Nov 1980	12:14
Pis	15 Mar 1980	01:09	Leo	13 Jul 1980	01:03	Aqu	13 Nov 1980	21:08
Ari	17 Mar 1980	00:40	Vir	15 Jul 1980	10:11	Pis	16 Nov 1980	03:19
Tau	19 Mar 1980	00:13	Lib	17 Jul 1980	21:54	Ari	18 Nov 1980	06:21
Gem	21 Mar 1980	01:48	Sco	20 Jul 1980	10:32	Tau	20 Nov 1980	06:50
Can	23 Mar 1980	06:55	Sag	22 Jul 1980	21:41	Gem	22 Nov 1980	06:26
Leo	25 Mar 1980	15:58	Cap	25 Jul 1980	05:44	Can	24 Nov 1980	07:18
Vir	28 Mar 1980	03:51	Aqu	27 Jul 1980	10:33	Leo	26 Nov 1980	11:24
Lib	30 Mar 1980	16:48	Pis	29 Jul 1980	13:10	Vir	28 Nov 1980	19:37
			Ari	31 Jul 1980	14:52			
Sco	2 Apr 1980	05:20	Tau	2 Aug 1980	16:54	Lib	1 Dec 1980	07:12
Sag	4 Apr 1980	16:33	Gem	4 Aug 1980	20:09	Sco	3 Dec 1980	19:59
Cap	7 Apr 1980	01:41	Can	7 Aug 1980	01:12	Sag	6 Dec 1980	07:56
Aqu	9 Apr 1980	07:58	Leo	9 Aug 1980	08:23	Cap	8 Dec 1980	18:11
Pis	11 Apr 1980	11:05	Vir	11 Aug 1980	17:54	Aqu	11 Dec 1980	02:34
Ari	13 Apr 1980	11:39	Lib	14 Aug 1980	05:31	Pis	13 Dec 1980	09:02
Tau	15 Apr 1980	11:10	Sco	16 Aug 1980	18:14	Ari	15 Dec 1980	13:19
Gem	17 Apr 1980	11:42	Sag	19 Aug 1980	06:07	Tau	17 Dec 1980	15:35
Can	19 Apr 1980	15:12	Cap	21 Aug 1980	15:10	Gem	19 Dec 1980	16:39
Leo	21 Apr 1980	22:52	Aqu	23 Aug 1980	20:31	Can	21 Dec 1980	18:02
Vir	24 Apr 1980	10:12	Pis	25 Aug 1980	22:42	Leo	23 Dec 1980	21:34
Lib	26 Apr 1980	23:08	Ari	27 Aug 1980	23:10	Vir	26 Dec 1980	04:32
Sco	29 Apr 1980	11:33	Tau	29 Aug 1980	23:41	Lib	28 Dec 1980	15:04
						Sco	31 Dec 1980	03:35

Moon Signs

1981

Sag	2 Jan 1981	15:40	Ari	1 May 1981	06:56	Sco	2 Sep 1981	21:10
Cap	5 Jan 1981	01:39	Tau	3 May 1981	06:58	Sag	5 Sep 1981	09:23
Aqu	7 Jan 1981	09:11	Gem	5 May 1981	06:00	Cap	7 Sep 1981	21:47
Pis	9 Jan 1981	14:41	Can	7 May 1981	06:17	Aqu	10 Sep 1981	07:57
Ari	11 Jan 1981	18:43	Leo	9 May 1981	09:41	Pis	12 Sep 1981	14:32
Tau	13 Jan 1981	21:44	Vir	11 May 1981	16:55	Ari	14 Sep 1981	17:54
Gem	16 Jan 1981	00:16	Lib	14 May 1981	03:24	Tau	16 Sep 1981	19:29
Can	18 Jan 1981	03:07	Sco	16 May 1981	15:37	Gem	18 Sep 1981	20:58
Leo	20 Jan 1981	07:20	Sag	19 May 1981	04:13	Can	20 Sep 1981	23:39
Vir	22 Jan 1981	14:02	Cap	21 May 1981	16:19	Leo	23 Sep 1981	04:08
Lib	24 Jan 1981	23:45	Aqu	24 May 1981	02:59	Vir	25 Sep 1981	10:28
Sco	27 Jan 1981	11:48	Pis	26 May 1981	11:03	Lib	27 Sep 1981	18:39
Sag	30 Jan 1981	00:10	Ari	28 May 1981	15:42	Sco	30 Sep 1981	04:52
			Tau	30 May 1981	17:09			
Cap	1 Feb 1981	10:35	Gem	1 Jun 1981	16:47	Sag	2 Oct 1981	16:59
Aqu	3 Feb 1981	17:54	Can	3 Jun 1981	16:38	Cap	5 Oct 1981	05:48
Pis	5 Feb 1981	22:20	Leo	5 Jun 1981	18:42	Aqu	7 Oct 1981	17:00
Ari	8 Feb 1981	01:00	Vir	8 Jun 1981	00:26	Pis	10 Oct 1981	00:30
Tau	10 Feb 1981	03:10	Lib	10 Jun 1981	09:55	Ari	12 Oct 1981	03:59
Gem	12 Feb 1981	05:50	Sco	12 Jun 1981	21:54	Tau	14 Oct 1981	04:42
Can	14 Feb 1981	09:42	Sag	15 Jun 1981	10:30	Gem	16 Oct 1981	04:41
Leo	16 Feb 1981	15:10	Cap	17 Jun 1981	22:20	Can	18 Oct 1981	05:51
Vir	18 Feb 1981	22:34	Aqu	20 Jun 1981	08:35	Leo	20 Oct 1981	09:34
Lib	21 Feb 1981	08:12	Pis	22 Jun 1981	16:43	Vir	22 Oct 1981	16:04
Sco	23 Feb 1981	19:54	Ari	24 Jun 1981	22:16	Lib	25 Oct 1981	00:56
Sag	26 Feb 1981	08:28	Tau	27 Jun 1981	01:15	Sco	27 Oct 1981	11:37
Cap	28 Feb 1981	19:45	Gem	29 Jun 1981	02:20	Sag	29 Oct 1981	23:47
Aqu	3 Mar 1981	03:49	Can	1 Jul 1981	02:56	Cap	1 Nov 1981	12:44
Pis	5 Mar 1981	08:11	Leo	3 Jul 1981	04:47	Aqu	4 Nov 1981	00:48
Ari	7 Mar 1981	09:47	Vir	5 Jul 1981	09:26	Pis	6 Nov 1981	09:50
Tau	9 Mar 1981	10:22	Lib	7 Jul 1981	17:41	Ari	8 Nov 1981	14:36
Gem	11 Mar 1981	11:42	Sco	10 Jul 1981	05:01	Tau	10 Nov 1981	15:43
Can	13 Mar 1981	15:05	Sag	12 Jul 1981	17:34	Gem	12 Nov 1981	14:59
Leo	15 Mar 1981	21:02	Cap	15 Jul 1981	05:18	Can	14 Nov 1981	14:36
Vir	18 Mar 1981	05:19	Aqu	17 Jul 1981	15:00	Leo	16 Nov 1981	16:32
Lib	20 Mar 1981	15:30	Pis	19 Jul 1981	22:24	Vir	18 Nov 1981	21:53
Sco	23 Mar 1981	03:13	Ari	22 Jul 1981	03:42	Lib	21 Nov 1981	06:32
Sag	25 Mar 1981	15:50	Tau	24 Jul 1981	07:17	Sco	23 Nov 1981	17:36
Cap	28 Mar 1981	03:51	Gem	26 Jul 1981	09:41	Sag	26 Nov 1981	05:59
Aqu	30 Mar 1981	13:13	Can	28 Jul 1981	11:40	Cap	28 Nov 1981	18:51
			Leo	30 Jul 1981	14:20			
Pis	1 Apr 1981	18:40	Vir	1 Aug 1981	18:54	Aqu	1 Dec 1981	07:08
Ari	3 Apr 1981	20:24	Lib	4 Aug 1981	02:24	Pis	3 Dec 1981	17:14
Tau	5 Apr 1981	20:03	Sco	6 Aug 1981	12:58	Ari	5 Dec 1981	23:46
Gem	7 Apr 1981	19:47	Sag	9 Aug 1981	01:21	Tau	8 Dec 1981	02:29
Can	9 Apr 1981	21:34	Cap	11 Aug 1981	13:19	Gem	10 Dec 1981	02:29
Leo	12 Apr 1981	02:37	Aqu	13 Aug 1981	22:54	Can	12 Dec 1981	01:40
Vir	14 Apr 1981	10:56	Pis	16 Aug 1981	05:33	Leo	14 Dec 1981	02:08
Lib	16 Apr 1981	21:37	Ari	18 Aug 1981	09:48	Vir	16 Dec 1981	05:37
Sco	19 Apr 1981	09:38	Tau	20 Aug 1981	12:42	Lib	18 Dec 1981	12:58
Sag	21 Apr 1981	22:14	Gem	22 Aug 1981	15:17	Sco	20 Dec 1981	23:38
Cap	24 Apr 1981	10:30	Can	24 Aug 1981	18:16	Sag	23 Dec 1981	12:10
Aqu	26 Apr 1981	20:55	Leo	26 Aug 1981	22:09	Cap	26 Dec 1981	00:58
Pis	29 Apr 1981	03:55	Vir	29 Aug 1981	03:31	Aqu	28 Dec 1981	12:52
			Lib	31 Aug 1981	11:03	Pis	30 Dec 1981	22:59

Moon Signs

1982

Ari	2 Jan 1982	06:32	Vir	1 May 1982	23:45	Pis	2 Sep 1982	16:09
Tau	4 Jan 1982	11:00	Lib	4 May 1982	06:32	Ari	5 Sep 1982	00:22
Gem	6 Jan 1982	12:47	Sco	6 May 1982	15:23	Tau	7 Sep 1982	06:26
Can	8 Jan 1982	13:00	Sag	9 May 1982	02:16	Gem	9 Sep 1982	10:56
Leo	10 Jan 1982	13:21	Cap	11 May 1982	14:49	Can	11 Sep 1982	14:17
Vir	12 Jan 1982	15:37	Aqu	14 May 1982	03:43	Leo	13 Sep 1982	16:45
Lib	14 Jan 1982	21:17	Pis	16 May 1982	14:44	Vir	15 Sep 1982	18:56
Sco	17 Jan 1982	06:45	Ari	18 May 1982	22:02	Lib	17 Sep 1982	22:03
Sag	19 Jan 1982	18:59	Tau	21 May 1982	01:20	Sco	20 Sep 1982	03:32
Cap	22 Jan 1982	07:49	Gem	23 May 1982	01:53	Sag	22 Sep 1982	12:30
Aqu	24 Jan 1982	19:24	Can	25 May 1982	01:38	Cap	25 Sep 1982	00:30
Pis	27 Jan 1982	04:48	Leo	27 May 1982	02:27	Aqu	27 Sep 1982	13:20
Ari	29 Jan 1982	11:57	Vir	29 May 1982	05:42	Pis	30 Sep 1982	00:16
Tau	31 Jan 1982	17:02	Lib	31 May 1982	12:02			
Gem	2 Feb 1982	20:19	Sco	2 Jun 1982	21:11	Ari	2 Oct 1982	08:04
Can	4 Feb 1982	22:17	Sag	5 Jun 1982	08:31	Tau	4 Oct 1982	13:07
Leo	6 Feb 1982	23:49	Cap	7 Jun 1982	21:11	Gem	6 Oct 1982	16:38
Vir	9 Feb 1982	02:15	Aqu	10 Jun 1982	10:06	Can	8 Oct 1982	19:38
Lib	11 Feb 1982	07:01	Pis	12 Jun 1982	21:42	Leo	10 Oct 1982	22:43
Sco	13 Feb 1982	15:15	Ari	15 Jun 1982	06:19	Vir	13 Oct 1982	02:08
Sag	16 Feb 1982	02:44	Tau	17 Jun 1982	11:04	Lib	15 Oct 1982	06:22
Cap	18 Feb 1982	15:35	Gem	19 Jun 1982	12:32	Sco	17 Oct 1982	12:20
Aqu	21 Feb 1982	03:13	Can	21 Jun 1982	12:12	Sag	19 Oct 1982	21:02
Pis	23 Feb 1982	12:07	Leo	23 Jun 1982	11:57	Cap	22 Oct 1982	08:37
Ari	25 Feb 1982	18:16	Vir	25 Jun 1982	13:36	Aqu	24 Oct 1982	21:34
Tau	27 Feb 1982	22:30	Lib	27 Jun 1982	18:29	Pis	27 Oct 1982	09:10
			Sco	30 Jun 1982	03:01	Ari	29 Oct 1982	17:24
						Tau	31 Oct 1982	22:02
Gem	2 Mar 1982	01:49	Sag	2 Jul 1982	14:25	Gem	3 Nov 1982	00:21
Can	4 Mar 1982	04:47	Cap	5 Jul 1982	03:14	Can	5 Nov 1982	01:58
Leo	6 Mar 1982	07:49	Aqu	7 Jul 1982	16:02	Leo	7 Nov 1982	04:09
Vir	8 Mar 1982	11:27	Pis	10 Jul 1982	03:34	Vir	9 Nov 1982	07:39
Lib	10 Mar 1982	16:33	Ari	12 Jul 1982	12:47	Lib	11 Nov 1982	12:45
Sco	13 Mar 1982	00:17	Tau	14 Jul 1982	18:59	Sco	13 Nov 1982	19:41
Sag	15 Mar 1982	11:03	Gem	16 Jul 1982	22:01	Sag	16 Nov 1982	04:51
Cap	17 Mar 1982	23:46	Can	18 Jul 1982	22:44	Cap	18 Nov 1982	16:20
Aqu	20 Mar 1982	11:51	Leo	20 Jul 1982	22:35	Aqu	21 Nov 1982	05:19
Pis	22 Mar 1982	20:59	Vir	22 Jul 1982	23:20	Pis	23 Nov 1982	17:41
Ari	25 Mar 1982	02:35	Lib	25 Jul 1982	02:45	Ari	26 Nov 1982	03:05
Tau	27 Mar 1982	05:38	Sco	27 Jul 1982	09:58	Tau	28 Nov 1982	08:30
Gem	29 Mar 1982	07:43	Sag	29 Jul 1982	20:47	Gem	30 Nov 1982	10:34
Can	31 Mar 1982	10:08						
Leo	2 Apr 1982	13:36	Cap	1 Aug 1982	09:35	Can	2 Dec 1982	10:57
Vir	4 Apr 1982	18:17	Aqu	3 Aug 1982	22:16	Leo	4 Dec 1982	11:26
Lib	7 Apr 1982	00:26	Pis	6 Aug 1982	09:22	Vir	6 Dec 1982	13:32
Sco	9 Apr 1982	08:32	Ari	8 Aug 1982	18:19	Lib	8 Dec 1982	18:10
Sag	11 Apr 1982	19:06	Tau	11 Aug 1982	00:58	Sco	11 Dec 1982	01:34
Cap	14 Apr 1982	07:40	Gem	13 Aug 1982	05:21	Sag	13 Dec 1982	11:26
Aqu	16 Apr 1982	20:16	Can	15 Aug 1982	07:39	Cap	15 Dec 1982	23:14
Pis	19 Apr 1982	06:18	Leo	17 Aug 1982	08:39	Aqu	18 Dec 1982	12:11
Ari	21 Apr 1982	12:21	Vir	19 Aug 1982	09:39	Pis	21 Dec 1982	00:54
Tau	23 Apr 1982	14:57	Lib	21 Aug 1982	12:22	Ari	23 Dec 1982	11:32
Gem	25 Apr 1982	15:47	Sco	23 Aug 1982	18:20	Tau	25 Dec 1982	18:36
Can	27 Apr 1982	16:43	Sag	26 Aug 1982	04:10	Gem	27 Dec 1982	21:47
Leo	29 Apr 1982	19:08	Cap	28 Aug 1982	16:41	Can	29 Dec 1982	22:11
			Aqu	31 Aug 1982	05:22	Leo	31 Dec 1982	21:32

Moon Signs

1983

Vir	2 Jan 1983	21:49	Cap	1 May 1983	11:01	Can	2 Sep 1983	02:51
Lib	5 Jan 1983	00:45	Aqu	3 May 1983	23:08	Leo	4 Sep 1983	04:46
Sco	7 Jan 1983	07:16	Pis	6 May 1983	11:42	Vir	6 Sep 1983	04:35
Sag	9 Jan 1983	17:13	Ari	8 May 1983	22:14	Lib	8 Sep 1983	04:13
Cap	12 Jan 1983	05:25	Tau	11 May 1983	05:35	Sco	10 Sep 1983	05:48
Aqu	14 Jan 1983	18:25	Gem	13 May 1983	10:02	Sag	12 Sep 1983	11:08
Pis	17 Jan 1983	07:01	Can	15 May 1983	12:47	Cap	14 Sep 1983	20:33
Ari	19 Jan 1983	18:07	Leo	17 May 1983	15:00	Aqu	17 Sep 1983	08:44
Tau	22 Jan 1983	02:34	Vir	19 May 1983	17:36	Pis	19 Sep 1983	21:28
Gem	24 Jan 1983	07:38	Lib	21 May 1983	21:11	Ari	22 Sep 1983	09:09
Can	26 Jan 1983	09:27	Sco	24 May 1983	02:17	Tau	24 Sep 1983	19:11
Leo	28 Jan 1983	09:09	Sag	26 May 1983	09:27	Gem	27 Sep 1983	03:23
Vir	30 Jan 1983	08:34	Cap	28 May 1983	19:06	Can	29 Sep 1983	09:23
			Aqu	31 May 1983	06:59			
Lib	1 Feb 1983	09:47	Pis	2 Jun 1983	19:40	Leo	1 Oct 1983	12:52
Sco	3 Feb 1983	14:32	Ari	5 Jun 1983	06:58	Vir	3 Oct 1983	14:14
Sag	5 Feb 1983	23:29	Tau	7 Jun 1983	15:03	Lib	5 Oct 1983	14:41
Cap	8 Feb 1983	11:33	Gem	9 Jun 1983	19:36	Sco	7 Oct 1983	16:05
Aqu	11 Feb 1983	00:39	Can	11 Jun 1983	21:31	Sag	9 Oct 1983	20:20
Pis	13 Feb 1983	13:00	Leo	13 Jun 1983	22:21	Cap	12 Oct 1983	04:30
Ari	15 Feb 1983	23:44	Vir	15 Jun 1983	23:38	Aqu	14 Oct 1983	15:59
Tau	18 Feb 1983	08:29	Lib	18 Jun 1983	02:36	Pis	17 Oct 1983	04:40
Gem	20 Feb 1983	14:50	Sco	20 Jun 1983	07:59	Ari	19 Oct 1983	16:17
Can	22 Feb 1983	18:30	Sag	22 Jun 1983	15:55	Tau	22 Oct 1983	01:46
Leo	24 Feb 1983	19:45	Cap	25 Jun 1983	02:08	Gem	24 Oct 1983	09:08
Vir	26 Feb 1983	19:48	Aqu	27 Jun 1983	14:06	Can	26 Oct 1983	14:45
Lib	28 Feb 1983	20:30	Pis	30 Jun 1983	02:50	Leo	28 Oct 1983	18:49
						Vir	30 Oct 1983	21:31
Sco	2 Mar 1983	23:51	Ari	2 Jul 1983	14:46	Lib	1 Nov 1983	23:30
Sag	5 Mar 1983	07:14	Tau	5 Jul 1983	00:03	Sco	4 Nov 1983	01:53
Cap	7 Mar 1983	18:28	Gem	7 Jul 1983	05:40	Sag	6 Nov 1983	06:08
Aqu	10 Mar 1983	07:29	Can	9 Jul 1983	07:49	Cap	8 Nov 1983	13:31
Pis	12 Mar 1983	19:46	Leo	11 Jul 1983	07:53	Aqu	11 Nov 1983	00:10
Ari	15 Mar 1983	05:59	Vir	13 Jul 1983	07:42	Pis	13 Nov 1983	12:39
Tau	17 Mar 1983	14:03	Lib	15 Jul 1983	09:10	Ari	16 Nov 1983	00:35
Gem	19 Mar 1983	20:18	Sco	17 Jul 1983	13:38	Tau	18 Nov 1983	10:04
Can	22 Mar 1983	00:51	Sag	19 Jul 1983	21:31	Gem	20 Nov 1983	16:44
Leo	24 Mar 1983	03:42	Cap	22 Jul 1983	08:10	Can	22 Nov 1983	21:09
Vir	26 Mar 1983	05:17	Aqu	24 Jul 1983	20:26	Leo	25 Nov 1983	00:18
Lib	28 Mar 1983	06:48	Pis	27 Jul 1983	09:10	Vir	27 Nov 1983	03:01
Sco	30 Mar 1983	09:57	Ari	29 Jul 1983	21:19	Lib	29 Nov 1983	05:56
Sag	1 Apr 1983	16:19	Tau	1 Aug 1983	07:35	Sco	1 Dec 1983	09:40
Cap	4 Apr 1983	02:29	Gem	3 Aug 1983	14:41	Sag	3 Dec 1983	14:56
Aqu	6 Apr 1983	15:05	Can	5 Aug 1983	18:08	Cap	5 Dec 1983	22:28
Pis	9 Apr 1983	03:29	Leo	7 Aug 1983	18:36	Aqu	8 Dec 1983	08:39
Ari	11 Apr 1983	13:35	Vir	9 Aug 1983	17:48	Pis	10 Dec 1983	20:52
Tau	13 Apr 1983	20:57	Lib	11 Aug 1983	17:50	Ari	13 Dec 1983	09:15
Gem	16 Apr 1983	02:13	Sco	13 Aug 1983	20:44	Tau	15 Dec 1983	19:31
Can	18 Apr 1983	06:13	Sag	16 Aug 1983	03:33	Gem	18 Dec 1983	02:22
Leo	20 Apr 1983	09:25	Cap	18 Aug 1983	13:59	Can	20 Dec 1983	06:01
Vir	22 Apr 1983	12:11	Aqu	21 Aug 1983	02:25	Leo	22 Dec 1983	07:43
Lib	24 Apr 1983	15:03	Pis	23 Aug 1983	15:08	Vir	24 Dec 1983	09:01
Sco	26 Apr 1983	19:04	Ari	26 Aug 1983	03:07	Lib	26 Dec 1983	11:18
Sag	29 Apr 1983	01:28	Tau	28 Aug 1983	13:36	Sco	28 Dec 1983	15:26
			Gem	30 Aug 1983	21:47	Sag	30 Dec 1983	21:43

1984

Cap	2 Jan 1984	06:06		Gem	2 May 1984	16:00		Sag	1 Sep 1984	16:29
Aqu	4 Jan 1984	16:30		Can	4 May 1984	23:24		Cap	3 Sep 1984	22:55
Pis	7 Jan 1984	04:33		Leo	7 May 1984	04:42		Aqu	6 Sep 1984	08:11
Ari	9 Jan 1984	17:14		Vir	9 May 1984	08:00		Pis	8 Sep 1984	19:24
Tau	12 Jan 1984	04:35		Lib	11 May 1984	09:53		Ari	11 Sep 1984	07:46
Gem	14 Jan 1984	12:38		Sco	13 May 1984	11:21		Tau	13 Sep 1984	20:32
Can	16 Jan 1984	16:46		Sag	15 May 1984	13:50		Gem	16 Sep 1984	08:24
Leo	18 Jan 1984	17:48		Cap	17 May 1984	18:42		Can	18 Sep 1984	17:35
Vir	20 Jan 1984	17:34		Aqu	20 May 1984	02:55		Leo	20 Sep 1984	22:46
Lib	22 Jan 1984	18:06		Pis	22 May 1984	14:08		Vir	23 Sep 1984	00:17
Sco	24 Jan 1984	21:04		Ari	25 May 1984	02:38		Lib	24 Sep 1984	23:40
Sag	27 Jan 1984	03:12		Tau	27 May 1984	14:12		Sco	26 Sep 1984	23:04
Cap	29 Jan 1984	12:12		Gem	29 May 1984	23:21		Sag	29 Sep 1984	00:32
Aqu	31 Jan 1984	23:10								
				Can	1 Jun 1984	05:53		Cap	1 Oct 1984	05:27
Pis	3 Feb 1984	11:21		Leo	3 Jun 1984	10:17		Aqu	3 Oct 1984	14:03
Ari	6 Feb 1984	00:02		Vir	5 Jun 1984	13:26		Pis	6 Oct 1984	01:19
Tau	8 Feb 1984	12:03		Lib	7 Jun 1984	16:02		Ari	8 Oct 1984	13:50
Gem	10 Feb 1984	21:37		Sco	9 Jun 1984	18:47		Tau	11 Oct 1984	02:27
Can	13 Feb 1984	03:18		Sag	11 Jun 1984	22:26		Gem	13 Oct 1984	14:12
Leo	15 Feb 1984	05:08		Cap	14 Jun 1984	03:47		Can	15 Oct 1984	23:58
Vir	17 Feb 1984	04:31		Aqu	16 Jun 1984	11:41		Leo	18 Oct 1984	06:40
Lib	19 Feb 1984	03:39		Pis	18 Jun 1984	22:17		Vir	20 Oct 1984	09:54
Sco	21 Feb 1984	04:44		Ari	21 Jun 1984	10:39		Lib	22 Oct 1984	10:30
Sag	23 Feb 1984	09:22		Tau	23 Jun 1984	22:36		Sco	24 Oct 1984	10:07
Cap	25 Feb 1984	17:49		Gem	26 Jun 1984	08:02		Sag	26 Oct 1984	10:43
Aqu	28 Feb 1984	05:01		Can	28 Jun 1984	14:07		Cap	28 Oct 1984	14:05
				Leo	30 Jun 1984	17:29		Aqu	30 Oct 1984	21:13
Pis	1 Mar 1984	17:28		Vir	2 Jul 1984	19:27		Pis	2 Nov 1984	07:49
Ari	4 Mar 1984	06:06		Lib	4 Jul 1984	21:26		Ari	4 Nov 1984	20:19
Tau	6 Mar 1984	18:08		Sco	7 Jul 1984	00:28		Tau	7 Nov 1984	08:52
Gem	9 Mar 1984	04:28		Sag	9 Jul 1984	05:02		Gem	9 Nov 1984	20:09
Can	11 Mar 1984	11:46		Cap	11 Jul 1984	11:22		Can	12 Nov 1984	05:30
Leo	13 Mar 1984	15:19		Aqu	13 Jul 1984	19:41		Leo	14 Nov 1984	12:32
Vir	15 Mar 1984	15:45		Pis	16 Jul 1984	06:09		Vir	16 Nov 1984	17:06
Lib	17 Mar 1984	14:51		Ari	18 Jul 1984	18:25		Lib	18 Nov 1984	19:28
Sco	19 Mar 1984	14:49		Tau	21 Jul 1984	06:51		Sco	20 Nov 1984	20:30
Sag	21 Mar 1984	17:40		Gem	23 Jul 1984	17:09		Sag	22 Nov 1984	21:34
Cap	24 Mar 1984	00:36		Can	25 Jul 1984	23:42		Cap	25 Nov 1984	00:18
Aqu	26 Mar 1984	11:08		Leo	28 Jul 1984	02:40		Aqu	27 Nov 1984	06:05
Pis	28 Mar 1984	23:36		Vir	30 Jul 1984	03:28		Pis	29 Nov 1984	15:33
Ari	31 Mar 1984	12:12								
Tau	2 Apr 1984	23:54		Lib	1 Aug 1984	04:02		Ari	2 Dec 1984	03:41
Gem	5 Apr 1984	10:03		Sco	3 Aug 1984	06:03		Tau	4 Dec 1984	16:19
Can	7 Apr 1984	17:58		Sag	5 Aug 1984	10:29		Gem	7 Dec 1984	03:22
Leo	9 Apr 1984	22:59		Cap	7 Aug 1984	17:24		Can	9 Dec 1984	11:55
Vir	12 Apr 1984	01:09		Aqu	10 Aug 1984	02:25		Leo	11 Dec 1984	18:07
Lib	14 Apr 1984	01:28		Pis	12 Aug 1984	13:12		Vir	13 Dec 1984	22:34
Sco	16 Apr 1984	01:41		Ari	15 Aug 1984	01:27		Lib	16 Dec 1984	01:50
Sag	18 Apr 1984	03:43		Tau	17 Aug 1984	14:12		Sco	18 Dec 1984	04:26
Cap	20 Apr 1984	09:10		Gem	20 Aug 1984	01:29		Sag	20 Dec 1984	06:58
Aqu	22 Apr 1984	18:26		Can	22 Aug 1984	09:18		Cap	22 Dec 1984	10:21
Pis	25 Apr 1984	06:25		Leo	24 Aug 1984	12:58		Aqu	24 Dec 1984	15:47
Ari	27 Apr 1984	19:01		Vir	26 Aug 1984	13:31		Pis	27 Dec 1984	00:18
Tau	30 Apr 1984	06:29		Lib	28 Aug 1984	12:56		Ari	29 Dec 1984	11:49
				Sco	30 Aug 1984	13:23				

Moon Signs

1985

Tau	1 Jan 1985	00:35	Lib	1 May 1985	21:20	Ari	1 Sep 1985	05:41
Gem	3 Jan 1985	11:58	Sco	3 May 1985	21:16	Tau	3 Sep 1985	17:27
Can	5 Jan 1985	20:16	Sag	5 May 1985	20:55	Gem	6 Sep 1985	06:26
Leo	8 Jan 1985	01:26	Cap	7 May 1985	22:12	Can	8 Sep 1985	18:09
Vir	10 Jan 1985	04:39	Aqu	10 May 1985	02:38	Leo	11 Sep 1985	02:25
Lib	12 Jan 1985	07:13	Pis	12 May 1985	10:56	Vir	13 Sep 1985	06:51
Sco	14 Jan 1985	10:07	Ari	14 May 1985	22:25	Lib	15 Sep 1985	08:32
Sag	16 Jan 1985	13:47	Tau	17 May 1985	11:22	Sco	17 Sep 1985	09:16
Cap	18 Jan 1985	18:28	Gem	19 May 1985	23:59	Sag	19 Sep 1985	10:40
Aqu	21 Jan 1985	00:38	Can	22 May 1985	11:03	Cap	21 Sep 1985	13:49
Pis	23 Jan 1985	09:02	Leo	24 May 1985	19:52	Aqu	23 Sep 1985	19:11
Ari	25 Jan 1985	20:05	Vir	27 May 1985	02:05	Pis	26 Sep 1985	02:50
Tau	28 Jan 1985	08:52	Lib	29 May 1985	05:39	Ari	28 Sep 1985	12:42
Gem	30 Jan 1985	20:59	Sco	31 May 1985	07:06			
Can	2 Feb 1985	05:58	Sag	2 Jun 1985	07:32	Tau	1 Oct 1985	00:34
Leo	4 Feb 1985	11:00	Cap	4 Jun 1985	08:33	Gem	3 Oct 1985	13:35
Vir	6 Feb 1985	13:08	Aqu	6 Jun 1985	11:52	Can	6 Oct 1985	01:57
Lib	8 Feb 1985	14:10	Pis	8 Jun 1985	18:46	Leo	8 Oct 1985	11:31
Sco	10 Feb 1985	15:48	Ari	11 Jun 1985	05:23	Vir	10 Oct 1985	17:08
Sag	12 Feb 1985	19:08	Tau	13 Jun 1985	18:10	Lib	12 Oct 1985	19:11
Cap	15 Feb 1985	00:27	Gem	16 Jun 1985	06:44	Sco	14 Oct 1985	19:12
Aqu	17 Feb 1985	07:35	Can	18 Jun 1985	17:21	Sag	16 Oct 1985	19:05
Pis	19 Feb 1985	16:37	Leo	21 Jun 1985	01:30	Cap	18 Oct 1985	20:35
Ari	22 Feb 1985	03:42	Vir	23 Jun 1985	07:31	Aqu	21 Oct 1985	00:55
Tau	24 Feb 1985	16:26	Lib	25 Jun 1985	11:46	Pis	23 Oct 1985	08:27
Gem	27 Feb 1985	05:10	Sco	27 Jun 1985	14:36	Ari	25 Oct 1985	18:47
			Sag	29 Jun 1985	16:29	Tau	28 Oct 1985	06:58
						Gem	30 Oct 1985	19:58
Can	1 Mar 1985	15:22	Cap	1 Jul 1985	18:21	Can	2 Nov 1985	08:30
Leo	3 Mar 1985	21:26	Aqu	3 Jul 1985	21:36	Leo	4 Nov 1985	19:02
Vir	5 Mar 1985	23:41	Pis	6 Jul 1985	03:40	Vir	7 Nov 1985	02:16
Lib	7 Mar 1985	23:46	Ari	8 Jul 1985	13:20	Lib	9 Nov 1985	05:51
Sco	9 Mar 1985	23:47	Tau	11 Jul 1985	01:43	Sco	11 Nov 1985	06:30
Sag	12 Mar 1985	01:29	Gem	13 Jul 1985	14:22	Sag	13 Nov 1985	05:51
Cap	14 Mar 1985	05:54	Can	16 Jul 1985	00:52	Cap	15 Nov 1985	05:52
Aqu	16 Mar 1985	13:11	Leo	18 Jul 1985	08:24	Aqu	17 Nov 1985	08:25
Pis	18 Mar 1985	22:50	Vir	20 Jul 1985	13:28	Pis	19 Nov 1985	14:43
Ari	21 Mar 1985	10:19	Lib	22 Jul 1985	17:09	Ari	22 Nov 1985	00:42
Tau	23 Mar 1985	23:05	Sco	24 Jul 1985	20:15	Tau	24 Nov 1985	13:06
Gem	26 Mar 1985	12:00	Sag	26 Jul 1985	23:12	Gem	27 Nov 1985	02:07
Can	28 Mar 1985	23:11	Cap	29 Jul 1985	02:20	Can	29 Nov 1985	14:22
Leo	31 Mar 1985	06:50	Aqu	31 Jul 1985	06:25			
Vir	2 Apr 1985	10:23	Pis	2 Aug 1985	12:34	Leo	2 Dec 1985	00:58
Lib	4 Apr 1985	10:52	Ari	4 Aug 1985	21:43	Vir	4 Dec 1985	09:12
Sco	6 Apr 1985	10:10	Tau	7 Aug 1985	09:40	Lib	6 Dec 1985	14:32
Sag	8 Apr 1985	10:18	Gem	9 Aug 1985	22:30	Sco	8 Dec 1985	16:55
Cap	10 Apr 1985	12:57	Can	12 Aug 1985	09:26	Sag	10 Dec 1985	17:12
Aqu	12 Apr 1985	19:03	Leo	14 Aug 1985	16:56	Cap	12 Dec 1985	16:59
Pis	15 Apr 1985	04:30	Vir	16 Aug 1985	21:13	Aqu	14 Dec 1985	18:14
Ari	17 Apr 1985	16:17	Lib	18 Aug 1985	23:43	Pis	16 Dec 1985	22:51
Tau	20 Apr 1985	05:11	Sco	21 Aug 1985	01:50	Ari	19 Dec 1985	07:36
Gem	22 Apr 1985	17:59	Sag	23 Aug 1985	04:35	Tau	21 Dec 1985	19:40
Can	25 Apr 1985	05:25	Cap	25 Aug 1985	08:24	Gem	24 Dec 1985	08:44
Leo	27 Apr 1985	14:08	Aqu	27 Aug 1985	13:31	Can	26 Dec 1985	20:43
Vir	29 Apr 1985	19:23	Pis	29 Aug 1985	20:24	Leo	29 Dec 1985	06:43
						Vir	31 Dec 1985	14:42

1986

Sign	Date	Time	Sign	Date	Time	Sign	Date	Time
Lib	2 Jan 1986	20:44	Pis	2 May 1986	14:30	Leo	1 Sep 1986	01:07
Sco	5 Jan 1986	00:43	Ari	4 May 1986	23:01	Vir	3 Sep 1986	10:04
Sag	7 Jan 1986	02:46	Tau	7 May 1986	09:58	Lib	5 Sep 1986	16:32
Cap	9 Jan 1986	03:41	Gem	9 May 1986	22:25	Sco	7 Sep 1986	21:11
Aqu	11 Jan 1986	05:01	Can	12 May 1986	11:17	Sag	10 Sep 1986	00:39
Pis	13 Jan 1986	08:39	Leo	14 May 1986	23:14	Cap	12 Sep 1986	03:27
Ari	15 Jan 1986	16:03	Vir	17 May 1986	08:43	Aqu	14 Sep 1986	06:06
Tau	18 Jan 1986	03:13	Lib	19 May 1986	14:39	Pis	16 Sep 1986	09:27
Gem	20 Jan 1986	16:11	Sco	21 May 1986	17:01	Ari	18 Sep 1986	14:34
Can	23 Jan 1986	04:13	Sag	23 May 1986	16:56	Tau	20 Sep 1986	22:26
Leo	25 Jan 1986	13:46	Cap	25 May 1986	16:14	Gem	23 Sep 1986	09:13
Vir	27 Jan 1986	20:50	Aqu	27 May 1986	16:59	Can	25 Sep 1986	21:44
Lib	30 Jan 1986	02:09	Pis	29 May 1986	20:55	Leo	28 Sep 1986	09:38
						Vir	30 Sep 1986	18:56
Sco	1 Feb 1986	06:18	Ari	1 Jun 1986	04:42	Lib	3 Oct 1986	01:01
Sag	3 Feb 1986	09:30	Tau	3 Jun 1986	15:45	Sco	5 Oct 1986	04:34
Cap	5 Feb 1986	12:01	Gem	6 Jun 1986	04:26	Sag	7 Oct 1986	06:47
Aqu	7 Feb 1986	14:35	Can	8 Jun 1986	17:15	Cap	9 Oct 1986	08:52
Pis	9 Feb 1986	18:32	Leo	11 Jun 1986	05:10	Aqu	11 Oct 1986	11:45
Ari	12 Feb 1986	01:21	Vir	13 Jun 1986	15:17	Pis	13 Oct 1986	16:03
Tau	14 Feb 1986	11:38	Lib	15 Jun 1986	22:36	Ari	15 Oct 1986	22:13
Gem	17 Feb 1986	00:16	Sco	18 Jun 1986	02:34	Tau	18 Oct 1986	06:35
Can	19 Feb 1986	12:37	Sag	20 Jun 1986	03:34	Gem	20 Oct 1986	17:15
Leo	21 Feb 1986	22:23	Cap	22 Jun 1986	02:59	Can	23 Oct 1986	05:37
Vir	24 Feb 1986	04:57	Aqu	24 Jun 1986	02:50	Leo	25 Oct 1986	18:02
Lib	26 Feb 1986	09:06	Pis	26 Jun 1986	05:12	Vir	28 Oct 1986	04:19
Sco	28 Feb 1986	12:05	Ari	28 Jun 1986	11:35	Lib	30 Oct 1986	11:02
			Tau	30 Jun 1986	21:54			
Sag	2 Mar 1986	14:51	Gem	3 Jul 1986	10:31	Sco	1 Nov 1986	14:18
Cap	4 Mar 1986	17:55	Can	5 Jul 1986	23:18	Sag	3 Nov 1986	15:18
Aqu	6 Mar 1986	21:42	Leo	8 Jul 1986	10:54	Cap	5 Nov 1986	15:48
Pis	9 Mar 1986	02:48	Vir	10 Jul 1986	20:49	Aqu	7 Nov 1986	17:28
Ari	11 Mar 1986	10:03	Lib	13 Jul 1986	04:39	Pis	9 Nov 1986	21:30
Tau	13 Mar 1986	20:03	Sco	15 Jul 1986	09:57	Ari	12 Nov 1986	04:14
Gem	16 Mar 1986	08:22	Sag	17 Jul 1986	12:33	Tau	14 Nov 1986	13:24
Can	18 Mar 1986	21:03	Cap	19 Jul 1986	13:09	Gem	17 Nov 1986	00:26
Leo	21 Mar 1986	07:37	Aqu	21 Jul 1986	13:17	Can	19 Nov 1986	12:45
Vir	23 Mar 1986	14:38	Pis	23 Jul 1986	14:59	Leo	22 Nov 1986	01:24
Lib	25 Mar 1986	18:22	Ari	25 Jul 1986	20:02	Vir	24 Nov 1986	12:44
Sco	27 Mar 1986	20:04	Tau	28 Jul 1986	05:11	Lib	26 Nov 1986	20:57
Sag	29 Mar 1986	21:20	Gem	30 Jul 1986	17:18	Sco	29 Nov 1986	01:11
Cap	31 Mar 1986	23:25						
Aqu	3 Apr 1986	03:11	Can	2 Aug 1986	06:03	Sag	1 Dec 1986	02:07
Pis	5 Apr 1986	09:03	Leo	4 Aug 1986	17:26	Cap	3 Dec 1986	01:28
Ari	7 Apr 1986	17:11	Vir	7 Aug 1986	02:43	Aqu	5 Dec 1986	01:23
Tau	10 Apr 1986	03:36	Lib	9 Aug 1986	10:03	Pis	7 Dec 1986	03:48
Gem	12 Apr 1986	15:50	Sco	11 Aug 1986	15:35	Ari	9 Dec 1986	09:49
Can	15 Apr 1986	04:41	Sag	13 Aug 1986	19:16	Tau	11 Dec 1986	19:10
Leo	17 Apr 1986	16:08	Cap	15 Aug 1986	21:21	Gem	14 Dec 1986	06:41
Vir	20 Apr 1986	00:22	Aqu	17 Aug 1986	22:44	Can	16 Dec 1986	19:09
Lib	22 Apr 1986	04:49	Pis	20 Aug 1986	00:52	Leo	19 Dec 1986	07:43
Sco	24 Apr 1986	06:15	Ari	22 Aug 1986	05:27	Vir	21 Dec 1986	19:30
Sag	26 Apr 1986	06:15	Tau	24 Aug 1986	13:37	Lib	24 Dec 1986	05:04
Cap	28 Apr 1986	06:40	Gem	27 Aug 1986	01:00	Sco	26 Dec 1986	11:04
Aqu	30 Apr 1986	09:06	Can	29 Aug 1986	13:39	Sag	28 Dec 1986	13:18
						Cap	30 Dec 1986	12:53

1987

Aqu	1 Jan 1987	11:54	Can	2 May 1987	07:39	Cap	2 Sep 1987	17:03
Pis	3 Jan 1987	12:37	Leo	4 May 1987	20:06	Aqu	4 Sep 1987	18:21
Ari	5 Jan 1987	16:51	Vir	7 May 1987	08:06	Pis	6 Sep 1987	18:36
Tau	8 Jan 1987	01:13	Lib	9 May 1987	17:28	Ari	8 Sep 1987	19:34
Gem	10 Jan 1987	12:39	Sco	11 May 1987	23:07	Tau	10 Sep 1987	22:58
Can	13 Jan 1987	01:18	Sag	14 May 1987	01:40	Gem	13 Sep 1987	05:54
Leo	15 Jan 1987	13:44	Cap	16 May 1987	02:36	Can	15 Sep 1987	16:22
Vir	18 Jan 1987	01:14	Aqu	18 May 1987	03:42	Leo	18 Sep 1987	04:50
Lib	20 Jan 1987	11:08	Pis	20 May 1987	06:23	Vir	20 Sep 1987	17:12
Sco	22 Jan 1987	18:30	Ari	22 May 1987	11:23	Lib	23 Sep 1987	03:57
Sag	24 Jan 1987	22:34	Tau	24 May 1987	18:38	Sco	25 Sep 1987	12:29
Cap	26 Jan 1987	23:41	Gem	27 May 1987	03:55	Sag	27 Sep 1987	18:48
Aqu	28 Jan 1987	23:16	Can	29 May 1987	14:59	Cap	29 Sep 1987	23:07
Pis	30 Jan 1987	23:25						
Ari	2 Feb 1987	02:10	Leo	1 Jun 1987	03:25	Aqu	2 Oct 1987	01:50
Tau	4 Feb 1987	08:53	Vir	3 Jun 1987	15:55	Pis	4 Oct 1987	03:39
Gem	6 Feb 1987	19:23	Lib	6 Jun 1987	02:22	Ari	6 Oct 1987	05:34
Can	9 Feb 1987	07:54	Sco	8 Jun 1987	09:04	Tau	8 Oct 1987	08:58
Leo	11 Feb 1987	20:20	Sag	10 Jun 1987	11:51	Gem	10 Oct 1987	15:04
Vir	14 Feb 1987	07:25	Cap	12 Jun 1987	12:04	Can	13 Oct 1987	00:31
Lib	16 Feb 1987	16:44	Aqu	14 Jun 1987	11:45	Leo	15 Oct 1987	12:34
Sco	19 Feb 1987	00:03	Pis	16 Jun 1987	12:55	Vir	18 Oct 1987	01:05
Sag	21 Feb 1987	05:08	Ari	18 Jun 1987	16:56	Lib	20 Oct 1987	11:48
Cap	23 Feb 1987	07:56	Tau	21 Jun 1987	00:09	Sco	22 Oct 1987	19:40
Aqu	25 Feb 1987	09:08	Gem	23 Jun 1987	09:54	Sag	25 Oct 1987	00:56
Pis	27 Feb 1987	10:07	Can	25 Jun 1987	21:22	Cap	27 Oct 1987	04:32
			Leo	28 Jun 1987	09:51	Aqu	29 Oct 1987	07:26
			Vir	30 Jun 1987	22:33	Pis	31 Oct 1987	10:19
Ari	1 Mar 1987	12:37	Lib	3 Jul 1987	09:53	Ari	2 Nov 1987	13:40
Tau	3 Mar 1987	18:11	Sco	5 Jul 1987	18:02	Tau	4 Nov 1987	18:02
Gem	6 Mar 1987	03:26	Sag	7 Jul 1987	22:03	Gem	7 Nov 1987	00:16
Can	8 Mar 1987	15:24	Cap	9 Jul 1987	22:42	Can	9 Nov 1987	09:10
Leo	11 Mar 1987	03:53	Aqu	11 Jul 1987	21:49	Leo	11 Nov 1987	20:45
Vir	13 Mar 1987	14:54	Pis	13 Jul 1987	21:36	Vir	14 Nov 1987	09:28
Lib	15 Mar 1987	23:33	Ari	16 Jul 1987	00:01	Lib	16 Nov 1987	20:47
Sco	18 Mar 1987	05:56	Tau	18 Jul 1987	06:04	Sco	19 Nov 1987	04:46
Sag	20 Mar 1987	10:31	Gem	20 Jul 1987	15:32	Sag	21 Nov 1987	09:15
Cap	22 Mar 1987	13:47	Can	23 Jul 1987	03:13	Cap	23 Nov 1987	11:31
Aqu	24 Mar 1987	16:17	Leo	25 Jul 1987	15:49	Aqu	25 Nov 1987	13:12
Pis	26 Mar 1987	18:45	Vir	28 Jul 1987	04:25	Pis	27 Nov 1987	15:40
Ari	28 Mar 1987	22:12	Lib	30 Jul 1987	15:58	Ari	29 Nov 1987	19:36
Tau	31 Mar 1987	03:46						
Gem	2 Apr 1987	12:17	Sco	2 Aug 1987	01:07	Tau	2 Dec 1987	01:06
Can	4 Apr 1987	23:33	Sag	4 Aug 1987	06:46	Gem	4 Dec 1987	08:13
Leo	7 Apr 1987	12:03	Cap	6 Aug 1987	08:50	Can	6 Dec 1987	17:20
Vir	9 Apr 1987	23:26	Aqu	8 Aug 1987	08:36	Leo	9 Dec 1987	04:40
Lib	12 Apr 1987	08:04	Pis	10 Aug 1987	08:01	Vir	11 Dec 1987	17:30
Sco	14 Apr 1987	13:39	Ari	12 Aug 1987	09:10	Lib	14 Dec 1987	05:39
Sag	16 Apr 1987	17:00	Tau	14 Aug 1987	13:39	Sco	16 Dec 1987	14:39
Cap	18 Apr 1987	19:20	Gem	16 Aug 1987	21:59	Sag	18 Dec 1987	19:32
Aqu	20 Apr 1987	21:45	Can	19 Aug 1987	09:19	Cap	20 Dec 1987	21:07
Pis	23 Apr 1987	01:02	Leo	21 Aug 1987	21:57	Aqu	22 Dec 1987	21:20
Ari	25 Apr 1987	05:40	Vir	24 Aug 1987	10:22	Pis	24 Dec 1987	22:10
Tau	27 Apr 1987	12:06	Lib	26 Aug 1987	21:35	Ari	27 Dec 1987	01:06
Gem	29 Apr 1987	20:43	Sco	29 Aug 1987	06:48	Tau	29 Dec 1987	06:36
			Sag	31 Aug 1987	13:22	Gem	31 Dec 1987	14:29

Moon Signs

1988

Can	3 Jan 1988	00:17	Sco	1 May 1988	01:38	Gem	2 Sep 1988	08:12
Leo	5 Jan 1988	11:47	Sag	3 May 1988	08:51	Can	4 Sep 1988	15:37
Vir	8 Jan 1988	00:35	Cap	5 May 1988	13:53	Leo	7 Sep 1988	02:15
Lib	10 Jan 1988	13:16	Aqu	7 May 1988	17:36	Vir	9 Sep 1988	14:48
Sco	12 Jan 1988	23:37	Pis	9 May 1988	20:38	Lib	12 Sep 1988	03:51
Sag	15 Jan 1988	05:58	Ari	11 May 1988	23:23	Sco	14 Sep 1988	16:06
Cap	17 Jan 1988	08:14	Tau	14 May 1988	02:22	Sag	17 Sep 1988	02:24
Aqu	19 Jan 1988	08:01	Gem	16 May 1988	06:31	Cap	19 Sep 1988	09:43
Pis	21 Jan 1988	07:26	Can	18 May 1988	13:06	Aqu	21 Sep 1988	13:41
Ari	23 Jan 1988	08:31	Leo	20 May 1988	22:52	Pis	23 Sep 1988	14:50
Tau	25 Jan 1988	12:37	Vir	23 May 1988	11:12	Ari	25 Sep 1988	14:29
Gem	27 Jan 1988	20:02	Lib	25 May 1988	23:48	Tau	27 Sep 1988	14:29
Can	30 Jan 1988	06:11	Sco	28 May 1988	10:05	Gem	29 Sep 1988	16:43
			Sag	30 May 1988	16:56			
Leo	1 Feb 1988	18:06	Cap	1 Jun 1988	20:57	Can	1 Oct 1988	22:40
Vir	4 Feb 1988	06:54	Aqu	3 Jun 1988	23:33	Leo	4 Oct 1988	08:31
Lib	6 Feb 1988	19:35	Pis	6 Jun 1988	02:00	Vir	6 Oct 1988	21:01
Sco	9 Feb 1988	06:41	Ari	8 Jun 1988	05:03	Lib	9 Oct 1988	10:03
Sag	11 Feb 1988	14:34	Tau	10 Jun 1988	09:02	Sco	11 Oct 1988	21:57
Cap	13 Feb 1988	18:36	Gem	12 Jun 1988	14:15	Sag	14 Oct 1988	07:57
Aqu	15 Feb 1988	19:24	Can	14 Jun 1988	21:19	Cap	16 Oct 1988	15:44
Pis	17 Feb 1988	18:43	Leo	17 Jun 1988	06:57	Aqu	18 Oct 1988	21:04
Ari	19 Feb 1988	18:35	Vir	19 Jun 1988	19:03	Pis	20 Oct 1988	23:57
Tau	21 Feb 1988	20:51	Lib	22 Jun 1988	07:57	Ari	23 Oct 1988	00:58
Gem	24 Feb 1988	02:43	Sco	24 Jun 1988	18:58	Tau	25 Oct 1988	01:22
Can	26 Feb 1988	12:12	Sag	27 Jun 1988	02:16	Gem	27 Oct 1988	02:56
Leo	29 Feb 1988	00:12	Cap	29 Jun 1988	05:59	Can	29 Oct 1988	07:28
						Leo	31 Oct 1988	16:04
Vir	2 Mar 1988	13:06	Aqu	1 Jul 1988	07:29	Vir	3 Nov 1988	04:01
Lib	5 Mar 1988	01:31	Pis	3 Jul 1988	08:33	Lib	5 Nov 1988	17:03
Sco	7 Mar 1988	12:26	Ari	5 Jul 1988	10:37	Sco	8 Nov 1988	04:46
Sag	9 Mar 1988	20:57	Tau	7 Jul 1988	14:27	Sag	10 Nov 1988	14:05
Cap	12 Mar 1988	02:30	Gem	9 Jul 1988	20:16	Cap	12 Nov 1988	21:11
Aqu	14 Mar 1988	05:07	Can	12 Jul 1988	04:08	Aqu	15 Nov 1988	02:36
Pis	16 Mar 1988	05:41	Leo	14 Jul 1988	14:11	Pis	17 Nov 1988	06:33
Ari	18 Mar 1988	05:45	Vir	17 Jul 1988	02:17	Ari	19 Nov 1988	09:12
Tau	20 Mar 1988	07:05	Lib	19 Jul 1988	15:21	Tau	21 Nov 1988	11:02
Gem	22 Mar 1988	11:22	Sco	22 Jul 1988	03:12	Gem	23 Nov 1988	13:12
Can	24 Mar 1988	19:27	Sag	24 Jul 1988	11:40	Can	25 Nov 1988	17:19
Leo	27 Mar 1988	06:53	Cap	26 Jul 1988	16:06	Leo	28 Nov 1988	00:53
Vir	29 Mar 1988	19:48	Aqu	28 Jul 1988	17:24	Vir	30 Nov 1988	12:00
			Pis	30 Jul 1988	17:23			
Lib	1 Apr 1988	08:04	Ari	1 Aug 1988	17:53	Lib	3 Dec 1988	00:55
Sco	3 Apr 1988	18:25	Tau	3 Aug 1988	20:24	Sco	5 Dec 1988	12:50
Sag	6 Apr 1988	02:27	Gem	6 Aug 1988	01:43	Sag	7 Dec 1988	21:54
Cap	8 Apr 1988	08:18	Can	8 Aug 1988	09:53	Cap	10 Dec 1988	04:06
Aqu	10 Apr 1988	12:09	Leo	10 Aug 1988	20:26	Aqu	12 Dec 1988	08:25
Pis	12 Apr 1988	14:23	Vir	13 Aug 1988	08:45	Pis	14 Dec 1988	11:53
Ari	14 Apr 1988	15:46	Lib	15 Aug 1988	21:51	Ari	16 Dec 1988	15:03
Tau	16 Apr 1988	17:31	Sco	18 Aug 1988	10:10	Tau	18 Dec 1988	18:11
Gem	18 Apr 1988	21:11	Sag	20 Aug 1988	19:53	Gem	20 Dec 1988	21:43
Can	21 Apr 1988	04:05	Cap	23 Aug 1988	01:47	Can	23 Dec 1988	02:35
Leo	23 Apr 1988	14:34	Aqu	25 Aug 1988	04:04	Leo	25 Dec 1988	09:58
Vir	26 Apr 1988	03:15	Pis	27 Aug 1988	04:01	Vir	27 Dec 1988	20:27
Lib	28 Apr 1988	15:36	Ari	29 Aug 1988	03:29	Lib	30 Dec 1988	09:09
			Tau	31 Aug 1988	04:23			

Moon Signs

1989

Sco	1 Jan 1989	21:33	Ari	2 May 1989	11:50	Lib	2 Sep 1989	01:48
Sag	4 Jan 1989	07:11	Tau	4 May 1989	11:55	Sco	4 Sep 1989	14:23
Cap	6 Jan 1989	13:12	Gem	6 May 1989	12:04	Sag	7 Sep 1989	02:50
Aqu	8 Jan 1989	16:30	Can	8 May 1989	14:21	Cap	9 Sep 1989	13:12
Pis	10 Jan 1989	18:30	Leo	10 May 1989	20:23	Aqu	11 Sep 1989	20:01
Ari	12 Jan 1989	20:36	Vir	13 May 1989	06:30	Pis	13 Sep 1989	23:06
Tau	14 Jan 1989	23:36	Lib	15 May 1989	19:07	Ari	15 Sep 1989	23:38
Gem	17 Jan 1989	03:57	Sco	18 May 1989	07:47	Tau	17 Sep 1989	23:23
Can	19 Jan 1989	09:57	Sag	20 May 1989	18:51	Gem	20 Sep 1989	00:17
Leo	21 Jan 1989	18:02	Cap	23 May 1989	03:53	Can	22 Sep 1989	03:51
Vir	24 Jan 1989	04:32	Aqu	25 May 1989	11:00	Leo	24 Sep 1989	10:45
Lib	26 Jan 1989	17:01	Pis	27 May 1989	16:13	Vir	26 Sep 1989	20:32
Sco	29 Jan 1989	05:48	Ari	29 May 1989	19:25	Lib	29 Sep 1989	08:15
Sag	31 Jan 1989	16:29	Tau	31 May 1989	20:59			
Cap	2 Feb 1989	23:28	Gem	2 Jun 1989	22:03	Sco	1 Oct 1989	20:53
Aqu	5 Feb 1989	02:50	Can	5 Jun 1989	00:18	Sag	4 Oct 1989	09:29
Pis	7 Feb 1989	03:52	Leo	7 Jun 1989	05:28	Cap	6 Oct 1989	20:44
Ari	9 Feb 1989	04:18	Vir	9 Jun 1989	14:30	Aqu	9 Oct 1989	05:06
Tau	11 Feb 1989	05:45	Lib	12 Jun 1989	02:31	Pis	11 Oct 1989	09:36
Gem	13 Feb 1989	09:23	Sco	14 Jun 1989	15:11	Ari	13 Oct 1989	10:40
Can	15 Feb 1989	15:40	Sag	17 Jun 1989	02:11	Tau	15 Oct 1989	09:52
Leo	18 Feb 1989	00:33	Cap	19 Jun 1989	10:41	Gem	17 Oct 1989	09:20
Vir	20 Feb 1989	11:34	Aqu	21 Jun 1989	16:56	Can	19 Oct 1989	11:10
Lib	23 Feb 1989	00:05	Pis	23 Jun 1989	21:36	Leo	21 Oct 1989	16:48
Sco	25 Feb 1989	12:56	Ari	26 Jun 1989	01:06	Vir	24 Oct 1989	02:16
Sag	28 Feb 1989	00:28	Tau	28 Jun 1989	03:45	Lib	26 Oct 1989	14:11
			Gem	30 Jun 1989	06:08	Sco	29 Oct 1989	02:56
						Sag	31 Oct 1989	15:22
Cap	2 Mar 1989	08:56	Can	2 Jul 1989	09:19	Cap	3 Nov 1989	02:46
Aqu	4 Mar 1989	13:35	Leo	4 Jul 1989	14:38	Aqu	5 Nov 1989	12:08
Pis	6 Mar 1989	14:58	Vir	6 Jul 1989	23:05	Pis	7 Nov 1989	18:24
Ari	8 Mar 1989	14:36	Lib	9 Jul 1989	10:30	Ari	9 Nov 1989	21:07
Tau	10 Mar 1989	14:26	Sco	11 Jul 1989	23:09	Tau	11 Nov 1989	21:09
Gem	12 Mar 1989	16:17	Sag	14 Jul 1989	10:30	Gem	13 Nov 1989	20:19
Can	14 Mar 1989	21:28	Cap	16 Jul 1989	19:01	Can	15 Nov 1989	20:52
Leo	17 Mar 1989	06:13	Aqu	19 Jul 1989	00:34	Leo	18 Nov 1989	00:47
Vir	19 Mar 1989	17:39	Pis	21 Jul 1989	04:06	Vir	20 Nov 1989	08:55
Lib	22 Mar 1989	06:24	Ari	23 Jul 1989	06:40	Lib	22 Nov 1989	20:25
Sco	24 Mar 1989	19:10	Tau	25 Jul 1989	09:10	Sco	25 Nov 1989	09:13
Sag	27 Mar 1989	06:53	Gem	27 Jul 1989	12:15	Sag	27 Nov 1989	21:29
Cap	29 Mar 1989	16:24	Can	29 Jul 1989	16:32	Cap	30 Nov 1989	08:26
Aqu	31 Mar 1989	22:43	Leo	31 Jul 1989	22:42			
Pis	3 Apr 1989	01:36	Vir	3 Aug 1989	07:19	Aqu	2 Dec 1989	17:42
Ari	5 Apr 1989	01:50	Lib	5 Aug 1989	18:28	Pis	5 Dec 1989	00:47
Tau	7 Apr 1989	01:08	Sco	8 Aug 1989	07:05	Ari	7 Dec 1989	05:11
Gem	9 Apr 1989	01:32	Sag	10 Aug 1989	19:02	Tau	9 Dec 1989	06:58
Can	11 Apr 1989	04:58	Cap	13 Aug 1989	04:16	Gem	11 Dec 1989	07:15
Leo	13 Apr 1989	12:32	Aqu	15 Aug 1989	09:58	Can	13 Dec 1989	07:49
Vir	15 Apr 1989	23:40	Pis	17 Aug 1989	12:45	Leo	15 Dec 1989	10:42
Lib	18 Apr 1989	12:31	Ari	19 Aug 1989	13:59	Vir	17 Dec 1989	17:19
Sco	21 Apr 1989	01:12	Tau	21 Aug 1989	15:11	Lib	20 Dec 1989	03:46
Sag	23 Apr 1989	12:37	Gem	23 Aug 1989	17:39	Sco	22 Dec 1989	16:18
Cap	25 Apr 1989	22:14	Can	25 Aug 1989	22:14	Sag	25 Dec 1989	04:37
Aqu	28 Apr 1989	05:32	Leo	28 Aug 1989	05:12	Cap	27 Dec 1989	15:10
Pis	30 Apr 1989	10:02	Vir	30 Aug 1989	14:30	Aqu	29 Dec 1989	23:37

Moon Signs

1990

Pis	1 Jan 1990	06:10	Leo	1 May 1990	00:10	Aqu	1 Sep 1990	20:50
Ari	3 Jan 1990	10:56	Vir	3 May 1990	07:18	Pis	4 Sep 1990	04:05
Tau	5 Jan 1990	14:03	Lib	5 May 1990	17:28	Ari	6 Sep 1990	08:22
Gem	7 Jan 1990	16:01	Sco	8 May 1990	05:22	Tau	8 Sep 1990	10:55
Can	9 Jan 1990	17:52	Sag	10 May 1990	17:56	Gem	10 Sep 1990	13:05
Leo	11 Jan 1990	21:03	Cap	13 May 1990	06:21	Can	12 Sep 1990	15:53
Vir	14 Jan 1990	02:58	Aqu	15 May 1990	17:30	Leo	14 Sep 1990	19:52
Lib	16 Jan 1990	12:18	Pis	18 May 1990	01:52	Vir	17 Sep 1990	01:19
Sco	19 Jan 1990	00:16	Ari	20 May 1990	06:31	Lib	19 Sep 1990	08:34
Sag	21 Jan 1990	12:43	Tau	22 May 1990	07:42	Sco	21 Sep 1990	18:06
Cap	23 Jan 1990	23:26	Gem	24 May 1990	07:00	Sag	24 Sep 1990	05:52
Aqu	26 Jan 1990	07:24	Can	26 May 1990	06:34	Cap	26 Sep 1990	18:36
Pis	28 Jan 1990	12:50	Leo	28 May 1990	08:30	Aqu	29 Sep 1990	05:53
Ari	30 Jan 1990	16:34	Vir	30 May 1990	14:09			
Tau	1 Feb 1990	19:27	Lib	1 Jun 1990	23:31	Pis	1 Oct 1990	13:41
Gem	3 Feb 1990	22:12	Sco	4 Jun 1990	11:22	Ari	3 Oct 1990	17:41
Can	6 Feb 1990	01:27	Sag	6 Jun 1990	23:59	Tau	5 Oct 1990	19:06
Leo	8 Feb 1990	05:51	Cap	9 Jun 1990	12:11	Gem	7 Oct 1990	19:47
Vir	10 Feb 1990	12:14	Aqu	11 Jun 1990	23:08	Can	9 Oct 1990	21:30
Lib	12 Feb 1990	21:10	Pis	14 Jun 1990	07:59	Leo	12 Oct 1990	01:17
Sco	15 Feb 1990	08:34	Ari	16 Jun 1990	13:54	Vir	14 Oct 1990	07:21
Sag	17 Feb 1990	21:07	Tau	18 Jun 1990	16:42	Lib	16 Oct 1990	15:27
Cap	20 Feb 1990	08:29	Gem	20 Jun 1990	17:14	Sco	19 Oct 1990	01:24
Aqu	22 Feb 1990	16:52	Can	22 Jun 1990	17:09	Sag	21 Oct 1990	13:09
Pis	24 Feb 1990	21:48	Leo	24 Jun 1990	18:25	Cap	24 Oct 1990	02:02
Ari	27 Feb 1990	00:16	Vir	26 Jun 1990	22:43	Aqu	26 Oct 1990	14:13
			Lib	29 Jun 1990	06:47	Pis	28 Oct 1990	23:20
						Ari	31 Oct 1990	04:13
Tau	1 Mar 1990	01:43	Sco	1 Jul 1990	18:01	Tau	2 Nov 1990	05:31
Gem	3 Mar 1990	03:38	Sag	4 Jul 1990	06:35	Gem	4 Nov 1990	05:06
Can	5 Mar 1990	07:02	Cap	6 Jul 1990	18:39	Can	6 Nov 1990	05:07
Leo	7 Mar 1990	12:25	Aqu	9 Jul 1990	05:06	Leo	8 Nov 1990	07:24
Vir	9 Mar 1990	19:47	Pis	11 Jul 1990	13:28	Vir	10 Nov 1990	12:49
Lib	12 Mar 1990	05:09	Ari	13 Jul 1990	19:36	Lib	12 Nov 1990	21:09
Sco	14 Mar 1990	16:25	Tau	15 Jul 1990	23:28	Sco	15 Nov 1990	07:39
Sag	17 Mar 1990	04:56	Gem	18 Jul 1990	01:31	Sag	17 Nov 1990	19:39
Cap	19 Mar 1990	17:01	Can	20 Jul 1990	02:44	Cap	20 Nov 1990	08:31
Aqu	22 Mar 1990	02:30	Leo	22 Jul 1990	04:29	Aqu	22 Nov 1990	21:06
Pis	24 Mar 1990	08:08	Vir	24 Jul 1990	08:18	Pis	25 Nov 1990	07:31
Ari	26 Mar 1990	10:15	Lib	26 Jul 1990	15:19	Ari	27 Nov 1990	14:05
Tau	28 Mar 1990	10:26	Sco	29 Jul 1990	01:39	Tau	29 Nov 1990	16:37
Gem	30 Mar 1990	10:43	Sag	31 Jul 1990	14:00			
Can	1 Apr 1990	12:51	Cap	3 Aug 1990	02:08	Gem	1 Dec 1990	16:22
Leo	3 Apr 1990	17:50	Aqu	5 Aug 1990	12:18	Can	3 Dec 1990	15:28
Vir	6 Apr 1990	01:42	Pis	7 Aug 1990	19:54	Leo	5 Dec 1990	16:00
Lib	8 Apr 1990	11:45	Ari	10 Aug 1990	01:12	Vir	7 Dec 1990	19:39
Sco	10 Apr 1990	23:18	Tau	12 Aug 1990	04:54	Lib	10 Dec 1990	03:01
Sag	13 Apr 1990	11:48	Gem	14 Aug 1990	07:41	Sco	12 Dec 1990	13:28
Cap	16 Apr 1990	00:14	Can	16 Aug 1990	10:12	Sag	15 Dec 1990	01:44
Aqu	18 Apr 1990	10:51	Leo	18 Aug 1990	13:11	Cap	17 Dec 1990	14:34
Pis	20 Apr 1990	17:57	Vir	20 Aug 1990	17:33	Aqu	20 Dec 1990	02:59
Ari	22 Apr 1990	20:57	Lib	23 Aug 1990	00:18	Pis	22 Dec 1990	13:47
Tau	24 Apr 1990	21:02	Sco	25 Aug 1990	09:57	Ari	24 Dec 1990	21:44
Gem	26 Apr 1990	20:12	Sag	27 Aug 1990	21:57	Tau	27 Dec 1990	02:08
Can	28 Apr 1990	20:40	Cap	30 Aug 1990	10:22	Gem	29 Dec 1990	03:25
						Can	31 Dec 1990	03:02

Moon Signs

1991

Leo	2 Jan 1991	02:55	Cap	3 May 1991	03:55	Gem	1 Sep 1991	03:02
Vir	4 Jan 1991	04:57	Aqu	5 May 1991	16:51	Can	3 Sep 1991	06:19
Lib	6 Jan 1991	10:34	Pis	8 May 1991	04:03	Leo	5 Sep 1991	08:13
Sco	8 Jan 1991	19:59	Ari	10 May 1991	11:33	Vir	7 Sep 1991	09:35
Sag	11 Jan 1991	08:06	Tau	12 May 1991	15:07	Lib	9 Sep 1991	11:52
Cap	13 Jan 1991	21:00	Gem	14 May 1991	16:02	Sco	11 Sep 1991	16:43
Aqu	16 Jan 1991	09:04	Can	16 May 1991	16:14	Sag	14 Sep 1991	01:15
Pis	18 Jan 1991	19:23	Leo	18 May 1991	17:30	Cap	16 Sep 1991	13:04
Ari	21 Jan 1991	03:27	Vir	20 May 1991	21:01	Aqu	19 Sep 1991	01:57
Tau	23 Jan 1991	09:00	Lib	23 May 1991	03:08	Pis	21 Sep 1991	13:19
Gem	25 Jan 1991	12:06	Sco	25 May 1991	11:42	Ari	23 Sep 1991	21:55
Can	27 Jan 1991	13:23	Sag	27 May 1991	22:22	Tau	26 Sep 1991	03:59
Leo	29 Jan 1991	14:04	Cap	30 May 1991	10:41	Gem	28 Sep 1991	08:25
Vir	31 Jan 1991	15:44				Can	30 Sep 1991	11:58
Lib	2 Feb 1991	20:03	Aqu	1 Jun 1991	23:41	Leo	2 Oct 1991	14:58
Sco	5 Feb 1991	04:02	Pis	4 Jun 1991	11:35	Vir	4 Oct 1991	17:45
Sag	7 Feb 1991	15:23	Ari	6 Jun 1991	20:24	Lib	6 Oct 1991	21:01
Cap	10 Feb 1991	04:16	Tau	9 Jun 1991	01:11	Sco	9 Oct 1991	02:01
Aqu	12 Feb 1991	16:16	Gem	11 Jun 1991	02:36	Sag	11 Oct 1991	09:59
Pis	15 Feb 1991	01:58	Can	13 Jun 1991	02:17	Cap	13 Oct 1991	21:10
Ari	17 Feb 1991	09:11	Leo	15 Jun 1991	02:11	Aqu	16 Oct 1991	10:04
Tau	19 Feb 1991	14:24	Vir	17 Jun 1991	04:03	Pis	18 Oct 1991	21:52
Gem	21 Feb 1991	18:10	Lib	19 Jun 1991	09:02	Ari	21 Oct 1991	06:33
Can	23 Feb 1991	20:56	Sco	21 Jun 1991	17:19	Tau	23 Oct 1991	11:54
Leo	25 Feb 1991	23:13	Sag	24 Jun 1991	04:16	Gem	25 Oct 1991	15:08
Vir	28 Feb 1991	01:51	Cap	26 Jun 1991	16:49	Can	27 Oct 1991	17:37
			Aqu	29 Jun 1991	05:47	Leo	29 Oct 1991	20:20
						Vir	31 Oct 1991	23:47
Lib	2 Mar 1991	06:03	Pis	1 Jul 1991	17:51	Lib	3 Nov 1991	04:13
Sco	4 Mar 1991	13:09	Ari	4 Jul 1991	03:33	Sco	5 Nov 1991	10:09
Sag	6 Mar 1991	23:36	Tau	6 Jul 1991	09:51	Sag	7 Nov 1991	18:21
Cap	9 Mar 1991	12:14	Gem	8 Jul 1991	12:41	Cap	10 Nov 1991	05:16
Aqu	12 Mar 1991	00:30	Can	10 Jul 1991	13:02	Aqu	12 Nov 1991	18:06
Pis	14 Mar 1991	10:10	Leo	12 Jul 1991	12:35	Pis	15 Nov 1991	06:33
Ari	16 Mar 1991	16:37	Vir	14 Jul 1991	13:13	Ari	17 Nov 1991	16:07
Tau	18 Mar 1991	20:40	Lib	16 Jul 1991	16:35	Tau	19 Nov 1991	21:48
Gem	20 Mar 1991	23:37	Sco	18 Jul 1991	23:42	Gem	22 Nov 1991	00:22
Can	23 Mar 1991	02:27	Sag	21 Jul 1991	10:17	Can	24 Nov 1991	01:25
Leo	25 Mar 1991	05:43	Cap	23 Jul 1991	22:55	Leo	26 Nov 1991	02:38
Vir	27 Mar 1991	09:41	Aqu	26 Jul 1991	11:49	Vir	28 Nov 1991	05:12
Lib	29 Mar 1991	14:50	Pis	28 Jul 1991	23:34	Lib	30 Nov 1991	09:47
Sco	31 Mar 1991	22:02	Ari	31 Jul 1991	09:19			
Sag	3 Apr 1991	07:59	Tau	2 Aug 1991	16:31	Sco	2 Dec 1991	16:33
Cap	5 Apr 1991	20:20	Gem	4 Aug 1991	20:54	Sag	5 Dec 1991	01:33
Aqu	8 Apr 1991	08:59	Can	6 Aug 1991	22:46	Cap	7 Dec 1991	12:41
Pis	10 Apr 1991	19:17	Leo	8 Aug 1991	23:09	Aqu	10 Dec 1991	01:26
Ari	13 Apr 1991	01:48	Vir	10 Aug 1991	23:35	Pis	12 Dec 1991	14:18
Tau	15 Apr 1991	05:05	Lib	13 Aug 1991	01:53	Ari	15 Dec 1991	01:05
Gem	17 Apr 1991	06:41	Sco	15 Aug 1991	07:34	Tau	17 Dec 1991	08:09
Can	19 Apr 1991	08:18	Sag	17 Aug 1991	17:11	Gem	19 Dec 1991	11:20
Leo	21 Apr 1991	11:05	Cap	20 Aug 1991	05:34	Can	21 Dec 1991	11:54
Vir	23 Apr 1991	15:30	Aqu	22 Aug 1991	18:27	Leo	23 Dec 1991	11:39
Lib	25 Apr 1991	21:37	Pis	25 Aug 1991	05:51	Vir	25 Dec 1991	12:25
Sco	28 Apr 1991	05:34	Ari	27 Aug 1991	15:00	Lib	27 Dec 1991	15:38
Sag	30 Apr 1991	15:42	Tau	29 Aug 1991	21:59	Sco	29 Dec 1991	22:04

Moon Signs

1992

Sag	1 Jan 1992	07:30	Tau	1 May 1992	19:09	Sag	3 Sep 1992	00:52
Cap	3 Jan 1992	19:09	Gem	4 May 1992	00:28	Cap	5 Sep 1992	10:07
Aqu	6 Jan 1992	07:59	Can	6 May 1992	04:09	Aqu	7 Sep 1992	22:08
Pis	8 Jan 1992	20:52	Leo	8 May 1992	07:07	Pis	10 Sep 1992	10:56
Ari	11 Jan 1992	08:22	Vir	10 May 1992	09:56	Ari	12 Sep 1992	23:02
Tau	13 Jan 1992	17:00	Lib	12 May 1992	13:05	Tau	15 Sep 1992	09:47
Gem	15 Jan 1992	21:53	Sco	14 May 1992	17:15	Gem	17 Sep 1992	18:40
Can	17 Jan 1992	23:25	Sag	16 May 1992	23:23	Can	20 Sep 1992	00:58
Leo	19 Jan 1992	22:56	Cap	19 May 1992	08:13	Leo	22 Sep 1992	04:18
Vir	21 Jan 1992	22:23	Aqu	21 May 1992	19:44	Vir	24 Sep 1992	05:08
Lib	23 Jan 1992	23:44	Pis	24 May 1992	08:25	Lib	26 Sep 1992	04:55
Sco	26 Jan 1992	04:33	Ari	26 May 1992	19:52	Sco	28 Sep 1992	05:44
Sag	28 Jan 1992	13:21	Tau	29 May 1992	04:15	Sag	30 Sep 1992	09:35
Cap	31 Jan 1992	01:08	Gem	31 May 1992	09:18			
Aqu	2 Feb 1992	14:09	Can	2 Jun 1992	11:57	Cap	2 Oct 1992	17:29
Pis	5 Feb 1992	02:50	Leo	4 Jun 1992	13:35	Aqu	5 Oct 1992	04:53
Ari	7 Feb 1992	14:14	Vir	6 Jun 1992	15:28	Pis	7 Oct 1992	17:37
Tau	9 Feb 1992	23:35	Lib	8 Jun 1992	18:33	Ari	10 Oct 1992	05:36
Gem	12 Feb 1992	06:08	Sco	10 Jun 1992	23:27	Tau	12 Oct 1992	15:48
Can	14 Feb 1992	09:30	Sag	13 Jun 1992	06:29	Gem	15 Oct 1992	00:08
Leo	16 Feb 1992	10:14	Cap	15 Jun 1992	15:50	Can	17 Oct 1992	06:36
Vir	18 Feb 1992	09:47	Aqu	18 Jun 1992	03:19	Leo	19 Oct 1992	11:00
Lib	20 Feb 1992	10:05	Pis	20 Jun 1992	16:00	Vir	21 Oct 1992	13:27
Sco	22 Feb 1992	13:13	Ari	23 Jun 1992	04:03	Lib	23 Oct 1992	14:39
Sag	24 Feb 1992	20:27	Tau	25 Jun 1992	13:27	Sco	25 Oct 1992	16:05
Cap	27 Feb 1992	07:34	Gem	27 Jun 1992	19:13	Sag	27 Oct 1992	19:29
Aqu	29 Feb 1992	20:34	Can	29 Jun 1992	21:41	Cap	30 Oct 1992	02:19
Pis	3 Mar 1992	09:10	Leo	1 Jul 1992	22:15	Aqu	1 Nov 1992	12:44
Ari	5 Mar 1992	20:06	Vir	3 Jul 1992	22:38	Pis	4 Nov 1992	01:12
Tau	8 Mar 1992	05:05	Lib	6 Jul 1992	00:28	Ari	6 Nov 1992	13:19
Gem	10 Mar 1992	12:03	Sco	8 Jul 1992	04:54	Tau	8 Nov 1992	23:18
Can	12 Mar 1992	16:49	Sag	10 Jul 1992	12:18	Gem	11 Nov 1992	06:49
Leo	14 Mar 1992	19:20	Cap	12 Jul 1992	22:16	Can	13 Nov 1992	12:18
Vir	16 Mar 1992	20:13	Aqu	15 Jul 1992	10:03	Leo	15 Nov 1992	16:23
Lib	18 Mar 1992	20:55	Pis	17 Jul 1992	22:44	Vir	17 Nov 1992	19:28
Sco	20 Mar 1992	23:21	Ari	20 Jul 1992	11:07	Lib	19 Nov 1992	22:03
Sag	23 Mar 1992	05:13	Tau	22 Jul 1992	21:35	Sco	22 Nov 1992	00:52
Cap	25 Mar 1992	15:09	Gem	25 Jul 1992	04:44	Sag	24 Nov 1992	05:01
Aqu	28 Mar 1992	03:45	Can	27 Jul 1992	08:08	Cap	26 Nov 1992	11:39
Pis	30 Mar 1992	16:23	Leo	29 Jul 1992	08:39	Aqu	28 Nov 1992	21:20
			Vir	31 Jul 1992	08:01			
Ari	2 Apr 1992	03:03	Lib	2 Aug 1992	08:18	Pis	1 Dec 1992	09:23
Tau	4 Apr 1992	11:17	Sco	4 Aug 1992	11:17	Ari	3 Dec 1992	21:48
Gem	6 Apr 1992	17:33	Sag	6 Aug 1992	17:57	Tau	6 Dec 1992	08:16
Can	8 Apr 1992	22:18	Cap	9 Aug 1992	04:01	Gem	8 Dec 1992	15:36
Leo	11 Apr 1992	01:46	Aqu	11 Aug 1992	16:07	Can	10 Dec 1992	20:05
Vir	13 Apr 1992	04:09	Pis	14 Aug 1992	04:51	Leo	12 Dec 1992	22:47
Lib	15 Apr 1992	06:10	Ari	16 Aug 1992	17:11	Vir	15 Dec 1992	00:56
Sco	17 Apr 1992	09:10	Tau	19 Aug 1992	04:09	Lib	17 Dec 1992	03:33
Sag	19 Apr 1992	14:41	Gem	21 Aug 1992	12:35	Sco	19 Dec 1992	07:20
Cap	21 Apr 1992	23:41	Can	23 Aug 1992	17:36	Sag	21 Dec 1992	12:43
Aqu	24 Apr 1992	11:39	Leo	25 Aug 1992	19:15	Cap	23 Dec 1992	20:05
Pis	27 Apr 1992	00:19	Vir	27 Aug 1992	18:46	Aqu	26 Dec 1992	05:43
Ari	29 Apr 1992	11:12	Lib	29 Aug 1992	18:11	Pis	28 Dec 1992	17:28
			Sco	31 Aug 1992	19:39	Ari	31 Dec 1992	06:07

Moon Signs

1993

Tau	2 Jan 1993	17:30	Lib	3 May 1993	01:19	Ari	2 Sep 1993	21:21
Gem	5 Jan 1993	01:41	Sco	5 May 1993	01:57	Tau	5 Sep 1993	10:09
Can	7 Jan 1993	06:10	Sag	7 May 1993	03:35	Gem	7 Sep 1993	22:15
Leo	9 Jan 1993	07:49	Cap	9 May 1993	07:51	Can	10 Sep 1993	07:36
Vir	11 Jan 1993	08:21	Aqu	11 May 1993	15:44	Leo	12 Sep 1993	12:50
Lib	13 Jan 1993	09:31	Pis	14 May 1993	02:51	Vir	14 Sep 1993	14:19
Sco	15 Jan 1993	12:43	Ari	16 May 1993	15:24	Lib	16 Sep 1993	13:44
Sag	17 Jan 1993	18:31	Tau	19 May 1993	03:16	Sco	18 Sep 1993	13:15
Cap	20 Jan 1993	02:47	Gem	21 May 1993	13:06	Sag	20 Sep 1993	14:54
Aqu	22 Jan 1993	13:01	Can	23 May 1993	20:38	Cap	22 Sep 1993	19:54
Pis	25 Jan 1993	00:48	Leo	26 May 1993	02:02	Aqu	25 Sep 1993	04:19
Ari	27 Jan 1993	13:28	Vir	28 May 1993	05:46	Pis	27 Sep 1993	15:13
Tau	30 Jan 1993	01:36	Lib	30 May 1993	08:18	Ari	30 Sep 1993	03:29
Gem	1 Feb 1993	11:13	Sco	1 Jun 1993	10:23	Tau	2 Oct 1993	16:13
Can	3 Feb 1993	16:56	Sag	3 Jun 1993	13:02	Gem	5 Oct 1993	04:26
Leo	5 Feb 1993	18:51	Cap	5 Jun 1993	17:26	Can	7 Oct 1993	14:41
Vir	7 Feb 1993	18:29	Aqu	8 Jun 1993	00:40	Leo	9 Oct 1993	21:32
Lib	9 Feb 1993	17:58	Pis	10 Jun 1993	10:57	Vir	12 Oct 1993	00:34
Sco	11 Feb 1993	19:24	Ari	12 Jun 1993	23:14	Lib	14 Oct 1993	00:47
Sag	14 Feb 1993	00:09	Tau	15 Jun 1993	11:18	Sco	16 Oct 1993	00:01
Cap	16 Feb 1993	08:21	Gem	17 Jun 1993	21:11	Sag	18 Oct 1993	00:24
Aqu	18 Feb 1993	19:05	Can	20 Jun 1993	04:05	Cap	20 Oct 1993	03:43
Pis	21 Feb 1993	07:12	Leo	22 Jun 1993	08:26	Aqu	22 Oct 1993	10:50
Ari	23 Feb 1993	19:50	Vir	24 Jun 1993	11:18	Pis	24 Oct 1993	21:18
Tau	26 Feb 1993	08:11	Lib	26 Jun 1993	13:46	Ari	27 Oct 1993	09:39
Gem	28 Feb 1993	18:52	Sco	28 Jun 1993	16:37	Tau	29 Oct 1993	22:20
			Sag	30 Jun 1993	20:28			
Can	3 Mar 1993	02:15	Cap	3 Jul 1993	01:49	Gem	1 Nov 1993	10:12
Vir	7 Mar 1993	05:52	Aqu	5 Jul 1993	09:15	Can	3 Nov 1993	20:24
Lib	9 Mar 1993	04:46	Pis	7 Jul 1993	19:10	Leo	6 Nov 1993	04:06
Sco	11 Mar 1993	04:40	Ari	10 Jul 1993	07:11	Vir	8 Nov 1993	08:46
Sag	13 Mar 1993	07:34	Tau	12 Jul 1993	19:37	Lib	10 Nov 1993	10:41
Cap	15 Mar 1993	14:29	Gem	15 Jul 1993	06:06	Sco	12 Nov 1993	10:59
Aqu	18 Mar 1993	00:53	Can	17 Jul 1993	13:06	Sag	14 Nov 1993	11:21
Pis	20 Mar 1993	13:11	Leo	19 Jul 1993	16:47	Cap	16 Nov 1993	13:35
Ari	23 Mar 1993	01:51	Vir	21 Jul 1993	18:24	Aqu	18 Nov 1993	19:08
Tau	25 Mar 1993	13:59	Lib	23 Jul 1993	19:40	Pis	21 Nov 1993	04:28
Gem	28 Mar 1993	00:47	Sco	25 Jul 1993	22:01	Ari	23 Nov 1993	16:30
Can	30 Mar 1993	09:13	Sag	28 Jul 1993	02:13	Tau	26 Nov 1993	05:14
			Cap	30 Jul 1993	08:27	Gem	28 Nov 1993	16:47
Leo	1 Apr 1993	14:20	Aqu	1 Aug 1993	16:37	Can	1 Dec 1993	02:16
Vir	3 Apr 1993	16:10	Pis	4 Aug 1993	02:44	Leo	3 Dec 1993	09:32
Lib	5 Apr 1993	15:54	Ari	6 Aug 1993	14:39	Vir	5 Dec 1993	14:42
Sco	7 Apr 1993	15:32	Tau	9 Aug 1993	03:22	Lib	7 Dec 1993	18:03
Sag	9 Apr 1993	17:10	Gem	11 Aug 1993	14:46	Sco	9 Dec 1993	20:04
Cap	11 Apr 1993	22:25	Can	13 Aug 1993	22:45	Sag	11 Dec 1993	21:39
Aqu	14 Apr 1993	07:36	Leo	16 Aug 1993	02:42	Cap	14 Dec 1993	00:07
Pis	16 Apr 1993	19:33	Vir	18 Aug 1993	03:40	Aqu	16 Dec 1993	04:52
Ari	19 Apr 1993	08:14	Lib	20 Aug 1993	03:35	Pis	18 Dec 1993	13:00
Tau	21 Apr 1993	20:07	Sco	22 Aug 1993	04:28	Ari	21 Dec 1993	00:19
Gem	24 Apr 1993	06:27	Sag	24 Aug 1993	07:46	Tau	23 Dec 1993	13:04
Can	26 Apr 1993	14:45	Cap	26 Aug 1993	13:58	Gem	26 Dec 1993	00:45
Leo	28 Apr 1993	20:39	Aqu	28 Aug 1993	22:42	Can	28 Dec 1993	09:45
Vir	30 Apr 1993	23:59	Pis	31 Aug 1993	09:19	Leo	30 Dec 1993	15:59

Moon Signs

1994

Vir	1 Jan 1994	20:14	Aqu	1 May 1994	16:35	Leo	2 Sep 1994	15:36
Lib	3 Jan 1994	23:31	Pis	4 May 1994	00:48	Vir	4 Sep 1994	20:33
Sco	6 Jan 1994	02:29	Ari	6 May 1994	12:02	Lib	6 Sep 1994	22:56
Sag	8 Jan 1994	05:34	Tau	9 May 1994	00:50	Sco	9 Sep 1994	00:26
Cap	10 Jan 1994	09:16	Gem	11 May 1994	13:43	Sag	11 Sep 1994	02:25
Aqu	12 Jan 1994	14:26	Can	14 May 1994	01:26	Cap	13 Sep 1994	05:44
Pis	14 Jan 1994	22:04	Leo	16 May 1994	10:57	Aqu	15 Sep 1994	10:43
Ari	17 Jan 1994	08:42	Vir	18 May 1994	17:30	Pis	17 Sep 1994	17:31
Tau	19 Jan 1994	21:22	Lib	20 May 1994	20:54	Ari	20 Sep 1994	02:30
Gem	22 Jan 1994	09:34	Sco	22 May 1994	21:50	Tau	22 Sep 1994	13:48
Can	24 Jan 1994	18:55	Sag	24 May 1994	21:43	Gem	25 Sep 1994	02:41
Leo	27 Jan 1994	00:37	Cap	26 May 1994	22:18	Can	27 Sep 1994	15:11
Vir	29 Jan 1994	03:38	Aqu	29 May 1994	01:20	Leo	30 Sep 1994	00:54
Lib	31 Jan 1994	05:34	Pis	31 May 1994	08:04			
Sco	2 Feb 1994	07:49	Ari	2 Jun 1994	18:31	Vir	2 Oct 1994	06:39
Sag	4 Feb 1994	11:15	Tau	5 Jun 1994	07:14	Lib	4 Oct 1994	08:55
Cap	6 Feb 1994	16:02	Gem	7 Jun 1994	20:03	Sco	6 Oct 1994	09:22
Aqu	8 Feb 1994	22:17	Can	10 Jun 1994	07:21	Sag	8 Oct 1994	09:47
Pis	11 Feb 1994	06:23	Leo	12 Jun 1994	16:28	Cap	10 Oct 1994	11:45
Ari	13 Feb 1994	16:49	Vir	14 Jun 1994	23:15	Aqu	12 Oct 1994	16:10
Tau	16 Feb 1994	05:20	Lib	17 Jun 1994	03:47	Pis	14 Oct 1994	23:19
Gem	18 Feb 1994	18:05	Sco	19 Jun 1994	06:20	Ari	17 Oct 1994	08:56
Can	21 Feb 1994	04:27	Sag	21 Jun 1994	07:32	Tau	19 Oct 1994	20:34
Leo	23 Feb 1994	10:46	Cap	23 Jun 1994	08:37	Gem	22 Oct 1994	09:27
Vir	25 Feb 1994	13:26	Aqu	25 Jun 1994	11:10	Can	24 Oct 1994	22:15
Lib	27 Feb 1994	14:06	Pis	27 Jun 1994	16:44	Leo	27 Oct 1994	09:04
			Ari	30 Jun 1994	02:07	Vir	29 Oct 1994	16:20
						Lib	31 Oct 1994	19:45
Sco	1 Mar 1994	14:43	Tau	2 Jul 1994	14:23	Sco	2 Nov 1994	20:19
Sag	3 Mar 1994	16:54	Gem	5 Jul 1994	03:12	Sag	4 Nov 1994	19:46
Cap	5 Mar 1994	21:25	Can	7 Jul 1994	14:17	Cap	6 Nov 1994	20:02
Aqu	8 Mar 1994	04:15	Leo	9 Jul 1994	22:42	Aqu	8 Nov 1994	22:49
Pis	10 Mar 1994	13:10	Vir	12 Jul 1994	04:48	Pis	11 Nov 1994	05:04
Ari	12 Mar 1994	23:59	Lib	14 Jul 1994	09:14	Ari	13 Nov 1994	14:44
Tau	15 Mar 1994	12:27	Sco	16 Jul 1994	12:34	Tau	16 Nov 1994	02:44
Gem	18 Mar 1994	01:28	Sag	18 Jul 1994	15:09	Gem	18 Nov 1994	15:41
Can	20 Mar 1994	12:52	Cap	20 Jul 1994	17:30	Can	21 Nov 1994	04:21
Leo	22 Mar 1994	20:38	Aqu	22 Jul 1994	20:39	Leo	23 Nov 1994	15:32
Vir	25 Mar 1994	00:12	Pis	25 Jul 1994	01:57	Vir	26 Nov 1994	00:07
Lib	27 Mar 1994	00:46	Ari	27 Jul 1994	10:31	Lib	28 Nov 1994	05:22
Sco	29 Mar 1994	00:15	Tau	29 Jul 1994	22:13	Sco	30 Nov 1994	07:21
Sag	31 Mar 1994	00:42						
Cap	2 Apr 1994	03:38	Gem	1 Aug 1994	11:04	Sag	2 Dec 1994	07:13
Aqu	4 Apr 1994	09:46	Can	3 Aug 1994	22:21	Cap	4 Dec 1994	06:42
Pis	6 Apr 1994	18:51	Leo	6 Aug 1994	06:31	Aqu	6 Dec 1994	07:52
Ari	9 Apr 1994	06:09	Vir	8 Aug 1994	11:41	Pis	8 Dec 1994	12:25
Tau	11 Apr 1994	18:47	Lib	10 Aug 1994	15:06	Ari	10 Dec 1994	21:04
Gem	14 Apr 1994	07:47	Sco	12 Aug 1994	17:56	Tau	13 Dec 1994	08:56
Can	16 Apr 1994	19:40	Sag	14 Aug 1994	20:53	Gem	15 Dec 1994	21:59
Leo	19 Apr 1994	04:44	Cap	17 Aug 1994	00:18	Can	18 Dec 1994	10:24
Vir	21 Apr 1994	09:57	Aqu	19 Aug 1994	04:34	Leo	20 Dec 1994	21:12
Lib	23 Apr 1994	11:39	Pis	21 Aug 1994	10:28	Vir	23 Dec 1994	06:01
Sco	25 Apr 1994	11:18	Ari	23 Aug 1994	18:55	Lib	25 Dec 1994	12:26
Sag	27 Apr 1994	10:49	Tau	26 Aug 1994	06:13	Sco	27 Dec 1994	16:17
Cap	29 Apr 1994	12:06	Gem	28 Aug 1994	19:07	Sag	29 Dec 1994	17:45
			Can	31 Aug 1994	07:00	Cap	31 Dec 1994	17:57

Moon Signs

1995

Aqu	2 Jan 1995	18:39	Gem	1 May 1995	11:53	Sag	1 Sep 1995	16:56
Pis	4 Jan 1995	21:50	Can	4 May 1995	00:44	Cap	3 Sep 1995	19:44
Ari	7 Jan 1995	04:57	Leo	6 May 1995	12:54	Aqu	5 Sep 1995	21:47
Tau	9 Jan 1995	15:58	Vir	8 May 1995	22:32	Pis	8 Sep 1995	00:09
Gem	12 Jan 1995	04:57	Lib	11 May 1995	04:29	Ari	10 Sep 1995	04:14
Can	14 Jan 1995	17:20	Sco	13 May 1995	06:53	Tau	12 Sep 1995	11:22
Leo	17 Jan 1995	03:36	Sag	15 May 1995	06:58	Gem	14 Sep 1995	21:48
Vir	19 Jan 1995	11:39	Cap	17 May 1995	06:35	Can	17 Sep 1995	10:15
Lib	21 Jan 1995	17:53	Aqu	19 May 1995	07:40	Leo	19 Sep 1995	22:19
Sco	23 Jan 1995	22:31	Pis	21 May 1995	11:41	Vir	22 Sep 1995	08:01
Sag	26 Jan 1995	01:36	Ari	23 May 1995	19:13	Lib	24 Sep 1995	14:49
Cap	28 Jan 1995	03:26	Tau	26 May 1995	05:46	Sco	26 Sep 1995	19:20
Aqu	30 Jan 1995	05:03	Gem	28 May 1995	18:07	Sag	28 Sep 1995	22:30
			Can	31 May 1995	06:59			
Pis	1 Feb 1995	08:06	Leo	2 Jun 1995	19:17	Cap	1 Oct 1995	01:10
Ari	3 Feb 1995	14:13	Vir	5 Jun 1995	05:46	Aqu	3 Oct 1995	03:59
Tau	6 Feb 1995	00:09	Lib	7 Jun 1995	13:11	Pis	5 Oct 1995	07:35
Gem	8 Feb 1995	12:43	Sco	9 Jun 1995	17:03	Ari	7 Oct 1995	12:42
Can	11 Feb 1995	01:16	Sag	11 Jun 1995	17:49	Tau	9 Oct 1995	20:05
Leo	13 Feb 1995	11:30	Cap	13 Jun 1995	17:05	Gem	12 Oct 1995	06:09
Vir	15 Feb 1995	18:51	Aqu	15 Jun 1995	16:52	Can	14 Oct 1995	18:20
Lib	18 Feb 1995	00:00	Pis	17 Jun 1995	19:13	Leo	17 Oct 1995	06:46
Sco	20 Feb 1995	03:55	Ari	20 Jun 1995	01:30	Vir	19 Oct 1995	17:11
Sag	22 Feb 1995	07:12	Tau	22 Jun 1995	11:36	Lib	22 Oct 1995	00:14
Cap	24 Feb 1995	10:10	Gem	25 Jun 1995	00:02	Sco	24 Oct 1995	04:06
Aqu	26 Feb 1995	13:14	Can	27 Jun 1995	12:56	Sag	26 Oct 1995	05:56
Pis	28 Feb 1995	17:16	Leo	30 Jun 1995	01:01	Cap	28 Oct 1995	07:15
						Aqu	30 Oct 1995	09:24
Ari	2 Mar 1995	23:31	Vir	2 Jul 1995	11:35	Pis	1 Nov 1995	13:18
Tau	5 Mar 1995	08:51	Lib	4 Jul 1995	19:54	Ari	3 Nov 1995	19:21
Gem	7 Mar 1995	20:55	Sco	7 Jul 1995	01:17	Tau	6 Nov 1995	03:35
Can	10 Mar 1995	09:40	Sag	9 Jul 1995	03:37	Gem	8 Nov 1995	13:55
Leo	12 Mar 1995	20:27	Cap	11 Jul 1995	03:43	Can	11 Nov 1995	01:57
Vir	15 Mar 1995	03:54	Aqu	13 Jul 1995	03:21	Leo	13 Nov 1995	14:37
Lib	17 Mar 1995	08:17	Pis	15 Jul 1995	04:37	Vir	16 Nov 1995	02:01
Sco	19 Mar 1995	10:52	Ari	17 Jul 1995	09:24	Lib	18 Nov 1995	10:16
Sag	21 Mar 1995	12:57	Tau	19 Jul 1995	18:20	Sco	20 Nov 1995	14:39
Cap	23 Mar 1995	15:31	Gem	22 Jul 1995	06:23	Sag	22 Nov 1995	15:56
Aqu	25 Mar 1995	19:09	Can	24 Jul 1995	19:16	Cap	24 Nov 1995	15:48
Pis	28 Mar 1995	00:18	Leo	27 Jul 1995	07:06	Aqu	26 Nov 1995	16:15
Ari	30 Mar 1995	07:26	Vir	29 Jul 1995	17:12	Pis	28 Nov 1995	18:59
Tau	1 Apr 1995	16:58	Lib	1 Aug 1995	01:23	Ari	1 Dec 1995	00:52
Gem	4 Apr 1995	04:49	Sco	3 Aug 1995	07:29	Tau	3 Dec 1995	09:40
Can	6 Apr 1995	17:40	Sag	5 Aug 1995	11:13	Gem	5 Dec 1995	20:34
Leo	9 Apr 1995	05:15	Cap	7 Aug 1995	12:51	Can	8 Dec 1995	08:44
Vir	11 Apr 1995	13:37	Aqu	9 Aug 1995	13:28	Leo	10 Dec 1995	21:24
Lib	13 Apr 1995	18:20	Pis	11 Aug 1995	14:47	Vir	13 Dec 1995	09:26
Sco	15 Apr 1995	20:12	Ari	13 Aug 1995	18:41	Lib	15 Dec 1995	19:08
Sag	17 Apr 1995	20:51	Tau	16 Aug 1995	02:26	Sco	18 Dec 1995	01:05
Cap	19 Apr 1995	21:54	Gem	18 Aug 1995	13:40	Sag	20 Dec 1995	03:12
Aqu	22 Apr 1995	00:39	Can	21 Aug 1995	02:23	Cap	22 Dec 1995	02:46
Pis	24 Apr 1995	05:50	Leo	23 Aug 1995	14:12	Aqu	24 Dec 1995	01:52
Ari	26 Apr 1995	13:41	Vir	25 Aug 1995	23:50	Pis	26 Dec 1995	02:46
Tau	28 Apr 1995	23:53	Lib	28 Aug 1995	07:15	Ari	28 Dec 1995	07:06
			Sco	30 Aug 1995	12:50	Tau	30 Dec 1995	15:21

Moon Signs

1996

Gem	2 Jan 1996	02:29	Sco	2 May 1996	12:41	Tau	1 Sep 1996	12:21
Can	4 Jan 1996	14:56	Sag	4 May 1996	16:04	Gem	3 Sep 1996	19:08
Leo	7 Jan 1996	03:30	Cap	6 May 1996	17:53	Can	6 Sep 1996	05:29
Vir	9 Jan 1996	15:29	Aqu	8 May 1996	19:39	Leo	8 Sep 1996	17:54
Lib	12 Jan 1996	01:54	Pis	10 May 1996	22:29	Vir	11 Sep 1996	06:28
Sco	14 Jan 1996	09:29	Ari	13 May 1996	03:00	Lib	13 Sep 1996	17:51
Sag	16 Jan 1996	13:23	Tau	15 May 1996	09:24	Sco	16 Sep 1996	03:19
Cap	18 Jan 1996	14:06	Gem	17 May 1996	17:47	Sag	18 Sep 1996	10:29
Aqu	20 Jan 1996	13:14	Can	20 May 1996	04:16	Cap	20 Sep 1996	15:11
Pis	22 Jan 1996	13:03	Leo	22 May 1996	16:28	Aqu	22 Sep 1996	17:39
Ari	24 Jan 1996	15:37	Vir	25 May 1996	04:58	Pis	24 Sep 1996	18:43
Tau	26 Jan 1996	22:17	Lib	27 May 1996	15:32	Ari	26 Sep 1996	19:45
Gem	29 Jan 1996	08:42	Sco	29 May 1996	22:29	Tau	28 Sep 1996	22:24
Can	31 Jan 1996	21:10						
Leo	3 Feb 1996	09:45	Sag	1 Jun 1996	01:41	Gem	1 Oct 1996	04:02
Vir	5 Feb 1996	21:22	Cap	3 Jun 1996	02:28	Can	3 Oct 1996	13:15
Lib	8 Feb 1996	07:29	Aqu	5 Jun 1996	02:45	Leo	6 Oct 1996	01:11
Sco	10 Feb 1996	15:34	Pis	7 Jun 1996	04:19	Vir	8 Oct 1996	13:48
Sag	12 Feb 1996	20:57	Ari	9 Jun 1996	08:23	Lib	11 Oct 1996	00:59
Cap	14 Feb 1996	23:28	Tau	11 Jun 1996	15:11	Sco	13 Oct 1996	09:44
Aqu	16 Feb 1996	23:59	Gem	14 Jun 1996	00:16	Sag	15 Oct 1996	16:06
Pis	19 Feb 1996	00:09	Can	16 Jun 1996	11:08	Cap	17 Oct 1996	20:36
Ari	21 Feb 1996	01:59	Leo	18 Jun 1996	23:21	Aqu	19 Oct 1996	23:50
Tau	23 Feb 1996	07:08	Vir	21 Jun 1996	12:06	Pis	22 Oct 1996	02:22
Gem	25 Feb 1996	16:14	Lib	23 Jun 1996	23:36	Ari	24 Oct 1996	04:50
Can	28 Feb 1996	04:10	Sco	26 Jun 1996	07:52	Tau	26 Oct 1996	08:11
			Sag	28 Jun 1996	11:59	Gem	28 Oct 1996	13:35
			Cap	30 Jun 1996	12:46	Can	30 Oct 1996	21:57
Leo	1 Mar 1996	16:47	Aqu	2 Jul 1996	12:05	Leo	2 Nov 1996	09:16
Vir	4 Mar 1996	04:12	Pis	4 Jul 1996	12:07	Vir	4 Nov 1996	21:56
Lib	6 Mar 1996	13:39	Ari	6 Jul 1996	14:42	Lib	7 Nov 1996	09:27
Sco	8 Mar 1996	21:04	Tau	8 Jul 1996	20:44	Sco	9 Nov 1996	18:01
Sag	11 Mar 1996	02:31	Gem	11 Jul 1996	05:52	Sag	11 Nov 1996	23:25
Cap	13 Mar 1996	06:07	Can	13 Jul 1996	17:08	Cap	14 Nov 1996	02:43
Aqu	15 Mar 1996	08:15	Leo	16 Jul 1996	05:31	Aqu	16 Nov 1996	05:14
Pis	17 Mar 1996	09:50	Vir	18 Jul 1996	18:16	Pis	18 Nov 1996	08:00
Ari	19 Mar 1996	12:16	Lib	21 Jul 1996	06:13	Ari	20 Nov 1996	11:34
Tau	21 Mar 1996	16:59	Sco	23 Jul 1996	15:42	Tau	22 Nov 1996	16:12
Gem	24 Mar 1996	01:00	Sag	25 Jul 1996	21:22	Gem	24 Nov 1996	22:20
Can	26 Mar 1996	12:06	Cap	27 Jul 1996	23:16	Can	27 Nov 1996	06:37
Leo	29 Mar 1996	00:36	Aqu	29 Jul 1996	22:47	Leo	29 Nov 1996	17:29
Vir	31 Mar 1996	12:13	Pis	31 Jul 1996	22:01			
Lib	2 Apr 1996	21:25	Ari	2 Aug 1996	23:06	Vir	2 Dec 1996	06:10
Sco	5 Apr 1996	03:56	Tau	5 Aug 1996	03:34	Lib	4 Dec 1996	18:23
Sag	7 Apr 1996	08:21	Gem	7 Aug 1996	11:49	Sco	7 Dec 1996	03:37
Cap	9 Apr 1996	11:29	Can	9 Aug 1996	22:57	Sag	9 Dec 1996	08:57
Aqu	11 Apr 1996	14:09	Leo	12 Aug 1996	11:29	Cap	11 Dec 1996	11:13
Pis	13 Apr 1996	16:59	Vir	15 Aug 1996	00:07	Aqu	13 Dec 1996	12:14
Ari	15 Apr 1996	20:43	Lib	17 Aug 1996	11:54	Pis	15 Dec 1996	13:44
Tau	18 Apr 1996	02:06	Sco	19 Aug 1996	21:49	Ari	17 Dec 1996	16:55
Gem	20 Apr 1996	09:54	Sag	22 Aug 1996	04:47	Tau	19 Dec 1996	22:10
Can	22 Apr 1996	20:25	Cap	24 Aug 1996	08:21	Gem	22 Dec 1996	05:17
Leo	25 Apr 1996	08:44	Aqu	26 Aug 1996	09:10	Can	24 Dec 1996	14:14
Vir	27 Apr 1996	20:48	Pis	28 Aug 1996	08:49	Leo	27 Dec 1996	01:09
Lib	30 Apr 1996	06:26	Ari	30 Aug 1996	09:15	Vir	29 Dec 1996	13:44

1997

Sign	Date	Time	Sign	Date	Time	Sign	Date	Time
Lib	1 Jan 1997	02:31	Pis	1 May 1997	12:49	Vir	1 Sep 1997	04:27
Sco	3 Jan 1997	13:00	Ari	3 May 1997	14:59	Lib	3 Sep 1997	17:29
Sag	5 Jan 1997	19:26	Tau	5 May 1997	17:04	Sco	6 Sep 1997	06:09
Cap	7 Jan 1997	21:53	Gem	7 May 1997	20:21	Sag	8 Sep 1997	16:53
Aqu	9 Jan 1997	21:59	Can	10 May 1997	02:13	Cap	11 Sep 1997	00:21
Pis	11 Jan 1997	21:51	Leo	12 May 1997	11:33	Aqu	13 Sep 1997	04:09
Ari	13 Jan 1997	23:22	Vir	14 May 1997	23:43	Pis	15 Sep 1997	04:58
Tau	16 Jan 1997	03:40	Lib	17 May 1997	12:26	Ari	17 Sep 1997	04:24
Gem	18 Jan 1997	10:53	Sco	19 May 1997	23:10	Tau	19 Sep 1997	04:21
Can	20 Jan 1997	20:28	Sag	22 May 1997	06:50	Gem	21 Sep 1997	06:38
Leo	23 Jan 1997	07:50	Cap	24 May 1997	11:50	Can	23 Sep 1997	12:34
Vir	25 Jan 1997	20:26	Aqu	26 May 1997	15:19	Leo	25 Sep 1997	22:13
Lib	28 Jan 1997	09:20	Pis	28 May 1997	18:17	Vir	28 Sep 1997	10:27
Sco	30 Jan 1997	20:47	Ari	30 May 1997	21:17	Lib	30 Sep 1997	23:32
Sag	2 Feb 1997	04:50	Tau	2 Jun 1997	00:39	Sco	3 Oct 1997	11:56
Cap	4 Feb 1997	08:43	Gem	4 Jun 1997	04:54	Sag	5 Oct 1997	22:41
Aqu	6 Feb 1997	09:20	Can	6 Jun 1997	11:02	Cap	8 Oct 1997	07:03
Pis	8 Feb 1997	08:33	Leo	8 Jun 1997	19:58	Aqu	10 Oct 1997	12:27
Ari	10 Feb 1997	08:29	Vir	11 Jun 1997	07:43	Pis	12 Oct 1997	14:58
Tau	12 Feb 1997	10:57	Lib	13 Jun 1997	20:35	Ari	14 Oct 1997	15:24
Gem	14 Feb 1997	16:53	Sco	16 Jun 1997	07:50	Tau	16 Oct 1997	15:16
Can	17 Feb 1997	02:13	Sag	18 Jun 1997	15:38	Gem	18 Oct 1997	16:26
Leo	19 Feb 1997	13:52	Cap	20 Jun 1997	20:01	Can	20 Oct 1997	20:46
Vir	22 Feb 1997	02:38	Aqu	22 Jun 1997	22:20	Leo	23 Oct 1997	05:10
Lib	24 Feb 1997	15:22	Pis	25 Jun 1997	00:09	Vir	25 Oct 1997	16:59
Sco	27 Feb 1997	02:55	Ari	27 Jun 1997	02:38	Lib	28 Oct 1997	06:04
			Tau	29 Jun 1997	06:23	Sco	30 Oct 1997	18:15
Sag	1 Mar 1997	11:59	Gem	1 Jul 1997	11:35	Sag	2 Nov 1997	04:26
Cap	3 Mar 1997	17:38	Can	3 Jul 1997	18:32	Cap	4 Nov 1997	12:30
Aqu	5 Mar 1997	19:53	Leo	6 Jul 1997	03:45	Aqu	6 Nov 1997	18:33
Pis	7 Mar 1997	19:56	Vir	8 Jul 1997	15:21	Pis	8 Nov 1997	22:33
Ari	9 Mar 1997	19:32	Lib	11 Jul 1997	04:20	Ari	11 Nov 1997	00:43
Tau	11 Mar 1997	20:38	Sco	13 Jul 1997	16:20	Tau	13 Nov 1997	01:45
Gem	14 Mar 1997	00:49	Sag	16 Jul 1997	01:01	Gem	15 Nov 1997	03:05
Can	16 Mar 1997	08:51	Cap	18 Jul 1997	05:45	Can	17 Nov 1997	06:32
Leo	18 Mar 1997	20:08	Aqu	20 Jul 1997	07:28	Leo	19 Nov 1997	13:38
Vir	21 Mar 1997	08:59	Pis	22 Jul 1997	07:59	Vir	22 Nov 1997	00:33
Lib	23 Mar 1997	21:34	Ari	24 Jul 1997	09:03	Lib	24 Nov 1997	13:29
Sco	26 Mar 1997	08:41	Tau	26 Jul 1997	11:54	Sco	27 Nov 1997	01:42
Sag	28 Mar 1997	17:39	Gem	28 Jul 1997	17:04	Sag	29 Nov 1997	11:27
Cap	31 Mar 1997	00:05	Can	31 Jul 1997	00:38			
Aqu	2 Apr 1997	03:58	Leo	2 Aug 1997	10:27	Cap	1 Dec 1997	18:38
Pis	4 Apr 1997	05:42	Vir	4 Aug 1997	22:15	Aqu	3 Dec 1997	23:57
Ari	6 Apr 1997	06:19	Lib	7 Aug 1997	11:16	Pis	6 Dec 1997	04:06
Tau	8 Apr 1997	07:20	Sco	9 Aug 1997	23:49	Ari	8 Dec 1997	07:23
Gem	10 Apr 1997	10:29	Sag	12 Aug 1997	09:43	Tau	10 Dec 1997	09:59
Can	12 Apr 1997	17:03	Cap	14 Aug 1997	15:41	Gem	12 Dec 1997	12:35
Leo	15 Apr 1997	03:22	Aqu	16 Aug 1997	17:58	Can	14 Dec 1997	16:25
Vir	17 Apr 1997	16:00	Pis	18 Aug 1997	18:00	Leo	16 Dec 1997	22:58
Lib	20 Apr 1997	04:35	Ari	20 Aug 1997	17:44	Vir	19 Dec 1997	09:00
Sco	22 Apr 1997	15:18	Tau	22 Aug 1997	18:57	Lib	21 Dec 1997	21:34
Sag	24 Apr 1997	23:30	Gem	24 Aug 1997	22:57	Sco	24 Dec 1997	10:06
Cap	27 Apr 1997	05:32	Can	27 Aug 1997	06:10	Sag	26 Dec 1997	20:06
Aqu	29 Apr 1997	09:49	Leo	29 Aug 1997	16:19	Cap	29 Dec 1997	02:47
						Aqu	31 Dec 1997	06:58

Moon Signs

1998

Pis	2 Jan 1998	09:55	Leo	2 May 1998	09:50	Cap	1 Sep 1998	02:21
Ari	4 Jan 1998	12:43	Vir	4 May 1998	19:46	Aqu	3 Sep 1998	09:19
Tau	6 Jan 1998	15:52	Lib	7 May 1998	08:18	Pis	5 Sep 1998	12:46
Gem	8 Jan 1998	19:42	Sco	9 May 1998	21:09	Ari	7 Sep 1998	13:51
Can	11 Jan 1998	00:43	Sag	12 May 1998	08:47	Tau	9 Sep 1998	14:16
Leo	13 Jan 1998	07:45	Cap	14 May 1998	18:38	Gem	11 Sep 1998	15:40
Vir	15 Jan 1998	17:31	Aqu	17 May 1998	02:29	Can	13 Sep 1998	19:20
Lib	18 Jan 1998	05:44	Pis	19 May 1998	08:02	Leo	16 Sep 1998	01:48
Sco	20 Jan 1998	18:34	Ari	21 May 1998	11:04	Vir	18 Sep 1998	10:52
Sag	23 Jan 1998	05:24	Tau	23 May 1998	12:05	Lib	20 Sep 1998	21:57
Cap	25 Jan 1998	12:37	Gem	25 May 1998	12:25	Sco	23 Sep 1998	10:21
Aqu	27 Jan 1998	16:26	Can	27 May 1998	13:59	Sag	25 Sep 1998	23:03
Pis	29 Jan 1998	18:08	Leo	29 May 1998	18:37	Cap	28 Sep 1998	10:28
Ari	31 Jan 1998	19:20				Aqu	30 Sep 1998	18:52
Tau	2 Feb 1998	21:25	Vir	1 Jun 1998	03:21	Pis	2 Oct 1998	23:21
Gem	5 Feb 1998	01:09	Lib	3 Jun 1998	15:16	Ari	5 Oct 1998	00:30
Can	7 Feb 1998	06:57	Sco	6 Jun 1998	04:05	Tau	6 Oct 1998	23:57
Leo	9 Feb 1998	14:57	Sag	8 Jun 1998	15:33	Gem	8 Oct 1998	23:44
Vir	12 Feb 1998	01:09	Cap	11 Jun 1998	00:49	Can	11 Oct 1998	01:49
Lib	14 Feb 1998	13:17	Aqu	13 Jun 1998	08:02	Leo	13 Oct 1998	07:25
Sco	17 Feb 1998	02:12	Pis	15 Jun 1998	13:30	Vir	15 Oct 1998	16:53
Sag	19 Feb 1998	13:54	Ari	17 Jun 1998	17:22	Lib	18 Oct 1998	04:02
Cap	21 Feb 1998	22:28	Tau	19 Jun 1998	19:47	Sco	20 Oct 1998	16:36
Aqu	24 Feb 1998	03:09	Gem	21 Jun 1998	21:26	Sag	23 Oct 1998	05:15
Pis	26 Feb 1998	04:41	Can	23 Jun 1998	23:39	Cap	25 Oct 1998	17:04
Ari	28 Feb 1998	04:41	Leo	26 Jun 1998	04:04	Aqu	28 Oct 1998	02:42
			Vir	28 Jun 1998	11:55	Pis	30 Oct 1998	08:56
			Lib	30 Jun 1998	23:04			
Tau	2 Mar 1998	05:00	Sco	3 Jul 1998	11:44	Ari	1 Nov 1998	11:25
Gem	4 Mar 1998	07:14	Sag	5 Jul 1998	23:22	Tau	3 Nov 1998	11:11
Can	6 Mar 1998	12:27	Cap	8 Jul 1998	08:26	Gem	5 Nov 1998	10:11
Leo	8 Mar 1998	20:45	Aqu	10 Jul 1998	14:51	Can	7 Nov 1998	10:40
Vir	11 Mar 1998	07:35	Pis	12 Jul 1998	19:21	Leo	9 Nov 1998	14:33
Lib	13 Mar 1998	19:57	Ari	14 Jul 1998	22:44	Vir	11 Nov 1998	22:37
Sco	16 Mar 1998	08:50	Tau	17 Jul 1998	01:33	Lib	14 Nov 1998	09:57
Sag	18 Mar 1998	20:55	Gem	19 Jul 1998	04:17	Sco	16 Nov 1998	22:40
Cap	21 Mar 1998	06:42	Can	21 Jul 1998	07:42	Sag	19 Nov 1998	11:11
Aqu	23 Mar 1998	12:59	Leo	23 Jul 1998	12:49	Cap	21 Nov 1998	22:44
Pis	25 Mar 1998	15:41	Vir	25 Jul 1998	20:34	Aqu	24 Nov 1998	08:42
Ari	27 Mar 1998	15:48	Lib	28 Jul 1998	07:14	Pis	26 Nov 1998	16:13
Tau	29 Mar 1998	15:06	Sco	30 Jul 1998	19:44	Ari	28 Nov 1998	20:32
Gem	31 Mar 1998	15:38				Tau	30 Nov 1998	21:51
Can	2 Apr 1998	19:09	Sag	2 Aug 1998	07:47	Gem	2 Dec 1998	21:29
Leo	5 Apr 1998	02:36	Cap	4 Aug 1998	17:17	Can	4 Dec 1998	21:28
Vir	7 Apr 1998	13:25	Aqu	6 Aug 1998	23:29	Leo	6 Dec 1998	23:56
Lib	10 Apr 1998	02:04	Pis	9 Aug 1998	03:03	Vir	9 Dec 1998	06:21
Sco	12 Apr 1998	14:55	Ari	11 Aug 1998	05:10	Lib	11 Dec 1998	16:43
Sag	15 Apr 1998	02:51	Tau	13 Aug 1998	07:04	Sco	14 Dec 1998	05:16
Cap	17 Apr 1998	13:03	Gem	15 Aug 1998	09:46	Sag	16 Dec 1998	17:47
Aqu	19 Apr 1998	20:40	Can	17 Aug 1998	13:55	Cap	19 Dec 1998	04:54
Pis	22 Apr 1998	01:04	Leo	19 Aug 1998	20:00	Aqu	21 Dec 1998	14:15
Ari	24 Apr 1998	02:29	Vir	22 Aug 1998	04:21	Pis	23 Dec 1998	21:44
Tau	26 Apr 1998	02:08	Lib	24 Aug 1998	15:02	Ari	26 Dec 1998	03:02
Gem	28 Apr 1998	01:56	Sco	27 Aug 1998	03:25	Tau	28 Dec 1998	06:04
Can	30 Apr 1998	03:57	Sag	29 Aug 1998	15:54	Gem	30 Dec 1998	07:21

Moon Signs

1999

Can	1 Jan 1999	08:15	Sag	2 May 1999	07:35	Gem	2 Sep 1999	05:24
Leo	3 Jan 1999	10:31	Cap	4 May 1999	20:11	Can	4 Sep 1999	08:09
Vir	5 Jan 1999	15:49	Aqu	7 May 1999	07:39	Leo	6 Sep 1999	11:28
Lib	8 Jan 1999	00:53	Pis	9 May 1999	16:14	Vir	8 Sep 1999	15:56
Sco	10 Jan 1999	12:48	Ari	11 May 1999	20:51	Lib	10 Sep 1999	22:16
Sag	13 Jan 1999	01:22	Tau	13 May 1999	21:55	Sco	13 Sep 1999	07:08
Cap	15 Jan 1999	12:27	Gem	15 May 1999	21:07	Sag	15 Sep 1999	18:34
Aqu	17 Jan 1999	21:10	Can	17 May 1999	20:39	Cap	18 Sep 1999	07:12
Pis	20 Jan 1999	03:39	Leo	19 May 1999	22:38	Aqu	20 Sep 1999	18:37
Ari	22 Jan 1999	08:24	Vir	22 May 1999	04:15	Pis	23 Sep 1999	02:49
Tau	24 Jan 1999	11:51	Lib	24 May 1999	13:29	Ari	25 Sep 1999	07:32
Gem	26 Jan 1999	14:28	Sco	27 May 1999	01:04	Tau	27 Sep 1999	09:49
Can	28 Jan 1999	16:56	Sag	29 May 1999	13:36	Gem	29 Sep 1999	11:20
Leo	30 Jan 1999	20:15						
			Cap	1 Jun 1999	02:04	Can	1 Oct 1999	13:31
Vir	2 Feb 1999	01:37	Aqu	3 Jun 1999	13:35	Leo	3 Oct 1999	17:12
Lib	4 Feb 1999	09:56	Pis	5 Jun 1999	22:58	Vir	5 Oct 1999	22:39
Sco	6 Feb 1999	21:06	Ari	8 Jun 1999	05:07	Lib	8 Oct 1999	05:51
Sag	9 Feb 1999	09:37	Tau	10 Jun 1999	07:42	Sco	10 Oct 1999	15:01
Cap	11 Feb 1999	21:08	Gem	12 Jun 1999	07:47	Sag	13 Oct 1999	02:18
Aqu	14 Feb 1999	05:56	Can	14 Jun 1999	07:13	Cap	15 Oct 1999	15:02
Pis	16 Feb 1999	11:38	Leo	16 Jun 1999	08:07	Aqu	18 Oct 1999	03:15
Ari	18 Feb 1999	15:05	Vir	18 Jun 1999	12:13	Pis	20 Oct 1999	12:30
Tau	20 Feb 1999	17:28	Lib	20 Jun 1999	20:10	Ari	22 Oct 1999	17:40
Gem	22 Feb 1999	19:53	Sco	23 Jun 1999	07:17	Tau	24 Oct 1999	19:24
Can	24 Feb 1999	23:08	Sag	25 Jun 1999	19:50	Gem	26 Oct 1999	19:33
Leo	27 Feb 1999	03:44	Cap	28 Jun 1999	08:11	Can	28 Oct 1999	20:09
			Aqu	30 Jun 1999	19:18	Leo	30 Oct 1999	22:47
Vir	1 Mar 1999	10:04	Pis	3 Jul 1999	04:33	Vir	2 Nov 1999	04:07
Lib	3 Mar 1999	18:34	Ari	5 Jul 1999	11:19	Lib	4 Nov 1999	11:56
Sco	6 Mar 1999	05:21	Tau	7 Jul 1999	15:20	Sco	6 Nov 1999	21:45
Sag	8 Mar 1999	17:45	Gem	9 Jul 1999	16:59	Sag	9 Nov 1999	09:14
Cap	11 Mar 1999	05:53	Can	11 Jul 1999	17:26	Cap	11 Nov 1999	21:59
Aqu	13 Mar 1999	15:30	Leo	13 Jul 1999	18:25	Aqu	14 Nov 1999	10:44
Pis	15 Mar 1999	21:28	Vir	15 Jul 1999	21:39	Pis	16 Nov 1999	21:18
Ari	18 Mar 1999	00:11	Lib	18 Jul 1999	04:19	Ari	19 Nov 1999	03:55
Tau	20 Mar 1999	01:08	Sco	20 Jul 1999	14:30	Tau	21 Nov 1999	06:25
Gem	22 Mar 1999	02:05	Sag	23 Jul 1999	02:47	Gem	23 Nov 1999	06:13
Can	24 Mar 1999	04:33	Cap	25 Jul 1999	15:07	Can	25 Nov 1999	05:28
Leo	26 Mar 1999	09:22	Aqu	28 Jul 1999	01:53	Leo	27 Nov 1999	06:18
Vir	28 Mar 1999	16:34	Pis	30 Jul 1999	10:26	Vir	29 Nov 1999	10:11
Lib	31 Mar 1999	01:49						
Sco	2 Apr 1999	12:48	Ari	1 Aug 1999	16:46	Lib	1 Dec 1999	17:29
Sag	5 Apr 1999	01:07	Tau	3 Aug 1999	21:07	Sco	4 Dec 1999	03:35
Cap	7 Apr 1999	13:38	Gem	6 Aug 1999	23:56	Sag	6 Dec 1999	15:27
Aqu	10 Apr 1999	00:22	Can	8 Aug 1999	01:52	Cap	9 Dec 1999	04:12
Pis	12 Apr 1999	07:33	Leo	10 Aug 1999	03:55	Aqu	11 Dec 1999	16:57
Ari	14 Apr 1999	10:44	Vir	12 Aug 1999	07:21	Pis	14 Dec 1999	04:16
Tau	16 Apr 1999	11:06	Lib	14 Aug 1999	13:24	Ari	16 Dec 1999	12:28
Gem	18 Apr 1999	10:39	Sco	16 Aug 1999	22:40	Tau	18 Dec 1999	16:44
Can	20 Apr 1999	11:28	Sag	19 Aug 1999	10:31	Gem	20 Dec 1999	17:38
Leo	22 Apr 1999	15:06	Cap	21 Aug 1999	22:58	Can	22 Dec 1999	16:51
Vir	24 Apr 1999	22:04	Aqu	24 Aug 1999	09:47	Leo	24 Dec 1999	16:31
Lib	27 Apr 1999	07:46	Pis	26 Aug 1999	17:49	Vir	26 Dec 1999	18:33
Sco	29 Apr 1999	19:12	Ari	28 Aug 1999	23:07	Lib	29 Dec 1999	00:15
			Tau	31 Aug 1999	02:39	Sco	31 Dec 1999	09:36

2000

Sag	2 Jan 2000	22:31	Ari	1 May 2000	01:52	Sco	2 Sep 2000	06:55	
Cap	5 Jan 2000	11:23	Tau	3 May 2000	05:53	Sag	4 Sep 2000	15:08	
Aqu	7 Jan 2000	23:51	Gem	5 May 2000	07:22	Cap	7 Sep 2000	02:46	
Pis	10 Jan 2000	10:57	Can	7 May 2000	08:13	Aqu	9 Sep 2000	15:43	
Ari	12 Jan 2000	19:47	Leo	9 May 2000	10:01	Pis	12 Sep 2000	03:33	
Tau	15 Jan 2000	01:36	Vir	11 May 2000	13:41	Ari	14 Sep 2000	12:58	
Gem	17 Jan 2000	04:23	Lib	13 May 2000	19:27	Tau	16 Sep 2000	20:04	
Can	19 Jan 2000	05:00	Sco	16 May 2000	03:16	Gem	19 Sep 2000	01:21	
Leo	21 Jan 2000	04:57	Sag	18 May 2000	13:09	Can	21 Sep 2000	05:15	
Vir	23 Jan 2000	06:06	Cap	21 May 2000	01:00	Leo	23 Sep 2000	07:59	
Lib	25 Jan 2000	10:09	Aqu	23 May 2000	13:59	Vir	25 Sep 2000	10:01	
Sco	27 Jan 2000	18:00	Pis	26 May 2000	02:05	Lib	27 Sep 2000	12:21	
Sag	30 Jan 2000	05:17	Ari	28 May 2000	11:05	Sco	29 Sep 2000	16:29	
			Tau	30 May 2000	16:00				
Cap	1 Feb 2000	18:09	Gem	1 Jun 2000	17:33	Sag	1 Oct 2000	23:50	
Aqu	4 Feb 2000	06:30	Can	3 Jun 2000	17:29	Cap	4 Oct 2000	10:42	
Pis	6 Feb 2000	17:01	Leo	5 Jun 2000	17:45	Aqu	6 Oct 2000	23:32	
Ari	9 Feb 2000	01:16	Vir	7 Jun 2000	19:57	Pis	9 Oct 2000	11:34	
Tau	11 Feb 2000	07:19	Lib	10 Jun 2000	00:59	Ari	11 Oct 2000	20:49	
Gem	13 Feb 2000	11:21	Sco	12 Jun 2000	08:55	Tau	14 Oct 2000	03:04	
Can	15 Feb 2000	13:44	Sag	14 Jun 2000	19:17	Gem	16 Oct 2000	07:17	
Leo	17 Feb 2000	15:10	Cap	17 Jun 2000	07:26	Can	18 Oct 2000	10:36	
Vir	19 Feb 2000	16:53	Aqu	19 Jun 2000	20:25	Leo	20 Oct 2000	13:41	
Lib	21 Feb 2000	20:21	Pis	22 Jun 2000	08:50	Vir	22 Oct 2000	16:51	
Sco	24 Feb 2000	02:58	Ari	24 Jun 2000	18:54	Lib	24 Oct 2000	20:29	
Sag	26 Feb 2000	13:10	Tau	27 Jun 2000	01:16	Sco	27 Oct 2000	01:23	
Cap	29 Feb 2000	01:44	Gem	29 Jun 2000	03:58	Sag	29 Oct 2000	08:40	
						Cap	31 Oct 2000	19:01	
Aqu	2 Mar 2000	14:13	Can	1 Jul 2000	04:08	Aqu	3 Nov 2000	07:39	
Pis	5 Mar 2000	00:28	Leo	3 Jul 2000	03:37	Pis	5 Nov 2000	20:11	
Ari	7 Mar 2000	07:53	Vir	5 Jul 2000	04:19	Ari	8 Nov 2000	06:01	
Tau	9 Mar 2000	12:59	Lib	7 Jul 2000	07:46	Tau	10 Nov 2000	12:10	
Gem	11 Mar 2000	16:45	Sco	9 Jul 2000	14:48	Gem	12 Nov 2000	15:26	
Can	13 Mar 2000	19:50	Sag	12 Jul 2000	01:05	Can	14 Nov 2000	17:50	
Leo	15 Mar 2000	22:42	Cap	14 Jul 2000	13:27	Leo	16 Nov 2000	19:18	
Vir	18 Mar 2000	01:48	Aqu	17 Jul 2000	02:25	Vir	18 Nov 2000	22:15	
Lib	20 Mar 2000	05:56	Pis	19 Jul 2000	14:42	Lib	21 Nov 2000	02:34	
Sco	22 Mar 2000	12:18	Ari	22 Jul 2000	01:07	Sco	23 Nov 2000	08:32	
Sag	24 Mar 2000	21:43	Tau	24 Jul 2000	08:42	Sag	25 Nov 2000	16:32	
Cap	27 Mar 2000	09:50	Gem	26 Jul 2000	12:59	Cap	28 Nov 2000	02:56	
Aqu	29 Mar 2000	22:33	Can	28 Jul 2000	14:28	Aqu	30 Nov 2000	15:25	
			Leo	30 Jul 2000	14:22				
Pis	1 Apr 2000	09:10	Vir	1 Aug 2000	14:27	Pis	3 Dec 2000	04:21	
Ari	3 Apr 2000	16:20	Lib	3 Aug 2000	16:31	Ari	5 Dec 2000	15:15	
Tau	5 Apr 2000	20:27	Sco	5 Aug 2000	22:05	Tau	7 Dec 2000	22:24	
Gem	7 Apr 2000	22:57	Sag	8 Aug 2000	07:30	Gem	10 Dec 2000	01:49	
Can	10 Apr 2000	01:15	Cap	10 Aug 2000	19:43	Can	12 Dec 2000	02:47	
Leo	12 Apr 2000	04:15	Aqu	13 Aug 2000	08:42	Leo	14 Dec 2000	03:08	
Vir	14 Apr 2000	08:18	Pis	15 Aug 2000	20:40	Vir	16 Dec 2000	04:29	
Lib	16 Apr 2000	13:35	Ari	18 Aug 2000	06:42	Lib	18 Dec 2000	08:00	
Sco	18 Apr 2000	20:35	Tau	20 Aug 2000	14:29	Sco	20 Dec 2000	14:11	
Sag	21 Apr 2000	05:57	Gem	22 Aug 2000	19:53	Sag	22 Dec 2000	22:57	
Cap	23 Apr 2000	17:46	Can	24 Aug 2000	22:58	Cap	25 Dec 2000	09:53	
Aqu	26 Apr 2000	06:41	Leo	27 Aug 2000	00:16	Aqu	27 Dec 2000	22:24	
Pis	28 Apr 2000	18:05	Vir	29 Aug 2000	00:54	Pis	30 Dec 2000	11:25	
			Lib	31 Aug 2000	02:33				

Moon Signs

2001

Ari	1 Jan 2001	23:12	Vir	2 May 2001	03:15	Pis	2 Sep 2001	01:31
Tau	4 Jan 2001	07:55	Lib	4 May 2001	05:49	Ari	4 Sep 2001	13:57
Gem	6 Jan 2001	12:42	Sco	6 May 2001	09:00	Tau	7 Sep 2001	01:16
Can	8 Jan 2001	14:07	Sag	8 May 2001	14:05	Gem	9 Sep 2001	10:39
Leo	10 Jan 2001	13:43	Cap	10 May 2001	22:10	Can	11 Sep 2001	17:08
Vir	12 Jan 2001	13:26	Aqu	13 May 2001	09:19	Leo	13 Sep 2001	20:14
Lib	14 Jan 2001	15:05	Pis	15 May 2001	22:00	Vir	15 Sep 2001	20:38
Sco	16 Jan 2001	20:02	Ari	18 May 2001	09:39	Lib	17 Sep 2001	19:59
Sag	19 Jan 2001	04:35	Tau	20 May 2001	18:28	Sco	19 Sep 2001	20:27
Cap	21 Jan 2001	15:56	Gem	23 May 2001	00:10	Sag	22 Sep 2001	00:03
Aqu	24 Jan 2001	04:42	Can	25 May 2001	03:41	Cap	24 Sep 2001	07:48
Pis	26 Jan 2001	17:37	Leo	27 May 2001	06:11	Aqu	26 Sep 2001	19:04
Ari	29 Jan 2001	05:34	Vir	29 May 2001	08:37	Pis	29 Sep 2001	07:49
Tau	31 Jan 2001	15:19	Lib	31 May 2001	11:41			
Gem	2 Feb 2001	21:53	Sco	2 Jun 2001	15:55	Ari	1 Oct 2001	20:06
Can	5 Feb 2001	00:58	Sag	4 Jun 2001	21:58	Tau	4 Oct 2001	07:00
Leo	7 Feb 2001	01:19	Cap	7 Jun 2001	06:22	Gem	6 Oct 2001	16:11
Vir	9 Feb 2001	00:34	Aqu	9 Jun 2001	17:19	Can	8 Oct 2001	23:17
Lib	11 Feb 2001	00:46	Pis	12 Jun 2001	05:52	Leo	11 Oct 2001	03:53
Sco	13 Feb 2001	03:51	Ari	14 Jun 2001	18:02	Vir	13 Oct 2001	05:57
Sag	15 Feb 2001	11:03	Tau	17 Jun 2001	03:37	Lib	15 Oct 2001	06:25
Cap	17 Feb 2001	21:58	Gem	19 Jun 2001	09:40	Sco	17 Oct 2001	07:02
Aqu	20 Feb 2001	10:53	Can	21 Jun 2001	12:39	Sag	19 Oct 2001	09:47
Pis	22 Feb 2001	23:44	Leo	23 Jun 2001	13:54	Cap	21 Oct 2001	16:11
Ari	25 Feb 2001	11:18	Vir	25 Jun 2001	14:57	Aqu	24 Oct 2001	02:26
Tau	27 Feb 2001	21:04	Lib	27 Jun 2001	17:10	Pis	26 Oct 2001	14:54
			Sco	29 Jun 2001	21:28	Ari	29 Oct 2001	03:13
						Tau	31 Oct 2001	13:46
Gem	2 Mar 2001	04:35	Sag	2 Jul 2001	04:13	Gem	2 Nov 2001	22:11
Can	4 Mar 2001	09:23	Cap	4 Jul 2001	13:21	Can	5 Nov 2001	04:43
Leo	6 Mar 2001	11:28	Aqu	7 Jul 2001	00:32	Leo	7 Nov 2001	09:32
Vir	8 Mar 2001	11:43	Pis	9 Jul 2001	13:04	Vir	9 Nov 2001	12:47
Lib	10 Mar 2001	11:47	Ari	12 Jul 2001	01:34	Lib	11 Nov 2001	14:52
Sco	12 Mar 2001	13:43	Tau	14 Jul 2001	12:11	Sco	13 Nov 2001	16:44
Sag	14 Mar 2001	19:16	Gem	16 Jul 2001	19:24	Sag	15 Nov 2001	19:50
Cap	17 Mar 2001	05:01	Can	18 Jul 2001	22:54	Cap	18 Nov 2001	01:40
Aqu	19 Mar 2001	17:35	Leo	20 Jul 2001	23:41	Aqu	20 Nov 2001	10:55
Pis	22 Mar 2001	06:27	Vir	22 Jul 2001	23:28	Pis	22 Nov 2001	22:51
Ari	24 Mar 2001	17:42	Lib	25 Jul 2001	00:08	Ari	25 Nov 2001	11:19
Tau	27 Mar 2001	02:49	Sco	27 Jul 2001	03:17	Tau	27 Nov 2001	22:04
Gem	29 Mar 2001	09:59	Sag	29 Jul 2001	09:44	Gem	30 Nov 2001	06:02
Can	31 Mar 2001	15:22	Cap	31 Jul 2001	19:15			
Leo	2 Apr 2001	18:53	Aqu	3 Aug 2001	06:52	Can	2 Dec 2001	11:28
Vir	4 Apr 2001	20:45	Pis	5 Aug 2001	19:29	Leo	4 Dec 2001	15:14
Lib	6 Apr 2001	21:56	Ari	8 Aug 2001	08:03	Vir	6 Dec 2001	18:10
Sco	9 Apr 2001	00:02	Tau	10 Aug 2001	19:22	Lib	8 Dec 2001	20:56
Sag	11 Apr 2001	04:47	Gem	13 Aug 2001	03:57	Sco	11 Dec 2001	00:08
Cap	13 Apr 2001	13:21	Can	15 Aug 2001	08:53	Sag	13 Dec 2001	04:29
Aqu	16 Apr 2001	01:10	Leo	17 Aug 2001	10:23	Cap	15 Dec 2001	10:48
Pis	18 Apr 2001	13:59	Vir	19 Aug 2001	09:52	Aqu	17 Dec 2001	19:42
Ari	21 Apr 2001	01:16	Lib	21 Aug 2001	09:18	Pis	20 Dec 2001	07:08
Tau	23 Apr 2001	09:54	Sco	23 Aug 2001	10:50	Ari	22 Dec 2001	19:44
Gem	25 Apr 2001	16:10	Sag	25 Aug 2001	15:59	Tau	25 Dec 2001	07:11
Can	27 Apr 2001	20:48	Cap	28 Aug 2001	01:02	Gem	27 Dec 2001	15:37
Leo	30 Apr 2001	00:23	Aqu	30 Aug 2001	12:47	Can	29 Dec 2001	20:38
						Leo	31 Dec 2001	23:07

Moon Signs

2002

Vir	3 Jan 2002	00:33	Aqu	3 May 2002	05:42	Can	1 Sep 2002	22:12
Lib	5 Jan 2002	02:23	Pis	5 May 2002	16:45	Leo	4 Sep 2002	03:34
Sco	7 Jan 2002	05:40	Ari	8 May 2002	05:21	Vir	6 Sep 2002	05:15
Sag	9 Jan 2002	10:57	Tau	10 May 2002	17:31	Lib	8 Sep 2002	04:56
Cap	11 Jan 2002	18:17	Gem	13 May 2002	04:03	Sco	10 Sep 2002	04:47
Aqu	14 Jan 2002	03:41	Can	15 May 2002	12:32	Sag	12 Sep 2002	06:43
Pis	16 Jan 2002	14:59	Leo	17 May 2002	18:51	Cap	14 Sep 2002	11:48
Ari	19 Jan 2002	03:34	Vir	19 May 2002	22:59	Aqu	16 Sep 2002	19:54
Tau	21 Jan 2002	15:46	Lib	22 May 2002	01:17	Pis	19 Sep 2002	06:17
Gem	24 Jan 2002	01:25	Sco	24 May 2002	02:37	Ari	21 Sep 2002	18:10
Can	26 Jan 2002	07:15	Sag	26 May 2002	04:19	Tau	24 Sep 2002	06:63
Leo	28 Jan 2002	09:29	Cap	28 May 2002	07:54	Gem	26 Sep 2002	19:25
Vir	30 Jan 2002	09:39	Aqu	30 May 2002	14:35	Can	29 Sep 2002	06:00
Lib	1 Feb 2002	09:44	Pis	2 Jun 2002	00:37	Leo	1 Oct 2002	12:55
Sco	3 Feb 2002	11:35	Ari	4 Jun 2002	12:50	Vir	3 Oct 2002	15:50
Sag	5 Feb 2002	16:21	Tau	7 Jun 2002	01:05	Lib	5 Oct 2002	15:50
Cap	8 Feb 2002	00:08	Gem	9 Jun 2002	11:27	Sco	7 Oct 2002	14:57
Aqu	10 Feb 2002	10:14	Can	11 Jun 2002	19:14	Sag	9 Oct 2002	15:20
Pis	12 Feb 2002	21:52	Leo	14 Jun 2002	00:38	Cap	11 Oct 2002	18:44
Ari	15 Feb 2002	10:24	Vir	16 Jun 2002	04:22	Aqu	14 Oct 2002	01:51
Tau	17 Feb 2002	22:56	Lib	18 Jun 2002	07:10	Pis	16 Oct 2002	12:06
Gem	20 Feb 2002	09:48	Sco	20 Jun 2002	09:42	Ari	19 Oct 2002	00:12
Can	22 Feb 2002	17:15	Sag	22 Jun 2002	12:41	Tau	21 Oct 2002	12:55
Leo	24 Feb 2002	20:34	Cap	24 Jun 2002	17:01	Gem	24 Oct 2002	01:16
Vir	26 Feb 2002	20:46	Aqu	26 Jun 2002	23:36	Can	26 Oct 2002	12:08
Lib	28 Feb 2002	19:46	Pis	29 Jun 2002	09:00	Leo	28 Oct 2002	20:18
							Vir	31 Oct 2002	00:57
Sco	2 Mar 2002	19:51	Ari	1 Jul 2002	20:48	Lib	2 Nov 2002	02:26
Sag	4 Mar 2002	22:55	Tau	4 Jul 2002	09:15	Sco	4 Nov 2002	02:09
Cap	7 Mar 2002	05:47	Gem	6 Jul 2002	19:59	Sag	6 Nov 2002	02:01
Aqu	9 Mar 2002	15:56	Can	9 Jul 2002	03:35	Cap	8 Nov 2002	03:58
Pis	12 Mar 2002	03:56	Leo	11 Jul 2002	08:06	Aqu	10 Nov 2002	09:27
Ari	14 Mar 2002	16:33	Vir	13 Jul 2002	10:39	Pis	12 Nov 2002	18:41
Tau	17 Mar 2002	05:00	Lib	15 Jul 2002	12:38	Ari	15 Nov 2002	06:36
Gem	19 Mar 2002	16:18	Sco	17 Jul 2002	15:12	Tau	17 Nov 2002	19:22
Can	22 Mar 2002	01:04	Sag	19 Jul 2002	19:01	Gem	20 Nov 2002	07:24
Leo	24 Mar 2002	06:12	Cap	22 Jul 2002	00:25	Can	22 Nov 2002	17:46
Vir	26 Mar 2002	07:42	Aqu	24 Jul 2002	07:39	Leo	25 Nov 2002	01:58
Lib	28 Mar 2002	07:03	Pis	26 Jul 2002	17:04	Vir	27 Nov 2002	07:40
Sco	30 Mar 2002	06:20	Ari	29 Jul 2002	04:38	Lib	29 Nov 2002	10:52
			Tau	31 Jul 2002	17:16			
Sag	1 Apr 2002	07:48	Gem	3 Aug 2002	04:45	Sco	1 Dec 2002	12:14
Cap	3 Apr 2002	12:59	Can	5 Aug 2002	12:59	Sag	3 Dec 2002	12:57
Aqu	5 Apr 2002	22:06	Leo	7 Aug 2002	17:26	Cap	5 Dec 2002	14:38
Pis	8 Apr 2002	09:57	Vir	9 Aug 2002	19:02	Aqu	7 Dec 2002	18:53
Ari	10 Apr 2002	22:39	Lib	11 Aug 2002	19:37	Pis	10 Dec 2002	02:46
Tau	13 Apr 2002	10:54	Sco	13 Aug 2002	21:00	Ari	12 Dec 2002	13:57
Gem	15 Apr 2002	21:55	Sag	16 Aug 2002	00:25	Tau	15 Dec 2002	02:42
Can	18 Apr 2002	06:59	Cap	18 Aug 2002	06:14	Gem	17 Dec 2002	14:41
Leo	20 Apr 2002	13:18	Aqu	20 Aug 2002	14:16	Can	20 Dec 2002	00:28
Vir	22 Apr 2002	16:33	Pis	23 Aug 2002	00:10	Leo	22 Dec 2002	07:47
Lib	24 Apr 2002	17:21	Ari	25 Aug 2002	11:47	Vir	24 Dec 2002	13:03
Sco	26 Apr 2002	17:14	Tau	28 Aug 2002	00:30	Lib	26 Dec 2002	16:52
Sag	28 Apr 2002	18:12	Gem	30 Aug 2002	12:43	Sco	28 Dec 2002	19:40
Cap	30 Apr 2002	22:03				Sag	30 Dec 2002	22:00

Moon Signs

2003

Cap	2 Jan 2000	00:42	Gem	3 May 2003	04:26	Sag	2 Sep 2003	19:31
Aqu	4 Jan 2003	04:56	Can	5 May 2003	16:41	Cap	4 Sep 2003	22:51
Pis	6 Jan 2003	11:57	Leo	8 May 2003	02:44	Aqu	7 Sep 2003	03:14
Ari	8 Jan 2003	22:14	Vir	10 May 2003	09:29	Pis	9 Sep 2003	09:07
Tau	11 Jan 2003	10:47	Lib	12 May 2003	12:40	Ari	11 Sep 2003	17:08
Gem	13 Jan 2003	23:06	Sco	14 May 2003	13:12	Tau	14 Sep 2003	03:49
Can	16 Jan 2003	08:54	Sag	16 May 2003	12:42	Gem	16 Sep 2003	16:31
Leo	18 Jan 2003	15:27	Cap	18 May 2003	13:03	Can	19 Sep 2003	05:06
Vir	20 Jan 2003	19:30	Aqu	20 May 2003	16:01	Leo	21 Sep 2003	15:01
Lib	22 Jan 2003	22:22	Pis	22 May 2003	22:41	Vir	23 Sep 2003	21:02
Sco	25 Jan 2003	01:08	Ari	25 May 2003	08:58	Lib	25 Sep 2003	23:47
Sag	27 Jan 2003	04:25	Tau	27 May 2003	21:31	Sco	28 Sep 2003	00:51
Cap	29 Jan 2003	08:29	Gem	30 May 2003	10:30	Sag	30 Sep 2003	01:56
Aqu	31 Jan 2003	13:44						
Pis	2 Feb 2003	20:54	Can	1 Jun 2003	22:26	Cap	2 Oct 2003	04:21
Ari	5 Feb 2003	06:44	Leo	4 Jun 2003	08:23	Aqu	4 Oct 2003	08:45
Tau	7 Feb 2003	18:58	Vir	6 Jun 2003	15:49	Pis	6 Oct 2003	15:20
Gem	10 Feb 2003	07:44	Lib	8 Jun 2003	20:28	Ari	9 Oct 2003	00:07
Can	12 Feb 2003	18:18	Sco	10 Jun 2003	22:37	Tau	11 Oct 2003	11:05
Leo	15 Feb 2003	01:02	Sag	12 Jun 2003	23:11	Gem	13 Oct 2003	23:44
Vir	17 Feb 2003	04:21	Cap	14 Jun 2003	23:38	Can	16 Oct 2003	12:39
Lib	19 Feb 2003	05:47	Aqu	17 Jun 2003	01:42	Leo	18 Oct 2003	23:39
Sco	21 Feb 2003	07:08	Pis	19 Jun 2003	06:56	Vir	21 Oct 2003	07:00
Sag	23 Feb 2003	09:45	Ari	21 Jun 2003	16:05	Lib	23 Oct 2003	10:25
Cap	25 Feb 2003	14:11	Tau	24 Jun 2003	04:14	Sco	25 Oct 2003	11:07
Aqu	27 Feb 2003	20:24	Gem	26 Jun 2003	17:12	Sag	27 Oct 2003	10:54
			Can	29 Jun 2003	04:51	Cap	29 Oct 2003	11:37
						Aqu	31 Oct 2003	14:41
Pis	2 Mar 2003	04:25	Leo	1 Jul 2003	14:11	Pis	2 Nov 2003	20:52
Ari	4 Mar 2003	14:29	Vir	3 Jul 2003	21:14	Ari	5 Nov 2003	06:02
Tau	7 Mar 2003	02:35	Lib	6 Jul 2003	02:19	Tau	7 Nov 2003	17:28
Gem	9 Mar 2003	15:36	Sco	8 Jul 2003	05:42	Gem	10 Nov 2003	06:13
Can	12 Mar 2003	03:10	Sag	10 Jul 2003	07:47	Can	12 Nov 2003	19:09
Leo	14 Mar 2003	11:04	Cap	12 Jul 2003	09:20	Leo	15 Nov 2003	06:47
Vir	16 Mar 2003	14:50	Aqu	14 Jul 2003	11:38	Vir	17 Nov 2003	15:35
Lib	18 Mar 2003	15:42	Pis	16 Jul 2003	16:13	Lib	19 Nov 2003	20:40
Sco	20 Mar 2003	15:37	Ari	19 Jul 2003	00:20	Sco	21 Nov 2003	22:22
Sag	22 Mar 2003	16:32	Tau	21 Jul 2003	11:47	Sag	23 Nov 2003	22:02
Cap	24 Mar 2003	19:48	Gem	24 Jul 2003	00:41	Cap	25 Nov 2003	21:31
Aqu	27 Mar 2003	01:50	Can	26 Jul 2003	12:21	Aqu	27 Nov 2003	22:48
Pis	29 Mar 2003	10:25	Leo	28 Jul 2003	21:15	Pis	30 Nov 2003	03:25
Ari	31 Mar 2003	21:04	Vir	31 Jul 2003	03:25			
Tau	3 Apr 2003	09:19	Lib	2 Aug 2003	07:47	Ari	2 Dec 2003	11:56
Gem	5 Apr 2003	22:22	Sco	4 Aug 2003	11:11	Tau	4 Dec 2003	23:29
Can	8 Apr 2003	10:34	Sag	6 Aug 2003	14:10	Gem	7 Dec 2003	12:25
Leo	10 Apr 2003	19:52	Cap	8 Aug 2003	17:02	Can	10 Dec 2003	01:10
Vir	13 Apr 2003	01:04	Aqu	10 Aug 2003	20:23	Leo	12 Dec 2003	12:39
Lib	15 Apr 2003	02:40	Pis	13 Aug 2003	01:19	Vir	14 Dec 2003	22:05
Sco	17 Apr 2003	02:15	Ari	15 Aug 2003	09:00	Lib	17 Dec 2003	04:45
Sag	19 Apr 2003	01:51	Tau	17 Aug 2003	19:52	Sco	19 Dec 2003	08:18
Cap	21 Apr 2003	03:20	Gem	20 Aug 2003	08:40	Sag	21 Dec 2003	09:14
Aqu	23 Apr 2003	07:58	Can	22 Aug 2003	20:43	Cap	23 Dec 2003	08:55
Pis	25 Apr 2003	16:02	Leo	25 Aug 2003	05:47	Aqu	25 Dec 2003	09:13
Ari	28 Apr 2003	02:54	Vir	27 Aug 2003	11:25	Pis	27 Dec 2003	12:10
Tau	30 Apr 2003	15:25	Lib	29 Aug 2003	14:40	Ari	29 Dec 2003	19:08
			Sco	31 Aug 2003	16:59			

Moon Signs

2004

Tau	1 Jan 2004	06:01	Lib	1 May 2004	19:01	Tau	3 Sep 2004	01:16
Gem	3 Jan 2004	18:57	Sco	3 May 2004	21:37	Gem	5 Sep 2004	11:24
Can	6 Jan 2004	07:37	Sag	5 May 2004	22:07	Can	7 Sep 2004	23:49
Leo	8 Jan 2004	18:37	Cap	7 May 2004	22:16	Leo	10 Sep 2004	12:04
Vir	11 Jan 2004	03:36	Aqu	9 May 2004	23:47	Vir	12 Sep 2004	22:15
Lib	13 Jan 2004	10:36	Pis	12 May 2004	03:52	Lib	15 Sep 2004	05:53
Sco	15 Jan 2004	15:31	Ari	14 May 2004	11:02	Sco	17 Sep 2004	11:24
Sag	17 Jan 2004	18:17	Tau	16 May 2004	20:56	Sag	19 Sep 2004	15:29
Cap	19 Jan 2004	19:23	Gem	19 May 2004	08:46	Cap	21 Sep 2004	18:35
Aqu	21 Jan 2004	20:10	Can	21 May 2004	21:34	Aqu	23 Sep 2004	21:09
Pis	23 Jan 2004	22:29	Leo	24 May 2004	10:06	Pis	25 Sep 2004	23:55
Ari	26 Jan 2004	04:06	Vir	26 May 2004	20:50	Ari	28 Sep 2004	03:57
Tau	28 Jan 2004	13:46	Lib	29 May 2004	04:21	Tau	30 Sep 2004	10:24
Gem	31 Jan 2004	02:17	Sco	31 May 2004	08:06			
Can	2 Feb 2004	15:02	Sag	2 Jun 2004	08:51	Gem	2 Oct 2004	19:54
Leo	5 Feb 2004	01:48	Cap	4 Jun 2004	08:12	Can	5 Oct 2004	07:53
Vir	7 Feb 2004	10:01	Aqu	6 Jun 2004	08:10	Leo	7 Oct 2004	20:22
Lib	9 Feb 2004	16:11	Pis	8 Jun 2004	10:39	Vir	10 Oct 2004	06:59
Sco	11 Feb 2004	20:56	Ari	10 Jun 2004	16:49	Lib	12 Oct 2004	14:30
Sag	14 Feb 2004	00:34	Tau	13 Jun 2004	02:36	Sco	14 Oct 2004	19:09
Cap	16 Feb 2004	03:13	Gem	15 Jun 2004	14:43	Sag	16 Oct 2004	21:57
Aqu	18 Feb 2004	05:26	Can	18 Jun 2004	03:36	Cap	19 Oct 2004	00:06
Pis	20 Feb 2004	08:26	Leo	20 Jun 2004	16:04	Aqu	21 Oct 2004	02:37
Ari	22 Feb 2004	13:45	Vir	23 Jun 2004	03:08	Pis	23 Oct 2004	06:13
Tau	24 Feb 2004	22:30	Lib	25 Jun 2004	11:48	Ari	25 Oct 2004	11:24
Gem	27 Feb 2004	10:22	Sco	27 Jun 2004	17:11	Tau	27 Oct 2004	18:37
Can	29 Feb 2004	23:11	Sag	29 Jun 2004	19:14	Gem	30 Oct 2004	04:10
Leo	3 Mar 2004	10:16	Cap	1 Jul 2004	19:00	Can	1 Nov 2004	15:52
Vir	5 Mar 2004	18:17	Aqu	3 Jul 2004	18:21	Leo	4 Nov 2004	04:31
Lib	7 Mar 2004	23:29	Pis	5 Jul 2004	19:26	Vir	6 Nov 2004	15:59
Sco	10 Mar 2004	03:02	Ari	8 Jul 2004	00:04	Lib	9 Nov 2004	00:21
Sag	12 Mar 2004	05:56	Tau	10 Jul 2004	08:50	Sco	11 Nov 2004	05:04
Cap	14 Mar 2004	08:51	Gem	12 Jul 2004	20:44	Sag	13 Nov 2004	06:55
Aqu	16 Mar 2004	12:10	Can	15 Jul 2004	09:39	Cap	15 Nov 2004	07:32
Pis	18 Mar 2004	16:25	Leo	17 Jul 2004	21:55	Aqu	17 Nov 2004	08:39
Ari	20 Mar 2004	22:29	Vir	20 Jul 2004	08:43	Pis	19 Nov 2004	11:38
Tau	23 Mar 2004	07:09	Lib	22 Jul 2004	17:38	Ari	21 Nov 2004	17:10
Gem	25 Mar 2004	18:34	Sco	25 Jul 2004	00:06	Tau	24 Nov 2004	01:15
Can	28 Mar 2004	07:22	Sag	27 Jul 2004	03:46	Gem	26 Nov 2004	11:25
Leo	30 Mar 2004	19:06	Cap	29 Jul 2004	04:56	Can	28 Nov 2004	23:10
			Aqu	31 Jul 2004	04:53			
Vir	2 Apr 2004	03:44	Pis	2 Aug 2004	05:34	Leo	1 Dec 2004	11:49
Lib	4 Apr 2004	08:50	Ari	4 Aug 2004	09:00	Vir	3 Dec 2004	23:59
Sco	6 Apr 2004	11:23	Tau	6 Aug 2004	16:26	Lib	6 Dec 2004	09:44
Sag	8 Apr 2004	12:50	Gem	9 Aug 2004	03:32	Sco	8 Dec 2004	15:42
Cap	10 Apr 2004	14:33	Can	11 Aug 2004	16:19	Sag	10 Dec 2004	17:53
Aqu	12 Apr 2004	17:32	Leo	14 Aug 2004	04:29	Cap	12 Dec 2004	17:41
Pis	14 Apr 2004	22:24	Vir	16 Aug 2004	14:48	Aqu	14 Dec 2004	17:09
Ari	17 Apr 2004	05:23	Lib	18 Aug 2004	23:08	Pis	16 Dec 2004	18:23
Tau	19 Apr 2004	14:42	Sco	21 Aug 2004	05:36	Ari	18 Dec 2004	22:52
Gem	22 Apr 2004	02:09	Sag	23 Aug 2004	10:07	Tau	21 Dec 2004	06:52
Can	24 Apr 2004	14:55	Cap	25 Aug 2004	12:45	Gem	23 Dec 2004	17:31
Leo	27 Apr 2004	03:13	Aqu	27 Aug 2004	14:07	Can	26 Dec 2004	05:37
Vir	29 Apr 2004	12:58	Pis	29 Aug 2004	15:33	Leo	28 Dec 2004	18:13
			Ari	31 Aug 2004	18:45	Vir	31 Dec 2004	06:32

Moon Signs

2005

Lib	2 Jan 2005	17:18	Pis	2 May 2005	15:42	Vir	2 Sep 2005	20:55
Sco	5 Jan 2005	00:57	Ari	4 May 2005	19:35	Lib	5 Sep 2005	08:51
Sag	7 Jan 2005	04:43	Tau	7 May 2005	01:01	Sco	7 Sep 2005	19:09
Cap	9 Jan 2005	05:09	Gem	9 May 2005	08:28	Sag	10 Sep 2005	03:01
Aqu	11 Jan 2005	04:06	Can	11 May 2005	18:20	Cap	12 Sep 2005	07:55
Pis	13 Jan 2005	03:50	Leo	14 May 2005	06:16	Aqu	14 Sep 2005	10:01
Ari	15 Jan 2005	06:26	Vir	16 May 2005	18:46	Pis	16 Sep 2005	10:24
Tau	17 Jan 2005	13:07	Lib	19 May 2005	05:29	Ari	18 Sep 2005	10:43
Gem	19 Jan 2005	23:24	Sco	21 May 2005	12:46	Tau	20 Sep 2005	12:48
Can	22 Jan 2005	11:41	Sag	23 May 2005	16:37	Gem	22 Sep 2005	18:06
Leo	25 Jan 2005	00:20	Cap	25 May 2005	18:10	Can	25 Sep 2005	03:10
Vir	27 Jan 2005	12:23	Aqu	27 May 2005	19:09	Leo	27 Sep 2005	15:02
Lib	29 Jan 2005	23:11	Pis	29 May 2005	21:09	Vir	30 Sep 2005	03:43
Sco	1 Feb 2005	07:50	Ari	1 Jun 2005	01:08	Lib	2 Oct 2005	15:23
Sag	3 Feb 2005	13:19	Tau	3 Jun 2005	07:19	Sco	5 Oct 2005	01:02
Cap	5 Feb 2005	15:31	Gem	5 Jun 2005	15:35	Sag	7 Oct 2005	08:27
Aqu	7 Feb 2005	15:25	Can	8 Jun 2005	01:46	Cap	9 Oct 2005	13:42
Pis	9 Feb 2005	14:59	Leo	10 Jun 2005	13:39	Aqu	11 Oct 2005	17:04
Ari	11 Feb 2005	16:21	Vir	13 Jun 2005	02:21	Pis	13 Oct 2005	19:05
Tau	13 Feb 2005	21:18	Lib	15 Jun 2005	13:57	Ari	15 Oct 2005	20:39
Gem	16 Feb 2005	06:17	Sco	17 Jun 2005	22:21	Tau	17 Oct 2005	23:04
Can	18 Feb 2005	18:12	Sag	20 Jun 2005	02:43	Gem	20 Oct 2005	03:44
Leo	21 Feb 2005	06:54	Cap	22 Jun 2005	03:51	Can	22 Oct 2005	11:41
Vir	23 Feb 2005	18:43	Aqu	24 Jun 2005	03:36	Leo	24 Oct 2005	22:48
Lib	26 Feb 2005	04:58	Pis	26 Jun 2005	04:03	Vir	27 Oct 2005	11:27
Sco	28 Feb 2005	13:19	Ari	28 Jun 2005	06:51	Lib	29 Oct 2005	23:13
			Tau	30 Jun 2005	12:45			
Sag	2 Mar 2005	19:28	Gem	2 Jul 2005	21:25	Sco	1 Nov 2005	08:28
Cap	4 Mar 2005	23:10	Can	5 Jul 2005	08:07	Sag	3 Nov 2005	14:54
Aqu	7 Mar 2005	00:48	Leo	7 Jul 2005	20:10	Cap	5 Nov 2005	19:16
Pis	9 Mar 2005	01:32	Vir	10 Jul 2005	08:56	Aqu	7 Nov 2005	22:30
Ari	11 Mar 2005	03:03	Lib	12 Jul 2005	21:08	Pis	10 Nov 2005	01:22
Tau	13 Mar 2005	07:05	Sco	15 Jul 2005	06:50	Ari	12 Nov 2005	04:22
Gem	15 Mar 2005	14:44	Sag	17 Jul 2005	12:33	Tau	14 Nov 2005	08:02
Can	18 Mar 2005	01:43	Cap	19 Jul 2005	14:24	Gem	16 Nov 2005	13:10
Leo	20 Mar 2005	14:16	Aqu	21 Jul 2005	13:54	Can	18 Nov 2005	20:42
Vir	23 Mar 2005	02:09	Pis	23 Jul 2005	13:12	Leo	21 Nov 2005	07:09
Lib	25 Mar 2005	11:58	Ari	25 Jul 2005	14:23	Vir	23 Nov 2005	19:41
Sco	27 Mar 2005	19:28	Tau	27 Jul 2005	18:54	Lib	26 Nov 2005	07:56
Sag	30 Mar 2005	00:55	Gem	30 Jul 2005	03:02	Sco	28 Nov 2005	17:32
						Sag	30 Nov 2005	23:30
Cap	1 Apr 2005	04:47	Can	1 Aug 2005	13:52	Cap	3 Dec 2005	02:41
Aqu	3 Apr 2005	07:30	Leo	4 Aug 2005	02:09	Aqu	5 Dec 2005	04:35
Pis	5 Apr 2005	09:45	Vir	6 Aug 2005	14:53	Pis	7 Dec 2005	06:44
Ari	7 Apr 2005	12:28	Lib	9 Aug 2005	03:07	Ari	9 Dec 2005	10:02
Tau	9 Apr 2005	16:49	Sco	11 Aug 2005	13:33	Tau	11 Dec 2005	14:46
Gem	11 Apr 2005	23:55	Sag	13 Aug 2005	20:46	Gem	13 Dec 2005	20:59
Can	14 Apr 2005	10:03	Cap	16 Aug 2005	00:11	Can	16 Dec 2005	05:01
Leo	16 Apr 2005	22:16	Aqu	18 Aug 2005	00:37	Leo	18 Dec 2005	15:18
Vir	19 Apr 2005	10:25	Pis	19 Aug 2005	23:52	Vir	21 Dec 2005	03:38
Lib	21 Apr 2005	20:25	Ari	22 Aug 2005	00:02	Lib	23 Dec 2005	16:25
Sco	24 Apr 2005	03:24	Tau	24 Aug 2005	02:58	Sco	26 Dec 2005	03:02
Sag	26 Apr 2005	07:45	Gem	26 Aug 2005	09:43	Sag	28 Dec 2005	09:42
Cap	28 Apr 2005	10:31	Can	28 Aug 2005	19:57	Cap	30 Dec 2005	12:33
Aqu	30 Apr 2005	12:53	Leo	31 Aug 2005	08:14			

2006

Aqu	1 Jan 2006	13:14	Can	1 May 2006	16:17	Cap	2 Sep 2006	15:33
Pis	3 Jan 2006	13:44	Leo	4 May 2006	01:18	Aqu	4 Sep 2006	19:14
Ari	5 Jan 2006	15:44	Vir	6 May 2006	13:20	Pis	6 Sep 2006	19:56
Tau	7 Jan 2006	20:09	Lib	9 May 2006	02:09	Ari	8 Sep 2006	19:23
Gem	10 Jan 2006	02:58	Sco	11 May 2006	13:23	Tau	10 Sep 2006	19:30
Can	12 Jan 2006	11:50	Sag	13 May 2006	21:55	Gem	12 Sep 2006	22:00
Leo	14 Jan 2006	22:30	Cap	16 May 2006	03:58	Can	15 Sep 2006	03:54
Vir	17 Jan 2006	10:48	Aqu	18 May 2006	08:18	Leo	17 Sep 2006	13:16
Lib	19 Jan 2006	23:48	Pis	20 May 2006	11:38	Vir	20 Sep 2006	01:07
Sco	22 Jan 2006	11:27	Ari	22 May 2006	14:23	Lib	22 Sep 2006	14:06
Sag	24 Jan 2006	19:36	Tau	24 May 2006	17:00	Sco	25 Sep 2006	02:53
Cap	26 Jan 2006	23:29	Gem	26 May 2006	20:19	Sag	27 Sep 2006	14:15
Aqu	29 Jan 2006	00:08	Can	29 May 2006	01:34	Cap	29 Sep 2006	22:59
Pis	30 Jan 2006	23:32	Leo	31 May 2006	09:52			
Ari	1 Feb 2006	23:46	Vir	2 Jun 2006	21:17	Aqu	2 Oct 2006	04:23
Tau	4 Feb 2006	02:32	Lib	5 Jun 2006	10:08	Pis	4 Oct 2006	06:32
Gem	6 Feb 2006	08:32	Sco	7 Jun 2006	21:39	Ari	6 Oct 2006	06:32
Can	8 Feb 2006	17:33	Sag	10 Jun 2006	06:04	Tau	8 Oct 2006	06:04
Leo	11 Feb 2006	04:44	Cap	12 Jun 2006	11:17	Gem	10 Oct 2006	07:06
Vir	13 Feb 2006	17:13	Aqu	14 Jun 2006	14:31	Can	12 Oct 2006	11:22
Lib	16 Feb 2006	06:08	Pis	16 Jun 2006	17:05	Leo	14 Oct 2006	19:38
Sco	18 Feb 2006	18:11	Ari	18 Jun 2006	19:53	Vir	17 Oct 2006	07:15
Sag	21 Feb 2006	03:36	Tau	20 Jun 2006	23:22	Lib	19 Oct 2006	20:19
Cap	23 Feb 2006	09:14	Gem	23 Jun 2006	03:49	Sco	22 Oct 2006	08:53
Aqu	25 Feb 2006	11:13	Can	25 Jun 2006	09:48	Sag	24 Oct 2006	19:52
Pis	27 Feb 2006	10:55	Leo	27 Jun 2006	18:08	Cap	27 Oct 2006	04:46
			Vir	30 Jun 2006	05:14	Aqu	29 Oct 2006	11:15
						Pis	31 Oct 2006	15:09
Ari	1 Mar 2006	10:19	Lib	2 Jul 2006	18:05	Ari	2 Nov 2006	16:46
Tau	3 Mar 2006	11:23	Sco	5 Jul 2006	06:13	Tau	4 Nov 2006	17:04
Gem	5 Mar 2006	15:38	Sag	7 Jul 2006	15:12	Gem	6 Nov 2006	17:46
Can	7 Mar 2006	23:38	Cap	9 Jul 2006	20:24	Can	8 Nov 2006	20:46
Leo	10 Mar 2006	10:42	Aqu	11 Jul 2006	22:45	Leo	11 Nov 2006	03:34
Vir	12 Mar 2006	23:23	Pis	13 Jul 2006	23:59	Vir	13 Nov 2006	14:19
Lib	15 Mar 2006	12:12	Ari	16 Jul 2006	01:39	Lib	16 Nov 2006	03:14
Sco	17 Mar 2006	23:58	Tau	18 Jul 2006	04:44	Sco	18 Nov 2006	15:46
Sag	20 Mar 2006	09:41	Gem	20 Jul 2006	09:38	Sag	21 Nov 2006	02:14
Cap	22 Mar 2006	16:35	Can	22 Jul 2006	16:27	Cap	23 Nov 2006	10:24
Aqu	24 Mar 2006	20:20	Leo	25 Jul 2006	01:25	Aqu	25 Nov 2006	16:40
Pis	26 Mar 2006	21:32	Vir	27 Jul 2006	12:36	Pis	27 Nov 2006	21:20
Ari	28 Mar 2006	21:30	Lib	30 Jul 2006	01:27	Ari	30 Nov 2006	00:29
Tau	30 Mar 2006	22:01						
Gem	2 Apr 2006	00:50	Sco	1 Aug 2006	14:07	Tau	2 Dec 2006	02:26
Can	4 Apr 2006	07:14	Sag	4 Aug 2006	00:12	Gem	4 Dec 2006	04:05
Leo	6 Apr 2006	17:24	Cap	6 Aug 2006	06:19	Can	6 Dec 2006	07:00
Vir	9 Apr 2006	05:58	Aqu	8 Aug 2006	08:46	Leo	8 Dec 2006	12:53
Lib	11 Apr 2006	18:46	Pis	10 Aug 2006	09:10	Vir	10 Dec 2006	22:31
Sco	14 Apr 2006	06:08	Ari	12 Aug 2006	09:22	Lib	13 Dec 2006	11:00
Sag	16 Apr 2006	15:18	Tau	14 Aug 2006	11:00	Sco	15 Dec 2006	23:41
Cap	18 Apr 2006	22:12	Gem	16 Aug 2006	15:07	Sag	18 Dec 2006	10:09
Aqu	21 Apr 2006	02:54	Can	18 Aug 2006	22:03	Cap	20 Dec 2006	17:38
Pis	23 Apr 2006	05:43	Leo	21 Aug 2006	07:33	Aqu	22 Dec 2006	22:48
Ari	25 Apr 2006	07:11	Vir	23 Aug 2006	19:07	Pis	25 Dec 2006	02:43
Tau	27 Apr 2006	08:27	Lib	26 Aug 2006	08:01	Ari	27 Dec 2006	06:03
Gem	29 Apr 2006	10:58	Sco	28 Aug 2006	20:55	Tau	29 Dec 2006	09:08
			Sag	31 Aug 2006	07:59	Gem	31 Dec 2006	12:16

Moon Signs

2007

Can	2 Jan 2007	16:14	Sco	1 May 2007	11:40	Tau	1 Sep 2007	06:35
Leo	4 Jan 2007	22:15	Sag	3 May 2007	23:47	Gem	3 Sep 2007	08:30
Vir	7 Jan 2007	07:18	Cap	6 May 2007	10:20	Can	5 Sep 2007	12:08
Lib	9 Jan 2007	19:15	Aqu	8 May 2007	18:47	Leo	7 Sep 2007	17:59
Sco	12 Jan 2007	08:07	Pis	11 May 2007	00:30	Vir	10 Sep 2007	02:10
Sag	14 Jan 2007	19:10	Ari	13 May 2007	03:48	Lib	12 Sep 2007	12:32
Cap	17 Jan 2007	02:48	Tau	15 May 2007	03:48	Sco	15 Sep 2007	00:37
Aqu	19 Jan 2007	07:15	Gem	17 May 2007	03:34	Sag	17 Sep 2007	13:20
Pis	21 Jan 2007	09:47	Can	19 May 2007	04:38	Cap	20 Sep 2007	00:50
Ari	23 Jan 2007	11:52	Leo	21 May 2007	08:57	Aqu	22 Sep 2007	09:17
Tau	25 Jan 2007	14:28	Vir	23 May 2007	17:26	Pis	24 Sep 2007	13:53
Gem	27 Jan 2007	18:09	Lib	26 May 2007	05:16	Ari	26 Sep 2007	15:22
Can	29 Jan 2007	23:17	Sco	28 May 2007	18:11	Tau	28 Sep 2007	15:17
			Sag	31 May 2007	06:06	Gem	30 Sep 2007	15:34
Leo	1 Feb 2007	06:14	Cap	2 Jun 2007	16:08	Can	2 Oct 2007	17:57
Vir	3 Feb 2007	15:34	Aqu	5 Jun 2007	00:14	Leo	4 Oct 2007	23:28
Lib	6 Feb 2007	03:15	Pis	7 Jun 2007	06:24	Vir	7 Oct 2007	08:03
Sco	8 Feb 2007	16:09	Ari	9 Jun 2007	10:25	Lib	9 Oct 2007	18:57
Sag	11 Feb 2007	04:00	Tau	11 Jun 2007	12:28	Sco	12 Oct 2007	07:13
Cap	13 Feb 2007	12:40	Gem	13 Jun 2007	13:24	Sag	14 Oct 2007	19:58
Aqu	15 Feb 2007	17:34	Can	15 Jun 2007	14:46	Cap	17 Oct 2007	08:02
Pis	17 Feb 2007	19:29	Leo	17 Jun 2007	18:25	Aqu	19 Oct 2007	17:51
Ari	19 Feb 2007	20:06	Vir	20 Jun 2007	01:46	Pis	22 Oct 2007	00:00
Tau	21 Feb 2007	21:03	Lib	22 Jun 2007	12:44	Ari	24 Oct 2007	02:23
Gem	23 Feb 2007	23:43	Sco	25 Jun 2007	01:26	Tau	26 Oct 2007	02:06
Can	26 Feb 2007	04:48	Sag	27 Jun 2007	13:22	Gem	28 Oct 2007	01:12
Leo	28 Feb 2007	12:30	Cap	29 Jun 2007	23:04	Can	30 Oct 2007	01:50
Vir	2 Mar 2007	22:32	Aqu	2 Jul 2007	06:23	Leo	1 Nov 2007	05:48
Lib	5 Mar 2007	10:25	Pis	4 Jul 2007	11:51	Vir	3 Nov 2007	13:45
Sco	7 Mar 2007	23:16	Ari	6 Jul 2007	15:56	Lib	6 Nov 2007	00:47
Sag	10 Mar 2007	11:36	Tau	8 Jul 2007	18:54	Sco	8 Nov 2007	13:18
Cap	12 Mar 2007	21:33	Gem	10 Jul 2007	21:10	Sag	11 Nov 2007	01:58
Aqu	15 Mar 2007	03:51	Can	12 Jul 2007	23:40	Cap	13 Nov 2007	14:00
Pis	17 Mar 2007	06:30	Leo	15 Jul 2007	03:44	Aqu	16 Nov 2007	00:28
Ari	19 Mar 2007	06:41	Vir	17 Jul 2007	10:40	Pis	18 Nov 2007	08:13
Tau	21 Mar 2007	06:15	Lib	19 Jul 2007	20:54	Ari	20 Nov 2007	12:22
Gem	23 Mar 2007	07:06	Sco	22 Jul 2007	09:18	Tau	22 Nov 2007	13:17
Can	25 Mar 2007	10:50	Sag	24 Jul 2007	21:29	Gem	24 Nov 2007	12:29
Leo	27 Mar 2007	18:04	Cap	27 Jul 2007	07:21	Can	26 Nov 2007	12:08
Vir	30 Mar 2007	04:27	Aqu	29 Jul 2007	14:13	Leo	28 Nov 2007	14:24
			Pis	31 Jul 2007	18:40	Vir	30 Nov 2007	20:45
Lib	1 Apr 2007	16:43	Ari	2 Aug 2007	21:42	Lib	3 Dec 2007	07:01
Sco	4 Apr 2007	05:35	Tau	5 Aug 2007	00:16	Sco	5 Dec 2007	19:30
Sag	6 Apr 2007	17:56	Gem	7 Aug 2007	03:01	Sag	8 Dec 2007	08:10
Cap	9 Apr 2007	04:35	Can	9 Aug 2007	06:36	Cap	10 Dec 2007	19:50
Aqu	11 Apr 2007	12:21	Leo	11 Aug 2007	11:42	Aqu	13 Dec 2007	06:01
Pis	13 Apr 2007	16:38	Vir	13 Aug 2007	19:03	Pis	15 Dec 2007	14:14
Ari	15 Apr 2007	17:46	Lib	16 Aug 2007	05:04	Ari	17 Dec 2007	19:51
Tau	17 Apr 2007	17:10	Sco	18 Aug 2007	17:13	Tau	19 Dec 2007	22:37
Gem	19 Apr 2007	16:51	Sag	21 Aug 2007	05:44	Gem	21 Dec 2007	23:13
Can	21 Apr 2007	18:50	Cap	23 Aug 2007	16:19	Can	23 Dec 2007	23:18
Leo	24 Apr 2007	00:39	Aqu	25 Aug 2007	23:34	Leo	26 Dec 2007	00:53
Vir	26 Apr 2007	10:24	Pis	28 Aug 2007	03:33	Vir	28 Dec 2007	05:44
Lib	28 Apr 2007	22:44	Ari	30 Aug 2007	05:24	Lib	30 Dec 2007	14:38

Moon Signs

2008

Sco	2 Jan 2008	02:32	Ari	2 May 2008	11:49	Lib	1 Sep 2008	12:45
Sag	4 Jan 2008	15:13	Tau	4 May 2008	12:57	Sco	3 Sep 2008	21:03
Cap	7 Jan 2008	02:42	Gem	6 May 2008	12:17	Sag	6 Sep 2008	08:11
Aqu	9 Jan 2008	12:12	Can	8 May 2008	12:03	Cap	8 Sep 2008	20:44
Pis	11 Jan 2008	19:44	Leo	10 May 2008	14:11	Aqu	11 Sep 2008	08:19
Ari	14 Jan 2008	01:22	Vir	12 May 2008	19:49	Pis	13 Sep 2008	17:04
Tau	16 Jan 2008	05:12	Lib	15 May 2008	04:46	Ari	15 Sep 2008	22:38
Gem	18 Jan 2008	07:29	Sco	17 May 2008	15:59	Tau	18 Sep 2008	01:56
Can	20 Jan 2008	09:05	Sag	20 May 2008	04:18	Gem	20 Sep 2008	04:17
Leo	22 Jan 2008	11:21	Cap	22 May 2008	16:55	Can	22 Sep 2008	06:49
Vir	24 Jan 2008	15:48	Aqu	25 May 2008	04:51	Leo	24 Sep 2008	10:14
Lib	26 Jan 2008	23:36	Pis	27 May 2008	14:37	Vir	26 Sep 2008	14:52
Sco	29 Jan 2008	10:35	Ari	29 May 2008	20:51	Lib	28 Sep 2008	21:06
Sag	31 Jan 2008	23:08	Tau	31 May 2008	23:17			
Cap	3 Feb 2008	10:51	Gem	2 Jun 2008	23:05	Sco	1 Oct 2008	05:26
Aqu	5 Feb 2008	20:09	Can	4 Jun 2008	22:16	Sag	3 Oct 2008	16:14
Pis	8 Feb 2008	02:45	Leo	6 Jun 2008	23:01	Cap	6 Oct 2008	04:48
Ari	10 Feb 2008	07:17	Vir	9 Jun 2008	03:02	Aqu	8 Oct 2008	17:02
Tau	12 Feb 2008	10:33	Lib	11 Jun 2008	10:56	Pis	11 Oct 2008	02:30
Gem	14 Feb 2008	13:19	Sco	13 Jun 2008	21:53	Ari	13 Oct 2008	08:06
Can	16 Feb 2008	16:12	Sag	16 Jun 2008	10:19	Tau	15 Oct 2008	10:30
Leo	18 Feb 2008	19:52	Cap	18 Jun 2008	22:51	Gem	17 Oct 2008	11:25
Vir	21 Feb 2008	01:07	Aqu	21 Jun 2008	10:33	Can	19 Oct 2008	12:41
Lib	23 Feb 2008	08:45	Pis	23 Jun 2008	20:31	Leo	21 Oct 2008	15:35
Sco	25 Feb 2008	19:05	Ari	26 Jun 2008	03:48	Vir	23 Oct 2008	20:40
Sag	28 Feb 2008	07:22	Tau	28 Jun 2008	07:50	Lib	26 Oct 2008	03:48
			Gem	30 Jun 2008	09:02	Sco	28 Oct 2008	12:48
						Sag	30 Oct 2008	23:41
Cap	1 Mar 2008	19:32	Can	2 Jul 2008	08:53	Cap	2 Nov 2008	12:13
Aqu	4 Mar 2008	05:24	Leo	4 Jul 2008	09:16	Aqu	5 Nov 2008	01:00
Pis	6 Mar 2008	11:51	Vir	6 Jul 2008	12:05	Pis	7 Nov 2008	11:41
Ari	8 Mar 2008	15:22	Lib	8 Jul 2008	18:31	Ari	9 Nov 2008	18:26
Tau	10 Mar 2008	17:13	Sco	11 Jul 2008	04:35	Tau	11 Nov 2008	21:04
Gem	12 Mar 2008	18:54	Sag	13 Jul 2008	16:50	Gem	13 Nov 2008	21:11
Can	14 Mar 2008	21:38	Cap	16 Jul 2008	05:20	Can	15 Nov 2008	20:53
Leo	17 Mar 2008	02:04	Aqu	18 Jul 2008	16:40	Leo	17 Nov 2008	22:08
Vir	19 Mar 2008	08:25	Pis	21 Jul 2008	02:07	Vir	20 Nov 2008	02:13
Lib	21 Mar 2008	16:45	Ari	23 Jul 2008	09:21	Lib	22 Nov 2008	09:20
Sco	24 Mar 2008	03:06	Tau	25 Jul 2008	14:13	Sco	24 Nov 2008	18:54
Sag	26 Mar 2008	15:11	Gem	27 Jul 2008	16:55	Sag	27 Nov 2008	06:14
Cap	29 Mar 2008	03:42	Can	29 Jul 2008	18:11	Cap	29 Nov 2008	18:47
Aqu	31 Mar 2008	14:32	Leo	31 Jul 2008	19:22			
Pis	2 Apr 2008	21:53	Vir	2 Aug 2008	22:00	Aqu	2 Dec 2008	07:44
Ari	5 Apr 2008	01:26	Lib	5 Aug 2008	03:29	Pis	4 Dec 2008	19:22
Tau	7 Apr 2008	02:19	Sco	7 Aug 2008	12:27	Ari	7 Dec 2008	03:43
Gem	9 Apr 2008	02:27	Sag	10 Aug 2008	00:10	Tau	9 Dec 2008	07:51
Can	11 Apr 2008	03:43	Cap	12 Aug 2008	12:41	Gem	11 Dec 2008	08:33
Leo	13 Apr 2008	07:29	Aqu	14 Aug 2008	23:55	Can	13 Dec 2008	07:40
Vir	15 Apr 2008	14:07	Pis	17 Aug 2008	08:45	Leo	15 Dec 2008	07:23
Lib	17 Apr 2008	23:10	Ari	19 Aug 2008	15:09	Vir	17 Dec 2008	09:37
Sco	20 Apr 2008	10:00	Tau	21 Aug 2008	19:37	Lib	19 Dec 2008	15:24
Sag	22 Apr 2008	22:07	Gem	23 Aug 2008	22:48	Sco	22 Dec 2008	00:37
Cap	25 Apr 2008	10:46	Can	26 Aug 2008	01:18	Sag	24 Dec 2008	12:13
Aqu	27 Apr 2008	22:26	Leo	28 Aug 2008	03:51	Cap	27 Dec 2008	00:56
Pis	30 Apr 2008	07:10	Vir	30 Aug 2008	07:18	Aqu	29 Dec 2008	13:42

Moon Signs

2009

Pis	1 Jan 2009	01:26	Leo	1 May 2009	01:56	Aqu	1 Sep 2009	04:43
Ari	3 Jan 2009	10:48	Vir	3 May 2009	05:37	Pis	3 Sep 2009	16:58
Tau	5 Jan 2009	16:45	Lib	5 May 2009	10:52	Ari	6 Sep 2009	03:14
Gem	7 Jan 2009	19:11	Sco	7 May 2009	17:48	Tau	8 Sep 2009	11:17
Can	9 Jan 2009	19:13	Sag	10 May 2009	02:50	Gem	10 Sep 2009	17:16
Leo	11 Jan 2009	18:41	Cap	12 May 2009	14:09	Can	12 Sep 2009	21:19
Vir	13 Jan 2009	19:33	Aqu	15 May 2009	03:01	Leo	14 Sep 2009	23:39
Lib	15 Jan 2009	23:31	Pis	17 May 2009	15:16	Vir	17 Sep 2009	00:56
Sco	18 Jan 2009	07:21	Ari	20 May 2009	00:28	Lib	19 Sep 2009	02:27
Sag	20 Jan 2009	18:30	Tau	22 May 2009	05:40	Sco	21 Sep 2009	05:52
Cap	23 Jan 2009	07:18	Gem	24 May 2009	07:33	Sag	23 Sep 2009	12:44
Aqu	25 Jan 2009	19:56	Can	26 May 2009	07:58	Cap	25 Sep 2009	23:19
Pis	28 Jan 2009	07:12	Leo	28 May 2009	08:45	Aqu	28 Sep 2009	12:06
Ari	30 Jan 2009	16:24	Vir	30 May 2009	11:18			
Tau	1 Feb 2009	23:07	Lib	1 Jun 2009	16:17	Pis	1 Oct 2009	00:25
Gem	4 Feb 2009	03:13	Sco	3 Jun 2009	23:44	Ari	3 Oct 2009	10:19
Can	6 Feb 2009	05:05	Sag	6 Jun 2009	09:24	Tau	5 Oct 2009	17:33
Leo	8 Feb 2009	05:43	Cap	8 Jun 2009	21:00	Gem	7 Oct 2009	22:46
Vir	10 Feb 2009	06:38	Aqu	11 Jun 2009	09:52	Can	10 Oct 2009	02:47
Lib	12 Feb 2009	09:33	Pis	13 Jun 2009	22:31	Leo	12 Oct 2009	06:02
Sco	14 Feb 2009	15:51	Ari	16 Jun 2009	08:50	Vir	14 Oct 2009	08:45
Sag	17 Feb 2009	01:54	Tau	18 Jun 2009	15:19	Lib	16 Oct 2009	11:30
Cap	19 Feb 2009	14:25	Gem	20 Jun 2009	18:00	Sco	18 Oct 2009	15:23
Aqu	22 Feb 2009	03:06	Can	22 Jun 2009	18:12	Sag	20 Oct 2009	21:50
Pis	24 Feb 2009	13:59	Leo	24 Jun 2009	17:50	Cap	23 Oct 2009	07:39
Ari	26 Feb 2009	22:23	Vir	26 Jun 2009	18:47	Aqu	25 Oct 2009	20:07
			Lib	28 Jun 2009	22:25	Pis	28 Oct 2009	08:44
						Ari	30 Oct 2009	18:56
Tau	1 Mar 2009	04:33	Sco	1 Jul 2009	05:19	Tau	2 Nov 2009	01:43
Gem	3 Mar 2009	08:58	Sag	3 Jul 2009	15:11	Gem	4 Nov 2009	05:52
Can	5 Mar 2009	12:06	Cap	6 Jul 2009	03:08	Can	6 Nov 2009	08:42
Leo	7 Mar 2009	14:24	Aqu	8 Jul 2009	16:03	Leo	8 Nov 2009	11:23
Vir	9 Mar 2009	16:34	Pis	11 Jul 2009	04:43	Vir	10 Nov 2009	14:30
Lib	11 Mar 2009	19:46	Ari	13 Jul 2009	15:39	Lib	12 Nov 2009	18:22
Sco	14 Mar 2009	01:23	Tau	15 Jul 2009	23:28	Sco	14 Nov 2009	23:24
Sag	16 Mar 2009	10:22	Gem	18 Jul 2009	03:40	Sag	17 Nov 2009	06:22
Cap	18 Mar 2009	22:19	Can	20 Jul 2009	04:51	Cap	19 Nov 2009	16:01
Aqu	21 Mar 2009	11:06	Leo	22 Jul 2009	04:27	Aqu	22 Nov 2009	04:11
Pis	23 Mar 2009	22:07	Vir	24 Jul 2009	04:23	Pis	24 Nov 2009	17:07
Ari	26 Mar 2009	06:03	Lib	26 Jul 2009	06:26	Ari	27 Nov 2009	04:10
Tau	28 Mar 2009	11:08	Sco	28 Jul 2009	11:57	Tau	29 Nov 2009	11:33
Gem	30 Mar 2009	14:35	Sag	30 Jul 2009	21:11			
Can	1 Apr 2009	17:30	Cap	2 Aug 2009	09:09	Gem	1 Dec 2009	15:23
Leo	3 Apr 2009	20:32	Aqu	4 Aug 2009	22:08	Can	3 Dec 2009	17:00
Vir	6 Apr 2009	00:02	Pis	7 Aug 2009	10:34	Leo	5 Dec 2009	18:07
Lib	8 Apr 2009	04:22	Ari	9 Aug 2009	21:22	Vir	7 Dec 2009	20:06
Sco	10 Apr 2009	10:24	Tau	12 Aug 2009	05:49	Lib	9 Dec 2009	23:48
Sag	12 Apr 2009	19:01	Gem	14 Aug 2009	11:24	Sco	12 Dec 2009	05:31
Cap	15 Apr 2009	06:27	Can	16 Aug 2009	14:12	Sag	14 Dec 2009	13:26
Aqu	17 Apr 2009	19:19	Leo	18 Aug 2009	14:56	Cap	16 Dec 2009	23:32
Pis	20 Apr 2009	06:54	Vir	20 Aug 2009	15:00	Aqu	19 Dec 2009	11:39
Ari	22 Apr 2009	15:07	Lib	22 Aug 2009	16:12	Pis	22 Dec 2009	00:42
Tau	24 Apr 2009	19:45	Sco	24 Aug 2009	20:17	Ari	24 Dec 2009	12:38
Gem	26 Apr 2009	22:02	Sag	27 Aug 2009	04:17	Tau	26 Dec 2009	21:25
Can	28 Apr 2009	23:38	Cap	29 Aug 2009	15:44	Gem	29 Dec 2009	02:12
						Can	31 Dec 2009	03:45

Moon Signs

2010

Leo	2 Jan 2010	03:40	Cap	2 May 2010	11:00	Gem	1 Sep 2010	01:17
Vir	4 Jan 2010	03:52	Aqu	4 May 2010	21:51	Can	3 Sep 2010	07:48
Lib	6 Jan 2010	05:57	Pis	7 May 2010	10:32	Leo	5 Sep 2010	10:43
Sco	8 Jan 2010	11:00	Ari	9 May 2010	22:27	Vir	7 Sep 2010	10:51
Sag	10 Jan 2010	19:09	Tau	12 May 2010	07:46	Lib	9 Sep 2010	10:00
Cap	13 Jan 2010	05:53	Gem	14 May 2010	14:16	Sco	11 Sep 2010	10:21
Aqu	15 Jan 2010	18:16	Can	16 May 2010	18:44	Sag	13 Sep 2010	13:52
Pis	18 Jan 2010	07:16	Leo	18 May 2010	22:05	Cap	15 Sep 2010	21:30
Ari	20 Jan 2010	19:35	Vir	21 May 2010	00:57	Aqu	18 Sep 2010	08:34
Tau	23 Jan 2010	05:38	Lib	23 May 2010	03:49	Pis	20 Sep 2010	21:14
Gem	25 Jan 2010	12:09	Sco	25 May 2010	07:16	Ari	23 Sep 2010	09:46
Can	27 Jan 2010	14:59	Sag	27 May 2010	12:15	Tau	25 Sep 2010	21:15
Leo	29 Jan 2010	15:08	Cap	29 May 2010	19:43	Gem	28 Sep 2010	07:09
Vir	31 Jan 2010	14:22				Can	30 Sep 2010	14:43
Lib	2 Feb 2010	14:42	Aqu	1 Jun 2010	06:06	Leo	2 Oct 2010	19:19
Sco	4 Feb 2010	17:54	Pis	3 Jun 2010	18:32	Vir	4 Oct 2010	20:58
Sag	7 Feb 2010	01:04	Ari	6 Jun 2010	06:48	Lib	6 Oct 2010	20:50
Cap	9 Feb 2010	11:43	Tau	8 Jun 2010	16:39	Sco	8 Oct 2010	20:51
Aqu	12 Feb 2010	00:23	Gem	10 Jun 2010	23:08	Sag	10 Oct 2010	23:09
Pis	14 Feb 2010	13:22	Can	13 Jun 2010	02:49	Cap	13 Oct 2010	05:16
Ari	17 Feb 2010	01:29	Leo	15 Jun 2010	04:53	Aqu	15 Oct 2010	15:23
Tau	19 Feb 2010	11:53	Vir	17 Jun 2010	06:40	Pis	18 Oct 2010	03:50
Gem	21 Feb 2010	19:45	Lib	19 Jun 2010	09:12	Ari	20 Oct 2010	16:21
Can	24 Feb 2010	00:26	Sco	21 Jun 2010	13:13	Tau	23 Oct 2010	03:28
Leo	26 Feb 2010	02:06	Sag	23 Jun 2010	19:09	Gem	25 Oct 2010	12:46
Vir	28 Feb 2010	01:51	Cap	26 Jun 2010	03:21	Can	27 Oct 2010	20:13
			Aqu	28 Jun 2010	13:51	Leo	30 Oct 2010	01:36
Lib	2 Mar 2010	01:31	Pis	1 Jul 2010	02:08	Vir	1 Nov 2010	04:50
Sco	4 Mar 2010	03:11	Ari	3 Jul 2010	14:43	Lib	3 Nov 2010	06:17
Sag	6 Mar 2010	08:36	Tau	6 Jul 2010	01:27	Sco	5 Nov 2010	07:15
Cap	8 Mar 2010	18:12	Gem	8 Jul 2010	08:48	Sag	7 Nov 2010	09:27
Aqu	11 Mar 2010	06:41	Can	10 Jul 2010	12:36	Cap	9 Nov 2010	14:36
Pis	13 Mar 2010	19:42	Leo	12 Jul 2010	13:52	Aqu	11 Nov 2010	23:32
Ari	16 Mar 2010	07:30	Vir	14 Jul 2010	14:14	Pis	14 Nov 2010	11:23
Tau	18 Mar 2010	17:28	Lib	16 Jul 2010	15:23	Ari	16 Nov 2010	23:57
Gem	21 Mar 2010	01:26	Sco	18 Jul 2010	18:41	Tau	19 Nov 2010	11:02
Can	23 Mar 2010	07:14	Sag	21 Jul 2010	00:48	Gem	21 Nov 2010	19:44
Leo	25 Mar 2010	10:37	Cap	23 Jul 2010	09:38	Can	24 Nov 2010	02:12
Vir	27 Mar 2010	11:55	Aqu	25 Jul 2010	20:37	Leo	26 Nov 2010	07:00
Lib	29 Mar 2010	12:20	Pis	28 Jul 2010	08:59	Vir	28 Nov 2010	10:32
Sco	31 Mar 2010	13:41	Ari	30 Jul 2010	21:40	Lib	30 Nov 2010	13:14
Sag	2 Apr 2010	17:51	Tau	2 Aug 2010	09:11	Sco	2 Dec 2010	15:42
Cap	5 Apr 2010	02:07	Gem	4 Aug 2010	17:53	Sag	4 Dec 2010	18:58
Aqu	7 Apr 2010	13:50	Can	6 Aug 2010	22:47	Cap	7 Dec 2010	00:16
Pis	10 Apr 2010	02:46	Leo	9 Aug 2010	00:21	Aqu	9 Dec 2010	08:30
Ari	12 Apr 2010	14:29	Vir	11 Aug 2010	00:00	Pis	11 Dec 2010	19:39
Tau	14 Apr 2010	23:53	Lib	12 Aug 2010	23:42	Ari	14 Dec 2010	08:13
Gem	17 Apr 2010	07:07	Sco	15 Aug 2010	01:26	Tau	16 Dec 2010	19:47
Can	19 Apr 2010	12:37	Sag	17 Aug 2010	06:33	Gem	19 Dec 2010	04:36
Leo	21 Apr 2010	16:40	Cap	19 Aug 2010	15:17	Can	21 Dec 2010	10:20
Vir	23 Apr 2010	19:23	Aqu	22 Aug 2010	02:37	Leo	23 Dec 2010	13:49
Lib	25 Apr 2010	21:15	Pis	24 Aug 2010	15:10	Vir	25 Dec 2010	16:13
Sco	27 Apr 2010	23:28	Ari	27 Aug 2010	03:48	Lib	27 Dec 2010	18:37
Sag	30 Apr 2010	03:35	Tau	29 Aug 2010	15:34	Sco	29 Dec 2010	21:49

CLAIRE PETULENGRO

Year Ahead 2003

Aries, Taurus, Gemini, Cancer, Leo, Virgo, Libra, Scorpio, Sagittarius, Capricorn, Aquarius, Pisces

PAN BOOKS   £3.50 EACH

Let Claire Petulengro, renowned celebrity astrologer, reveal what the stars have in store for you in 2003

Whether you're looking for a broad overview of the entire year, the flavour of each month, or a more detailed daily examination of what to expect, this well-organized handbook will provide you with the advance information you need to make the most of your life. With her trademark wit and style, Claire divulges what 2003 will bring in terms of your love life, career, finances, health, luck and family. Sun signs aren't the only factor to take into account, however, so use the ready reckoner to look up your moon sign and find out how your emotional side will react to the year's events. With monthly astrological facts, your favourite celebrities' birthdays and information on the life-changing effects of the Saturn return, this is your one-stop reference for every day of the New Year.

CLAIRE PETULENGRO

Health Signs

PAN BOOKS   £5.99

*A fresh, vital new look at natural health from Britain's
most exciting young astrologer*

Your sign dictates your health needs, just as it shapes your
personality and how you approach life. Consult *Health Signs*
for a tailor-made programme advising on which vitamins you
need to boost, what your superfoods are, what to avoid, and
how to prevent and heal the ailments you are prone to.

Claire has researched and surveyed hundreds of people to
support the knowledge she has from a lifetime's experience in
astrology and of Romany lore with sound medical findings.

CLAIRE PETULENGRO

Diet Signs

PAN BOOKS   £5.99

The healthy eating and weight management plan to suit who you really are!

Claire Petulengro is the UK's freshest new astrologer, down to earth and compellingly accurate. In *Diet Signs* she explains the link between the stars and the way you relate to food, giving you the information to handle your diet wisely, and what to be aware of when YOU try to lose weight.

There's a tailor-made plan for Fire Signs (Aries, Leo, Sagittarius), Earth Signs (Taurus, Virgo, Capricorn), Air Signs (Gemini, Libra, Aquarius) and Water Signs (Cancer, Scorpio, Pisces) – encompassing healthy eating, exercise, foods you'll love and foods you should avoid, and simple, nutritious recipes to keep you on track. Did you know that Taureans and Librans really go for sweet foods – so they should try and manage their intake of these foods rather than try to cut them out and fail – and Geminis and Virgos are most likely to be vegetarian? Pisces tend to retain water, and won't stand the same sort of regimen as Virgos. Be realistic, come to understand your body's needs through the forces that govern it, and discover your star diet for life.

OTHER PAN BOOKS
AVAILABLE FROM PAN MACMILLAN

CLAIRE PETULENGRO
HEALTH SIGNS   0 330 39317 0   £5.99
DIET SIGNS   0 330 37405 2   £5.99

RITA ROGERS
SOUL MATES   0 330 39078 3   £6.99
MYSTERIES   0 330 39079 1   £6.99

LINDA GOODMAN
SUN SIGNS   0 330 23390 4   £9.99
STAR SIGNS   0 330 30344 9   £7.99

All Pan Macmillan titles can be ordered from our website,
www.panmacmillan.com, or from your local bookshop
and are also available by post from:

Bookpost, PO Box 29, Douglas, Isle of Man IM99 1BQ
Credit cards accepted. For details:
Telephone: 01624 677237
Fax: 01624 670923
E-mail: bookshop@enterprise.net
www.bookpost.co.uk

Free postage and packing in the United Kingdom

Prices shown above were correct at the time of going to press.
Pan Macmillan reserve the right to show new retail prices on covers
which may differ from those previously advertised in the text
or elsewhere.